# Classic Russian Cooking

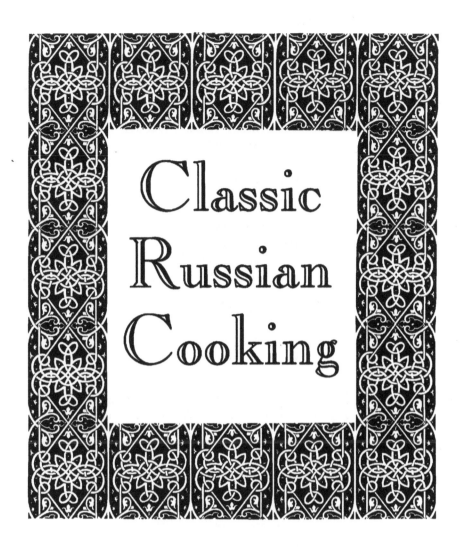

# Classic Russian Cooking

Elena Molokhovets'
*A Gift to Young Housewives*

TRANSLATED, INTRODUCED, AND ANNOTATED BY
JOYCE TOOMRE

INDIANA UNIVERSITY PRESS • BLOOMINGTON & INDIANAPOLIS

**Indiana-Michigan Series in Russian and East European Studies**
Alexander Rabinowitch and William G. Rosenberg,
*general editors*

This book is a publication of

Indiana University Press
Office of Scholarly Publishing
Herman B Wells Library 350
1320 East 10th Street
Bloomington, Indiana 47405 USA

www.indiana.edu/~ipress

First paperback edition 1998
© 1992 by Joyce Toomre
All rights reserved

The paper used in this publication meets the minimum requirements of American
National Standard for Information Sciences—Permanence of Paper for Printed
Library Materials, ANSI Z39.48-1984.

Manufactured in the United States of America

**Library of Congress Cataloging-in-Publication Data**

Toomre, Joyce Stetson.
    Classic Russian cooking : Elena Molokhovets' A gift to young
housewives / translated, introduced, and annotated by Joyce Toomre.
        p.      cm. — (Indiana-Michigan series in Russian and East
European studies)
    Includes bibliographical references and index.
    ISBN 0-253-36026-9 (cl). — 0-253-21210-3 (pbk)
    1. Cookery, Russian.   I. Molokhovets, Elena, b. 1831. Podarok
molodym khoziaikam.   1992.   II. Title.   III. Series.
TX723.3.T66   1992
641.5947—dc20                                          91-46254

4   5   6   7   18   17   16   15   14

To Alar, *with love*

# Contents

# ELENA MOLOKHOVETS' *A GIFT TO YOUNG HOUSEWIVES*

Contents　　　　　　　　　　　　　ix

# Acknowledgments

For the last decade I have made a nuisance of myself peppering nearly everyone I met with questions as I struggled to understand the world of Elena Molokhovets. Scholarship is always collaborative; it is built on the work of others, past and present. Few scholars do their best work in isolation, and I for one have been particularly blessed in my associates. It is my happy duty now to acknowledge with gratitude those organizations, colleagues, friends, and family members who have helped me piece together the mosaic that culminated in this book.

Donald Fanger started it all by sending me Simon Karlinsky's article on Molokhovets. Even so, the project would have been unthinkable without the support of the Russian Research Center at Harvard University; I am deeply indebted to its Executive Committee for providing me with unparalleled opportunities to pursue my research. Colleagues at the Center have provided a wonderful mix of friendly support along with expert advice and guidance. In particular I want to thank Adam Ulam, John Malmstad, William Mills Todd III, Sanford Lieberman, John Le Donne, Catherine Chvany, Patricia Herlihy, Mark Field, David Powell, Robert Rothstein, Tibor Vais, Musya Glants, Susan Gardos, Edith Haber, Sonia Ketchian, and of course Mary Towle, long at the hub of the Center's activities.

The libraries of Harvard University with their magnificent collections made it feasible to undertake this research; their knowledgeable staffs made it a pleasure. I especially want to thank Hugh Olmsted at Widener Library, Roger Stoddard at Houghton Library, Jean Boise at the Farlow Library, and Eva Jonas at the Museum of Comparative Zoology Library. My work on Molokhovets began and ended in the Schlesinger Library with its stunning culinary collection. Patricia King, the director, and her entire staff went out of their way time and again to be helpful. Also at the Schlesinger, Barbara Haber endlessly counseled, cajoled and comforted me; the book is better for her guidance and I am richer for having such a friend and colleague.

Key contributions were made to this work also by the librarians at the University of Illinois at Urbana-Champaign. In particular, I want to thank Helen Sullivan and Larry Miller, who were resourceful in locating all sorts of rare and unusual materials, and June Pachuta Farris, now at the University of Chicago, who obtained for me a microfilm of the first edition of Molokhovets' book. My time in their care at the Illinois Summer Research Laboratories on Russia and Eastern Europe was very well spent. Likewise in Illinois, I benefited from the annual Workshops on Women in Slavic Cultures that were organized so ably by my good friend and mentor in Slavic Studies, Mary Zirin.

The staffs at the British Library, the Bibliothèque nationale, and the Slavic Division of the New York Public Library were all most helpful. Leonard Beck, a former curator of Special Collections at the Library of Congress, readily shared with me his fund of information on matters Russian and culinary. He was as comfortable with the Yudin collection and those magnificent volumes that were once part of the Russian Imperial Library as he was with the Bitting and Pennell gastronomic collections. His impish erudition added special zest to my visits to the Library; in his retirement, he is sorely missed.

Baryara Arutunova, also now retired, but formerly a member of Harvard's Slavic Department, was exceptionally generous in loaning to me for several years her copy of the Berlin edition of *A Gift to Young Housewives*. This clearly printed text not only saved my eyesight but allowed me to resolve numerous inconsistencies aggravated by fuzzy photocopies. Ernst Birsner of Verlag Aenne Burda in Germany very kindly provided me with a fine copy of his newly acquired and extremely rare German translation of Molokhovets. Thanks also are due to Friederike F. Seligman for her enthusiastic collaboration in the early stages of this project; the present translation of the "Author's Introduction" is derived from her work, and so is that of "An Evening Tea." Also in the early days, Becky Saika-Wilson, a former student in one of my classes and now an editor at Houghton Mifflin, labored over ur-drafts of nearly all the chapters, cutting them down to size intelligently—and ruthlessly. The book benefited greatly from her attention and I learned more than I had ever taught.

Other people helped in other ways. Alan Davidson has been an avid supporter from the beginning; he encouraged me to undertake this translation and advised me shrewdly along the way. This is also the time to tip my hat and acknowledge the enormous contribution he has made to the field of culinary history through his founding and editing of *Petits Propos Culinaires*. Without those little journals, my work would have been much harder. Three steadfast friends, Martha Robert, Meryle Evans, and Marge Leibenstein, were always ready to discuss some arcane point of culinary history or simply to lend a sympathetic ear. I also want to thank Barbara Kirshenblatt-Gimblett for her assistance with Baumkuchen and with Molokhovets' Jewish recipes, Frances Cattermole-Tally for locating folk beliefs in the preparation of vinegar, Karen Hess for information about isinglass and her words of general encouragement, Carolyn Payne for translating the French passages, Bart Germond for sharing his expertise on cows and milking from his vantage point as Regional Dairy Specialist with the University of Massachusetts Cooperative Extension, and Nahum Waxman for his sage advice about the world of publishing.

Without the help of experts, I never could have groped my way safely through

Molokhovets' cupboard of chemicals. In that respect, I am particularly grateful to Ruth Tanner, Shirley Cohen, and Harold Goldwhite—and to Ruth Lynden-Bell, who patiently sorted out all the final details. For technical assistance of another kind, I want to thank Edward T. Wilcox who introduced me to the marvels of personal computers, floppy disks, and state-of-the-art clattery printers. Lynn Visson, Olga Orechwa, Anne Odom, Florence Trefethen, Katherine Keenum, Elizabeth Silins, Barbara Kuck, Kay Fleischer, Netta Davis, Linda McCoy, Joan Nathan, Anne Mendelsohn, Jeanne Lesem, and Nancy Harmon Jenkins were also helpful, each in her own special way. An extra word of thanks is due to the members of the Culinary Historians of Boston; in many ways they have furthered my education in culinary matters; and Patricia Kelly, a former president, assisted with the proofreading and helped to create the index. The Senior Common Room at Adams House under the leadership of Robert and Jana Kiely has likewise been a source of inspiration and encouragement; I have cherished the witty and impassioned exchanges among its members.

The guidance of native Russian speakers was also essential for this translation. This book would have foundered without the many patient hours of explanation that Ella Gorlov, Tibor and Helen Vais, Snegana Tempest, and Musya Glants were willing to put into it. At times I may not have known enough to have asked the right questions, but that is my fault, not theirs.

The influence of two close friends and colleagues, Barbara Ketcham Wheaton and Darra Goldstein, permeates this book. Almost every page bears witness to their copious comments, probing questions, and funny asides. Each an expert in her own field, those two bombarded me from different directions, and though I groaned at their queries, their scrutiny was keenly appreciated. My fellow Slavists Ron LeBlanc and Diana Greene read only my long introduction, but there they too made numerous helpful suggestions.

To Janet Rabinowitch at Indiana University Press go my heartfelt thanks for helping me finish this project. Her deep knowledge of Russian culture and her editorial experience have been invaluable assets. Together with Roberta Diehl from the same Press, she worked very hard to turn an unwieldy manuscript into the book that is before you. I am enormously grateful to them both.

No scholar could ask for a more loyal squadron of boosters than the younger generation of Toomres—Lars, his wife Niña, Erik, and Anya. Near or far they never neglected to ask after Molokhovets. Finally I turn to my husband, Alar, who was inundated with details even without asking. His probity and meticulousness have inspired my scholarship while his ready laughter and acuity of mind have made him a boon companion lo these many years. In return for his endurance, support, and trust, I offer him this book.

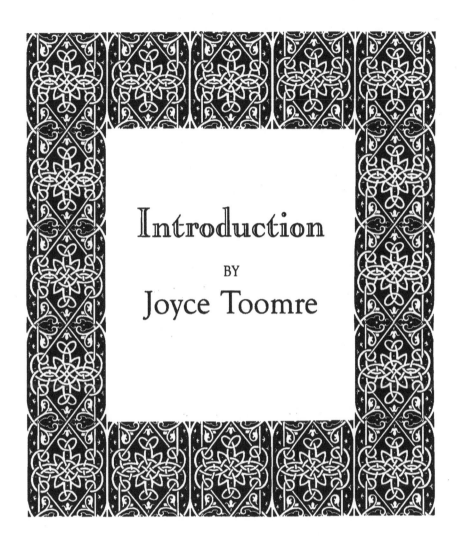

# Introduction

## BY
## Joyce Toomre

All cookbooks start as manuals of instruction, but some develop an extra richness as they age. In such books, it is the asides or the glimpses of another culture that come to captivate us as much as their antiquated directions for frying an egg or roasting a pig. Embedded in the language of every recipe are assumptions about the reader and his or her milieu, skills, and resources. A *collection* of recipes is even more informative, both for what it includes and for what it omits. Recipes are rooted in time and space; essentially static, they function as snapshots of a culture. Like translations, they usually serve the needs of a particular group of people in a particular locale. With rare exceptions, they do not move easily from place to place or from one generation to another.

*A Gift to Young Housewives* is one of those exceptions. For more than half a century, from the emancipation of the serfs in 1861 to the onset of the Bolshevik revolution in 1917, Elena Molokhovets oversaw the successive editions of her book. Her volume was a treasured asset in many families where it was handed down from one generation to another and even carried into exile. Her name (pronounced Ma-la-hah-VYETS) became a household word and passed into the culture of the period. Chekhov parodied her menus in one of his early humorous sketches, "Kalendar' *Budil'nika*" [*Alarm-clock*'s Calendar], by offering a series of absurd daily menus. One of them, for journalists, consisted of eight courses: (1) a glass of vodka, (2) daily *shchi* with yesterday's kasha, (3) 2 glasses of vodka, (4) suckling pig with horseradish, (5) 3 glasses of vodka, (6) horseradish, cayenne pepper, and soy sauce, (7) 4 glasses of vodka, and (8) 7 bottles of beer.[1] Another spoof of Molokhovets, this time of her Easter table, was published by the Russian writer and poet Nadezhda Teffi in 1912.[2] By Soviet times, Molokhovets and her recipes were no longer a laughing matter. She became a symbol of bourgeois decadence to Communist ideologues and the object of envy in a time of food shortages in a poem by the Soviet poet Arsenij Tarkovskij who, to quote Alan Davidson, "devised for her a fate worthy of Dante's *Inferno*." Instead of preparing crayfish bordelaise or imperial aspics, she sits under an icy rock face reciting her culinary "Testament" while in one hand she holds an insatiable worm and in the other—her skull mumbling in a colander (*"tvoj cherep mjamlit v durkhshlage"*).[3]

After the revolution, the Soviets never reprinted the book in its entirety, but within several months after the collapse of the Soviet Union new reprints of the full text of *A Gift to Young Housewives* were being hawked on the streets of Moscow. In the late 1980s articles about Molokhovets accompanied by some of her recipes appeared in the Moscow newspaper *Vechernjaja Moskva* [Evening Moscow].[4] Two small collections from *A Gift to Young Housewives* were published in Moscow in 1989. One booklet contains recipes for sweet dishes such as waffles, sweet pies, ice creams, tortes, and mazurkas. Recipes in the other booklet are limited to fast day dishes and to *kuliches* and *paskhas,* which are an integral part of the traditional Easter table. This odd selection showing the extremes of austerity and lavishness of the Russian kitchen seems to be tied to the resurgence of religious activity in the Soviet Union.[5]

Molokhovets' cookbook is encyclopedic; it describes a cuisine and culture that have now vanished and for that reason alone it deserves to be more widely available. She was writing for inexperienced housewives at a time when Russian cuisine was at its zenith. Her culinary standards were high, but she knew the value of a kopeck. I hope this translation will introduce readers to Russian cuisine in all its simplicity and in all its glory. Like the original, it is meant to be used in the kitchen. Readers with a Slavic background will find in these pages many dishes that they have heard about from their grandmothers. Aside from practicing cooks, the book should also interest Slavists, social historians, and culinary historians.

This Introduction is intended to help the reader understand the cultural significance of the dishes. It is not a history of Russian cookery per se, but rather an impressionistic reconstruction of household conditions based on anecdotes and scraps of evidence taken from a wide variety of sources. The systematic documentation of these issues must be left to others. My aim throughout has been to provide enough background information for the text to be appreciated by one group of readers while not belaboring the obvious for another. The Introduction also synthesizes Molokhovets' views on household management. These cover a wide range of topics—everything from her opinions on feeding the servants and entertaining guests to her detailed instructions for growing mushrooms in the cellar, constructing a bed for the cook in the kitchen, and preserving grapes in one of the second floor rooms.

Since beginning work on this book, my views of Russian culinary history have changed dramatically. I began by regarding the kitchen activities in Tsarist Russia as quaint and backward, but with time I realized that the Russians shared many domestic and culinary problems with other rural preindustrial societies and solved them in similar ways. Thus, wherever possible, I have pointed out analogies with English, Western European, and American practices. In the Introduction I have been lavish in the use of notes, partly because my audience is so diverse and partly to provide guidance for further research. All books mentioned in the notes are listed in the bibliography. I have appended notes to individual recipes only when I wanted to bring some particular issue to the reader's attention or to explain some point that might not be immediately obvious. I have provided introductory commentary for just a few of the separate chapters, inasmuch as the basic information about Russian dishes is available elsewhere and to expound on it further would require another volume. My essay only suggests some of the main topics in Russian culinary history; I hope it will inspire other scholars to carry the research forward.

The first edition of Molokhovets I read was the twentieth (published in 1897), since it was the only one available at the Harvard University Library. Several years later, the library staff at the University of Illinois at Urbana-Champaign obtained a microfilm of the first edition, published in 1861, which allowed me to follow the growth and development of Molokhovets' work. (The differences between the early and late editions are discussed later in this Introduction.) After comparing different editions of Molokhovets' book, I found that there are distinct advantages to working with a later edition of a cookbook. As Elizabeth David, the preeminent modern English writer on cookery, has noted, "first editions . . . wouldn't be anything like as interesting to serious students of cookery as later ones, in which the authors themselves have made revisions, corrected errors, added new recipes, brought cooking methods up to date, and incorporated recently introduced ingredients."[6]

The twentieth edition of *A Gift to Young Housewives* consists of approximately 800 pages of very small type. Except for a few diagrams, there are no illustrations. The present translation includes about a quarter of the original recipes, each of which is numbered according to the 1897 edition. Although some colleagues have objected to my abridging the text on the grounds of intellectual integrity, the repetitive nature of many of the recipes made it feasible, if not entirely desirable, to do so. With jams or syrups, for instance, Molokhovets often repeated the same recipe, changing only the kind of fruit. She similarly repeated herself in most of the fast day recipes. Chapter 40—Fast Day Ices, Compotes, and *Kissels*—is no more than a list of numbered recipe titles referring the reader back to the appropriate recipe in Chapter 14 with the admonition to substitute fish glue for gelatin.

I began by roughly translating the entire text. Although I knew which recipes had to be included because of special culinary or cultural considerations, it was not easy to assure a balanced selection. My goal was to put together a group of recipes that seemed interesting from a contemporary American viewpoint, but at the same time demonstrated the full range of Russian ingredients and techniques. I also tried to keep the same proportion of recipes that had been carried over from the first edition. Molokhovets' habit of following a longish basic recipe with several derivations considerably eased the process of deciding what to include and what to omit. Nevertheless, each chapter had its agonizing moments. (A full list of recipes appears at the end of the book.) Once the recipes were selected, I settled down to turning them into something approaching idiomatic English. Along the way, I checked out puzzling terms with native Russian speakers and obscure culinary processes with cooks and historians.

Like humans, cookbooks tend to expand with age. Often the first edition of a

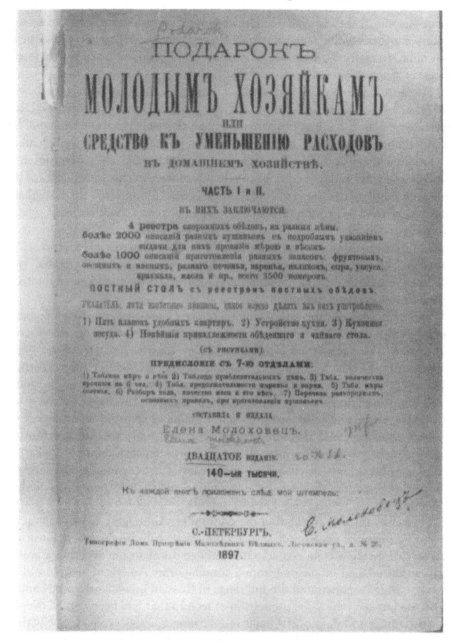

Title page of the twentieth edition of Elena Molokhovets'
*Podarok molodym khozjajkam* [*A Gift to Young Housewives*]
(St. Petersburg, 1897).

cookbook is quite slender while successive editions grow ever larger. Elena Molokhovets' cookbook fits that pattern. The first edition began with fifteen hundred

recipes, the twentieth edition of 1897 (upon which the present translation is based) had grown to thirty-two hundred and eighteen, while the last Russian edition of the book, published in Berlin in the 1920s, finished by adding another thousand recipes.

*A Gift to Young Housewives* reflects the basic division of Russian cuisine by providing recipes for both meat days and fast days. In later editions, Molokhovets reformulated the main chapters for soups, sauces, vegetables, fish, desserts, etc., into parallel chapters with recipes for fast days. Preserving stores for winter was an important feature of Russian household management, and Molokhovets included several chapters on making wine, jams, vinegars, and *kvass*. In addition, she described various cuts of meat and gave hints for cooking, prices, and measurements. She suggested menus for grand occasions, daily menus for three levels of income, fast day menus, and menus for servants and for children. She provided sample floor plans for summer homes and apartments as well as suggestions for arranging the kitchen. She also listed equipment and utensils useful in the kitchen and dining room and gave directions for setting the table for dinner or for tea.

## Development of Cookbooks in Russia

Cookbooks, as such, became common in Russia only in the 1840s. The best early source for establishing the history of Russian cuisine comes not from a cookbook, but from a manual of domestic literature. The *Domostroj* [Domestic management], which dates from the mid sixteenth century, is a prescriptive book with a very conservative ideology that outlines proper behavior toward the church and state as well as toward family and servants.[7] It includes religious, moral, and domestic precepts for almost all facets of life—everything from how to behave in church (stand up straight without wriggling or shifting from one foot to another) to how to brew beer. The *Domostroj* belongs to that common European genre of manuals of which the fourteenth century French text *Le ménagier de Paris* is one of the best known examples.[8] Domestic manuals became popular in Russia in the late seventeenth century and continued to be published through the eighteenth century. Early works of this type were based upon Polish translations of Greek and Latin originals. Later, translations from German texts appeared, such as Florinus' *Ekonomiia* [Agricultural and household management], which was published in 1738.[9]

Household manuals were another source for cookbooks. These differed from the domestic manuals in that the emphasis was not on religious and moral themes but on the practical problems of managing one's estate or farm. Cooking, for the writers of these manuals, was a task like any other and did not receive much special attention. Kitchen chores simply blended into the daily and seasonal press of activity common to all preindustrial rural households. In such circumstances, a chapter or two of recipes was sufficient; just as important were the instructions on tending the orchard, keeping bees, and handling the livestock. Manuals of this type were published right through the nineteenth century and were available up to the eve of the Russian Revolution in 1917. A good example is the *Nastol'naja kniga* [Manual], which was distributed as a free supplement to the magazine *Zhivopisnoe obozrenie* [Pictorial review] in 1895. In addition to a chapter devoted to recipes and another to preserves, the editors included a list of male and female Orthodox names as well as a list of saint's days according to the Old Style and New Style Calendars; instructions for managing fields, meadows, and forests; veterinary advice for cattle, birds, and dogs; and directions for building a house and installing one's own telegraph system.[10] Even Molokhovets expanded her cookbook in 1880 to include sections on personal health and hygiene, the care of sick adults and children, and the care, feeding, and diseases of domestic birds and animals. This new material, however, seems never to have been as popular as her recipes and was not reprinted with later editions of her cookbook.[11]

Cookbooks began to be published in Russia in the last decades of the eighteenth century. Sergej Drukovtsev's book *Povarennye zapiski* [Cooking notes], which was published in Moscow in 1779, probably deserves to be considered the first although it contains only very limited descriptions of Russian peasant dishes and Russian national dishes. With directions so minimal that they verge on the enigmatic, it is hard to envision the dishes, much less recreate them. Another problem is that Drukovtsev only numbered his recipes without giving them names, which would have been much more useful for the historian.

During the 1780s and 1790s several German and French cookery books were translated into Russian. Most of these translations were rather free-form, omitting large sections of the original work and adding new material that was considered more suitable for Russian conditions. Among the most important of the books translated was Menon's *La cuisinière bourgeoise,* first published in Paris in 1746. This was translated by Nikolaj Jatsenkov and was published in Russia in 1790–91 as *Novejshaja i polnaja povarennaja kniga* [The newest complete cookery book]. Several original collections of recipes were published in the 1790s as well. Nikolaj Petrovich Osipov (1751–1799), for instance, published the *Starinnaja russkaja khozjajka, kljuchnitsa i strjapukha* [Old-time Russian mistress of the household, housekeeper, and cook] in 1790 and *Novyj i polnyj rossijskoj khozjajstvennoj vinokur* [The new and complete Russian domestic vintner] in 1796. The *Old-time Russian Mistress of the Household, Housekeeper, and Cook* is a miscellany of household hints and recipes, all arranged alphabetically. By beginning with directions for cleaning diamond objects and then explaining how to distinguish true diamonds from false, Osipov gave an unexpectedly vivid glimpse of his intended audience, which clearly was wealthy and educated. Only later did he turn to more prosaic matters like the making of barberry jam or the bleaching of linen. In 1795–1797, Vasilij Alekseevich Levshin (1746–1826) published an important culinary dictionary; in 1800, Pankrat Sumarokov (1765–1814), the nephew of the well-known author, published another.[12]

Aside from these various antiquarian considerations, the first author of really popular cookbooks in Russia was Katerina Alekseevna Avdeeva (1789–1865), the elder sister of the well-known journalist and man of letters Nikolaj Alekseevich Polevoj (1796–1846). The cookbooks of this prolific author were well reviewed and went through numerous editions. The cost of this popularity was that she was beset by imitators and plagiarizers. In 1851 she published a declaration acknowledging authorship of only the following four cookbooks: *Ruchnaja kniga russkoj opytnoj khozjajki* [Handbook of an experienced Russian mistress of the household] (1842); *Karmannaja povarennaja kniga* [The pocket cookbook] (1846); *Rukovodstvo dlja khozjaek, kljuchnits, ekonomok i kukharok* [Handbook for the mistress of the household, the housekeeper, steward, and cook] (1846); and *Ekonomicheskij leksikon* [Steward's lexicon], written with her son and published in 1848.[13] Her books remained popular after her death and imitations continued to be published until well into the 1870s when her name and works were finally eclipsed by the success of Molokhovets' cookbook.

*A Gift to Young Housewives* seems to have been an instant success when it appeared in 1861; by 1917, 295,000 copies had been printed. Such steadfast popularity and wide circulation of a cookbook were unprecedented in Russia, although not unknown elsewhere in Europe. Numerous editions of a single title have always been the hallmark of an exceptional cookbook, wherever and whenever this occurred.[14] In France, Louis Audot's *La cuisinière de la campagne et de la ville: ou, La nouvelle cuisine économique* was first published in Paris in 1818; the 72nd edition of the same book appeared in 1894.[15] In Germany, Henriette Davidis' *Praktisches Kochbuch für die gewöhnliche und feinere Küche . . .* was first published in Bielefeld in 1851, while the 45th edition appeared in 1910. The most outstanding English cookery book of the eighteenth century was Hannah Glasse's *The Art of Cookery, Made Plain and Easy*, which first appeared in London in 1747 and was still being published nearly a century later.[16] Two important English books in the nineteenth century were Eliza Acton's *Modern Cookery for Private Families*, which was first published in London in 1845 and continued to be published until 1914,[17] and Isabella Beeton's *Book of Household Management*, which first appeared in parts in 1859–61 (as *Beeton's Book of Household Management*) and which is still being published, although the contents and format have changed radically. In American culinary literature, the best modern examples are Fannie Farmer's *The Boston Cooking-School Cook Book*, first published in 1895 and reprinted as recently as 1965, and Irma Rombauer's *Joy of Cooking*, first published in 1931 and still one of the most popular cookbooks on the market. Of all the works cited, *A Gift to Young Housewives* is exceptional in that the original author was still editing her work half a century later.

The devoted following of the Molokhovets book is partly due to its intrinsic worth and partly to historical accident. The first factor should not be underestimated. Quite simply, the book is a very good manual with excellent recipes. It is comprehensive, logically organized, and unpretentious; it accomplishes its goals with a minimum of fuss and bother and very little extraneous material. This by itself is much, but it is not the stuff of legends. For that, we have to thank the Bolsheviks. *A Gift to Young Housewives* was published in 1861, the same year that the serfs were freed; it was at this time that Lev Tolstoy was writing *War and Peace*.[18] Molokhovets continued to edit successive editions of her cookbook right through the end of the century until the fall of the Romanovs and collapse of the Tsarist Empire in 1917. Since that time, the book has taken on an added significance. Old copies have become family heirlooms and they are treasured, often as the last tangible remnant of a vanished way of life. With the passage of time, however, Soviet citizens have tended to view Molokhovets and her world less with nostalgia than with disbelief. The horrific shortages and hardships that they have suffered over the past seventy years have virtually eradicated the notion of plenty. When I tell Soviet émigrés what book I have been translating, almost without exception they break out laughing and, through guffaws, repeat the same advice from Molokhovets, "When unexpected guests arrive, send the servant down into the cold cellar for hazel grouse or a ham." They almost explode with laughter at such ridiculous advice, since they have no adequate housing, let alone servants, cold cellars, or provisions to store. That a mere cookbook could provoke such universal black humor among Soviets tells volumes about the genre as historical witness and the failure of the Soviet system to respond to the needs of its citizens.

The genesis of *A Gift to Young Housewives* has become shrouded in senti-mentalism. It is commonly repeated among Soviet émigrés that the husband of Elena Molokhovets collected her recipes and had them published for her as a surprise in honor of her thirtieth name day. I have even heard it argued that the husband, rather than the wife, was the true author of this successful cookbook. According to Elena Molokhovets herself, the story is simpler and more plausible, although less romantic. In the Introduction to the 1914 edition, she stated that *she published* her cookbook for the first time in 1861 and that *she gave* it (my emphasis in both cases) the title *A Gift to Young Housewives*. Several pages later she quoted with evident approval a description of herself as having been an active and educated young woman who loved to plan the meals for her family and who began to compose and transcribe recipes for various dishes. When a full assortment of these recipes had been gathered, her husband, who enjoyed the fruits of her efforts, wanted to publish them in honor of her name day.[19] In other words, she was already collecting and organizing the recipes when her husband proposed having them published. There is no hint of surprise in her story, rather a suggestion of encouragement and cooperation between husband and wife. Permission to publish the book was granted by the St. Petersburg censor on 9 August 1860, well before her thirtieth name day on 21 May 1861. The original edition did not include her name or even her initials.

# Introduction

## Biography of Elena Ivanovna Molokhovets

Very little is known about the author, just the bare bones of her biography. As far as we know, she left no diaries or correspondence. Molokhovets, née Burman, was born in 1831 in Archangel into a military family. She attended the school run by the Imperial Educational Society for Noble Girls.[20] Her husband was an architect who worked for the Kursk provincial government; he died sometime before 1907. Their surname is unusual and, according to Molokhovets, was limited to members of the immediate family, all of whom were descended from a single source.

The author and her husband had ten children, nine sons and a daughter who died in 1909. The eldest son was already a retired general in 1911, the time of the jubilee edition of her cookbook.[21] Another son, a naval engineer, died in action during the Russo-Japanese war of 1905 and was buried at sea.[22] Several of her grandsons attended military school. The date of Molokhovets' death is unknown. She may have lived for a few years beyond the jubilee celebrations of her book, only to die unnoticed in the tumult of the revolution. Otherwise it is hard to explain the absence of any obituaries or notices of her death.[23]

In the Introduction to the 1914 edition, Molokhovets gave some details about the genesis of the book, its reception by the public, and the problems she had with plagiarizers. Like Avdeeva before her, Molokhovets was harassed by imitators. Beginning with the second edition, she tried to ward off these predators by having each copy of her book stamped with her initials. This attempt at proving authenticity by establishing her own "Good Housekeeping Seal of Approval," as it were, apparently failed, because she used her full name for the fourth edition three years later . She did this with some reluctance, partly because she wanted to protect her privacy. The intellectual and cultural climate of nineteenth-century Russia was not hospitable to women writers, which caused many of them to sign their works only with their initials or to use a pseudonym, often choosing a male name. Given these traditions, Molokhovets was understandably upset when her friends told her that street-hawkers were calling her a "well-known authoress" and using her name to mislead the public into buying discounted and forged cookbooks, passed off as authentically hers. Aside from the injustice of it all, she was indignant that people might think that she herself had abetted the vendors in singing her praises in the streets. Pushed to exasperation, she revealed her own deep political conservatism by protesting that these spurious works were not only a personal affront, they "were humiliating for the virtue of our Orthodox government."[24]

Molokhovets seems to have been somewhat ambivalent about her accomplishment, noting that "the compilation of a cookery book is far removed from real writing." Most educated Russian women of her generation were uninterested in acquiring domestic skills, preferring instead to give their energies to cultural pursuits or philanthropic activities, while the idealistic younger women of the 1860s, the so-called *nigilistki* (female nihilists), were contemptuous of most bourgeois ideals. These young women "wanted to cut through every polite veneer, to get rid of all conventional sham, to get to the bottom of things."[25] They fled from their families to work in the cities or among the peasants in remote villages. Not for them were such mundane goals as learning to bake a perfect baba. The ideals of these young nihilists must have been anathema to Molokhovets, who seems to have been an unassuming woman dedicated to her family and who, particularly in her later years, became increasingly conservative and outspoken in her support of the Orthodox Church and the Tsar. These views are shown not only in her pamphlets and writings (see Bibliography), but also in the letters she included in the 1914 Introduction, most of which came from the privileged members of society, a professor's wife, the widow of a lieutenant general, an archpriest, a marshal of the nobility, a certain Princess Anna and—more modestly—the captain of a gunboat on the Volga.

Whatever Molokhovets' reservations may have been about admitting her authorship, it is clear that by the time of the jubilee celebrations she was justifiably proud of the service she had rendered her compatriots through her cookbook. She seemed to have liked the sobriquet that was given her, *baba-povarikha* (old woman-cook), as well as the image of herself as the bountiful housekeeper in Gogol's early short story "The Old World Landowners." With evident satisfaction she repeatedly quoted the same lines from reviewers (who in turn seemed to plagiarize each other shamelessly): "On this day it is no sin for young and old housewives to honor the venerable jubilarian who could have written ten worthless novels, but preferred instead to create a single good and useful book." Although the sound culinary advice and the tastiness of Molokhovets' recipes were appreciated, her readers stressed the usefulness of her book to the family and to society. Since these same readers firmly believed that thrift and skillful domestic management led to family happiness, they were grateful to Molokhovets for providing instruction for young and inexperienced housewives. One correspondent wrote that "a good kitchen is . . . not an object of luxury. It is a token of the health and well-being of the family, upon which all the remaining conditions of life depend." The maintenance of the family's physical and spiritual welfare was, of course, the woman's task. For some of Molokhovets' readers, family happiness seemed to consist of little more than a well-fed, contented husband. The editorial staff of *Novoe vremja* [New time], for instance, noted that "she had nurtured and fattened up exactly 250,000 Russian husbands for exactly that number of copies of her book had been printed."[26]

No summary of the letters included in the 1914 Introduction would be complete without reference to the ladies of the Smolensk Society.[27] According to the testimony of the members, *A Gift to Young Housewives* saved many families that otherwise would have been destroyed by drunkenness and loose living. Thanks to Molokhovets' advice, these young women created such cozy homes that their husbands and fathers had not been tempted to run off to "restaurants and cafés with their dangerous enticements that break down the family."[28] Such ideas, of course, were not uniquely Russian. Similar sentiments were expressed, for example, in an article in the *New England Kitchen Magazine* for October 1897. According to that essay, a cooking teacher in San Francisco asked her pupils to describe the benefits of cooking lessons, and was delighted when "a 'serious, sweet-faced' little girl promptly explained that 'if we knew how to cook lots of nice things, and what kinds of foods were "healthy," the men and boys would like to stay home more, and not go to saloons so much.' "[29] The Smolensk ladies firmly believed in the virtues of domesticity. They closed their letter by dismissing "the unhappy priestesses of fashion and light-minded gaiety" and noted that "among those who have signed this address you will not find anyone who is emancipated from domestic work. For us, the rational thriftiness of bees is more appealing."

## Influence of the Russian Orthodox Church

The Russian Orthodox Church had a profound influence on the formation of cuisine in Tsarist Russia. Up until the Bolshevik Revolution in 1917, Russian cooking developed along two parallel tracks with separate foods for meat days and for fast days. Since Orthodox believers were required to fast nearly two hundred days per year, the cuisine developed into a diet of opposites with frequent alterations between fasting and feasting.[30]

The Church prescribed four major fasts per year, the most important of which was the seven-week Great Fast preceding Easter. The Trinity or Whitsun Fast lasted from eight to forty-two days; it began fifty days after Easter and continued until June 29, which was the Feast of Peter and Paul. The third fast of a fortnight's duration preceded the Assumption of the Virgin in mid-August. The Christmas or Advent Fast lasted for forty days; it began November 15 and ended on December 25. In addition, all Wednesdays and Fridays were treated as fast days except that fasting was prohibited during Easter week, Whitsun week, and the twelve days after Christmas.[31]

On these fast days it was forbidden to eat any meat or meat products, including eggs, milk, and cheese. The truly devout—as well as the wretchedly poor—also gave up fish. Wine and spirits were sometimes given up, but more often not. Finally, it should be noted that travelers to Russia in the seventeenth century told of sugar being proscribed because it was refined with animal products.[32] Two hundred years later, these rules were still in place, but signs of erosion were apparent, especially among the upper classes. Most people still fasted rigorously, but much less frequently. Fishless meals, in particular, were on the decline. Indeed, fasting had become associated with fish, not the absence of it. And by the nineteenth century, all traces of the prohibition against sugar had vanished.[33]

Alphonse Petit, a French chef who worked in Russia for twelve years in the mid nineteenth century as *chef de cuisine* for Count Panin, then minister of justice, observed that the fasts did not dampen in the least the Russian penchant for entertaining. Providing a suitably elegant fast day dinner, however, put quite a burden on the chef, especially for anyone unfamiliar with the Russian culinary tradition.[34] A brief glance at one of Petit's fast day menus shows how elaborate those dinners could be.

*Potage rossolnick d'esturgeon*
*Coulibiac aux siguis*
*Aspic de sterlets sauce raifort*
*Côtelettes de poisson à la pojarski*
*Lentilles à la maître-d'hôtel*
*Perches frites*
*Compote de poires et prunes*[35]

The fast day menus in *A Gift to Young Housewives* allow us to reconstruct the basic pattern of fasting in a prosperous but not aristocratic household by showing us who fasted, how frequently, and what was consumed. Typical fast day menus for the family were as follows:

*Mushroom and sturgeon marrow pirog*
*Sturgeon head soup*
*Potatoes with herring*
*Cranberry kissel*

*Plum soup with wine*
*Pike in yellow sauce*
*Potato cutlets with mushroom sauce*
*Compote made with odds and ends*

While Molokhovets followed the strict rules of Orthodox fasting, her meals were not particularly abstemious. No more than three or four dishes were served at these dinners, but the Lenten fast was not seen as an excuse for belt tightening. Her use of imported ingredients and expensive native ones—oranges, lemons, dried fruits, nuts, sturgeon, and wines—put these meals well beyond the means of ordinary folk. By the twentieth edition of 1897, fast day meals became even more luxurious with such dishes as sterlet with truffles, salmon *en papillote*, apple *pirog à la reine*, and toast points with apricot purée and Madeira.[36]

Fasting was apparently more important for the servants than it was for the family. Fully half of the space allotted to menus for the servants was devoted to fast day dishes. By contrast, in the first edition of Molokhovets, the family's meat day dishes outnumbered its fast day dishes by perhaps as much as one hundred to one. The servants' diet, not surprisingly, was poorer and more monotonous than the family's, but both master and servant ate a number of the same dishes. These included soups like mixed meat soup, borshch, sauerkraut *shchi*, potato soup, dried pea soup, and cold spinach soup with salmon, as well as such homely standbys as thick buckwheat kasha, fried fish, fried potatoes, and vinaigrette—a kind of potato and beet salad.

The opposite side of fasting, of course, is feasting. The meaning of each is intensified by the existence of the other. The apex of the Russian ecclesiastical calendar was the progression from Butter Week, or Carnival, through the Great Lenten Fast to the joyous celebration of Easter. Butter Week was traditionally a gay, frivolous holiday, the time for a last fling of intense merrymaking before people settled down to the somber austerities of Lent. Great fairs were held, theaters were erected, and steep ice hills for sliding were constructed for the amusement of the people. Everyone took part in the festivities; part of the annual orgy was to consume vast quantities of blini (yeast-leavened pancakes) smothered in butter and sour cream, two favorite ingredients that were banished from the Russian table during Lent. The feasting continued for a full week; forks were put down only at the pealing of the midnight bells announcing the commencement of the Great Fast. For seven weeks, the devout consumed no meat, eggs, or dairy products. Then, again at the stroke of midnight, the privations ended and people gave themselves over to the celebration of Easter and the keenly anticipated pleasures of the Easter table (see the Easter menu at the end of Mealtimes and Menus).

### Eastern Influence on Russian Cuisine

Russian foodways have been influenced from the East almost since the dawn of recorded history; to this day the cuisines of Central Asia and the Caucasus are still affecting culinary developments in European Russia. Despite the significance of these Eastern influences, they have not received much attention in the scholarly literature.[37] According to the Soviet food historian N. I. Kovalev, the Russians learned the art of making raised bread from the Scythian nomads, who came from Central Asia and who ruled southern Russia for over three hundred years from the seventh century B.C. The Scythians were displaced by the Sarmatians, another nomadic tribe from central Asia, who ruled until the beginning of the third century A.D. It was during the Scytho-Sarmatian period that Greek civilization developed around the Black Sea and in the Russian steppe. Instead of destroying the Greek colonies, the Scythians and the Sarmatians traded vigorously with the Greeks.[38] I suspect that if the Scythians did not discover the secret of leavened bread themselves, they may have learned about it from the Greeks before passing it on to the Russians. Going back one link in the chain, the Greeks had acquired the skill from the Egyptians, who already had professional millers and bakers by about 2000 B.C.[39]

Another Eastern influence on the old Russian diet was koumiss or fermented mare's milk. The nutritive value of koumiss was known since ancient times to many Asian people, especially the Kazakhs, Kirgiz, and Bashkirs. The Greek historian Herodotus reported in the fifth century B.C. that the Scythian nomads regularly made *koumiss* and carefully guarded the secret of its production. In the old Russian chronicles, *koumiss* was called *mlechnoe vino* (milk wine), a name which corresponded to the old medical term for this drink, *vinum lactis*.[40] Despite the widespread appreciation for the curative properties of mare's milk in early times, as well as more recently, the Orthodox Church forbade the eating of horse flesh or the drinking of mare's milk in the seventeenth century; at that period, those items, among others, were considered *pogano* or unclean.[41]

The next major contact with the East that affected Russian cuisine occurred nearly a thousand years later with the opening of trade with Constantinople in A.D. 945 and the introduction into Russia of rice and such spices as cloves and pepper. More important for Russian cuisine, however, was the Mongol invasion in 1237. Mostly Turkic in origin, but known generally as Tartars, these invaders subjugated the native population for the next two and a half centuries. Despite their generally destructive impact upon Russian society, the Tartars enriched the Russian cuisine in several important ways, most significantly by reopening the old Silk Road to China which allowed the introduction of new spices; some of them, notably saffron and cinnamon, ultimately became central flavoring elements in Russian cuisine.[42] The Englishman Samuel Collins, who lived in Moscow from 1660 to 1669 as personal physician to Tsar Alexis, the father of Peter the Great, noted that cinnamon was "the Aroma Imperiale" and that the Tsar liked to drink a little cinnamon water at his meals, or "oyl [*sic*] of Cinnamon in his small beer."[43]

Even more important than the spices, the Tartars brought with them from China the art of fermenting cabbage to make sauerkraut.[44] Cabbage, of course, had long been an important vegetable in northern Europe, but the Russians had not developed the skill for preserving it in salt or brine. Once introduced by the Tartars, fermented cabbage or sauerkraut quickly became a dietary staple throughout northern and central Europe. According to the Polish scholar Anna Kowalska-Lewicka, fermented vegetables were so important to the Poles and their Eastern neighbors that the Lithuanians even "worshipped a god of pickled food called Roguszys."[45] The Russians may not have actually worshipped sauerkraut and other pickled vegetables, but their cuisine is unthinkable without them. Indeed, the Russian peasants mostly survived on a diet of kasha and *shchi*, made of sauerkraut, not fresh cabbage.

As historians well know, the subjugation in the sixteenth century of the Mongol khanates of Kazan (1552–57) and Astrakhan (1556), and of Siberia (1582) had far-reaching political and economic consequences for the Muscovite state. Pointing to the impact of these developments on culinary history, Darra Goldstein has suggested that with the annexation of these vast territories "Eastern foods were more substantially integrated into the Russian national cuisine."[46] As the Russian explorers and settlers spread out into these fertile new lands, they had to adapt their diet to local circumstances; in time some of these foods lost their novelty and became fundamental components of the Russian kitchen.

Tea was the most significant of these new foodstuffs, but this beverage caught on very slowly in Russia, partly because of its scarcity and expense, but also because the Russians were suspicious of foreign novelties. In 1638, gifts of tea were sent by the Mongol Khan to the Russian Court, but Tsar Mikhail Fedorovich reputedly "objected that tea was an unknown and superfluous article in Russia" and that he would prefer the equivalent in sables.[47] After its introduction in the mid seventeenth century, tea remained scarce until 1725 when the establishment of Kiakhta as a trading post on the Sino-Russian border boosted Russian imports.[48] The long overland route—which in the 1860s still took one to two hundred days—and the frequent disruptions in trade kept the price high and delayed the spread of tea drinking in Russia for another hundred years.[49] Although imports rose sharply at the beginning of the eighteenth century, prices tumbled significantly only with the opening of the Chinese commercial ports to Russian traders in the late 1860s. Once the Kiakhta monopoly on the tea trade was broken, the demand for the newer, cheaper varieties (the so-called Canton teas) soared, turning tea into a serious rival of *kvass* as the Russian national beverage.

Despite the wider availability of tea, peasants were puzzled enough by the unfamiliar product for the subject to turn up in songs of the period. One such song tells of an unlucky house serf who was ordered to prepare tea by his master, and not knowing what to do with the leaves, seasoned the brew with pepper, onion, and parsley, the traditional Russian seasonings. When he was abused for his concoction, he decided it was because he forgot the salt.[50] Regardless of such incidents, cheap teas began to circulate ever more widely and, after the 1870s, even began to displace spirits among the working classes. According to Smith and Christian, "It was in the late nineteenth century, too, that 'for tea' (*na chai, na chaek*), rather than 'for vodka,' became the set expression for a tip."[51]

The romance of Russian tea drinking is intimately associated with the samovar. After its introduction in the late eighteenth century, the samovar was quickly adopted by the Russian gentry and became an integral part of their tea-drinking ritual.[52] The preparation of the samovar and the sound of its hissing became as culturally laden in Russian literature as the teakettle whistling on the hob in English literature. The origins of the samovar are unclear. In appearance it resembles an English urn for serving tea, but with its internal tube for burning charcoal, its construction is more like a Mongolian hot pot. Some scholars have speculated that the Russian samovar was probably modeled after "the Western European wine fountain which had a similar shape and also a central cylinder which held ice to keep the surrounding wine cool."[53] The samovar became a common motif in nineteenth-century Russian painting; splendid examples can be seen in Vladimir Makovskij's painting "A Gathering of the Nightingale Watchers" (1872–73) and Vasilij Maksimov's "All in the Past" (1889).[54]

Unlike the samovar, the Eastern origin of noodles and ravioli-like preparations

in Russia is less debatable. Both the words and the products show their Eastern roots. The Russian word for noodles, *lapsha*, comes from Turkic instead of "the Germanic *nudel* from which both the English *noodle* and French *nouille* derive."[55] According to Kovalev, the word for small Siberian dumplings, *pel'meni*, comes from Finno-Ugric while their shape and fillings resemble the Central Asian *chuchvar* and *manti*, the Turkish *borek*, and the Georgian *khinkali*.[56] Only *vareniki*, another type of filled dumpling, show their Slavic origins directly since the name derives from the verb *varit'*, to boil. *Vareniki* are prevalent in the Ukraine and are more likely to have entered Russia across the Polish border from Eastern Europe and Austria-Hungary. Vermicelli and macaroni were both later imports from Western Europe. Dal', the great Russian lexicographer of the nineteenth century, defined *vermishel'* (vermicelli) as *ital'janskaja lapsha* (Italian noodles) and *makarony* (macaroni) as *trubchataja lapsha* (tubular noodles) or *ital'janskaja trubki* (Italian tubes).[57]

With the incorporation of the Mongol khanates into the Muscovite state, the Russians finally acquired new and fairly dependable sources of fresh and dried fruits, some of which were unfamiliar to them. In addition to fresh lemons, raisins,

Opposite: Mid-nineteenth-century Russian samovar.
Copper with silver chasing. From *Russkie samovary*
(Leningrad, 1971). Above: Samovar in the shape of
a cock, from a print by N. Nikonov. From *Motivy
russkoj arkhitektury* (St. Petersburg, 1879).

dried apricots, and figs were all adopted at this time.[58] Watermelons, perhaps because of their size, were slower to reach Moscow. We know that three hundred melons were sent from Astrakhan to the capital in 1658.[59] These apparently pleased Tsar Alexis, who loved rare plants and tried to obtain them from other countries, because in 1660 he issued an ukase ordering the cultivation of watermelons in southern Russia.[60] Despite this encouragement from the Tsar, watermelons could not have been very common in the seventeenth century, even at Court. Soon after Peter I became Tsar in 1682, he was presented with a watermelon at Kamyshin, a town on the Volga River, and reputedly he was astonished that such fruits were produced on Russian soil.[61]

Two other non-Western borrowings deserve mention. One was the introduction of a whole range of very sweet new desserts and sweetmeats such as fruit drops, halvah, and Turkish delight. Also introduced were new jams made from vegetables, preparations like carrots preserved with honey and ginger, and radishes in treacle or syrup.[62] These Eastern influences are reflected in Molokhovets' recipes for Carrots in syrup (#2089, 2090, 2631), Walnuts in syrup (#2087), and Lettuce stalks preserved with ginger (#1986). Her numerous recipes utilizing rose petals come from the same tradition.

Spit-roasted meats are one of the oldest methods of cooking. For Russians, shashlik—pieces of lamb or mutton impaled on a skewer or sword and roasted over an open fire—was associated with the Caucasian mountain tribesmen and became popular in Russia after the conquest of the Caucasus in the nineteenth century, when the region began to be romanticized in the works of Pushkin, Lermontov, and Byron.[63] European and Russian travelers then began to flock to the Caucasus and Central Asia, and there is hardly a memoir that does not testify to the excellence of the melons and the savoriness of the shashlik. Alexandre Dumas, no admirer of Russian cooking, waxed eloquent over a delicious shashlik prepared for him by a poor Armenian family in Astrakhan.[64] Of the few dishes for mutton or lamb included by Molokhovets, only Turkish pilaf (#741, 741a) and Mutton shashlik (#742) show an Eastern influence.

### French Influence on Russian Cuisine

In the early eighteenth century, Peter the Great instituted a series of reforms to end his country's isolation. One unanticipated result was a decisive change in Russian cuisine, at least for the upper classes. According to the Soviet food historian V. V. Pokhlebkin, both the upper and lower classes in Russia had formerly eaten the same kind of national dishes, although to be sure the upper classes had always eaten a wider variety of better foods. With the opening of Peter's "window to the West," however, a sharp divergence occurred. The lower classes retained their traditional dishes, while the Court and nobility began to accept unfamiliar foods along with new Western ideas. The first important foreign influences on Russian cuisine were German and Dutch, followed by Swedish. Soon thereafter French culture became predominant in Russia, in the kitchen as well as the drawing room.[65]

Russian cuisine was transformed by the French chefs who began to stream into the country after Peter's reforms to work for wealthy Russian families, mostly the nobility. These chefs introduced new dishes, but more importantly their expertise and skill with native Russian ingredients revolutionized Russian dining. An early arrival was Formay, a chef employed by two Empresses, Anna Ivanovna (1730–1740) and Elizaveta Petrovna (1741–1761).[66] More chefs found employment during the reign of Catherine the Great (1762–1796), a noted Francophile, and by the beginning of the next century, anyone in Russia with social pretensions had hired a French chef. Martha Wilmot, a young Irish woman who lived in the household of Princess Dashkova from 1803 to 1808, wrote home from St. Petersburg about the Russian infatuation with everything French. "For example, everything is shocking for dinner that is not dress'd by a French Cook, every Boy & girl awkward who are not Educated by French People, every dress inelegant that is not

Parisien, etc. etc."[67] Indeed, like the old Countess from Pushkin's *The Queen of Spades* who asked in astonishment, "Are there any Russian novels?" visitors to Russia began to wonder, "Are there any Russian dishes?"[68]

No discussion of French chefs in Russia would be complete without reference to Antonin Carême, the greatest of all French chefs in the nineteenth century. More is made of his relation with the Russian court, however, than the facts support. Contrary to many accounts, he never worked in Tsar Alexander's kitchens in St. Petersburg. His influence on the development of Russian cuisine was primarily indirect, either through his writings or through his followers. He worked for the Tsar only while the latter was in Paris for the peace negotiations in 1814 and 1815 and later during the Congress of Aix-la-Chapelle in 1818. The Tsar admired Carême's work and several times offered him employment at the palace in St. Petersburg, offers that Carême did not immediately accept. When Carême finally decided to go to Russia, he arrived just as the Tsar was departing for an extended visit to Archangel; under palace regulations, he could not be hired until the Tsar's return. Carême used his free time to explore the capital and the palace kitchens, where he discovered that due to past abuses by the staff, a rigorous surveillance of all the kitchen personnel had been instituted. Carême was profoundly disillusioned by what he saw and, not wishing to associate with the corrupt staff nor submit to such humiliating vigilance, the chef, ignoring all entreaties to stay, decided to return to France almost immediately.[69]

French cooking was so prevalent among the upper classes that there were not enough French-born chefs to fill the demand. Wealthy Russians began to send their serfs to work under French chefs in Moscow and St. Petersburg, and a few were even sent to France for their training. Some of these peasants were allowed to work in the city, provided they remitted to their masters the required *obrok* or quitrent, which was a payment in kind or in money. Others were sold after they had completed their training.[70] Count Rostov in Tolstoy's *War and Peace*, for instance, spoke with satisfaction of paying a thousand rubles for Taras, a serf who prepared savory hazel grouse sautéed in Madeira for his daughter Natasha's name day dinner.[71]

The French influence on Russian cuisine was primarily a matter of technique and of refining native Russian dishes. Russian soups, for instance, had long been an important part of the meal, sometimes the only part. Most were filling, thick, and heavy like *shchi*, unlike the new French soups of puréed vegetables and light, clear broth. The Russians traditionally served large pieces of meat, either roasted or baked, while the French preferred to sauté small pieces of meat or game. The French not only vastly expanded the Russian repertory of sauces, but they also introduced an entirely new range of light, airy desserts including creams, zephyrs, and mousses. Most of these innovations required new techniques of preparing, cooking, and combining ingredients. Extensive chopping and puréeing became fashionable and only the wealthy could support such a labor-intensive cuisine. After all, in the days before electric appliances, a great deal of skill and persever-

Left: Dacha executed in pastillage, a mixture of sugar and gum tragacanth, by Marie Antonin Carême. From Carême, *Le Patissier pittoresque* (Paris, 1854). Right: Architectural drawing for a Russian dacha, 1840. From Pavel A. Mukhanov, *Portfel' dlja khozjaev, ili kurs sel'skoj arkhitektury*, vol. 2 (Moscow, 1840), by permission of the Department of Printing and Graphic Arts, The Houghton Library, Harvard University.

ance were required to make the fish quenelles, the reduced stocks, and the other smooth, puréed foods which were (and still are) the hallmark of French haute cuisine.

Despite the appeal of French cuisine, it was not always accepted, even by the Tsar. When Alexander I went to Paris for the peace negotiations in 1815, he chose to make a symbolic gesture by having Carême prepare and serve to the diplomats on several different occasions that most quintessential of all Russian dishes, cabbage soup. This was not a case of not appreciating French cuisine; it was a matter of emphasizing his nationality.[72] Ideological battles were still being fought over a bowl of soup nearly a century later when Chekhov's protagonist in "Glupyj frantsuz" [The foolish Frenchman] orders a bowl of consommé for himself, while he watches a Russian who he assumes is trying to commit suicide by consuming stack after stack of hot blini.[73]

## Mealtimes and Menus

Traditionally the pattern of Russian mealtimes was dictated by the agricultural cycle. Farming was hard work, and most people ate four and sometimes five meals a day, depending upon the season. The first was *zavtrak* or breakfast, often taken by peasants before dawn; this was followed by *poldnik*—the word means midday, but the meal was a kind of second breakfast; *obed* or dinner was the main meal; and the day finished with *uzhin* or supper.[74] By the nineteenth century, increased urbanization and the influence of European customs caused a change in eating patterns, at least for wealthier Russians. For these people, the day might start with tea or coffee; *zavtrak* now became a kind of light early lunch, "the purpose of which was not to satisfy hunger but to awaken the appetite";[75] and *obed*, the main meal, was served in mid-afternoon. Molokhovets, for instance, directed that the dough for *pirozhki* and babas be started at eight or nine o'clock in the morning so that the pastries would be ready for dinner at three or four in the afternoon (Remarks, Chapter 17). Guests left promptly after dinner, often attending another round of parties in the evening.[76] The day concluded with supper or an evening tea that was more or less elaborate depending upon the presence or absence of guests. (Molokhovets' description of an evening tea precedes the recipes, below.)

As we turn from progression to content, from the "when" to the "what" of Russian meals, we need to look at period menus, a useful resource that is often overlooked by social historians. In this respect, few collections of menus match those provided by Molokhovets. She included monthly menus for grand occasions plus daily menus for six to eight persons divided into three categories according to the cost. In addition, she provided lists of dishes suitable for children, for hors d'oeuvres (*zakuski*)., and for breakfast, or really lunch (*zavtrak*). She finished with menus for the servants for both meat days and fast days. As a group, the Molokhovets menus are valuable in that they demonstrate the shape of Russian meals under various shades of French influence; they show class differences or what was expendable for economic reasons; they indicate what was available seasonally and how much reliance was placed upon imported foodstuffs; they reveal the extent of the influence of the Eastern Orthodox Church on eating patterns of that period and for that class; and they show what foods were served at holidays, particularly Butter Week and Easter.

On the micro scale, even a single menu can be instructive. The language it is written in, the order of serving, the choice of foods, the methods of preparation (which in turn reveal so much about the equipment in the kitchen and the skill of its staff), the source of the ingredients, the prices—even the incongruities and misspellings—are all part of the story. Taken in this light, menus could be traps for the unwary and were especially treacherous for the socially uninitiated. Russian families with culinary pretensions wrote their menus in French, but these efforts sometimes resulted in either fractured French or mangled Russian. The Parisian-trained Russian chef Radetskij was so dismayed by these linguistic howlers that he composed a series of thirty paired menus, later expanded to ninety, to demonstrate the correct culinary equivalents in French and in Russian.[77] The anonymous author of one imitation of Molokhovets' book, on the other hand, was concerned with more basic problems. In his or her opinion, the writing of menus should be done by the mistress of the household herself; it was too important a task to be delegated to servants. Like Molokhovets, her imitator advised that the same major ingredient should appear only once per meal, that heavy and light dishes should be alternated, and that the same dish should not be served two days in a row. "It was a mistake," the author warned, "to try and serve provisions when they first came into season and as soon as they appeared in the market. A menu planned on those principles would never be good, just expensive. The entire art of menu planning was to know what was best and cheapest."[78]

Economy, however, is relative; and although Molokhovets suffered from what I call the "Save that bit of string" syndrome, she clearly knew how to entertain. Her very human principle was to splurge for guests, but economize for the family. Since sour cream and fresh caviar, the traditional accompaniments for blini during Butter Week, were rather expensive, she advised cutting corners for the family and servants. One thrifty practice was to curdle a mixture of sour cream and milk; another was to beat sour cream into pressed caviar (which was less expensive than fresh) until it became "smooth like thick, fresh caviar" (Remarks, Russian Pancakes, Chapter 11). Such cheeseparing, however, was not for guests. Russians were noted for their hospitality and Molokhovets was no exception. For a formal dinner for twenty-five, she allotted 40 to 60 silver rubles, not including the wine.[79]

### Menu for April

*Oxtail soup and Purée of asparagus soup*
*Yeast-leavened pirozhki with brains*
*Pirozhki of puff-pastry with fish stuffing*
*Spanish wine: Sherry, Madeira, or Marsala*

*Beef in the English style*
*Red wine*

*Fish pâté made from eels, burbot, or crayfish*
*Porter or ale*

*Spinach or other greens, garnished*
*Wine: Rhine, Château-d'Yquem, or Haut-sauternes*

*Pudding of sieved rice or Biscuit with Sabayon sauce*
*Sweet wine: German "Weinstein" or Malaga*[80]

*Champagne sorbet*

# Introduction

*Home-style roast veal with cheese or cherries, or game*
*"Vegetable salad"*[81]
*Champagne*

*Mosaic or pineapple gelatin*
*Liqueurs*

*Fruit*
*Coffee and tea*

Although alcohol was an important part of these formal occasions, its use significantly increased their cost, especially as imported wines were much more expensive than domestic wines.[82] Etiquette, moreover, required that each wine be served in its own distinctive glass, an additional expense that must have been bemoaned by many a housewife besides the frugal author of the imitation of *A Gift to Young Housewives*. Nevertheless, that writer bowed to the current vogue by strongly advising the purchase of blue and other colored glasses that could be passed after dinner for rinsing the mouth.[83] As for the serving of wine, Molokhovets recommended warming wine by placing the bottle in hot sand before dinner and chilling champagne in metal buckets with ice. The bottles of champagne, she said, "must be uncorked skillfully, without noise and without splashing those seated at the table."[84]

Despite the large amount of wine and champagne consumed at formal occasions, no Russian dinner was complete without vodka. And the grander the occasion, the greater the assortment of flavored vodkas offered. Radetskij's formal dinners, for instance, began with *zakuski* and a selection of vodkas in the living room. The variety is bewildering, but presumably no one was expected to taste them all, nor indeed was it likely that all of them would have been served at any one occasion. Nevertheless, he suggested offering guests a choice of white orange, red orange, bitter orange, mint, almond, peach, bitter English, clove, raspberry, cherry, ratafia, bitter Spanish, balsamic, Danzig, rose, anise, wormwood, gold, cinnamon, lemon, caraway, and Crimean vodka, plus Holland gin, cognac, and arrack.[85] Flavored vodkas were usually made at home rather than purchased and many families had their favorite traditional recipes. Molokhovets included nearly seventy recipes for preparing vodkas, brandies, and wines at home. (See Chapters 22 and 23 for details.) Between collecting the honey from the apiary, gathering the fruits and herbs from the garden and the forest, and then distilling, fermenting, and aging the products, making these drinks demanded a great deal of skill, equipment, storage space, and, most of all—time. These drawbacks notwithstanding, homemade liqueurs and flavored vodkas were an important component of the culture, so much so that the tradition of flavoring vodkas at home is still practiced by Soviet families today.[86]

The sheer number of daily menus provided by Molokhovets dwarfs those provided for grand occasions. Her first group of daily menus cost an average of four to six silver rubles per meal and consisted of five or six "luxurious" dishes. These meals usually started with *zakuski* although they were not mentioned on the menus—probably because it was too obvious. The first course was frequently soup accompanied by a dish made with grains such as *pirozhki*, dumplings, or kasha. A cold course, often fish or poultry in aspic, was next, followed by some sort of meat dish. The dinner ended with dessert.

## SAMPLE MENUS

*January 1: Pie stuffed with brains and fish; Bouillon with boiled dumplings; Sterlet in champagne; Stuffed turkey with marinated cherries; and Wine gelatin or Cream torte*

*February 17 (Butter Week): Puréed artichoke soup; Beef in the Portuguese style or "Gourmet" cutlets; Plum pudding; Roast stuffed chicken with "vegetable salad"; and Orange mousse*

*(See above, Influence of the Russian Orthodox Church, for Lenten menus)*

*May 1: Bouillon with sorrel or spinach leaves; Pirozhki stuffed with mushrooms or brains; Turkey in aspic; Crayfish soufflé; Roast duck with "vegetable salad"; and Coffee ice cream and Pistachio torte*

*June 15: Fish pie, Bouillon with crayfish dumplings; Stewed pike; Green peas garnished with crayfish tails; Roast veal or chicken; and Cold berry soup*

*August 1: Bouillon and pirozhki stuffed with rice and root vegetables; Fish aspic with "vegetable salad" and green sauce; Chestnut pudding; Roast or fried snipe with "vegetable salad"; and Ice cream with maraschino liqueur*

*September 15: Puréed turnip soup with duck; Ground beef cutlets; Dumplings with cheese and sour cream; Fried whole veal liver with "vegetable salad"; Boiled milk cream with vanilla and whipped cream*

*November 1: Clear bouillon with croutons; A whole stuffed fried fish chilled in aspic; Rice pudding with crayfish or without; Roast or fried home-style hazel grouse with "vegetable salad"; Cream plombir garnished with oranges in syrup*

*December 1: Bouillon with root vegetables, cabbage, and potatoes; A whole stuffed boiled fish chilled in aspic; Hazel grouse soufflé; Roast or fried hare with marinated beets; Various fruits and berries in gelatin*

For the next group of menus, Molokhovets simply advised the reader to omit one course, thereby reducing the annual cost to an average of three to five silver rubles per dinner. The third group of menus was more modest; it consisted of only three, or sometimes four, dishes and cost an average of two to four silver rubles per meal. What is notable about this last group is their heavy reliance on carbohydrates and grains. For instance, for February 4, she suggested serving Bouillon with potato dumplings, Boiled beef with Italian macaroni, and either Rice or Wheat pudding for dessert; the next day's menu began with a meatless Soup of

Easter table with paskha and kulich. Paper, watercolor, and ink by Boris M. Kustodiev. From *Rus': Russkie tipy B. M. Kustodieva* (1923).

puréed potatoes, followed by Sautéed slices of spit-roasted beef served with puréed lentils, and finished with Deep-fried fritters made with yeast dough.

For Butter Week and Easter, Molokhovets provided only one set of menus instead of three. Then as now, holidays apparently were a time when people would spread as lavish a table as they could afford.

### Easter Table

*Paskha, Kulich, Babas, Mazurkas, Pljatski, Tortes*
*Decorated eggs*
*Lamb made from butter*
*Boar's head, Baked ham*
*Boiled freshly salted ham, Stuffed turkey*
*Cold roast hare, Roast veal, Wood grouse*
*Cold roast antelope or venison, Roast elk, Roast marinated beef*
*Stuffed suckling pig*
*Bread, horseradish, mustard, vinegar, olive oil*
*Various vodkas and wines*
*Cress salad on wooden statuettes; summer-house from cress*
*Baumkuchen*

### Table Service and Settings

For most people, the serving of a grand dinner is nearly as important as what is served. Part of the aesthetic pleasure of the occasion is the spectacle of the service, how the table is laid and the manner in which the dishes are presented. Although variations exist, the basic choice is whether to display a group of dishes on the table or to serve them sequentially. A banquet is expensive to produce whatever the mode of service, but the manner of presentation determines whether more resources are allocated to preparing the food in the kitchen or serving it in the dining room.

Fashions in table service come and go. Medieval banquets in Western Europe began with a fanfare. After a ritual hand-washing, the guests were seated and only then were a succession of dishes brought to the table, each heralded with a further flourish of trumpets.[87] By the seventeenth century, the emphasis had shifted in

Europe from the medieval idea of sequential service to a static display of dishes arranged on the table in an artful pattern. This new mode of serving became known as *service à la française*.

To produce a grand dinner of three courses in the French style called for tremendous organization in the kitchen plus a skilled overseer in the dining room to arrange the table. It did not, however, require a large staff for serving the food or an extraordinary outlay for dishes, glassware, and cutlery. For the first two courses, numerous platters of fish, poultry, meat, vegetables, salad, and some sweets were set out; the final course consisted of sweet dishes, fruit, and nuts. The entire table was cleared between courses. Since visual considerations predominated, the individual platters had to be attractive in their own right and contribute to the design as a whole.[88] This meant that the serving platters might be removed, but were not passed. Guests helped themselves to what was near at hand; otherwise they either did without or relied on a helpful neighbor to convey a choice morsel that was beyond their reach. The sumptuous array of dishes was not only delectable to behold, but allowed the diners to gauge their consumption according to what choices were available, confident that no unwelcome surprises were waiting in the wings.

Europeans accustomed to the French service were dismayed when they attended Russian court banquets in the seventeenth century. The lavishness of these banquets was legendary, but the dishes and the Russian mode of service were completely unfamiliar. As one German envoy glumly noted,

> there were neither spoons nor plates on the tables; they first served vodka and exceedingly tasty white bread, then they served various dishes of food, mostly hashes, but badly cooked; among them was a huge pie filled with small fish; the dishes were not served all at once, but one at a time: there were very many of them, but all tasteless, partly from an excessive amount of oil, partly from the honey which the Muscovites use instead of sugar.[89]

The emphasis at Russian feasts was less on elegance than on abundance of food; they were often marathon events lasting eight or more hours. Commonly as many as two hundred dishes were served during the progression of eight or ten courses, each of which featured a single type of preparation such as roasted wild fowl, salted fish, or an assortment of blini or *pirogs*. It would be interesting to know when this custom of serving a sequence of dishes began in Russia and whether it developed within the country or was a foreign borrowing. Nevertheless, by the late eighteenth century, the order of courses had become codified. The meal began with hot dishes (hot soups), followed by cold dishes (cold soup or fish or meat in aspic), roasts (meat or poultry), flesh (boiled or fried fish), savory pies, kasha, and sweet pastries. Sweetmeats were the final course.[90]

With the emphasis upon French culture at the court of Catherine the Great, it is not surprising that the Russian nobility and upper classes were also interested in learning about the French service. Levshin included several detailed monthly menus in his *Slovar' povarennyj* with diagrams for setting the table and arranging the dishes according to the French plan. The dishes themselves were both French and Russian. Most of the meals were divided into four courses, each having nearly as many dishes as people. For instance, at a supper for twenty-four guests in January, twenty-nine dishes plus twelve plates of oysters were served at the first course. This included six different soups and, rather incongruously, two jugs of flowers. The second course had twenty-four dishes mostly of fish or poultry including dishes of carp, salmon, trout, sturgeon, perch, turkey, pheasant, hazel grouse, duck, and pigeons. Another twenty-four dishes appeared for the third course, along with eight different sauces. These were mainly platters of roasted domestic and wild fowl, but also included eight different salads and six bowls of oranges. The meal closed with a final twenty-six assorted platters. Among them were a savory ham pie, a wild boar's head, four dishes of truffles including two cooked in the Italian style and two piled up into pyramids, boiled crayfish, two platters of asparagus, apples in the Portuguese style, a *génoise*, two dishes of blancmange, a pistachio cream, and a chocolate cream. This menu was not exceptional; the others described by Levshin were similarly lavish, scaled according to the number of guests.[91]

The French service was not popular with the Russians, who preferred their own traditions. In 1810 the Russian ambassador to France turned the cultural tables, as it were, by introducing Parisians to dinners served in the Russian style, or *service à la russe*.[92] Instead of placing whole roasts on the table as formerly, meats were now carved at a sideboard and divided into individual portions before being served to the guests; also the dishes and cutlery were cleared by servants after each course and replaced with clean ones. People appreciated the heightened taste of the food which now could be served at the right temperature and at its peak of readiness, but they did not rush to embrace the new Russian service. For one thing, it was visually less appealing than the traditional French service. Also, as Philip Hone, a former mayor of New York, complained in 1838, "one does not know how to choose, because you are ignorant of what is coming next, or whether anything more is coming."[93] Cost was another issue. England's Isabella Beeton considered the Russian service inappropriate for modest households because it required too many dishes and too many servants to carry off properly.

> Dinners *à la Russe* are scarcely suitable for small establishments; a large number of servants being required to carve, and to help the guests; besides there being a necessity for more plates, dishes, knives, forks, and spoons, than are usually to be found in any other than a very large establishment. Where, however, a *service à la Russe* is practicable, there is, perhaps, no mode of serving a dinner so enjoyable as this.[94]

Molokhovets clearly adhered to this tradition, at least for her formal meals, which were served in the Russian style with just one or perhaps two dishes per course (see Mealtimes and Menus in this Introduction). Although her everyday menus are composed as if they were divided into courses, it is not clear how family meals were served. By the 1870s and 1880s the new Russian manner of serving finally became widely accepted in Europe thanks in part to the efforts of a few influential French chefs who had worked in Russia, such as Urbain Dubois. World War I marked the end of the old *service à la française* as of so much else; its demise, according to Charles Ranhofer, the former chef of Delmonico's Restaurant in New York, was due to greatly reduced kitchen staffs in wealthy private homes and to a new taste for a less ostentatious style of living.[95] The name, however, has survived, albeit with a totally new meaning. Ironically enough, French service now means a formal dinner with individual dishes served sequentially—otherwise known as *service à la russe*.

In wealthy Russian households like that of Molokhovets, mealtimes were formal occasions orchestrated according to strict patterns. That Molokhovets included such detailed instructions for setting the table is another small indication that her society was in a state of flux. Etiquette books are inherently prescriptive and often appear when a society and its institutions begin to change markedly; the books are a way of imposing standards when people find the old rules inapplicable but are unsure of the new ones. This was exactly the case in Russia after the emancipation of the serfs; it was a time when the gentry began to lose their former wealth and influence, extended families began to break up into smaller units, and new commercial and professional classes began to develop in the urban centers. The tables of the wealthy were set according to prescribed rules that required a full complement of dishes, glasses, and utensils with the importance of the event determining the elaborateness of the setting. The aesthetics of the day called for a symmetrical and precise laying of the table antithetical in spirit to the impromptu, casual meals that are so common in contemporary American society.[96] Also, households were larger a century ago. Several generations of the family usually lived together under one roof augmented by numerous children (Molokhovets had ten), various impoverished female relatives, a few governesses and tutors, and a steady stream of visitors.[97] With all these people to serve, punctuality at meals must have been somewhat of an issue. Molokhovets' imitator stated unequivocally that "the hours for mealtimes must be set and invariable to avoid chaos. Otherwise," that writer warned, "the servants would never know when to serve what and, because of the unwarranted bustle while preparing the dishes, would waste provisions and firewood unnecessarily."[98]

Dining rooms were usually heated by a separate stove, or even two if the room was very large. Tending these stoves required considerable attention—firewood had to be supplied, ashes had to be emptied, and the fire lit and nurtured at the appropriate time.[99] Standards of comfort, however, are relative. Most English travelers complained of the stuffiness of Russian interiors during the winter, but Lady Londonderry came across the opposite situation—verily the Russian equivalent of our modern air-conditioned restaurants.

Introduction

> We dined at Monsieur Laval's, an old Frenchman who has been fifty or sixty years
> in Russia and had married a great heiress. He has a magnificent house on the
> English Quay, with a very fine collection of pictures. The dinner was *tres recherché*
> but the dining room was exceedingly cold and I was told this was a precaution that
> gourmands take that they may the better enjoy their dinner and be able to eat a
> greater quantity.[100]

Like other cookbook writers of the period, Molokhovets included precise instructions for setting the table for *zakuski*, dinners, and suppers as well as the evening tea. In most cases she described both formal and less formal presentations. *Zakuski* were to be set out on a round table near the door of the dining room or in an adjacent room. A lazy susan divided into compartments was desirable for a formal presentation while on less formal occasions it was permissible to set individual bowls around the table provided they were arranged symmetrically. Several pitchers of vodka, each with its own label, were placed on a tray with glasses in the center of the table. On more formal occasions, four decanters, each surrounded by a matching set of glasses, were set out on the table, one decanter at each point of the compass. The care with which the plates, napkins, and utensils were displayed also signaled the importance of the event.

Formal dinners were expensive affairs, and the table appointments were correspondingly lavish.[101] According to Molokhovets, the table was to be covered with a cloth of "blazing whiteness" with illumination provided by candelabra or lamps. The centerpiece should be a glass or silver étagère filled with fruit, candies, and fresh flowers. Molokhovets suggested filling the bottom level with oranges, mandarins, and bunches of grapes, the next layer with apples, pears, and more grapes, the third layer with candies, and the top layer with "a luxurious bouquet" of fresh or artificial flowers such as lilacs, lily-of-the-valley, or fuchsias and greens.[102] Several vases of decreasing size filled with more flowers were placed on either side of the étagère in addition to a small vase of fresh flowers at each setting or at least in front of the honored guest, such as the person whose name day it was.[103] For simpler dinners, pots of live flowers such as hyacinths were sometimes used. Molokhovets advised decorating the pots with colored cigarette papers—light rose, light green, or even white—and matching ribbons. Alternatively, the flower pots could be inserted into overturned Chinese lampshades which could be purchased for just 15 kopecks a pair. This profusion of fresh fruits and flowers could be horrendously expensive, but it was an indulgence that Molokhovets shared with many of her compatriots. Given their long, harsh winters, the Russian love of flowers, a trait that is still apparent today, is understandable. The popular illustrated magazines *Niva* and *Nov'* regularly included articles on the culture of household plants and numerous books on the subject were published in nineteenth-century Russia.[104] Chapters on the maintenance and display of house plants and flowers were also occasionally included in household manuals and cookbooks. Molokhovets' imitator, for instance, devoted a major portion of the book to gardening and house plants. This book recommended distributing flowers

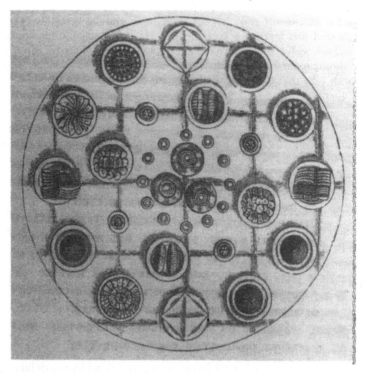

Top: Table set for serving zakuski. Bottom: Table set for a formal
dinner. From Molokhovets, 1897.

around the house, especially near the stove in the dining room, so that their odor
would permeate the room during dinner—which may seem an unusually extrava-

gant touch for this otherwise frugal author, but in fact this writer was as interested in flowers as in food, notwithstanding the purloined title of the book.[105]

At formal dinners monogrammed napkins were folded so that with one end tucked under the dinner plate the monogram would hang down over the edge of the table. A small plate to the left of the main plate was intended for bread and for the *pirozhki* served with the soup. Ideally each guest was provided with a small 1 kopeck roll of finely ground wheat flour, a 1 kopeck French roll, and a slice of black bread. Crystal or silver knife rests were only used on informal occasions; they were unnecessary at more formal dinners since the dirty utensils were collected after each course and replaced with clean ones. Small saltcellars or a pair of them with salt and pepper were set out at every place or every other place.[106] Pitchers of water and bottles or jugs of wine were also placed on the table for those who wanted it. Additional wines, beer, *kvass*, and mead were arranged on a table near the door next to another table holding the clean plates and extra utensils needed for the meal. Servants were expected to collect the soiled plates and utensils and immediately replace them with clean ones. Shortly after diners left the table, black coffee was served in another room, accompanied by minute wineglasses of sweet liqueur.

Fads played a role in table service as in other aspects of life. Molokhovets disparaged the recent affectation of eating all sweet dishes, even ice cream, with a fork instead of a spoon. She expected that the fashion would "soon change because it is not only awkward, but even harmful to compel many lovers of ice cream to swallow it too cold. And," she added, "a fork is worthless if the ice cream has melted only slightly." This vogue of serving very cold ice cream was in part a result of the Victorian rage for using elaborate molds. The foods when unmolded were aesthetically pleasing, but the unnatural shapes could be controlled only by adjusting the temperature, adding gelatin, or some combination of the two. These frozen presentations were difficult to serve and were liable to slide around disconcertingly, hence Molokhovets' instructions for lining the platter with a clean white napkin before unmolding the ice cream.[107]

## Image of a Russian Household

A good cookbook is more than the sum of its parts, more than a simple stringing together of individual recipes. In the case of *A Gift to Young Housewives*, the aggregate of recipes vividly shows the effort required to run a prosperous household in nineteenth-century Russia. Although traces of city life are evident in the later editions of the book, reflecting Molokhovets' move from Kursk to St. Petersburg, the primary image is that of a large rural household staffed by an army of servants. The sense of plenitude that emanates from the book is one of its most appealing features. Its pastoral overtones suggest a better and simpler life, insulated from the cares of the city. It is a vision of an idyllic countryside where circumstances are expansive rather than cramped or constrained. What we find is

Detail from "All in the Past." Oil on canvas by V. M. Maksimov, 1889.
State Tretjakov Gallery, Moscow.

a domestic world untouched by political issues, a society where there is no unrest among the former serfs, no threat of anarchy, no assassination of the Tsar. Ignorance, hardship, and poverty are all muted. This is a magic realm overflowing with the bounty of nature, a land where the fields and orchards yield abundant crops, the woods and marshes reverberate with the sound of game, and the ponds and rivers teem with fish. Even the harvest is gathered effortlessly. Or so it seems.

The simplicity and serenity of the above images, which provide the implicit backdrop of Molokhovets' world, are as misleading as they are beguiling. Life was never that easy, especially in a premodern household where the domestic work was long and onerous. Even in a wealthy or prosperous family, someone had to prepare the food and put it on the table. This involved tasks and skills that we now have all but forgotten. Survival depended on preserving the harvest and storing it away for consumption during the long winter months. Every day had its tasks, but the basic rhythm of the household was seasonal and was dominated more by the calendar than the clock. To produce a meal today demands almost no forethought and little effort beyond a quick trip to the store to purchase the ingredients, followed by a hasty preparation, which often entails no more than chopping, heating, or chilling. The source of water is not an issue, the heating of the stove is not a problem. By contrast, most households of the nineteenth century, Russian or otherwise, relied on ingredients that were domestically produced and preserved. Store-bought goods were luxuries; usually they were purchased reluctantly and used sparingly. And water, stoves, and storage were all issues to be reckoned with.[108]

## Water

The presence or absence of running water made an enormous difference to the running of a household, as did the quality of the water and its temperature. Molokhovets often added a modifier to the word "water" in her recipes by calling for "rain water," "well water," "river water," or even "warm water." The use of these attributes signaled that the source of the water was important and that it was not to be taken for granted. Both the temperature and the composition of the water varied according to its source. The threat of contamination was always an issue, of course, but beyond that pond water was liable to be muddy and stagnant, well water might be too hard, and river water might be unavailable at certain seasons either because it froze in the winter or dried up in the summer.

When making a syrup for Rose blossom jam, Molokhovets directed the reader to cook sugar with rosewater, "or lacking that, ordinary river water" (#1959). When preserving lemons, she soaked them in [well] water for twelve days, then "covered them with cold river water and cooked them until they could be pierced with a straw" (#1970). After soaking dry-cured stockfish in an alkaline solution for four days and then in a mixture of water and quicklime for a fifth day, she soaked the fish for a final day "in river water, changing the water thrice during the day" (#969). Molokhovets preferred river water over well water. That may have been a feature of the particular locality where she lived, but wells were often problematic since they were so susceptible to contamination.[109] According to Molokhovets, scraped beets should be marinated "in a vat of river water, or lacking that, well water" (#2603). Similarly, "Soft river water must be used to prepare mead. In an extreme case, well water may be used, but it must be soft enough for soap to lather and suitable for washing linens" (#2218). She mentioned spring water (*kljuchevaja voda*) only once, when she mixed it with vodka and honey to make ordinary vinegar (#2219). Rain water, surprisingly, was also mentioned only once when it was used for making Grain vinegar (#2224).

The temperature of the water was as important as its quality. After churning, the butter had to be "washed clean in water as warm as river water in the summer" (#2272). When preparing wheat starch, which was a long and arduous process, the grains were soaked for nine days, "covered at first with warm water (*letnjaja voda*) and then with cold water, each time using fresh water" (#2269). Water was heated either on the stove or in the samovar. Peaches, for instance, were scalded with "boiling water from the samovar" (#1967).

River water presented other problems. Sometimes it was so muddy that it was unfit for drinking, as when the ice broke up in the spring and during the heavy rains in autumn. This situation could be alleviated by constructing a cistern for clarifying the water, which amounted to little more than a wooden barrel filled with alternate layers of stones and fine sand.[110] An American cookbook of a slightly earlier period (1854) included an engraving of a metal cistern for filtering water for cooking or table use among the " 'requisite articles' for running a household in mid-nineteenth century America."[111] In the 1897 edition Molokhovets included floor plans for houses and apartments that showed taps for hot and cold water in the bathrooms. She advised that the water should either be piped in from the kitchen or stored in a tank near the stove in the bathroom and heated as required.[112] The use of taps within the household, however, did not necessarily imply running water any more than running water depends upon electricity. Nevertheless, its widespread distribution was not economically feasible before the advent of electric pumps. While some city dwellers in the late nineteenth century might have had water piped into the house, most rural folk were still dependent upon holding tanks filled with buckets of river water or well water.[113]

### Stoves and Ovens

The traditional Russian stove (*russkaja pech'*) was the focus of family life in rural Russia. Occupying nearly a quarter of the living space in a peasant home, these mammoth installations were used primarily for heating, but also for cooking and baking as well as drying fruit and making *kvass*. They were usually made of clay, less often of brick or stone; they weighed between one and two tons and rested on the ground in a corner of the room.[114] Their squarish flat tops provided a cozy niche for sleeping, a coveted place that was usually reserved for the elderly, the sick, and the very young in the family. Given the climate, a reliable source of warmth was not to be despised. Johann Kohl, a German who traveled around Russia in 1837, noted how the Russian peasants basked in the comfort of the stove.

> Round [the stove] are placed benches, where at their leisure the inmates may enjoy the luxury of increased heat, for to these denizens of the north the imbibing of caloric is among the highest of enjoyments. In the stove itself, a variety of niches and indentations are made, where various articles are laid to dry, and wet stockings and linen are constantly hanging about it. On the platform, at the top, lie beds, on which, wrapped up in their sheepskin cloaks, the inmates often abandon themselves to the twofold luxury of idleness and perspiration.[115]

These large structures burned fuel very efficiently. They were heated by lighting a wood fire within; cooking or baking began after the fire had burned down and the ashes and coals had been swept out or pushed to one side of the oven. Common equipment included long pokers (*kochergi*), bread peels or shovels (*lopaty*), and rods with a U-shaped fork at the end (*ukhvaty*) for lifting the ordinary earthenware cooking pots (*gorshki*).[116] Few stoves had chimney pipes, instead

Drawing of a large stove faced with ceramic tiles, Poltava Province, Ukraine. Although this model is unusually elaborate, the size and structure are typical of stoves found throughout Russia and Ukraine in the nineteenth century. From V. P. Samojlovich, *Narodnoe tvorchestvo v arkhitekture sel'skogo zhilishcha* (Kiev, 1961).

the exhaust and fumes were left to escape through a hole in the roof or chinks in the walls. Homes without chimneys were called black huts (*chernaja izba*), those with chimneys were called white huts (*belaja izba*). The risk of fire and suffocation due to noxious fumes was considerable, not to mention the discomfort of living with acrid smoke for six months in the year. As early as 1722, during the reign of Peter the Great, an ordinance was passed outlawing the construction of black huts, but they continued to be built throughout the nineteenth century.[117] Kovalev, citing the Russian historian O. M. Rakov, suggested that the Russian peasants kept their flueless stoves, not through conservatism, but because the smoke together with the heavy winter frosts offered a primitive but effective protection against infectious diseases.[118]

The traditional Russian stove also influenced the development of the national cuisine with its preponderance of soups, stews, and dishes that needed long, slow baking. Other processes like frying or sautéing that required quick adjustments of intense heat were impractical and rarely used in Russia before the introduction in the nineteenth century of wood and coal-burning metal stoves with their useful stove-top burners.[119] In 1797, the American inventor Benjamin Thompson, otherwise known as Count Rumford, published his important paper "On the Management of Fire and the Economy of Fuel," which resulted from his redesigning two large hospital kitchens in Verona in 1795. Rumford's "great contribution was to enclose the fires in a big insulated box." His changes so revolutionized kitchen stoves "that they were immediately seized on by hundreds of people all over Europe, and the Count himself suddenly became in great demand as a kitchen architect."[120] In 1802, George Bodley patented the closed range stove in England. By the 1820s these were being manufactured and by the 1840s these so-called kitcheners were widely used in English homes.[121] In Russia, the sixth edition (1848) of Katerina Avdeeva's popular cookbook, *Handbook of an Experienced Russian Mistress of the Household*, included a drawing of an enclosed metal range. According to Avdeeva, this new type of stove takes up so little space that it is "mostly preferred in those homes where there is hardly room for the cook to sit down." Other advantages, in her opinion, were that the stove top saved on cooking fuel and that the heat could be adjusted as needed.[122] The drawbacks of the new stove tops were that they could be used only for cooking and not for heating and that traditional Russian dishes like *kvass* or black bread could not be prepared in them. In the long run, the ease of operation which allowed a greater range of dishes to be prepared seems to have been the decisive factor in the adoption of the new stove tops, since by the end of the century they were widely used both in the cities and in the country.[123]

In *A Gift to Young Housewives* Molokhovets used both the traditional Russian stove and the newer and smaller metal range with its useful stove top. Despite the new equipment, the management of hot coals was still an important kitchen technique that could only be mastered by skill and experience. For best results, Molokhovets advised baking waffles over hot coals (Chapter 13, Remarks). She also grilled meat on a spit before hot coals (#637) and baked puddings after spreading live coals on the lid of the pot (#1170). Another important piece of equipment was the summer oven, which was located outside the main house in the garden or even in a separate summer kitchen. These were particularly common in the Ukraine and in Belorussia, less so in the northern regions of Great Russia. In hot weather when it was impractical to fire up the traditional Russian stove, Molokhovets used its oven as a handy place for storing jams and jellies (Chapter 20, Remarks). This was only possible, of course, when a summer oven was available for ordinary household tasks like baking bread, heating milk for cheese (#2296), baking tortes (#1596), and making apple leather (#2359).

Before gas and electric stoves became available, time had to be allowed for heating up a range or oven with either wood or coal.[124] While a Russian stove provided a long, steady heat with just a single daily firing, the metal ranges were lit only as they were needed for cooking. When making blini, for instance, Molokhovets directed that the stove be lit an hour before cooking (#1252). For *krendels* or *kuliches* made with yeast, she advised lighting the oven after setting the *krendels* to rise for the last time (#1812). According to the imitation *Gift to Young Housewives*, the decision about when to light the stove was too important a matter to be left to the discretion of the servants. The housewife should supervise this activity personally, the author warned, otherwise the stove would be lit either too soon or too late; as a result the rooms would be either too hot or too cold and the hostess would have to "treat her guests to meals that either were undercooked or overcooked."[125]

The ability to determine the temperature of an oven accurately was an important skill before the development of reliable oven thermometers. Usually Molokhovets tested the oven in time-honored ways by watching how quickly paper curled or flour browned.[126] The oven was still too hot for baking pastries if a sheet of paper placed in the middle of the oven immediately turned yellow and burned, but if the paper curled up and yellowed gradually, the pastry could be set in the oven with confidence (Chapter 15, Remarks). Occasionally Molokhovets was more specific, as when she noted that wheat bread should be baked at 60 degrees Reaumur or, in other words, "that the oven had to be much warmer for baking wheat bread than ordinary rye bread" (#2326). Experience and skill were crucial, however, since most of her advice was comparative. To bake Honey spice cakes, for instance, "the oven must be the same temperature as for baking white bread" (#1937); to preserve bottled cherries, the bottles should be set in the oven "after white bread has finished baking" and left there until the oven cools (#2085).

In general, Molokhovets used the Russian oven to process large quantities of raw ingredients harvested from the fields and gardens, produce that underscored her rural circumstances. Her frequent use of hay is redolent of the farm. To prepare stewed cabbage, she began by spreading straw on the oven floor "as soon as rye loaves are removed from the oven." After warning the reader that "the oven should not be too hot or the straw will burn," she set good, firm heads of cabbage on the straw one next to another and left them to stew in the closed oven (#2536). She also finished Real Vyborg *krendels* (a kind of bagel) by baking them on straw spread on the oven floor (#1892). She boiled jars of preserves wrapped in straw to prevent the bottles from knocking against each other (#2053); she tested cakes and fruit with wisps of straw to see if they were done (Chapter 17, Remarks); and she stored eggs and fruit on straw-lined shelves in the cold cellar (#2313 and 2335). She filtered raspberry *kvass* through a barrel filled with fresh straw (#2199), smoked fish over damp straw (#2651), and recommended the American custom of dipping peaches in paraffin before transporting them in chests filled with straw (#2510).

Some of the instructions in *A Gift to Young Housewives* concern artisan production more than preparations for an ordinary family meal. To brew large amounts of *kvass* and beer, for instance, required extensive facilities; the family kitchen would not have sufficed. *Kvass* was important in the peasant diet and was used in many recipes, but it called for a lengthy preparation since the dough for leavening needed to rise for twenty-four hours in a sealed oven (#2185). Beer was less commonly drunk, in part because its production was more costly and required skilled, attentive labor. The drying of the barley or oats on the oven floor was a critical but labor-intensive operation when making beer since the grain had to be constantly mixed with a wooden shovel "to prevent it from burning or roasting even slightly" (#2211). Drying oats for oat flour was another tedious and time-consuming chore. For several days in a row, the oats were dried on the oven floor, but each morning, they had to be swept out of the oven while a new fire was laid. When the oven had reached the proper temperature, the ashes were swept out and the oats were returned to the oven for another round of drying (#2267). Admittedly none of these were daily tasks, but all of them demanded a dedicated use of the stove, which would have precluded its availability for other purposes.

## Food Preservation and Storage

Before the introduction of mechanical refrigeration, ice houses were an important means of preserving food during the warm weather. The benefits of cold for preserving food had of course long been known. The Chinese harvested and stored ice more than a thousand years before the birth of Christ; the Greeks and Romans cooled their drinks with snow and the Romans even dug pits for the long-term storage of snow.[127] The practice of using ice to cool drinks was taken up again by the Italians and Spanish in the sixteenth century, followed by the Italian discovery of how to make water ices in the early seventeenth century. By the end of the century, ice cream had become popular among the upper classes in France and to a lesser extent in England, where the first published recipe for ice cream did not appear until 1718.[128] The popularity of the new frozen and chilled desserts increased the demand for ice among the wealthy and that, in turn, spurred the construction of ice houses. According to Elizabeth David, King Charles II of England had an ice house in Greenwich by 1662; another was built in 1666–67 "when a 'snow-well' was installed at St. James's Palace for the King's brother, James, Duke of York." The London ice house was sunk in the ground and thatched with straw and seems to have been modeled on those the Duke of York had seen while exiled abroad.[129]

By the eighteenth century, the well-to-do in England refrigerated a variety of foods, including meat, in their ice houses, but it was not until the nineteenth century that ice began to be so widely used that it became an important commercial commodity. Partly this was a matter of the growing industrialization and urbanization in Europe and America which meant that more foods had to be transported over longer distances just to feed the population. At the same time, a substantial number of people were changing their eating habits, relying less upon staple grains and more upon perishable foods that required refrigeration.[130] By the mid nineteenth century, large commercial ice houses were being built in English and American cities, while small-scale domestic ice houses continued to serve the needs of rural households. These domestic ice houses were usually dug into the side of the hill or were constructed as separate structures above the ground and away from the main house. Webster seems to have been one of the few English commentators to speculate on the convenience of connecting the ice house with the pantries of the main house or of placing it "in a cellar to which access might

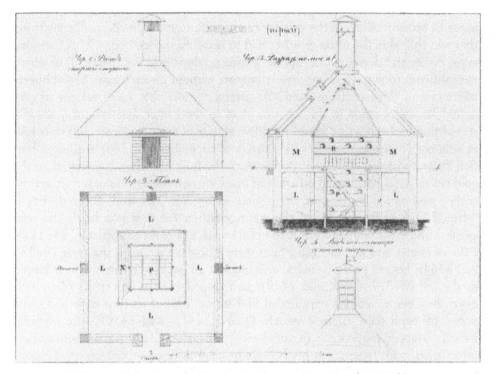

Architectural drawing of a Russian ice house. From Pavel A. Mukhanov,
*Portfel' dlja khozjaev*, vol. 2 (Moscow, 1840), by permission of the
Department of Printing and Graphic Arts, The Houghton Library,
Harvard University.

easily be had."[131] The ice houses were used only for chilling perishable foods and
for storing ice. In the American climate, three or four tons of ice were reckoned
enough "to last the largest household through the season."[132]

The Russians chilled and preserved their food and drink in ice houses long
before their counterparts in Western Europe. The first attested Russian use of the
word "ice house" (*lednik*) in 1482 predates the English by two centuries
(1687).[133] By the 1660s when the English king, Charles II, was building his first
ice house, the Russian Tsar had fifteen ice cellars for storing meat and fish and
more than thirty cellars for storing drinks. All of the "drinks in the cellars stood
on ice which was only changed in March each year."[134] Given the harsh extremi-
ties of their climate, it is not surprising that Russians of all classes became adept
at freezing foods. Frozen fish had long been a regular staple of the Russian winter
markets. By the nineteenth century, ordinary domestic households commonly
stored ice in a pit within their cold cellar (*pogreb*). Usually only large establishments had a separate building just for the storage of ice.[135]

Although Molokhovets says nothing about the construction of an ice house,
she obviously had one available and used it extensively. It must have been enor-

mous to accommodate all the provisions that she stored in it. Basically, anything that was chilled in the warm weather had to be set in the ice house. This included main dishes and desserts, but especially aspics, jellies, and ice cream, all of which were difficult to make and impossible to store without an ice house. Molokhovets was aware of these problems and was careful to note that more gelatin was required for aspics made in the summer than in the winter. For instance, she observed that four calf's feet would yield five glasses of aspic in winter, but only four in summer (Remarks, Chapter 9). Barrels of cucumbers (#2596) and most bottled fruits and juices were kept on ice until the frost and then transferred to the cold cellar. After bottling an infusion of black currant leaves, Molokhovets set the corked and tarred bottles on their sides in an iron box and directed that it "should be kept on ice during the warm weather. An iron box holds the cold better," she explained, "and in it the bottles are less likely to explode" (#2117). Pails of apples and jars of fresh plums were stored on ice until the frost (#2337 and 2364); kegs of pears, cherries, and melons, all packed separately, were buried in the ice (#2379, 2389, and 2420); and tinned copper saucepans filled with pears, oranges, or lemons were sealed and set on ice, but the moisture had to be wiped off each piece of fruit weekly (#2379, 2413, and 2439). Alternatively, lemons, wrapped individually in nonabsorbent paper, could be packed into a chest interspersed with fresh green birch branches before being stored on ice. Lemons packed in this manner required less attention, since they only had to be inspected every two to three weeks (#2437). The kegs of cherries buried in ice would keep as long as one and a half years, but the saucepan of lemons barely lasted three months. In one instance, Molokhovets combined a primitive method of canning with freezing by packing strawberries into tin cans and soldering on the lids with tin before burying the cans in ice (#2479). Aside from chilling prepared dishes and containers of fruit in the ice house, it was also used for storing dairy products, meat, and fish. Again, the quantities are impressive. Numerous barrels were buried in ice, filled with such stores as salted sturgeon, wild ducks, geese, marinated eels, snipe, salted hams, and corned beef (see Chapter 30).

Molokhovets also stored provisions in cold cellars, dry basements (*podval*), and wine cellars, with other small sheds and outbuildings being called into service as needed. Normally the cold cellar was a separate building that usually contained an ice pit, while the dry basement was dug out below the main living quarters of the family. Such industrious housekeeping brings up visions of the landowners in Gogol's *Dead Souls*, where Korobochka could let nothing go to waste and Pushkin's "store-rooms, warehouses, and drying sheds were cluttered with such a world of linens, cloths, sheepskins (both dressed and raw), dried fish of all sorts, and all kinds of vegetables and salted meat."[136] Reading through the list of Molokhovets' provisions, each with its own requirements for storage, one begins to understand the reason for the constant exhortations to unflagging vigilance that one finds in older books of household management. Just keeping track of the inventory must have been a major headache, never mind the regular inspection of goods, the wiping off of moisture from the saucepans of fruit, the upending of barrels of cherries, the picking off of rotten grapes, and the rotating of bacon flitches.

Many foods were buried in sand or earth for storage. Bottles of raspberry juice were overturned and buried up to their shoulders in dry sand (#2038) as were bottles of gooseberry juice. The latter would keep improving for two to three years until, finally, the gooseberry juice was "barely distinguishable from lemon juice" (#2045). Barrels of fermenting cherry brandy were buried in sand for three months (#2101); apple and honey drinks needed to mature for a year in the basement before they were fit to drink (#2123). Sparkling drinks (*shipovki*) required special care. According to Molokhovets, the corked and tarred bottles should be overturned and stored in sand for one to two months in a cold place, but not on ice. "During this time the wine will ferment and, if a bottle or two bursts, it proves that the sparkling wine is ready. If bad corks or ordinary bottles are used instead of champagne bottles," she warned, "most of the bottles will explode" (#2104). Jars of plums were buried one *arshin* deep (= 28 inches) in the earth in the basement, but if wooden kegs were used instead of jars, the kegs had to be covered with tar and submerged in water for storage (#2374). Smoked hams were wrapped with rags and buried as deeply as possible in a storage bin filled with rye (#2684).

In addition to the items that were buried in sand, heads of cabbage (#2528) and cauliflower (#2525) and strings of onions (#2550) were hung from the ceiling along with smoked hams and sausages. Shelves lined the walls and were covered with straw to hold apples, pears, and eggs. Tubs filled with nuts packed in damp sand were stored in the basement (#2452) along with barrels of vinegar and vats of cucumbers and sauerkraut. All these provisions were prepared in large quantities. One recipe for sauerkraut called for shredding sixty-five heads of cabbage (#2531). Beets were stacked in a high pyramid, with the roots to the center and each layer covered with enough sand to hide the tops of the beets (#2604). Carrots were treated the same way (#2630). Garden chicory was stored in the basement for the winter, but three weeks before it was wanted, it was placed in a box of earth, dampened, and set in a warm place to sprout (#2542). Mushrooms were also cultivated in the basement in the winter by planting them in a deep trench of horse manure (#2582).

Of all the provisions, none required more care than the wintering of fresh grapes. Molokhovets described two methods, one taken from a French newspaper, the other, described below, resembling instructions given in an article that appeared in *Nov'* in 1885.[137] The latter method for keeping grapes fresh until May required extensive resources since a room on the second floor of the house had to be given over entirely to the grapes, special shelves were necessary, and each bunch of grapes needed to be sealed in its own glass jar of water. In addition, the grapes required regular inspection and any spoiled grapes had to be "cut off carefully with a pair of scissors and immediately thrown away." The expense and trouble of storing grapes in this way were considerable but, according to Molokhovets, these grapes keep so well "that it is impossible to distinguish them from those just cut [from the vine], and therefore the price for them in both winter and spring is much higher than for grapes kept by other means" (#2410). This is the only instance in the book where Molokhovets speaks of selling agricultural produce. Hovering in the shadow of these elaborate instructions is the question of how the grapes were raised in the first place. Greenhouses or other special facilities are never mentioned in the book, but that does not prove that none were available.

In her book Molokhovets included several floor plans for model houses and apartments. Ample storage facilities were an important feature of these plans since even families who lived in cities or towns relied heavily on regular shipments of produce from their estates in the country. These raw materials admittedly had to be accommodated, but Molokhovets' concept of adequate storage space would dumbfound a modern New Yorker or Muscovite. For houses, she advised constructing the basement with a single door that could be entered only from the storeroom built directly above it. This arrangement she felt would be very convenient because it would allow the housewife, "even if she were not well,"[138] to monitor the gathering of the day's provisions while sitting comfortably at a desk in a heated room without the necessity of going down into the cold basement herself.

### Containers and Utensils

For purposes of discussion, the domestic equipment and utensils mentioned in *A Gift to Young Housewives* may be divided into two groups: storage containers and cooking utensils. Storage containers were rough and numerous; they included a variety of barrels, kegs, vats, tubs, jars, bottles, and carboys. Most were made of wood or glass but tin chests and wicker baskets were also used. The German traveler Kohl noted that the Russians had developed "a peculiar dexterity in wood-carving" and that "many household utensils which with us [Germans] are formed of clay or iron, are carved out of wood in Russia; such as pots, jugs, water-pitchers, etc."[139] Tubs of oak, maple, or even alder were preferred; resinous woods such as spruce or pine were avoided since they affected the flavor of butter and other delicate foods (#2272). The inventory of containers was necessarily large, partly because of the sheer volume of food preserved and partly because some foods, like salted fish and preserved fruits and juices, spoiled quickly after being exposed to the air; hence it was usually advisable to store foods in numerous small vessels rather than a few large ones. In addition, the absorbency of wooden containers limits their adaptability. Cucumber barrels could not be used for any other purpose (#2584) and a separate bread trough was required for each kind of dough (#2326). Fermentation was necessary to preserve the foods, but the process was unreliable and not well understood at this time.[140] What was understood, however, was that wooden vessels could not be interchanged without risk of spoiling the next batch of food. Taste was also a factor in the selection and utilization of storage containers. Fish barrels for this reason were useless for anything else and even these had to be renewed periodically.

Preparing the containers for long term storage required care and attention. The kegs for fermenting sauerkraut were washed and the interior chinks were sealed with a dough made from rye flour before the cabbage and brine were added (#2529). Barrels for storing apples or pears were steamed with black currant leaves (#2354); those for salting cucumbers were steamed with "pure water, dill, chervil, and other fragrant herbs" (#2584). Another method for salting cucumbers entailed covering the bottom of a barrel with a layer of dried and "very clean river sand" before filling the barrel with cucumbers. The process was finished by covering the cucumbers with currant leaves, topped by a final layer of sand (#2593). The sand, of course, kept out the air by sealing the barrel and thereby kept the cucumbers fresh even if somewhat gritty. Preserving with sugar presented a different problem. Since excess moisture caused mildew and spoilage, Molokhovets gave many hints for preserving jams and jellies and even advised washing the bottles for sugar syrups several weeks beforehand to allow time for them to dry thoroughly (Remarks, Chapter 20).

Molokhovets' *batterie de cuisine* was a curious combination of odds and ends and specialized equipment. As mentioned above in the discussion on Russian stoves, the basic cooking pot was the earthenware *gorshok*. Other basic utensils included stewpans, saucepans, skillets, and soup cauldrons. Molokhovets also called into service anything that was handy in the house or just outside the door. She stirred sauces with a bundle of twigs (#314), she measured and reduced liquids, especially soups and preserves, by notching sticks or spills (#v, 1), she cooled her babas on down pillows (Chapter 17, Remarks), and she used a flatiron in place of a salamander for browning meringue (#1441). The homely kitchen stool was another useful item which, when overturned and with a napkin tied to its legs, could be transformed into a giant strainer. If crystal-clear bouillon was needed for company, Molokhovets strained it twice through a napkin tied to the legs of an overturned stool, the second time after "lining a clean napkin with white blotting paper" (#14). The stool was upended again when it was time to make Rose syrup. In this case, boiling water was poured over a pound of trimmed fresh rose petals spread out in the napkin; for the best flavor, Molokhovets cautioned that "the rose petals should just be shaken from time to time, without being pressed" (#2030).

Special tasks like baking required special equipment such as an assortment of large and small tin pans as well as flat iron sheets and paper cases for pastry. Some of these pans must have been very large indeed, since a typical recipe for a baba ³⁄₄ *arshin* (21 inches) tall called for 1 pound of butter, 4 pounds of flour, and 70 egg yolks (#1726). For wine-making, Molokhovets used a spirit thermometer (#2142), numerous champagne bottles, and a great quantity of the best "velvety" corks (#2026). Sometimes she cooked vegetables in silver saucepans (#446), and she had special small skillets for making blini (#1208). She roasted coffee in a brazier (#1418), prepared chocolate in an iron mortar (#2171), and molded *paskha* in a hinged wooden form (#1900). Like her counterparts in England and America, Molokhovets was fascinated with gadgets, appending a list of the most useful at the end of later editions of her book. Among them she delighted in a novel meat grinder with eighteen removable blades called "the ordinary American" that could be purchased for 4 rubles 25 kopecks. She described a modern ice cream maker with interior paddles that churned the ice cream simply by cranking, thereby eliminating the necessity of removing the lid with the attendant danger of salt falling into the cream. The most exotic item among her list of utensils was a portable samovar. She made no pretense that it was useful in the kitchen, but she did point out that it was "especially practical for outings, for hunting, and for long journeys to uninhabited places" and that it could be "attached to the saddle or carried on one's shoulders instead of a knapsack."[141]

Pans for the stove top were another problem for the Russian housewife. For the translator, their nomenclature remains a problem. *Kastrjulja* is the general term for pan and included almost any size or shape except a frying pan (*skovorodka*), sauté pan (*sotejnik*), or soup kettle (*kotel*). In her list of kitchen equipment, Molokhovets used a nest of single-handled saucepans to illustrate the term, but a catalog of cookware printed in Odessa in 1897 included a great assortment of imported and domestic pots and pans under that name. Some had one handle, others two; some were high and narrow, others broad and low; some were convex, others had straight or flaring sides; and most had lids, but a few had a lip for pouring.[142] Several factors including durability, cost, and health had to be considered when choosing a pan. Nickel, aluminum, and silver pans were available at that time, as well as those made of copper, iron, and enameled cast-iron. Molokhovets preferred enameled pans over copper ones even though the enamel was fragile and was easily destroyed if an empty pan was placed on a hot stove.

Although copper pans were more durable, they were expensive and had to be handled with care since they were easily bent out of shape if allowed to become too hot. Moreover, it was widely believed at that time in Russia and elsewhere that copper pans had to be well-tinned to avoid serious food poisoning. According to Molokhovets, "a copper pan in constant use had to be retinned every two months."[143] The expense and inconvenience associated with the need for constant retinning were probably reason enough for her to advise against making soup in a copper pan (#i). Everyone from John Farley in *The London Art of Cookery* (8th edition, 1796) and Isabella Beeton in *The Book of Household Management* (1861) to Raida Varlamova in *Semejnyj magazin* [Family Magazine] (1856) all warned against the dangers of using untinned copper pans. The same general advice is still being given today, even though we now know that copper is not poisonous per se.[144] Problems arise, however, when copper reacts with certain acids causing a poisonous green verdigris to develop. *Clean* copper vessels, used properly, are apparently not harmful, but most of the early warnings were cognizant of the danger without understanding the details.[145] The common practice of cooking jams and jellies in untinned copper pans is safe because the large quantity of sugar used in preserving prevents the copper from reacting with the acid in the fruit.[146] Like many others, Molokhovets used a copper preserving pan for making jams and preserves, but she warned that "the jam must be cooled in a china basin. If left to stand in a copper vessel, the jam will take on a metallic taste harmful to the health and it will lose its natural color" (Remarks, Chapter 20).

Green pickles were a staple of the Russian diet, but they posed a special hazard since it was difficult to preserve their color by natural means. Some housewives went to extraordinary lengths to produce a pickle of the desired hue, but the results were often less than ideal. Store-bought pickles, on the other hand, were often an attractive—and unhealthy—shade of green, signaling that they had probably been prepared in an untinned copper vessel, making them "extremely harmful to your health." Molokhovets advised testing any cucumbers that seemed unnaturally green by piercing them with a clean steel needle; if the needle turned green, the cucumbers had been adulterated and should be discarded (#2601).[147]

### Servants

*A Gift to Young Housewives* appeared in 1861, the same year that the serfs were freed. The underlying assumption of the book is that many hands were available to assist in the myriad tasks that were necessary to preserve the foods for the household and prepare meals for the family and guests. Most servants at this period were illiterate and needed to be instructed in the performance of their duties. For prudent household management, Molokhovets advocated using accurate measurements in the kitchen, but lamented that the practice was not widespread and might seem "strange and even comic or awkward to carry out, especially for simple folk, such as our servants or cooks." Thus she recommended that the cook begin by learning to prepare the broth under the housewife's supervision and to her own specifications. Molokhovets' trick was to determine the amount of finished broth by pouring the requisite number of bowls of water into a pan. The level of liquid was then marked on a clean wooden splint or spill, more liquid was added to the pan and, finally, it was reduced to the level marked on the splint. This method, she claimed, would produce broth that would always be the desired strength without there being either too much or too little.[148]

Petty thievery was often a problem in large households where some members were better off and better fed than others. The counterfeit version of *A Gift to Young Housewives* suggested that the housewife should store her valuable china and silver in the buffet in the dining room and carry the key with her; failing that, it advised her to check the cabinet frequently to make sure "everything was in order."[149] Molokhovets discouraged frequent trips to the cold cellar for supplies as they disrupted work in the kitchen and made it difficult for the housewife to monitor the distribution of provisions. Fetching goods in a hurry from the dark basements and storage sheds was also a frequent source of accidents due to awk-ward, crowded conditions and poor lighting in those storage areas. Fires from unguarded and sputtering candles were another danger.

Domestic chores were onerous in preindustrial households; with no electricity, running water, or labor-saving devices, a servant's life was unenviable.[150] Food really was prepared from scratch, but not as we understand the term today. Most foodstuffs were grown locally and prepared at home by the consumer, which meant threshing the grain, slaughtering the animals, and cleaning the fish and game after trapping or shooting. Some tasks were disgusting, most were laborious or just tedious, and only a precious few were actually enjoyable. Among the most loathsome was butchering, a job that was clearly left for the servants. Neverthe-less, Molokhovets fully described the steps for dismembering a pig since she felt that every housewife should be knowledgeable about the process even if she did not want to watch it (Remarks on Pork, Chapter 31). Preparing beef stomachs for tripe was such a dirty job that Molokhovets advised scrubbing them down in the river (#666). Even after the initial preparation of the carcass, there was still a lot of work to be done since meat was often buried in the ground for tenderizing. Both the quality of the soil and the depth of the hole seemed to matter. Molokho-vets directed that veal be buried "two *arshins* deep in good earth for twelve hours" (#677); hams and wood grouse were similarly buried (#763, 846), and fresh cheese was placed in a shallow pit with its top covered with canvas to protect it from dirt. The hole was filled with soil which was trampled down by foot, and finally, a stone was placed on top as a marker (#2302). Only chicken seems to have been buried in sand (#807).

Other distasteful tasks included cleaning eels or skinning them after hanging them up by a string passed through their eyes with a needle (#109, 1106). To reclaim preserved fish that had mildewed, Molokhovets advised beating it with willow switches, which she claimed was "best done in a river or pond" (#2641).

By comparison, the process of making wheat starch—which involved tram-pling down the soaked and swollen grains in a trough with bare feet—was merely onerous (#2269). One curiously labor-intensive technique involved cleaning out the seeds from berries and fruit with a hairpin. Rose hips for jam were cleaned in this way, then swabbed dry with a scrap of linen (#1990–91). More surprisingly, tomatoes were treated in the same fashion (#494). "To preserve green goose-berries like sprigs of hops" (#1945) was an equally tedious process. Each berry was cut into four parts to resemble four leaves, the centers or seeds were removed with a penknife, and then four or five of the berries were threaded onto a twig from a currant bush. Only when the jar was filled with these embellished twigs did the process of preserving continue. Beating a cake batter "for a full hour without stopping" (e.g., #1728) sounds easy by comparison, until one realizes that these baba batters often contained seventy to ninety eggs.

In contrast to the chores described above and others like them, the opportu-nity to gather berries or mushrooms was a real treat. Sofya Kovalevskaya (1850–

1891), the renowned mathematician, described the great excitement among the servants and children in her parents' household when it was time to go into the forest to gather mushrooms.[151] Russian literature is full of similar scenes, one of the most notable occurring in Tolstoy's *Anna Karenina*, when Sergej Ivanovich, distracted in part by the beauty of the forest and the hunt for mushrooms, fails to propose to Varvara Andreevna. The heaps of mushrooms that were gathered on such excursions were salted and pickled and then set aside for the winter. The eating of these pickled mushrooms, which were so evocative of the forest, became a culture-laden act, almost an epic definition of Russianness. Natasha Rostova in Tolstoy's *War and Peace* showed herself a genuine Russian despite her Europeanized upbringing in part by appreciating a serf's offering of mushrooms "which seemed to her the most delicious in the world" and then by demonstrating her innate ability to execute the peasant dances to perfection. The same use of mushrooms as a cultural marker of the "good old days" in the Russian sense can be found in Pushkin's *Eugene Onegin*, Gogol's "The Old World Landowners," and Goncharov's *Oblomov*.[152]

Given all their hard labor, what respite was there for the servants? Aside from showing a slight concern with their spiritual well-being, Molokhovets does not give us much information. Mostly she was concerned with what they ate and that leftovers from the family meals be consumed. Any fat, for instance, that was left from roasting a goose (#828a) or hazel grouse (#858) was given to the servants the next day with their kasha, or, alternatively, it could be used for frying doughnuts (#828). She recommended making an inexpensive White grain *kvass* (#2184) which could be drunk by the servants and used in *shchi*. Any extra sediment left from making the *kvass*, she said, could be poured into the mash for the cows. Molokhovets did not think that roach was a very tasty or useful fish, but she did consider it "good for the servants' soup on fast days" (#2639).

Katerina Avdeeva, whose cookbooks were so successful in the 1840s, wrote that the usual diet for servants in Russia was *shchi* and kasha, with *pirogs* for holidays. Simple filling dishes, coarsely made with inferior ingredients, seemed to be her guiding principle. Cabbage dishes for the servants, for instance, utilized the weak, ill-formed heads and the tough outer leaves of the firmer heads. In exceptional cases, one pound of beef per person per day was used in making *shchi* but, she observed, "one-half pound per person still makes a good soup."[153] Her other suggestions included many traditional Russian dishes utilizing grains and offal such as potato soup made from a cow's udder, tripe soup, hot bran *kissel*, *varenets* (a boiled fermented milk pudding, whereby the milk was coaxed into forming successive skins or layers),[154] *salamata* (a kind of wheat gruel served with goose or other fat), rye blini made from scraps of leftover bread dough, and sheep's head and tripe boiled with kasha.

Molokhovets gave sample daily menus for the servants for both meat days and fish days. Although far from luxurious, they seem to be a step above those advocated by Avdeeva. Only one dish was served at breakfast, and that was usually potatoes—boiled, baked, or fried—served by themselves or with yogurt or fried eggs. Oatmeal, yogurt, milk, or hot wheat porridge were alternative suggestions. Dinner usually consisted of two dishes (for four servants): sauerkraut *shchi* and thick buckwheat kasha; borshch (made with 2 lbs of meat of the 2nd or 3rd grade) and dumplings made of 1st grade flour; oat or barley meatless soup with potatoes, plus roast beef and mashed potatoes; or soup made from root vegetables and either milk or 2 lbs meat and barley kasha. The holiday menus for the servants were much better, with the *pirogs* noted by Avdeeva still apparently in favor.

#1: *Breakfast: Pirog stuffed with sauerkraut*
*Dinner: Rossol'nik (made with 2 lbs meat for 4 persons) and fried liver and potatoes*

#2: *Breakfast: Pirog stuffed with kasha*
*Dinner: Borshch (made either with buttermilk or 2 lbs meat) and either wheat kasha or roast goose and potatoes*

#3: *Breakfast: Pirog stuffed with fresh cabbage*
*Dinner: Sorrel shchi and Roast suckling pig and potatoes*

#4: *Breakfast: Rice pirog*
*Dinner: Beef tripe soup with potatoes and roast pork with potatoes*

During Butter Week, the servants were given blini for breakfast every morning. The reader should be reminded that meat could be eaten by Orthodox believers only on one-third of the days of the year. For the rest of the days no meat or dairy products were allowed. Since it was more likely that servants would follow this strict dietary regime than members of the upper classes, the servants' diet was considerably more circumscribed than might appear from this discussion.[155]

Sleeping arrangements for the cook were often less than ideal. The problem was aggravated in city apartments where space was at a premium. According to the authors of *Nastol'naja kniga*, "A kitchen will only be clean if no one sleeps in it or does the laundry in it. But if it is impossible for the servants to sleep elsewhere than in the kitchen, their section should be partitioned off and best of all remote from the windows."[156] Nineteenth-century reformers in London and Paris were similarly concerned about the health of servants who had to spend almost all their time in the kitchen, "which often had the worst hygienic conditions of any room in the house or apartment." They feared that the servants, forced to work and live in such unhealthy surroundings, might contract tuberculosis or typhoid fever and transmit it to the families for whom they worked.[157] Molokhovets, it must be admitted, showed no concern for either the comfort or the health of the servants. She suggested constructing a niche in the wall for what we today call a Murphy bed, or in this case a plank which was kept out of sight during the day, then folded out at night to serve as a bed after spreading out a mattress filled with straw chaff or dried seaweed.[158] (See her section, "Arangement of the Kitchen.")

From the seventh edition onward, Molokhovets included floor plans for houses in the country and apartments in the city. (I have not seen the third through the sixth editions so I do not know when the floor plans first appeared.)

In every plan, space was allotted for a prayer room, where all the family, including the servants, could gather at least once a day in common prayer. It was important, she felt, that the head of the family daily lead everyone in prayers and by his own good example try to instill both in the family and the servants "an unlimited love of God and faith in His impartial justice and His charity towards mankind."[159]

## Health

For a book of this length, Molokhovets included few references to diet and health. Aside from a simple list of foods that were suitable for children (such as kashas, soups, simply prepared meats, and *kissels*), she only referred to children once in the text when she provided a recipe for beef bouillon intended for "weak children and adults who must lead an active life and be constantly on the go" (#5). Otherwise, she did not comment about dishes that might be good for the children or pleasing to them. This lack of information (I am tempted to say lack of concern) is especially surprising from a mother of ten children. Given her interest in food, one would have expected her to pay more attention to what the children were eating. Other Russian cookbooks did so. Both Levshin and Sumarokov, for instance, in the food dictionaries or encyclopedias that they compiled in the late eighteenth century showed a close interest in the effect of diet on health. And in the nineteenth century, Radetskij, who worked as *chef de cuisine* in various Russian noble households, recommended diluting mashed potatoes with milk to whatever consistency the children preferred. This touch, small as it was, undoubtedly mattered to the children in the family, but we find no analogous advice from Molokhovets.[160]

Although Molokhovets approved of beef bouillon—and gave a recipe that was especially suited for sick people—boiled beef, in her opinion, had no nutritional value since it had lost all its goodness to the cooking liquid (Chapter 5, Remarks). As for fish, she advised that while fresh fish was tasty and healthy, stale fish should be avoided (Chapter 7, Remarks); similarly, she warned against eating any eel that had not been cooked sufficiently (#99 and 932). The consumption of fat was not the issue in the nineteenth century that it is now, but Molokhovets did suggest omitting the butter when making toast and croutons for sick people (#176). She considered that milk taken from the morning's milking was best for sick people (#2308).[161] She recommended drinking a glass of rowanberry *kvass* daily to maintain good health (#2207). In her experience, convalescents liked a jam made with lingonberries and apples (#1987), and, finally, she recommended using dried raspberries as a sudorific to treat colds (#2446).

## Markets

Before the present century, what we ate was determined by the season and where we lived. Both the Church calendar and the climate underscored the seasonality of the diet in Russia. The German traveler Kohl speculated that the extremes of the Russian climate were "the cause of the decided and strictly maintained distinctions between the summer and the winter *cuisine*. Every season has its own soup, its own poultry, its own pastry. To many, a positive date for their enjoyment may be given. Fruit comes in on the 8th of August, ice on Easter Sunday."[162] Supplies for the winter began to arrive in Moscow and St. Petersburg in early December. Transportation of goods was always a problem in preindustrial Russia due to the lack of paved roads and the paucity of railway lines. It was, however, easier in the winter after the roads had frozen and were covered with snow.

> On the 6th of December, namely, neither sooner nor later, but on the feast of St. Nicholas, it is generally assumed that the snow track must be in a firm and proper condition for the winter. Among the Russians indeed almost all actions, but particularly those which relate to their household arrangements, are regulated, not according to nature, but according to certain festivals of the church, which are assumed to be the most suitable periods for certain arrangements to be made.[163]

Traveler after traveler remarked on the wealth of provisions that were brought to the winter market. At the end of the seventeenth century, both Johann-Georg Korb, who served as Secretary of the Austrian Legation at the court of Peter the

"A Fruit Seller's Shop, St. Petersburg." From *Illustrated London News*,
18 April 1874.

Great, and John Parkinson, an Oxford don, were fascinated by the bustle and activity of the Christmas preparations.

> Today, being the eve of our Lord's Nativity (old style), which is preceded by a Russian fast of seven weeks, all the markets and public thoroughfares are to be seen plenished to overflowing with flesh meats. Here you have an incredible multitude of geese; in another place such store of pigs, ready killed, that you would think it enough to last the whole year; the number of oxen killed is in proportion; fowl of every kind looked as if they had flown together from all Muscovy, and every part thereof, into this one city. It would be useless to attempt naming all the varieties: everything that one could wish for was to be had.[164]

> I [went] to the Newfski market, called so from being held in a spot not far from the convent of Alexander Newfski. It takes place always a few days before Xmas. The peasants from all the neighbouring districts bring beef, mutton, veal, pork, fowl, game, butter, and even hay, all except the last in a frozen state and from hence the people of Petersburg supply themselves with these articles for the winter. . . . The Perspective was crowded with sledges belonging to persons who were going to purchase or returning with their bargains. It was curious to see whole pigs in several of these sledges as stiff and upright as if they were stuffed. The Market itself which occupies a very large space, was entirely filled with the sledges of the peasants, in which the frozen meat either remained or was piled up against them. The pigs in particular were for the most part fixed upright round about the sledges.[165]

The market was just as lively a century later when visited by the British painter Robert Ker Porter.

> [On the frozen Neva] your astonished sight is arrested by a vast open square, containing the bodies of animals piled in pyramidal heaps on all sides. Cows, sheep, hogs, fowls, butter, eggs, fish are all stiffened into granite. . . . Their hardness is so extreme that the natives chop them up for the purchaser, like wood; and the chips of their carcasses fly off in the same way as splinters do from masses of timber or coal. A hatchet, the favourite instrument of the country, is used in the operation; as indeed it is generally applied to every other act of ingenuity or strength.[166]

Normally, these frozen provisions were enough for the entire winter and included a sufficient amount of fish to last through the Great Fast. An unseasonable thaw, therefore, was a disaster, as noted by the French painter Horace Vernet.

> The snow has melted; a constant fine rain bathes the streets. It's a calamity for the populace. In the winter, sledges bring in all St. Petersburg's provisions and on Christmas Day all the markets are full of meat, fish, and poultry that are frozen— the way to keep these commodities until Lent. Unhappily and unexpectedly a thaw has overtaken us and our foodstuffs, which are now nothing but carrion; it's a real debacle.[167]

As inviting as the market was on a cold winter day at the beginning of the season, it was another story during the annual spring thaw.

So long as the frost keeps all liquid matter in captivity, and so long as the snow, constantly renewed, throws a charitable covering over all the hidden sins of the place, so long the ploshtshod [= square] looks clean enough, but this very snow and frost prepare for the coming spring a spectacle which I would counsel no one to look upon, who wishes to keep his appetite in due order for the sumptuous banquets of St. Petersburg. Every kind of filth and garbage accumulates during the winter; and when at last the melting influence of spring dissolves the charm, the quantities of sheep's eyes, fish tails, crab shells, goat's hairs, fragments of meat, pools of blood, not to speak of hay, dung, and other matters, are positively frightful.[168]

## Ingredients

To turn from historical to more practical matters, as far as the ingredients are concerned, the modern reader should have no trouble cooking from this book. Molokhovets relied mostly on root vegetables, using the more tender vegetables only when they were in season. She preserved as many vegetables as possible for the winter months when few were available in the markets. Salad greens were a rarity and appeared on dining tables only in the early spring. Artichokes and asparagus were expensive vegetables, eaten mainly by the upper classes on special occasions. Eggplants and tomatoes, although known in Russia by this time, were not yet very popular. For a full list of ingredients in the book, see Appendix A. A number of Molokhovets' ingredients merit special comment.

### POTATOES

The introduction of potatoes into Russia is linked to the reign of Peter the Great, although the exact details are not known. The story goes that when the Tsar visited Holland at the end of the seventeenth century, he became interested in the plant and sent a sack of potatoes from Rotterdam to Count Sheremet'ev in Russia. Instrumental in promoting the potato was the Free Economic Society, which was founded in St. Petersburg in 1765. A Senate order that same year was aimed at encouraging more widespread cultivation of the new crop.[169] In 1770 Andrej Bolotov, known as Russia's first agronomist,[170] published his important paper "Primechanie o kartofele, ili zemljanykh jablokakh" [Remarks on the potato, or earth apples]. In 1797 a government ukase was issued ordering peasants to cultivate potatoes; to encourage compliance, allotments of arable land were increased for those who planted the new crop. The peasants, however, were suspicious of the potato, preferring instead to plant traditional crops such as rye.[171] The Old Believers (a group of Orthodox believers with a very conservative ideology), in particular, refused to eat the new root or to have anything to do with it, calling it "the Devil's Apple." In their view, eating the new food, which was not mentioned in the Bible, was akin "to eating the forbidden fruit of Eden."[172] By the beginning of the nineteenth century, potatoes had not yet been adopted by the Russian peasantry. Hardly known outside of the cities and the larger settlements, potatoes were still regarded as an exotic food of the privileged classes who consumed them in small amounts. In 1840, the government issued a new decree "ordering state peasants to plant a certain amount of potatoes on common lands." This decree led to "potato riots" by the peasants in about a dozen provinces, revolts that were only settled in 1843 when "the government gave up the attempt to spread the forced cultivation of potatoes, and began to use persuasion instead."[173] Despite the revolt, peasant resistance to eating potatoes dropped sharply during the disturbances. Thereafter, the plant moved from the kitchen garden to the open fields and became a staple of the Russian diet. Even in the first edition of her cookbook, Molokhovets included many recipes for the potato, treating it as a familiar and well-known vegetable. By the twentieth edition, potatoes had become standard fare for the servants and were served daily.

## TOMATOES

When tomatoes were brought from the New World to Europe, they were initially regarded as a decorative plant. They spread slowly from Spain to Italy and from there to the Middle East and Northern Europe. They became popular in northern France only at the end of the eighteenth century. According to food historian Rudolph Grewe, the tomato was still listed as an ornamental plant by the French seed company Andrieux-Vilmorin in its 1760 catalog; "not until the 1778 catalog was it listed as a vegetable."[174] In Russia, Andrej Bolotov was as instrumental in popularizing the tomato as he was in promoting the potato. In his 1784 article "O ljubovnykh jablochkakh" [On love-apples], Bolotov described the attractiveness of the fruit and refuted the belief that tomatoes were poisonous. In his opinion, they were perfectly safe to eat. He even suggested the idea, novel for that time, that the seeds could be started indoors and then transplanted to grow and ripen outside as the weather got warmer.[175] What hindered the spread of tomatoes in nineteenth-century Russia was the expense associated with their cultivation in a cold climate, rather than the resistance of the people. By 1873, Katherine Guthrie mentioned seeing "brilliant crimson heaps of tomatoes" in the markets at Taganrog and Yalta. She also praised the national dish, *shchi*, which she said was excellent: "—all sorts of vegetables, tomatoes and potatoes preponderating, are boiled in mutton broth, along with barley."[176] Contrary to Guthrie's testimony, tomatoes in *shchi* are usually considered an innovation of the twentieth century, where they augment the basic sourness of the soup.[177] Molokhovets did not add tomatoes to any of her *shchi* recipes. In fact, she rarely served them as a vegetable or used them as a component in other dishes. She suggested serving boiled pike or cod with tomato sauce (#898, 974), but otherwise did not cook fish with tomatoes; by contrast, almost every fish entry—and there must be hundreds—in the contemporary Soviet *Commercial Encyclopedia* of nine volumes dutifully records the fact that fish, whatever it may be, is available "preserved in tomato sauce."[178]

## ASPARAGUS

Adam Olearius, the oft-quoted Saxon member of a trade commission that visited Russia between 1633–39, remarked on the wide variety of fruits and vegetables available in the Moscow market, including "asparagus as thick as a thumb."[179] Captain John Perry, a former British naval officer, lived and worked in Russia from 1698 to 1712. An avid traveler, he reported from the Crimea that "Asparagus, the best I ever eat, grows so thick that you may in some places mow it down."[180] Despite these reports of the succulence of the native spears, asparagus has remained a rare and costly commodity, perhaps even more so today than in Molokhovets' time. At the turn of the nineteenth century, Martha Wilmot told of attending the Governor General's ball "given for the birth Day of the Empress Elizabeth. There was a lottery where every Lady drew a prize. I got a bunch of Asparagus which open'd and gave me Verses & Sweetmeats."[181] Asparagus was obviously more available by the time Molokhovets was writing, but she still used it sparingly, mostly as garnishes, but also in soup and as a vegetable served with various sauces (#72, 447–452). Molokhovets also preserved asparagus by salting (#2619). In the parodic poem by Tarkovskij cited earlier, the Soviet poet wistfully recalled Molokhovets' luxurious dishes, including bream with asparagus in its jaw.[182]

## FRUITS

Of the several categories of fruits used by Molokhovets, the orchard fruits—apples, pears, and cherries—were the oldest and most common. These fruits were the basis of the traditional Russian desserts that were commonly served before pastry, cakes, and creams were introduced from Western Europe. Next in importance are native berries, those so-called gifts of the forest that are so beloved in Russian folklore. Kovalevskaja, the Russian mathematician, wrote movingly of this edible natural wealth in her memoirs.

> [The forest] had inexhaustible stores of riches of every sort. There were numberless varieties of game: hares, black grouse, hazel grouse, partridge. All a hunter had to do was walk in and shoot. Even the clumsiest, with only an old flintlock for a rifle, could count on getting a bagful. And in summer there was no end to the different kinds of berries. First to appear would be the wild strawberries which, it is true, ripen a bit later in the woods than in the fields, but then are much juicier and more fragrant. Almost before the strawberries were gone the bilberries would make their appearance, and then the stone-fruit, the raspberries, the cranberries.
>
> And then, before you realized it, the nuts would be ripening, and after that the mushroom harvest would begin. Even in summer one might find a good many brown-caps and orange-caps, but autumn was the real season for the "milkies," the "rusties," and the prized "whites."[183]

Another category is the "exotica," including the melons from the East we have already discussed. The group of fruits that made the greatest impression on foreigners, however, were those that were grown in hothouses. The natural growing season in Russia was so short that wealthy members of the nobility developed very elaborate hothouses for growing rare and tropical fruits, as Martha Wilmot testified.

> as to fruits, there is a display beyond every thing I have seen elsewhere of the Kind which is not surprising when one recollects that hothouses are a necessary of life here and those too on so prodigal a scale that I have often walk'd thro' ranges of Pine Apples in a line of a hundred at each side seperated in Pots to introduce at the Desert, totally independent of what is to be found in the bed of the Orangerie.[184]

Great care and expenditure were lavished on these systems, and the results apparently were breathtaking, in appearance, in taste—and in cost. Dumas reported that, according to hearsay, every January Potemkin sent Catherine the Great a basket of cherries worth ten thousand rubles.[185] Lady Londonderry wrote on the same theme:

> I called on the Stroganovs where I was received with a kindness and cordiality at all times that made me invariably feel welcome. The Count talking of the severity of the climate told me what appears astonishing, that the gardeners (who are principally German) so well understand the management of the hothouses that any dish of fruit may be ordered for a particular day; for example, a plate of cherries commanded for any date in January would punctually be ready, "but," added the Count, "you have to pay 4 or 5 rubles for each cherry, and according to what you'd need to have, four or five hundred could amount to a dish costing 2,000 rubles."[186]

Carême was as impressed as any other foreigner when he saw the great systems of hothouses in Russia during his visit there during the summer of 1819. Although he admired the ingenuity which could produce such fine fruit—and he thought the Russian pineapples better than any that could be procured in France—he was depressed by a climate and social system that gave fine fruits to a few and denied them to the masses.[187] Molokhovets' elaborate method for preserving grapes (#2410) in an upstairs room seems to have been an amateur's answer to the professional resources of the nobility. Otherwise, one senses that she used fruits in season and preserved them for the winter without indulging much in the extravagance of growing or purchasing the hothouse varieties.

## MEAT

The overwhelming majority of Molokhovets' meat recipes were for beef. Veal and pork were not as common, while mutton or lamb was a distant fourth. Other meats were rarities. Most meat was slaughtered as needed on the estate; in the cities, meat was available in the markets.[188]

> The anatomical dissections of a Russian butcher are extremely simple. Bones and meat having been all rendered equally hard by the frost, it would be difficult to

attempt to separate the several joints. The animals are, accordingly, sawn up into a number of slices of an inch or two in thickness, and in the course of this operation a quantity of animal sawdust is scattered on the snow, whence it is eagerly gathered up by poor children, of whom great numbers haunt the market.[189]

Given these conditions, it is not surprising that connoisseurs like Carême were less than enthusiastic about what they saw in Russian markets.[190]

## WILD BIRDS

Wild birds were readily available and good.[191] At the end of the seventeenth century, Olearius mentioned that "birds were so plentiful that the Russians did not value them. The peasants got little for grouse, wild ducks and geese. Cranes, swans and small birds like thrushes and larks were not considered worth hunting and eating."[192] Plenty of birds were still apparent when Kohl visited Russia in the 1830s:

> It is astonishing what a quantity of these birds are yearly consumed at the luxurious tables of St. Petersburg. In winter the cold keeps the meat fresh, and at the same time facilitates its conveyance to market. The partridges come mostly from Saratoff, the swans from Finland; Livonia and Esthonia supply heath-cocks and grouse, and the wide steppes must furnish the trapp geese which flutter over their endless plains, where the Cossack hunts them on horseback, and kills them with his formidable whip. All these birds, as soon as the life-blood has flown, are converted into stone by the frost, and, packed up in huge chests, are sent for sale to the capital.[193]

Wild birds, like wild mushrooms, seem to have have been taken for granted by Molokhovets, perhaps because of their abundance. "When the summer's hunting yielded so many wild ducks that there was no room for them," she recommended packing the ducks in small barrels with salt and then burying the barrels in ice (#2641). To preserve domestic ducks, she advised slaughtering them after the first frost and then hanging them in the ice house "without removing their feathers or eviscerating them." This method was very practical, in her opinion, "because the ducks were always available and could be kept until Christmas without having to feed them" (#2638).

## FISH

Fish was a very important element in the Russian diet, mainly due to the many religious fasts, but also because the Russian rivers and lakes were so well stocked. This piscatory abundance, so well documented through the ages, has dropped off precipitously in the Soviet period. In the nineteenth century, most of the urban population in Moscow and Petersburg procured their fish in the winter from merchants who set up specially constructed vessels or shops on the frozen river. The French chef Alphonse Petit was among those who were impressed with the great variety and high quality of fish available for sale: "In St. Petersburg fish is sold from large barges that you find on the several different canals that cross the city. These fishmongers sell live fish, frozen fish (in the winter), salt fish, dried sturgeon marrow, isinglass, and caviar."[194] The river was obviously a busy place whatever the season, but especially in winter when some people even maintained their own fishing holes.

> [In Moscow] the remoter part of the river is cut open in trenches and lines of washerwomen bend over to wring their cloaths unconscious of the cold. Baskets as large as huts appear above the surface which contain the winter's fish plunged to a considerable depth beneath and each proprietor weekly visits his watry prison provident of the impending fast.[195]

The Marquis de Custine (1790–1857), a French aristocrat who visited Russia in 1839, described the role of the annual fair at Nizhnij-Novgorod in supplying enough fish for the fasting population of Moscow and St. Petersburg:

> I also traversed a city [each specialized section of the fairgrounds was called a city] destined solely as a receptacle for the dried and salted fish which are sent from the Caspian Sea for the Russian Lents. The Greek devotees are great consumers of these aquatic mummies. Four months of abstinence among the Muscovites enriches the Mohammedans of Persia and Tartary. This city of fishes is situated on the borders of the river: some of the fish are piled upon earth, the remainder lay within the holds of the vessels that brought them. The dead bodies, heaped together in millions, exhale, even in the open air, a disagreeable perfume.[196]

These "aquatic mummies" may have served the poor folk, for whom fresh fish was too expensive, but those with more money had more options. The gentry, for instance, often had ponds on their estates which assured them of an ample supply of fresh fish. It was not unusual for the greater part of a noble family's provisions to be sent to them in the city from their country estates, an example of which was described by Goncharov in his novel *Oblomov*, published in 1859.[197] Eugene Schuyler, who was the American consul in Moscow before he was appointed Secretary of the United States Legation at St. Petersburg in 1869, was knowledgeable about Russian customs and was one of the few foreigners who was favorably impressed by Russian cuisine. He had nothing but praise for the quality and variety of the fish that were available in the Russian markets, but the sterlet, that special fish which abounded in the Volga, was his favorite. In Schuyler's opinion, the sterlet was "the king not only of Russian fish, but of fish everywhere."[198] Dumas, on the other hand, was not convinced; like an epicurean curmudgeon, he grumbled that the sterlet was overpriced and overrated:

> Russia prides herself on her national *cuisine*, particularly on those dishes that no other country can offer, depending as they do upon ingredients found within her mighty empire and nowhere else in the world—sterlet soup, for instance. Russians are passionately fond of it, but the only remarkable thing about it, to my mind, is its cost—fifty or sixty francs in summer, three or four hundred in winter. Yet the

simple bouillabaisse one gets in Marseilles is much more to my liking. What makes sterlet soup so expensive? The transport charges!

The sterlet is found in certain rivers, chiefly the Volga and the Oka, and can live only in its native waters. The problem is to bring it, alive, the four or five hundred miles to St. Petersburg. (If it arrives dead, it is useless.) In summer there is no special difficulty. The fish travels in a tank of river water, shaded from the sun, extra supplies of the same water being carried in specially cooled jars. But in winter, with 30 degrees of frost, it's a very different matter, calling for a little furnace operated by a skilled man, to maintain the water always at the right temperature.

In the old days, before railways, great Russian lords kept special trucks, equipped with fish-tanks and slow ovens, to bring sterlet to St. Petersburg, for custom demands that the host shall show his guests the fish, alive and swimming, that, a quarter of an hour later, they will enjoy as soup. You may recall that the Romans did much the same, having their fish brought from Ostia to Rome by relays of swift slaves, changed every three miles, and the first delight of a real gourmet was to watch the rainbow colours change and fade from the scales of the fish as it died. The sterlet, however, has none of the iridescence of goldfish or mullet, for its skin is rough and spiky, like shagreen. Indeed, I maintain that the sterlet is simply a young sturgeon. Its flesh is insipid and greasy, and no Russian cook bothers to improve its flavour. A sauce that could do so has yet to be invented, and if one ever is, I predict it will be the creation of a French chef.[199]

## Cooking Techniques

Molokhovets was a good, practical cook; her suggestions were sound for the time, and some are still sensible in today's kitchen. To release the meat juices into soup broth, she recommended starting with cold water, but to seal the juices in the meat, she plunged it into boiling water (#iii). Similarly, she advised cooking small fish in boiling water, but starting large fish in cold water (#94). To tenderize chicken, she cooked it with a piece of crystal such as the stopper of a carafe (#47), and to tenderize beef, she added vodka to the cooking water (#xii). She used birch coals to improve the flavor of meat (#xii), to rid fish of its marshy taste (Chapter 7, Remarks), and to remove unpleasant odors from vodka (#2142). To reduce the odor of a turkey while it is roasting—an odor which she said many people found objectionable—she recommended placing a piece of fresh ginger in the cavity (Chapter 6, Remarks).

Freezing was widely used in Russia for preserving, which is hardly surprising given the climate. Molokhovets advised roasting beef without defrosting the meat (#641) and boiling frozen fish by starting it in cold water (Chapter 7, Remarks). When making sausages, she noted that "some people freeze the meat to make it easier to chop, but frozen meat loses its taste and juiciness" (#2692). According to Molokhovets, Siberians made *pel'meni* in great quantities and froze them until they were needed (#1289). She froze cranberries before crushing them to make juice or cranberry leather (#2040, 2470).

Molokhovets gave many recipes for yeast doughs. She hardly used baking powder and quick breads were not part of her repertory, but she used yeast for making breads, *kuliches*, and pastry for *pirogs* and *pirozhki*. One of her methods was to tie up the yeast dough in a clean cloth leaving plenty of room for it to expand, and then to submerge the entire bundle in a tub of cold water for several hours or overnight (#1032, 1779). According to Elizabeth David, this is a very old but effective method of making bread. She calls it Peggy Tub Bread after the tub in which it was made (a Peggy tub was a variety of wash tub in Victorian times). James Beard referred to the method as "waterproofing."[200]

Although Molokhovets had no way of broiling foods (see section on Stoves and Ovens), she liked to roast meat or poultry wrapped in buttered paper in the oven or on a spit in front of a fire. In the mid eighteenth century, the English, who were noted for the excellence of their roasts, regularly protected their meats with buttered paper during spit-roasting.[201] Molokhovets not only wrapped the foods in paper, but she seemed to season the paper as well. For a spit-roasted capon, she sprinkled the wrapped bird with bread crumbs and juices from the meat "so it will brown" (#794), and for greyhens, she basted the paper with butter and sour cream (#846). This method of cooking in paper is somewhat analogous to the French technique of baking *en papillote* and clearly presages the fad of paper-bag cookery that broke out in England and America just before the First World War.[202]

Molokhovets did not devote much space to the appearance of her dishes. Although she frequently listed garnishes for the dishes, she did not say how the food was to be arranged. Sometimes her garnishes were simple and involved nothing more than inserting small bones or little pieces of parsley root or carrot into cutlets of ground meat or fish to make them resemble chops (#690, 919a). At other times she seemed to prefer fussy, vaguely geometrical presentations. Symmetry was her strong point, as evidenced in her directions for setting the table. (See above, section on Table Service and Settings, and Molokhovets' essay on Evening Tea.) Colored aspics and gelatins were a special delight, and she liked to use several different colors in one presentation, such as assembling a platter of assorted cold fish, each kind masked in a different colored gelatin (Remarks, Chapter 9), or combining layers of different colored gelatins and blancmanges in a mold for dessert (#1487).[203] Red and white sheets of gelatin could be purchased; alternatively, Molokhovets colored natural white aspic red with cochineal, yellow with saffron or burnt sugar, blue with cornflowers boiled in water, or green with puréed spinach (Chapter 9, Remarks; Chapter 14, Remarks for Gelatins). Molokhovets also garnished dishes with colored aspic, either chopped or cut into fancy shapes. For more elaborate presentations, she chilled aspics and desserts in a combination of small and large molds that could be arranged in intricate patterns.

Molokhovets liked clusters of fruit, such as gooseberries or currants, preserved on their stems. Perhaps the difficulty of the preparation, the demonstration of virtuosity, appealed to her (#1945, 1957, 2495). Even the simplest *pirozhki* are fussy to make, but Molokhovets, who used the term loosely to mean any tidbit that accompanied the soup, gave several recipes for *pirozhki* that were particularly labor-intensive. In one case, she filled crayfish shells with a brain forcemeat and covered the edges of the shells with puff pastry (#264); in another, she baked vermicelli in small tins, cut off the top, removed the soft interior, and filled the interior with an onion cheese sauce (#262).

Containers seemed to be an important part of the ethos. This may have been an extension of all the *pirogs* and *pirozhki* in the cuisine, or it may have been an expression of a larger aesthetic sense whereby it was unseemly for an object to sprawl without clearly defined limits.[204] When serving Sturgeon with bechamel sauce (#967), she covered the border of the platter with a rim of pastry. More elaborately, she often prepared a grid of pastry so that several kinds of vegetables could be served on the same platter, each in its own compartment. She either baked the grid of dough on a separate sheet in the oven, or she affixed parallel strips of dough on the platter and, after baking it, arranged the vegetables in the compartments (#382).

Eggshells were another useful container. She split hard-boiled eggs in half lengthwise, scooped out the eggs, chopped them, and mixed with other ingredients. The shells were then filled with this mixture and browned in the oven before serving with soup (#219). For dessert, she served orange gelatin "eggs" molded in blown eggshells. This required blowing out the eggs after making a small hole in the shells. They were filled with liquid gelatin, presumably by means of a syringe, chilled, and peeled before serving (#1496). Her recipe for Baked goose eggs is similar, but even trickier to execute. After blowing out the eggs, she turned the contents into scrambled eggs, which she sieved and mixed with bread crumbs, seasonings, and several raw chicken eggs. This mixture she injected back into the shells "with a fine hypodermic needle or syringe." The eggs were baked before serving (#1279).

Once in a while Molokhovets went to extra trouble with the presentation of her dishes. To serve a roast pheasant, she reassembled the bird in the classic manner of *haute cuisine*, affixing its head mounted on a short stick, decorating its neck with a paper ruff, and reattaching its tail feathers (#853). She suggested making paper boxes for pastries and lining the boxes with white and rose cigarette paper, curled into a ruff (Remarks, Polish Cakes, Chapter 17). Spice cakes for the Christmas tree were cut out as deer and horses and either frosted with white icing or gilded (#1928). To adorn tortes and platters of fruit and grapes, Molokhovets dipped fresh roses into a cherry glue (= gelatin?) and dried them in the sun (#2476).

Special skills were needed to prepare blini and babas. Molokhovets urged care and patience in making these dishes, but admitted that even experienced cooks occasionally met with failure. Babas were especially temperamental. To prevent unnecessary noise or drafts which would cause them to fall, Molokhovets advised keeping everyone out of the kitchen while they were baking. The last line of her directions for a 72-egg-yolk baba, appropriately named Capricious Baba, summed up the problem: "This baba is extraordinarily tasty when it succeeds, but it rarely succeeds" (#1750). The preserving of foods and the making of wines, vinegars, and *kvass*, all required specialized techniques, but for these, the reader is referred to the individual chapters.

## Comparison between First and Twentieth Editions

A quick summary of the differences between the editions shows that the later work is longer, fancier, and addressed to a more prosperous reader. The language, the methods, and the ingredients have all been "gussied up." The French influences are stronger and the cooking techniques are more refined, or at least more explicit. The later edition also includes more archaic recipes, although their inclusion should not be unduly emphasized. A comparison of the two meat charts neatly illustrates the differences between the editions, with the later diagram subdivided into smaller parts than the earlier one.

What began in 1861 as a volume of 1,500 recipes divided among twenty-two chapters had more than doubled by the twentieth edition in 1897. Numbers alone do not tell the whole story, however. With certain notable exceptions, the first edition is more complete than it might seem because Molokhovets included variations within a recipe in the first edition, but assigned a number to each variation in the twentieth edition, whether or not she gave full instructions. Also in the first edition, she often concluded a recipe by saying, "This may be made for fast days by substituting vegetable oil for butter," whereas in the later edition the phrase was expanded into a recipe and assigned a number.

Except for directions on preserving fish and poultry, the complete range of recipes was included in the first edition. Of the original twenty-two chapters, fourteen grew by more than 60 percent in the later edition. In several instances, a few recipes served as the nucleus of a full chapter later on. This happened with *paskhas*, gingerbreads, vodkas, *kvass*, vinegars, butter and cheese, and bread. The original chapter on Fruit and Vegetable Preserves was later expanded and divided into two separate chapters. The three chapters that grew the least were Tortes (11%), Ice Creams, Mousses, *Kissels*, and Compotes (22%), and Mazurkas and Other Small Pastries (29%). In addition, the fast day recipes were gathered into a new set of chapters parallel to the butter- or meat-based recipes.

The growth, rather than reduction, of the preserving sections is puzzling. These foods were among the most traditional in the Russian kitchen, but they were the most time-consuming to prepare. They also required bulky equipment and extensive storage space. Molokhovets must have been aware of the problems associated with these preparations since she herself had moved from Kursk to St. Petersburg and, to judge from her remarks, from a large house to the more limited quarters of a city apartment. Despite the obvious difficulty of preparing such recipes in urban conditions, there was still a demand for them. With the breakup of the large extended families in the countryside and the general growth of the urban population, there were more young women who needed guidance on how to make these dishes, even if they did not prepare many of them. More isolated in the city, a young woman had few resources for information, whereas previously she could have turned to her mother, aunts, or cousins for advice. Tolstoy's description of jam-making in the country in *Anna Karenina* captured the essence of this informal exchange among women, a traditional "rite of passage" that was being lost even as he wrote.[205]

The vast majority of the recipes that appeared in the first edition are still recognizable in the late editions. The changes, for the most part, were small but fell into a clear pattern affecting measurements, ingredients, techniques, and language. Although Molokhovets always measured with a combination of weights and volumes, she later preferred to measure by volume. What had been ⅛ lb sugar became ¼ glass; ½ lb flour became 1½ glasses flour (#1712).

The ingredients used in the later edition were both richer and more varied. She increased the number and variety of her sauces; those for Ground beef cutlets grew from 7 to 41 (#659). She also added suggestions for sauces when there were none before even as she moved away from the idea of interchangeable sauces and began to indicate specific sauces for specific fish dishes and special sweet syrups for particular soufflés and ice creams. Honey was replaced by sugar in many of the later recipes, notably in those for gingerbreads (#1412, Chapter 19). Also, the sheer amount of sugar increased with time; for small amounts it sometimes even was doubled. Although one might argue about the effect on any given recipe, the greater intake of sugar by the Russians was not exceptional; it formed part of a broad pattern whereby increased sugar consumption seemed to accompany industrialization in Western Europe, Great Britain, and the United States.[206] For jams and jellies, Molokhovets used a slightly heavier sugar syrup in the later editions by changing the ratio of sugar to water. Instead of using 2 lbs of sugar and 1½ glasses of water for each pound of berries, she reduced the amount of water in the later recipes to 1 glass (#1941, 1949). Grapes, quince, and ginger were some of the new ingredients that she preserved in sugar; she also found new uses for familiar fruits such as plums, black currants, melons, and whortleberries.

Spices were used with more discretion in the later edition. In particular, Molokhovets halved the amount of cloves, allspice, and bay leaves that she used in her pâtés and aspics (#1060, 1079). At the same time, she increased the amount of basic protein in these recipes, adding half again as much meat or fish, and sometimes doubling the number of eggs (Chapter 8). In the later edition, cochineal was replaced as a coloring agent by red gelatin (#1079). She used truffles with a certain abandon even in the early edition, but later on she took to soaking them in Madeira before using them; by the same token, she frequently added sherry and Madeira to her sauces where there was none before (#1069, 1062, 1080). The later edition is also replete with obvious French garnishes like cocks' combs, asparagus tips, and crayfish. These turn up especially as garnishes for the soups and for aspics (#43, 63).

The balance and flavor of aspics, one of the crowning glories of the Russian cold table, changed noticeably over the period in which Molokhovets was writing. In general, the spices were reduced and the solids increased. The amount of liquid for the aspic was increased as well, but its distinctive sourness began to be muted. Whereas the early edition called for ½ glass or more of vinegar or lemon juice "so the aspic will be pleasantly sour" (Chapter 9, Remarks), half that amount of vinegar was used in the 1897 edition, and it was supplemented by sherry and sugar, both of which were new to aspics in the later edition.

The cooking techniques were not so much changed as refined in the later editions. For instance, in her *Pirog* with sauerkraut and fish, she mixed the two main ingredients together in the early version, but layered the sauerkraut and fish in the later version (#1044). In the 1897 edition, she boned more meats for her *pirogs* and she tended to use more purées, on occasion even filling a pie with alternate layers of different purées (#1072). Many of the early instructions were expanded slightly later on, all with the aim of improving the cooking.

The names of Molokhovets' recipes were plain and descriptive; she did not "Frenchify" them or otherwise indulge in the nomenclature of haute cuisine. She expanded the occasional recipe name in the later edition, sometimes by including new alternatives, but usually just to describe the underlying recipe more accurately. For instance, "Boiled beef with stewed mushrooms" became "Boiled beef with stewed or fried boletus mushrooms, saffron milk-cap mushrooms, milk-agaric mushrooms, or morels" (#547).

### Issues of Translation

In transliterating from the Russian, I followed the Library of Congress system, except I have used a "j" to indicate soft vowels. I used standard English spelling for familiar Russian proper names (Tolstoy instead of Tolstoj), but I transliterated unfamiliar proper names. For older materials, I have quoted Russian and English titles, names, and text exactly as they appeared on the printed page without modernizing the orthography. Some of these forms may look odd to the modern reader—especially since Molokhovets' spelling was somewhat inconsistent—but they are not modern typographical errors.

The names of foreign dishes are often untranslatable. Pastries are a particular problem in this regard. I have tried to assign an English name or descriptive title to as many recipes as possible, but this was not always feasible. For cultural reasons, I decided not to translate the names of common Russian dishes like *shchi, kvass, pirozhki, kissel,* and *kulich.* Readers are urged to look at the recipes to determine the basic preparations. Some of Molokhovets' subheadings contained only one or two recipes. If none of them was included in this translation, I omitted the subheading from the text. All the subheadings, however, are in the Complete List of Recipes. To avoid confusion, I also deleted the letters by which Molokhovets designated the subheadings.

Since this translation contains only a quarter of the original recipes, I deleted many of Molokhovets' numbered references to specific recipes in favor of just using the name of the dish. For example, instead of specifying Carrots #383, I simply referred to puréed carrots. The loss of the numbers I hope is balanced by lessening the aggravation caused by directing the reader to numerous recipes that were not included in this translation. Occasionally I had to add a sentence or two of explanation from the relevant recipe. These additions, like any other explanatory comments, I placed in square brackets.

Molokhovets' book was designed as a practical manual for young housewives for use in the kitchen, not in the library. Molokhovets was pragmatic, but she was no great stylist. Thus I have made no attempt to capture the cadence of her prose, which is often repetitive, sometimes ambiguous, and occasionally contradictory. If she had an editor, it is not apparent. Some mistakes went uncorrected for half a century; others were rectified only to be replaced by new ones. In keeping with Molokhovets' original intention, I have translated this book by focusing on the needs of the practicing cook, rather than on those of the historian or Slavist. This has meant expanding the text, compressing it, and occasionally even changing the sequence of instructions. All this has been done in the name of clarity, in order to highlight the logical progression of steps in each recipe. Although I have not "modernized" the recipes for today's cook, I have taken more liberty with the text than I consider permissible with a piece of literature, but Molokhovets herself recognized the limitations of the genre, that "the compilation of a cookbook was far removed from real writing."[207]

Sometimes I did no more than eliminate Molokhovets' wordiness. At other times, my editing was more radical.

Linguists who are interested in tracking the development of Russian verb usage might well want to examine the text of *A Gift to Young Housewives*. Over the years, Molokhovets changed the aspect of many of the verbs and increasingly chose to use perfective over imperfective verbs. All the other grammatical changes pale by comparison. Teachers of Russian should consider giving their students some recipes to translate. The following instructions for cutting up a turkey illustrate the flexibility of Russian verbal prefixes (#1083):

> Ochistit' indejku. Krylyshki i nozhki *otrezat'*, *razrezat'* vdol' khrebta, vynut' ostorozhno vse kosti, chtoby ne *prorezat'* kozhitsy . . . (Clean the turkey, cut off the wings and feet, cut along the backbone, and carefully remove all the bones without piercing the skin.)

On a more general plane, certain distinctions that we make in English are unavailable in Russian. *Khleb* broadly means bread or grain, but as used by Molokhovets can mean either a loaf of bread or a roll. Guided by the context, I have mostly translated *khleb* as "roll," especially when it appears as "1 *khleb*" in a list of ingredients, such as for stuffing. *Maslo*, if unqualified, means either butter or oil, whereas the meaning of *slivochnoe maslo* (butter), *rastitel'noe maslo* (vegetable oil), or *provanskoe maslo* (olive oil) is unmistakable. If the meaning was not clear, I chose "butter" rather than oil since it is preferable for most cooking and was favored by the Russians who usually resorted to oil only for economic or religious reasons.

No one doubts that color plays an important role in the kitchen, both for the cooking of the food and its presentation. When the perception of color is a cultural issue, however, it must be dealt with by the translator. Molokhovets, for instance, was inordinately fond of red (*krasnyj*), whereas the culinary palette of the Anglo-Saxon world is dominated by hues of yellow and brown. Molokhovets heated milk until reddish skins formed (#1904). She also spoke of frying "until red" (#1024b) and prepared Red bouillon (#2) and Red sauce (#278). Since Americans fry "until golden" and produce brown bouillons and sauces instead of red, I have adjusted the text accordingly.

Molokhovets distinguished between three major types of pans, a *gorshok* (an earthenware pot somewhat resembling a New England beanpot), a *skovorodka* (a frying pan), and a *kastrjulja* (a saucepan or stewing pan). Only the last term is problematical because it embraces such a large range of shapes and sizes of pots and pans, all of which have distinct names in the culinary lexicon in French if not in English. Using quantity and context as a guide, I tried to use the stewpan for larger preparations and save the saucepan for smaller ones, but sometimes such distinctions were impossible and the choice became purely arbitrary.

The single most troublesome word for the translator of a Russian cookbook is the verb *zharit'*, an expansive cooking term which functions much like the German verb *backen*. It can mean to roast, broil, fry, or grill and it is impossible to distinguish among those meanings without a context. Once in a while Molokhovets even used *zharit'* to indicate stewing and braising, i.e., cooking in a covered pan in a small amount of liquid, although most of the time she used the ordinary Russian verb for stewing, *tushit'*. For a further discussion of her unusual usage, see my notes in Chapter 5. Although neither the Russians nor the Germans seem to be bothered by this linguistic loophole, I remain uncomfortable with that degree of flexibility. For me, it matters whether one is talking about roast potatoes or fried potatoes, roast chicken or fried chicken, but I have found no solution to this particular conundrum.

The occasional word has disappeared from the language or changed its meaning. The most troubling phrase was *anglijskij perets* or English pepper. Searching for this was somewhat analogous to what I imagine a scholar in the twenty-first or twenty-second century will feel when trying to track down "English mustard," which also is not a normal dictionary entry. None of the usual references was any help in my search; I had just about decided that this phrase meant a particularly fine grade of black pepper that had been imported from London—because Molokhovets usually listed it in the phrase "5 ordinary peppercorns and 10 English peppercorns"—when Robert Rothstein, a Slavic linguist who specializes in Polish, told me that the term meant allspice. In a Polish dictionary, he had found that *pieprz angielski* is "the dried fruit of the plant *Myrta pimenta*, used as a spice and medicine."[208] The key word here is *pimenta*, which is the normal word for allspice outside the United States.[209] With that clue, it was an easy matter to establish the meaning in nineteenth-century Russian. Russians currently use *dushistyj perets* or *jamajskij perets* (fragrant pepper or Jamaican pepper) for allspice.[210]

*Sardel'ka* is a misleading word. Nowadays it means a thick, short sausage, but the old meaning of the word, according to Dal' and Ushakov, was sardine.[211] That at least saved me from mashing up sausages in Molokhovets' sauces (#283, 342), but the Canadian ichthyologist W. E. Ricker tells us that *sardel'ki* really means Black Sea sprats (*Sprattus sprattus phalericus*).[212] They are part of the herring family (*Clupeidae*) and are related to the Baltic sprat; their usual length is 8–11 cm. and they weigh 5 to 9 g. on the average. Although sardines (*Sardina pilchardus pilchardus*) come from the same family, they weigh from 30 to 60 g. and measure from 10.5 to 17.5 cm. in length.[213] Sprats are preserved in salt, and like salted anchovies would impart an intense flavor to a sauce. Canned sardines are much blander. For the most part I have translated *sardina* and *sardinka* as sardines and *sardel'ka* as Black Sea sprats. However, given the fuzziness of the language and inconsistency of Molokhovets' usage, the choice ultimately is a matter of taste, and that is best left to the individual reader.

This short list of difficult words would not be complete without mention of *khozjajka*, as in the title of this book—*Podarok molodym khozjajkam*. The word really means something like "mistress of the household" or a female owner or proprietress, but those terms either lack the full range of meaning or they sound awkward or archaic in English. I have therefore opted for the word "housewife," although that choice suffers also from being both too limited and too modern for the Russian.

The careful reader will note occasional inconsistencies between the text of a recipe and the list of ingredients. Sometimes an ingredient is not carried over from one section of the recipe to another and sometimes the amounts are inconsistent. These are errors and omissions in the original text. I have eliminated as many of the errors as possible by comparing different editions, but if a mistake persisted, I left it as is. I marked any unresolved inconsistencies with a *sic* enclosed by square brackets. Molokhovets did not finish every recipe with a list of ingredients— indeed some recipes, especially in the later chapters of the book, had none. If a list of ingredients was included, I placed it at the end of the recipe even if this meant transposing a few final lines or short paragraphs. Molokhovets usually listed the primary ingredient first, followed by other ingredients as they occurred in the body of the recipe. She used parentheses to indicate optional ingredients. My order of ingredients varies slightly but insignificantly from hers; otherwise I have not added anything or tampered with her lists of ingredients except for correcting small misprints. Before using any of her recipes, readers are advised to check thoroughly both the text of the recipe and the list of ingredients.

Introduction

## Measurements and Conversions

Butter the size of a walnut (#339), ginger the size of a thimble (#734), and lemon salt the size of 1/2 a pea (#1568) are all measurements used by Molokhovets that are redolent of another era. She broke off dough the size of a chicken's egg or of a wild apple (#1294, 1847) and, according to the circumstances, rolled it out to the thickness of a finger (#1658), the blunt edge of a knife (#1667), or of 2 silver ruble coins (#1866). This kind of measurement based on familiar comparisons worked well for an experienced cook in Molokhovets' society, as does the modern American usage of #2 cans or a packet of dried onion soup mix. Once such a frame of reference is lost, however, it becomes difficult or impossible to reproduce the recipe. Butter the size of an egg may not be precise enough for modern standards, but it is still understandable, and in most cases a little butter more or less will not unduly affect the outcome of the recipe. More of a problem is her habit of calling for a "5 kopeck roll" or "half a French roll"; even knowing that a 5 kopeck roll weighed about 180 grams, or 2/5 of a U.S. pound, we can only speculate how much bread was represented by a 3 kopeck or a 1 kopeck roll. Were the prices strictly proportional to the amount of bread or was an inferior grade of flour used in the cheaper roll? I was unable to determine, but the search for the answer seems as elusive as the task the cook or historian a century hence will face when trying to reproduce an American recipe based on "ingredients" composed of commercial products long since vanished from the scene. Fortunately, such culturally bound directions are exceptional for Molokhovets, who was ahead of her time in trying to provide precise, accurate measurements for most of her recipes.

Molokhovets used a combination of weight and volume measurements, as Americans do today. In the first edition, her basic unit was by weight, but in the later editions, units of volume predominated. The Russian *stakan*, or glass, when filled with water weighed one-half pound. Like the cup used in American cookery, it was convenient to use, but was awkward to convert into weights. A pound of sugar, for instance, filled two glasses, but a pound of flour filled three. She did include scales in her kitchen inventory, but I find it telling that an otherwise extensive catalog of kitchen implements published in Odessa in 1897 did not.[214] This issue of why some societies moved toward measuring by volume and others by weight is an interesting one. Karen Hess, one of America's preeminent culinary historians, has rightly protested that "measuring flour by the cup is ludicrously inaccurate," and has speculated that "the American habit of measuring all ingredients by the cup may be blamed on frontier life where scales were cumbersome but a cup was always to hand."[215] At first hearing, this explanation sounds plausible for Russia as well as America, but it still leaves unexplained why other nations with their own rural and educational problems managed to adopt a more rational system of weights in the kitchen.

The Table of Weights and Measures (Appendix B) is intended as a guideline for the practicing cook. I chose not to convert the original units in the recipes into either metric or U.S. units. This was primarily a matter of aesthetics to avoid a text littered with such ungainly terms as .615 liter (= 1 bottle), 4.26 grams (= 1 *zolotnik*), or 1.75 inches (= 1 *vershok*). Another factor was that even after conversion, approximations are still necessary. When modernizing a historical recipe many factors come into play, and it seemed better to allow each cook to exercise his or her own judgment when it came time for adjustments and practical applications. Except for baking, which requires more exact measurements, slight variations will not matter. After all, most traditional and inventive cooking is based upon using what is available and in making intelligent substitutions. I based my conversions upon the following measurements:

### Basic Metric and U.S. Conversions

1 liter = 1.06 U.S. liquid quarts
1 liter = 1000 grams
1 U.S. quart = 896 grams
1 U.S. pound = 453.6 grams

In some cases, the converted values will not match exactly because I have combined several sources and, in particular, have used Elizabeth David's system of converting quarts and liters into grams which is very useful for making further conversions into the Russian system. She allows 1000 grams to each liter and 896 grams to each quart; this works extremely well except that it results in 1 liter equaling 1.12 quarts instead of the international standard of 1.06. With apologies to readers other than Americans, I used the term "U.S. pounds" only as a way of distinguishing between Russian and non-Russian pounds; it should not be taken as an example of rampant nationalism.[216]

### Advice to Modern Cooks

People ask me if I have tried out all the recipes in this book. The simple answer is no, but those that I have tried have worked well. My job has been to translate the recipes, not to modernize them, which is an entirely different task. Most of Molokhovets' recipes are straightforward and can be prepared readily in today's kitchen, but some, such as the instructions for making wheat starch (#2269), are of purely historical interest. We need to know how these older processes were carried out but, thank goodness, we need not repeat them. Nor is the idea of stringing an eel up by its eyes (#928) very appealing. I am quite content to begin my work with an eel that I know less intimately, one that has been skinned and cleaned by the fishmonger. Between the extremes of, on the one hand, recipes that require little or no adaptation and, on the other hand, those that are impractical or impossible to execute in contemporary conditions, there is another group that challenges a cook's ingenuity. Mostly these involve antiquated techniques. The cook who attempts to modernize a recipe should read it very carefully, envisioning the entire process and trying to understand the rationale for each step. Measurements are an important issue. Most of them are straightforward, but two, namely "pound" and "spoon," are "false friends" in that they do not really mean what they seem. Cooks should consult the Table of Weights and Measures before embarking on any recipe.

The use of historical recipes is one thing, but the production of a full meal, faithful to its period in every detail, is quite another. Period meals are best undertaken as a joint venture. Not only is the work too much for a single individual, but the dialogue that develops as people tackle the problems and devise solutions is a very valuable part of the experience. For the last ten years as a member of the Culinary Historians of Boston, I have participated in the agony and orgy of "The Annual Period Banquet," when members of the group attempt to recreate, as closely as possible, dishes from earlier periods, from Jeffersonian America to ancient Rome. Reliable period recipes in a language that the participants can read are the *sine qua non*. It sounds obvious, but it can be a major stumbling block since culinary historians, unlike practicing anthropologists, are primarily dependent on written sources. Historical menus are an intractable problem and often are impossible to execute either because of cost or the lack of a crucial component, such as adequate facilities, necessary skills, or even a key ingredient. With a bow toward expediency, the Culinary Historians have devised their own menus, feeling free to omit dishes that no one cares to recreate, or adding those that sound particularly appealing. The only stricture is that all the recipes must be appropriate to the time and place.

Reproducing isolated historical recipes on an occasional basis is much simpler than trying to put together a full-scale period meal. Although there are pitfalls, the problems of a single recipe are usually not insurmountable. Ingredients and cooking techniques are the overriding issues. Ingredients which were not available to a particular society at a given period should not be used. Allowance must be made for how those ingredients have changed over time. Gertrude Stein may have felt that a "Rose is a rose is a rose is a rose," but the same cannot be said for apples or many another product of the orchard or barnyard.[217] The older products may or may not have been better, but it is quite likely that they were different.

Cooking techniques also change with time. An awareness of these changes and a strategy to compensate for them is probably the most critical factor when modernizing a historical recipe. While some dishes now can be made more swiftly and expeditiously using modern kitchen equipment, the integrity of others is closely linked to a special process or piece of equipment no longer at hand. The Russian stove is a good example. Its virtues and drawbacks were discussed earlier. An example closer to home is the effort required to produce a traditional French baguette in an ordinary American stove.[218] Older recipes often omit crucial details like the amount of a spice or how long something should cook. Even when a recipe includes all pertinent details, and even when we follow those instructions closely, we cannot be sure of reproducing the exact taste and texture of the original. There is much that we do not know, such as the strength of the spices or the quality of the meat. We taste with late twentieth century palates, shaped by our own habits, experiences, and prejudices. We may be shocked, for instance, by the excessive use of salt, fat, and sugar in Molokhovets' recipes. Although we may choose to adjust her recipes, we should be aware that the cost of compromise is the loss of historical authenticity.

With few exceptions, most of the ingredients used by Molokhovets are readily available in American markets. One exception is *viziga*, or the dried spinal cord of the sturgeon, which is sometimes available in speciality shops that carry caviar. Since there is no substitute for this item, just omit it and continue with the recipe. Admittedly, the dish will lack the special savor that the sturgeon marrow provides, but informants have told me that this is a blessing in disguise.[219] Although caviar is available, I doubt that many readers will want to use it to clarify bouillon as Molokhovets recommended. Many more wild birds were eaten in nineteenth-century Russia than are available in American cities today. Special mail order sources can be tapped for these birds, but judicious substitutions will probably still be necessary. The varieties of freshwater fish that the Russians took from their rivers and streams in Tsarist times are usually not available in America today. For substitutions, consult any standard book of fish cookery.[220] The Russian butcher cut his meat in different ways than we do (see diagram of beef cuts in Chapter 5). Twentieth-century American meat is moister, fatter, and more tender than that used by Molokhovets, which means that cooking times along with the amount of liquid used in stews must be adjusted. The domesticated fowls she cooked were tougher, leaner, and often smaller than our own. She usually used a 3-pound turkey in her recipes and she gave instructions for carving a 5-pound turkey into twenty servings (#785 and Chapter 6, Remarks). Eggs were smaller as well. Before embarking on one of her 70-egg baba recipes (even if you reduce the ingredients by a third as she suggests), compare the figure given by Molokhovets, that is 6 eggs = 1 glass, with the number of eggs it takes to fill an American measuring cup.

It is important to consider what the food tastes like, even though it may be hard to pin down. When we compare the ingredients available to us and to Molokhovets, we have to conclude that while some of our products were better, so were some of hers, like poultry and game. Her free-range chickens scrabbled for feed in the yard and her wild boars devoured nuts in the forest; our chickens and pigs are raised in crowded batteries where movement is all but impossible. Not only the animal but the flavor suffers from this confinement.[221] On the other hand, some modern products are better, partly because some of hers were a long time on the road, and partly because of the widespread adulteration of comestibles in the nineteenth century. Cookbooks of the period were full of methods for detecting spurious additions. Adulterated pickles especially plagued Molokhovets.

Some fruits and vegetables that were rarities for Molokhovets have since become commonplace, thanks to technological developments such as improved transportation and better control over systems of heating and refrigeration. Tomatoes are one example and pineapples another. Americans may love to hate their commercially grown tomatoes, but they may have hated Molokhovets' puny green bullets even more. Pineapples were introduced into Russia in the eighteenth century during the reign of Empress Elizaveta. From the beginning they were a symbol of luxury and Western culture.[222] They were always grown in hothouses and it was difficult to force the plants to bear fruit. Because they were so rare, Molokhovets used them economically, making a little go a very long way. When cooking Pineapple preserves, she said, "The more pineapple the better, but if proportions of only ¼ pineapple and ¾ apples are used, the preserves still will be very tasty and will resemble real pineapple preserves" (#1983).

Modern Russians clearly have no difficulty understanding even the most archaic of Molokhovets' preparations. Those without a Slavic heritage must make a greater leap of faith to experiment with these recipes. I advise starting with something simple and gradually working up to the more complicated dishes, relying on one's own experience and judgment. Be prepared for mistakes! The occasional catastrophe makes success that much more delectable.

# NOTES

1. Anton Pavlovich Chekhov, *Polnoe sobranie sochinenij i pisem v tridtsati tomakh* [Complete collected works and letters in thirty volumes] (Moscow: Nauka, 1974–1982), I, 153.

2. Teffi was the pseudonym of Nadezhda Aleksandrovna Buchinskaja (1872–1952). Her piece was entitled, "Paskhal'nýe sovety molodym khozjajkam" [Easter advice to young housewives]. See also Darra Goldstein, *A la Russe: A Cookbook of Russian Hospitality* (New York: Random House, 1983), 124. For a brief description of Teffi's work, see *Handbook of Russian Literature*, ed. Victor Terras (New Haven: Yale University Press, 1985), 465.

3. Tarkovskij's poem "Elena Molokhovets" appeared in part IV of his collection *Pered snegom* [Before the snow, 1941–1966]. See Arsenij Aleksandrovich Tarkovskij, *Stikhotvorenija* [Poems] (Moscow: Khudozhestvennaja literatura, 1974), 120–121; and Alan Davidson, *North Atlantic Seafood* (London: Macmillan, 1979), 340.

4. E.g., 10 February 1989.

5. *Podarok molodym khozjajkam. 400 original'nykh retseptov sladkikh bljud* [A gift to young housewives. 400 original recipes for sweet dishes] (Vosproizvedeno s izdanija 1904 goda. Moscow, n.d. [1989]). The second is *Iz kulinarnykh sovetov grafini Eleny Molokhovets: Vegetarianskij stol; Postnyj stol; Kulichi i paskhi* [Culinary advice from Countess Elena Molokhovets: vegetarian dishes; fast day dishes; *kuliches* and *paskhas*] (Moscow: Khudozhestvennaja literatura, 1989). The Soviets turned Molokhovets into a countess for this second pamphlet, an elevation without apparent basis except that she was listed as Helene von Molochowetz on the title page of the 1877 Leipzig edition of her book.

6. Elizabeth David, "Hunt the Ice Cream," *Petits Propos Culinaires [1]* (1979), 8.

## DEVELOPMENT OF COOKBOOKS IN RUSSIA

7. Aleksandr Sergeevich Orlov, *Domostroj: Izsledovanie, pt. 1* [Domestic management: Research, part 1] (Moscow: Sinodal'naja tip., 1917; rpt. The Hague: Europe Printing, 1967). The last third of the work contains directions for managing the household and the preparation and storage of food.

8. *Le Ménagier de Paris*, ed. Georgina E. Brereton and Janet M. Ferrier (New York: Oxford University Press, 1981). A good short discussion of the relation between the *Domostroj* and the European domestic book is found in Carolyn Johnston Pouncy, "The *Domostroi* as a Source for Muscovite History" (Ph.D. diss., Stanford University, 1985): 154–165.

9. [Florinus, Franciscus Philippus], pseud., *Ekonomija* [Agricultural and household management] (St. Petersburg: Akademija nauk, 1738).

10. *Nastol'naja kniga. Raznyja neobkhodimyja spravochnyja svedenija* [Manual. Various essential pieces of infomation] (St. Petersburg: S. Dobrodeev, 1895).

11. *Podarok molodym khozjajkam. Domashnee, gorodskoe i sel'skoe khozjajstvo, gigiena i meditsina, zakljuchajushchaja v sebe 3000 domashnikh sredstv ot razlichnykh boleznej vzroslykh i detej i 1000 ukazanij na ukhod, otkarmlivanie i bolezni domashnikh ptits i zhivotnykh.* [Gift to young housewives. Domestic and urban housekeeping, agriculture, hygiene, and medicine, including 3000 domestic remedies for treating various adult and childhood illnesses and 1000 instructions for the care and feeding of domestic birds and animals, also the curing of their diseases.] part III. Circa 1880.

12. Vasilij Alekseevich Levshin, *Slovar' povarennyj, prispeshnichij, kanditerskij i distilljator-*

*skij, soderzhashchij po azbuchnomu porjadku podrobnoe i vernoe nastavlenie k prigotovleniju vsjakago roda kushan'ja iz frantsuzskoj, nemetskoj, gollandskoj, ispanskoj i anglijskoj povarni* [An alphabetical dictionary of cooking, general assistance, confectionary, and distilling, containing detailed and reliable instructions for preparing all sorts of French, German, Dutch, Spanish, and English dishes] (Moscow: Univ. tip., 1795–1797), and Pankratij Platonovich Sumarokov, *Istochnik zdravija, ili Slovar' vsekh upotrebitel'nykh snedej, priprav i napitkov iz trekh tsarstv prirody izvlekaemykh* [Source of health, or Dictionary of all common foods, seasonings, and beverages derived from the three realms of nature] (Moscow: Univ. tip., 1800).

13. Nikolaj Nikolaevich Golitsyn, *Bibliograficheskij slovar' russkikh pisatel'nits* [Bibliographical dictionary of Russian women writers] (St. Petersburg: V. C. Valashev, 1889), 5–7.

14. I am indebted to Barbara Wheaton for her helpful comments on the publishing history of individual cookbooks. Many of the citations in this paragraph stem from her suggestions.

15. The first edition of Audot's book was published in 1818 without indication of authorship; according to Leonard Beck, it was not until the fortieth edition (1860) that Audot was listed "as both publisher and author for the first time." See Leonard Beck, "La Cuisine moderne" in *Two "Loaf-Givers"* (Washington, D.C.: Library of Congress, 1984), 208.

16. According to Virginia Maclean, the last certain edition of Hannah Glasse's work was published in 1843, although there may have been a later edition in 1852. See Maclean's bibliography, *A Short-title Catalogue of Household and Cookery Books published in the English Tongue 1701–1800* (London: Prospect Books, 1981), 59–61.

17. Elizabeth David, the doyenne of English food writers and culinary historians, wrote that Miss Acton's work was so widely plagiarized that "it is difficult to find any standard cookery compendium of the latter part of the Victorian era . . . which do[es] not include a quantity of Miss Acton's recipes," few of which were ever acknowledged. See the Introduction to *The Best of Eliza Acton*, ed. Elizabeth Ray (London: Longmans, Green, 1968; London: Penguin Books, 1974), xxv.

18. It is generally accepted that Tolstoy began work on *War and Peace* in late 1860 and that the book was published in several parts between 1865 and 1869. Victor Shklovsky, *Lev Tolstoy* (Moscow: Progress Publishers, 1978), 355.

19. Elena Molokhovets, *Podarok molodym khozjajkam*, 28th ed. (St. Petersburg: Pervaja SPB Trudovaja Artel', 1914), iii and vi.


## BIOGRAPHY OF ELENA IVANOVNA MOLOKHOVETS

20. The dedication of the anonymous first edition of *A Gift to Young Housewives* reads as follows: "A former pupil dedicates this work to her friends and the other pupils of the Imperial Educational Society for Noble Girls."

21. *Novoe vremja* [New time], 20 May 1911, 4.

22. *Podarok*, 28th ed. (1914), viii.

23. I am grateful to Richard Seitz of the Slavic and East European Library at the University of Illinois at Urbana-Champaign for his assistance in searching for notices of Molokhovets' death. In the absence of any solid evidence to the contrary, Seitz hypothesizes, and I concur, that Molokhovets was still alive in late 1916 or 1917 since Vengerov included her date of birth, but not her date of death, in his collection of materials for a dictionary of Russian writers. This is a fragile supposition, but it seems plausible. See Semen Afanas'evich Vengerov, *Istochniki slovarja russkikh pisatelej* [Sources for a dictionary of Russian writers] (St. Petersburg: Tip. imper. akademii nauk, 1900–1917), IV, 400, 128–129. The 29th edition was passed by the censor in September 1916 and was published in 1917.

24. *Podarok*, 28th ed. (1914), iv.

25. Nicholas V. Riasanovsky, *A History of Russia*, 4th ed. (New York: Oxford University Press, 1984), 381.

26. *Podarok*, 28th ed. (1914), vi, viii, and v.

27. I have no further information about this society. The group may have been organized for philanthropic purposes, but the letter from the members shows that socializing was important as well.

28. *Podarok*, 28th ed. (1914), vii.

29. Quoted by Laura Shapiro in *Perfection Salad* (New York: Farrar, Straus & Giroux, 1986), 137–138.

## INFLUENCE OF THE RUSSIAN ORTHODOX CHURCH

30. Readers interested in this subject should consult two important books on the influence of the Roman Church on medieval eating habits: Bridget Ann Henisch's *Fast and Feast: Food in Medieval Society* (University Park: Pennsylvania State University Press, 1976) and Caroline W. Bynum's *Holy Feast and Holy Fast: The Religious Significance of Food to Medieval Women* (Berkeley: University of California Press, 1987).

31. Anatolij Vasil'evich Belov, *Kogda zvonjat kolokola* [When the bells ring] (Moscow: Sovetskaja Rossija, 1977), 321–322.

32. Samuel Collins, *The present state of Russia, in a letter to a friend at London; written by an eminent person residing at the Great Tsars court at Moscow for the space of nine years* (London: Dorman Newman, 1671). The prohibition against sugar would not have significantly affected the diet of many people since sugar at that time was made only from the cane; the much cheaper process of extracting sugar from sugar beets was not developed until the early nineteenth century. Because imported cane sugar was prohibitively expensive, honey was the traditional sweetener used in Russian cooking. The cost of fish in the fasting season was much more of a problem.

33. My analysis of cookbook menus for "Three Hundred Years of Russian Fasting: Foreign Perceptions vs. Native Practice" showed that the influence of the Church was waning in the late nineteenth century, at least as it affected the diet of the middle and upper classes. This paper was presented at the Eighth International Conference on Ethnological Food Research held in Philadelphia in June 1990; the conference proceedings will be published by the Balch Institute for Ethnic Studies.

34. Alphonse Petit, *La Gastronomie en Russie* (Paris: Chez l'auteur, 1860), frontispiece; iii; and 9.

35. Petit, *La Gastronomie en Russie*, 203.

36. *Podarok*, 20th ed. (1897), 199–204. All references are to this edition unless noted otherwise.

## EASTERN INFLUENCE ON RUSSIAN CUISINE

37. One notable exception is Darra Goldstein's article "The Eastern Influence on Russian Cuisine," in *Current Research in Culinary History: Sources, Topics, and Methods* (Boston: Culinary Historians of Boston, 1986) 20–26. Although our emphases sometimes differ, my essay basically follows Goldstein's outline. For the purposes of this discussion, "East" is used in a very broad sense to include Arab and Mongol cultures as well as Chinese—in fact anywhere except Western Europe, the Americas, Africa, and Oceania.

38. Nikolaj Ivanovich Kovalev, *Russkaja kulinarija* [Russian cooking] (Moscow: Ekonomika, 1972), 8–9, 14; and Nicholas V. Riasanovsky, *A History of Russia*, 13–15.

39. Don and Patricia Brothwell, *Food in Antiquity* (New York: Frederick A. Praeger, 1969), 95; and William J. Darby, Paul Ghalioungui, and Louis Grivetti, *Food: The Gift of Osiris* (London: Academic Press, 1977), II, 501–502.

40. The Herodotus reference is cited in *Kumys i shubat* [Fermented mare's milk and fermented camel's milk] (Alma-Ata: Kajnar, 1979), 66. This book contains a discussion of the restorative properties of *koumiss* and offers as evidence many comments (unfortunately undocumented) from early travelers, and from literary figures such as Pushkin, Aksakov, Tolstoy, and Chekhov. See pp. 66–85.

41. Collins, *The Present State of Russia*, 13–14.

42. Goldstein, "The Eastern Influence," 21.

43. Collins, *The Present State of Russia*, 62.

44. According to the *Rites of Chou*, a Chinese text from the third or fourth century B.C.,

the royal household employed 62 vegetable picklers (in addition to 61 employees who specialized in meat pickling). At that period the Chinese were pickling leeks, rape turnip, watershield, mallow, water dropwort, arrow bamboo shoots, and bamboo shoots. David Knechtges, "A Literary Feast: Food in Early Chinese Literature," *Journal of the American Oriental Society*, vol. 106, no. 1 (Jan.–Mar. 1986), 49–50. The earliest surviving Chinese agricultural encyclopedia, the *Qimin Yaoshu*, written in the sixth century A.D., devoted a full chapter to the process of fermenting vegetables, called *zu*, and of these recipes nearly 40% could be classified as "sauerkraut." The title of this important agricultural text has been variously translated as *Essential Ways for Living of the Common People* or *Essential Techniques for the Peasantry*. Françoise Sabban, "Insights into the Problem of Preservation by Fermentation in 6th Century China," in *Food Conservation: Ethnological Studies*, ed. Astri Riddervold and Andreas Ropeid (London: Prospect Books, 1988), 45–47, 53.

45. Anna Kowalska-Lewicka, "The Pickling of Vegetables in Traditional Polish Peasant Culture," in *Food Conservation: Ethnological Studies*, ed. Riddervold and Ropeid, 33.

46. Goldstein, "The Eastern Influence," 22.

47. R. E. F. Smith, "Whence the Samovar?" *Petits Propos Culinaires*, 4 (February 1980), 57.

48. R. E. F. Smith, *Peasant Farming in Muscovy* (Cambridge: Cambridge University Press, 1977), 76. What was a footnote in *Peasant Farming* became an article in 1980 and an entire chapter in Smith and Christian's later work. For a thorough discussion of the history of the tea trade in Russia, see R. E. F. Smith and David Christian, *Bread and Salt: A Social and Economic History of Food and Drink in Russia* (Cambridge: Cambridge University Press, 1984), 228–247. Anne Fitzpatrick included some good material on the nineteenth-century tea trade in her new book *The Great Russian Fair: Nizhnii Novgorod, 1840–90* (London: Macmillan, 1990), especially pp. 47–56.

49. Fitzpatrick, *The Great Russian Fair*, 50, 55. Smith and Christian estimated that "perhaps less than 1 lb (0.45 kg) of leaf tea a year was available to members of gentry families in the late eighteenth century." Smith and Christian, *Bread and Salt*, 246, 234.

50. Ljubov' Fedorovna Zakharova and Eva Iosifovna Tolchinskaja, *Puteshestvie v stranu Kulinariju* [Journey in Culinary Land], 2nd ed. (Kishinev: Timpul, 1987), 142. Unfortunately, the authors did not cite the source of the song.

51. Smith and Christian, *Bread and Salt*, 236–237. Alexandre Dumas commented on the prevalence of the plea "na tchay" during his trip to Russia in 1858, saying, "the Russian begs 'for tea' at every opportunity, without having done anything to deserve reward, without rhyme or reason, save the hope that perhaps he may be given it." *Alexandre Dumas' Adventures in Czarist Russia*, tr. Alma Elizabeth Murch (Westport, Conn.: Greenwood Press, 1961), 61.

52. The center of the samovar-making industry in Russia was Tula, where the first known samovar workshop was set up in 1778. Smith and Christian, *Bread and Salt*, 240. According to Dix, the close association of tea drinking with the samovar in Russia showed the gentry origins of the custom. Samovars were costly items and even in the late nineteenth century only the rich peasants could afford them. See Graham Dix, "Non-Alcoholic Beverages in Nineteenth Century Russia," *Petits Propos Culinaires*, 10 (March 1982), 24. Dumas, on the other hand, observed that "no home is so poor that it has no samovar." Dumas, *Adventures in Czarist Russia*, 61. Since I tend to side with Dix and discount Dumas' testimony, I consider the relatively well known Russian photograph of the late nineteenth century showing Russian peasants sitting outside at a table playing the balalaika and about to enjoy tea from a samovar exceptional enough to be somewhat misleading. See *In the Russian Style*, ed. Jacqueline Onassis (New York: Viking Press, 1976), 171.

53. Dix, "Non-Alcoholic Beverages," 24. For a clear diagram of a samovar with its working parts, see Genevra Gerhart, *The Russian's World: Life and Language* (New York: Harcourt Brace Jovanovich, 1974), 65–66.

54. Both of these paintings are in the State Tretyakov Gallery in Moscow; reproductions are included in *Russia, The Land, The People: Russian Painting, 1850–1910* (Washington, D.C. and Seattle: Smithsonian Institution Traveling Exhibition Service in association with University of Washington Press, 1986), 58–59, 62–63.

55. Goldstein, "The Eastern Influence," 23.

56. Nikolaj Ivanovich Kovalev, *Rasskazy o russkoj kukhne* [Tales of a Russian kitchen] (Moscow: Ekonomika, 1984), 128. Although I have no evidence to the contrary, I would have more confidence in Kovalev's assertion about *pel'meni* if it were substantiated with information about the historical development of these Eastern pastries. There could be many reasons for the similarity of the modern varieties, without the Russian pastries having evolved from those in Central Asia.

57. Vladimir Ivanovich Dal', *Tolkovyj slovar' zhivago velikorusskago jazyka* (1880; rpt. Moscow: Russkij jazyk, 1989), II, 290 and I, 181.

58. Vil'jam Vasil'evich Pokhlebkin, *Natsional'nye kukhni nashikh narodov* [The national dishes of our people] (Moscow: Pishchevaja promyshlennost', 1980), 9.

59. Smith and Christian, *Bread and Salt*, 252.

60. Nikolaj Ivanovich Guba, *Tainy shchedrogo stola* [Secrets of a lavish table], 2nd ed. (Dnepropetrovsk: Promin', 1978), 229.

61. Taisija Grigor'evna Gutsaljuk, *Ot arbuza do tykvy* [From watermelon to pumpkin] (Alma-Ata: Kajnar, 1989), 27. Anecdotes like this are hard to evaluate and track down. Although it seems unlikely that Peter would not have known about the cultivation of watermelons along the Volga, it is true that Peter's father had died when the boy was only four and that Peter had had other things on his mind in the intervening years besides rare plants.

62. Pokhlebkin, *Natsional'nye kukhni*, 9; Goldstein, "The Eastern Influence," 24.

63. Goldstein, "The Eastern Influence," 24.

64. Dumas, *Adventures in Czarist Russia*, II, 20–21.

## FRENCH INFLUENCE ON RUSSIAN CUISINE

65. Pokhlebkin, *Natsional'nye kukhni*, 10.

66. Lesley Chamberlain, "Ideology and the Growth of a Russian School of Cooking," in *Oxford Symposium Papers* (London: Prospect Books, 1982), 188; and Christopher Marsden, *Palmyra of the North: The First Days of St. Petersburg* (London: Faber & Faber, 1942), 130.

67. Martha and Catherine Wilmot, *The Russian Journals of Martha and Catherine Wilmot*, ed. The Marchioness of Londonderry and H. Montgomery Hyde (1934; rpt. New York: Arno Press & The New York Times, 1971), 216. Here and elsewhere, I have retained the spelling and punctuation of the original.

68. Aleksandr Sergeevich Pushkin, *Polnoe sobranie sochinenij* (Leningrad: Akademija nauk SSSR, 1937–59), VIII, 232. For English readers, see *The Queen of Spades* in *The Poems, Prose and Plays of Pushkin* ed. Avrahm Yarmolinsky (New York: Modern Library, 1936 and 1964), 562. At a time when French culture had nearly overwhelmed native Russian culture, Pushkin asked and answered the Countess' question at the same time. Although strictly speaking *The Queen of Spades* is not a novel, Pushkin demonstrated new possibilities for Russian prose by writing this novella.

69. Antonin Carême, *Le maître d'hôtel français* (Paris: Didot, 1822), II, 101. For a full discussion of Carême's employment, see Louis Rodil, *Antonin Carême de Paris, 1783–1833* (Paris: Editions Jeanne Laffitte, 1980), 26–30, 36.

70. An Englishwoman who resided in Russia for a decade in the mid nineteenth century gave two good examples of this unfortunate system; in one, the cook was the victim, but in the other, the gluttonous master was outwitted by his wily serf. See *An Englishwoman in Russia by a Lady Ten Years Resident in That Country* (New York: Charles Scribner, 1855), 141–142 and 144–145.

71. Lev Nikolaevich Tolstoj, *Polnoe sobranie sochinenij* (Moscow: Gosudarstvennoe izd. khudozhestvennoj literatury, 1928–1958), IX, 68. This reference is found in vol. I, part I, section 17 of the Russian edition, but part I, section 14 of the Garnett translation. See *War and Peace*, tr. Constance Garnett (New York: Modern Library, Random House, n.d.), 48.

72. Antonin Carême, *Le maître d'hôtel français*, 111–145. This of course was not the only traditional dish or soup served at these dinners. *La soupe froide à la Russe* and *Le potage de poissons à la Russe*, which presumably were *botvin'ja* and fish *ukha* respectively, were also served. Neither of these dishes, however, carries quite the symbolic weight of *shchi*, which is caught in

the folk expression *Shchi da kasha—pishcha nasha.* Unfortunately, the zest of the original is lost in translation, which in English rather lamely reads, "Cabbage soup and kasha, those are our foods."

73. Chekhov, *Polnoe sob. soch.,* III, 386–389.


## MEALTIMES AND MENUS

74. N. I. Kovalev, *Rasskazy o russkoj kukhne,* 279–280. Also see entry for "vyt'" in Dal', *Tolkovyj slovar',* I, 322.

75. *Podarok molodym khozjajkam i neopytnym khozjaevam* [Gift to young and inexperienced housewives] (St. Petersburg: Dom prizrenija maloletnikh bednykh, 1874), 9. For this reason, the author advised serving nothing but salted *zakuski* and cold meats. The only hot dishes deemed suitable for the meal were soft-boiled eggs, meat patties, and beefsteaks. This anonymous book (hereafter referred to as Anon., *Podarok*) was among the many that tried to capitalize on the success of Elena Molokhovets' cookbook, *Podarok molodym khozjajkam,* that was first published in 1861. In the Introduction to the 1914 edition of her book, Molokhovets gave many details about this flood of plagiarisms.

76. Martha Wilmot objected to the early dinner hour of the Russians since it effectively put an end to all useful daytime activities. "I do not like the practise they have here of dining at three o'clock and separating *before tea* [her emphasis], so that by half after five or six, unless you are engag'd to some party, you return home gaping for your amusement your Scandal and your tea—but the practice is universal . . . " *Russian Journals,* 29.

77. I. M. Radetskij, *Al'manakh gastronomov* [Almanac for gastronomes] (St. Petersburg: Tip. shtaba otdel'nago korpusa vnutrennej strazhi, 1852), 2–61. The second revised edition was published in St. Petersburg in 1877.

78. Anon., *Podarok,* 13. Most of Molokhovets' advice on menu planning appeared in the Berlin, Parabola edition (p. 38), but was not included in the editions published in Russia as late as the twentieth in 1897.

79. These meals, obviously, were both lavish and expensive. By contrast, note that when the St. Petersburg Public Lectures [for women] opened in January 1870, the cost was 25 rubles per semester to attend evening lectures four times a week. Similarly, when Guerrier's Courses [also for women] opened in Moscow in 1872, they cost 50 rubles per year. Christine Johanson, *Women's Struggle for Higher Education in Russia, 1855–1900* (Kingston and Montreal: McGill-Queen's University Press), 39, 49.

80. I have not been able to identify the German wine more specifically.

81. The Russian word is *salat.* Rather than referring to a green lettuce salad like the one customary in America, it usually indicated a salad of marinated vegetables or even marinated fruits. See Recipes #880–897 for examples.

82. Although much has been written about Russian and Soviet consumption of alcohol, I do not know of any thorough history of Russian and Soviet wines, either in Russian or in English. An excellent beginning was made, however, with the publication of the three-volume *Entsiklopedija vinogradarstva* [Encyclopedia of viticulture] (Kishinev: Glavnaja redaktsija Moldavskoj Sovetskoj Entsiklopedii, 1986). For a brief discussion of the development of the champagne industry in Russia, see my article, "Russia and Champagne," *Wine and Spirits,* vol. 7, no. 3 (June 1988), 26–27.

83. Anon., *Podarok,* 8. I have found only one other reference to this custom. After describing a large dinner party that was given in Moscow, an English businessman's wife finished by adding, "There is one custom that might well be entirely abolished. Each person washes his mouth out after dinner, and after having well rinsed it, empties its contents into the finger-glass; it certainly is not pleasant to see a whole party thus employed." *An Englishwoman in Russia,* 98–99.

84. *Podarok,* II, 304.

85. Radetskij, *Al'manakh gastronomov,* ii–iii.

86. For an exposition of drinks and drinking customs in nineteenth-century Russia, see

Patricia Herlihy, "'Joy of the Rus': Rites and Rituals of Russian Drinking," *Russian Review*, vol. 50 (April 1991), 131–147.

## TABLE SERVICE AND SETTINGS

87. Henisch, *Fast and Feast*, 209.

88. Barbara Ketcham Wheaton, *Savoring the Past: The French Kitchen and Table from 1300 to 1789* (Philadelphia: University of Pennsylvania Press, 1983), 138.

89. G. Peyerle in N. G. Ustryalov, *Skazanija sovremennikov o Dmitrii Samozvantse* [Contemporaries' tales about the false Dmitrij] (St. Petersburg, 1831–34), Vol. 2, 58–59. Cited in Smith and Christian, *Bread and Salt*, 115–116.

90. Pokhlebkin, *Natsional'nye kukhni*, 10.

91. Levshin, *Slovar' povarennyj*, V, 373–376.

92. Gerard Brett, *Dinner Is Served: A History of Dining in England, 1400–1900* (London: Rupert Hart-Davis, 1968), 119.

93. Patrick Dunne and Charles L. Mackie, "Clio's Table: Dining in the French Fashion" *Historic Preservation* (Jan.–Feb. 1991), 63.

94. Mrs. Isabella Beeton, *The Book of Household Management* (London: S. O. Beeton, 1861; Facsimile rpt. New York: Farrar, Straus & Giroux, 1977), 955.

95. Charles Ranhofer, *The Epicurean* (1893; rpt. New York: Dover, 1971), 9.

96. My comments are limited strictly to upper-class meals eaten indoors in the dining room. Picnics and outings were much more informal by their standards, but not necessarily by ours. See the photographs entitled "A country picnic of Grand Duchess Maria Pavlovna, 1913" in *A Portrait of Tsarist Russia: Unknown Photographs from the Soviet Archives* (New York: Pantheon Books, 1989), 92–93, and "Luncheon at Belenkow, an estate of the Miklashevski family in Ekaterinoslav Province, c. 1900" in Marvin Lyons, *Russia in Original Photographs, 1860–1910* (Boston: Routledge & Kegan Paul, 1977), 88.

97. The plight of unmarried adult women in Tsarist Russia was made more difficult by their not being allowed to have their own passports. Females were listed on their father's passport until they married and thereafter on their husband's. One result of this archaic system was that single women found it very difficult to support themselves and usually remained dependent upon their families or wealthier relatives. After the emancipation of the serfs, many gentry families became impoverished making it difficult or impossible to continue support of these women. This shrinking of the extended family was another impetus toward providing educational opportunities for women. For more on this issue, see Christine Johanson, *Women's Struggle*, 26 and Barbara Engel, *Mothers and Daughters: Women of the Intelligentsia in Nineteenth-Century Russia* (Cambridge: Cambridge University Press, 1983). 20–42.

98. Anon., *Podarok*, 13.

99. The anonymous author of *Podarok molodym khozjajkam* outlined the duties involved and advised the housewife to supervise the care of the stoves herself, otherwise the work would never be done properly (168–170).

100. *Russian Journal of Lady Londonderry, 1836–37*, ed. W. A. L. Seaman and J. R. Sewell (London: John Murray, 1973), 112.

101. *Podarok*, I, 5.

102. *Podarok*, II, 302.

103. In Tsarist Russia, children in Orthodox familes were named after saints who were listed in a calendar that had been approved by the Eastern Orthodox Church. Thereafter, the child celebrated not his or her date of birth but the date on which the saint was listed in the calendar. This was called a name day. Thus, a girl named Larissa who was born in December celebrated not her birthday, but her name day on March 26.

104. A few examples from Vol'f's *Katalog* (1830–1870) include Berar, *Rukovodstvo k soderzhaniju komnatnykh rastenij v zdorovom i tsvetushchem sostojanii, s polnym ob"jasneniem sposoba ukhoda za kazhdym tsvetkom* [Guide to keeping house plants healthy and flowering, with full instructions for caring for each plant] (St. Petersburg, 1852); *Komnatnyj sadovnik, ili nastavlenie razvodit' raznyja rastenija, tsvety i derev'ja v sadu, tsvetnike, balkone i osoblivo v*

*komnatakh na oknakh. S kratkim ponjatiem ob organizatsii rastenij* [Room or household gardener, or instructions for cultivating various plants, flowers and trees in the garden, flower beds, on balconies, and especially in windows of rooms. With brief ideas for the organization of plants] (Moscow, 1827); Kurtoa-Zherar, *Prakticheskoe rukovodstvo k proizrashcheniju tsvetov v komnatakh i pr.* [Practical guide to the growing of flowers in rooms, etc.] (St. Petersburg, 1861); and *Nastavlenie prakticheskoe k soderzhaniju tsvetov i derev'ev v komnatakh* [Practical instructions for maintaining flowers and trees indoors] (Moscow, 1855). See *Katalog russkago otdelenija knizhnago magazina Mavrikija Osipovicha Vol'fa* [Catalog of the Russian department of M. O. Vol'f's bookstore] (St. Petersburg: Tip. M. O. Vol'fa, 1872), 5544, 5990, 6031, and 6188.

105. Anon., *Podarok*, 6–7. The composition of this book is quite different from Molokhovets' book of similar title. Whereas her entire book was devoted to food with very few references to flowers and none to houseplants, this author gave equal space to flowers and food. The book also contained a long section on maintaining health and concluded with instructions on sewing and knitting.

106. Lady Londonderry, who visited Russia during 1836–1837, mentioned the absence of saltcellars at formal dinners. "There is a general and ancient superstition of ill luck attending accidents with salt and in some old Russian families it is shaped and piled on the table so that everyone may carry off a little while no one can upset it." *Russian Journal of Lady Londonderry*, 70.

107. *Podarok* II, 303. Serving ice cream on a napkin was neither novel nor particularly Russian. See Mrs. Beeton, *The Book of Household Management*, 650 (#1290—Iced Apple Pudding from a French Recipe, after Carême) and Ranhofer, *The Epicurean*, 982–985 (#3434–3444). One should also consider the aesthetic ideal, especially in America at this period, of containing and controlling the food which the white napkin served to accentuate. For more on this issue see Laura Shapiro's *Perfection Salad*. Elaborate tinned copper molds were an important part of the *batterie de cuisine* in late nineteenth century Russia as well as in Europe, England, and America. Molokhovets used them, and illustrations of these molds were included in many nineteenth-century cookbooks including Ranhofer's *The Epicurean* and *Ices Plain and Fancy* ed. Barbara Ketcham Wheaton (rpt. of Mrs. A. B. Marshall's *Book of Ices*, London: Marshall's School of Cookery, n.d. [1885]; New York: Metropolitan Museum of Art, 1976). For more on the subject of copper molds, see David W. Miller, "Technology and the Ideal: Production Quality and Kitchen Reform in Nineteenth-Century America" in *Dining in America, 1850–1900*, ed. Kathryn Grover (Amherst: University of Massachusetts Press, 1987), 47–84.

## IMAGE OF A RUSSIAN HOUSEHOLD

108. The traditional importance of water and stoves to the family's well-being is evident in Russian folklore with its many popular beliefs about water spirits and household demons, some of which made their home in the family's stove. Although no hint of these superstitions appears in the pages of *A Gift to Young Housewives*, the reader should be aware of their wide acceptance among Russian peasants, for whom these lively spirits were an integral part of the household.

## WATER

109. According to Jonathan Periam, the American author of *The Home and Farm Manual*, "no well-water is entirely safe, unless means have been taken to keep out surface drainage, and they are liable to be contaminated by the seepage, from sewers, the out-houses or the barnyard. . . . The earth is always honey-combed with the borings of insects and small animals, which always carry their burrows to the nearest water, generally the well. Seepage once entering these cavities inevitably finds its way to the well. Unfortunately, the most deadly germs are often not to be detected by the taste or smell. For this reason, many persons prefer cistern water [rain water collected in a cistern] to that from the well. When danger is suspected from wells, the water should always be boiled. No filtering will take out the deadly germs. Indeed, half the

disease of the world would be avoided if all the water drunk was first boiled." Periam, *The Home and Farm Manual* (1884; rpt. New York: Greenwich House, 1984), 733.

110. Anon., *Podarok*, 6.

111. Jan Longone, "A Sufficiency and No More, A Graphic Description of the American Kitchen of the 1850s," *American Magazine and Historical Chronicle* (published by the Clements Library, University of Michigan), vol. 3, no. 1 (Spring–Summer 1987), 28–31.

112. *Podarok*, II, 312–313.

113. Robert A. Caro, the biographer of Lyndon B. Johnson, wrote movingly of Johnson's accomplishment in bringing electricity to the Hill Country in Texas in the late 1930s and early 1940s. It is not easy for today's urban dweller to understand just how hard life was without running water, but Caro, quoting figures from the U.S. Department of Agriculture, painted a vivid picture of the difficulties. "The average farm family uses two hundred gallons of water a day," he said. "That's seventy-three thousand gallons, or three hundred tons, a year. And it all had to be lifted by these women, one bucket at a time," and carried by means of yokes thrown across their shoulders, "so that they could carry one of the heavy buckets on each side." Caro, "Lyndon Johnson and the Roots of Power" in *Extraordinary Lives: The Art and Craft of American Biography*, ed. William Zinsser (Boston: Houghton Mifflin, 1986), 205–206.

## STOVES AND OVENS

114. Smith described pre-Mongol stoves which were supported by posts or built on a solid frame over a small pit. He also clearly summarized the traditional positioning of the stove, which varied according to region but was always in a corner of the room. See R. E. F. Smith, "The Russian Stove," *Oxford Slavonic Papers*, New Series, vol. XVIII (1985), 86, 91.

115. Unlike many other travelers to Russia in the nineteenth century, Kohl spoke Russian. His detailed account of what he saw is a pleasure to read since little escaped the notice of this seasoned German traveler who admired the Russians and their way of life, even their stoves. Johann George Kohl, *Russia* (1842; rpt. New York: Arno Press & The New York Times, 1970), 45.

116. David Lyle, *The Book of Masonry Stoves: Rediscovering an Old Way of Warming* (Andover, Mass.: Brick House Publishing, 1984), 91. See also Gerhart's *The Russian's World*, 63–66, for a good description of the Russian stove and its traditional utensils accompanied by drawings clearly labeled in Russian. Mention of the poker would not be complete without directing readers to Zoshchenko's humorous sketch built around the irregular declension of the noun *kocherga*. See Mikhail Zoshchenko, "Kochergà" [The Poker], in *Scenes from the Bathhouse and Other Stories of Communist Russia*, tr. Sidney Monas (Ann Arbor: Ann Arbor Paperbacks, University of Michigan Press, 1962), 169–172.

117. Smith, "The Russian Stove," 100.

118. Kovalev, *Rasskazy o russkoj kukhne*, 39–40.

119. Smith suggested that if semispherical dome-shaped stoves really were used in premodern Russia, then "vessels placed over the smoke-hole in such stoves" might have been used for frying and boiling (Smith and Christian, *Bread and Salt*, 15). Even if Smith's hypothesis is correct for the early period, neither of these cooking techniques became integrated into the national cuisine. Frying, in particular, was seen as a novel technique when it was "reintroduced" by foreign chefs in the eighteenth century. For a further discussion of stoves, see Smith and Christian, *Bread and Salt*, 13–23.

120. Sanborn C. Brown, *Benjamin Thompson, Count Rumford* (Cambridge, Mass.: MIT Press, 1979; pb. ed., 1981), 152–154. For Rumford's essay "On the Management of Fire and the Economy of Fuel," see Volume II, *Practical Applications of Heat*, in *The Collected Works of Count Rumford*, ed. Sanborn C. Brown (Cambridge, Mass.: The Belknap Press of Harvard University Press, 1968–1970), 309–477.

121. John Seymour, *Forgotten Household Crafts* (New York: Alfred A. Knopf, 1987) 30–33.

122. To be more precise, the heat could be raised more quickly than with a Russian stove; rapid lowering of the heat was not possible before the advent of the gas stove. Katerina Avdeeva, *Ruchnaja kniga russkoj opytnoj khozjajki*, 6th ed. (St. Petersburg: Tip. voenno-

uchebnykh zavedenij, 1848), 192; Appendix, Plate 5. Balky stoves were a perennial problem in Russia well into the twentieth century. When the hero of Pasternak's novel *Doktor Zhivago* discusses the malfunctioning stove in his Moscow apartment with his colleague, he is told that "Getting a stove to work isn't like playing the piano, it takes skill." Boris Pasternak, *Doktor Zhivago* (Ann Arbor: University of Michigan Press, 1958), 190).

123. *Nastol'naja kniga*, 294. These arguments about the pros and cons of the foods that could be prepared in the Russian stove and on the new stove tops recall the polemics raging between the Westernizers and Slavophiles in that period. Tolstoy took up this theme in *Anna Karenina*, where he used food preferences to signal the political views of his characters. See Lynn Visson, "Kasha vs. Cachet Blanc: The Gastronomic Dialectics of Russian Literature" in *Russianness: Studies on a Nation's Identity*, ed. Robert L. Belknap (Ann Arbor, Mich.: Ardis, 1990), 60–73.

124. The first proper gas range was designed by James Sharp in 1816, but gas ranges did not become popular for domestic use in England until the 1890s. Apparently the first recorded use of gas for cooking was by Albert Winsor, a German, at a dinner party in 1802, but Winsor did not develop his idea further. See Nell du Vall, *Domestic Technology: A Chronology of Developments* (Boston: G. K. Hall, 1988), 113–116. Initially the English were wary of the new-fangled gas ranges. Alexis Soyer, the preeminent French chef of London's Reform Club in the 1840s, was one of the first to appreciate their advantages and gave cooking demonstrations to promote their use in commercial kitchens.

125. Anon., *Podarok*, 168.

126. Similarly, the popular American cooking teacher of the late nineteenth century, Sarah Tyson Rorer (1849–1937), used to lament the absence of a dependable oven thermometer. Like Molokhovets, she too suggested that her students throw some flour onto the oven floor to determine the temperature of the oven. If the flour browned in fifteen seconds, the oven was ready for meat but too hot for cakes. The oven was ready for bread if the flour "browned quickly without taking fire," or if she could hold her hand in the oven to the count of twenty. She added comfortingly that experience would help in knowing when the oven was ready. Emma Siefrit Weigley, *Sarah Tyson Rorer* (Philadelphia: American Philosophical Society, 1977), 123.

## FOOD PRESERVATION AND STORAGE

127. Thomas Webster, assisted by Mrs. Parkes, *An Encyclopaedia of Domestic Economy* (London: Longman, Brown, Green, and Longmans, 1847), 667. See also Oscar Anderson, *Refrigeration in America: A History of a New Technology and Its Impact* (Princeton: Princeton University Press for the University of Cincinnati, 1953), 5–6.

128. Elizabeth David, "Savour of Ice and of Roses," *Petits Propos Culinaires*, 8 (June 1981), 10; and W. S. Stallings, Jr., "Ice Cream and Water Ices in 17th and 18th Century England," *Petits Propos Culinaires*, 3 (Supplement) [1979], 2–3.

129. Elizabeth David, "Fromages Glacés and Iced Creams," *Petits Propos Culinaires*, 2 (August 1979), 24; and Mark Girouard, *Life in the English Country House* (New York: Penguin Books, 1980), 262. See also Sylvia P. Beamon and Susan Roaf, *The Ice-Houses of Britain* (London: Routledge, 1990). Unfortunately, this impressive book appeared too late to influence the present discussion.

130. C. Anne Wilson, *Food and Drink in Britain* (London: Constable, 1973), 103; and Anderson, *Refrigeration in America*, 7–8.

131. Webster and Parkes, *An Encyclopaedia of Domestic Economy*, 673.

132. *Goodholme's Domestic Cyclopaedia of Practical Information*, ed. Todd S. Goodholme (New York: C. A. Montgomery, 1887), 301. Periam expressed the requirements by volume: "A cube of ice of eight feet . . . will keep perfectly and supply a moderate family for a year, . . . a cube of ice twelve feet square will supply an ordinary farm dairy, and one of sixteen feet a large creamery." *The Home and Farm Manual*, 410–411.

133. *Slovar' russkogo jazyka XI–XVII vv* [Dictionary of the Russian language from the 11–17th centuries], vol. 8 (Moscow: Nauka, 1975–1988), 194, and *The Compact Edition of the Oxford English Dictionary*, 2 vols. (Oxford: Oxford University Press, 1971), I, 1365.

134. Smith and Christian, *Bread and Salt*, 122–125. Smith was quoting from Grigorij Karpovich Kotoshikhin, *O Rossii v tsarstvovanie Alekseja Mikhajlovicha* (1859; rpt., Oxford: Clarendon Press, Oxford University Press, 1980), 112–116, 128–129.

135. Avdeeva clearly described a cold cellar, one half of which contained the ice house and the other half shelves for storing fruits, vegetables, and other preserves. Avdeeva, *Ruchnaja kniga*, II, 165–167. See also *Nastol'naja kniga*, 307–308.

136. Nikolaj Vasilievich Gogol', *Polnoe sobranie sochinenij* (Moscow: Izd. Akademii nauk SSSR, 1937–1952), VI, 117. English readers should refer to Bernard Guerney's translation of *Dead Souls* (New York: Rinehart, 1942 and 1948), 131.

137. *Nov'*, vol. 3 (1885), 499. The French method, which is considerably less tedious, is apparently still practiced in Bulgaria today. According to the Bulgarian food ethnologist Lilija Radeva, "vine branches with bunches of grapes are hung in a cool draughty place, their cut ends smeared with melted bees' wax which after hardening cuts off the air supply." Lilija Radeva, "Traditional Methods of Food Preserving among the Bulgarians," in *Food Conservation: Ethnological Studies*, ed. Astri Riddervold and Andreas Ropeid (London: Prospect Books, 1988), 40.

138. *Podarok*, vii and II, 308.


## CONTAINERS AND UTENSILS

139. Kohl, *Russia*, 196.

140. In the late 1850s, Louis Pasteur began to unravel the mysteries of fermentation, both its beneficial and harmful effects, but it took some time for the knowledge to spread to the ordinary housewife in France, much less in Russia. For more on the history of fermentation, see Harold McGee, *On Food and Cooking* (New York: Charles Scribner's Sons, 1984).

141. *Podarok*, II, 327–328, 331. The new ice cream maker was introduced in Russia toward the end of the nineteenth century. Although Molokhovets regarded it favorably, it could not have been very common since she still carried forward from the first edition her instructions for preparing ice cream in the time-honored way by removing the lid and stirring the cream by hand. See her Remarks on Ice Cream, Chapter 14.

142. *Izvlechenie iz obshchago kataloga s risunkami na kukhonnuju posudu"* (Odessa: Tip. E. I. Fesenko, 1897), 3–6, 23. That modern English nomenclature is no better can be seen from Lynne Howard Frazer's account of recataloging the cooking equipment in the Colonial Williamsburg Foundation's collection. See "Calling the Kettle a Pot: Reviving Eighteenth Century Cooking Equipment Nomenclature," *Petits Propos Culinaires*, 26 (July 1987), 40–53.

143. *Podarok*, II, 321.

144. John Farley's stern warning from the eighth edition of *The London Art of Cookery* (London: J. Scatcherd and J. Whitaker, 1796) was quoted by Alan Davidson in "The Use of Copper in Cooking," *Petits Propos Culinaires*, 2 (August 1979), 20–21. See also Isabella Beeton, *The Book of Household Management*, 1085; Raida Varlamova, *Semejnyj magazin* [Family magazine] (Moscow: Tip. A. Evrennova, 1856), 215–218; and Irma S. Rombauer and Marion Rombauer Becker, *Joy of Cooking* (New York: Bobbs-Merrill, 1963), 139.

145. According to Harold McGee, the problem with copper is not that it is absolutely poisonous, but that the human body excretes only small amounts of copper. As the metal builds up in the body, it may cause gastrointestinal problems and ultimately damage the liver: "No one will be poisoned by the occasional zabaglione whipped in a copper bowl, but clearly copper is not a good candidate for everyday cooking." McGee, *On Food and Cooking*, 623. Perhaps not surprisingly, the Copper Development Association in England takes the other side, holding that "pure copper is not poisonous unless consumed in abnormally large quantities" and that a person "could not consume such quantities by eating food cooked in copper pans." They further claim that "a protective coating has . . . been adopted for copper cookware to prevent any foods becoming adversely flavoured . . . and not, as is commonly believed, as a provision against toxicity." Davidson, "The Use of Copper in Cooking," 22.

146. Davidson, "The Use of Copper in Cooking," 22.

147. Charles Ranhofer, chef of Delmonico's Restaurant in New York in the late nineteenth century, who elsewhere recommended using tinned copper pans, nevertheless included a recipe

for salted cornichons that were finished by being boiled briefly with spices in a mixture of half water and half vinegar in an untinned copper basin. They were then poured into a large jar or barrel and left to marinate in the spiced vinegar for several days before serving. I suppose the danger was minimal because the pickles were only allowed to "bubble for a few minutes" before being removed from the fire. Ranhofer, *The Epicurean*, 227, 194.

## SERVANTS

148. *Podarok*, I, viii.

149. Anon., *Podarok*, 7.

150. Hardships, however, are relative; and household servants usually had an easier life than the field hands. At least they were protected from the elements and, with ready access to the landowner's food and provisions, they were less likely to go hungry.

151. Sofya Kovalevskaya, *A Russian Childhood*, tr. Beatrice Stillman (New York: Springer-Verlag, 1978), 84–92.

152. Tolstoy, *Polnoe sob. soch.*, XIX, 123–139 (for English readers: *Anna Karenina*, part 6, chapters i–v); Tolstoy, *Polnoe sob. soch.*, X, 261–269 (this reference is found in vol. 2, part IV, section VII of the Russian edition, but part 7, section VII, p. 476 of Garnett's English transtion); Pushkin, *Polnoe sob. soch.*, VI, 45–46 (chapter II, stanza 32); and Gogol, *Polnoe sob. soch.*, II, 27. English readers should consult *Mirgorod*, tr. David Magarshack (New York: Farrar, Strauss & Cudahy, 1962), 17. For more on the role of mushrooms in Russian culture, see V. P. Wasson and R. Gordon Wasson, *Mushrooms, Russia and History* (New York: Pantheon, 1957). The cultural prominence of the mushroom in Russian cuisine may also be seen as another small facet of the Westernizer/Slavophile controversy in nineteenth century Russia. See Visson, "Kasha vs. Cachet Blanc."

153. Avdeeva, *Ruchnaja kniga*, I, 220.

154. Dal' considered that *varenets*, in the form of a boiled milk pudding, was of Eastern origin (Dal', *Tolkovyj slovar'*, I, 166). Kovalevskaja mentioned visiting an Old Believer's cottage during her mushroom hunt, where she was offered *varenets* and other traditional Russian foods that she otherwise never got to eat (Kovalevskaja, *A Russian Childhood*, 89–90). Although it was considered somewhat old-fashioned or declassé by the 1860s, Molokhovets included two recipes (#1559, 1560) for this traditional dish. A related dish called cabbage cream was prepared from clotted cream in early seventeenth century England. According to the English food historian C. Anne Wilson, "the skins of cream were lifted carefully from the bowls with a skimmer, and were built up in a dish 'round and high like a cabbage.' Sugar and rosewater were sprinkled between the layers" (Wilson, *Food and Drink in Britain*, 169).

155. For more on this subject see Toomre, "Three Hundred Years of Russian Fasting."

156. *Nastol'naja kniga*, 293.

157. Theresa M. McBride, *The Domestic Revolution: The Modernisation of Household Service in England and France 1820–1920* (New York: Holmes & Meier, 1976), 52–53.

158. All sorts of natural products were used to stuff mattresses in the nineteenth century, provoking a good deal of discussion about the merits of various alternatives. In the opinion of Lydia Maria Child, "Barley straw is the best for beds; dry corn husks, slit into shreds, are far better than straw." Child, *The American Frugal Housewife* (rpt. of 12th edition, 1833; Cambridge, Mass.: Applewood Books in Cooperation with Old Sturbridge Village, n.d.), 16.

159. *Podarok*, II, 307–308.

## HEALTH

160. I. M. Radetskij, *Khozjajka, ili Polnejshee rukovodstvo k sokrashcheniju domashnikh raskhodov* [Mistress of the household, or, the most complete guide to reducing household expenses] (St. Petersburg: M. O. Vol'f, [187–?]), 11. The title of Sumarokov's work, *Istochnik zdravija* [The source of health], clearly indicated his biases, but even Levshin regularly included medical remarks in his *Slovar' povarennogo* [Dictionary of cookery] as part of his discussion and description of individual foods.

161. Despite the popular belief that the morning's milk is higher in butterfat than milk from the evening's milking, analyses show that there is almost no difference. If anything, the butterfat is marginally higher at night, but the difference does not show up regularly nor is it statistically significant. Molokhovets' preference for the morning's milk may have had more to do with storage conditions than the quality of milk itself. Given the lack of refrigeration, even though ice houses were available, the bacteria content of the milk would have been higher if it was held overnight, plus it would have begun to turn sour.

## MARKETS

162. Kohl, *Russia*, 136.

163. Ibid., 61.

164. Johann-Georg Korb, *Diary of an Austrian Secretary of Legation* (1863; rpt. London: Frank Cass, 1968), 216–217.

165. John Parkinson, *A Tour of Russia, Siberia and the Crimea 1792–1794* (London: Frank Cass, 1971), 71. After being defeated in his bid for the presidency of Magdalen College in 1791, Parkinson accompanied Edward Wilbraham-Bootle during the latter's tour of Russia from 1792 to 1794.

166. Quoted in Francesca Wilson, *Muscovy: Russia through Foreign Eyes, 1553–1900* (London: George Allen & Unwin, 1970), 181.

167. Amédée Durande, *Joseph, Carle et Horace Vernet: Correspondance et Biographies* (Paris: J. Hezel, [1863]), 226. Horace Vernet (1789–1863) was a noted French painter who spent the year 1842 in Russia at the invitation of Nicholas I. This quote is taken from one of the letters that Vernet sent to his wife from Russia, extracts of which appeared in *La Presse* (nos. 8–11) in April 1856.

168. Kohl, *Russia*, 60.

## INGREDIENTS

169. *Bul'ba: Entsiklopedicheskij spravochnik po vyrashchivaniju, khraneniju, pererabotke i ispol'zovaniju kartofelja* [Tubers: Encyclopedic guide for the cultivation, storage, treatment, and use of potatoes] (Minsk: Izd. "Belorusskoj sovetskoj entsiklopedi" imeni Petrusja Brovki, 1988), 9–10.

170. John Halit Brown, "A Provincial Landowner: A. T. Bolotov (1738–1833)," (Ph.D. diss., Princeton University, 1977), 100.

171. *Bul'ba*, 9–10.

172. Redcliffe Salaman, *The History and Social Influence of the Potato* (1949; rpt. Cambridge: Cambridge University Press, 1986), 116. The British art critic Katherine Guthrie, who visited Russia in the summer of 1873, also mentioned the resistance of the Old Believers to the potato, which was regarded by that time as somewhat ludicrous. Katherine Blanche Guthrie, *Through Russia: From St. Petersburg to Astrakhan and the Crimea* (1874; rpt. New York, Arno Press and the New York Times, 1970), 234.

173. Smith and Christian, *Bread and Salt*, 280, 283.

174. Rudolf Grewe, "The Arrival of the Tomato in Spain and Italy: Early Recipes," *Journal of Gastronomy*, vol. 3, no. 2 (Summer 1987), 78.

175. Zhanna Ivanovna Orlova, *Vse ob ovoshchakh* [All about vegetables], 2nd ed. (Moscow: Agropromizdat, 1986), 95. According to Orlova, the original article by Bolotov appeared in *Ekonomicheskij magazin* [Economic magazine], 1784, ch. XIX.

176. Guthrie, *Through Russia*, II, 112–113; II, 183; I, 203.

177. For further discussion of *shchi*, see Pokhlebkin, *Natsional'nye kukhni*, 18–19; and Joyce Toomre, "A Short History of 'Shchi,'" in *Proceedings of the Oxford Symposium on Food & Cookery 1984 & 1985* (London: Prospect Books, 1986), 62–69.

178. *Tovarnyj slovar'* [Commercial dictionary] (Moscow: Gosudarstvennoe izd. torgovoj literatury, 1957–1959), VIII, 833–834.

179. Cited by Wilson, *Muscovy*, 71.

180. Ibid., 109.

181. Wilmot, *Russian Journals*, III, 320.

182. Tarkovskij, *Stikhotvorenija*, 120. Tarkovskij was known for his personal and artistic integrity. His poem with its recounting of unobtainable and all but forgotten dishes is another poignant indictment of the Soviet regime.

183. Kovalevskaya, *A Russian Childhood*, 84–85.

184. Wilmot, *Russian Journals*, 226–227.

185. Dumas, *Adventures in Czarist Russia*, 53.

186. *Russian Journal of Lady Londonderry, 1836-7*, 92.

187. Carême, *Le maître d'hôtel français*, 109–110.

188. Obviously meat was sold in Russian markets both in winter and summer. The Russian summer markets, however, were not very different from other European markets and hence made less of an impression on visitors than did the frozen carcasses of the Russian winter markets.

189. Kohl, *Russia*, 59–60.

190. Carême, *Le maître d'hôtel français*, 103.

191. Carême was unusual in considering the wild birds in Russia neither as varied nor as tasty as those found in France. *Le maître d'hôtel français*, 104.

192. Wilson, *Muscovy*, 71.

193. Kohl, *Russia*, 56–57.

194. Petit, *La Gastronomie en Russie*, 18.

195. Wilmot, *Russian Journals*, 222.

196. The Marquis de Custine, *Empire of the Czar: A Journey through Eternal Russia* (New York: Doubleday, 1989), 520. This new edition of Custine's work with its foreword by Daniel J. Boorstin is a reprint of the Longman edition of 1843, which was an English translation of the three-volume French original *La Russie en 1839*.

197. Ivan Aleksandrovich Goncharov, *Sobranie sochinenij* [Collected works] (Moscow: Gosudarstvennoe izd. khudozhestvennoj literatury, 1952–55), IV, 488. English readers should refer to *Oblomov*, tr. Natalie Duddington (New York: E. P. Dutton, 1960), 495. Oblomov, the protagonist, remembered the family estate, Oblomovka, as a veritable Garden of Eden where the land yielded a profusion of raw ingredients that were regularly transformed into a multitude of delectable dishes for the dinner table.

198. Eugene Schuyler, "Diner à la Russe, 1868," *Petits Propos Culinaires*, 28 (April 1988), 25.

199. Dumas, *Adventures in Czarist Russia*, 97–98.


COOKING TECHNIQUES

200. Elizabeth David, *English Bread and Yeast Cookery* (New York: Viking Press, 1980), 126, 311–312, and James Beard, *Beard on Bread* (New York: Alfred A. Knopf, 1973), 142–144.

201. Glasse, *The Art of Cookery*, 3–4; *William Verrall's Cookery Book: First Published 1759* (rpt. Lewes, East Sussex: Southover Press, 1988), 56; and John Farley, *The London Art of Cookery* (1783; rpt. Lewes, East Sussex: Southover Press, 1988), 52–54. Farley copied Hannah Glasse in his directions for spit-roasting beef and veal with buttered paper; his directions for spit-roasting venison differed from hers although both used buttered paper. Ude gave a recipe for spit-roasting a loin of veal under buttered paper in the early nineteenth century; Mary Randolph recommended the same method in America; and Mrs. Beeton was still roasting venison under buttered paper in 1861, the same year that Molokhovets' book was published. See Louis Eustache Ude, *The French Cook* (1828; rpt. New York: Arco Publishing, 1978), 77–78; Mary Randolph, *The Virginia Housewife*, notes by Karen Hess (1828; rpt. Columbia: University of South Carolina Press, 1984), 23–25; and Beeton, *The Book of Household Management*, 532 (Recipe 1049).

202. A regular spate of books on paper bag cookery appeared around 1911 in England and the United States, some of which were written to promote the use of paper bags produced by specific companies. The best known of these books is Nicholas Soyer, *Soyer's Paper-Bag Cookery*

(New York: Sturgis & Walton, 1911). Soyer gave a recipe for broiling in a paper bag, but none for roasting on a spit. Elizabeth Driver in her bibliography also included Countess Vera Serkoff, *Paper-Bag Cookery* (London: C. Arthur Pearson, 1911), noting that she was listed as Vyera Syerkova in the British Museum catalog. Elizabeth Driver, *A Bibliography of Cookery Books Published in Britain, 1875–1914* (London: Prospect Books in association with Mansell Publishing, 1989), 570.

203. Delight in colored foods has a long history; they were especially popular in the Middle Ages when the appearance of food seemed to matter more than the taste. See Henisch, *Fast and Feast*, 99–101, 105–106; Wilson, *Food and Drink in Britain*, esp. 287–288; and Wheaton, *Savoring the Past*, 15–16. For an account of the fad of color-coordinated meals which American women pursued at the turn of the twentieth century, see Shapiro, *Perfection Salad*, 84–85. Sarah Tyson Rorer prepared some bizarre special meals such as a political campaign supper that featured a head of blue cabbage hollowed out and filled with red tomato aspic, served with white mayonnaise. She also organized a violet lunch beginning with cream of purple cabbage soup and ending with grape sherbet (Weigley, *Sarah Tyson Rorer*, 70–71). Barbara Kirshenblatt-Gimblett touched on the same theme in her article "The Kosher Gourmet in the Nineteenth-Century Kitchen: Three Jewish Cookbooks in Historical Perspective," *Journal of Gastronomy*, vol. 2, no. 4 (Winter 1986/1987), 75.

204. Shapiro, *Perfection Salad*, 96–102.

## COMPARISON BETWEEN FIRST AND TWENTIETH EDITIONS

205. Tolstoy, *Polnoe sob. soch.*, XIX, 125–130; English readers should consult part 6, chapter 2.

206. See Sidney W. Mintz, *Sweetness and Power* (New York: Penguin Books, 1985); and Harvey Levenstein, *Revolution at the Table: The Transformation of the American Diet* (New York: Oxford University Press, 1988), 32–33.

## ISSUES OF TRANSLATION

207. *Podarok*, 28th ed. (1914), iv.

208. *Slownik języka polskiego* [Dictionary of the Polish language], (Warsaw: Wiedza Powszechna, 1958–    ), VI, 324–325.

209. Frederic Rosengarten, *The Book of Spices* (Wynnewood, Pa.: Livingston Publishing Co, 1969), 87–88.

210. *Tovarnyj slovar'*, VIII, 833–834.

211. For a good modern description of these sausages with an illustration, see *Tovarnyj slovar'*, IX, 1021–1022. Also see Dal', *Tolkovyj slovar'*, IV, 138; and Ushakov, *Tolkovyj slovar'*, III, 52.

212. W. E. Ricker, *Russian-English Dictionary for Students of Fisheries and Aquatic Biology*, Bulletin 183 (Ottawa: Fisheries Research Board of Canada, 1973), 99–100, 216–217.

213. *Tovarnyj slovar'*, VII, 1020; and Alan Davidson, *Mediterranean Seafood*, 2nd ed. (London: Penguin Books, 1981), 41–44.

## MEASUREMENTS AND CONVERSIONS

214. *Izvlechenie iz obshchago kataloga s risunkami na kukhonnuju posudu.*

215. Mary Randolph, *The Virginia Housewife*, 297.

216. David, *English Bread and Yeast Cookery*, 233–235. I have taken most of the Russian-English conversions directly from *Dictionary of Russian Historical Terms from the Eleventh Century to 1917*, compiled by Sergei G. Pushkarev, ed. George Vernadsky and Ralph T. Fisher, Jr. (New Haven: Yale University Press, 1970), 195. Molokhovets' Table of Weights and Measures is found in *Podarok*, ix–xi. Another useful book is William D. Johnstone, *For Good Measure: A Complete Compendium of International Weights and Measures* (New York: Avon Books, 1977). For U.S. and British conversions, see Rombauer and Becker, *Joy of Cooking*, 546–548.

# Notes

## ADVICE TO MODERN COOKS

217. *Sacred Emily*, 1913. Cited in John Bartlett, *Familiar Quotations*, 15th ed. (Boston: Little, Brown, 1980), 752:8.

218. There are almost as many solutions to the problem of producing an acceptable loaf in the American kitchen as there are American cookbook authors.

219. Alan Davidson thinks otherwise. "It looks unprepossessing—small white curled-up knobbly fragments—but is considered a great delicacy, and the taste and texture which it gives to pie fillings are distinctive and delicious." Davidson then quotes Molokhovets' directions for preparing *viziga:* " 'Remove the spinal cords of a sturgeon, wash them and wipe them dry, and hang them out on a string to dry. When they are half dry, wind them into balls, like a skein of threads, tie them together and dry them out over the stove.' " See *North Atlantic Seafood*, 349. One of the anomalies of Molokhovets' work is that directions for drying *viziga*, which surely was more of a commercial than a domestic operation, were included in the late Berlin edition (II, 196, 4056), but not in any of the Russian editions up to and including the twentieth.

220. Recommended books include A. J. McClane and Arie deZanger, *The Encyclopedia of Fish* (New York: Holt, Rinehart & Winston, 1977); Bruce Beck, *The Official Fulton Fish Market Cookbook* (New York: E. P. Dutton, 1989); Ruth A. Spear, *Cooking Fish and Shellfish* (Garden City, N.Y.: Doubleday, 1980); and Alan Davidson *Seafood: A Connoisseur's Guide and Cookbook* (New York: Simon & Schuster, 1989).

221. For a discussion of the history of the chicken industry, see Margaret Visser, "Chicken: From Jungle Fowl to Patties," in *Much Depends on Dinner* (New York: Grove Press, 1986), 115–154.

222. Marsden, *Palmyra of the North*, 131. The golden pineapple ("*I ananasom zolotym*") of Pushkin's *Eugene Onegin* is the most famous example in Russian literature of the fruit being used as a cultural symbol. (*Polnoe sob. soch.*, VI, 11; English readers see chapter I, stanza 16.) The pineapple carries a more explicit message of Western decadence in Goncharov's novel *Oblomov*. (*Sob. soch.*, IV, 398, 447, 450; for readers of Duddington's English translation, see 404, 455, 457.)

# Appendix A: Ingredients by Category

Listed here are ingredients that appear in Molokhovets' recipes. The ingredients are given in alphabetical order without reference to the frequency with which they were used. Most were used daily, some only for guests, others very rarely, and a few—like Limburger cheese and pigeons' eggs—were mentioned without being used. Although I have tried to make these lists as complete as possible, a few items may have escaped my notice.

## VEGETABLES

artichokes, asparagus, beans, beets, Brussels sprouts, cabbage (Savoy, green, red, and seedlings), carrots, celery root, chestnuts, chicory, chives, cress, cucumbers, eggplant, goose-foot (orach), green onions, Jerusalem artichokes, kohlrabi, leeks, lettuce, nettles, onions, parsley root, parsnips, peas, potatoes, pumpkin, radishes, rutabaga, shallots, tomatoes, turnip.

## FRUITS

apples, apricots, barberries, blackberries, cantaloupe, cherries, cloudberries, cranberries, currants (red, white, and black), gooseberries, grapes, greengages, lemons, lingonberries, Mazzard cherries, oranges (bitter and sweet), peaches, pears, pineapples, plums, quinces, raspberries, rose hips, rowanberries, Siberian crabapples, stone brambles, strawberries (wild and cultivated), watermelon.

## FLOWERS, SEEDS, AND NUTS

sweet and bitter almonds, coconut, hazelnuts, jasmine, mignonette, nasturtiums, orange blossoms, peanuts, pistachios, poppy seeds, roses, sesame seeds, sunflower seeds, walnuts.

## SPICES, HERBS, AND FLAVORINGS

allspice, anise, bayleaf, bergamot oil, black pepper, canella, capers, cardamom, caraway seeds, cayenne pepper, chervil, cinnamon, cloves, coriander, dill, fenugreek, garlic, ginger, green parsley, hops, horseradish, juniper berries, mace, marjoram, mint, mustard, nutmeg, oak bark, orange flower water, orris root, *pois de senteur*, purslane, rosemary, rosewater, saffron, sage, salt, savory, star anise, sweet flag, tarragon, tormentilla cinquefoil, tragacanth, vanilla, wormwood.

GRAINS

barley, buckwheat, maize, millet, oats, rice, rye, semolina, wheat.

MEATS

beef, chamois, elk, hare, mutton, pork, suckling pig, veal, venison, wild boar.

DOMESTIC BIRDS

capon, chicken, duck, turkey.

CHEMICALS

alum, bicarbonate of soda, chloride of lime, cream of tartar, lye, magnesia, potash, quicklime, salicylic acid, saltpeter, slaked lime, tartar, vitriol.

WINES, SPIRITS, AND LIQUEURS

ale, Alicante, Alkermes, arrack, beer, bishop, bitter pale ale, Bordeaux, brandy, Burgundy, Cahors wine, Canary wine, champagne, Château d'Yquem, cherry liqueur, cider, Crimean vodka, Curaçao, Cypriot wine, dessert wine, Graves wine, Jamaican rum, Kirschwasser, Kümmel, *kvass*, Limpopo (a Finnish drink), Madeira, Malaga, Maraschino liqueur, Marsala, mead, Médoc, mulled wine, Muscat de Lunel, orgeat, pear liqueur, plum brandy, Port, porter, punch, ratafia, red wine, Rhine wine, rum, Sauternes, sherry, Spanish wine, sparkling wine, sweet wine, Tokay wine, vodka.

MISCELLANEOUS INGREDIENTS

baker's yeast, birch sap, bran, butter, chicken eggs, chocolate, cochineal, cocoa, coffee, cream, currants, dates, dried apricots, Dutch cheese, farmer's cheese, fat for frying, Finnish butter, flour, gelatin, gherkins, goose eggs, hempseed oil, herb tea, isinglass, Limburger cheese, lime honey, macaroni, malt, mustard oil, nut oil, olive oil, olives, Parmesan cheese, pickles, pigeon eggs, poppy seed oil, raisins, rennet, Russian butter, salt cod, sour cream, "soy" sauce, Stilton cheese, stockfish, sturgeon marrow (*viziga*), sultanas, Swiss cheese, tea, tomato paste, treacle, truffles, vermicelli, vinegar, whey, wort, yeast, yellow tea, yogurt.

### Fish

| *Russian* | *Latin* | *English* |
| --- | --- | --- |
| anchous | Engraulis | anchovy |
| belorybitsa | Stenodus leucichthys leucichthys | salmon, white |

1. Black Sea herring. 2. Caspian herring. 3. White salmon. 4. Sterlet. 5. Russian sturgeon. 6. Beluga. 7. Sevrjuga. 8. Zander. From *Entsiklopedicheskij slovar* (St. Petersburg, 1898).

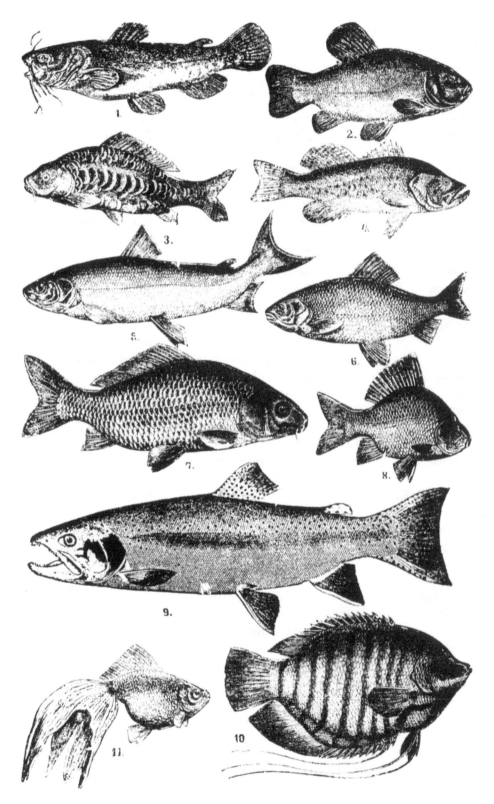

1. American sheatfish. 2. Tench. 3. Mirror carp. 4. American perch-trout. 5. Whitefish.
6. Ide. 7. Carp. 8. Crucian. 9. Trout. 10. Gourami. 11. Telescope fish.
From *Entsiklopedicheskij slovar'* (St. Petersburg, 1898).

| Russian | Latin | English |
|---|---|---|
| beluga | Huso huso | beluga |
| ersh | Acerina cernua | ruff, pope |
| forel' | Salmo fario | trout |
| kambala, rechnaja | Platichthys flesus | flounder |
| karas' | Carassius vulgaris | crucian (carp) |
| karp | Cyprinus carpio | carp |
| kharius | Thymallus vexillifer | grayling |
| kil'ka | Sprattus sprattus balticus | sprat, Baltic |
| korjushka | Osmerus eperlanus | smelt, European |
| leshch | Abramis brama | bream |
| lin' | Tinca vulgaris tinca | tench |
| losos' | Salmo salar | salmon, Atlantic |
| minoga | Petromyzon fluviatilis | lamprey |
| nalim | Lota lota lota | burbot, eel pout |
| navaga | Eleginus navaga | navaga |
| okun' | Perca fluviatilis | perch |
| osetr | Acipenser guldenstadti | sturgeon, Russian |
| peskar' | Gobio gobio | gudgeon |
| rak | Astacus leptodactylus | crayfish |
| rjapushka | Corregonus albula | cisco |
| sardel'ka | Sprattus sprattus phaler-icus | sprat, Black Sea |
| sardina | Sardina pilcharus pilchardus | sardine, Atlantic |
| sel'd', seledka | Clupea harengus harengus | herring |
| seljava (= rjapushka) | Coregonus albula | cisco, vendace |
| semga (= losos') | Salmo salar | salmon, Atlantic |
| shchuka | Esox lucius | pike |
| sig | Coregonus lavaretus | whitefish |
| skumbrija | Scomber scombrus | mackerel, Atlantic |
| snetok | Osmerus eperlanus eperlanus, spirinchus | smelt, sparling |
| sterljad' | Acipenser ruthenus | sterlet |
| sudak | Stizostedion lucioperca | zander, pike-perch |
| syrm' | Vimba vimba | vimba, zarthe |
| treska | Gadus morhua | cod |
| ugor' | Anguilla anguilla | eel |

## Mushrooms

| | | |
|---|---|---|
| belyj grib | Boletus edulis | cep, edible boletus |
| borovik | Boletus edulis | cep, edible boletus |
| gruzd' | Lactarius piperatus | milk-agaric |
| krasnyj grib | Leccinum aurantiacum | orange-cap boletus, Aspen mushroom |
| masljanik | Boletus luteus | yellow-brown boletus |
| ryzhik | Lactarius deliciosus | saffron milk-cap |
| shampin'on | Agaricus campestris | common field mushroom |
| smorchok | Morchella | morel |
| volnushka | Lactarius torminosus | wooly milk-cap |

## Wild Fowl

| | | |
|---|---|---|
| bekas | Gallinago gallinago | common snipe |
| drozd | Turdus sp. | thrush |
| fazan | Phasianus colchicus | pheasant |
| glukhar' | Tetrao urogallus | capercaillie |
| kulik-vorobej | Calidris minuta | sandpiper, little stint |
| kuropatka | Perdix perdix | partridge |
| perepel | Coturnix coturnix | quail |
| rjabchik | Tetrastes bonasia | hazel grouse or hazel hen |
| svistunok | Anas crecca | teal |
| teterev | Lyrurus tetrix | black grouse |
| teterka | Lyrurus tetrix | greyhen, f. of black grouse |
| val'dshnep | Scolopax rusticola | woodcock |
| zhavoronok | Alauda arvensis | skylark |

# Appendix B: Weights and Measures

UNITS OF LIQUID VOLUME

1 glass = ⅓ bottle = 205 grams = ½ Russian lb = .46 U.S. pint or slightly less
   than 1 U.S. liquid cup (= 225 grams or about ½ U.S. lb)
1 bottle = 3 glasses = 0.615 liter = 615 grams = 0.69 U.S. quart
1 *shtof* = 2 bottles = 1.23 liters = 1.3 U.S. quarts
1 *chetvert'* = ¼ bucket = 3.08 liters = 3.26 U.S. quarts
1 bucket/pail (*vedro*) = 10 *shtofy* = 12.3 liters = 3.25 U.S. gallons
1 barrel (*bochka*) = 40 buckets = 492 liters = 131.5 U.S. gallons

UNIT OF DRY MEASURE

1 *garnets* = 12 glasses = 2400 grams = 5.29 U.S. pounds[1]

UNITS OF LENGTH

1 *vershok* = 4.4 centimeters = 1.75 inches
1 *arshin* = 71.1 centimeters = 28 inches
1 *versta* = 1.067 kilometers = 0.663 miles

UNITS OF WEIGHT

1 *zolotnik* = 4.26 grams = about 1 U.S. teaspoon (= 5 grams)
1 *lot* = 12.85 grams = about ½ ounce = about 1 U.S. tablespoon (= 14 grams)
1 pound (Russian) = 96 *zolotniki* = 409 grams = 0.9 U.S. pounds
1 pood = 40 Russian pounds = 16.38 kilograms = 36.113 U.S. pounds

MISCELLANEOUS UNITS OF MEASUREMENTS

1 Russian spoon (*lozhka*) = between 3.2 and 3.6 U.S. tablespoons
1 teaspoon = 1 U.S. teaspoon[2]
1 wineglass = ¼ glass[3]

EQUIVALENTS PROVIDED BY MOLOKHOVETS

1 lb flour = 3 glasses
1 lb fine sugar = 2 glasses
1 lb sugar in pieces = 3 glasses = 32 pieces

## Appendix B: Weights and Measures

1 piece sugar = 1 *lot* = 12.85 grams
1 level silver tablespoon fine sugar = 1 *lot* = 1 piece
1 lb white French rolls = 2¼ 5 kopeck rolls
16 ground rusks = 1 glass
1 glass rusks = 1 French 5 kopeck roll
1 glass grated roll = ½ French roll
12 egg yolks = 1 glass
6 eggs = 1 glass
1 kopeck dry yeast = 3 *zolotniki*[4] [= about 1 U.S. tablespoon]

### Notes

1. *Podarok*, 20th ed., ixx. Most modern dictionaries define *garnets* as a Russian dry measure that equals 3.28 liters, but at 2280 grams, this would convert into 8.02 Russian pounds and 7.23 U.S. pounds, whereas Molokhovets clearly states that "¼ pail of flour, that is, 1 *garnets* = 5 pounds" (ibid., xi). Using the table above based primarily on Pushkarev's figures, ¼ pail yields 15 glasses which equals 3075 grams or 7.52 Russian pounds. Despite Molokhovets' inconsistency, it seems best not to tamper with her figures in this instance.

2. These conversions are derived from Molokhovets who allows 9 spoons of flour or 8 spoons of butter to 1 pound. Without any written confirmation, I have assumed that 1 Russian teaspoon equals 1 U.S. teaspoon. This seems to work in the recipes that I have tried, but readers are urged to exercise caution in these spoon conversions because Molokhovets is far from consistent in her own usage. The qualifier for the noun is the crucial component and, if omitted, the result can be disastrous, such as when she directed the reader to add 1 spoon (*lozhka*) of salt to a sauce.

3. *Podarok*, 20th ed., Recipe #935.

4. Ibid., part II, 14 (Chapter 17, Remarks on Yeast Cakes and *Kuliches*).

# Appendix C: Glossary

ALMONDS

The almond is closely related to the plum and peach; one variety is bitter (*Amygdalus communis*, var. *amara*), and the other is sweet (*Ac.*, var. *dulcis*). Molokhovets' dessert recipes often specify bitter as well as sweet almonds to supplement and intensify the flavor. The bitter variety, the sale of which is banned in the United States, contains a significant amount of cyanogens that can lead to cyanide poisoning. Instead of bitter almonds, almond flavoring may be used to supplement and intensify the flavor of sweet almonds.

ALUM

A whitish, transparent mineral salt, chemically a double sulfate of aluminum and potassium (potassium aluminum sulfate). Alum is very astringent and is widely used in industry to help clarify, harden, and purify other materials. Alum is also used as a mordant (fixative) for dyes. It has long been considered an adulterant when added to bread for its whitening action. Molokhovets used alum in many of her pickle recipes as it helped to make the pickles crunchy. She also added alum to the dyes when coloring Easter eggs. (For other examples of adding alum to pickles, see *Martha Washington's Booke of Cookery*, 169.)

AMOURETTES

*Amourettes* is the French name for the spinal marrow of beef, mutton, or veal. After poaching and seasoning the marrow, Molokhovets mostly used *amourettes* in sauces or for garnishing vegetables. See Chapter 4 for her basic preparation.

APPLES

Apples were the single most important fruit in Molokhovets' book. Usually she distinguished only between sweet and sour apples, but she did name the following varieties: Ananasnye, Anisovskie, Antonov, Arabskie, Jantarnye, Korobovki, Krymskie, Limonnye, Oportovskie, Renet, Stekljannye, and Titovskie. All of them, with the exception of Ananasnye and Korobovki (and the Renet, which was not a Russian apple), were among the 300 varieties of apples that were imported by the U.S. Department of Agriculture in 1870 with the aim of improving the American stock of winter apples. Molokhovets favored the popular Antonov, a sourish winter apple that kept very well. (Ragan, *Nomenclature of the Apple*, 25–29, 121, 169, 178, and 311; and Beach, *The Apples of New York*, 25–26.)

BERGAMOT OIL

Although bergamot can refer to a variety of either orange or pear, Molokhovets probably used an oil made from pears. Not only were pears much more common in nineteenth-century Russia, but none of the standard Russian dictionaries (Dal', Ushakov, Ozhegov, and *The Oxford Russian-English Dictionary*) mentions oranges under the entry for bergamot. Macura, the sole exception, mentions oranges and omits any reference to pears. (Macura, *Russian-English Botanical Dictionary*, 43.)

## Appendix C: Glossary

### BICARBONATE OF SODA

A carbonate that is one of the two essential components of baking powder, the other being an acid, traditionally cream of tartar or tartaric acid, but nowadays often acid phosphates. The two combine when mixed with water or milk to form carbon dioxide (a gas) which causes the dough to rise. This process, known as leavening, is due to the production of carbon dioxide *either* by a living agent (yeast) *or* by a chemical reaction of a carbonate with an acid. Sodium bicarbonate is convenient because it is cheap and is a fine powder so can readily be mixed with the flour. Some recipes are sufficiently acid that no additional acid is needed; some use sour milk. Chemical leavening was common in America (see *Potash*), but was not much used in Russia, where traditional yeast doughs were still preferred. Molokhovets gave only three recipes for quick dough (#1816, 2797, and 3187). To retain the color of green vegetables, she added baking soda to the boiling water. (For a lucid discussion of chemical leavening, see David, *English Bread and Yeast Cookery*, 515–519; see McGee, *On Food and Cooking*, 176–178, for the problems associated with cooking vegetables with baking soda.)

### BLADDER

Before storing her jams and preserves, Molokhovets covered each jar with a bladder. Animal bladders, sheep, ox, and pig, had been used since the mid eighteenth century in England to give an airtight seal. Hannah Glasse covered her jars of preserves with a bladder and then a leather. (This example from Glasse's 1747 cookbook predates the *Oxford England Dictionary* citation ascribing the first usage to Mrs. Raffald's 1769 *English Housekeeper*.) According to Alan Davidson, the bladder provided a good seal, but was "porous when wet, and not very strong," whereas the leather fastened over it "would give much greater protection against possible assaults by mice, insects etc." Molokhovets sometimes covered the bladder with paper, but never mentioned leather. Since she gives the impression of heavy traffic through her storerooms and close monitoring of the provisions, perhaps she felt the added protection was unnecessary. (Glasse, *Art of Cookery*, 132–133, 177.)

### BUTTER

The word *maslo* can mean either butter or oil. I translated it according to the context, using butter in most instances and oil only for fast day dishes. For Molokhovets, *slivochnoe maslo* meant butter made from fresh cream; *chukhonskoe maslo*, or Finnish butter, was made from sour cream (cf. #2272); and Russian butter was a processed and clarified butter, somewhat similar to the Indian *ghee* (cf. #2291). Where Molokhovets specified Finnish butter, I did also; ordinary butter made with fresh cream, I mostly left without attribution.

### CANELLA

Sometimes called canella bark, wild or white cinnamon. Canella is the dried inner bark of a West Indian tree (*Canella alba*); it was probably imported into Russia with allspice, which came from Jamaica. Canella smells somewhat like an inferior cinnamon but, unlike true cinnamon, it is very spicy and burns the mouth after a short time. Molokhovets used canella to flavor Clove vodka (#2149). (Mrs. Grieve, *A Modern Herbal*, 203.)

### CAPERS

The true caper is the unexpanded flower bud of *Capparis spinosa*, a small perennial bush that grows wild around the Mediterranean but that can also be grown from cuttings as an annual in northern climates. Nowadays capers are cultivated in the Transcaucasian republics, in Central Asia, and in the Crimea. According to Brokgaus and Efron, Caucasian pickled capers harvested from a perennial grass, *Capparis herbacea W.*, were as good as imported capers. Nasturtium seeds were and still are widely used as a substitute for capers. Molokhovets included two recipes for pickling nasturtium seeds (#2620, 2621). (*Entsiklopedicheskij slovar'*, Vol. 27, 361; Rybak, Romanenko, and Korableva, *Prjanosti*, 121.)

## CAVIAR

Molokhovets dispensed caviar with a lavishness that we now find hard to believe. She used it to clear bouillon, in sauces, and with sauerkraut, although the primary consumption of caviar was always with blini during Butter Week, the last week before Lent. The cheapness and easy availability of caviar made such prodigality possible; according to Brokgauz and Efron, the price of caviar in Russia in the early 1890s varied from 60 kopecks to 4 rubles per pound. Caviar proper is strictly the processed salted roe of the sturgeon. In general, the less salted the caviar, the more valuable and perishable it is. Fresh, barely salted caviar from the beluga sturgeon is the finest, but it is very perishable. Pressed salted caviar, compressed to reduce its liquid and packed in barrels or tins, keeps better and is less expensive than fresh caviar. *Malosol* caviar with a salt content of 3–4% is the best of the compressed black caviars. (*Entsiklopedicheskij slovar'*, Vol. 24, 905–907; Georgacas, *Ichthyological Terms*, 148–149; and McClane and deZanger, *Encyclopedia of Fish*, 59–65.)

## CHEESE

Molokhovets used cheese extensively in her recipes. Those specified were Dutch (undifferentiated), Parmesan, Stilton, and Swiss. Limburger cheese was mentioned, but not used in a recipe. Despite the influence of French cuisine on the Russian kitchen, Molokhovets did not refer to French cheeses, either as a class or individually, not even Roquefort. The cheese most commonly used in these recipes is *tvorog*, made at home from curdled sour milk. It is smooth, creamy, and slightly sour (#2296). American commercially made cottage cheese, if pressed with weights overnight to remove excess moisture, is a passable substitute, but farmer's cheese, which has a denser texture, is preferable.

## CHEMICALS

Molokhovets, who was always busy with her baking and preserving, needed a full cupboard of chemicals. Aside from salt and vinegar, these included alum, bicarbonate of soda, chloride of lime, cream of tartar, lye, magnesia, potash, quicklime, salicylic acid, saltpeter, slaked lime, tartar, and vitriol. Most of these chemicals are still used in household products, but since the names have become unfamiliar to American readers, I have described their use in separate entries.

## CHLORIDE OF LIME

Calcium hypochlorite, commonly called bleaching powder. It is used as a bleaching agent for fabrics and as a disinfectant. Molokhovets used 5 kopecks worth to clean a burned stockpot and then saved the water to bleach yellowed linen (#i).

## COCHINEAL

Cochineal is a dyestuff made from the dried bodies of the female *Dactylopius coccus*, syn. *Coccus cacti*, a scale insect that feeds on cacti. It was used to give a reddish or purple coloring in cooking and as the source of carmine pigment. Molokhovets gave two recipes for preparing cochineal, one a powder and the other a liquid extract (#2635–2636). By the 1897 edition, she tended to substitute red gelatin for cochineal, possibly due to the new factories in St. Petersburg that had begun to manufacture gelatin. See *Gelatin*.

Appendix C: Glossary

## CREAM OF TARTAR

Potassium hydrogen tartrate. Molokhovets used cream of tartar as the acidic component of the leavening agent for baking (see *Bicarbonate of Soda*) and for preparing fizzy drinks, either instant lemonade (#2181), or fermented wines (#2108 and 2117). Both of her recipes for cochineal also required cream of tartar.

## FENUGREEK

Molokhovets only called for fenugreek (*Triogonella foenum-graecum*) once, in her recipe for Real green cheese (#2307a). To flavor and color the cheese in this recipe, Molokhovets mixed horseradish leaves with the pounded and sieved leaves of the fenugreek plant. According to Rybak et al., the Swiss have long added fenugreek to their cheeses, both for its odor and color. (The dried leaves are bitter and have a strong aroma not unlike lovage or celery.) Fenugreek is grown in Transcaucasia, the southern part of European Russia, and western Siberia. Fenugreek is an important component of the Georgian spice mixture *khmeli-suneli*. (Mrs. Grieve, *A Modern Herbal*, 299; Norman, *Book of Spices*, 59; and Rybak, Romanenko and Korableva, *Prjanosti*, 76.)

## FLOUR

When Molokhovets was writing, rye flour was more commonly used than wheat. Six grades of rye flour and three of wheat were available in Russian markets at the end of the nineteenth-century. The first grade of wheat flour was *krupchatka*, the second *pervach* (the leavings after the first and second millings), and the third grade *vybojka*. The first grade, the finest and whitest, used 18.9% of the grain, while each successive milling gave a coarser and darker flour. (*Entsiklopedicheskij slovar'*, Vol. 39, 147, 169.) Molokhovets used all three grades of wheat flour, the finest for her own baking, the second grade when baking *pirogs* for the servants, and the third grade for thickening the servants' *shchi*. She also baked a smoked veal leg in a dough made from third grade flour (#2659).

## GELATIN

In home cooking, gelatin is usually prepared by boiling animal bones, particularly calves' feet and heads. In nineteenth-century Russia, commercial gelatin was usually sold in sheets and that is what Molokhovets used. As far as I know, the first granulated gelatin was produced in America in October 1893 by the Knox Gelatin Company, following a suggestion of the popular Philadelphian cooking teacher, Sarah Tyson Rorer. (Weigley, *Sarah Tyson Rorer*, 95.) One of the earliest Russian gelatin factories, if not the first, was founded in St. Petersburg in 1887 by the Swiss confectioner Moritz Conradi (1831–1887), the same man who had founded a chocolate factory in St. Petersburg in 1857. At the end of the century there were three gelatin factories in St. Petersburg and another in the Crimea. (Kaiser, *Fast ein Volk von Zuckerbäkern?* 77, 147, 162; 22, 741.) See also *Isinglass*.

## GREENS AND ROOT VEGETABLES

Molokhovets used the word "greens" in the overlapping sense of both vegetables and garnishes. Greens could mean vegetables in general or almost anything that garnished or accompanied the main dish. In a more limited sense, greens referred to any green vegetable, but particularly leafy greens like sorrel, spinach, and beet tops. She also garnished many dishes with greens, by which she meant freshly chopped green herbs, most commonly fresh parsley and dill, but also chervil and tarragon. The reader will have to be guided by custom and by his or her own sense of appropriateness. Molokhovets' use of "root vegetables" was similarly expansive. Although normally limited to onion, carrot, turnip, parsley root, celery root, and leek, the term could include almost any vegetable except leafy greens and fresh herbs. Parsley root, also called

Hamburg or turnip-rooted parsley, is faintly aromatic and tastes slightly sweet. Long valued as a flavoring for stews and soups, this root is nowadays not often seen in American or European shops. Parsnips are a good substitute. (Grieve, *A Modern Herbal*, 611–613; and Fitzgibbon, *Food of the Western World*, 317.)

## HERBS AND SPICES

Aside from onions, garlic, and leeks, green parsley and dill along with salt and pepper were the basic seasonings used by Molokhovets. Allspice (English pepper), cinnamon, cloves, nutmeg, and mace were all used, but of these allspice was the most important. Altogether, the range of herbs used by Molokhovets was much wider than those currently available in Russia. She used cayenne pepper occasionally, but very sparingly. For a full list of spices and herbs mentioned in *A Gift to Young Housewives*, see Appendix A, Ingredients by Category.

## HUNGARIAN PLUMS

*Prunus domestica.* A plum widely cultivated in Russia's southern, southwestern, and western provinces and as far north as St. Petersburg. It was especially common in the provinces of Bessarabia and Poltava, which were called *slivovoju zhitneitsej* (plum granaries). The color and characteristics vary according to the variety. One of the most common has a violet colored fruit (*Prune Queutsche de Hongrie, Hauszwetsche*), which is used for a special kind of jam, *povidla*, for eaux de vie, of which slivovitz is the most well known, and for drying into prunes. (*Entsiklopedicheskij slovar'*, Vol. 10, 870–871; Vol. 59, 357–358.)

## ISINGLASS OR FISH GLUE

A very pure form of gelatin made from the inner membrane of the sturgeon's air bladder. (Georgacas, *Ithyological Terms*, 149–150.) Isinglass was in great demand in nineteenth-century Russia since gelatin could not be used for fast day dishes. (See *Gelatin*.) According to Thomas Webster and Mrs. Parkes, who were writing in 1847, "The best isinglass is brought from Russia; some of an inferior kind is brought from North and South America, and the East Indies. The several varieties may be had from the wholesale dealers in isinglass in London." (Webster and Parkes, *Encyclopaedia of Domestic Economy*, 362.)

## LYE

Potassium hydroxide (caustic potash) or sodium hydroxide (caustic soda). Lye is an important strong alkali that was originally made by boiling wood ashes in water, filtering, and concentrating the solution by further boiling. This produces potash (potassium carbonate) which was treated with slaked lime (calcium hydroxide) to give lye. Molokhovets used lye to soften the flesh of dried stockfish (#969) and as a leavening agent for Quick pastry rings (#1890). Although lye is considered too dangerous to use directly nowadays, it still serves several useful purposes in baking: it fixes colors such as in chocolate, it tenderizes baked goods, and it neutralizes a too-acid bread dough. Lye also gives texture and taste to pretzels.

## MAGNESIA

Magnesium oxide. Molokhovets added magnesia to rectify wheat flour that had begun to sour (#2634).

## MUSTARD

Brokgauz and Efron described three varieties of mustard that were available in nineteenth-century Russia, black (*Brassica nigra*), Sareptskaja (*Brassica juncea*), and white (*Sinapis alba*).

The *Sareptskaja* mustard, mentioned frequently by Molokhovets, at that time grew only in India and in the southern steppes of Russia, which is why I suppose she called it "local" mustard. Also known as Russian mustard within Russia, *Brassica juncea* used to be called Indian or oriental mustard in the West, but is now called brown mustard. Although formerly *Brassica juncea* was not cultivated commercially in North America, it is now grown much more widely mainly because of the ease of harvesting it mechanically. As far as I can tell, the color of *Brassica juncea* must be in the eyes of the beholder. Brokgauz and Efron described two varieties of *Sareptskaja* mustard, white or yellow and red or black (this presumably describes the color of the seeds, but it is not entirely clear); other Russian sources refer to *Sareptskaja* mustard as blue (*sizaja*), while Western sources mostly describe the seeds as brown. (*Entsiklopedicheskij slovar'*, Vol. 17, 346–349; *Tovaryny slovar'*, Vol. 2, 314–319; Rybak, Romanenko, and Korableva, *Prjanosti*, 33–34; Anufriev, Kirillova, and Kiknadze, *Sousy i spitsii*, 83–85; Norman, *Book of Spices*, 23–25; Stone, *The Mustard Cookbook*, 9–10; Garland, *Book of Herbs and Spices*, 162–163; and *Sturtevant's Edible Plants of the World*, 107.)

## OAK BARK

Oak bark and leaves contain tannins, which have a bitter, astringent taste. Molokhovets added a piece of oak bark to her dough when making sweet and sour rye bread (#2330), oak leaves to the barrel when salting cucumbers (#2583), oak chips to Berry vinegar (#2228), and a decoction of oak bark when salting cucumbers in a pumpkin (#2598).

## OAKUM AND TOW

Oakum is the coarse part of flax; tow, the fiber of flax, hemp, or jute prepared for spinning. Molokhovets recommended using oakum and tow as packing materials to preserve apples from the winter's cold (#2341). The picking of oakum, the loose fiber from old ropes, was often done by convicts and inmates in English workhouses and jails in the nineteenth century. It was a practice that Dickens soundly condemned in his novels.

## ORRIS ROOT

Corruption of iris root; the dried rhizomes of three species of Iris, *I. germanica*, *I. pallida*, and *I. florentina*. The dried roots formerly were used medicinally, but are primarily valued now by the perfume industry because of their violet-like oil. To a lesser extent, they are used in the manufacture of confectionery and cordials. In the past wines and brandies were perfumed with the root; also, a piece of root added to a keg of home-brewed beer reputedly kept the beer from going stale. Mrs. Grieve, quoting a Dr. Rhind (*History of the Vegetable Kingdom*, 1868), noted that the root was "much used in Russia to flavour a drink made of honey and ginger which is sold in the streets" (437). The best dried root was nearly white, lesser grades yellow or darker colors. Molokhovets used orris root when cleansing the odor from spirits (#2142) and colored orris root when making Sweetened mead (#2213). ("Orris Root," *Bulletin of Miscellaneous Information*, Royal Botanic Gardens, Kew, No. 1, 1930, 91–93; Winton and Winton, *Structure and Composition of Foods*, IV, 196–197.)

## PEARS

For Molokhovets, pears were second only to apples in importance. She named the following varieties: Belaja, Beri, Bergamot, Bezsemjannaja, Dolgovetki, Gdanskaja, Sakharnaja, and Trubchevskaja. Of these, Bergamot was the most important.

## POPPY SEEDS

Poppy seeds were widely used in nineteenth-century Russia, both as seeds and pressed into oil. The seeds were cultivated mostly in Ukraine, Saratov, and Voronezh; they came in three or four colors, depending on the variety of the plants, white, brown, blue, or gray. Molokhovets decorated pastries with "variously colored poppy seeds" and, when making wafers, preferred to use gray rather than white seeds (#3084). (*Entsiklopedicheskij slovar'*, Vol. 35, 451–453; and Norman, *Book of Spices*, 49.)

## POTASH

Potassium carbonate, also called pearl ash; a forerunner of baking soda and the later American baking powders. Molokhovets used potash in many of her gingerbread (*prjaniki*) recipes. Gingerbreads are a very old Russian confection (see the Introduction to Chapter 19), but I do not know when the practice started in Russia of adding potash to the batter. The oldest printed mention of potash used as a leavener in baking that I am aware of is in a Dutch book of 1752, the translated title of which reads *A Dialogue between a Lady and a Pastrycook-Confiturier*; the first American recipes to call for pearl ash as a leavener appeared in Amelia Simmons' book *American Cookery*, 1796. Clearly the popular practice was much older than the printed record. (See Mendelson's query "Hartshorn Salt and Potash," 78–79 and Witteveen's response "Potash and Hartshorn Salt," 66–68.)

## QUICKLIME AND SLAKED LIME

Quicklime (calcium oxide) absorbs water to form slaked lime (calcium hydroxide), which is an important and cheap alkali. Molokhovets used quicklime and slaked lime to soften the textures of foods chemically and to absorb unwanted moisture. Prior to cooking watermelons, muskmelons, and pumpkins for preserves, Molokhovets soaked them in a quicklime solution (#2523). She also soaked stockfish in a quicklime solution after removing it from its bath of lye as part of the long process of making this dried fish edible (#969). To lower the humidity in the room where grapes were hung for the winter, Molokhovets set out barrels of quicklime (#2410). The ability of slaked lime to absorb moisture made it useful for keeping apples fresh (#2339) and storing eggs (#2314).

## RAISINS

Molokhovets used raisins (including a variety she called blue raisin), currants, and *kishmish*. *Kishmish*, which I have translated as sultanas, are small seedless fruits; most varieties are white or golden, but some are black. In the nineteenth century raisins and *kishmish* were imported from Persia, but dried fruits are now produced on a large scale in Central Asia. (*Entsiklopedija vinogradarstva*, III, 193.)

## SAGO

Sago is extracted from the pith of the Asian sago palm (*Sagus farinifera*). A single trunk will yield 600 pounds of the refined starch which is used for thickening soups, puddings, and gravies. After grinding, washing, and straining the pulp, the starch is dried into small pellets. The finest sago has a slightly reddish hue. Sago can sometimes be found in shops that sell Oriental spices and groceries, but it is not readily available in American supermarkets. Depending on the recipe, cornstarch or tapioca may be substituted. (Webster and Parkes, *Encyclopaedia of Domestic Economy*, 767; Fitzgibbon, *Food of the Western World*, 406; and Rombauer and Becker, *Joy of Cooking*, 500.)

## SALICYLIC ACID

Salicylic acid is widespread in nature and is found in the roots, leaves, blossoms, and fruits of many plants. The acid was first prepared in the laboratory in 1838, but it was not sold commercially on a large scale before new processes for its manufacture were developed in the 1870s. Molokhovets used salicylic acid to store butter (#2281) and eggs (#2315), and to rectify spoiled fish and meat (#2637 and Remarks, Chapter 31). By contrast, few American or British cookbook authors of the late nineteenth century mentioned salicyclic acid or took advantage of its antiseptic qualities. The primary use for the chemical today is in the preparation of aspirin and in salves and ointments for treating skin ailments. Its use as a preservative in foods is now outlawed in many countries.

## SALTPETER

Potassium nitrate. Saltpeter is an effective antibacterial agent and has been used to preserve meats and heighten their color and flavor since the sixteenth or seventeenth century. Molokhovets used it extensively for curing meat, but also for preserving vegetables and clarifying hempseed oil (#2258). (McGee, *On Food and Cooking*, 104, 508–511.)

## SARACHINSKOE WHEAT

*Sarachinskoe psheno* or *Saratsinskoe psheno* is the old, now obsolete, Russian term for rice. In the language of medieval knights and crusaders, *Saratsiny* or Saracens, referred to Muslins in general. From the Russian point of view, the basic Muslim grain was rice, hence the name. According to the *Oxford English Dictionary*, however, Saracen corn (remember the British term for "grain" is corn) comes from the sixteenth-century French term *blé sarrasin* and means buckwheat. The plot thickens with Molokhovets' usage: she used the term only thrice in her book, once each in Almond milk soup (#2764) and Stuffed turnips with sour-sweet sauce (#2876), in both cases where the expression could mean anything, and once for Mixed-grain pudding (#1164). The pudding recipe is enlightening but perplexing, since it called for oats, buckwheat, rice, and *sarachinskoe psheno*. Perhaps she regarded it as a special variety of rice or perhaps she really did mean wheat. (*Entsiklopedicheskij slovar'*, Vol. 56, 420 and Vol. 52, 811; Ushakov, *Tolkovyj slovar'*, III, 52; and *Oxford English Dictionary*, II, 106, 112.)

## SIPPETS, CROUTONS, AND RUSKS

Sippets, according to Alan Davidson, are "small sops of fried or toasted bread used to garnish broths, soups, gravy or meat." The word *grenki* in Russian can refer to sippets or croutons. The custom goes back to the Middle Ages when trenchers of bread served as plates and were meant to be eaten at the end of a meal (by the poor if not the diners themselves.) The two items differ in size and shape, but not in purpose—croutons are small cubes, sippets are usually flat slices of bread. Molokhovets used rusks for sops as well. In the United States, melba toast, Dutch rusks, and packaged croutons nowadays serve some of the same purposes. (Glasse, *Art of Cookery*, 200; for a discussion of sippets including both historical and modern preparations, see Spurling, *Elinor Fettiplace's Receipt Book*, 92–93.)

## SLAKED LIME

See *Quicklime*.

## SMOLENSK BUCKWHEAT

Finely ground buckwheat groats, about the size of poppy seeds. (Pokhlebkin, *O kulinarii*, 49.)

## SPIRIT THERMOMETER

Another name for a hydrometer, an instrument used for measuring the density of a liquid.

Although the use of hydrometers was first described in England by Robert Boyle in 1675, they were not developed further until the eighteenth century when they began to be used for industrial purposes and for measuring the strength of alcoholic spirits. Molokhovets advised using one to determine the strength of vodka after refining (#2142).

## STURGEON MARROW

In the late nineteenth century, sturgeon marrow (*viziga*) was prepared in fisheries located on the shores of the Caspian and Azov seas; at that time sturgeon marrow cost 34–36 rubles a pood in Astrakhan and nearly 40 rubles a pood in St. Petersburg. Sturgeon marrow is valued primarily for its gelatinous properties and is used almost exclusively as a component of the fish stuffing for coulibiac, *pirozhki*, *rassetgai*, etc. To prepare sturgeon marrow, soak it in water for several hours and boil in water for another 3 hours before combining it with other ingredients. In large urban centers in the United States and Europe, sturgeon marrow is sold in both powdered and dried forms. (*Entsiklopedicheskij slovar'*, Vol. 14, 720; *Tovarnyj slovar'*, II, 110–111; McClane and deZanger, *Encyclopedia of Fish*, 455.)

## SUGAR

The history of sweeteners in Russia is a movement from honey to cane sugar to beet sugar. The first factory for processing sugar cane was established in Russia in 1723. In the late eighteenth century, the production was so limited that consumption was effectively restricted to gentry families and even for them "less than ¼ lb of sugar was available per person per year" (Smith and Christian, *Bread and Salt*, 177, 234). That situation changed with the development of the process for extracting sugar from sugar beets. The first sugar beet factory in Russia was established in 1802 in Tula province; by 1897 there were 236 sugar beet factories in Russia. Private refineries were also built on large estates (*Entsiklopedicheskij slovar'*, Vol. 57, 13.)

The final stage of processing cane sugar was to pour the molten sugar syrup into large conical molds. After the syrup cooled and solidified, the cones were wrapped in heavy blue paper (in Russia, at least) and offered for sale. Pieces of sugar had to be cut from the cone, then chopped up or ground and sieved before the sugar could be used for cooking or for tea. Molokhovets, who bought her sugar in solid cones, often used pieces of sugar to scrape off the zest from oranges or lemons before pounding the flavored sugar and using it in the recipe. Granulated sugar (*sakharny pesok*) was also available and, because it was derived from sugar beets, was cheaper than cone sugar. Russians, however, preferred cone sugar; beet sugar, although whiter than the cones of cane sugar, tended to have an unpleasant aroma and aftertaste which made it less desirable for eating, cooking, or confectionery.

## SULTANAS

See *Raisins*.

## SWALLOWS' NESTS

The white-nest swiftlet (*Aerodramus fuciphagus*) and the black-nest swiftlet (*Aerodramus maximus*) make their nests using a glutinous substance from their salivary glands. Practically all saliva, the predigested protein and nutrients of these nests are said to be very nutritious and easily digestible. They have long been a very expensive delicacy in the Far East and have been highly prized, especially by the Chinese. Molokhovets noted that some people add an old swallow's nest to the barrel when making vinegar (#2223). Presumably she was talking about the nests of local swallows (*lastochki* of the family Hirunididae), not those of the exotic Asian swiftlets, but perhaps the nests contained just enough additional protein to quicken the formation of the mother of vinegar. (Cost, *Bruce Cost's Asian Ingredients*, 171–173; and Vakki and Summers, "Nest Gatherers of Tiger Cave," 107–133.)

# Appendix C: Glossary

## SWEET FLAG

Sweet flag (*Acorus calamus*) is said to have originated in India and to have been introduced into Poland by the Tartars. It now grows all over the world, wherever there is wet, swampy ground, including European Russia, Eastern Siberia, and the Caucasus. Since ancient times, sweet flag has been used for medicinal purposes; the dried root is used for flavoring fruit preparations (compotes, mousses, *kissels*, and fruit soups), where it may replace bay leaves, ginger, or cinnamon. The fresh root is mostly candied. See Molokhovets' recipe (#2522) for dried sweet flag preserves, her only use of the root in *A Gift to Young Housewives*. (Mrs. Grieve, *A Modern Herbal*, 726–731; *Sturtevant's Edible Plants of the World*, 23; and Rybak, Romanenko, and Korableva, *Prjanosti*, 28–29.)

## TARTAR

Potassium bitartrate, a solid white byproduct of wine fermentation. Molokhovets added tartar to several of her recipes for vinegar, including that which was "quickly made" (#2229).

## TRAGACANTH

Tragacanth, also called gum dragon, is a gummy exudation obtained from the several species of shrubs of the genus *Astragalus*. According to Mrs. Grieve, "it is much used for the suspension of heavy insoluble powders to impart consistence to lozenges, being superior to gum arabic." Molokhovets used it for making gummy candies (#2524). Similarly, tragacanth was a primary ingredient, along with sugar and water, in the pastillage that was the basis of Carême's famous architectural *pièces montées*. (Mrs. Grieve, *A Modern Herbal*, 820; *Martha Washington's Booke of Cookery*, 292; and Carême, *Royal Parisian Pastrycook*, 366.]

## TREACLE

A thick, sweet syrup (called molasses in the U.S.) produced when sugar is refined. Treacle can also be made from the juices of other plants, including birch and sycamore trees, and from malt. Molokhovets' reference to potato treacle (#2427) is the only one I have seen, although McGee mentions a treacle from beets used for animal feed. (For an excellent discussion of the history of treacle see *Martha Washington's Booke of Cookery*, 201–202, 413; also McGee, *On Food and Cooking*, 391–392.)

## TRUFFLES, WHITE OR POLISH

This fragrant truffle (*Choiromyces meandriformis*) grows in the birch forests of Central Europe, just under the soil or, more rarely, on the surface. It was also commonly found in the environs of Moscow, where, according to Brokgauz and Efron, it used to be hunted with the aid of tame bears. Molokhovets used them to marinate goose rolls (#2648). (*Entsiklopedicheskij slovar'*, Vol. 67, 12; Phillips, *Mushrooms and Other Fungi of Great Britain and Europe*, 278–279; and Fedorov, *Griby*, 172, 174.)

## VITRIOL

Oil of vitriol is concentrated sulphuric acid. Molokhovets added it to Rose liqueur (#2154) and American raspberry jam (#1951), in both instances to intensify the red color.

## VIZIGA

See *Sturgeon Marrow*.

ELENA
MOLOKHOVETS'

A Gift

to Young

Housewives

# Author's Introduction
# to the First Edition

Cooking is an art unto itself. Without instruction or dedicated application, mastery of this art requires decades of experience. And a decade of inexperience can prove costly, especially to a young wife; as a result of such inexperience, fortunes can be dissipated and family discord may occur. Most of this is due to an inexperienced housewife who is unwilling to understand and occupy herself with running the household.

My aim and earnest wish is to warn of such dire consequences or, at least, to take steps to avoid them. If my book fulfills even half of my intentions and is useful to my female compatriots, my labors will have been rewarded and I will be completely happy.

I have composed this book exclusively for inexperienced young housewives so that they can quickly learn the principles of household economy and, with this knowledge, acquire a taste for its management.

This book has three goals.

First of all, I want to acquaint housewives with the kitchen and the household in general. With this in mind, I have described essential supplies for the larder and ways to prepare them; for example: rolls, rusks, jams, home-made beverages, various vegetable and fruit preserves, salted meat, fish, etc.

Second, I want to show the housewife how to reduce expenses and how she should dispense provisions from the storeroom. Therefore, wherever possible, I have given precise amounts for all the ingredients in the text of my recipes (calculated for 6 people). In many cases, I have appended a list of ingredients. Neither the mistress nor her cook can, without such a list, recall all the ingredients needed for a given dish and consequently must run continually to the larder to fetch one item or another. This is not only boring but also extremely difficult for the mistress and well-nigh impossible if she has a social life.

My third goal is to ease the creation of daily menus. For this purpose I have composed 800 menus divided into 5 categories: 4 lists of meat day meals, grouped by cost, and 1 list of fast day dishes.

When composing these menus, I deliberately chose seasonal supplies that are readily available and consequently less expensive. The recipes are designed for 6 people, so that a family of 6 (assuming normal appetites) will be satisfied with 3 or 4 dishes while 4 or 5 dishes will feed 8 people. This ratio may be decreased or increased as desired: To prepare a meal for 3 people, divide the proportions in half; for 2 people divide by one third; for 1 person divide by one sixth; for 9 or 12 people increase the proportion by one and a half, and so forth.

I have also added a list of dishes for breakfast and for *zakuski*, as well as those suitable for the children's breakfast and for the servants' meals.

This book will enable you to have continually good, tasty, healthy, and varied meals at a moderate cost, even if you lack an excellent cook. This goal can be achieved only through prudent economy, including the timely purchase and exact allocation of provisions. Measuring and weighing are essential not only for meat, butter, flour and the like, but even for water and milk. Accurate measuring, which is not yet practiced widely in Russia, may seem strange and even comic or awkward to carry out, especially for simple folk such as our servants or cooks. To control the daily distribution of ingredients, however, measuring is essential. Take Broth #1 as an example.

For 6–8 people, pour 6 full soup bowls of water into your usual soup pot and add 2–4 pounds of beef. Mark the height of the water on a clean, smoothly planed stick. Add more water and some salt, herbs, and spices and cook the broth over a low flame for at least three hours until the liquid has reduced to the mark on the stick. The strength of the broth depends on the amount of meat added. Frequently, however, a different scenario occurs: the cook pours water over the meat without bothering to measure the liquid and sets the pan, covered, to boil over quite a high flame. Right before the meal, when it is discovered that the broth has nearly boiled away, the cook adds more water measuring by his or her eye, which, being that of a simple person, often miscalculates. When this soup is poured into the tureen, you find there is double the amount of broth required; 6 bowls are served at the table, but the rest must be returned to the kitchen. This broth, furthermore, is not tasty but weak. Any groats in it would be lost.

Under such conditions, a dish may be tasteless even if the housewife has dispensed the provisions correctly; one might be tempted to blame the book, but that would be unjustified. As a precaution, therefore, each housewife should select several dishes to be prepared under her supervision, following the recipes exactly. If she likes the broth, prepared as indicated above, and it is strong enough, then she can demand of her cook (*povar ili kukharka*) that the soup always be as strong. The same warning applies to other dishes as well, such as *pirogs*. For fast day dough the proportions should be 3 pounds of finely ground flour to precisely 3 glasses of water mixed with yeast. If the water is measured by eye, $3\frac{1}{4}$ or $3\frac{1}{2}$ glasses may be added and consequently the flour will be insufficient.

By using this book, and taking account of local prices, the cost of a small dinner or evening meal may be established beforehand.

The housewife who wants to monitor the distribution of provisions indicated in this book should keep the following items in her larder:

(1) a silver tablespoon

(2) a copper or iron measure holding 1 *garnets* or ¼ pail; also, if possible, measures for ½ and ¼ *garnets*. These will make it easier to dispense milk, flour for rolls, etc.

(3) a medium size glass, about 2¼ *vershok* tall. This glass should contain exactly ½ pound of rice or water. 3 glasses equal ¼ *garnets* and will fill a large champagne bottle. Approximately 6 glasses equal 1 *shtof* and 12 equal 1 *garnets*.

# Evening Tea

When acquaintances gather for friendly conversation that does not last far beyond midnight, a late evening tea instead of a supper may be served by the housewife. The tea table is arranged as follows.

Spread a clean tablecloth on a long dinner table and set a samovar on a small side table at one end. In the middle of the long table place a tall vase filled with fruit, such as apples, pears, oranges, mandarin oranges, and grapes; on each side, place stacks of dessert plates and next to them silver or bone dessert knives.

On either side of the bowl arrange serving dishes (*sukharnitsa*), covered by napkins and filled with tea pastries: buns and babas made of egg whites, saffron, wheat flour, or almonds; English biscuits and small baked goods, either purchased or homemade.

Nearby set out small crystal plates with lemon slices, small carafes of rum, red wine, and cherry syrup, and bowls of sherbet,* cream, and sugar. On both sides of the table, place small stemmed crystal bowls of jam, to be added to the tea or eaten separately; on either side of the bowls, set out teaspoons and small crystal saucers for jam.

One of the bowls of jam may be replaced by orange slices; these bowls should be placed symmetrically at either end of the table, the jam at one end, the orange slices at the other. The oranges are prepared as follows. With a knife, carefully cut and remove the peel in 4 sections, reserving it to make candied orange peel. Using a sharp knife, slice the oranges so that they are slightly thicker than lemon slices; sprinkle the oranges with very fine sieved sugar. All this may be done in the morning to give the oranges time to absorb sugar.

Near the bowls of jam and oranges, place butter in crystal butter dishes and, next to them, crystal plates or butter dishes filled with flavored butters.

Along the length of the table near the butter, place large round wooden trays, covered with napkins and filled with thin slices of bread arranged in circles, with the long edges overlapping. For the outer ring use black bread; for the next, smaller one—French rolls; for the third—fine rye bread, sour-sweet rye, Swedish rye, or steamed bread; the fourth circle may include buns; and at the very center— slices of fine wheat bread (*sytnyj khleb*) standing upright.

Surround the bread tray with small plates of thinly sliced veal, ham, beef, breasts of hazel grouse, turkey or chicken, tongue, hare, Swiss cheese, Russian or homemade cheese, some grated green cheese, etc. Arrange all these foods symmetrically; for example, because cheese is light in color, fill the center of a platter with sliced cheese and surround it with darker slices of meat, placing ham on one

"Merchant's Wife at Tea," by Boris M.
Kustodiev, 1918. State Russian Museum,
St. Petersburg.

side and tongue on the other; in the same way, place sliced veal on one side, and turkey or hazel grouse on the other. Or, fill a plate with beef, another with cheese, a third with ham, a fourth with veal, etc.

The tongue should be fresh. If it is salted, bring it to a boil in water, pour off the water, and replace it with fresh boiling water. Bring the water to a boil twice. This water may also be poured off and replaced with fresh boiling water. Cook until done in this last water. However, to be good, the tongue should retain some salt. The poured-off waters, especially the last two, may be used for borshch or *shchi*.

Beef is best when marinated.

Butters to be served with tea may be prepared variously: sweet butter; Parmesan butter; lemon butter; butter with almonds, walnuts, or pistachios; hazel grouse butter.

Also, hare cheese; cream cheese; assorted cheeses; lemon cider for tea (for those who like to drink tea while holding sugar in their mouths [*vprikusku*]); orange cider; lemon sherbet; almond sherbet; raspberry sherbet; almond shell sherbet; syrups to accompany tea; liqueur for punch; punch for maids of honor; ladies' punch; mulled wine; dark and light cognac (from 1 ruble 15 kopecks to 6 rubles); and dark and light rum (from 1 ruble 15 kopecks to 3 rubles 50 kopecks).

*\*Sherbet, according to Molokhovets, was not a frozen dessert, but a boiled and hardened sweet confection taken with tea instead of lump sugar. See my note following #2032.*

# The Arrangement of the Kitchen

My book is intended to help housekeepers of modest means who must adjust to life's vicissitudes. In this chapter I suggest several ways to arrange small apartment kitchens where the Russian stove and, possibly, a cooking range are located. The latter must be fuel-efficient and covered with an iron hood (it may even be wooden, like those in the Ukraine). Attach the hood, painted with an oil-based paint, flush to the wall over the range and high enough so that you will not bump your head. Under the hood, make a small opening (about 10 inches square)* in the stove pipe for a draft of air. Place a ventilator in the opening and attach doors that can be closed when the range is not lit.

The hood is essential for the family's health; without it, the only way to rid the kitchen of fumes is to open doors onto a cold stairwell. But in that case, the servant will catch cold and drafts will blow through the apartment. On the other hand, if the staircase door is not opened, then all the fumes will penetrate the rooms to the detriment of the family's health. Even the walls will become saturated with this smoke and the apartment cannot be aired out until summer. For this reason, you must see that the hood over the range is constructed so that it draws a powerful current of air. This hood is especially important for small apartments; in large ones, the kitchen is usually far enough removed from the other rooms.

Paint the entire kitchen, including the ceiling, with a light oil-based paint.

Since cleanliness and spaciousness are essential, kitchen furniture should be kept to a minimum. A kitchen table with drawers and two or three stools are necessary, as well as a box for firewood. During the day this box can serve as a second table for dishes or as an ironing board. It should be 21 inches wide, 42 inches long, and 28 inches high. The top should lift up so it may be filled with wood each morning. The front should have small doors to allow easy removal of the wood during the day and the back should be open to facilitate cleaning. On either side of the box, attach drop leaves like those on some dining tables. The leaves should be supported by collapsible legs, so that they may be raised or lowered; one leaf up will turn the box into a table 70 inches long or, with both leaves up, 98 inches long.

The outer wall of the kitchen is ideal for built-in cupboards—one should be warm, the other cold with external ventilation. The cupboard doors should be thoroughly insulated to prevent cold drafts from leaking into the room and to protect the contents of the cupboards from the kitchen's heat. Of course, the larger the cupboard, the better, since it can hold more.

# The Arrangement of the Kitchen

If there is no other accommodation for the cook, construct a niche about 16 inches wide, 6½ feet long, and 7 feet high on a warm interior wall for her bed. For the bed, make two firm, sturdy, varnished shelves, each 14 inches wide and 6½ feet long; join the boards with hinges. Secure one length of board to the wall 21 inches from the floor and attach 3 or 4 legs, also on hinges, to the other plank. At night, open the cupboard doors, fold down the plank, stand it on its legs, and spread out the bedding, which is filled with chaff from straw or dried seaweed. During the day fold up the plank and legs with the bedding and close the cupboard.

A trunk may be placed under this bed shelf; the half which juts into the room may serve as a kitchen bench during the day. The cupboard doors should not extend to the very top; at least 21 inches should be left free to avoid stuffy air in the niche.

A small rack for dresses should be nailed to the wall of the niche at the foot of the bed, and at the head, a peg for a personal towel.

The interior of the niche should be painted with an oil-based paint.

In old houses it is often impossible to construct such a niche: the kitchen may be very small with nowhere to turn, nowhere even to place a second table, much less a bed. In such a case, order a large, simple, clean, and smooth table, or more exactly, a board to be made (35 inches wide and 7 feet long). Seven inches from each end, attach ordinary bench supports (no more than 7–10 inches high) instead of legs. During the daytime place this big bench on top of the servant's bed, covering it completely so that the bench can be used for storing dishes, ironing, or even preparing food if necessary. At night, stand the bench upright against a free wall. This is very useful in small apartments.

In addition, small benches and collapsible shelves with supports may be fastened to the kitchen walls.

Shelves for dishes are, of course, also necessary; all the shelves should be painted with an oil-based paint the same color as the kitchen and they should be decorated with paper cut-outs.

Towels, straining spoons, kitchen spoons, sieves, cutting boards for cleaning herring, etc., may be hung from nails, or preferably, from black metal pegs which cost from 3–5 kopecks a pair.

Cupboards for underwear, clothes, and linen may be built into the structural walls along the corridor. Small cupboards with drawers for various staples such as groats and macaroni may also be added.

These are the essentials of the kitchen.

*For this section only, I have converted Molokhovets' Russian measurements into American feet and inches.*

# 1
# Soups
## (Supy)

## HOT MEAT-BASED SOUPS
### (Supy mjasnye, gorjachie)

### REMARKS CONCERNING THE BASIC PREPARATION OF BOUILLON

#### i  Utensils for bouillon
*(Posuda dlja bul'ona)*

Bouillon, like soups, should not be made in a copper pan. It is essential to use a thoroughly clean clay, stoneware, or enameled cast-iron pot.* Two kettles should be used when preparing soup—one for the initial cooking of the bouillon, the other for seasoning the already strained bouillon.

*\*Note by Molokhovets: Guard against placing an empty pan on a hot stove. To clean a burned pan, strew 5 kopecks' worth of chloride of lime [bleaching powder] into the pot, fill with water, and boil this liquid until the pot is bleached white. Let the bleach water cool in the pan and then strain into a bottle.\*\* Wash the pan thoroughly in several waters.*

*\*\*Second note by Molokhovets: After yellowed linen is washed, it may be soaked in this water for fifteen minutes or longer until it whitens. It should then be rinsed thoroughly.*

#### ii  The quality of meat
*(Kachestvo mjasa)*

As for meat, the primary requirement is that it be very fresh, slaughtered two days earlier. It is best to use a smaller quantity of the best grade of meat. Before making soup, rinse the meat thoroughly in cold water under a faucet, removing any dust or dirt. To preserve the natural juices, be sure not to squeeze the meat.

#### iii  [No heading]

If rich, strong broth is desired and juicy beef or *bul'i* [beef boiled in bouillon]* is not needed for serving as a second course, place the meat in cold water to release the juices more easily. If a juicy piece of meat is wanted for the second course, plunge the meat into boiling water. The albumin cooks immediately and, like the white of a hard-boiled egg, forms a sort of rind around the outside which prevents the meat juices from escaping into the broth. Meat boiled in this manner consequently remains juicy.

*This term comes from the French word* bouilli. *See #xv in this section or recipes for boiled beef in Chapter 5.*

### iv  The quantity of beef
*(Kolichestvo govjadiny)*

To prepare enough bouillon to fill 6 deep soup plates, use 10–12 lbs of beef and bones. This amount is excessive,* however, since the bouillon will be excellent if made from only 6 lbs, allotting about 1 lb per person. For ordinary bouillon [for six] use 1¼ to 3 lbs beef with bones, or ⅙ to ½ lb (70–200 grams)** per person. With ½ lb or 200 grams per person, the bouillon will be very good. Do not make bouillon from less than ⅙ lb per person. For puréed soups and *shchi*, use proportionately less beef; for example, 2 to 2½ lbs per six servings, instead of 3.

*Molokhovets was generous to guests, but she always economized where she could. This aside to thriftiness is just the first of many examples in the book.*
** *The reference here to the metric system is rare for Molokhovets. Russia, along with sixteen other countries, signed the Metric Treaty in 1875. The system was authorized for optional use in Russia in 1899 and only became mandatory in the RSFSR in 1918 and for the entire USSR in 1925 (*Great Soviet Encyclopedia, *XVI, 215).*

### v  The quantity of water
*(Kolichestvo vody)*

For each soup bowl use 2½ glasses of water of which at least 1 glass must boil away. For 6 people, therefore, use 15 glasses or 5 bottles of water, from which 6 glasses or 2 bottles of water must boil away. Place the beef in the soup kettle and pour over it 6 full soup dishes or 9 glasses of water. Measure the height of the water with a clean, smoothly planed spill* or stick. Mark the stick and add the remaining water. Cook the bouillon for 3–4 hours, by which time it should be reduced to the mark on the stick.

*Spill is the English word for wooden splints or* luchinki, *which were widely used as a cheap source of lighting by Russian peasants and would have been readily available in the kitchen. In England and America they were kept in jars (called spill jars) next to the stove or the fireplace mantel.*

### vi  The order of cooking
*(Porjadok varki)*

First place the bouillon over a high flame, covering the kettle with a lid so that it will come to a boil quickly. Bring to a vigorous boil three times, then place the kettle over a low fire to simmer for 3–4 hours. Since it is better for the bouillon to boil from one side only,* it is a good idea to place under the non-boiling side of the pan a burner cover taken from the top of the stove.

*\*Almost all ranges in Russian kitchens during this period were either wood or coal burning. Only gas, which was not then available in ordinary homes, allows a rapid adjustment of the flame. Otherwise, to adjust the heat, pans were moved around physically from warmer to less warm parts of the stove top. See the section on stoves in the Introduction.*

### vii  Scum
*(Pena)*

It used to be that when bouillon had boiled briskly 2–3 times, the scum was removed immediately and completely with a skimmer. This same scum is now believed to contain the valuable nutrient albumin. It is not necessary, therefore, to remove it; but if it is removed, place it in a smaller pan with 2–3 glasses of the boiled bouillon. This pan should sit on the back edge of the stove to allow the scum to settle gradually. Within three to four hours, as it is absorbed into the bouillon, it will form a thin membrane, which can be discarded. The remaining bouillon should then be strained into the original bouillon.

### viii  Root vegetables
*(Koren'ja)*

After the scum has been removed and transferred to another smaller stewpan, as described above, salt the bouillon remaining in the large kettle and add root vegetables, such as a parsley root, 1–2 carrots, ½ celery root, ½ leek, a small rutabaga, a whole baked onion, a fried onion, and a dried mushroom. Cook this over a low fire for 3–4 hours, without adding water.

Since additional water must not be added to the bouillon, add the required amount of water all at once. Thereafter add only the strained bouillon that formerly contained the scum.

When the meat is ready and can be pierced easily with a fork, add 1 spoon of cold water to the bouillon. Set the stockpot aside for the bouillon to settle and remove the fat on top. Strain the bouillon through a sieve and then through a clean napkin, washed without soap, into another stewpan. Bring this to a boil, transfer it directly to a soup tureen, and garnish it with finely chopped dill.

[Numbers ix and x missing from the original]

### xi  The amount of salt
*(Kolichestvo soli)*

Use 3 full teaspoons of salt for bouillon for 6 persons. Should the soup happen to be salted twice, the mistake can be remedied as follows. Tie up in a clean cloth a glass of the very best fine-ground wheat flour or cleanly screened rice, and add this to the oversalted bouillon. The flour and rice will absorb the salt while boiling, but will cloud the bouillon slightly. Since this bouillon cannot be cleared, use it to prepare soup with Italian macaroni, thickening it with a liaison, that is, cream and egg yolks.

In extreme cases, pour off half the bouillon and reserve it for the next day. Dilute the remaining half of the oversalted bouillon with boiling water, add dry bouillon and 2 spoons of dried and compressed root vegetables, soaked first in water.* To prepare the reserved oversalted bouillon the next day, add water and half the usual amount of beef, without adding salt.

*See #2654 for dried bouillon and #2632 for dried vegetables and greens for soup.

### xii  How to correct unsavory bouillon resulting from inferior cuts of meat
*(Sredstvo ispravit' durnoj vkus bul'ona, proizshedshij ot durnago sorta mjasa)*

In case the meat is tough and of poor quality, cook it for another half hour after removing the scum from the bouillon. For 3 lbs of tough beef, add 2 tablespoons of vodka and cook until the odor of the vodka evaporates, by which time the beef will be tender.

If the beef is not completely fresh, add a clean birch coal to the bouillon as it cooks. The coal will absorb the offensive odor and taste.

### xiii  How to color a clear bouillon
*(Kak podtsvechivajut chistyj bul'on)*

To color a clear bouillon amber, follow one of these methods:

(1) In a small saucepan boil the skins from one or two onions in a small quantity of bouillon. When the skins have boiled thoroughly, strain the broth and add it to the rest of the bouillon.

(2) Finely chop a peeled onion and wrap it in a clean cloth. Wash it under a faucet several times, squeeze and drain it, and then fry the onion in ½ spoon butter. Dilute with bouillon, bring to a boil, and strain into the rest of the bouillon.

(3) Peel and finely slice an onion, fry in ½ spoon butter in a skillet until golden, add 2 to 3 spoons bouillon, and bring to a boil. Transfer everything,

including the onion, to the rest of the bouillon so that everything cooks together. Strain.

(4) Cut an unpeeled onion in half and a peeled and washed carrot lengthwise into thirds. Place the vegetables in a pan on top of the stove and fry them on all sides until they darken, being careful not to let them burn. Add to the bouillon and cook together.

(5) Pound a piece of sugar and pour onto a clean skillet. Moisten it with water and cook until it turns reddish-brown, but do not let it burn. Dilute with 2–3 spoons water, bring to a boil, and strain into the bouillon.

(6) Cut off ½ lb of lean meat from the 3 lbs of beef intended for the soup. Mince it with a finely chopped onion and carrot. Fry the beef, onion, and carrot in a dry saucepan, without adding butter, stirring constantly and browning on all sides. Pour in boiling water and boil thoroughly. Combine with the rest of the bouillon, continue cooking, and then strain.

### xiv To clarify bouillon
*(Kak ochishchat' bul'on, chtoby byl prozrachen)*

Bouillon for formal dinners must be strained through a fine sieve and napkin and also be clarified as follows. Beat a raw egg white and add it to the boiling bouillon. When the egg has thoroughly boiled, strain the soup through a hair sieve, or still better, through a napkin that has been washed without soap. The napkin should first be moistened in cold water, squeezed out, and tied to an overturned stool. [Place a pan under the napkin to collect the strained bouillon.]

If the bouillon must be clear as crystal, strain it a second time, lining the napkin with white blotting paper.

To clarify a large quantity of bouillon, finely chop ½–1 lb beef and pass it once through a meat grinder. Mix the ground beef with 1–2 glasses of cold, unboiled water and pour the mixture into the boiling bouillon. Boil for at least 30 minutes and strain through a napkin and blotting paper as indicated above.

Sometimes ½ lb of picked-over spinach leaves or finely chopped dill is added to clarified bouillon. The greens are placed in the soup tureen and the boiling bouillon is poured over them.

If serving the bouillon in cups, omit the greens and serve *pirozhki* instead.

### xv The kinds of beef usually used for soup
*(Sorta govjadiny, upotrebljaemye na sup voobshche)*

Soup may be prepared from various cuts of beef, according to circumstance. For example:

a) For clear, strong bouillon use beef round (*bedro*). For a thinner bouillon, use beef from the rump, round, or shank, etc. (*ssek, kostrets, oguzok, podbederok,* and *buldyshka*).*

b) If the beef for the bouillon (or *bul'i* as it is called) will be served as a second course, use 5–6 lbs of sirloin. For a lesser quality *bul'i*, use the end cut of the rump or round. In that case, prepare soup for two days. The first day serve the boiled beef as a second course, and the next day with some sort of sauce, or in stew.

*Each country and region usually has a particular style for cutting up animal carcasses. With unfamiliar cuts and non-equivalent names, the choosing and naming of an appropriate cut of meat outside of one's own culture is an exercise in frustration. A series of fascinating diagrams on the local cuts of meat in various cities in late Tsarist Russia is contained in Ignat'ev, Mjasovedenija dlja kulinarnykh shkol. For guidance on Molokhovets' terminology, see her diagram of beef in Chapter 5.*

### xvi [The basic recipe for a clear, strong bouillon for all kinds of soups]

The type of beef may be varied according to the kind of soup.

The root vegetables mentioned are small, and therefore the parsley root, celery root, and leek should be chopped into 2–3 pieces. Since root vegetables add flavor, it is better to add more rather than fewer of these.

I usually put the onion and bay leaf in parentheses in the list of ingredients because not everyone likes them. They should be added as desired.

Use good regular butter or Finnish butter* in *shchi* and other soups.

The recipes are intended to make enough soup to fill 6 deep soup dishes; if necessary, this amount will be sufficient for 8 people. Consequently for clear bouillon #1 and #2, etc: For 6–8 people, use 3–4 lbs of beef; for 9–12 people, 6 lbs; for 13–18 people, 9 lbs; and for 19–24 people, 12 lbs.

Above all, add bones to the bouillon and any leftover scraps from veal, turkey, or chicken intended for the main course.

Increase the proportions similarly for other soups and *shchi*.

INGREDIENTS (*for 6 persons*)

| | |
|---|---|
| 3 lbs beef | 1 parsley root |
| 15 glasses water or 5 bottles reduced to 9 glasses or 3 bottles | ½ leek |
| | ½ celery root |
| 3 teaspoons salt | ½ rutabaga |
| Not less than ½ lb of basic root vegetables, such as: | 1 dried mushroom |
| | 1 onion |
| 1–2 carrots | handful of dill |

*See "Butter" in Glossary.*

[*Translator's note:* In earlier editions, the recipes above were included in Molokhovets' general Introduction. Later, she reformulated her remarks to resemble recipes and added them to the chapter on soups, but failed to renumber the other recipes.]

## [1] Clear bouillon
### (Bul'on chistyj)

Prepare as just indicated in the Remarks. Thus, for 6–8 persons, take 3–4 lbs of fresh beef rump, round, or chuck, and wash it in cold water to remove any dust or dirt, taking care not to squeeze the meat. Place the beef in a stoneware pot or stockpot reserved for soup and add 2 onions and 6 full plates, or 9 glasses, of cold water. Measure with a spill or stick, [mark the height of the liquid,] and add another 6 glasses of water. Let the soup come to a boil over a high flame, skim the bouillon, and then simmer over a low flame for 3–4 hours until reduced to the mark on the spill. As directed in the Remarks, transfer the beef to another stewpan 30 minutes before dinner. Remove the bouillon from the fire, add 1 spoon cold water, and let the soup settle completely until it is clear and transparent. Skim off any fat and carefully strain through a clean napkin, pouring off the clear bouillon.

Rinse out the stewpan in which the bouillon cooked and pour back the strained bouillon. Add the rinsed beef and the peeled and washed root vegetables (2 carrots, 1–2 parsley roots, ½ leek, ½ celery root) and cook.

If the bouillon has to be very clear and transparent, clarify it with egg whites, caviar,* or raw beef as indicated in the Remarks.

To serve, strain into a soup bowl and garnish with finely chopped parsley and dill.

*Remarks:* All or part of the following may be added to this bouillon, according to taste and circumstance. When meat or poultry is prepared for another dish, add the scraps to the bouillon, especially any bits of veal, the head and feet of chickens and turkeys, and the crushed bones from yesterday's bouillon. The more of these the better. Cook all this in the bouillon from the very beginning so that the scum can be removed; then strain. Some people add 1–2 baked rather than raw onions; or 1–2 dried, cleaned mushrooms; or a beef kidney; or ½ tablespoon of the best dried green peas, washed. Two hours before serving, you may add a rutabaga to the bouillon. Forty-five minutes before serving, you may add additional carrots, parsley roots, or celery roots to the basic root vegetables. Some people add 1–2 whole cloves or ground nutmeg. Cook until just before serving and then strain.

To serve, this bouillon may be varied as follows:** clear, only with dill and parsley, with all kinds of *pirozhki* and stuffed shells; with croutons or sippets; with carrots and spinach leaves, halved and blanched in salted boiling water for a few minutes (¼ lb spinach and 2 carrots, sliced evenly); with *Frikadellen* [small meatballs] or quenelles (use ¼ lb beef for the meatballs) or *kletski* [a kind of dumpling]; or with kasha made from Smolensk groats; noodles; *lazanki* [small dumplings boiled in bouillon or salted water]; semolina; rice kasha, rice *pirozhki*, or croquettes; sago; oats; pearl barley; carefully cut root vegetables and *pirozhki* or potatoes; root vegetables and cabbage; Brussels sprouts and meatballs; green peas, cauliflower, and asparagus; dried vegetables; or *pel'meni* [dumplings].

INGREDIENTS

3–4 lbs beef
2 onions
1–2 carrots
½ leek
½ celery root
1–2 parsley roots

parsley and dill

*To clarify the bouillon*
2 egg whites, or
¼ lb pressed caviar,* or
½ lb beef

* To clarify the soup, Molokhovets used pressed caviar, which is of second quality. Pressed caviar contains broken eggs and is darker in color than first quality caviar. See Glossary for more on caviar. The protein in the caviar as in the egg white or beef serves to precipitate the minute particles suspended in the bouillon. From a modern point of view, this seems like an extravagant use for caviar, but it does strongly suggest that caviar must have been much cheaper and more readily available a century ago than it is today.

**Soup accompaniments came in many guises and from many different sources as can be seen from this list, with its German Frikadellen and kletski (from Polish, from the Middle High German Klotz), its French quenelles, its Italian lazanki (from Polish from the Italian lazagne), its Siberian pel'meni (with Finno-Ugric roots), and its adopted lapsha (from Turkic). (Vasmer, Etimologiches-kij slovar', II, 249; and Preobrazhensky, Etymological Dictionary, 315.)

### 4 Bouillon for sick people*

*(Bul'on dlja bol'nykh)*

Prepare the following bouillon for very weak, sick people. Finely chop ¼ lb of the highest quality, tender rump beef without any fat. Place in a champagne bottle,** cork the bottle, and set it in a kettle or large stewpan with water on top of the stove. Boil it from morning until dinnertime. These proportions will yield one teacup of strong bouillon. Strain and salt lightly before serving.

*In the later undated German edition, this recipe is called "English meat tea for sick people."
**Russians in Tsarist times had an inordinate fondness for champagne, a taste that is still shared by modern Soviets. The debris left from their legendary debauches meant that there was an ample supply of good, strong bottles readily available for use in the kitchen and still room or cold cellar. See Chapters 22 and 23 for other examples. (Toomre, "Russia and Champagne," 26–27.)

### 5 Bouillon with rum for weak children and adults who must lead an active life and "be constantly on the go"

*(Bul'on s romom dlja slabykh detej i vzroslykh, kotorye prinuzhdeny vesti dejatel'nyju zhizn' i byt' v postojannom dvizhenii)*

Crush the bones from an ox foot and shin and boil them over a low fire for 3 hours. If the foot is large, add enough water to completely fill four soup plates. Then remove the bones and boil them in half the amount of fresh water, so that there will be altogether 2 glasses to mix with the first bouillon. Boil it thoroughly for 15 minutes and strain. This bouillon may be kept in a cold place for 3 days in bottles, corked with paper.

Remove the meat from the bones and mix with a roll and parsley to make small meatballs. When serving the bouillon, pour a teaspoon of rum into each soup bowl. This bouillon is very healthy for weak children and adults as indicated above.

## 6  Beef bouillon for breakfast for sick people

*(Bul'on iz govjadiny k zavtraku dlja bol'nago)*

Cut a half pound of good, tender, lean beef into small pieces and place in a small stoneware pot. Cover with 1½ glasses of water and bring to a boil twice. Add salt, strain, and serve. Add the beef which remains to the general stockpot and recook it with the beef intended for that day's soup at dinner.

## 9  French julienne soup*

*(Sup frantsuzskij zhjul'en)*

Prepare an ordinary bouillon from 3–4 lbs beef and root vegetables and strain as indicated in the Remarks. Dry ½ lb rye bread [in the oven] until brown, pour over enough bouillon to cover the bread, and set aside for at least an hour, covered. Then pour off the bouillon from the bread and strain it. Meanwhile, cut up like vermicelli 1 large carrot, 1 kohlrabi or young sweet turnip, 1 celery root, and 6–8 spears of asparagus. Add 1 spoon of dried green peas, rinse all the vegetables and peas, and cook in the original, strained bouillon. Just before serving, add the reserved bread bouillon and sprinkle with 50 spinach leaves. The chopped root vegetables may be fried lightly in ½ spoon butter before adding them to the bouillon, in which case cook them in the bouillon for half an hour.

INGREDIENTS

| | |
|---|---|
| 3–4 lbs beef | 1 kohlrabi or young turnip |
| 2 carrots | 50 spinach leaves |
| 1 parsley root | 6–7 [sic] spears asparagus |
| 1 celery root | 1 spoon dried green peas |
| 1 leek | ½ lb rye bread |
| ½ spoon butter | |

*Although Molokhovets called this French soup, its origin was not necessarily French. Neither* the rye bread bouillon nor the dried green peas were part of the classic French preparation. As is the case in other cuisines, the Russian notion of a foreign dish was often idiosyncratic.

## 11 Windsor soup made from calf's feet*

*(Sup vindzor iz teljach'ikh nozhek)*

Prepare a bouillon with 3–4 lbs beef but no root vegetables. Strain the bouillon. Trim and wash thoroughly 4 calf's feet, cook them in salted water and at least ½ glass vinegar, which is essential. Remove the meat from the bones. In separate pans of bouillon, cook ½ glass of pearl barley and ⅙ lb broken** Italian macaroni. Mix ½ spoon flour with 1 spoon butter and dilute with a little bouillon. Boil this roux thoroughly, add the cooked pearl barley, and rub it all through a fine sieve. Dilute the purée with the strained beef bouillon, add ½ glass of cream mixed with 2 egg yolks, and sprinkle with Parmesan cheese. Reheat, stirring, until very hot. Add to the soup tureen the boiled macaroni, the veal meat cut into even pieces, and a wineglass or two of sauternes. Sprinkle with cayenne pepper, add the bouillon, and serve.

Use the leftover bouillon from the calf's feet for aspic.

*Pirozhki* made from puff pastry and *pirozhki* in crayfish shells are served with this soup.

INGREDIENTS

| | |
|---|---|
| 3–4 lbs beef | ½ glass sauternes*** |
| 4 calf's feet | ½ glass cream |
| ½ glass pearl barley | 2 egg yolks |
| 1 [sic] spoon flour | cayenne pepper |
| 1 spoon butter | ⅛ lb Parmesan cheese |
| ⅙ lb Italian macaroni | |

*Francatelli, *Queen Victoria's chef, published a recipe for Calf's Feet Soup à la Windsor in 1846. He garnished the soup with small quenelles of chicken breast, but did not include the barley used by Molokhovets (see Francatelli, The Modern Cook, 126–127).

** The nomenclature for pasta shapes and sizes is far from standardized, but in general the term macaroni, from the Italian maccheroni, refers to a group of long, hollow noodles that vary in size and thickness. While Americans today mostly think of macaroni as elbow-shaped pasta, the term referred to long, tubular noodles in both nineteenth-century America and Russia.

***One half glass equaled two wineglasses. See Table of Weights and Measures for conversions.

## 16 Salted cucumber soup or rassol'nik

*(Sup iz solenykh ogurtsov ili razsol'nik)*

Prepare a bouillon as usual from 2½ to 3 lbs of beef and add, if desired, 1 beef kidney. Add root vegetables, spices, and 2–3 dried mushrooms. Boil and strain. Peel, slice, and cook 6 small salted cucumbers [in the bouillon]. If necessary, add some cucumber brine to make it pleasantly sour. Slice the kidney into small pieces and place in the soup tureen with some greens. Pour on the bouillon and serve.

Sometimes ½ to 1½ glasses of sour cream are added to this soup. Also, you may cook a few potatoes in the bouillon and thicken the soup with flour.

INGREDIENTS

| | |
|---|---|
| 2½ to 3 lbs beef | 2–3 dried mushrooms |
| (1 beef kidney) | 6 small salted cucumbers with brine |
| 1 parsley root | (½ to 1½ glass sour cream) |
| 1 celery root | 12 potatoes |
| 1 leek | 1 spoon flour |
| 1–2 bay leaves | [greens] |

## 18  Cherry soup with Smolensk buckwheat

*(Sup iz vishen' so smolenskimi krupami)*

Prepare a bouillon from 2½ lbs of beef and strain.

Stone ripe cherries and place the cherries in a saucepan with 1 lb veal, a piece of cinnamon, cardamom, and ½ spoon butter. Cover with bouillon and simmer over a low fire until well stewed. Pound the cherry stones in a mortar, pour on bouillon, and cook separately in a small, covered saucepan for 15 minutes. Strain through a fine sieve into the cherries, add ½ lb of grated sour-sweet bread and a little bouillon, and cook until the mixture thickens. Just before serving, rub the cherry mixture through a sieve, dilute with bouillon, add sugar and salt to taste, and mix with fluffy Smolensk buckwheat kasha.

INGREDIENTS

| | |
|---|---|
| 2½ lbs beef | ½ lb bread |
| 1 carrot | ½ spoon butter |
| 1 parsley root | 2 cardamom pods |
| ½ celery root | |
| ½ leek | *For the kasha* |
| 1 lb, or 3 glasses, cherries | ½ glass Smolensk groats* |
| cinnamon | 1 egg |
| 1 lb veal | ¾ glass water |
| salt | 1 spoon butter |
| ½ glass sugar | |

*For a description of Smolensk groats or buckwheat, see the Glossary.*

## 20  Italian soup with macaroni

*(Sup ital'janskij s makaronami)*

Prepare a bouillon with 3 pounds of beef and root vegetables and strain the bouillon. Break ⅓ pound Italian macaroni into even pieces, cook in boiling water, drain in a coarse sieve, and rinse with cold water. Transfer the macaroni to a stewpan, cover with the bouillon, and simmer over a low fire. Beat 2 egg yolks in a small saucepan, sprinkle with grated Parmesan cheese, and dilute with 1 glass of boiled cream. Just before serving, dilute the cream and eggs with 2 glasses of hot bouillon, stirring constantly. Heat until very hot, strain through a fine sieve into the bouillon, and add ½ spoon butter, salt, and a little ground white pepper. Put the cooked macaroni in a soup tureen, cover with the bouillon, and serve.

INGREDIENTS

| | |
|---|---|
| 3 lbs beef | 1 glass cream |
| 2 carrots | 2 egg yolks |
| 1 parsley root | ½ spoon butter |
| 1 celery root | 3 white peppercorns |
| 1 leek | ⅛ lb Parmesan cheese |
| ⅓ lb Italian macaroni | |

## 29  Sauerkraut *shchi*

*(Shchi iz kapusty kisloj)*

Prepare a bouillon in the usual way from 3 lbs fatty beef, using chuck, rump, or brisket. Or, use 2 lbs beef and 1 lb ham with dried mushrooms and spices. Strain the bouillon. Squeeze the excess liquid from 2 glasses of sauerkraut, chop, and fry until tender with 1 finely chopped onion and ground black pepper in 1½ spoons butter or, better yet, rendered beef or pork fat. Pour in the bouillon, add 1 spoon flour mixed with water, and boil until tender. When the meat and cabbage are done, serve the soup with the boiled sliced ham or beef.

Serve this *shchi* with one of the following: sour cream, fried or boiled sausages, fried thick buckwheat kasha, pancake loaf, or pancake *pirozhki* made with a stuffing from the mushrooms that were boiled in the *shchi* and buckwheat kasha.

INGREDIENTS

| | |
|---|---|
| 2 lbs beef | 1½ spoons butter |
| 1 lb ham | (5 black peppercorns) |
| 3–4 dried mushrooms | 1 spoon flour |
| (2 onions) | 1–1½ glasses sour cream |
| 5–10 allspice | 1–2 bay leaves |
| 2 glasses, or 1 lb, sauerkraut | |

### 31  Ukrainian borshch

*(Borshch malorossijskij)*

Prepare bouillon #1 from 3 lbs of fatty beef or fresh pork, or from beef with smoked ham. Omit the root vegetables, but add a bay leaf and allspice. Strain the bouillon. An hour before serving add a little fresh cabbage, cut into pieces. Cook, stirring in beet brine or grain *kvass* to taste or about 2 spoons vinegar. Meanwhile thoroughly wash and boil 5 red beets, but do not peel or cut them; that is, boil them separately in water without scraping. Remove them when tender, peel, and grate. Stir 1 spoon of flour into the beets, add them to the bouillon with some salt, and bring to a boil twice. Put parsley in a soup tureen (some people add the juice of a grated raw beet) and pour in the hot borshch. Add salt to taste. Sprinkle with black pepper, if desired, and serve with the sliced beef, pork, or ham; or with fried sausages, meatballs, or mushroom buns. This borshch may also be served with fried buckwheat kasha, pancake pie with beef stuffing, or plain pancakes.

### 39  Fresh mushroom soup

*(Sup s svezhimi gribami)*

Prepare a bouillon from 3 lbs of beef and spices. Strain the bouillon. An hour before dinner, blanch a dish of clean, fresh mushrooms in boiling water. These may be boletus mushrooms, yellow-brown boletus [*Boletus luteus*], saffron milk-cap or milk-agaric, but not woolly milk-caps. Fry the blanched mushrooms and an onion in butter and sprinkle them with 1 spoon of flour. Pour on bouillon, add 6–9 potatoes, and cook [until tender]. Add a handful of minced green onions, some salt, and sour or fresh cream. Boil thoroughly, pour into a soup tureen, and serve strewn with greens and black pepper.

INGREDIENTS

| | |
|---|---|
| 3 lbs beef | 1–2 spoons of butter |
| root vegetables | 1 spoon flour |
| a plateful of fresh mushrooms | ½–1 glass sour or sweet cream |
| 6–9 potatoes | 1–2 onions |
| handful of green onions | black pepper |
| greens | |

### 42  Suckling pig soup

*(Sup iz porosenka)*

Prepare a bouillon as usual, using 3 lbs of suckling pig and some root vegetables and spices. Strain the bouillon. In a separate pan boil until soft ½ glass barley with 1 spoon butter. Beat the barley until white, add sour cream, dilute with bouillon, and bring to a boil. Serve strewn with parsley and dill. This soup may be served with meat balls made from the kidneys, but the suckling pig should be served separately with horseradish and sour cream.

INGREDIENTS

| | |
|---|---|
| 3–4 lbs suckling pig | 1–3 bay leaves |
| 2 carrots | ½ glass of pearl barley |
| 1 parsley root | 1–1½ glasses sour cream |
| 1 celery root | parsley and dill |
| 1 onion | 10–15 allspice |
| 1 leek | |

### 43  Oxtail soup

*(Sup iz bychach'ikh khvostov)*

Wash 3 oxtails and blanch them in boiling water. Cook in bouillon made with yesterday's bones, adding 1 carrot, 1 parsley root, 1 parsnip, 1 celery root, 1 leek, and 1 seeded slice of lemon. Strain the bouillon.

Place 1 halved carrot, 1 onion, and ½ spoon butter in a stewpan. Add 5–6 lbs beef and fry until brown, but do not let it burn. Cover with water and cook for 2 hours. Lightly fry 2 spoons flour with 1½ spoons butter, dilute with bouillon, and boil thoroughly. Sauté 2 sliced celery roots and add these to the bouillon with the oxtails, which have been cut at the joints. Remove the fillets from a large raw chicken and mince and pound them. Add ½ French roll, 1 egg, ⅛ lb butter, and salt. Rub this mixture through a fine sieve, form into small meatballs, and fry them until golden in ⅛ lb butter. Add the meatballs to the bouillon with ½ lb veal sweetbreads, 12–20 cocks' combs, boiled separately, 15 field mushrooms, ½ glass of tomatoes (the purchased red purée from tomatoes),* and ¼ lb of picked-over sorrel. Bring to a boil, and add 1 glass of strong Madeira and salt to taste. Serves 12.

For 6 people use 1 oxtail, 1–2 lbs beef, 1 small chicken, etc.

INGREDIENTS

| | |
|---|---|
| 3 oxtails | 5–6 lbs beef |
| 2 carrots | 1 carrot |
| 1 parsley root | 1 onion |
| 1 celery root | 2 celery roots |
| 1 leek | 2 spoons flour |
| 1 parsnip | 1 large chicken |
| 1 lemon slice | 1 egg |

½ French roll
½ lb sweetbreads
12–20 cocks' combs
15 field mushrooms

½ glass tomatoes
¼ lb picked-over sorrel
1 glass of strong Madeira
5 spoons, or ⅝ lb butter

*Although Molokhovets used the word jabloko, meaning apple, she undoubtedly meant tomatoes since applesauce is not a reasonable substitute for tomato purée. What happened, I suspect, is that she dropped the word zolotye, inadvertently or otherwise, from zolotye jabloki, a literal translation of the Italian pomi d'oro or golden apples. Tomat has become the usual word for tomato in modern Russian, while pomidor is used less frequently.*

## 48  Chicken soup with stuffed morels

*(Sup iz kuritsy s farshirovannymi smorchkami)*

Prepare a bouillon from a 3 lb chicken (or use two small chickens with 1 lb of beef bones). Before cooking the chicken, remove one fillet from the breast to make forcemeat. Chop and pound the fillet and add ½ spoon butter, a little salt, nutmeg, ⅛ wineglass of Rhine wine, 1 egg, and enough flour to thicken the mixture slightly. Wash 18 to 24 large morels thoroughly, cut off the stems and, where possible, stuff the morels with this forcemeat. Boil the morels in strong bouillon in a separate saucepan. Strain the bouillon, which may be thickened with butter and flour. Bring it to a boil and add ½ glass of cream with 2 egg yolks. Heat until very hot, stirring, and then strain into a soup tureen. Add the stuffed morels.

INGREDIENTS

1 large chicken
1 lb or more beef bones
½ carrot
½ celery root
½ parsley root
dill and parsley
1 spoon butter
nutmeg

⅛ wineglass Rhine wine
1 egg
2 spoons flour
1 spoon butter
18–24 morels
½ glass cream
2 egg yolks

## 54  Goose blood soup

*(Sup krovjanoj iz gusja)*

Prepare soup [bouillon] from goose gizzards. Add 2 onions, 10 black peppercorns, 1–2 bay leaves, and about 2 glasses of beet brine. Cook until the meat is done and strain. Dried pears and dried or fresh apples may be used instead of the brine. In a stoneware bowl mix 1 glass of grated bread with the blood from a whole goose, dilute with the strained bouillon, and rub through a colander. Heat on top of the stove, stirring constantly until very hot, but do not boil.

With the goose soup serve stuffed goose neck,* prepared as follows: remove the bones from the neck, leaving the skin in one piece. Boil the goose liver and mix with 1 spoon raw goose fat, ½ French roll soaked and squeezed out, allspice, and ¼ onion. Chop everything fine and stir in 2 raw eggs, salt, and nutmeg. Stuff the neck, tie the skin at both ends, and place in the boiling strained bouillon. Cook, cool, cut into pieces, and add to the soup tureen.

INGREDIENTS

½ goose and goose blood
2 onions
5 allspice and 5 black peppercorns
1–2 bay leaves
1 glass grated rye bread
5–10 dried pears, or 5–10 dried or
    fresh apples, or beet brine

2 eggs
1 spoon goose fat
½ French roll
¼ onion
1–2 black peppercorns
salt
nutmeg

*For the forcemeat*
goose liver

*Stuffed goose neck is a regional speciality in several parts of Europe, including the foie gras regions of Alsace and Périgord. The skin, of course, serves as a giant sausage casing. East European Jewish cooks make a version called* helzel, *although they do not make blood soup, which is contrary to the Jewish dietary laws. A twentieth-century Polish-Jewish version of a stuffed goose neck that added ground veal and omitted Molokhovets' onion appears in* The Jews of Poland, *originally published in French in 1929. The same recipe appears in modern Polish cookbooks. See de Pomiane,* The Jews of Poland, *170–171, and Czerny,* Polish Cookbook, *265.*

## 56  Crayfish soup

*(Sup iz rakov)*

Prepare a bouillon as usual, using 3 lbs beef, root vegetables, and spices. Cook 40 medium crayfish in salted water with dill. Clean the claws and tails. Finely pound half the tails and all the claws and use them to make the following stuffing. Beat 4 eggs with parsley and dill, pour into a pan with ½ spoon melted butter, and make a runny omelet. Set aside and add salt, nutmeg, the pounded crayfish tails and claws, 3–4 spoons of pounded rusks or ½ French roll moistened and squeezed dry, parsley, dill, and 2 raw egg yolks. Mix everything together and stuff the backs of the dry, clean crayfish shells.

Pound the remaining shells as finely as possible, pour them into a saucepan, and add 1½ spoons butter. Fry, stirring, until the mixture darkens, and then sprinkle with 1½ to 2 spoons flour. Mix, dilute with the bouillon, and boil. Strain and add the stuffed shells and the remaining crayfish tails. Bring to a boil twice and add ½–1½ glass sour cream. Serve.

*Remarks:* When crayfish are expensive, economize by not adding them to this soup, but instead use them that same day to prepare crayfish sauce.

Instead of using flour, pearl barley or rice boiled separately in bouillon may be added to the soup tureen together with the remaining tails and some dill. Pour in the soup, stir, and serve.

To flavor the soup, some people add 2–3 seeded lemon slices or ¼–½ glass of table wine.

The stuffing may be varied as follows. Finely pound all the cleaned claws and half the tails. Mix with 2 spoons of finely pounded rusks, ½ glass of rice boiled in bouillon, parsley, and dill. Add 2 raw eggs, 1 spoon butter, salt, and nutmeg. Dilute with ½ glass or more of whole milk or cream, but not too much—the forcemeat should be rather thick. Fill the crayfish shells, add to the bouillon, and bring to a boil.

This stuffing is also made from buckwheat groats or millet, which first must be washed and scalded with boiling water and then rinsed in cold water. Cook with butter in a small quantity of water. Let it cool, then mix with an egg and butter and stuff the crayfish shells. Use 1 glass of groats in all, ½ glass for the stuffing and ½ glass for the soup.

INGREDIENTS

| | |
|---|---|
| 3 lbs beef or veal | 5–6 eggs |
| 2 carrots | parsley and dill |
| 1 parsley root | salt |
| 1 celery root | 2 spoons butter |
| 1 leek | nutmeg |
| (1 onion) | 3–4 spoons rusks, or ½ French roll |
| 40 crayfish | ½ glass flour |
| 5–10 allspice | ½–1½ glasses sour cream |
| (1–2 bay leaves) | (½ glass rice or pearl barley) |

## 57  Mixed meat soup, or *soljanka*

*(Seljanka mjasnaja)*

Prepare a bouillon in the usual way, with 1 or 2 lbs of beef, root vegetables, pepper, and a bay leaf. Strain and, when the bouillon is done, add a plateful of meat, cut into small cubes. Use a little of each of the following: boiled or roast beef, veal, chicken, ham, goose, duck, and sausage.

Finely chop 1 onion and fry in 1 spoon of fresh butter. Sprinkle with 1 spoon flour, fry lightly, and dilute with bouillon. Add 2 cubed, salted cucumbers, 12 olives, 6–12 field mushrooms [*Agaricus campestris* or *Psalliota campestris*], 6–12 marinated saffron milk-caps, and 6–12 salted milk-agaric mushrooms, scalded with boiling water.* Or add fresh white mushrooms, saffron milk-caps, yellow-brown boletus [*Boletus luteus*] or milk-agaric mushrooms. Before using fresh mushrooms, they must be cleaned, scalded with boiling water, and cooked separately, skimming the liquid. Add 1–2 glasses of cucumber brine and fresh cabbage scalded with boiling water. When all this is ready, add it to the rest of the bouillon containing the assorted meats. Pour in ½ to 1 glass of sour cream or thick fresh cream and bring to a boil. To serve, sprinkle the soup tureen with finely chopped parsley and dill, and for those who like it, a good handful of finely chopped green onions.

INGREDIENTS

[Listed as follows in a single paragraph]:
From 1–3 lbs beef, less than a full plate of various meats, root vegetables, an onion, spices, 1 spoon butter, 1 spoon flour, less than a full plate of various fresh or marinated mushrooms, 12 olives, 2 salted cucumbers, 1–2 glasses of cucumber brine, ¼ head of fresh cabbage, ½–1 glass of fresh sour or sweet cream, dill, parsley, and green onions.

*See Chapter 29 for directions on marinating and salting mushrooms.

## MEAT-BASED PURÉED SOUPS
### (Supy-pjure mjasnye)

*Remarks about puréed soups made from pulses and vegetables:* Use root vegetables from which puréed soups are prepared, such as carrots, turnips, rutabagas, and Jerusalem artichokes. Wash them and, without peeling or slicing them, put them in warm water. Bring them just to a boil; this will remove the raw, bitter taste. Drain them immediately in a sieve. Now peel and wash the vegetables, cut them into small cubes, and place them in a stoneware pot. Cover with boiling water or bouillon. Boil them until they are completely soft, rub them through a colander, and dilute with the remaining bouillon. Thicken the purée with a liaison; that is, beat 2 egg yolks with ½ glass of cream, strain the eggs and cream, and add to the puréed soup. Heat until the soup is very hot, but not boiling, as this would curdle the eggs. The liaison keeps the vegetable purée from settling or separating from the bouillon and gives the soup a smooth consistency. The liaison serves the same purpose in puréed pulse soups, as well.

*Remarks about puréed game soups:* For puréed soups made with wildfowl, chicken, hare, etc., the game must first be fried in butter. Remove the meat from the bones, pound it thoroughly, sprinkle 1 spoon flour over the meat, and add a little bouillon. Boil until soft, rub through a colander, and dilute with the remaining bouillon. Add 2 egg yolks mixed with ½ glass of cream as indicated in the previous remarks about puréed vegetable soups and heat until very hot, but do not boil.

## 58  Puréed bread soup with wine*

*(Sup pjure iz khleba s vinom)*

Finely crumble ¾ lb of the soft part of stale rye bread and stew in a covered saucepan with 2 spoons butter. Dilute with an ordinary bouillon made from 3 lbs of beef and root vegetables and rub the mixture through a fine sieve. Add 1 glass of Madeira or sherry before serving.

To give the soup a good, dark color, caramelize about 2 pieces of fine sugar in a small skillet, dilute with bouillon, and then pour in the wine. A liaison may also be added. Heat the soup, stirring, until it is very hot, and serve.

INGREDIENTS

| | |
|---|---|
| 3 lbs beef | 1 leek |
| allspice | 1 glass Madeira or sherry |
| ¼ lb butter | 1–2 pieces sugar |
| 1 carrot | (2 egg yolks) |
| ¾ lb rye bread | (½ glass cream) |
| 1 celery root | |

* *This recipe is similiar to the French* Soupe panade au gras *except that Molokhovets used rye instead of white bread.*

## 60  Puréed chicken soup with crayfish tails and cauliflower

*(Sup pjure iz kuritsy s rakovymi shejkami, i tsvetnoju kapustoju)*

Cook 2–3 lbs beef and root vegetables in the usual manner over a low fire. In a separate pan boil ½ glass rice or pearl barley in bouillon until soft. Fry the chicken, let it cool, and remove the meat from the bones. Mince the meat and pound it in a stone mortar, adding bouillon gradually. Mix with the barley kasha, rub through a fine sieve, add butter and salt, and dilute with the strained bouillon. Before serving pour in ½ glass of cream mixed with 2 egg yolks. Heat, stirring, until very hot, but do not boil. Place crayfish tails and cauliflower, each cooked separately, in a soup tureen [and pour on the hot soup].

Croutons, stuffed olives, or *pirozhki* made from puff pastry are served with this soup.

INGREDIENTS

| | |
|---|---|
| 1 chicken | 1 carrot |
| 1–3 lbs beef | 1 leek |

1 parsley root
1 celery root
½ glass rice, or ½ glass pearl barley
2 egg yolks

½ glass cream
(30–40 crayfish tails)
1–2 heads of cauliflower

### 64  Puréed hazel grouse or pheasant soup with champagne

*(Sup pjure iz rjabchikov ili fazanov s shampanskim)*

Prepare a bouillon as usual from 3 lbs beef, 1 lb veal bones, and root vegetables. Strain the bouillon.

Fry 2 hazel grouse [*Tetrastes bonasia*], 2 snipe, 1 pheasant, or 2 woodcocks in butter. Chop up with a knife, pound in a mortar, and pour on bouillon. Add ½ spoon flour mashed with butter, boil thoroughly, pass through a sieve, and dilute with bouillon. Stir in a strained liaison (2 egg yolks beaten with ½ glass cream) and heat until the soup is very hot. Pour in ½ bottle of champagne when serving at the table. Add meat quenelles and asparaigus, each boiled separately.

This soup is served with sardine sippets, *pirozhki* made from puff pastry, or *pirozhki* in crayfish shells.

INGREDIENTS

3 lbs beef
1 lb veal bones
2 carrots
1 parsley root
1 celery root
1 leek

2 hazel grouse, 2 snipe, 1 pheasant, or
  2 woodcocks
2 spoons butter
½ spoon flour
½ bottle champagne
½ teaspoon mace
parsley and dill

### 69  Puréed fresh cucumber soup

*(Sup pjure iz svezhikh ogurtsov)*

Prepare a bouillon as usual from 3 lbs veal with root vegetables. Strain the bouillon.

Peel and slice 5 cucumbers and cook in salted boiling water. Drain them in a colander, rinse with cold water, and put in a soup tureen. Peel, quarter, and seed 5 more cucumbers and put them in a saucepan. Add ¼ lb of boiled ham, 1 onion, 1–2 cloves, and some rich bouillon. Cook over a low fire until tender, add ½ spoon butter mixed with 1 spoon flour, and boil thoroughly. Remove the ham before serving and rub the soup through a fine sieve into a saucepan. Dilute with bouillon and place on the edge of the stove to settle. Skim off the fat and pour in ½ glass of thick cream mixed with 2 egg yolks. Heat until the soup is very hot, stirring constantly so that it does not boil. Add salt, pepper, and dill to taste.

Serve with croutons made from white bread.

INGREDIENTS

| | |
|---|---|
| 3 lbs veal | ¼ lb boiled ham |
| 2 carrots | ½ spoon butter |
| 1 parsley root | 1 spoon flour |
| 1 leek | ½ glass thick cream |
| 2 onions | 2 egg yolks |
| 1 celery root | dill |
| 10 medium cucumbers | salt and pepper |

## 77　Puréed mushroom soup with ruff

*(Sup pjure iz shampin'onov i ershej)*

Prepare a bouillon from 3 lbs beef, 1 lb veal, and root vegetables. Strain the bouillon. Fillet 20 ruff,* wash the bones, and add the bones to the bouillon with ¼ lb rice, 10 field mushrooms, and 1 spoon butter. Pour on a little bouillon, boil until soft, and rub through a sieve. Dilute with the remaining bouillon, set the pan of soup in a saucepan of boiling water, and stir as often as possible to prevent the purée from settling. Skin the fish, cook the fillets in bouillon, and transfer them to the soup tureen. Mix 2 egg yolks and ½ glass thick cream, strain, and dilute with 1 glass of soup. Place on top of the stove and heat, stirring, until very hot. Dilute with the rest of the soup and garnish with parsley and dill.

INGREDIENTS

| | |
|---|---|
| 3 lbs beef | 20 ruff |
| 1 lb veal | 10 field mushrooms |
| 2 carrots | ¼ lb rice, or ½ glass |
| 1 parsley root | ⅛ lb butter |
| 1 celery root | 2 egg yolks |
| 1 leek | ½ glass cream |
| 10–15 allspice | greens |

*Ruff (Acerina cernua) is a European freshwater species of perch. Pike, pike-perch, or yellow perch may be substituted in America.*

## 80　Puréed tomato soup

*(Sup pjure iz pomidorov)*

Prepare a bouillon from 2 lbs beef, 1 lb veal, ½ chicken, and root vegetables. Strain the bouillon.

Chop very ripe tomatoes, put them in a saucepan, add 1 spoon butter, and stew until done. Stir in 2 spoons flour, dilute with bouillon, and boil thoroughly. Rub through a sieve and pour in sour cream.

Instead of flour, it is better to use well-boiled pearl barley. It is also good to add ½ glass of white table wine. Or, instead of the wine and barley, add 2 egg yolks mixed with ½ glass of fresh cream as indicated in the opening Remarks.

Serve this soup with puff-pastry *pirozhki* with brains, croutons, or best of all, stuffed green tomatoes [see recipe below].

INGREDIENTS

| | |
|---|---|
| 2 lbs beef | 3–5 tomatoes, or ¼ glass prepared |
| 1 lb veal | thick purée |
| ½ chicken | 2 spoons flour, or ½ glass pearl barley |
| 2 carrots | 1 spoon butter |
| (1 onion) | ½ to 2 glasses sour cream |
| 1 parsley root | parsley and dill |
| 1 celery root | (½ glass white wine) |
| 1 leek | (2 egg yolks) |
| | (½ glass cream) |

## 80a  Stuffed green tomatoes

### *(Pomidory farshirovannye)*

Finely mince ½ lb of veal and pound it in a mortar with ⅛ lb washed butter,* 1 raw egg, and ½ French roll moistened in milk and squeezed out. Add salt, 6 ground allspice, and nutmeg. Rub the mixture through a fine sieve. Scoop out the interior of green tomatoes (about 18 if they are very small) and fill the cavities with this forcemeat. Pour on bouillon and simmer, covered, over a low fire. Transfer to the soup tureen.

This soup may also be prepared without meat, using all the other ingredients as indicated above.

*Freshly churned butter is thoroughly washed to remove all traces of buttermilk, so that the butter will keep well.*

## 83  Fresh pea and pigeon soup*

### *(Sup iz svezhago gorokha i golubej)*

Prepare a soup from fresh peas, which must be shelled and cooked in salted boiling water. Cook the pigeons separately in meat bouillon with a bunch of parsley and marjoram. Place fried slices of white bread, the peas, and the pigeons in the soup tureen, pour on the strained bouillon, and sprinkle with a little nutmeg.

*Except for the addition of nutmeg and the absence of lettuce, Molokhovets' recipe is remarkably similar to La Varenne's* Potage de Pigeons aux pois verts, *published in 1651. Fresh peas were the rage of high society at the court of Louis XIV. (See Wheaton,* Savoring the Past, *136–137; also La Varenne,* Le cuisinier françois, *123.)*

### 89 Puréed oatmeal soup in the style of Hamburg

*(Sup pjure gamburgskij s ovsjanoju krupoju)*

Prepare a bouillon in the usual manner with 3 lbs of beef. Add oatmeal to the bouillon, boil until the oatmeal is soft, strain, and rub through a fine sieve. Add 2 wineglasses of rum, a little sugar, lemon zest, ½ glass each currants and grated almonds, and a piece of cinnamon. Bring the soup to a boil. Beat 2 egg yolks and ½ glass of cream, strain, and stir 2–3 spoons of the oatmeal soup into the eggs and cream. Pour liaison into the rest of the soup, stirring briskly, heat until very hot, and serve.

## FISH SOUPS

*(Supy rybnye)*

*Remarks:* For remarks about fish, see Chapter 7.

### 90 Mixed fish soup, or Fish *soljanka*

*(Seljanka rybnaja)*

A thin fish *soljanka* is prepared as follows: Finely chop 1 onion and fry in 2 spoons animal fat. Sprinkle with 1½ spoons flour, fry lightly, and dilute with water. Add about 3 lbs raw fish cut into small pieces, such as sturgeon, white sturgeon, and whitefish, an equal amount of each. Add a bay leaf, pepper, 10 olives, 10 finely sliced field mushrooms, 2 salted cucumbers, and a little fresh cabbage or sauerkraut, previously scalded with boiling water. Bring to a boil several times so that the fish cooks. Add cucumber brine to taste and bring to a boil. Add sour cream, strew with greens, and serve.

INGREDIENTS

| | |
|---|---|
| 3 lbs of various fish | 10 field mushrooms |
| ⅛–¼ lb butter | 1 bay leaf |
| 1½ spoons flour | pepper |
| 1 onion | about 1–2 glasses cucumber brine |
| 10 olives | ½–1 glass fresh sour or thick sweet |
| ½ lb or more fresh cabbage, or | cream |
| sauerkraut | 2 salted cucumbers |

## 91  Crucian borshch

*(Borshch iz karasej)*

Prepare a bouillon from 1 carrot, 1 parsley root, 1 celery root, ½ onion, 10–15 allspice, 2–3 bay leaves, and 2–3 mushrooms. Strain the bouillon, add ½ lb each washed sauerkraut and peeled, grated beets, and cook. Fry ½ finely chopped onion until golden in 2 spoons olive oil or ⅛ lb butter, mix with 1 spoon flour, and add to the borshch. Pour in the beet brine. Dip 1½ or 2 lbs crucians,* that is, 6–8 pieces, into flour or rusk crumbs and fry thoroughly in butter. Add to the borshch just before serving and bring to the boil once.

Serve with dumplings or with fish forcemeat.

INGREDIENTS

| | |
|---|---|
| 1½–2 lbs crucians | 2–3 mushrooms |
| 2 carrots | ½ lb beets |
| 1 parsley root | ½ lb sauerkraut |
| 1 celery root | about 1½ glasses beet brine |
| 1 onion | 1 spoon flour, or 2–3 rusks to dip the |
| 10–15 allspice | crucians |
| 2–3 bay leaves | ¼ lb Finnish butter |

*The crucian, sometimes called crucian carp, is a small (12 inch) freshwater fish of a deep yellow color. Native to Central Europe, it closely resembles a carp, which can be substituted for crucian in these recipes. Its French name is carassin; lean varieties are called Prussian carp.*

## 99  Eel and green pea soup

*(Sup iz ugrja i zelenago goroshka)*

Clean 3–4 lbs eel* and cut into pieces. Prepare a bouillon from root vegetables such as ½ parsley root, ½ celery root, 1–2 onions, 5–6 black peppercorns, 12 shallots, and about 2–3 glasses of shelled peas. Bring to a boil and remove the scum until the bouillon is clear. Add the pieces of eel and boil for almost 45 minutes, because eel is very harmful if it is insufficiently cooked. Garnish with parsley just before serving.

INGREDIENTS

| | |
|---|---|
| 3–4 lbs eel | 12 shallots |
| ½ parsley root | pepper |
| ½ celery root | 1 bay leaf |
| 1–2 onions | greens |
| 2–3 glasses shelled peas | |

*The relevant directions are as follows: "Remove the skin from a 3–4 lb eel, or wash it thoroughly with sand without removing the skin because a skinned eel is much less flavorful. Clean the eel, rub the interior cavity with salt, and dry with a clean napkin."*

### 101 Soup with smelts and sauerkraut

*(Sup so snetkami ili\* kisloju kapustoju)*

Squeeze [the excess liquid from] 1½ lbs shredded or chopped sauerkraut and boil with 1 onion and 2–3 bay leaves. Fry 1 spoon flour in 1 spoon butter and, if desired, a finely chopped onion. Add to the soup and boil thoroughly. Remove the heads from 1 lb of smelts, wash the fish in several changes of water, salt them lightly, and set aside for an hour. Then add them to the bouillon and cook until done, approximately 15 minutes.

INGREDIENTS

| | |
|---|---|
| 1½ lbs sauerkraut | pepper |
| 1 lb smelts | a bay leaf |
| 1 spoon flour | 1 onion |
| 1 spoon butter | |

*This "or" was corrected to "and" in the later German edition.*

### 103 Clear fish soup with ruff, burbot, perch, pike, whitefish, tench, or sturgeon

*(Ukha iz ershej, nalima, okunej, shchuki, siga, lina, osetra)*

Just as a meat bouillon is tastier when it has more meat, so an *ukha* is tastier with more fish. For a very good *ukha* for 6–8 persons, that is for 6–8 soup bowls, use no less than 6 lbs of fish. For a moderate quality, use 3 lbs of fish.

Prepare a bouillon from root vegetables and spices, adding, if possible, 3 lbs of ruff. Cook for an hour until completely tender. Then strain the bouillon, add 3 lbs of some sort of fish, skinned, boned, and cut into pieces, and boil until the fish is done. Use burbot, perch, pike, whitefish, tench, or sturgeon, etc. To serve, add greens and several lemon slices. Sauternes or champagne may also be added.

*Remarks:* The tastiest *ukha* is prepared from very fresh fish, just caught and cleaned. If a fish lies around, even for just a few hours, the *ukha* does not taste nearly as good as when a freshly caught fish is used. If starting with a lively fish, neither spices nor root vegetables need be added, only an onion. If the fish is already half-dead (lit.: sleepy or drowsy, *sonnaja*), add a parsley root, a celery root, a leek, and even spices as indicated above. If using burbot, do not add root vegetables, but boil the roe with the bouillon to give the *ukha* a special flavor. Mash the raw, soft fish roe and discard the membrane before adding the roe to the soup. Only add the roe if a live burbot is available.

INGREDIENTS

| | |
|---|---|
| (3 lbs ruff) | 10–20 allspice |
| 3 lbs larger fish | 1–2 bay leaves |
| ½ parsley root | parsley and dill |
| ½ celery root | (½ seeded lemon) |
| 2 onions | (½–1 glass sauternes or champagne) |

# BUTTER-BASED SOUPS (WITHOUT MEAT)
## (Supy masljanye (bez mjasa))

*Remarks:* These are prepared like meat-based soups, but without meat. Instead, use good Finnish butter or fresh butter and add more sour cream, mushrooms, etc. Instead of bouillon, use 9–12 glasses of water.

### 115  Green pea soup with or without tortoise

(Sup iz zelenago gorokha s cherepakhoj ili bez neja [masljanyj])

Remove 1 tortoise from its shell. Detach and discard the head and legs, clean the rest of the meat, and boil with salt and root vegetables. Strain the bouillon, reserving the meat. Pour part of the tortoise bouillon onto 4 glasses of ripe peas and boil until the peas are tender. Rub the peas through a fine sieve and dilute with bouillon to the desired consistency. Add the tortoise, cut into pieces, and 1 parsley root and 1 leek, both fried in butter. Bring the soup to a boil, sprinkle with greens, and serve.

If the soup is prepared without the tortoise, serve sippets of white or finely ground rye bread separately.

INGREDIENTS

| | |
|---|---|
| 1 tortoise | 2 onions |
| 2 carrots | 10–15 peppercorns |
| 1 parsley root | 4 glasses ripe, fresh, shelled peas |
| 1 leek | ⅛ lb Finnish butter |
| 1 celery root | dill and parsley |

### 119a  Meatless borshch with sour cream

(Borshch bez mjasa so smetanoju)

Prepare a bouillon from root vegetables and dried boletus mushrooms [*Boletus edulis*]. Strain the bouillon. Bake 2 lbs of beets, peel them, and finely grate. Place the beets in a stewpan, cover with the vegetable bouillon, pour in beet brine, boiled separately, and sour cream, and heat until the soup is very hot. Add salt, black pepper, greens, and finely shredded mushrooms. Serve with fried buckwheat groats.

INGREDIENTS

| | |
|---|---|
| 1 parsley root | 5–6 black peppercorns |
| 1 leek | parsley and dill |
| 2 celery roots | 2 lbs beets |
| 2 onions | beet brine |
| 10–15 allspice | 1/8 lb dried boletus mushrooms |
| 2–3 bay leaves | 1 or 2 glasses sour cream |

### 121  Sorrel and spinach* shchi (butter-based)

*(Shchi iz shchavelja popolam so shpinnatom—masljanyja)*

Prepare a bouillon from root vegetables, dried mushrooms, dill, and fine-ground barley. Strain the bouillon. Chop the mushrooms fine and fry them in 1 spoon butter and 1 finely chopped onion. Add 1 spoon flour, pour in the strained bouillon, and boil thoroughly.

Meanwhile, pick over 1½–2 lbs of sorrel, wash until clean, and drain in a coarse sieve. Chop in a wooden bowl, transfer the sorrel with its juice to a stoneware pot, bring it to a boil in its own juice, and cook until done. Transfer to the general bouillon and bring to a boil. To serve, add sour cream and dill. Serve hard-boiled eggs, *pirozhki*, or fried kasha separately.

INGREDIENTS

| | |
|---|---|
| 1½–2 lbs sorrel | 1–2 onions |
| a few root vegetables | 1 spoon flour |
| 1 onion | ½–2 glasses sour cream |
| 1 spoon butter | dill |
| 1/8 lb dried mushrooms | |

*Although spinach is not mentioned in the recipe proper, the name of the recipe indicates that the soup may also be prepared using equal parts of sorrel and spinach.*

### 122  Lentil soup

*(Sup iz chechevitsy)*

Stew 2 glasses of lentils, covered, in 1 spoon butter and a little water, but do not add salt. Rub the lentils through a fine sieve. Fry 1 onion in 1 spoon butter, dilute with the soup, and bring to a boil. Mix 2 egg yolks with ½ glass of cream, strain, and stir into the soup. Heat until very hot, but do not boil. Add salt and serve with croutons or sippets.

### 128 Oatmeal soup with prunes or raisins

*(Ovsjanka s chernoslivom ili izjumom)*

Wash 1 glass of good oatmeal and cook in a covered stewpan with 10 glasses of water, removing the scum. Add 1–2 spoons butter and a little salt. Reduce the soup to the consistency of good, thick cream, let it settle, and pour off the liquid, or rub it all through a colander. Meanwhile, in a separate saucepan, boil ½ lb of the best French prunes or raisins and place them in the soup tureen. Cover with the oat purée and serve with croutons. For sick people the croutons are dried in the oven, usually without butter. The broth from the prunes may be served separately for those who wish to pour it into the oatmeal porridge.

## MILK SOUPS

*(Supy molochnye)*

### 133 Milk soup with almond noodles

*(Molochnyj sup s mindal'noju lapsheju)*

Bring 9 glasses of milk to a boil. Prepare homemade noodles with almond milk. To prepare the almond milk, scald ⅛ lb, or ½ glass, of almonds with boiling water. Peel the almonds and pound them finely, adding 1 spoon of water. Mix, add more water, and strain though a napkin to obtain ¼ glass of almond milk. To prepare the noodles, mix together 1 egg, a little sugar, ½ lb of flour, [and the almond milk]. Pour the noodles into the boiling milk, [cook until tender,] and serve.

### 140 Milk soup with chopped dough

*(Molochnyj sup s rublennym testom)*

Prepare a dough that is not too stiff from 2 glasses of the very best flour, 1 egg, some salt, and not more than 1 glass of salted water. Chop up the dough quite finely with a knife, or better yet, pinch it off with your hands. Bring 9 glasses of milk to a boil, add the cut-up dough, and bring to a boil 2–3 times. Add salt and 1–2 spoons butter.

### 141  Milk soup with pumpkin

*(Molochnyj sup s tykvoju)*

Peel and seed half of a good, medium-size pumpkin. Cut the flesh into even pieces, place in a stewpan, and barely cover the pumpkin with water. Place the pan on the fire, covered, bring to a boil, and immediately drain in a fine sieve. Then pour on 2–3 glasses of fresh, boiled water or milk, add ½ French roll without crusts, and boil until soft. Rub through a colander, dilute with 3 bottles of boiled milk, and bring to a boil. Add salt and 1–2 spoons butter, or add sugar and ½ cup finely pounded sweet almonds.

## SWEET, HOT SOUPS FROM MILK, BEER, WINE, AND BERRIES

*(Supy gorjachie sladkie iz moloka, piva, vina i jagod)*

### 142  Milk soup with meringue

*(Sup molochnyj s meringoju)*

Beat 6 egg whites into a foam and stir in 1 glass of sugar pounded with ¼ vanilla bean or a little cinnamon. Bring 9 glasses of whole milk to a boil. Using a spoon, drop the beaten egg whites into the milk so that they resemble large dumplings. Bring to a boil* and, using a slotted spoon, arrange the meringues on a deep dish. Cover with the milk and serve.

This soup is sometimes served cold.

INGREDIENTS

| | |
|---|---|
| 9 glasses milk | 1 glass fine sugar |
| 6 eggs | cinnamon or vanilla |

*Contrary to Molokhovets' instructions, it is preferable just to simmer the meringues until firm. If actually boiled, they will turn rubbery. This "soup" resembles the French dessert Oeufs à la neige, the only difference being that in the French version the milk is used to make a custard before it is poured over the poached egg whites.*

### 144  Ersatz chocolate milk soup

*(Sup molochnyj na maner shokoladnago)*

On a clean skillet fry ¾ glass of fine-ground, previously dried flour. Stir constantly until the flour darkens, only watch that it does not burn. Meanwhile, bring to a boil 9 glasses of whole milk with a piece of vanilla (one *vershok* long) and 6 pieces of sugar. Add the fried flour to the milk, boil thoroughly, and remove from the fire. Beat 2–3 egg yolks with 6 pieces of fine sugar until the egg yolks whiten. Dilute with several spoons of warm milk, then pour the egg yolks into the remaining milk, or chocolate, beating with a whisk. Heat on the fire until the mixture begins to steam, but do not boil. Pour into a soup tureen and serve with biscuits or sugared rusks.

### 147 Sago soup with wine

*(Sup iz sago s vinom)*

Cover ¾ glass of red or white sago with cold water, set aside for 2 hours, and then drain the sago in a coarse sieve. Transfer the sago to a stewpan, cover with a large quantity of boiling water, and cook, stirring, until half done. Drain in a coarse sieve and rinse with cold water. When the sago has drained completely, pour it into a stewpan and cover with 7 glasses of boiling water. Add ½–¾ lb of sugar, a little lemon zest, a piece of cinnamon, and 2–3 cloves. Cook until done, that is, until the sago is soft and transparent. Five minutes before serving, pour in 1–3 glasses red wine and add, as desired, 1 glass of barberry, red currant, or cherry juice. Bring to a boil and pour into a soup tureen over dry sippets or rusks.

INGREDIENTS

| | |
|---|---|
| ¾ glass sago | 2–3 cloves |
| 1–3 glasses red wine | 1 glass barberry, red currant, or cherry |
| ½–¾ lb sugar | juice |
| ¼ lemon | ½ *vershok* cinnamon |

### 150 Fresh apple soup

*(Sup iz svezhikh jablok)*

Peel, core, and quarter sweet apples. Cook in water with sugar, a piece of cinnamon, and lemon zest. Add 2 full spoons of potato flour diluted gradually with ½ glass water and bring to a boil, stirring. When serving, 1–3 glasses of white table wine may be added with the juice of ½ lemon. The peels from the fresh apples should be cooked separately and strained into the soup when serving.

INGREDIENTS

| | |
|---|---|
| 12–15 apples | 1–3 glasses wine |
| a piece of cinnamon | 1 full spoon potato flour |
| ½ lemon | 1–2 glasses sugar |

### 152 Soup from various fresh berries with sour cream and wine

*(Sup iz raznykh svezhikh jagod so smetanoju i vinom)*

Purée 6 glasses of picked-over wild strawberries, raspberries, currants, or lingonberries. Add ½ or ¾ lb sugar, 1 glass each of very fresh sour cream and wine, and 3–4 glasses of boiled water. Mix everything together and heat, but do not boil. Serve with rusks or pâte à choux.

INGREDIENTS

3 lbs berries
1 glass sour cream

1 glass wine
1½–2 glasses sugar pieces

### 159 Beer soup with sour cream

*(Sup iz piva so smetanoju)*

Mix together fresh sour cream, egg yolks, butter, sugar, and ½ teaspoon salt. Dilute with light beer and set the pan on the fire, stirring, until very hot, but do not boil. Immediately pour into a soup tureen over pieces of wheat bread, either cut into cubes or made into croutons. Separately, serve farmer's cheese cut into small cubes.*

INGREDIENTS

2 bottles beer
2–3 glasses sour cream
1 spoon butter
2–3 egg yolks

3–6 pieces of sugar
bread from sifted flour
farmer's cheese

*Syr iz tvoroga, *which is often translated as cottage cheese, is firmer than the usual American cottage cheese. A better modern substitute is farmer's cheese.*

# COLD SOUPS
*(Supy kholodnye)*

### 161 Polish kholodnik with sour cream

*(Kholdnik pol'skij so smetanoju)*

Mash a handful of dill and chives with salt. Wash young beet greens and several very small young beets and cook them in salted water. Drain the beets and greens in a colander, chop them fine and put them in the soup tureen (there should be a full glass of greens). Add 2–5 glasses of very fresh sour cream and dilute with the same amount of grain *kvass* or cooled boiled water. Add hard-boiled eggs, cut into several pieces, cubed fresh cucumbers, crayfish tails, lemon slices, salt, a little pepper, and a piece of ice.

INGREDIENTS

| | |
|---|---|
| 1 lb young beet greens | 3 cucumbers |
| handful of dill | 30 crayfish |
| 2–5 glasses sour cream | 3 eggs |
| (grain *kvass*) | ½ lemon |
| (black pepper) | salt |
| [several small beets] | |

### 164  Fast-day *okroshka* from odds and ends

*(Okroshka postnaja iz raznostej)*

Peel and slice fresh or salted cucumbers, marinated mushrooms, marinated salted milk-agaric mushrooms,* woolly milk-caps, saffron milk-caps, and apples, both fresh and marinated. Plums, cherries, peaches, and marinated grapes may also be added. Boil and peel potatoes, beets, and green beans, using in all a full plateful. Place all this in a soup tureen. Just before dinner, mix a small spoon of prepared *Sareptskaja* mustard** and some salt in a stoneware dish and add 1 spoon of olive oil, drop by drop, until the mustard turns into a thick sauce. Dilute with 3 bottles of sour *shchi* or *kvass* and add salt, pepper, green onion, parsley, and dill. Stir everything together and add a piece of ice.

*It is odd that Molokhovets called for mushrooms that were both marinated and salted since they are two quite different processes. See Chapter 29.
**See Glossary.

### 165  Cold spinach soup with salmon

*(Botvin'ja)*

Clean and wash sorrel, cook the sorrel in its own juice, and rub through a fine sieve. Boil spinach or young beet greens in salted water until tender, finely chop, and mix with the sorrel. Add a couple of cubed cucumbers, dill, green onions, greens, salt, and fine sugar or treacle. Dilute with sour *shchi* and add ice. Cook a fresh salmon (*lososina ili semga*), white salmon, or whitefish in boiling water and add the fish to the soup when serving at the table. Serve with grated horseradish. Sherry or champagne may be added and also crayfish tails.

INGREDIENTS

½ lb sorrel

1 lb spinach or 1½ lbs young beet
  greens

3 [sic] cucumbers

green onion

dill

3–6 pieces of sugar, or ½ glass or
  more treacle

2–3 bottles sour *shchi*

2 lbs fresh salmon, white salmon, or
  whitefish

horseradish

(25 crayfish tails)

salt

### 170 Cold raspberry or wild or cultivated strawberry soup

*(Kholodets zavarnoj iz maliny, zemljaniki ili klubniki)*

Beat 6 egg yolks and ½ lb sugar until white, dilute with 2 bottles cream, and stir on top of the stove until the mixture thickens, but do not boil. Strain and cool, stirring. Dilute with sieved berry purée, cool, and pour into the soup tureen. Strew with 2 handfuls of berries from which the soup was prepared.

INGREDIENTS

6 egg yolks

½–1 lb sugar

2 bottles cream

2–3 lbs berries

Drop scoops of ice cream into the soup like dumplings and serve quickly before the ice cream melts. This soup is served on summer evenings at outdoor parties.

### 172 Cold chocolate soup

*(Kholodets shokoladnyj)*

Beat 6 egg yolks with ½ lb sugar until white and stir in 2 bottles of cream. Break ¼ to ½ lb of chocolate into pieces, dissolve in 2 glasses of milk, and bring to the boil. Add the chocolate and milk to the cream mixture and heat, stirring, until very hot. Strain, cool, and serve with ice cream.

INGREDIENTS

2 bottles cream

1 *vershok* vanilla

6 egg yolks

½ lb or 1 glass fine sugar

¼–½ lb chocolate

(biscuits or ice cream)

1 glass milk

# 2

# Soup Accompaniments

*(Prinadlezhnosti k supu)*

*Remarks:* Indicated proportions are for 6–8 persons. For 9–12 persons, increase the proportions by 1½. For 13–15 persons, double the proportions. For 16–18 persons, increase the proportions by 2½. For 19–24 persons, triple the proportions.

## 176 Croutons of white bread

*(Grenochki iz belago khleba)*

Cut a French roll into small, even cubes. Melt butter in a skillet, stir in the cubes of bread, and dry them out in the oven. These croutons may also be dried in the oven without butter, in which case they are especially good for sick people.

INGREDIENTS

1 or 1½ French rolls (⅝ lb)
1 spoon (⅛ lb) Finnish butter or 2
   spoons olive oil

## 177 Sippets with forcemeat and Parmesan cheese

*(Grenochki s mjasnym farshem i parmezanom)*

Chop 1 lb beef or veal, boiled or fried, with an onion, stir in 2 spoons of grated roll, and fry in 1 spoon butter. Beat in 1 egg and add 2 spoons sour cream and a little salt. Spread this mixture on slices of a roll, sprinkle with Parmesan cheese, and dry out slightly in the oven on a baking sheet* greased with butter.

INGREDIENTS

1 lb cooked meat
1 onion
2 spoons grated roll, or ¼ French roll

1½ spoons butter
1 egg
2 spoons sour cream

1 to 1½ French rolls                    ⅛ lb grated Parmesan

Alternatively, thinly slice the roll, remove the crusts, and, using a small feather,** paint the slices with melted butter. Place on a baking sheet, sprinkle with cheese, and bake.

INGREDIENTS

1 French roll                           ⅛–¼ lb Parmesan cheese
⅛–¼ lb butter

*Instead of Molokhovets' term "iron sheet," I have opted to use the more common American expression "baking sheet."
**In rural circumstances, feathers were readily available and were used in the kitchen where we now use a pastry brush. Feathers, however, do the job very nicely and are still preferred for applying delicate glazes on fragile pastry without leaving a mark.

### 179  Meatballs from veal kidneys

(Frikadel'ki iz teljach'ikh pochek)

Scald 2 veal kidneys, remove the membranes, chop fine, and add salt. Fry 1 finely chopped medium onion in 1 spoon butter, mix with the kidneys, and add 2–3 ground rusks. Beat in 2 eggs, 2 spoons sour cream, and a little pepper. Using a mortar and pestle, pound the mixture thoroughly. Sprinkle with salt and nutmeg, form into balls, and roll in rusk crumbs. Just before serving, drop the balls into bouillon. Meatballs may also be made from the kidneys of suckling pigs and served with suckling pig soup.

INGREDIENTS

2 veal kidneys                          2 eggs
1 onion                                 2 spoons sour cream
1 spoon butter                          pepper
6 rusks                                 nutmeg

### 181  Cheese balls from ordinary, Dutch, or Swiss cheese

(Frikadel'ki iz prostago, gollandskago, ili shvejtsarskago syru)

Grate ¼ lb cheese, add 1 spoon butter, and pound in a mortar. Beat in 2 eggs and add 1 spoon sour cream and ½ French roll moistened in milk and squeezed out. Form into balls, dip into rusk crumbs, and, like all other meatballs and dumplings, boil them separately in bouillon in a small stewpan. When cooked, remove the balls with a slotted spoon and cool. Halve each one with a sharp knife and place in the soup tureen. Pour the bouillon in which they were boiled through a napkin into the soup tureen and add more bouillon. Serve the cheese balls in clear bouillon, in soup with sour cream, or in puréed soups.

INGREDIENTS

| | |
|---|---|
| ¼ lb cheese | ½ of a 5 kopeck French roll |
| 2 eggs | 1 spoon sour cream |
| 1 spoon butter | 3–4 rusks |

### 182  Forcemeat or quenelles

*(Mjasnoj farsh ili knel')*

Finely chop ¾ lb boned beef or veal. Fry ½ finely chopped onion in butter, mix with the beef, and add salt, 1 egg, ¼ French roll moistened and squeezed out, ground allspice, black pepper, nutmeg, and 1 spoon butter or thick sour cream. Pound all this and rub through a sieve. Shape into a thin sausage, wrap in a clean cloth, tie with thread, and boil in bouillon. Cool and cut into thin slices. Drop into the bouillon and serve.

INGREDIENTS

| | |
|---|---|
| ¾ lb beef or veal | 1 spoon butter |
| ½ onion | allspice |
| 1 egg | black pepper |
| ¼ of a 5 kopeck French roll | nutmeg |
| salt | |

### 189  Herring forcemeat

*(Farsh iz sel'dej)*

Soak 2 good Scottish herring overnight in water, tea, *kvass*, or milk. Skin, bone, and chop fine. Fry lightly with a finely chopped onion in 1 spoon butter, transfer to a stoneware bowl, and cool. Add 2 eggs, 2 spoons sour cream, a little black pepper, and ground rusks sufficient to hold the mixture together. Use a teaspoon moistened in boiling water to drop pieces of forcemeat into potato soup.

### 190  Stuffed olives

*(Olivki farshirovannyja)*

Finely chop ¼ lb veal or ¼ lb chicken fillet. Add the moistened, soft center of a French roll, ½ spoon butter, nutmeg, and 1 egg. Pound in a mortar and add salt. Stuff olives and cook in bouillon.

INGREDIENTS

¼ lb veal or chicken                    1 egg
¼ of a 5 kopeck French roll            ½ spoon butter
nutmeg

### 192  Kasha from Smolensk groats

*(Kasha iz smolenskikh krup)*

Bring water to a boil and add salt. Sprinkle on 1¼ glass of Smolensk groats to make a moderately thick kasha. Add nutmeg, if desired. Turn onto a plate, smooth down, and let cool. Cut into small cubes like croutons, dumplings (*lazanki*), or half-moons. Just before serving, drop into the bouillon.

INGREDIENTS

1¼ glasses (½ lb) Smolensk groats       (nutmeg for those who like it)
salt

### 200  Almond noodles

*(Lapsha mindal'naja)*

Scald ⅛ lb (or ⅓ glass) of sweet almonds with boiling water, let them stand, and then remove the skins. Pound the nuts in a mortar, adding 1–2 spoons water, mix, and strain through a cloth. Pour the almond milk back into the mortar with the crushed almonds and pound again. Strain and squeeze again until ¼ glass of liquid is obtained. Add 2 raw eggs, 2–3 pieces of sugar, and ½ lb of the very best flour. Mix into a stiff dough, roll out until thin, and let it dry slightly. Cut with a knife into strips three fingers wide. Stack the strips, sprinkling them lightly with flour to prevent them from sticking together. Shred as fine as possible and spread the noodles on a large sieve to dry out. Drop into milk soup, i.e., boiling milk, and boil until cooked. Or fry the shredded noodles in butter, and dry on blotting paper before adding them to sweet soup.

### 201  Dumplings

*(Lazanki)*

Prepare a dough from 1½ glasses flour, 1 egg, and ⅓ glass water.* Cut into small cubes and drop into bouillon or first cook separately in boiling water.

*In this recipe, the proportions of liquid to flour changed over time. For the same amount of flour, the first through seventh editions called for no liquid except the egg. This edition (the 20th) adds ⅓ glass water, and the later undated edition printed in Germany used 1 egg, 2 egg yolks, and 2½ spoons water.

### 203 Carefully cut vegetables

*(Tochenye koren'ja)*

Strain bouillon. Add nicely cut root vegetables* that have been boiled separately in bouillon, such as 2 carrots, 2–3 thin parsley roots, 1 celery root, 8–10 stalks of asparagus, and 1 head of cauliflower. Or sprinkle on 2 full tablespoons of dried root vegetables. Begin cooking these root vegetables only a half hour before dinner, as they will lose their aroma if they cook longer.

*This recipe is interesting primarily for the quantity of vegetables added to the bouillon. Also, as used here, the term "root vegetables" suggests a more elastic category than the usual carrot, onion, and parsley or celery root. Molokhovets' use of the term "greens" is similarly expansive. See "Greens" in Glossary.*

### 209 Boiled dumplings

*(Kletski zavarnyja)*

Bring to a boil ¼ glass of butter and ½ glass of milk to make a total of ¾ glass. Sprinkle on ½ glass flour, stirring briskly, and cook until the mixture leaves the sides of the pan, at least half an hour. Remove from the heat, and that very moment, add 2–3 eggs to the hot dough. Immediately drop the dumplings by the teaspoon into boiling, strained bouillon, moistening the spoon in hot water each time. Parsley may be added to the dough. Cook, covered, until the dumplings rise to the surface, and serve.

INGREDIENTS

| | |
|---|---|
| ⅛ lb butter | ½ glass milk |
| ½ glass flour | 2–3 eggs |

### 214 Rice dumplings

*(Kletski risovyja)*

Bring ½ glass rice to a boil, drain in a colander, and rinse with cold water. Transfer to a stewpan and add a little salt, pepper, nutmeg, 1 parsley root, and 1 onion studded with 4 cloves. Pour on bouillon and cook, covered, over a low fire until tender. Remove the parsley root and onion with cloves.

Finely chop, like grains of rice, 1 small parsley root, 1 leek, 1 small carrot, and some turnip. Cover with bouillon, cook until tender, drain in a fine sieve, and add to the boiled rice. Mix and beat in 1 egg. Form dumplings with a spoon and set on a plate in a cold place. When cool, dip in a [beaten] egg and grated roll crumbs.* Five minutes before serving, fry in fat or in butter. Drain the dumplings in a napkin or on blotting paper and drop into bouillon.

INGREDIENTS

| | |
|---|---|
| ½ glass rice | 1 leek |
| pepper | 1 carrot |
| nutmeg | 1 turnip |
| 1 parsley root | 2 eggs |
| 1 onion | 3 rusks* |
| 4 cloves | fry in ¾ glass fat |
| 1 small parsley root | |

*The inconsistency between roll crumbs and rusk crumbs is in the original. Molokhovets seems to have used either, or whatever was readily available.

## 219 Stuffed eggs

### (Farshirovannyja jajtsa)

Boil 6 to 8 eggs until hard. Drop them into cold water and cut them in half lengthwise with a very sharp knife, being careful not to spoil or damage the shells. Remove the eggs from the shells and chop them fine. Melt 1 spoon butter in a saucepan, add the eggs, and mix. Add salt, chopped parsley and dill, a little pepper, 1 crushed rusk, and a raw egg. Fill the shells with this mixture, strew the tops with rusk crumbs, drizzle on butter, and brown in the oven. Serve with sorrel or spinach *shchi*.

INGREDIENTS

| | |
|---|---|
| 6–8 eggs | 2–3 peppercorns |
| ⅛ lb butter | 2–3 rusks |
| parsley | salt |

## 220 Meat or mushroom dumplings

### (Ushki i pel'meni s mjasnym ili gribnym farshem)

Prepare a stiff dough from 1½ glasses of flour and 2 eggs. Roll it out thin and cut into squares, making about 35 pieces. Put a little stuffing on each square and first fold it into a triangular *pirozhok*,* then seal the ends and fry in ½ glass of melted butter or olive oil.

*For meat stuffing:* Finely chop 1 medium onion, fry in 1 spoon butter, and add finely chopped raw or cooked beef or veal. Add salt and pepper and again fry slightly. A hard-boiled egg may be added.

*For mushroom stuffing:* Finely chop ⅛ lb dried mushrooms that have been boiled in bouillon. Fry in 1 spoon butter together with a finely chopped onion. Add salt.

Since the *ushki*, or dumplings, are served with mushroom soup, you will need nearly ⅜ lb of mushrooms in all; use ⅛ lb for the *ushki* and add the remaining mushrooms, shredded, to the soup.

INGREDIENTS

*For dough*
1½ glasses (½ lb) flour
2 eggs
½ glass melted butter or fast day oil

*For the meat stuffing*
¾ lb beef or veal
⅛ lb butter
1 onion

salt and pepper
(1 hard-boiled egg)

*For the mushroom stuffing*
⅛ lb dried mushrooms
1 onion
1 spoon (⅛ lb) butter, or 2 spoons
   olive oil
salt and pepper

   *These triangular pastries were shaped to resemble an ear* (ukho), *from which the name* ushki *derives.*

# PIROZHKI
## (Pirozhki)

*Remarks:* Pirozhki are prepared from puff pastry, short pastry (*sdobnyj* and *razsypchatyj*), and from boiled and yeast doughs, directions for which are given in Chapter 8.

### 221  Puff pastry for pirozhki
#### (Sloenoe testo dlja pirozhkov)

Prepare a dough from ½ glass water (8 silver tablespoons)* and 2 glasses of flour, of which ¼ glass should be set aside for dusting the table. Roll out the dough to the thickness of half a finger.

Wash ½ lb fresh butter in very cold water, and mash it with a spoon until smooth and free of lumps. Squeeze the butter several times in a napkin until no water remains.

Place this butter on a flat round of dough. The butter must be half as large as the rolled out circle of pastry. Cover the butter with the edges of the dough, pinch it, and roll into an oblong flat cake on a small, clean, separate, smooth board. Cover with a napkin and put in a cold place for 15 minutes. Then fold the dough in three, roll it out, cover with a napkin, and stand in a cold place for another 15 minutes. Repeat in the same manner 6 more times so that the dough will be folded 18 times. This will take nearly 2 hours. It is essential that the rolling out and resting of puff pastry be done in a cold place so that the butter does not melt, but neither should it freeze.

When the oven is ready, thinly roll out the dough and cut it into long strips, the width of one and a half fingers. Wrap them around special little sticks made for this purpose to shape the *pirozhki* into a horn of plenty, or cornucopia. (The sticks are 2½ *vershok* long, 1 finger's width at one end and 2 fingers' width at the other.) Paint the *pirozhki* with a beaten egg. All this should be done in a cold place, and then they should immediately be placed in a hot oven. When they are done, remove them from the little stick and fill them with a hot stuffing, prepared beforehand. If the *pirozhki* cool, return them to the oven for another 5 minutes.

Serve the *pirozhki* sprinkled with fried green parsley, prepared as follows: Lightly mix 3 handfuls of parsley leaves with 1 spoon hot butter. Place in the oven, being careful that the parsley only dries out and does not burn. Or put a glass of cooking fat into a stewpan and heat it until it smokes. Wash 3 handfuls of parsley, squeeze dry in a napkin, and drop into the hot fat for 2 minutes. Stir, remove with a slotted spoon, and drain on a coarse sieve. Sprinkle with salt. When the parsley has dried out a little, strew it onto the *pirozhki*.

*Pirozhki* from puff pastry may also be made into circles, in which case the dough should not be rolled out so thin. Using a cutter, stamp out 15 circles. In the middle of each, mark a medium-sized circle, cutting through only half the thickness of the dough. Paint with egg and immediately place in a hot oven. When the *pirozhki* are ready, pry off the incised [inner] circles with a knife. Stuff the *pirozhki*, cover with the small circles, and serve. Only half the indicated amounts of stuffing are needed for these *pirozhki* because there is less space to fill.

Or bake the *pirozhki* in the shape of books. That is, place ½ spoon or more of stuffing on the rolled out pastry, cover with the other half, and bake.

When preparing puff pastry with 5 pounds of flour, 1 or 2 eggs may be added to the dough.

INGREDIENTS

| | |
|---|---|
| 2 glasses (⅔ lb) flour | 1 egg for painting the tops of the |
| ½ lb butter | *pirozhki* |

*This conversion makes the silver tablespoon half the size of the ordinary Russian tablespoon and thus equivalent to the modern American tablespoon (= 14 g).*

### 227 Puff pastry *pirozhki* with crayfish forcemeat

*(Sloenye pirozhki s rakovym farshem)*

Remove the tails and large claws from 20 boiled crayfish. Chop the tails and claws and fry with 1 spoon flour in 1 spoon crayfish butter. Add about 2 spoons sour cream, salt, and nutmeg, mix, and bring to a boil. When cool, beat in 2 egg yolks and heat. As soon as the mixture thickens, stuff puff pastry *pirozhki* shaped like books, and bake as above.

INGREDIENTS

20 crayfish  
⅛ lb crayfish butter  
1 spoon flour  
about 2 spoons sour cream  
salt  
nutmeg

2 egg yolks  

*For the puff pastry*  
½ lb butter  
2 glasses flour  
1 egg to paint the *pirozhki*

### 232 Meat buns to be served with bouillon or beef

*(Rod mjasnykh pyshek k bul'onu ili k zharkomu-govjadine)*

Chop 2 lbs of tender beef, add salt and 2–3 chopped onions, and fry lightly in 1 spoon butter, watching that the mixture does not burn. Then remove from the saucepan and chop like dough [i.e., in any direction]. Add 2 spoons good quality flour, a little pepper, and ½ a nutmeg or more. Return to the saucepan and pour on bouillon until the stuffing resembles a thick kasha boiled soft. Bring to a boil about 3 times. (If it is too liquid, bring to a boil several more times.) Transfer to a stoneware bowl and cool on ice. When the mixture is cool, form into balls, flat cakes, or any other convenient shape. Dip these in eggs and rusk crumbs or in crushed, dry, fast day rolls. Repeat this process 3 times, each time dipping the balls in crumbs, painting with egg, and letting them dry. After the third time, fry in Russian butter [i.e., clarified butter] like buns (*pyshki*) and serve with soup, or use them to surround beef prepared for a second course.

INGREDIENTS

2 lbs beef  
⅛ [lb] butter  
about 2–3 onions  
2 spoons flour  
1 lb Russian butter or fat

½ nutmeg  
2 teaspoons salt  
2–3 eggs  
1 glass rusk crumbs  
[pepper]

### 233 Fried yeast *pirozhki* with brain forcemeat

*(Pirozhki iz testa na drozhzhakh, zharenye v fritjure, s mozgami)*

Prepare the dough from a full glass of warm water or milk, 1 *zolotnik* of dry yeast, and half of the flour [i.e., 2 glasses]. Let the dough rise in a warm place, then beat thoroughly with a wooden spatula. Sprinkle on salt, and beat in 2 eggs or 3 egg yolks. Add 1 spoon butter and enough flour to make a dough that is sufficiently thick. Stuff the *pirozhki* and place them on a table dusted with flour. When they have risen, fry in melted butter or fat.

Prepare the brain stuffing as follows: Plunge the brains from 2 calf's heads into boiling water with vinegar and salt. Boil, remove from the water, cool, and chop fine. Fry ½ spoon flour in 1 spoon butter, add the brains, and strew with a little ground pepper, nutmeg, or mace. Pour in about 2 spoons bouillon or 1 spoon sour cream and mix.

If the *pirozhki* are needed for dinner, that is, at four o'clock, then prepare the dough in the morning between eight and nine o'clock.

INGREDIENTS

*For the dough*
1 or 2 *zolotniki* dry yeast
1½ lbs (4 glasses) flour
2 eggs or 3 egg yolks
⅛ lb butter
1 glass water or milk
½ lb butter or cooking fat

*For the brain stuffing*
1 beef or 2 calf's brains
½ spoon flour
nutmeg
pepper and salt
⅛ lb butter

### 241  Pirozhki with rice, sturgeon marrow, and eggs

*(Pirozhki s risom, vizigoju i jajtsami)*

Soak ⅛ lb sturgeon marrow overnight in water. Pour off the water the next day, cover with fresh water, and cook until tender with ½ parsley root, ½ onion, salt, and allspice. Drain in a sieve, then chop fine. Add salt, allspice, 2–3 finely chopped eggs, ¾ glass of fluffy boiled rice, 1 spoon butter, 1 spoon rich bouillon, and greens. Mix and stuff *pirozhki* made from dough recipes in Chapter 8.

### 247  Pirozhki with fresh mushrooms

*(Pirozhki so svezhimi gribami)*

Take a plateful of young boletus (*borovik*) mushroom caps and cut each into 2–4 pieces. Put in a saucepan, sprinkle with salt, a little pepper, parsley, and dill, and place on the fire. When the mushrooms have released their juices and have completely wilted, add 1 spoon good Finnish butter and about 2 spoons very fresh sour cream. Boil thoroughly, but not too much—only until the mushrooms are no longer raw. Remove them from the fire and cool on ice. Use to fill *Pirozhki* in Chapter 8.

## 250 **Pirozhki stuffed with smoked pork fat, another way***

*(Shpek-kukhen drugim manerom)*

Finely chop 1 pound of smoked pork fat. Mix with a finely chopped onion, black pepper, allspice, dill, 1 raw egg, and, if desired, a little marjoram. Prepare a yeast dough (see Chapter 8) and form into small buns, stuffing them with the prepared filling. Take 1 glass of melted butter, dip each little bun into the butter, and place them side by side in a saucepan, one next to another. Cover the pan and, when the buns have risen, place in a hot oven. Serve them turned out onto a platter.

*\*Horst Scharfenberg, a contemporary writer on German cookery, gives a recipe that is similar to Molokhovets' called Courland Bacon Rolls, Courland being a stretch of the Baltic coastline. The finishing of the rolls is different, however. Whereas Molokhovets dipped hers in melted butter before the rising and baking, Scharfenberg paints his with beaten egg yolks and sprinkles them with caraway seeds. (See Scharfenberg, The Cuisines of Germany, 129.)*

## 254 **A pie of meat-stuffed *pirozhki***

*(Pirozhki v korzhe s mjasnym farshem)*

Dissolve yeast and prepare a dough from it. In addition, prepare 2 flat cakes of short pastry, using 1 lb flour, ½ glass of cold water, ½ teaspoon salt, 2 eggs, and ¼ lb butter. First mix the flour with the water, salt, and eggs, then add a piece of very fresh Finnish butter and knead the dough thoroughly—the longer, the better. From the prepared, raised yeast dough, make small *pirozhki*-like dumplings (*vareniki*). Stuff them with beef filling and let them rise. When they have risen, place one of the two flat cakes of short pastry on a skillet. Top with small *pirozhki* of yeast dough, set back to back in pairs, painting each with butter, so that they do not stick to one another. When they are all arranged, paint the top with butter and cover with the other flat cake of short pastry. Pinch the edges all around, paint with egg, and place in a hot oven. If the upper and lower crusts are not to be eaten, make them from a simple dough of flour and water, and just paint them with egg. Serve with soup.

INGREDIENTS

*For the short pastry*
1 lb flour
2 eggs
¼ lb butter

*For the yeast dough*
1 glass milk
1½ lb flour

⅓ lb butter
2 eggs

*For the stuffing*
1 lb beef
1 onion
⅛ lb butter
(⅛ lb butter to paint the *pirozhki*)

### 256  Pirozhki from pancakes with brains

*(Pirozhki iz blinov s mozgami)*

Bake thin pancakes as indicated in Chapter 11. Take the brains from 2 calf's heads or 1 beef head, remove the veins, and wash in cold water. Mix ⅛ lb butter with the brains, add salt, and fry in a saucepan, stirring, until they whiten. Add parsley and dill and mix. Spread some of this stuffing on each pancake, roll into a tube, and dip into egg or the leftover batter and rusk crumbs. Fry in butter.

INGREDIENTS

*For the pancakes*
3 glasses milk
2 glasses flour
2 eggs
-----------
⅛ lb butter, to fry the pancakes
1 egg

6 rusks

*For the stuffing*
brains
salt
⅛ lb butter
parsley and dill

### 259  Pirozhki-buns stuffed with carrots in bechamel sauce

*(Pirozhki-bulochki farshirovannye beshemelem iz slivok s morkov'ju)*

Take 12–18 small, oblong buns, either homemade or purchased. Cut off the tops and carefully remove the soft interiors. Stuff with carrots in bechamel sauce and sprinkle with grated cheese. Replace the tops, paint with butter, and sprinkle with more cheese. Using a feather, moisten the tops with rich bouillon and bake in the oven for 5 minutes.

To prepare the bechamel, [melt] ½ spoon butter, [stir in] ½ glass of flour, and dilute with 1½ glasses cream. Boil, stirring, until thickened. Add a boiled carrot, cut into pieces, and mix.

INGREDIENTS

12–18 small buns
1 carrot
⅛ lb butter

1½ glasses cream or milk
⅛ lb cheese
½ glass flour

### 262  Pirozhki made from vermicelli

*(Pirozhki iz vermisheli)*

Boil in salted water ½ lb purchased vermicelli or homemade noodles, prepared only from [flour and] eggs without water. Drain in a sieve. Melt 1 spoon butter in a saucepan and stir in the noodles, salt, 2 eggs, and 2 spoons grated cheese. Grease small tin molds with butter and sprinkle with rusk crumbs. Fill with the prepared vermicelli and bake. Carefully remove the upper browned crusts and a little vermicelli from the middle of each *pirozhok*. Fill the cavities with the following mixture: Melt ½ spoon butter and stir in ½ finely chopped onion and ¼ glass flour. Fry, add 1 glass sour cream, and bring to a boil. Let the sauce cool, beat in 2 egg yolks, and add 2 spoons grated cheese and some lemon juice. [Stuff the *pirozhki*,] replace the top crusts, and warm in the oven for several minutes.

INGREDIENTS

½ lb vermicelli, or 2 eggs and ½ glass
    flour
2 spoons grated cheese
2 eggs
1½ spoons butter
3–4 rusks

*For the ragout*
½ spoon butter
1 onion
1 spoon flour
2 egg yolks
2 spoons cheese
1 glass sour cream

## 266 "Pirozhki," or Eggs baked in crayfish shells

*(Pirozhki iz vypusknykh jaits v rakovinakh)*

Grease 6–9 crayfish shells with butter made from herrings, sardines, or sprats. Take 6–9 fresh eggs and carefully break 1 egg into each crayfish shell. Sprinkle with Dutch or any other cheese mixed with 1 spoon ground rusk crumbs. Drizzle with butter and place in a hot oven for several minutes until the eggs are set and the tops begin to brown.

INGREDIENTS

6–9 eggs
3–4 spoons sardine butter
1½-2 spoons cheese
2–4 rusks
½ spoon butter
[6–9 crayfish shells]

*For herring or sardine butter*
1 herring
1 apple
1 onion
nearly ⅛ lb rye bread
1½ spoons butter
nutmeg

# 3

# Sauces

*(Sousy ili podlivki)*

*Remarks concerning sauces or flour-based gravies:* For 6–8 persons, prepare 2½ glasses of sauce. Most sauces are made as follows. In a stoneware pot, melt ⅛ lb or 1 tablespoon of the very best ordinary butter or Finnish butter, add 1 full spoon of wheat flour, and fry, stirring lightly. Dilute with 3 glasses of strained meat, fish, or mushroom bouillon, boil thoroughly, and strain. Then add the remaining [ingredients] and ¼–¾ teaspoon salt, depending upon the other ingredients. These sauces should not be watery. Part of the sauce should be poured over the beef, fish, pudding, etc., and the remainder served in a sauceboat.

The proportions are intended to serve 6–8 persons. For 9–12 persons, increase the proportions by 1½. For 13–18 persons, double the proportions. For 19–24 persons, increase the proportions by 2½. When increasing the proportions, the dish should be served on two platters, and the sauce in two sauceboats.

In order to make a sauce quickly, it is useful to prepare enough butter with flour, fried flour, and caramelized sugar to last at least two weeks. These special sauce components follow.

### 269  Roux for white sauces*

*(Zagotovka masla s mukoju dlja belykh sousov)*

Bring to a boil 1 lb fresh Finnish butter, let it stand, and pour off the clear oil into a saucepan. Pour 2 glasses flour into the oil, stirring with a spoon, bring to a boil several times, and pour into a glazed pot. Store in a cold place and use as necessary for white sauces. For a sauce for 6 persons, use about 2 full spoons.

*La Varenne published in 1651 the earliest French recipe for a roux, a mixture which he advised making in quantity so that it would be available as needed. He cooked the flour in pork fat rather than butter, added onions, and then stored the mixture in an earthen pot. (Wheaton, Savoring the Past, 116.)

### 270  Caramelized sugar for dark sauces

*(Zagotovka zhzhenago sakhara dlja temnykh sousov)*

Moisten ½ lb of sugar pieces with water, place the pieces in a clean skillet, and heat the pan on top of the stove until the sugar melts and darkens. Add a little boiling water, bring to a boil, and pour into a pot. Use for dark sour-sweet sauces, adding about ½ spoon at a time. Reheat the sugar slightly before using.

### 271  Fried flour for sauces

*(Zagotovka podzharenoj muki dlja sousov)*

Sprinkle dry wheat flour onto a clean skillet, place over a low fire, and stir with a spoon until the flour browns. Remove from the fire and stir until cool. Pour into a dry jar and store in a dry place.

Before using, mix 1 spoon of this flour with 1 spoon Finnish butter and bring to a boil. This flour is used for strong, dark sauces.

### 272  Essence for strong sauces

*(Essentsija dlja krepkikh sousov)*

Mix together 1½ glasses sherry, 1 wineglass of strong tarragon vinegar, 12 cleaned sprats, a little pepper, ½ grated nutmeg, several whole cloves, a piece of horseradish, the zest of a lemon, and 2–3 sliced parsley roots. Place on top of the stove, boil until the sprats are cooked through, and rub through a fine sieve. Pour into a bottle, cool, and cork tightly. When preparing a strong sauce for fish, duck, capon, wild fowl, pork kidneys, lamb patties, pâté, etc., simply boil 1 spoon fried flour with 1½ spoons butter and dilute with 2 glasses bouillon and 1–2 spoons of this essence, according to taste. A little caramelized sugar may be added, then bring the sauce to a boil, strain, and pour over the dish.

### 272a  [Beef] essence for coloring bouillon and sauces

*(Eshche essentsija dlja podkrashivan'ja bul'ona i sousov)*

Cut 1 lb beef into pieces. Place 1 spoon butter in a saucepan with 1 chopped onion, 1 carrot, 1 celery root, 1 parsley root, 1 bay leaf, add the beef, and fry until everything has browned. Pour in 2 glasses water and bring to a full boil. Strain into a bottle and cork. When needed, add this essence to a sauce, 1–2 spoons at a time.

### 273  Browned butter with rusk crumbs*

*(Rumjanoe maslo s sukharjami)*

Melt fresh Finnish butter in a saucepan, bring it to a boil, and add ground rusk crumbs. Fry until the crumbs and the butter are browned and have thickened somewhat. This butter is poured over the root vegetables used to garnish boiled beef, cauliflower, macaroni, vermicelli, etc.

*For the 1920s German edition, the name was changed to Polish sauce. In Europe and America, this mixture is known now as a garnish á la polonaise, often with the addition of sieved hard-boiled egg yolks mixed with chopped parsley.*

### 274 Sardine or sprat butter

*(Maslo iz sardelek)*

Rinse a half pound of sprats in water, pound in a mortar, and add ½ lb melted, pure Finnish butter. Beat until white and pass through a sieve. Serve with capon, fried beefsteak (*tonkij filej*), etc. This may be stored in a cold place for 2–3 months.

## SAUCES FOR MEAT DISHES

*(Podlivki k mjasnym kushan'jam)*

### 275 Ordinary sauce

*(Sous obyknovennyj)*

Stir 3 glasses of bouillon into 1 spoon of ready-prepared butter mixed with flour, add salt, and boil for about 2 hours. Strain and sprinkle with chopped green onion. Serve with roast or boiled beef, patties, or pancake pudding, etc.

### 277 Another sauce for roast and boiled beef, patties, and pancake pudding

*(Eshche sous k zharenoj i razvarnoj govjadine, k kotletam i blinchatomy pudingu)*

Bake 2–3 onions. Peel the onions, slice thin, and fry lightly with butter. Stir in fried flour and dilute with 3 glasses of bouillon. Any juices released from the meat may also be added. Cook about 2 hours and strain. Sprinkle on sugar and add enough vinegar, apple soy, or lemon or gooseberry juice to give the sauce a pleasant sour-sweet taste. Bring to a boil several times, pour over the roast or other meats or serve separately in a sauceboat.

INGREDIENTS

| | |
|---|---|
| 2–4 onions | vinegar |
| 1 spoon fried flour | a lemon |
| 1–2 spoons butter | gooseberry juice or apple soy |
| 4–5 pieces of sugar | |

### 278 Brown sauce

*(Sous krasnyj)*

Mix ½ glass of fried flour with 1½ spoons butter and dilute with 2 glasses of bouillon to make nearly 3½ glasses of sauce for serving. Boil thoroughly and strain. Add prepared caramelized sugar or meat essence, bring to a boil, and strain through a fine sieve. Add about 3 pieces of sugar, lemon juice, and 1 full spoon capers, marinated mushrooms, or cornichons, cut lengthwise. Or, add *amourettes** boiled in water with vinegar or ½ seeded and sliced lemon. Bring the sauce to a boil once more and, while still hot, pour it over patties, roast ducks, suckling pig, turkey, capon, beef, or eel.

INGREDIENTS

½ glass fried flour
caramelized sugar
½ lemon
1 full spoon capers
Or, 1 full spoon cornichons

Or, marinated mushrooms
Or, *amourettes*
½–2 wineglasses table wine may be
 added

*Amourettes is the French name for the spinal marrow of beef, mutton, or veal. Somewhat like calf's brains in taste and consistency, amourettes, even if boiled in vinegar, are an unlikely substitute for the capers, marinated mushrooms, or cornichons mentioned in the recipe. Cf. Chapter 4 for the basic preparation of amourettes.*

### 281 Sauce for cold beef

*(Sous k kholodnomu zharkomu)*

Mash 3 hard-boiled egg yolks with 1 spoon olive oil. Add 2 teaspoons prepared mustard, 1 teaspoon fine sugar, ½ an onion, grated or very finely chopped, ½ herring, skinned and boned, ½ glass cream, and vinegar to taste. Mix thoroughly and pour over cold, sliced beef, which has been roasted or boiled.

INGREDIENTS

1 spoon olive oil
3 eggs
2 teaspoons mustard
1–2 pieces sugar

½ herring
½–1 onion
½ glass cream
vinegar

### 282 Salted cucumber sauce

*(Sous iz solenykh ogurtsov)*

Cut salted cucumbers into small oblong pieces. [Mix] ½ glass of fried flour with butter and 1 teaspoon finely chopped parsley. Dilute with 2 glasses bouillon, boil thoroughly, and strain. Add ½ glass cucumber brine and, if desired, mushroom bouillon and a little caramelized sugar. Bring to a boil.

Serve with boiled beef, or on fast days with herring and potato patties.

INGREDIENTS

3–6 salted cucumbers
½ glass fried flour
1–2 spoons butter
parsley

½ glass or more cucumber brine
(a small piece of sugar)
2–3 mushrooms
caramelized sugar

## 286  Mushroom sauce

*(Sous iz shampin'onov)*

Clean 6 large, fresh mushrooms and drop into clean water. Melt ½ spoon butter in a saucepan and add the mushrooms, 1 glass bouillon, and the juice from 1 lemon slice. Bring to a boil, remove the mushrooms, and slice them. Fry 1 spoon flour in 1 spoon butter, dilute with 2 glasses of bouillon, boil for 2 hours, and strain through a fine sieve. Add salt, 1 wineglass sherry, and the mushrooms and the sauce in which they were cooked and bring the sauce to a boil. About 2 spoons sour cream may also be added.

INGREDIENTS

6 mushrooms
2 spoons butter
1 spoon flour
½–2 spoons sour cream

1 wineglass sherry
salt
1 lemon slice

## 287  Sweet and sour sauce with raisins for tongue, calf's feet, carp, bream, etc.

*(Sous kislosladkij s izjumom k jazyku, teljach'im nozhkam, karpu, leshchu i pr.)*

Fry 1 full spoon of fried flour in 2 spoons butter and dilute with bouillon (a wineglass of wine may be added, if desired). Boil for 2 hours and strain. Stir in caramelized sugar and lemon juice and bring to a boil. Before serving, add 3–4 halved and seeded lemon slices, about 3–4 pieces of sugar, ½ glass of washed raisins, and, if desired, a few almonds. Bring to a boil once more.

If serving this sauce with fish, dilute it with fish bouillon; on fast days substitute any kind of fast day oil for the butter.

INGREDIENTS

| | |
|---|---|
| 1 spoon flour | ½ glass raisins |
| 1½ [*sic*] spoons butter | (¼ glass almonds) |
| 3–4 pieces sugar | (1 wineglass wine) |
| ½ lemon | caramelized sugar |

### 290 Onion sauce with caraway for lamb and patties

*(Sous iz lukovits s tminom k baranine i kotletam)*

Slice 5–6 onions, add 3 glasses boiling bouillon, boil, and rub through a sieve. Lightly fry 1 spoon flour in 2 spoons butter, dilute with a glass of bouillon, boil thoroughly, and strain. Mix the sauce with 2 glasses of the strained onion purée, add 1½ teaspoons caraway seeds and some caramelized sugar, and bring to a boil several times. Serve with roast lamb or patties.

INGREDIENTS

| | |
|---|---|
| 5–6 onions | caramelized sugar |
| 2 spoons butter | Add, if desired, a small spoon of |
| 1 spoon fried flour | mustard or vinegar |
| 1½ teaspoons caraway seeds | |

### 294 White sauce for boiled veal, chicken, or turkey, or even for fish

*(Sous beljy k varenoj teljatine, kuritse ili indejke i dazhe rybam)*

Mix ⅔ glass flour with 1½ spoons melted butter, fry lightly, and dilute with 3 glasses of strained turkey or chicken bouillon. Boil for 2 hours and strain. Add sour cream and, if desired, about 2 spoons marinated gooseberries. Bring to a boil and sprinkle on salt and 1 teaspoon finely chopped parsley or dill. Pour over the meat and serve in a deep platter or, if desired, in a sauceboat with boiled potatoes.

There should be at least 4 glasses of sauce.

INGREDIENTS

| | |
|---|---|
| 1½ spoons butter | (15–20 marinated gooseberries) |
| ⅔ glass flour | (parsley, dill) |
| 1–1½ glasses sour cream | [3 glasses bouillon] |

### 297 Horseradish sauce with currants for boiled beef

*(Sous iz khrena s korinkoju k varenoj govjadine)*

Dilute ½ spoon butter and ¼ spoon flour with 2 glasses of bouillon, boil thoroughly, and strain. Add ½ glass of washed currants and bring to a boil. Add 6 spoons grated horseradish and 1 seeded lemon slice, bring to a boil again, and serve with boiled beef.

INGREDIENTS

| | |
|---|---|
| horseradish | 1 spoon olive oil, or ½ spoon butter |
| ¼ spoon flour | 1 lemon slice |
| ½ glass currants | |

### 299 Cherry sauce for roast boar, chamois, etc.*

*(Sous iz vishen' k zharenomu veprju, serne i pr.)*

Heat ¾ glass cherry purée sweetened with honey or sugar mixed with 1½ glasses of the pan juices from the same roast with which the sauce is to be served. Add 2–3 pieces of sugar, ½ *vershok* stick cinnamon, 4–5 coarsely ground cloves, and 1 teaspoon potato flour mixed with 1 spoon water. Bring to a boil and rub through a fine sieve. Add ½ glass Madeira and pour over the sliced, roasted meat.

INGREDIENTS

| | |
|---|---|
| ¾ glass cherry purée | ½ *vershok* stick cinnamon |
| ½ glass Madeira | 1 teaspoon potato flour |
| 2–3 pieces sugar | 5–6 cloves |

*This sauce resembles the traditional Cumberland sauce served with cold game and made from currant jelly, port wine, vinegar, cherries, lemon, and orange. A chef at the Hanoverian court apparently dedicated this sauce to the Duke of Cumberland (1845–1923), the son of King George V of Hanover (1819–1878). (Küchen-Lexikon, 104.) Prior to this time, however, the sauce existed under other, more descriptive names.*

### 302 Strong sauce

*(Krepkij sous)*

Cut up 1 lb beef. Place the beef in a saucepan with ½ lb pork fat and root vegetables and fry until brown. Add 3 glasses water, boil for 30 minutes, and strain. Fry ½ spoon butter with ½ spoon flour, dilute with this bouillon, and boil thoroughly. Add 1½ *lots** of finely crushed dried bouillon, a little lemon juice, and salt. Bring to a boil, remove from the stove, and set aside. Remove the fat from the top and strain the sauce.

If serving this sauce with the main meat course, use 2 glasses of sauce in which the meat was cooked instead of 1 lb of beef as indicated above.

If preparing this sauce for pâté, add ½ glass Madeira, 4–5 truffles, and *amourettes*.

INGREDIENTS

| | |
|---|---|
| 1 lb beef | ½ spoon butter |
| ¼ lb pork fat | 1½ *lots* dried bouillon |
| ½ celery root | ----------- |
| 1 onion | |
| ½ spoon flour | *If the sauce is prepared for pâté, add* |
| juice from ½ lemon | ½ glass Madeira |
| 1 carrot | 4–5 truffles |
| ½ leek | |

*\*See Appendix, Weights and Measures, for equivalents.*

### 303  Tomato sauce

(*Sous iz pomidorov*)

Slice 2–3 very ripe, rather large tomatoes and discard the seeds. Stew the tomatoes in butter, pouring on bouillon, rub them through a fine sieve, and add sugar. Mix 1 spoon butter with 1 spoon flour, add the tomatoes and salt, and dilute as necessary with bouillon. Boil thoroughly and pour over beef, boiled lamb, boiled turkey, or chicken.

INGREDIENTS

| | |
|---|---|
| 2–3 tomatoes | 1 spoon flour |
| 2–3 pieces sugar | 1–2 spoons butter |

### 305  Bechamel made from cream

(*Beshemel' iz slivok*)

Knead 1 spoon, or ⅛ lb, Finnish butter with ¾ glass flour, dilute with ½ glass strong bouillon, and boil thoroughly, gradually adding 1½ glasses cream or whole milk. Add salt and boil, stirring, until thickened. Watch that the sauce does not burn. Strain, let it cool completely, and then beat in 2–3 egg yolks mixed with 1 spoon cream. Add a pinch of nutmeg, if desired. Use this bechamel to cover meat that is almost cooked—veal, turkey, or even beef. Sprinkle with grated cheese and set in the oven for 15 minutes to brown lightly. Partially slice the nearly cooked veal roast without cutting it through completely. These proportions should make enough sauce to spread the bechamel over the veal slices and to mask the top also.

INGREDIENTS

| | |
|---|---|
| 1 spoon butter | ½ glass bouillon |
| ¾ glass flour | (Parmesan cheese) |
| 1½ glasses cream | (nutmeg) |
| 2–3 egg yolks | |

## 311 French truffle sauce for roasts

*(Sous frantsuzskij iz trjufelej k zharkomu)*

In an uncovered saucepan, fry until brown 1–2 lbs beef, ½ lb finely chopped pork fat, 2 onions, root vegetables (one of each), a bay leaf, and allspice. Pour on water and boil for 1 hour. Fry ½ spoon butter with ½ spoon flour, dilute with the prepared bouillon, and boil, stirring. Strain through a fine sieve, remove the fat from the sauce, and add ½ glass Madeira, 6 sliced French truffles, and 5 cornichons, sliced lengthwise. Boil for 15 minutes, add salt if necessary, and serve with the main meat dish or duck pâté.

INGREDIENTS

| | |
|---|---|
| 1–2 lbs beef | ½ spoon flour |
| ½ lb pork fat | ½ spoon butter |
| 2 onions | ½ glass Madeira |
| 1 carrot | 6 truffles |
| ½ celery root | 5 cornichons |
| ½ parsley root | ½ leek |
| 1 bay leaf | allspice |

## 312 *Sareptskaja* mustard

*(Sareptskaja gorchitsa)*

Add a little fine sugar to the very best *Sareptskaja* mustard, infuse with boiling water, and mix until smooth.

Or, mash 1 glass of the very best *Sareptskaja* mustard with 2 spoons sugar, infuse with boiling water, and mix until smooth. Add 2 spoons each olive oil and vinegar.

Or, for every 3 spoons *Sareptskaja* [mustard] powder, add 2 spoons olive oil, a cup of cold water, and a little salt. Bring to a boil and serve.

# SAUCES FOR VEGETABLES
## *(Sousy k ovoshcham)*

### 314 Yellow sauce for asparagus, rutabagas, or turnips
#### *(Sous zheltyj k sparzhe, brjukve, repe)*

Bring to a boil 1 spoon butter, ¾ glass cream, and 1½ glasses of the water in which the asparagus or rutabagas were boiled. Cool slightly. Mix 5 egg yolks with 2 spoons sugar and dilute with a little of the sauce. Stir the yolks and sugar into the remainder of the sauce and beat with a whisk or simply mix over the fire until it is steaming hot, but do not boil.

INGREDIENTS

5 eggs
¾ glass cream

2–3 pieces sugar

# FISH SAUCES
## *(Podlivki k rybam)*

### 320 Walnut sauce for fish and carp*
#### *(Sous iz gretskikh orekhov k rybe k [sic] karpu)*

Finely pound 20 very fresh walnuts in a mortar, adding water gradually. Mix with 1 full teaspoon prepared *Sareptskaja* mustard and add a little salt, hard-boiled egg yolks mashed with olive oil, 1 spoon sieved rusks, and ½ glass vinegar. Mix thoroughly and pour over boiled or baked fish. Prepare the sauce just before serving.

INGREDIENTS

20 walnuts, that is, ½ lb nuts
1 spoon olive oil
2 egg yolks
1 spoon rusk crumbs

1 full spoon sugar, or about 2–3 pieces
½ glass vinegar
1 full teaspoon prepared mustard

*A similar recipe appears occasionally in modern Soviet cookbooks as Walnut and Rusk Sauce (Sous orekhovyj sukharnyj). (See Kulakova, Kholodnye bljuda i zakuski, 132.) Aside from the walnuts, Molokhovets' mild sauce is closer to a French vinaigrette than the Georgian walnut sauces, Garo and Satsivi, which include garlic, red pepper, spices, and herbs. For examples of the latter, see Chamberlain, The Food and Cooking of Russia, 157, 159.*

### 327 Sauce for boiled salmon, burbot, or eel with olives, capers, etc.

*(Sous k varenoj lososine, semge, nalimu ili ugrju, s olivkami, kaportsami i t. p.)*

Fry ½ glass flour in 1½ spoons butter and dilute with 2½ to 3 glasses strained fish bouillon. Mix, boil thoroughly, and strain. Add 1 small jar of olives, capers, or marinated mushrooms with their juice, or a lemon, or a little of each. Bring to a boil, add salt and finely chopped parsley and dill, and pour over the fish on a platter.

INGREDIENTS

| | |
|---|---|
| 1½ spoons butter | 1 small jar olives, or capers, or |
| ½ glass flour | marinated mushrooms, or ½ lemon |
| | parsley and dill |

### 331 Butter with eggs*

*(Maslo s jajtsami)*

Melt ⅓ lb butter or more, add 3–4 finely chopped hard-boiled eggs, and bring to a boil. Dilute, as desired, with either bouillon or cream. Pour over boiled whitefish, perch, pike, or cod, or serve separately in a sauceboat.

*Today, with the addition of chopped parsley and lemon juice or mustard, this is called Polish or Polish egg sauce. (See Ranhofer, The Epicurean, 303; Guba and Lazarev, Kulinarija, 75.)*

### 333 Sprat sauce

*(Sous iz sardelek)*

Melt 1 spoon butter in a saucepan, add small cut-up sprats and finely chopped onions, and bring to a boil. Add cream and a little bouillon, bring to a boil again, and cool slightly. Beat in egg yolks and heat, stirring, until very hot, but do not boil.

INGREDIENTS

| | |
|---|---|
| 1 spoon butter | 4 small sprats |
| 1–2 onions | 1 glass cream |
| 2–3 egg yolks | |

### 335 Tartar sauce*

*(Sous tatarskij)*

Beat 5 raw egg yolks with sugar and 1½ spoons olive oil until white. Add ½ glass or more of vinegar and 1 glass of finely grated horseradish. Mix.

INGREDIENTS

5 egg yolks                              1½ spoons olive oil
1–2 spoons sugar                         vinegar
horseradish

*The traditional French sauce by this name combines mayonnaise with green herbs and some-
times gherkins and capers. The horseradish seems to have been an innovation of Molokhovets which
survived even until the 1920s German edition. Meanwhile, Aleksandrova-Ignat'eva in 1912 used
the name to refer to the traditional French sauce, as did modern Soviet writers. (See Aleksandrova-
Ignat'eva, Prakticheskija osnovy kulinarnago iskusstva, 439–440; and Guba and Lazarev, Kulinarija, 76.)*

### 340  Almond milk sauce for fish

*(Sous k rybe s mindal'nym molokom)*

Place 4–5 egg yolks in a saucepan with ⅓–½ lb butter, 2 tablespoons vinegar,
½ glass thin almond milk, and 2 teaspoons fine sugar. Set the pan on top of the
stove and stir it constantly until the sauce steams, but do not let it boil.

## SAUCES FOR COLD FISH, ASPICS, AND PÂTÉS

*(Podlivki k kholodnym rybam, zalivnym, maionezam i pashtetam)*

### 342  Cold sprat sauce for fish and meat aspics

*(Sous kholodnyj iz sardelek k rybnym i mjasnym zalivnym)*

Mix 2 spoons olive oil, salt, 1 full spoon sugar, and 3–4 spoons vinegar. Pound
7–8 washed and boned sprats in a mortar with 4 hard-boiled egg yolks, mix with
the olive oil, and dilute with tarragon vinegar.

INGREDIENTS

2 spoons olive oil                       7–8 small sprats
salt                                     4 eggs
2–3 pieces sugar                         vinegar

### 343  Mixed sauce for cold fish

*(Sous sbornyj k rybam kholodnym)*

Steep 2 teaspoons of *Sareptskaja* mustard in 2 spoons boiling water. Add 6
raw or boiled and sieved egg yolks, 6 pieces sugar, 2 spoons olive oil, salt,
nearly 1 glass of vinegar, 1 hard-boiled egg, 1 peeled fresh cucumber, cut into

small cubes, marinated mushrooms, 1 finely chopped green onion, dill, 2 spoons capers, and 1 spoon olives, stoned and finely chopped. Serve with cold fish or aspics.

INGREDIENTS

2 teaspoons *Sareptskaja* mustard
6 egg yolks
2 spoons olive oil
1 egg
marinated mushrooms
1 spoon olives

1 glass vinegar
1 fresh cucumber
1 green onion
dill
2 spoons capers
6 pieces sugar

### 349 Crayfish sauce for pâtés

*(Sous iz rakov k pashtetam)*

Bring to a boil ½ spoon crayfish butter, 1 teaspoon flour, and 1½ glasses cream. Wash and shred 6 morels, place in a saucepan, cook them in their own juice until done, and add them to the cream sauce. Add a handful of finely chopped asparagus, boiled in salted water, and several crayfish tails. Boil the sauce thoroughly, stirring. Serve, sprinkled with salt and a little black pepper.

INGREDIENTS

6 morels
3 stalks asparagus
1½ glasses cream
1 teaspoon flour

½ spoon crayfish butter
6–12 crayfish tails
salt
pepper

# SAUCES FOR PUDDINGS

*(Podlivki k pudingam)*

### 352 Plum sauce for pudding

*(Sous iz sliv k pudingu)*

Boil 30 plums and spices, if desired (½ *vershok* stick cinnamon or 5–6 cloves), in water. Rub the plums through a fine sieve, mix with ¼ lb sugar and ½ or 1 glass table wine, bring to a boil. Add 1 teaspoon potato flour mixed with 1 spoon water and bring to a boil again, stirring.

INGREDIENTS

30 plums
½ *vershok* stick cinnamon, or 5–6
  cloves

½ glass sugar
½–1 glass wine
1 teaspoon potato flour

### 356  Vanilla sauce from milk or cream for pudding or cauliflower

*(Sous iz moloka ili slivok s vanil'ju k pudingu ili tsvetnoj kapuste)*

Bring to a boil 2 glasses cream or whole milk mixed with sugar. Add, if desired, ½ *vershok* vanilla, shaved and tied in a cloth, or cinnamon. Beat in 5 egg yolks and mix thoroughly. Place on top of the stove, stirring, until thickened, but do not boil. Strain and pour over a pudding or cauliflower.

INGREDIENTS

2 glasses cream, milk, or sour cream
3–4 pieces sugar

4–5 egg yolks
½ *vershok* vanilla, or cinnamon

### 357  Cranberry sauce for pudding

*(Sous iz kljukvy k pudingu)*

Cover ⅔ glass of cranberries with a little water, add ½ *vershok* stick cinnamon, and bring to a boil. Strain, beating with a spoon. Add sugar to 2½ glasses of this juice and bring to a boil. Cool and pour over the pudding. Or, add 2 teaspoons potato flour mixed with 1 spoon water and bring the sauce to a boil, stirring briskly for 3–4 minutes. Pour over the pudding and serve the remainder in a sauceboat.

INGREDIENTS

⅔ glass cranberries
½ *vershok* stick cinnamon

½ glass sugar
(2 teaspoons potato flour)

### 358  Sabayon sauce for pudding and cauliflower

*(Sabaion k pudingu i tsvetnoj kapuste)*

Grind 6 pieces of sugar and beat with 6 egg yolks until the mixture whitens. Stir in ½ glass each Madeira and water and add 1–2 seeded lemon slices. Place on top of the stove and beat constantly over a low fire with a whisk until the sabayon begins to rise. Then place the saucepan over a high flame. When the sauce rises and foams, immediately pour it over the pudding or other prepared dish and serve. One glass of light table wine may be substituted for the Madeira and water.

For 7 to 10 people, use 1½ the proportions; for 11 to 18 people, double the proportions.

INGREDIENTS

½ or 1 glass wine            6 pieces sugar
6 egg yolks                  1–2 lemon slices

### 359  Chocolate sauce for pudding and rice patties

*(Sous shokoladnyj k pudingu i risovym kotletam)*

Beat until white 2 egg yolks and fine sugar, sprinkle on ⅓ [grated] chocolate bar, and mix all this with 2 glasses of boiled milk that has cooled slightly. Place on top of the stove and beat until thickened, but do not boil. Pour the hot sauce over the pudding.

Or, mix ½ spoon butter with ½ spoon flour and dilute with a glass water. Boil thoroughly and strain. Sprinkle on ¼ lb chocolate, dilute with 2 glasses water, and add ¼ glass sugar. Mix thoroughly, and bring to a boil.

INGREDIENTS

2 glasses milk or cream       2–3 pieces sugar
2 egg yolks                   ⅓ chocolate bar

### 361  Poppy seed or hempseed* milk

*(Makovoe moloko ili konopljannoe)*

Scald 2 glasses of white or, better yet, gray poppy seeds with boiling water. Let them settle, then pour off the water. Scald again with boiling water, pour the water off, wash the seeds in cold water, and drain them in a fine sieve. Transfer to a stoneware bowl and grind with a wooden pestle until all the seeds are crushed. When the poppy seeds have whitened, pour in 2–3 glasses of boiled water. Mix, strain, squeeze the seeds, and add 2–4 pieces of sugar.

*Scholars surmise that the native home of hempseed was probably near the Caspian Sea. Herodotus reported that the Scythians cultivated it and ever since that time, it has been popular in Russia and Poland. Although hemp (Cannabis sativa) is, of course, the source of marijuana, the seeds are crushed for oil and are also parched and eaten. (Sturtevant's Edible Plants, 132.) Even in exile, the Lithuanians prepare salted hempseeds as a dip for hot potatoes or for sprinkling on rye bread. And, following Molokhovets, they still use poppy seed milk to pour over dry biscuits. (See Popular Lithuanian Recipes, 8th ed., 117–118, 19.)*

### 362 Excellent rum sauce for puddings

*(Prevoskhodnyj sous s romom k pudingam)*

Mix together 1 spoon each of very fresh butter and very good flour, dilute with a glass of water, and boil for at least 2 hours.* Strain and add ¾ glass white table wine, ½ glass of fine sugar, and 1 wineglass cognac. Squeeze the juice of ½ lemon and add enough water to make 2½ glasses in all. Add the lemon and water to the sauce and boil lightly. This sauce may be poured over all the puddings traditionally served with sabayon sauce. During Lent, use olive or nut oil instead of butter.

INGREDIENTS

| | |
|---|---|
| 1 spoon butter | ¾ glass table wine |
| 1 spoon flour | ½ glass fine sugar |
| ½ lemon | 1 wineglass rum [sic] |

*The liquid would evaporate long before two hours had elapsed. In a later version of this recipe, Molokhovets both increased the water by ½ glass and prudently advised the reader just to "boil the sauce thoroughly." It is not clear from the instructions whether she substituted cognac for the rum or whether she intended that both should be used.*

### 365 Sauce from apple skins and cores

*(Sous iz jablochnoj kozhitsy i serdtseviny)*

If preparing apple pudding or apple fritters, for example, rinse the discarded skins and cores and boil them in 2–3 glasses of water with a *vershok* of stick cinnamon. Strain and add ½ glass each sugar and cranberry water. Boil thoroughly and thicken with ½ spoon potato flour, mixed with cold water. Bring to a boil and serve. Strain the sauce, if lumpy.

### 368 Batter

*(Kljar)*

Mix 1 glass flour with 5 egg yolks, salt, and 6 spoons cream or milk. Fold in beaten egg whites. Pieces of boiled veal leg or mutton patties, for example, are first dipped in batter and then fried.

# 4

# Vegetables, Greens, and Garnishes

*(Kushan'ja iz ovoshchej i zeleni i raznye k nim garniry)*

## VEGETABLES AND GREENS
*(Ovoshchi i zelen')*

*Remarks concerning greens, vegetables, and roots:* To retain the color of any green vegetable, scald the greens with water or drop them directly into rapidly boiling, salted water. Better still, add ½ spoon baking soda to the boiling water. For example, when using spinach for soup, sauce, or puddings, first remove the stems, wash the leaves, and drain them in a coarse sieve until they dry slightly. Then plunge them into boiling water with baking soda, boil until tender, turn into a coarse sieve, and rinse with cold water. When the spinach has drained, rub it through a sieve into a stoneware pot, and immediately add a piece of butter. Just before serving, take a prepared bouillon from the fire, add the spinach, mix, and serve. Green beans are prepared exactly the same.

*Sorrel:* Pick over sorrel, that is, discard any spoiled leaves and tear off the stems completely. Wash the sorrel and drain it in a sieve. When the sorrel has drained and dried slightly, chop it in a wooden bowl and transfer the sorrel with its juice to a stoneware pot. Boil until done in its own juice, not adding any water at all. Add the leaves to strained, boiling bouillon. Or, rub them through a sieve, thicken with flour, and dilute with strained, boiling bouillon.

Young sorrel is less sour, therefore use more of it and less flour. If only old sorrel is available, use less of it and thicken the soup with a larger quantity of flour. Best of all, use half sorrel and half spinach, both for soups and for sauces.

*Sauerkraut* must always be boiled in a stoneware pot. Squeeze it out before boiling, but if it is too sour, wash it in water and then squeeze dry.

*Fresh cabbage:* No matter how the cabbage will be used, chop off the stalk. Cut the head into quarters, remove any spoiled leaves, and rinse the cabbage in cold water. If the cabbage is still young and tastes bitter, that is, before September, then drop it into boiling water and bring it once to a boil. From September onward, it is unnecessary to parboil the cabbage, but cook it directly in the bouillon instead.

*Carrots, turnips, rutabagas, etc.,* for soups and sauces are best only washed, but not peeled [lit., "not touched with a knife"].* Cover with warm water and bring to a boil only once in order to remove any dirt. Turn the vegetables into a sieve, then peel, wash, and cut up as required. Transfer to a stoneware pot, add 1–2 spoons fresh butter and a little bit of bouillon or milk. Stew, covered, in their own juice until ready. Add salt when they are done.

*Dried vegetables,* for example, peas, lentils, and kidney beans, must be soaked overnight in water at room temperature. The next day, cover with fresh, cold water and boil with 1 spoon baking soda until tender. Salt just before serving, because salting earlier will prevent them from becoming tender.

*Salted vegetables,* for example, kidney beans, must also soak overnight. The next day, boil them in fresh water; if this water seems too salty, pour it off and boil the beans in fresh water until tender.

It is impossible to give amounts for vegetables and greens, because some root vegetables are large and others are small, some are served alone and others with garnishes. Also, some greens are cleaner and fresher than others. Therefore, approximate proportions for 6–8 people are as follows. Use 3 lbs of carrots, turnips, rutabagas, etc., if ungarnished; if garnished, use 1 1/2–2 lbs. For greens such as spinach, sorrel, etc., use 4–5 lbs of unpicked-over leaves; if garnished, use about 2–3 lbs. Dried green peas and white beans are rarely eaten without garnishes, therefore 1/3–1/2 lb green peas is sufficient and 3/4–1 lb beans.

Add fresh butter or Finnish butter [i.e., not oil] to these vegetables.

The proportions are intended for 6–8 persons. For 9–12 persons, increase the proportions by 1 1/2. For 13–18 persons, double the proportions. For 19–24 persons, triple the proportions.

When the proportions are increased, serve on 2 platters. Sometimes several vegetables, separated by strips of [baked] dough, are served on a single platter; in that case prepare less than the indicated amount of any single vegetable.

*The instructions here are unclear, but I think Molokhovets means that one should never peel carrots, etc., when using them for soups and sauces. If using them as a separate vegetable, however, they should be peeled after parboiling.

# PEAS
## (Gorokh)

### 372  Green peas with cream

*(Gorokh zelenyj so slivkami)*

Shell 5 lbs peas or, if serving in the pod, remove the strings from only 2 1/2 lbs. Cut each pod in half, barely cover with water, add salt and sugar, and boil until

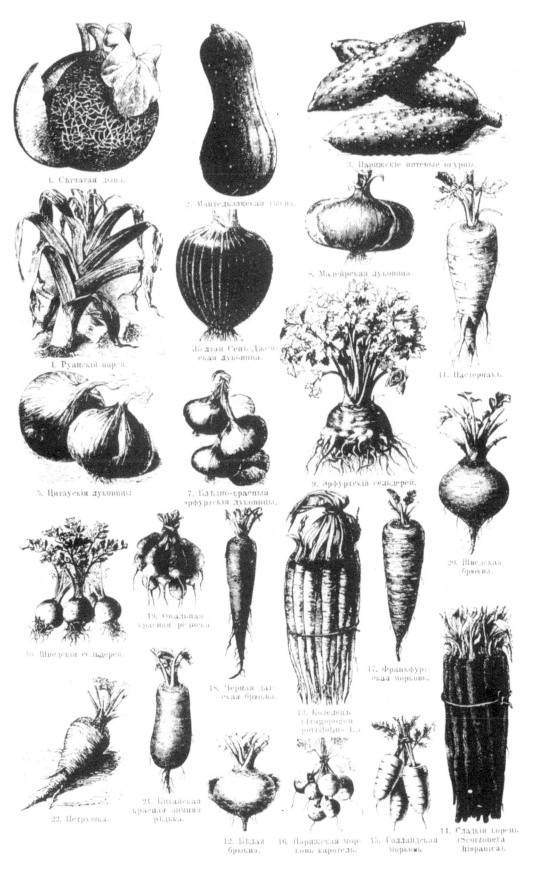

Vegetables. From *Entsiklopedicheskij slovar'* (St. Petersburg, 1898).

tender. Pour off the water, add 1–1½ glasses cream and ½ spoon flour creamed with 1 spoon butter, and boil thoroughly. Or, instead of the flour, add 3 egg yolks beaten with ½ glass cream and stir briskly. Heat the sauce until it is very hot, but do not let it boil.

INGREDIENTS

2–5 lbs pea pods
1½ glasses cream

3 egg yolks, or ½ spoon flour and 1
    spoon butter

### 375  Green peas with crayfish

*(Zelenyj gorokh s rakami)*

Prepare as indicated above, in #372. Thicken with a roux made from 1–2 spoons crayfish butter and ½ spoon flour. Arrange about 60 crayfish tails on top of the peas and garnish the platter with sippets.

### 376a  Dried green peas with mushroom patties

*(Zelenyj sushenyj goroshek s kotletami iz gribov)*

Soak 1½ glasses green peas in cold water. Pick over the peas, wash them, and pour into a saucepan. Fill the pan with water and, when it begins to boil, add some salt, 1 onion, and 1–2 pieces sugar. Boil until tender and turn out into a sieve. Boil ⅛ lb dried white mushrooms [Boletus edulis] in water and chop fine. Cook 1 glass rice until tender in water with salt, nutmeg, and a parsley root. Mix the rice with the mushrooms, form into patties, dip them in egg and crushed rusks, and fry in Finnish butter or poppy seed oil. Cream 1 teaspoon flour with 1 spoon butter and dilute with 1 glass of mushroom bouillon mixed with the drained juice from the green peas. Bring thoroughly to a boil and pour over the peas arranged on a platter. Garnish with the mushroom patties.

INGREDIENTS

1½ glasses, or ½ lb, green peas
2 onions
1–2 pieces sugar
1 glass rice
salt
pepper
1 parsley root
1 spoon butter

1 small spoon flour
½ glass olive or poppy seed oil, or 2
    spoons Finnish butter
(4–5 rusks)
(2 eggs)
nutmeg
⅛ lb mushrooms

## CARROTS
## *(Morkov')*

### 382 Carrots, turnips, potatoes, and cabbage with milk sauce

*(Morkov', repa, kartofel' i kapusta s molochnym sousom)*

Serve in a bowl with 4 compartments or on a platter divided into 4 sections by dough. To prepare the pastry, mix together 1 egg, 1 spoon water, and enough flour to make a stiff dough. Roll it out into a long strip, cut into two strips, and notch one edge attractively. Arrange the strips crisscross on the platter, paint them with egg, and brown in the oven. Remove from the oven and fill each section with a separate vegetable.

Prepare the dough for the dividers according to the size of the platter. It is best to bake the strips first on a sheet in the oven and then carefully transfer them to the platter.

Cut all the vegetables into small pieces, boil each vegetable separately in salted water until half cooked, and then drain. To each pan of vegetables, add 1 glass milk, or preferably cream, and ½ spoon butter mixed with ⅓ spoon flour. Boil each vegetable until done. Or, lightly fry the flour with the butter, pour on the cut-up raw vegetables, dilute with milk or cream, and boil until tender. Add salt, in which case more cream will be needed.

INGREDIENTS

1 glass chopped carrots
1 glass chopped turnip
1 small head cabbage, cut into
    sections

¼ *garnets* potatoes, sliced
2 spoons butter
1½ spoons flour
about 3 or 6 glasses milk or cream

## RUTABAGAS AND TURNIPS
## *(Brjukva i repa)*

### 391 Turnips or rutabagas with sweet stuffing

*(Repa ili brjukva so sladkim farshem)*

Boil 6–9 turnips or rutabagas in water. Cut off the tops and carefully scoop out the interior with a small spoon. Cream the pulp with 1 spoon butter and ⅔ glass or more whole milk or cream. Add ¼ grated French roll, salt, about 2–3 pieces sugar, (nutmeg, if desired,) ⅓ glass currants, and 1 egg yolk. Mix everything together and stuff the turnips or rutabagas. Replace the cut-off tops, strew with rusk crumbs, and bake in the oven. To serve, pour on Vanilla sauce.

Instead of ⅔ glass milk and ¼ French roll, ½ glass of semolina boiled in 1½ glasses of milk may be added.

INGREDIENTS

| | |
|---|---|
| 6–9 turnips or rutabagas | 2–3 pieces sugar |
| 1 spoon butter | (nutmeg) |
| ⅔ glass milk or cream | salt |
| 1 egg yolk | ⅓ glass currants |
| ½ stale French roll | ingredients for Vanilla sauce |

### 392 Turnips or rutabagas in Malaga sauce

*(Sous iz repy ili brjukvy s malagoju)*

Peel 6 turnips or small rutabagas. Cut each into several equal parts, trim the pieces to make them even, and drop them into salted boiling water. When they begin to boil, turn into a coarse sieve and rinse with cold water. Transfer the vegetables to a saucepan, add 1 spoon butter creamed with 1 spoon flour, and pour in about 2 glasses bouillon and 1 glass Malaga. Add 1 spoon sugar and boil, covered, over a high flame until the turnips are well-stewed and the liquid has reduced to the consistency of a sauce. Serve.

INGREDIENTS

| | |
|---|---|
| 6 turnips or small rutabagas | 1 spoon flour |
| 1 spoon butter | 1 glass Malaga |
| 1 piece sugar | (2 glasses bouillon) |

## KOHLRABI
## (Repnaja kapusta)

### 394 Kohlrabi

*(Repnaja kapusta (Kohlrabi))*

Peel the kohlrabi and cut into small half-moons or stars. Wash the pieces and pour into a saucepan. Add 2–3 spoons bouillon and 1–2 spoons butter creamed with ½ spoon flour and stew, covered. When the vegetables are tender, add some salt and sugar. Serve with beef patties, sippets, or fried udder or liver.

INGREDIENTS

| | |
|---|---|
| 2–3 lbs kohlrabi | 1–2 pieces sugar |
| 1–2 spoons butter | ½ spoon flour |

## PARSNIPS
## (Pasternak)

### 401  Parsnips in bouillon

*(Pasternak na bul'one)*

Peel and cut into even, oblong pieces. Barely cover the pieces with bouillon prepared from beef or mutton, salt, and root vegetables. Add an onion to the pan and boil the parsnips until tender. Thicken with ½ spoon flour creamed with ½ spoon butter and bring to a boil, diluting with bouillon if necessary. Serve with boiled beef.

## GREEN AND WHITE BEANS
## (Zelenaja i belaja fasol')

### 403  Green beans

*(Zelenaja fasol')*

Remove the ends from 2 lbs of young, green string beans. Wash and cut obliquely. Pour the beans into a crock, add ½ lb butter or more, cover the pot, and set in the oven to stew. Add salt after the beans have finished cooking. For flavoring, add a little fine sugar. Mix and return to the oven briefly. Serve with sippets made from white French bread, 1½ lbs corned beef, ham, the smoked and fried lower jaw of a wild boar, brains, patties, or tongue.

## SORREL, SPINACH, CRESS, GOOSEFOOT, AND RADISH TOPS
## (Shchavel', shpinat, salat, lebeda, red'kovnik)

### 408  Creamed sorrel

*(Sous iz shchavelja)*

Pick over 4–5 lbs sorrel and wash in several changes of cold water. Dry, chop fine in a wooden bowl, and transfer the sorrel and its juice to a stoneware pot. Cover the pot, boil the sorrel until tender in its own juice, and rub through a sieve. Return the sorrel to the pot and add about 1 teaspoon salt and 2–4 pieces of sugar. Cream 1 teaspoon flour with a small spoon of fresh butter or Finnish butter, which first may be fried with ½ finely chopped onion. Add the roux, with or without the onion, to the sorrel and boil thoroughly. If it is too thick, add bouillon or ½ or 1 glass very fresh sour cream. The sorrel may be mixed with spinach.

Serve with sippets made of white bread or bread made from sifted wheat (*belyj ili sytnyj khleb*). Or, serve with ham, poached eggs, patties, *amourettes*, omelets, fried liver, or fried slices of smoked ham. In that case, half the indicated amount of sorrel is sufficient.

INGREDIENTS

4–5 lbs sorrel before trimming, or 2½     1 spoon butter
   glasses marinated sorrel     1 teaspoon flour
2–4 pieces sugar     (½–1 glass fresh sour cream)

### 409 Creamed spinach

(*Sous iz shpinata*)

Pick over 4–5 lbs spinach, that is, tear off the stems entirely from the leaves. Wash the leaves in several changes of cold water to remove all the dirt and plunge them into a large quantity of salted, boiling water with 1 spoon baking soda. Boil until tender, drain in a fine sieve, and rinse with cold water. When the water has drained away, chop the spinach fine, rub through a fine sieve, transfer to a stoneware pot, and add 2–4 pieces sugar. Cream ½–1 spoon butter with 1 teaspoon flour, fry* thoroughly, and add to the spinach. Mix and, before serving, add a glass of raw (*syroj*) or boiled cream. Heat until it is very hot, but do not let it boil.

Serve with sippets, poached eggs, chopped [hard-boiled] eggs, omelets, fried liver, patties, smoked ham, or fried brains. In that case, half the indicated amount is sufficient.

INGREDIENTS

4–5 lbs spinach, before trimming     1 teaspoon flour
½–1 spoon butter     2–4 pieces sugar
1 glass cream

*Molokhovets used the verb prokipjatit', which means to boil thoroughly, but "fry" seems to describe the process more exactly since no additional liquid is added at this point.

## BEETS AND BEET GREENS
### (Svekla i svekol'nik)

### 415 Creamed beets

(*Sous iz svekly*)

Boil, or preferably bake, about 3 lbs beets. Peel and very finely chop. Fry 1 spoon finely chopped onion in 1½ spoons butter and add ¼ spoon flour and the beets. Mix everything together, add ¾ glass sour cream, salt, and 2–3 spoons vinegar and bring to a boil. Some people add sugar or honey.

To serve the beets with hare and black grouse, omit the flour and sour cream, but add several spoons of rich bouillon instead.

Garnish with sippets of white or sieved wheat bread (*sitnyj*), small sausages, patties, fried mutton breast, or smoked ham fried in butter. Cf. garnishes.

INGREDIENTS

| | |
|---|---|
| 3 lbs beets | vinegar |
| ⅓ [*sic*] spoon flour | salt |
| 1½ spoons butter | ¾ glass sour cream or bouillon |
| (½ onion, if desired) | |

## Cauliflower, Savoy Cabbage, and Brussels Sprouts
### (Tsvetnaja kapusta, ital'janskaja, brjussel'skaja)

### 417 Cauliflower

*(Tsvetnaja kapusta)*

Remove the leaves from a head of cauliflower and the membrane [from the stalks]. Soak the florets in cold water for an hour, then drop them into boiling, salted water. Add ½ spoon butter, cover the pan, and simmer on a low fire for 15 to 20 minutes. When the cauliflower is tender, drain it in a coarse sieve, and arrange on a small, deep platter with the stems of the cauliflower toward the center and the florets outwards.

To serve, pour on Polish sauce, that is, brown ½ lb butter and add 6 spoons stale, grated French bread. Serve when the sauce has browned and dried out slightly.

INGREDIENTS

| | |
|---|---|
| 3–6 heads of cauliflower, according to size | ½ spoon butter |
| | salt |

### 423 Italian or Savoy cabbage

*(Kapusta ital'janskaja ili safoj)*

Cut off the outer leaves and quarter the heads. Rinse and drop into salted boiling water. Let the water come to a boil twice and drain the cabbage. Line the bottom of a saucepan with several thin slices of pork fat, place the cabbage on top, and add 1 spoon butter. Cover with bouillon and boil until tender. Fry ½ spoon butter with 1 spoon flour, dilute with the bouillon, and boil thoroughly. Beat 2 egg yolks and dilute with the hot sauce, stirring briskly. Heat until very hot, but do not let it boil. Pour the sauce over the cabbage arranged on a platter.

INGREDIENTS

| | |
|---|---|
| 4 heads of Savoy cabbage | 1 spoon flour |
| 1½ spoons butter | (2 egg yolks) |
| ⅛ lb pork fat | salt |

## Ordinary Fresh Cabbage and Sauerkraut
### (Prostaja svezhaja i kislaja kapusta)

### 426  Fresh cabbage with butter and crumbs
#### · (Svezhaja belaja kapusta s maslom i sukharjami)

Remove the outer leaves from 1 head of cabbage and cut into 6–8 pieces. Drop into hot water, bring once to a boil, and drain in a coarse sieve. Lightly press the cabbage and spread it out evenly on the bottom of a saucepan. Cover with good bouillon, a few parsley leaves, and 1 onion. Cover the pan and boil until tender, but do not overcook. To serve this cabbage without sauce, pour browned butter with rusk crumbs over it.

Remove the outer leaves from a head of fresh cabbage and cut into quarters, at right angles, but not all the way through. Boil in salted water until the cabbage is completely tender, transfer the whole head onto a platter, and pour on browned butter with rusk crumbs.

### 429  Stewed sweet and sour cabbage
#### (Tushonaja kapusta kislo-sladkaja)

Remove the outer leaves from 1 large or 2 small heads of cabbage. Grate the cabbage, barely cover it with water, add 1 ½–2 spoons butter, and stew, covered. When the cabbage is almost tender, add a little sugar and vinegar, or preferably 2–3 peeled and finely chopped sour apples or apple juice. Remove the cover and boil away almost all the sauce until the cabbage browns slightly. It is usually served with fried small sausages and with goose.

### 430  Stuffed cabbage pudding
#### (Puding iz farshirovannoj kapusty)

Remove the outer leaves from 2 heads of cabbage, halve each head, and drop into salted boiling water. Bring once to a boil and turn into a sieve. Cut out the core, separate the leaves, sprinkle with salt and pepper, and place in a saucepan. Add a piece of ham, 1 carrot, and 2 onions studded with 4 cloves. Cover with bouillon and simmer over a low fire until done. Turn the cabbage into a sieve to drain and [reserve the bouillon]. Transfer the cabbage to a saucepan greased with butter, interlaying with stuffing and strewing with nutmeg. Pour in about 2 spoons bouillon, place a light weight [on top], and set in boiling water to steam. To serve, arrange on a platter and pour on brown sauce.

For the stuffing, clean a young chicken or use 1½ lbs veal or beef. Finely chop the meat and pound it in a mortar. Add a French roll soaked in milk and squeezed out, salt, pepper, nutmeg, and 1 spoon butter. Pound thoroughly again and rub through a fine sieve. If the mixture is too thick, add cream or bouillon.

## 432  French stuffed cabbage

*(Farshirovannaja kapusta po-frantsuzski)*

Remove the green leaves from 3–4 small heads of cabbage, halve each head, and drop into salted water. Let the cabbage come to a boil twice, drain in a coarse sieve and, when it has cooled, cut out the cores. Stuff a forcemeat between the leaves, fold each half into a kind of oblong head of cabbage, and tie it up with thread. Arrange the parcels of cabbage in a saucepan greased with ½ spoon butter and scatter several pieces of butter on top. Set the pan on coals, cover with a lid, and spread hot coals over the lid. Let the cabbage brown slightly.

For the stuffing, chop 1 piece of roast veal and mix with boiled, peeled crayfish claws and tails. Add 1 spoon chopped beef suet, ½ French roll soaked and squeezed out, ¾ glass sour cream, 1 egg yolk, 1 egg, 1 spoon crayfish butter, nutmeg, and salt. Mix thoroughly.

INGREDIENTS

3–4 small heads of cabbage
1 spoon butter

*For the stuffing*
veal, 1 lb or more
20–30 crayfish
1 spoon beef suet

½ white French roll
¾ glass sour cream
3 eggs
1 spoon crayfish butter
nutmeg
salt

## 438  Sauerkraut with caviar

*(Sous iz kapusty s ikroj)*

Boil 3 lbs shredded sauerkraut, adding only enough water to prevent it from burning. When it has cooked, drain in a coarse sieve. Melt ½ lb Finnish butter in a skillet, stir in the sauerkraut, and fry both together. Pour salted water over caviar that has just been removed from a fresh fish, mash it fine, mix with the sauerkraut, and let it boil thoroughly over the fire. The caviar will impart a fine flavor to the sauerkraut. This dish may be served with patties, small sausages, or fried fish. On fast days, substitute olive oil for the Finnish butter. Add enough caviar so that the sauerkraut appears as if it were strewn with poppy seeds.

INGREDIENTS

½ glass caviar                           3 lbs shredded sauerkraut
½ lb butter

### 439  Moscow sauerkraut and meat stew in a skillet, or Moscow *soljanka*

*(Moskovskaja seljanka na skovorode)*

This *soljanka* must be thick. Mostly it is eaten for breakfast, but at dinner, it should precede the bouillon.* Finely grate 1 onion, fry in ¼ lb butter, and stir in about 1½ lbs shredded sauerkraut. Stew, covered, until cooked, stirring so it does not burn. Sprinkle on ½ spoon flour, mix everything together, and transfer half the sauerkraut to a skillet. Add a layer of various kinds of cooked meat cut into small pieces, such as beef, veal, ham, chicken, various game, etc., and cover with the rest of the sauerkraut. Decorate the top with finely chopped salted cucumbers, cornichons, olives, marinated mushrooms and, if desired, truffles or small sausages. Pour on the sauce left from cooking the meat, brown in the oven, and serve from the same skillet.

Fresh cabbage may be used instead of sauerkraut, in which case, it should be shredded and dropped into boiling water. When it begins to boil, remove with a slotted spoon and place in a saucepan with butter. Add 2–3 finely chopped sour apples and stew until done.

INGREDIENTS

1½–2 lbs sauerkraut                      1 onion
¼ lb butter                              2 cucumbers
½ spoon flour                            10 cornichons
1½–2 lbs various meats                   10 olives
10 marinated mushrooms                   1–3 truffles

*It seems odd to serve this before bouillon. Perhaps Molokhovets considered it a substitute for zakuski. For more on menus and mealtimes, see the Introduction.*

## ASPARAGUS
### *(Sparzha)*

### 447 Asparagus with sabayon
*(Sparzha s sabaionom)*

Peel the asparagus, wash it, and cut off any stalks that are too long. Tie up in bundles with Holland string.* Boil in salted water until tender. Lay out on a fine sieve and remove the strings. When the water has drained off, transfer to a platter lined with a napkin, arrange with the tips to the middle, and cover with a napkin to keep warm.

Serve sabayon sauce separately.

*Since Holland cloth was any sturdy linen or cotton cloth, Holland string was presumably any plain, sturdy linen or cotton cord. The advice here was to avoid hemp, the ordinary Russian cord, which would have imparted an off taste to delicate foods like asparagus.*

## POTATOES
### *(Kartofel')*

### 455 Baked potatoes
*(Kartofel' pechenyj)*

Wipe off the potatoes without washing them. Bury them in the coals of a Russian stove or bake in the oven, turning frequently so that they do not burn. Serve for breakfast and pass salt and butter separately.

INGREDIENTS

3/4–1 *garnets* potatoes

### 468 Fried potatoes à la lyonnaise*
*(Zharenyj kartofel' à la lyonaise)*

Peel and wash 1 *garnets* potatoes, slice them, and rub them dry with a napkin. Melt fat, but definitely not butter, in a saucepan or a deep skillet. Bring it to a boil, add the potatoes, and fry them over a high fire, shaking the skillet. When the potatoes have browned, remove them with a slotted spoon so that the fat drains off. Then salt them and sprinkle with lemon juice, if desired. These crisp potatoes are extraordinarily tasty. Serve them with beef steak or other beef dishes. If serving them with beef steak, choose very small potatoes and serve them whole, not sliced.

To economize, the potatoes may be boiled first in water and quickly peeled before they cool. If they are large, slice them and fry in butter.

If serving the potatoes with roast meat, half the amount will be sufficient.

*Onions dominate Lyonnaise cuisine and are a critical ingredient in the classic French rendition of this dish. Molokhovets' version, lacking onions, is really misnamed. It is worth noting that a somewhat abbreviated version of this recipe appeared in her first edition under the heading "Fried potatoes," without the more pretentious, and inaccurate, phrase "à la lyonnaise."*

### 472  Potato pudding with ham

*(Puding kartofel'nyj s vetchinoju)*

Cream ¼ lb butter until white, beat in 3 eggs and 3 egg yolks, and add about 1½ glasses mashed, boiled potatoes and ½ lb finely chopped ham. Mix thoroughly and pile into a mold greased with butter. Set in the oven and, when the pudding is ready, turn it out onto a platter. Strew with cheese and pour on hot butter.

INGREDIENTS

| | |
|---|---|
| 2½ spoons butter | ½ lb ham |
| 6 eggs | ⅙ lb cheese |
| ½ *garnets* potatoes | 1–2 spoons butter |

### 474  Potatoes in bechamel sauce

*(Kartofel' pod beshemelem)*

Wash, boil, peel, and slice potatoes. Grease a tin or silver saucepan with butter, add a layer of potatoes, dot with pieces of butter, and strew with grated cheese. Then add another layer of potatoes, butter, and cheese. Pour on bechamel sauce, that is, mix ⅛ lb butter with ½ glass flour and dilute with 2½ glasses milk. Boil thoroughly several times and add salt. Beat in 2 eggs and add, if desired, greens. Pour over the potatoes and bake in the oven.

½ lb of thinly sliced ham may be added to the potatoes.

INGREDIENTS

| | |
|---|---|
| ⅔ *garnets* potatoes | 2 eggs |
| ⅜ lb butter | greens |
| ½ glass flour | ¼ lb cheese |
| 1 bottle milk | |

### 475  Potato pudding

*(Zapekanka ili kartofel'naja drachena)*

Peel, wash and boil about 4½ lbs (*os'mushka*)* potatoes until tender. Pour off the water and immediately mash the potatoes in the pan with a small wooden pestle until they are cool. Add salt and 1 full spoon butter and mix until they whiten. Stir in 1–1½ glasses milk, add 2–3 egg yolks or 1 egg, and mix again. Transfer to a sauté pan greased with butter, strew the top with rusk crumbs, and bake in a hot oven. Serve with roast meat, or better, for breakfast.

INGREDIENTS

| | |
|---|---|
| about 4½ lbs potatoes | 3 spoons butter |
| 1–3 eggs | 1–1½ glass milk |

*This word indicates ⅛ of a unit and here probably means ⅛ pood or about 4½ American lbs. The German translation of 1877 translated os'mushka as 1 garnets. See Table of Weights and Measures for more information.

### 479  Potatoes stuffed with mushrooms

*(Kartofel' farshirovannyj gribami)*

Finely chop cleaned and boiled fresh or dried boletus mushrooms. Fry 2 finely chopped leeks in 1 spoon butter and mix with the mushrooms. Add ½ grated French roll and 1 egg and mix thoroughly.

[Cut off the tops] of peeled and washed raw potatoes, hollow out the interiors, fill with the prepared stuffing, and replace the cut-off tops. Place in a saucepan and pour on ⅓ glass melted butter and ½ glass each of mushroom bouillon and regular bouillon. Cover and boil until tender.

INGREDIENTS

| | |
|---|---|
| 24 large potatoes | 2–3 allspice |
| ⅛ lb dried mushrooms, or ½ dish fresh mushrooms | 2 leeks |
| ¾ lb butter | ½ white French roll |
| 1 egg | [1 glass bouillon in all] |

### 482  Potatoes stuffed with sprats

*(Kartofel' farshirovannyj kil'kami)*

Select very large potatoes, peel them, and boil until half-cooked. Scoop out the interiors, [reserve the pulp,] and fill the potatoes with the following stuffing. Mash the reserved pulp and add morels boiled in bouillon and several finely chopped sprats. Mix and stuff the potatoes. Paint with egg, sprinkle with rusk crumbs, and fry in butter in a skillet. Serve with a sauce prepared from flour, butter, lemon juice, nutmeg, bouillon, and a little sour cream.

INGREDIENTS

about 24 large potatoes
6 morels
12 sprats
2 eggs
2–3 rusks
¼ lb butter

*For the sauce*
½ glass flour
⅓–½ glass sour cream
¼ lemon
1 spoon butter
nutmeg

### 484  Potatoes stuffed with forcemeat

*(Kartofel' farshirovannyj mjasnym farshem)*

Wash 24 large potatoes, peel thoroughly, and cut off a little from the bottom so they will stand upright. Cut off the tops and carefully hollow out the interior with a knife without piercing the walls. Drop into salted cold water, but be sure to bring it to a boil a couple of times. Remove the potatoes carefully with a slotted spoon, cool, and dip in egg and rusk crumbs. To prepare the stuffing, finely chop ½ lb raw, boiled, or roast veal or beef. Fry lightly in ½ spoon butter and add 5–6 fried morels, ¼ glass fresh sour cream, about 2 spoons bouillon, salt, pepper, and 3–4 ground rusks. Boil thoroughly. Stuff the potatoes, replace the cut-off tops, and bake in the oven in a sauté pan greased with butter. Drizzle butter on top.

When they have baked, the lids may be removed and replaced by boiled, halved crayfish tails. Sprinkle greens on top. These stuffed potatoes are mostly served for breakfast. To serve, pour on mushroom or sour cream sauce.

INGREDIENTS

24 large potatoes
½ lb meat
¼ lb butter
¼ glass sour cream
5–6 morels

3–4 rusks
(24 crayfish tails)
greens
ingredients for sauce

## MUSHROOMS
## (Griby)

### 488  Fried mushrooms

*(Griby zharenye)*

White, red (*krasnyj*),* and other mushrooms are prepared the same way, that is, clean and wash them and cut them up. Dip in flour. Melt ¼ lb butter in a skillet or a saucepan (if desired, fry 1 onion in the butter), add the mushrooms and some salt, and fry over a medium flame. Fry first on one side, then turn over and fry the other side. When the mushrooms are cooked, pour in ½ glass sour cream. Bring once to a boil, sprinkle with parsley and dill, and serve.

INGREDIENTS

| | |
|---|---|
| 1 full plate cleaned mushrooms | ½ glass sour cream |
| 1 spoon flour | (1 onion) |
| ¼ lb butter | pepper |
| parsley | salt |

*By white mushroom (belyj grib), Molokhovets meant Boletus edulis; red mushroom—Leccinum aurantiacum or Boletus aurantiacus—was the common name for podosinovik (lit.: under the aspen). Given the passion with which Russians hunt for wild mushrooms, it is surprising that Molokhovets included only nine named varieties in her recipes.

### 492 Morel sauce

*(Sous iz smorchkov)*

Clean sand and other impurities from morels, wash them in water until clean, finely shred, and drop into boiling, salted water. When the water begins to boil, turn the morels into a coarse sieve and rinse with cold water. Place in a saucepan with melted butter and fry until done. In a separate saucepan, bring to a boil ½ spoon butter and ½ spoon flour, dilute with 2–3 glasses bouillon, and bring to a boil 2 or 3 times until the sauce thickens. Add salt, nutmeg, lemon juice, and ⅛ lb butter or ½ glass sour cream. Mix with the morels and bring to a boil. Add chopped parsley and lemon juice. Serve with beef, veal breast, etc.

INGREDIENTS

| | |
|---|---|
| 2 lbs morels | ¼ lemon |
| ¼ lb Finnish butter | parsley |
| ½ spoon flour | salt |
| 1 spoon butter, or ½ glass sour cream | nutmeg |

### 492a Very tasty sauce from dried boletus mushrooms

*(Ochen' vkusnyj sous iz sushonykh belykh gribov)*

Wash 18–24 dried mushrooms and boil until almost cooked. Pour off the mushroom bouillon, which should be used the next day for borshch, sorrel *shchi*, or mushroom soup. Or, give the leftover bouillon to the servants. Pour 3 glasses of strained [meat] bouillon over the mushrooms and boil until done. Add 2–3 spoons fresh or sour cream, a little black pepper, and some salt. Serve, leaving the mushrooms whole as if they were fresh. Sprinkle with dill.

## TOMATOES
## (Pomidory)

### 494  Stuffed tomatoes or eggplants

*(Pomidory farshirovannye ili baklazhany)*

Make a small incision in large, ripe tomatoes and clean out the entire interior with a hairpin (*shpil'ka*). Fill with veal stuffing (if desired, mix this stuffing with boiled rice). After filling the tomatoes, dip them in flour and fry in butter in a skillet. Then transfer them to a saucepan, arranging them so that the stuffing will not fall out, pour on enough bouillon to barely cover them, and boil, but watch that they do not overcook. When they are done, pour on sour cream, bring once to a boil, and serve.

INGREDIENTS

| | |
|---|---|
| 12 large tomatoes | 1 onion |
| 1 spoon flour | 1 spoon butter |
| ¼ lb butter | 2 eggs |
| ½ glass sour cream | salt and pepper |

*For the stuffing*
1 lb veal

## LENTILS
## (Chechevitsa)

### 497  Lentil purée

*(Pjure iz chechevitsy)*

Pick over lentils, wash in warm water, and pour into a saucepan. Add raw ham, 2 peeled onions, 2 carrots, and 2 leeks. Cover with bouillon, bring to a boil, and set in the oven for 2 hours to stew until tender. Remove the ham and root vegetables and rub the lentils through a fine sieve. Fifteen minutes before serving, mix with butter and dilute with Malaga or bouillon that has been brought to a boil. Only then add salt to taste. Serve with sippets.

If serving with roast meat, 1 lb lentils will suffice. [In that case, reduce] the other ingredients proportionately.

INGREDIENTS

| | |
|---|---|
| 3 glasses, or, 1½ lbs lentils | ½ lb ham |
| 2 onions | ¼ [lb] butter |
| 2 carrots | (½ glass Malaga) |
| 2 leeks | |

## ARTICHOKES
### *(Artishoki)*

### 500 Artichokes with green peas and mushrooms

*(Artishoki s zelenym gorokhom i gribami)*

Clean and boil artichokes in salted water until tender. Boil shelled sugar peas in water, drain, and add butter to the peas. Serve with the artichokes, pouring butter fried with rusk crumbs over them. These artichokes may be stuffed with finely chopped fresh mushrooms, cooked in sour cream. Pour the mushrooms into the central cavity of each artichoke, interspersing some between the leaves.

INGREDIENTS

| | |
|---|---|
| about 15 artichokes | 3–4 rusks |
| 2 glasses shelled peas | ½ plate mushrooms |
| ½ lb butter | 1 spoon butter |
| 1 spoon sour cream | dill |

### 503 Artichokes with Hollandaise sauce

*(Artishoki s gollandskim sousom)*

Remove the green leaves from 15 artichokes and soak them in cold water for an hour. Boil in salted boiling water and let them cool. Remove some of the artichoke heart with a sharp knife and add to the sauce,* prepared as follows. Melt 1 spoon butter in a saucepan, stir in 1 spoon flour, and dilute with 1½ glasses bouillon. Boil thoroughly, stirring, and add nutmeg, a little lemon juice, and 2–3 beaten egg yolks, diluting them first with a little of the cooled sauce. Cook, stirring, until the sauce begins to emit steam. Add the artichokes to the sauce, heat, and serve.

*As with Tartar sauce, Molokhovets' version of this sauce differs significantly from the classic French Hollandaise.

## ONIONS
*(Luk)*

### 504 Stuffed onions in dough

*(Farshirovannyj luk v teste)*

Select several very large onions, wipe them without peeling, and drop them into boiling water for several minutes. Remove and let cool. Cut off the top and carefully scoop out the interior with a knife, leaving the outer wall intact. Add 5–6 more peeled, [raw] onions to the onion pulp removed from the interior. Cut up or finely chop all the onions together, pour the chopped onions into a saucepan, add ¾ glass cream, and boil until they are as soft as kasha. Rub through a sieve. Remove a fillet from a large young chicken, scrape it with a knife, and pound in a mortar. Add 4 eggs, ½ lb melted butter, 4 finely chopped sprats, a little grated cheese, a French roll (without the crust) soaked in milk and squeezed out, and a little salt and pepper. Add the onion purée, mix everything thoroughly, and fill the prepared onion shells.

After this, prepare short pastry, roll it out as thin as possible, and cut it into rectangles with a cutting wheel. Place a stuffed onion in the middle of each rectangle and fold up the four corners of dough to form four leaves, as it were, on top. Pinch the leaves together tightly in the middle and paint the sides with egg white, using a feather. Let them dry slightly and bake in a saucepan or small basin with fat, Russian butter, or half fat and half Russian butter.

Serve at the table with the following cream sauce. Melt 1 spoon butter in a saucepan, mix with 1 spoon flour, and dilute with 1½ glasses cream. Add a little salt, pepper, and, if desired, the juice of ½ lemon. Boil thoroughly and serve in a sauceboat.

## JERUSALEM ARTICHOKES
*(Zemljanyja grushi)*

### 507 Jerusalem artichokes

*(Zemljanyja grushi)*

Peel the artichokes as well as possible, dropping them immediately into cold water with vinegar. Wash and boil in salted water with a little vinegar. Add ½ spoon flour mixed with ½ spoon butter. To serve, arrange on a platter edged with pastry. Pour on butter with rusk crumbs or sabayon sauce.

INGREDIENTS

3–4 lbs Jerusalem artichokes                    vinegar

½ spoon butter  
½ spoon flour  
salt  

⅜ lb butter  
4–5 rusks  
Or sabayon sauce  

## APPLES
## *(Jabloki)*

### 509  Stewed apples for roast meat

*(Tushonyja jabloki k zharkomu)*

Peel, quarter, and core 6–10 apples. Place them in a saucepan and add 1 spoon butter, 2 spoons fine sugar, and 3–4 spoons water. Cover the pan and boil until tender. Serve with roast meat, such as beef, duck, or goose. Dried apples may also be used in this recipe.

INGREDIENTS

6–10 apples  
1 spoon butter  

2 spoons sugar

## PUMPKIN
## *(Tykva)*

### 511  Fried pumpkin

*(Tykva zharenaja)*

Peel and slice a pumpkin* and fry in butter. Fry ½ spoon flour in ½ spoon butter, add 1 glass sour cream, and bring to a boil. Pour the sauce over the pumpkin and serve.

*Pumpkins and squashes are often used interchangeably in Russian recipes. The same easy substitution, and confusion over nomenclature, existed in colonial New England.*

## CHESTNUTS
## *(Kashtany)*

### 513  Chestnuts in red wine sauce

*(Sous iz kashtanov s krasnym vinom)*

Peel chestnuts, scald, and remove the skins. Place in a saucepan and add ⅛ lb butter, salt, 1 glass bouillon, ½ glass red wine, ⅛ lb sugar, and a little dried bouillon. Boil until the chestnuts turn reddish-brown. Edge a platter with pastry. Make a thick dough by mixing together ½ lb flour and 2 eggs without water. Roll out as thin as possible and trim both edges evenly with a knife. Scallop one edge with the knife and paint the other edge with egg yolk. Surround the platter with the dough and paste it firmly to the bottom. Dry out slightly in the oven for 5 minutes. Transfer the chestnuts to the platter and pour on some of the same sauce in which they were boiled.

Chestnuts prepared in this manner may be served with beef dishes, in which case, use only half the indicated proportions.

INGREDIENTS

1 lb chestnuts
⅛ lb butter
½ glass red wine
about 3 pieces sugar
¹⁄₁₀ lb dried bouillon

*For the dough*
½ lb flour, that is 1½ glasses
2 eggs

# VARIOUS GARNISHES FOR DISHES OF GREENS AND ROOT VEGETABLES
### *(Raznye garniry dlja kushan'ev iz zeleni i koren'ev)*

### 516  Brain patties

*(Kotlety iz mozgov)*

Boil the brains from 2 calf's heads in salted water with vinegar, allspice, and a bay leaf. Rub through a fine sieve and add 3–4 spoons grated roll, a little allspice and black pepper, and a small finely chopped onion fried in ½ spoon butter. Add parsley, 2 egg yolks, and 1 egg. Mix everything together and form into patties. Dip each patty in egg, coat with rusk crumbs, and fry in butter.

These patties are served also with truffle sauce.

INGREDIENTS

2 pairs of calf's brains
vinegar
salt
a bay leaf
allspice and black pepper
5 eggs

parsley
½ onion
½ French roll
4–6 rusks
¼ lb butter

### 518 Fried udder

*(Vymja zharenoe)*

Boil until tender in salted water, slice, dip both sides in flour or rusk crumbs, and fry in butter (2 spoons butter, 2 spoons flour).

### 520 *Amourettes*

*(Amoretki)*

Drop the marrow from beef bones into boiling water for a very short time. Remove with a slotted spoon, cut up, and place in a saucepan. Barely cover with bouillon, add salt and ½ spoon butter, and bring to a boil over a high flame.

When the *amourettes* have browned, remove and use them to garnish spinach, sorrel, peas, etc.

### 527 Kidneys

*(Pochki)*

Boil 2 pork kidneys or 1 beef kidney in bouillon or water. Slice, dip in egg, and strew with 3–4 [ground] rusks or 2 spoons flour. Fry in 1 spoon butter.

### 529 Smoked lower jaw of a boar

*(Kopchenaja nizhnjaja cheljust' veprja)*

Thinly slice ¾–1 lb smoked meat from the lower jaw of a boar. Dip in egg and dried, grated, or ground crumbs made from rye or fine wheat bread and fry in 1 spoon butter. Use to garnish a platter of greens or root vegetables.

### 532 A pastry for garnishing vegetables

*(Rod pirozhnago dlja ogarnirovanija zeleni)*

Beat until white 6 egg yolks, ⅛ lb butter, and ¼ glass fine sugar. Add ½ lb flour and mix again. Turn the dough onto the table and roll out lightly to the thickness of a finger. Cut into various shapes, strew with sugar, and, using a feather, paint with butter. Bake in a moderate oven about 10 minutes to brown lightly.

### 534 Calf's liver sausages

*(Sosiski s farshem iz teljach'ej pechenki)*

Scald a calf's liver with boiling water, boil until half cooked, and let cool. Finely chop and add 1 spoon butter, ½ finely chopped onion fried in 1 spoon butter, ½ French roll moistened in water or milk and squeezed out, 1 spoon sour cream, 2 egg yolks, salt, 3 allspice, 3 black peppercorns, and nutmeg. Fill a beef intestine with this stuffing, as for sausages. Fry in the oven, pouring on ⅛ lb butter. Cut into pieces and use to garnish a platter of greens or root vegetables.

These sausages, as well as sausages made from buckwheat groats, may be served with *shchi*.

# 5

# Beef, Veal, Mutton, and Pork

## (Govjadina, teljatina, baranina, svinina)

## BEEF

### (Govjadina)

*Remarks:* Proportions are designed for 6–8 persons. For 9–12 persons, increase the proportions by 1½. For 13–18 persons, double the proportions. For 19–23 persons, triple the proportions. In the latter case serve the food on 2 platters.

For a good piece of boiled beef, use rump or round for the bouillon (*ssekgorbushka, oguzok, ili kostrets*)* For stewed beef, use rump or round. For cooked (*zharenyj*)** beef, use chuck or plate (*tonkij ili tolstyj kraj*). For roast beef, use the short loin or ribs (*filejnaja chast'*). For beef steaks, use the short loin or sirloin (*vnutrennyj filej ili vyrezka*). For cutlets use the short loin or sirloin, also short ribs, round, or chuck (*naruzhnyj filej, tonkij kraj, kostrets, ili tolstyj kraj*). For chopped beef or raw meat stuffing for *pirogs*, etc., use round or chuck (*ssek-seredina, bedro, perednaja lopatka, ili kostrets*).

In general boiled beef is served for reasons of economy rather than health since all the nourishment is boiled out of it. But those who prefer the taste of boiled beef, and not just to economize, should avoid the usual practice of putting meat into cold water. Instead, it should be put directly into boiling water so that the meat will contract and retain its juices.

When it has boiled, it may be sprinkled with crumbs and placed in a hot oven for a very short time.

---

*Since Russian and American cuts are not identical, I have included the Russian names so that readers can compare Molokhovets' diagram of meat cuts with those now used in America.

**The basic meaning of zharenyj is "cooked at a high temperature with fat but without liquid." Native speakers now prefer to translate zharenyj as fried, but Molokhovets used the word very loosely to indicate any of several cooking procedures which may or may not include frying. Under the heading "Cooked Beef" (Zharenaja Govjadina), she includes recipes that require boiling, baking or roasting, stewing, grilling, and spit-roasting. There are separate words or expressions to describe each of these processes unambiguously in Russian, but all of them are subsumed under the more general term zharenyj. For further discussion, see the section on "Cooked Beef."

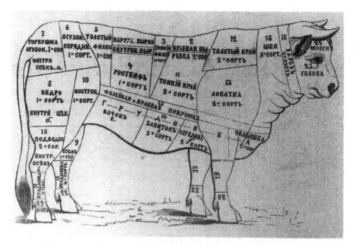

Diagram of cuts of beef. Most cuts are identified as
1st, 2nd, 3rd or 4th grade. From Molokhovets,
1897.

## BOILED BEEF
### (*Razvarnaja govjadina*)

### 538 Boiled beef garnished with root vegetables
#### (*Govjadina razvarnaja s garnirom iz koren'ev*)

(To serve 6–8 persons as a second course.) In order to have a good-sized piece
of boneless meat after cooking, prepare the bouillon from a piece of beef weighing
at least 6 lbs, but not less than 5 lbs. Wash and trim the meat and cook with root
vegetables as usual. Transfer the meat to a platter, slice, and surround with cabbage, attractively cut-up carrots, turnips, potatoes, and Italian macaroni. Each
vegetable should first be cooked in bouillon before being transferred to a saucepan
with 1 spoon butter. Then pour in 2 glasses rich bouillon, add salt, and set over a
low fire for ½ hour.

To serve, more butter browned with rusk crumbs may be poured over the
vegetables (¼ lb butter, 4–6 rusks).

INGREDIENTS

½ *garnets* potatoes
1 small head cabbage
1 turnip or rutabaga
[5–6 lbs beef]

2 carrots
1 spoon butter
salt

### 556 Boiled beef with piquant sauce

*(Govjadina razvarnaja s pikantnym sousom)*

Brown 1 spoon flour in 1 spoon melted butter, pour in 1 glass light berry vinegar and 1½ glasses bouillon, and boil thoroughly. Add a few cornichons, marinated white mushrooms, pickles, and some cayenne pepper. Bring to a boil and pour over the beef.

### 607 Fried boiled beef

*(Govjadina varenaja podzharenaja)*

Fry 1–2 finely chopped onions in 1 spoon butter. Add allspice and chopped parsley or dill, mix, and cool. Beat in 4 eggs and mix well. Slice beef that has been boiled in bouillon and dip each slice in the egg mixture. Place in a frying pan greased with butter, strew with grated bread crumbs, and brown in the oven. Remove from the oven and pour on the following sauce. Moisten and caramelize 2 pieces sugar, add 1 spoon water, and bring to a boil. Transfer to a saucepan and add 1 spoon butter, 1½ glasses bouillon, 1 scant spoon powdered *Sareptskaja* mustard, and some vinegar or about ½ glass wine. Mix, bring to a boil, and pour over the hot meat.

INGREDIENTS

| | |
|---|---|
| 1–2 onions | 2 pieces sugar |
| 2 spoons butter | parsley and dill |
| 1 scant spoon *Sareptskaja* mustard | several allspice berries |
| 4 eggs | ½ glass wine or vinegar |
| salt | 2–3 spoons grated bread |

## STEWED BEEF
### *(Tushonaja govjadina)*

### 608 Traveler's beef, or *Boeuf à la mode*

*(Dorozhnaja govjadina ili boeuf à la mode)*

Lard an 8 lb piece of beef rump (cf. Remarks) with pork fat cut into pieces as thick as a finger. Place the beef in an earthenware pot and add 1 bottle of red beer vinegar* and ½ bottle of Rhine wine vinegar or any good, ordinary wine vinegar. Add 25 allspice, 2 onions, 1 *zolotnik* cloves, and 5 bay leaves. Marinate the beef in the vinegar for 3 days, then add 1½ glasses cold water to the marinade, seal the pot with dough, and set in a hot oven for 4 hours. Remove the pot from the oven, pour off all the liquid, strain, and mix with 1 raw egg and 4 sheets of gelatin. If

there is not enough liquid to cover the beef, add some good brown bouillon.**
Bring to a boil 3 times, strain, pour over the beef, and cool. Beef prepared in this
manner may be taken on the road while traveling in the summer. It is very tasty
and will not spoil; also it is good as a snack at teatime.

INGREDIENTS

| | |
|---|---|
| 8 lbs beef | 2 onions |
| 1 lb pork fat | 1 zolotnik cloves |
| 1 bottle red beer vinegar | 2 [sic] bay leaves |
| ½ bottle ordinary wine vinegar | 4 leaves gelatin |
| 25 allspice | |

*Red beer vinegar was prepared by fermenting a mixture of soured beer, hot rye bread, black
treacle or molasses, and honey.
**Brown bouillon was a well-colored stock which Molokhovets obtained by browning the beef
with onions and carrots in the pan before adding water.

### 610  Italian *stufato*

(Stufat po-ital'janski)

Stud a good, tender 6 lb piece of beef with pork fat, garlic, peppercorns, and
cloves. Strew the meat with salt, tie it up firmly with stout cord, and place in a
glazed earthenware pot after greasing the interior with ¼ lb Finnish butter. Add 2
glasses red Médoc wine* and 5 bay leaves. Seal the pot securely with dough, set it
in the oven immediately after baking bread, and leave it there until the next
morning. Remove the dough and add another glass of Médoc. If there is not
enough liquid, add some meat bouillon. Add canned tomatoes and set the pot on
the edge of the stove to simmer slowly. At dinner time, remove the meat from the
pan, slice, and cover with the sauce in which it cooked. Instead of baking, *stufato*
may also be prepared entirely on top of the stove. To have it ready for dinner at 4
p.m., begin preparing it at 8 a.m. This will allow time for the pot, which must be
tightly sealed, to simmer slowly and constantly. Add the wine and tomatoes 2
hours before dinner. This is a real Italian *stufato* which is not widely known.

INGREDIENTS

| | |
|---|---|
| 6 lbs beef | 1 bottle Médoc |
| ¼ lb pork fat | ¼ lb butter |
| 2–3 cloves garlic | canned tomatoes |
| peppercorns | 5 bay leaves |
| cloves | |

*The use of Médoc, a French Bordeaux, in "a real Italian stufato" sounds faintly ludicrous to
the ears of modern purists. Why not an appropriate Italian wine? I do not know when Italian wines

*began to be imported into Russia, but the fact of the matter is that Molokhovets seemed to be unaware of them. See Appendix A for a full list of wines, spirits, and liqueurs mentioned in the book.*

### 613 Hussar's bake

*(Govjadina, pod nazvaniem gusarskaja pechen')*

Pound thoroughly a lean piece of boneless chuck. Salt the meat and cook on a spit or in the oven, basting it first with butter and then with its own juice. Slice diagonally and interlay with the following stuffing: Chop 2 onions, squeeze out the moisture, and mince the onions again until they are very fine. Mix the onions with 1 spoon butter, ⅛ lb grated Swiss cheese, a little pepper, salt, 2 egg yolks, and ½ lb grated white bread, or enough to form a rather thick mixture. Stir thoroughly, stuff the roast, and set the meat in a stewpan. Pour on the strained pan juices, cover the pot, and stew on the top of the stove or in the oven for ½ hour.

INGREDIENTS

| | |
|---|---|
| 3 lbs beef | ⅛ lb Swiss cheese |
| ¼ lb butter | ½ white French roll |
| 2 onions | 2 egg yolks |
| salt and pepper | |

### 615 Stewed beef with horseradish stuffing

*(Govjadina tushonaja s farshem iz khrena)*

Brown a piece of beef sirloin or chuck on a spit, basting with butter. Transfer the meat to a stewpan and add a variety of cut-up root vegetables and several slices of pork fat. Sprinkle with 2 small spoons vinegar and add 1½ glasses bouillon, 1 glass wine, and 4–5 cloves or some lemon zest. Cover the pan and stew on a low fire until tender. Using a knife, make several slits in the meat and stuff the gashes with grated horseradish fried in butter. Arrange the beef on a platter, skim the fat from the sauce, strain the sauce, and pour it over the meat.

The cost of this dish may be reduced by omitting the wine.

Instead of horseradish, the meat may be garnished with various root vegetables, such as 2 carrots, 1 parsley root, 1 rutabaga, and 2 onions, all attractively cut up. Boil the vegetables in water, drain, and finish cooking them with the broth from the meat. Cover the pan with a lid, boil up once or twice, and serve.

INGREDIENTS

| | |
|---|---|
| 3 lbs beef | 1 onion |
| 1 carrot | 1 leek |
| 1 parsley root | 2–3 bay leaves |
| 1 celery root | 4–5 cloves or zest from ½ lemon |

15–20 allspice

6 spoons grated horseradish

¼ lb pork fat

about ¼ lb butter

vinegar

(1 glass wine)

### 618 Stewed beef in an earthenware pot

*(Govjadina tushonaja v gorshke)*

Salt a piece of beef and lard it with ham or smoked tongue and pork fat. Place several slices of pork fat or butter, some root vegetables, and spices in an earthenware pot. Add the beef and pour in the wine and about 2 spoons vinegar, lemon juice, or gooseberry juice. Stew over a low fire, adding a little water as necessary so that the meat will cook on all sides. When the meat is tender, remove it from the pot and skim the fat from the sauce, adding more bouillon if necessary. Strain the sauce and pour over the meat. Garnish with potatoes, beets, red cabbage, saffron milk-cap mushrooms, boletus mushrooms, and carrots. Stew each of these vegetables separately in butter before adding to the meat.

INGREDIENTS

3 lbs beef

⅛ lb pork fat

¼ lb ham or smoked tongue

1 onion

1 celery root

1 carrot

1 parsley root

1–2 bay leaves

15–20 allspice

½–1 glass wine

vinegar, juice of ½ lemon, or

    gooseberry juice

¼ lb pork fat or ½ lb butter

*For garnishing*

root vegetables

mushrooms, etc.

### 620 Cold jellied beef

*(Kholodnoe zharkoe)*

Lard a piece of beef with pork fat, sprinkle with salt, and set the meat aside for an hour. Melt butter in a stewpan, add the beef, and set the pan on top of the stove, turning the meat frequently to brown on all sides. For 6–8 lbs of beef, add 2 cleaned and finely cut up calf's feet, 2–3 finely sliced carrots, 1 beet, several onions, 1 leek, 1 celery root, some allspice, and 2 bay leaves. Cover the vegetables with water and stew, covered, over a low fire for about 3 hours. Transfer the meat to a deep platter, strain the sauce, pour it over the meat, and set in a cold place to congeal. To serve, slice the beef with its jellied sauce.

INGREDIENTS

| | |
|---|---|
| 6–8 lbs meat | 2–3 onions |
| 2 calf's feet | 1 leek |
| 2–3 carrots | 1 celery root |
| ¼ lb butter | 10–15 allspice |
| 1 large beet | 1–2 bay leaves |

## COOKED BEEF
### (Zharenaja govjadina)

[*Translator's note:* The process described by the verb *zharit'*—the searing or cooking at high temperature with butter or fat but without liquids—is often translated as "frying," but is really a definition by exclusion and can mean almost anything as long as the meat is not cooked in a liquid. Possibilities include frying, grilling, broiling, roasting, baking, and spit-roasting. Under this same heading, however, Molokhovets also included recipes (18 out of 49, or 37% of the total) that call for cooking the beef in a liquid, either on top of the stove or in the oven. Some of these dishes require an initial or final browning, but others do not. Only eight recipes in this section (16% of the total) involve frying in the limited English sense. "Cooked" beef may sound like a very feeble translation, but I can think of no other word in English that is comprehensive enough to cover all the processes described in the recipes that follow.]

### 625  Beef served in a large roll
#### (Govjadina zharenaja v bol'shoj bulke)

Boil a 3–4 lb piece of tender beef in a small amount of water with 1 onion, 1 leek, 1 parsley root, salt, and a little pepper. When the meat has cooked and is at the peak of its juiciness, slice it.* Strain the bouillon in which the meat was cooked, skim off the fat, and bring the sauce to a boil. While the bouillon is boiling, melt ⅛ lb of Finnish butter in a small saucepan. Fry 1 chopped leek in the butter and when it is tender, add 1 spoon wheat flour and ½ glass sour cream. Mix everything together, cook thoroughly, and dilute with the bouillon in which the meat was cooked. Boil until the sauce thickens and then remove the pan from the fire. Mix 3 egg yolks well and gradually dilute with the hot sauce, stirring to prevent the eggs from curdling.

Bake a bun (*sdobnaja bulka*) large enough to contain all the beef with its sauce. Cut off the top of the bun and remove the soft interior. Butter the inside walls and strew with Dutch cheese or, preferably, Parmesan cheese. Then fill with layers of sliced beef, which should not be sliced until the last moment to prevent its drying out. Sprinkle each slice of beef with cheese and pour on some of the prepared sauce. Replace the top of the bun which was cut off earlier. Heat the filled bun in a hot oven for 30 minutes before serving. Do not remove the meat from the roll when serving, but eat it like a pâté en croûte (*pashtet*)** because the crust is very tasty. Pass the remaining sauce separately in a sauceboat.

INGREDIENTS

3–4 lbs beef
1 parsley root
1 leek
pepper
¼ lb butter
1 spoon flour
½ glass sour cream
3 egg yolks

2–3 spoons cheese

*Short pastry for the bun*
1½ lbs flour
⅛ lb butter
2–3 eggs
½ kopeck dry yeast
1¼ glasses milk

*Since the meat should be sliced at its juiciest, but not until needed, the timing of the cooking is more critical than it might appear (see the later instructions).*

**The Russian pashtet is related to the German Pasteten, which, in turn, can be dated back to the first French versions of about 1000 A.D. In the Middle Ages, these pastries and pies became an art in themselves and often were the high point of festivals and feasts of the period. In the nineteenth century, they became fashionable in Germany as they did in Russia. (Küchen-Lexikon, 364.)*

### 628 Superb meat, another way

(*Prevoskhodnoe zharkoe, drugim manerom*)

On the day before it is to be served, thoroughly pound a 5–6 lb piece of beef chuck with a wooden pestle and rub with 2 teaspoons fine salt and 1 small spoon finely ground black pepper. Place in an earthenware pot, cover, and set aside until the next day. Two hours before dinner, place the meat on a roasting pan and dot with pieces of good Russian butter, ¼ lb or more. After the meat has browned, add a little water. Serve the meat strewn with rusk crumbs.

This roast may be varied by serving with one of the following: fried potatoes or potato croquettes; rutabaga purée; onion purée; turnip purée; lentil purée; bean purée; stewed and fried mushrooms and morels; various stewed root vegetables; stewed cucumbers; celery root purée; carrot purée; chestnuts in sauce; chestnut purée; carrots and green peas; kohlrabi; bechamel sauce; Brussels sprouts; any fresh or marinated salad; apple compote; crayfish sauce; stewed apples; creamed pumpkin; buns (*pyshki*); stewed potatoes and sauce made from salted cucumbers; herring sauce; field mushroom sauce; sweet and sour onion sauce; cherry sauce; red currant sauce; strong sauce; dried mushroom sauce.

INGREDIENTS

3–5 lbs of chuck beef
¼ lb butter

salt and black pepper
3–4 rusks

## 630 Baked beef roll filled with eggs (used while hunting)

*(Govjadina zharenaja s jaichnitseju, upotrebljaemaja na okhote)*

Prepare an omelet from 6 eggs and boiled chopped ham, green onions, and butter. Lightly beat a tender piece of beef chuck with a rolling pin into a large thin cutlet, sprinkle with salt and pepper, and arrange the omelet on top. Roll up the meat to resemble an oblong bun, surround with small slices of pork fat or bits of butter, and place in the oven. To serve, slice and pour over Strong sauce #302.

INGREDIENTS

| | |
|---|---|
| 3 lbs tender beef | 6 eggs |
| ½ spoon butter | green onions |
| ½ lb boiled ham | salt and pepper |
| ¼ lb pork fat or butter | Strong sauce #302 |

## 632 English beef

*(Govjadina po-anglijski)*

Thoroughly pound a tender piece of beef, either ribs or sirloin, and marinate it for several days in a mixture of half water and half spiced vinegar. After removing the meat from the marinade, pierce or slit it in several places with a knife, and stuff the slits with beef suet chopped with salt, pepper, and cloves. Roast on a dripping pan, basting with the meat juices. Fry ½ spoon flour in 1 spoon butter, pour in bouillon, and add 2 spoons capers, ½ spoon white mushroom powder or truffles, ½ or 1 glass table wine, and several seeded lemon slices. Stir over the fire, skim off the fat, and dilute with the pan juices released from the beef. Bring the sauce to a boil and pour over the meat.

INGREDIENTS

| | |
|---|---|
| 3 lbs tender beef | 1 spoon butter |
| spiced vinegar | 1 spoon flour |
| ½ lb beef suet | 2 spoons capers |
| 4–5 cloves | ½ spoon mushroom powder |
| 4 black peppercorns | ½–1 glass wine |
| 6 allspice berries | ½ lemon |

## 635 Beef Stroganov with mustard

*(Govjadina po-strogonovski, s gorchitseju)*

Two hours before serving, cut a tender piece of raw beef into small cubes and sprinkle with salt and some allspice. Before dinner, mix together ¹/₁₆ lb (*polos'mushka*) butter and 1 spoon flour, fry lightly, and dilute with 2 glasses bouillon, 1 teaspoon of prepared *Sareptskaja* mustard, and a little pepper. Mix, bring to a boil, and strain. Add 2 tablespoons very fresh sour cream before serving. Then fry the beef in butter, add it to the sauce, bring once to a boil, and serve.*

INGREDIENTS

| | |
|---|---|
| 2 lbs tender beef | 2 spoons flour |
| 10–15 allspice | 2 tablespoons sour cream |
| ¼ lb butter | 1 teaspoon *Sareptskaja* mustard |
| salt | |

*Molokhovets' simple recipe did not endure. Already by 1912, Aleksandrova-Ignat'eva was teaching the students in her cooking classes to add finely chopped sautéed onions and tomato paste to the sauce, a practice which still turns up in modern Soviet and American recipes, with or without the addition of mushrooms. It is worth noting that Aleksandrova-Ignat'eva served this dish with potato straws, which have become the standard modern garnish for Beef Stroganov. (See Aleksandrova-Ignat'eva, Prakticheskija osnovy kulinarnago iskusstva, 611, 441; Guba and Lazarev, Kulinarija, 117; and Volokh, Art of Russian Cuisine, 266–268.)*

### 636 Beef filet, larded with truffles or anchovies

(*Govjadina-filej, shpikovannyj trjufeljami ili anchousami*)

Trim the veins and excess fat from a filet of beef, sprinkle with Madeira and lemon juice, strew with salt and ground pepper, and set the meat aside for 3 hours. Lard the filet with 5 truffles sliced into long, thin pieces, wrap the meat in buttered paper, and secure the meat onto a spit. Grill over a high flame, basting with butter, or bake in a roasting pan in the oven. After the meat has cooked, remove the paper and slice the meat. Arrange the sliced meat on a platter and pour on Strong sauce #302 made with the remaining truffle scraps and 2–3 additional truffles. Serve immediately at the table.

Instead of using truffles, a beef filet may be larded with anchovies and split lengthwise. Other boned pieces of beef may also be used.

INGREDIENTS

| | |
|---|---|
| 3 lbs beef | 2–3 spoons butter |
| 1 wineglass Madeira | 5 allspice berries |
| ½ lemon | 5 black peppercorns |
| 7–8 truffles or 10–20 anchovies | salt |

### 641 Roast beef

(*Rostbif*)

Salt 20 lbs well-marbled sirloin including the filet and bones and place in a sauté pan. Add 3–4 spoons butter and roast for nearly 2 hours in a hot oven, heated as for bread. Turn the meat occasionally to brown evenly and baste frequently with its own juices. Alternatively, the beef may be cooked on a spit. Serve the whole roast at the table or slice it. Garnish with small roasted or fried potatoes, grated horseradish, and Brussels sprouts. Skim the fat from the meat juices and pass the sauce separately in a sauceboat. If the meat is frozen, set it in the oven frozen without defrosting. This roast beef will be extraordinarily good, if, as it stands to reason, the meat is well-marbled and fresh. A piece of beef of this size will serve 18 persons for dinner.

INGREDIENTS

| | |
|---|---|
| 20 lbs beef | potatoes |
| 3–4 spoons butter | horseradish |

### 646 Beef steaks à la Hamburg, for breakfast (per portion)

*(Bifsteks po-gamburgski k zavtraku)*

Slice a piece of chuck. Do not pound the meat, but only trim the slices with a knife, brush them with olive oil, and strew with salt. At the same time, heat ½ spoon good butter on a small tin skillet. When the butter browns, add 1 spoon finely chopped onions, followed immediately by a slice of meat. When one side has browned, turn the meat over without pressing it with a knife. Spread 1 spoon of white or saffron milk-cap mushrooms stewed in butter on one half of the steak and place several small whole boiled potatoes on the other half. Drop an egg on each side and when the eggs just set, pour on 2 spoons of greatly reduced game bouillon. Serve at the table directly from the pan, setting the skillet on a small plate of the same size.

### 647a Grilled marinated beef strips

*(Basturli)*

Sprinkle salt and pepper on 3 lbs of beef sirloin. Marinate in vinegar for 48 hours and slice as for beef steaks. Thread the slices onto spits or iron skewers and grill, turning them over well-heated coals.

### 648 Cutlets in the Italian style

*(Govjadina v rode zrazov po-ital'janski)*

Slice beef into cutlets, each as thick as a finger. Pound well and sprinkle with salt. Fry lightly in a pan with 1½ spoons butter, an onion, and various root vegetables. Fry 2–3 spoons grated roll crumbs in ½ spoon butter, add 5–6 ground black peppercorns and 4 cloves. Spread the mixture over the meat, stack the cutlets one upon the other, and pour on wine, 1½ glasses bouillon, and the juice of ½ lemon. Cover the pan with a lid and stew until tender. Sprinkle on 1 spoon flour and add sour cream and capers. Replace the lid and cook on top of the stove for another 15 minutes. Strain the sauce, pour over the cutlets, and serve.

INGREDIENTS

| | |
|---|---|
| 3 lbs beef | ¼ lb butter |
| 1 onion | ½–1 glass wine |
| 1 carrot | ½ lemon |
| 1 parsley root | 1 spoon flour |
| 1 celery root | 2 spoons capers |
| 2–3 spoons grated roll crumbs | 4 cloves |
| 5–6 black peppercorns | [sour cream] |

## 651 Stewed beef cutlets

*(Klops)** *

Cut a piece of short loin or chuck into 6–9 pieces. Pound the pieces with a wooden mallet and then with the blunt edge of a knife. Sprinkle with salt and set aside for an hour or two. Grease the bottom of a stewpan with butter and add a bay leaf and allspice and top with the meat slices, sprinkling each with finely chopped onion and flour or grated, stale black bread. Add about 2 spoons water, cover, and stew until tender, shaking the stewpan to prevent the meat from burning, adding bouillon if necessary. To serve, turn out onto a platter and garnish with boiled potatoes. Add ½ glass sour cream to the sauce.

INGREDIENTS

| | |
|---|---|
| 2½ lbs tender beef | (½ glass sour cream) |
| 4 spoons finely chopped onion | 1 spoon butter |
| bay leaves | ¾ *garnets* potatoes |
| salt and pepper | ½ lb bread or ½ glass flour |

*This recipe is another of Molokhovets' misnomers. Klops, a German dish, are meatballs, usually made by combining several kinds of ground meat.

## 653 Ground beef patties with horseradish

*(Zrazy rublenyja s khrenom)*

Chop up a piece of beef, trimming off any veins. Beat in 2 egg yolks and 1 egg, mix well, and form into flat, round patties. Spread with horseradish fried with a grated roll in 1 spoon butter. Sprinkle with flour and a finely chopped onion, squeezed dry. Melt butter in a stewpan, add the patties, and fry on one side. Add about 2 glasses bouillon, cover the pan, and stew slowly. To serve, garnish the patties with fried or boiled potatoes and pour on the strained sauce.

Stewed sauerkraut may be spread on the patties instead of horseradish.

INGREDIENTS

3 lbs beef
3 eggs
3–4 spoons grated horseradish
3–4 spoons grated roll crumbs

1 onion
1 spoon flour
2–3 spoons butter
½ *garnets* potatoes

## 655 Lithuanian stuffed cutlets

*(Zrazy litovskija farshirovannyja)*

Slice a tender piece of beef into thin cutlets and pound them thoroughly. Sprinkle with salt and pepper and set aside for ½ hour. Fry 2 finely chopped onions in butter, mix with grated rye bread or a roll, and add salt, pepper, nutmeg, 4–8 chopped, boiled boletus or field mushrooms, and 1 egg. Mix together, spread some of this stuffing on each cutlet, and roll up into a tube (if you do not have the knack of rolling them neatly, tie each one with string). Sprinkle with flour and place them in a stewpan with rendered kidney fat or melted butter. Stew, covered, over a low flame. When they have browned on all sides, pour in about 2 glasses of bouillon. If the sauce boils away, then add some more.

One glass sour cream, a little mushroom bouillon, and a handful of grated rye bread crumbs may be added to this bouillon. Bring to a boil and pour over the cutlets on the platter. The cutlets should stew for a total of 45 minutes.

INGREDIENTS

2½ lbs boneless beef
salt and pepper
nutmeg
2 onions
½ spoon butter

½ white French roll or ¼ lb rye bread
⅛ lb mushrooms
1 egg
¼ lb kidney fat or butter
(½–1 glass sour cream)

## 665 Hunter's stew* from leftover beef with sauerkraut

*(Bigos iz ostavshejsja zharenoj govjadiny, s kisloju kapustoju)*

Line a saucepan with ¼ lb or more pork fat, add 3 glasses squeezed out, slightly soured cabbage [i.e., sauerkraut], and top with another ¼ lb pork fat or bacon. Pour on bouillon, cover with a lid, and stew. When the sauerkraut has half cooked, remove the pork fat and cut it into small cubes together with the pork skin. Mix with the cooked beef, game, etc., cut up in the same manner. Stir the cubed meat and pork fat into the sauerkraut, sprinkle with pepper, and add ½ spoon flour fried until golden with 1 spoon butter and a finely chopped onion. Stew, covered, until the sauerkraut browns slightly, stirring often with a spoon to prevent the sauerkraut from burning. When the sauce boils away, everything may be turned out onto a platter. Pour butter fried with finely pounded rusks over the sauerkraut and mixed meats, bake, and serve for breakfast or for dinner before the bouillon.**

*Bigos is a national dish of Poland and formerly was a great favorite on hunting expeditions. According to Lesley Chamberlain, bigos functioned "like 'cassoulet' in French cookery" and similarly made use of leftover meats rich in fat. (See Chamberlain, The Food and Cooking of Eastern Europe, 244.)*

**Normally bouillon or soup was the first course served at the table (the zakuski were served in another room while the guests were standing). Every once in a while, however, Molokhovets suggested serving a very heavy dish like this one before the lighter bouillon. Moscow sauerkraut and meat stew in a skillet (Chapter 4) is another example. Why such a heavy dish would be consumed before a light bouillon is a mystery to this commentator.*

## 666  Beef tripe

### (Volovij rubets)

Clean the tripe* as follows. Remove the tripe from the interior of a slaughtered ox, cow, or calf, not letting them touch the ground. Cut a small opening, remove the filth, and carefully turn inside out so that the dirty side is outside. Sew up the hole with a strong thread to prevent any filth from falling inside. Wash with a brush in water, changing the water frequently. Therefore, it is better to wash them in a river. Then drop them into moderately hot water, stirring with a spatula. When the black sputum begins to separate from the tripe, pour in cold water and clean them. Soak the tripe in cold water for 24 hours, changing the water every four hours. Then wash well and halve each piece lengthwise. Drop into boiling water, remove from the water, and scrape with a knife until completely clean. Spread the pieces out on a table to dry. Sprinkle with salt, pepper, and chopped ginger, and for those who like it, chopped garlic and field mushrooms. Wind into an oblong roll, tie up with thread, and surround with root vegetables and spices. Cover with cold water and bring to a boil. Then cover with a lid and transfer to a hot oven. Bake for four or more hours until tender and the sauce has reduced to the proper consistency. Remove from the oven, discard the threads, cut into pieces, and arrange on a platter. Pour butter on top and strew with grated bread and Parmesan cheese. Brown in a hot oven and serve.

*Tripe is the first and second stomach of a ruminant. Plain tripe is the first stomach, honeycomb is the second.*

# VEAL

## (Teljatina)

*Remarks:* In general, the same parts of the animal are used for veal as for beef, but they serve other purposes. The hindquarters, including the kidneys and two ribs, are used for roasts (*zharkoe*). The forequarters are sometimes used for roasts, but mostly for ground patties and herring casseroles (*forshmak*) and for stuffing pies. The bones are used for soup. The carcass between the forequarters and the hindquarters is divided into four parts. The lower half or breast is split lengthwise and is used for soups and sauces. The upper half or cutlet part is also split lengthwise, with each half yielding about 10 chops with bones. The head and feet are used for soups, sauces, and aspics. The tongue, being small, is served together with the head. The pluck, including the heart, is used for sauces and for stuffing pies. The liver is fried and used in sauces and for stuffing pies. The brains are used for sauces and in pies. The tripe is used for soup and sauces. The stomach, well-washed, salted, and dried, is used for making cheese, such as Dutch and Swiss. Calves' pelts should be stretched out on sticks, dried immediately, and then cured into leather.

The tastiest veal is from a 6-8 week old milk-fed (*otkormlennyj*) calf with white flesh.*

To assure an excellent, delicate flavor from a roasted hindquarter, soak the veal overnight in salted water (use two pounds of salt to a pail of water). But it is much better to bury the meat and keep it in the ground until just before cooking.

Veal is also soaked in milk, then washed in hot water and larded with fresh suet.

The French strew veal with pepper, salt, bay leaves, onion slices, and lemon, rub it with olive oil, and set it aside for several hours before cooking.

Cook the veal on a spit or in a roasting pan on crisscrossed birch twigs, basting as frequently as possible with its own juices. Cook for 1-2 hours according to size.

To prepare boiled veal for serving at the table, cut the meat into portions, wash it, and plunge it into boiling water. Bring to a boil twice, skim the liquid, and remove the veal. Let this water or bouillon settle. Meanwhile, rinse the meat in cold water and place it in a clean saucepan. After the bouillon has cleared, carefully strain it through a napkin over the meat so as not to disturb the sediment.

For a roast for 6-8 persons, use a small whole hindquarter weighing from 4½ to 5 pounds. If cutting off a single piece from a large hindquarter of 10 or more pounds, then cut off only a 3 lb piece. These portions are intended for 6-8 persons. For 9 to 12 persons, increase the proportions by 1½. For 13 to 18 persons, double the proportions. For 19 to 24 persons, triple the proportions.

*Only milk-fed veal has white flesh. If the animal has fed on anything other than milk, its flesh will have a pinkish cast from the iron in its diet.

### 674  Ordinary cooked veal

(Teljatina zharkoe obyknovennoe)

For this dish use a veal hindquarter including the kidneys and 2 ribs. Wash the meat, soak in salted water for several hours, and then douse it with vinegar. Sprinkle with salt and cook on a spit over a large fire, basting with 1–2 spoons butter according to the fatness of the veal. If cooking the veal in a roasting pan, then pour on several spoons water. Arrange a bed of crisscrossed birch twigs in the pan and place the meat on the twigs, turning it frequently and basting with butter (⅛ lb) so that it will be juicy and melt (razsypchata) in your mouth. Transfer the meat to a platter, strew with 2 grated rusks, and pour on the juices from the pan.

A piece of veal weighing 10–15 lbs should be cooked at least 1½ hours and if 4–5 lbs about ¾ hour. Serve with sauerkraut and other fresh and marinated salads. Any roast for 6–8 persons is better served whole at the table; if it is carved beforehand, it should be sliced with a sharp knife and the parts reassembled to give the appearance of a whole roast. The bones left over from the roast may be used to prepare soup, such as potato soup. 1–1½ pounds of beef may be added [to the bones] with root vegetables, ⅓ garnets potatoes, parsley, and dill.

Any leftover veal may be sliced the next day and sautéed in a skillet with 1 spoon butter. Pour bouillon over the meat and add the jellied sauce from the roast. To serve, strew with greens and serve very fresh sour cream in a separate bowl.

Or, slice the remaining roast veal the next day. Grease a tinned saucepan with butter, strew with rusk crumbs or a grated roll, add the veal slices, and sprinkle with chopped green onions and grated roll crumbs. Dot with Finnish butter, pour on 1 glass sour cream, and warm in the oven for 15 minutes before serving.

*Remarks:* The fatty caul sold with the hindquarter of veal and lamb may be used for preparing caul sausages (sal'niki).

### 677  Home-style spit-roasted veal

(Zharkoe teljatina po-amaterski)

(Proportions for 20–25 persons): Salt the hindquarter of a well-marbled calf in the evening, sew it up in a clean napkin* or piece of linen, and bury 2 arshins deep in the good earth. The next day, that is, 12 hours later, dig it up and remove the cloth but do not wash the veal. Grate about 4 glasses homemade white cheese, neither too fresh nor too fatty, and mix in several spoons sour cream and a generous amount of green onion, dill, and parsley. Cut the veal to the bone in three places and spread this thick stuffing between the slices. Skewer the slices together with thin birch spills so that the stuffing will not fall out when the meat is turned over. Lard the entire piece with pork fat and roast on a spit, basting with butter and the juices released from the meat and collected in a sauté pan placed beneath the spit. Transfer the meat to a platter, remove the spills, and strew with rusk crumbs. Serve with a salad of some kind.

INGREDIENTS

| | |
|---|---|
| 15–20 lbs veal | about 1 glass sour cream |
| ¾ lb pork fat | green onion |
| ½ lb butter | dill |
| 3–4 rusks, or bread crumbs | parsley |
| about 4 glasses cheese | |

*Formal, monogrammed linen napkins in nineteenth-century Europe were much larger than they are today. A square yard of cloth was not unusual.

## 680  Gourmet veal with caviar sauce

*(Gastronomicheskaja teljatina s sousom iz ikry)*

Using thin, long pieces of ham, pork fat, and lamprey, lard a good 3–4 lb piece of veal leg with each ingredient in several places. (Use marinated lamprey as for *zakuski*.)* Put the veal in a stewpan with thinly sliced onions, leeks, celery root, and parsley root. Pour in white wine (*vin de Graves*) and enough good bouillon to cover the meat. Add black peppercorns, allspice berries, and finely shredded lemon zest to the sauce. Cook the meat until tender, remove, slice, and arrange on a platter. Pour on the following sauce. Strain the remaining bouillon in which the meat was cooked and skim off the fat. Add fresh sturgeon caviar, or lacking that, good pressed caviar diluted with the bouillon. Add fresh butter, 1 spoon lemon juice, and about 1–2 *lots* dry bouillon. Bring this sauce to a boil, pour over the meat, and serve.

INGREDIENTS

| | |
|---|---|
| 3–4 lbs veal | 10 allspice |
| ½ lb ham | zest of ½ lemon |
| ½ lb pork fat | 2 full spoons sturgeon caviar |
| 10 pieces lamprey | 1 spoon butter |
| ½ celery root | ½ parsley root |
| 1 leek | ½ spoon lemon juice |
| 1¼ glasses wine (vin de Graves) | ⅛ lb dry bouillon |
| 10 black peppercorns | |

*To marinate freshly caught lamprey, the fish were dried thoroughly, rubbed with olive oil, and fried slightly. They were then packed in wooden vats with bay leaves and vinegar boiled with *allspice, pepper, and cloves. According to Alan Davidson, the lamprey is among "the most primitive of living vertebrates." The lamprey looks like an eel (although it is both jawless and boneless) and most eel recipes are also suitable for the lamprey. (Davidson, North Atlantic Seafood, 176–177.)*

### 682  Stewed veal with cherries

*(Zharkoe teljatina s vishnjami)*

Wash and lightly salt a boneless piece of veal from the hindquarter. Make about 20–30 slits with the point of a knife and insert one or two pitted cherries in each. When the veal is well-larded with cherries, place it in a sauté pan, pour on butter, and strew with finely ground cardamom and cinnamon. Brown in a hot oven, then baste again with butter, strew with flour, and return to the oven, covering with a lid. When the meat has half-cooked, add ½ glass each Madeira and cherry syrup, 1 glass bouillon, and some butter. Continue cooking, covered, and baste frequently with the sauce until the meat is done. Arrange the meat on a platter and pour on the sauce, adding several more spoons bouillon if necessary.

INGREDIENTS

| | |
|---|---|
| 3 lbs veal | ½ glass Madeira |
| 1½ glasses or ½ lb cherries | ½ glass cherry syrup |
| 2 whole cardamom pods | 2 spoons butter |
| ½ teaspoon cinnamon | 1 spoon flour |
| salt | |

### 684  Veal chops with piquant sauce

*(Teljach'i kotlety s ostrym sousom)*

Fry 9–10 veal chops as usual in ¼ lb good butter until they are lightly browned, but do not let them overcook. Remove the chops from the pan and set aside. Add 2 teacups good fresh sour cream and 1½ glasses of soup bouillon to the butter in the pan. Chop fine or grind into a paste 18 small sardines, or lacking them, some Reval sprats,* or even a good Dutch herring. Add the fish to the sauce, boil thoroughly, and then add the chops and boil for another 3 minutes. Turn out onto a platter. When ready to serve, the sardine paste should be so soft (*mjagkij*) and so well combined that it will not separate from the sauce.**

*\*Reval was the German name for Tallinn, the capital of Estonia. The Estonians are noted for the high quality of their fish curing, especially Baltic herring and sprats, which have long been a staple food of the people. Even today marinated sprats are considered an Estonian delicacy. For directions for preparing "Real Estonian Sprats," see Kalvik, Estonian Cuisine, 99; see 59–65 for recipes using Baltic herring and sprats. Alan Davidson also has a good discussion of the Baltic herring and sprats in Estonian cuisine. (Davidson, North Atlantic Seafood, 31, 356–357.)*

*\*\*This dish is reminiscent of the Italian vitello tonnato although I am not suggesting any influence. The only tenuous connection is that perhaps Francesco Leonardi, chef to Catherine the Great, helped the Russian court to appreciate veal as cooked by the Italians.*

### 691 [Ground] patties, another way

*(Kotlety drugim manerom)*

Trim any gristle from the veal and finely chop. Add salt, 2–3 ground allspice berries, ½ white French roll soaked in milk and squeezed dry or several boiled potatoes, and ½ spoon butter. Mix thoroughly and chop fine. Form into twelve patties and insert bones* if any are available. Dip in egg, strew with rusk crumbs, and fry in butter on both sides. Pour over brown sauce with truffles. Or serve with creamed beets, carrots, dried peas, or stewed mushrooms.

INGREDIENTS

| | |
|---|---|
| 2½ lbs veal | ½ white French roll, or 3–5 potatoes |
| salt | ¼ lb butter |
| 2–3 allspice | 5 rusks |
| 1–2 eggs | |

*When shaping minced meat into patties, Molokhovets usually added a piece of bone so that each finished piece resembled a chop. In the same manner, the French usually add a short piece of raw pasta to their version of Cutlets Pozharski.*

### 699 Boiled veal breast with raisins

*(Grudinka varenaja s izjumom)*

Cut a fairly lean veal breast into pieces, each with 2 ribs. Bring to a boil once and skim the liquid. Remove the pieces, rinse in cold water, and strew with salt. Strain the veal broth, return the meat to the strained broth, and boil with root vegetables and spices until tender. Fry ½ glass flour in 1½ spoons butter and dilute with 3–4 glasses of strained veal bouillon. Bring to a boil several times and add ½ glass of washed and picked over sultanas,* several seeded lemon slices, 1–2 lumps of sugar, and ¼ glass table wine. Add the veal to this sauce and bring to a boil once more.

INGREDIENTS

| | |
|---|---|
| 1 veal breast or 3 lbs veal shoulder | 1½ spoons butter |
| ½ celery root | ½ glass flour |
| ½ leek | ½ glass sultanas |
| 1 carrot | 1 wineglass table wine |
| ½ parsley root | ¼ lemon |
| 1–2 bay leaves | 1–2 pieces sugar |
| (5–10 allspice) | |

*The title of this recipe calls for raisins (izjum) but the body of the recipe calls for sultanas* (kishmish). *Raisins are dried from grapes that have seeds; sultanas are dried from seedless varieties. For more on raisins, see the Glossary.*

### 704 Fried calf's head and feet with brown sauce

*(Zharenaja teljach'ja golovka i nozhki pod krasnym sousom)*

Halve a cleaned calf's head and remove the brains, which should be set aside for another dish. Boil the head together with moderately large, cleaned calf's feet in salted water with pepper, bay leaves, root vegetables and vinegar, which is essential. Remove the head and feet when the meat is tender and rinse with cold water. Remove the bones, and slice the meat or cut it into pieces, and place the meat under a press. Salt when cooled and dip each piece in egg and crumbs, then fry in butter.

Pour on brown sauce made with wine or sweet and sour sauce. Continue to boil the remaining bouillon with the leftover bones, adding extra meat. Use this for some sort of aspic (*majonez* or *zalivnoe*). In summer this will make 6 glasses of aspic and in winter 9 glasses. Or cut up the meat from the boiled feet, dip each piece into batter, and fry in 2 spoons butter.

INGREDIENTS

| | |
|---|---|
| 1 calf's head and 2 feet or 6 feet without the head | 1 carrot |
| | 1 parsley root |
| 10–15 allspice | 1 celery root |
| 2–3 bay leaves | 1 leek |
| 6 rusks | (1 onion) |
| 2 eggs | 2–3 spoons butter |

### 708 Calf's head with prune sauce

*(Golovka teljach'ja s sousom iz chernosliva)*

Clean a calf's head as thoroughly as possible. Remove the bones, wash the meat, and boil with root vegetables, spices, and vinegar. Cut the meat into pieces. Fry 1 spoon flour in 1 spoon butter, dilute with 2 glasses bouillon, and bring to a boil. Caramelize 1 piece of sugar and mix everything together. Add 2 lumps of sugar, the juice of 1/2 lemon, and 1/2 lb of washed prunes. Boil until the prunes are tender. Prepare a vol-au-vent by making 1 recipe of puff pastry. Form the dough into a rimmed circle and bake. Then transfer the pastry to a platter. Fill the vol-au-vent with the meat cut from the calf's head or with a chicken and pour on the sauce.

Continue to boil the remaining bouillon with the leftover chopped bones, 1 lb of meat, and vinegar. Use the bouillon to prepare an aspic for *zalivnoe* or *majonez*. This amount of bouillon will yield 4 glasses in summer and 6 in winter.

INGREDIENTS

1 large calf's head, or 1 small head
  plus calf's feet
1 carrot
1 celery root
1 parsley root
1 spoon flour
⅛ lb butter

3 lumps sugar
½ lemon
½ lb, or 1½ glasses prunes

*For the puff pastry*
½ lb butter
2 glasses, or ⅔ lb flour


## 709 Brain sausages

*(Sosiski iz mozgov)*

Wash 2 calf's brains, bring them to a boil once in salted water, and then chop them fine. Remove the crusts from 5 rolls costing 1 kopeck each, soak them in cream or in milk and, without squeezing them, mix them with the brains. Pound everything together and add ¼ lb Finnish butter, salt, pepper, nutmeg, 8 egg yolks, and 1 glass cream. Mash everything together and stuff sausage casings half full with the mixture. Boil them and, just before serving, fry them.


## 714 Stewed calf's liver in sauce

*(Teljach'ja pechenka tushonaja pod sousom)*

Wash one large calf's liver in water, soak it for 4 hours in milk, and rinse it in water. Remove the outer membrane and slice it crosswise, each slice as thick as a finger. Pound the slices lightly with a wooden pestle and strew with a little salt, pepper, allspice, and cloves, all ground. Dredge each slice in flour on all sides and sauté in a skillet with butter so that the blood still runs when pierced with a fork. Transfer the pieces to a stewpan and cover with the following sauce: sauté ½ finely chopped onion in butter, add 1 spoon flour, and fry lightly. Add 1 glass bouillon, ½ glass wine, 2–3 pieces of sugar, 1½ *lots* dry bouillon, and 1 spoon lemon juice. Bring all this to a boil, stirring, then strain the sauce over the liver arranged in the stewpan. Set the pan over a low fire and bring to a boil two or three times. Serve with potatoes, cucumbers, and a salad made of shredded fresh cabbage and sauerkraut.

INGREDIENTS

1 large or 2 small calf's livers
milk
salt
3 peppercorns and 3 allspice
1 spoon lemon juice

½ onion
½ glass table wine
2–3 pieces sugar
1½ *lots* dry bouillon
2 spoons butter

### 715a  Fried veal tripe and brains in sauce

*(Teljachij rubets pod sousom s mozgami)*

Clean the tripe and boil in salted water until tender. Cut into several pieces and arrange on a plate. Cover with another plate, weight it with a stone, and set it aside for 1 hour. Then remove the weights, dip the pieces of tripe in egg, strew them with rusk crumbs, and fry in butter. Treat the brains similarly. Boil them in salted water, let them cool, and then slice. Dip in eggs and crumbs and cook in butter with vinegar. Arrange the tripe and brains in alternate rows on the platter.

Pour on Sauce #277, adding lemon juice and wine.

INGREDIENTS

| | |
|---|---|
| veal tripe | 2–3 eggs |
| brains from one head | 6–8 rusks |
| ¼ lb butter | |

### 720  Sweetbreads in sauce

*(Sladkoe mjaso pod sousom)*

Soak 2 lbs of sweetbreads in water for two hours, then cook for about 15 minutes in boiling water. Remove, rinse in cold water, discard the membrane, and lard all over with ¼ lb finely cut up pork fat. Meanwhile, melt 1½ spoons butter in a stewpan, add 1 grated onion, stir in ½ spoon flour, and fry lightly. Dilute with 1 glass bouillon and add ½ cup grated cheese, a little salt, pepper, nutmeg, and 1 glass cream. Add the sweetbreads, cover, and cook until tender. Transfer the sweetbreads to a platter and cover with the sauce. If desired, a handful of picked-over and finely chopped field mushrooms may be added to the sauce with cleaned crayfish tails and 1 spoon crayfish butter.

### 727  Kidney tartines

*(Tartiny iz pochek)*

Fry the veal kidneys in butter, then slice. Also slice white French bread, coat each side with melted butter, and top with a slice of kidney. Drizzle on the butter in which the kidneys were cooked and strew with grated Parmesan cheese. Drizzle on some more butter and brown in the oven. Transfer to a platter and pour on any sauce which has collected in the pan.

INGREDIENTS

| | |
|---|---|
| 2 veal kidneys | 2 spoons grated Parmesan cheese |
| 2 spoons butter | 1–1½ white French rolls, or ⅝ lb |

# MUTTON
## *(Baranina)*

*Remarks:* Just as veal should be white, so mutton should be dark red and fatty. It should be hung for at least 2 days. Soak it in whey or sprinkle it with vinegar the day before it is to be used. Roast it on a spit or in a dripping pan, on birch sticks, and set it directly in the hot oven to brown quickly and seal the juices. Do not cook it for more than an hour; it is ready when the meat begins to emit steam.

### 729   Ordinary roast mutton
#### *(Baranina zharkoe obyknovennoe)*

Pound well a tender 3 lb piece of mutton or a small hind quarter weighing about 4½ lbs. Soak and wash the meat and lard it with shallots or, for those who like it, garlic. Salt it and place on a sauté pan. Pour on about 2–3 spoons water and brown the meat slowly in the oven, basting often with its own juice. Degrease the sauce and serve with one of the following: thick buckwheat kasha, boiled from 1 lb groats; potato purée; onion sauce or onion purée; haricot beans (boil the beans in salted water until half-cooked, spoon the beans around the mutton, and finish roasting together); or some kind of salad.

### 732   Mutton, like chamois
#### *(Baranina na podobie serny)*

Hang a hind quarter of mutton in the cold cellar for 3–4 days, then trim off the fat and membranes. Boil together ¾ glasses each vinegar and beer with peppercorns, bay leaves, and 5–6 spoons of crushed juniper berries. Pour the hot liquid over the mutton and marinate for 5 days, each day turning the meat. Then, wash the meat in clean water and lard it with ½ lb of smoked pork fat. Fry the mutton on a dripping pan, pouring on 2 spoons of butter. When the meat is almost cooked, cover with sour cream and cook until the sour cream turns golden. Transfer the mutton to a platter, slice, and cover with the strained sauce.

INGREDIENTS

| | |
|---|---|
| a hind quarter of mutton | 10 bay leaves |
| vinegar | ½ lb smoked pork fat |
| ½ spoon allspice | 2 spoons butter |
| 5–6 spoons juniper berries | ½ glass sour cream |

### 736 Mutton chops fried in batter and garnished with onion purée

*(Baran'i kotlety, zharenyja v kljare i ogarnirovannyja pjure iz luka)*

Bring 1 glass of flour and ¼ lb of butter to a boil about 5 times, dilute with 1 bottle of whole milk, and boil thoroughly. Peel and slice 10 onions, add 2 glasses of bouillon, and boil until tender. Rub through a sieve and add the onion purée to the bechamel sauce. Boil thoroughly and add salt. To prepare the meat, slice the cutlet part of the mutton into serving pieces, leaving a little bone with each, pound the meat thoroughly, and trim off the veins. Melt ⅛ lb butter in a skillet, fry the chops on both sides, salt them, and place on a platter to cool. Meanwhile prepare some batter. Heat 1 lb of Russian butter or fat (*fritjur*) in a pan until it emits steam. Dip each chop in the batter and fry in the oil (3 or 4 pieces at a time). When they have browned, ring the chops around a platter and pour the onion purée into the center. Dissolve ⅛ lb of dried bouillon in ½ glass water, bring to a boil, and pour over the chops arranged on the platter.

INGREDIENTS

9 mutton chops
1 lb Russian butter or fat
⅛ lb butter
⅛ lb dried bouillon

*For the batter*
1 glass flour
6 spoons milk

5 eggs

*For the onion purée*
10 onions
1 glass flour
1 bottle milk
¼ lb butter

### 741a Another Turkish mutton pilaf

*(Eshche pilav turetskij iz baraniny)*

Boil a piece of fatty mutton, preferably from the breast, in water with root vegetables and a piece of dry bouillon. Form a border of pastry around a platter and bake. Boil rice in the mutton bouillon, adding prunes, if desired. When the rice cools, 2–3 egg yolks may be beaten in. Add ½ spoon butter, nutmeg, and salt and mix well. Spread part of the rice on the platter and top with alternate layers of mutton and rice, finishing with a layer of rice. Strew with rusk crumbs and brown in the oven.

INGREDIENTS

1 breast, or 2½ lbs mutton
1 carrot

½ parsley root
½ celery root

2 onions
10–12 allspice
1–2 bay leaves
1½–2 *lots* dry bouillon
1½ glass rice
(2–3 egg yolks)
1½ spoons butter

nutmeg
salt
3–4 dry rusks

*For the pastry border*
2 eggs
1⅓ glasses flour

## 746  Breast of mutton with caraway sauce

*(Grudinka baran'ja s sousom iz tmina)*

Boil a mutton breast until tender with salt and root vegetables. Fry 1 spoon flour in 1 spoon melted butter, stirring constantly. When the roux has cooked, add 1 spoon each caraway seeds and sugar, dilute with some of the bouillon in which the breast was cooked, add 2 spoons vinegar, and bring the sauce to a boil. Arrange the meat on a platter and pour on the thickened sauce.

INGREDIENTS

1 mutton breast
½ parsley root
½ celery root
½ leek
2 onions
salt
1 carrot

*For the sauce*
1 spoon butter
1 spoon flour
1 spoon caraway seeds
1 spoon sugar
vinegar

## 748  Mutton caul sausage

*(Sal'nik iz livera i pechenki baran'ej)*

Boil the mutton pluck* in water with root vegetables, drain in a coarse sieve, and chop fine. Add 2–3 eggs, grated bread crumbs, salt, allspice, black pepper-corns, 1 glass of chopped mutton fat, and ½ spoon butter fried with an onion. Line a stewpan with a mutton caul (the fatty membrane which covers the intes-tines of the sheep), and pile the prepared mixture on top. Bake in a moderate oven for 1 hour. To serve, turn out onto a plate like a pudding.

The mutton fat may be rendered before adding it to the forcemeat mixture in which case add about ⅔ glass mutton fat and substitute ½ glass currants for the butter with onions.

INGREDIENTS

mutton pluck

1 carrot

½ parsley root
½ celery root
1 onion
10–15 allspice
½ white French roll
2–3 eggs
allspice

black peppercorns
1 glass chopped mutton fat
(½ spoon butter plus onion, or ½
   glass currants)
mutton caul
salt

*The English and Russian collective terms for variety meats do not overlap exactly. While the Russian word liver includes lungs, heart, and spleen, the British word "pluck" includes the lungs, heart, and liver (sometimes with other viscera). Since Molokhovets also specified the liver for this recipe, I decided that "pluck" in this instance was a reasonable, if not quite exact, translation. For an excellent discussion of variety meats (with useful diagrams), see Grigson, The Art of Charcuterie, especially 310–311, 317–318.*

## SUCKLING PIG

### (Porosenok)

*Remarks:* Scald a suckling pig in rapidly boiling water, adding some cold water so that the skin does not come off with the bristles. Using this method, you can remove the bristles with a knife.

### 749  Roast stuffed suckling pig

#### (Zharenyj farshirovannyj porosenok)

Clean thoroughly a whole, small suckling pig and rub it with salt, both inside and out. Stuff the pig, sew it up, and cook on a spit over a large fire, basting frequently with 1–2 spoons of butter. Keep turning the pig until the outer skin is well browned.

A suckling pig may also be cooked in a dripping pan in the oven. Line the pan with crisscrossed birch sticks, place the suckling pig on top with its legs tucked in, and cook for a full hour, basting with butter (⅛ lb).

The stuffing is prepared as follows: Boil the liver and pluck of the suckling pig. Chop up the meat, pound it in a mortar, and rub through a fine sieve. Add 1 spoon butter, 3 egg yolks, currants, cloves, pepper, a little sugar, and ½ French roll soaked in water and squeezed out. Mix well and pound everything together. Stuff the suckling pig with this mixture. If you have a large (6–8 lb) suckling pig, cut off the head and feet, etc., which will weigh about 3 lbs. Use the cut-off parts for soup and stuff and roast the middle section as indicated above.

This suckling pig is sometimes served cold, especially on Easter Sunday. To stuff and roast a whole, large suckling pig, double the ingredients for the stuffing and add a piece of calf's liver.

Usually a roast suckling pig is stuffed with thick buckwheat kasha.

INGREDIENTS

1 suckling pig, 3–4 lbs
1–2 spoons butter for basting

*For stuffing*
liver and pluck
10 allspice
10 black peppercorns
⅛ lb butter

10 cloves
2–3 pieces sugar
2 eggs
½ glass currants
salt
½ French roll

# PORK

## (Svinina)

### 753a  Real fresh ham in hay dust with beer

*(Nastojashchaja buzhenina,\* v sennoj trukhe s pivom)*

Wash a leg of pork, wrap it in a napkin, and put it in a stewpan with cold water and 2 large handfuls of fresh, fragrant hay dust. Boil it up once or twice, then remove the pork from the napkin and place it in a stewpan. Add allspice and black peppercorns, 5–10 of each, 2–3 bay leaves, and the usual root vegetables, one of each kind. Pour in a bottle of dark (*chernoe*) beer; cover and stew until done. To serve, skim the fat from the sauce, thicken it with flour, and pour the sauce over the meat. Serve with chestnut sauce, stewed cabbage, or boiled potatoes.

INGREDIENTS

3–4 lbs pork
bottle of dark beer
5–10 black peppercorns

root vegetables, 1 of each
5–10 allspice

*\*Molokhovets defined buzhenina as "the hind quarter of a fresh unsalted boar (vepr'), which is cooked on a dripping pan like any other roast on two crisscrossed sticks." Vepr' means wild boar in Russian, but Molokhovets seemed to use the words for boar and pork (svinina) interchangeably, as in this recipe. I have followed her usage, although, gastronomically speaking, the flesh of the wild boar is considered a delicacy and preferred over that of the ordinary domestic pig. The freshly gathered hay obviously added to the flavor and aroma of this dish. Molokhovets used hay and straw extensively in the kitchen, for baking and smoking and as an indispensable part of her batterie de cuisine. See the Introduction under Stoves and Ovens for further examples.*

### 757  Fresh pork breast stuffed with cabbage and apples

*(Svezhaja svinaja grudinka, farshirovannaja kapustoju i jablokami)*

Wash a pork breast and chop or crack the bones [without detaching them from the meat]. Using a knife, make a slit between the bones and the meat and fill the cavity with the following stuffing. Shred a small head of fresh cabbage, add salt, and squeeze out the moisture, or use sauerkraut. Mix with 5 finely chopped sour apples and 1 spoon butter. Stuff the breast and sew it up. Strew with finely chopped onion, pour on 3 spoons of water, and roast in the oven.

INGREDIENTS

breast of pork
small head of fresh cabbage, or 2
   glasses sauerkraut

5 sour apples
1 spoon butter
1 onion

# HAM
## *(Vetchina)*

### 763  Boiled smoked ham

*(Varenaja kopchenaja vetchina)*

Soak a smoked ham overnight in cold water. The next morning, wash it in boiling water, wipe it clean with wheat bran, and rinse in cold water. Tie up in a napkin and cover with cold water. Boil over high heat at first, then reduce the fire. Watch that the meat does not overcook.

If the ham is to be served cold, let it cool in the water in which it boiled.

*Remarks:* If the ham is tough, then on the day before the ham is to be prepared, wrap it well in a towel or a napkin and bury it in dark, heavy earth for 12 hours. If it is salted, another 24 hours must be allowed for soaking in cold water and the water must be changed frequently. To cook the ham, boil it in several changes of water, each time adding a grated and sieved crust of black bread to the water. This will reduce the salt and remove any unpleasant odor from any meat. This method may be used with fish as well.

### 764  Baked smoked ham

*(Pechenaja kopchenaja vetchina)*

Soak overnight in cold water a large smoked leg, that is, the hind quarter of a pig. In the morning, wash it in boiling water, rub it clean with wheat bran, rinse in clean cold water, and wipe dry. Bake it with rye bread, that is, plaster it entirely with dough which is prepared for bread. Place the loaves of bread and the ham in the oven at the same time. Remove the ham when the loaves are done, but do not remove the dough from the ham until it cools. Then clean the ham with a knife, wipe it off, make a slit in the outer skin, peel it back, and stud the meat attractively with cloves in stripes or squares. Strew 1 teaspoon each of fine sugar and cinnamon over the ham. Set in the oven for several minutes until the sugar dissolves and the ham browns slightly. Ham prepared in this manner is served at the Easter table.

When, after several days, all the meat has been cut off, chop up the skin and the remaining bones into several pieces and put a little of each into borshch for flavor. Also add to *shchi* made from sorrel, nettles, spinach, etc.

### 766 Cold boar's head for the Easter table

*(Golova starago veprja i proch. zharkija, podavaemyja
kholodnymi na stol v den' Svetlago Khristova Voskresen'ja)*

Clean and boil a handsome smoked head of an old wild boar, following the directions given for boiled smoked ham. Place the head on a platter and decorate the ears and snout with attractively cut white paper and greens.

## CHAMOIS, VENISON, ELK, AND HARE

*(Serna, olenina, los', zajats)*

### 771 Stewed elk or chamois

*(Zharkoe los' ili serna)*

Pound a piece of elk or chamois, place in a glazed pot, and cover with cooled vinegar that has been boiled with salt and spices. Set the meat in a cold place, turning it each day. Remove the meat from the marinade, lard it with pork fat, and roll the meat in ground allspice or black peppercorns and in cloves and marjoram. Using a knife, make small slits in the meat with a knife and insert pieces of pork fat. Wrap the entire piece of meat with slices of pork fat, brown lightly in a hot oven, and then transfer the meat to a stewpan. Skim the fat from the pan juices and pour the juices over the meat. Add 1½ glasses vinegar, ½ glass wine, and a piece of dry bouillon. Cover tightly and stew over a low fire until tender. When the meat is cooked, transfer it to a platter to cool. Decorate with aspic or cover with the sauce in which the meat was stewed. If using the sauce, it must first be well reduced and then beaten on ice until it thickens.

## 776  Baked hare with sour cream

*(Zharkoe zajats so smetanoju)*

Lard a cleaned hare with pork fat, strew with salt, and place on a dripping pan. Cover with lumps of butter. When the hare is half cooked, begin to pour on sour cream. Cook until tender, cut into sections, and pour on the sauce. Usually creamed beets are served with this hare.

INGREDIENTS

| | |
|---|---|
| hare | vinegar |
| ¼ lb butter | ¼ lb pork fat |
| ½ glass sour cream | creamed beets |

# 6
# Domestic and Wild Birds and Salad Accompaniments

*(Domashnija ptitsy, dich' i raznye salaty k zharkomu)*

## DOMESTIC BIRDS
*(Domashnija ptitsy)*

*Remarks concerning domestic and wild birds:* To assure tender meat, birds must be slaughtered and hung in a cold place for several days before being used. For turkeys, hens (*kuritsa*), and capons, the following method is particularly good: pour 1 tablespoon of good vinegar down the throat of a turkey, or 1 dessertspoon for a hen or capon, and pen up the birds someplace where they can still move about. Slaughter them after 2 or 3 hours, but no sooner. Clean and immediately boil or fry them.* The meat of such birds will be exceptionally tender and tasty. Since birds grow unevenly, size is not a sure indication of age. Allow 3 lbs of cleaned and drawn bird for every 6 people; therefore allow 2 or 4 chickens (*tsyplenok*),** 1 or 2 ducks, or 1 or ½ turkey.

*Cook each bird as follows:* Roast a 5 lb turkey for 1½ hours in the oven or on a spit. Bake a young capercaillie*** for nearly an hour in the oven; an older bird for 1½ hours. Bake a young greyhen for about ½ hour, an older bird for nearly an hour. In a stewpan on top of the stove, cook a partridge for about 30 minutes or a chicken for about 15 minutes. Hazel grouse will take about 15 minutes. Geese require 2½ to 3 hours.

A slaughtered chicken must be soaked for a full hour in cold water, then plunged into hot but not boiling water. Singe to remove the feathers, draw, and wash the bird. A slightly larger bird need not be plunged into hot water.

After removing a hen or capon from the hot water, pluck and singe the bird. Eviscerate and set the bird aside for at least a day. Wash before using, rub with flour, etc. Place the gizzard under one wing, the liver under the other.**** Tie up with string and cook on a spit or in a stewpan.

Slaughter a turkey, and while the bird is still warm, pluck the feathers from the breast, backbone, and limbs; set aside the wings. Immediately draw the bird and set it aside for at least a day. When ready to use, clean, singe, wash thoroughly, and rub with wheat flour. Always save the head, feet, and wing tips for soup.

Young hens (*kura*) can be distinguished from old by their feet, knees, and necks. Young hens, turkeys, etc., always have thick feet, necks, and joints; older birds have thinner feet and necks, and the skin of the joints turns violet. In general, an old bird is not good for either soup or the main course (*zharkoe*).

A good turkey can always be recognized by its white skin and its fat.

Some people do not like the aroma of a turkey as it cooks; to reduce the odor, place a piece of ginger in the abdominal cavity before cooking.

A good goose will have fat that is white and transparent. Pluck the bird while still warm. Treat ducks in the same manner.

The skin on the breast of young pigeons will be light rose, whereas older pigeons will have dark violet skin and scrawny claws.

*How to carve a cooked bird for serving at the table:* A 5 lb turkey may be cut into 20 parts. To start, cut off the first and then the second joint of the legs, making 4 pieces. Then cut off the second joint of the wings. (Do not roast the wing tips, but save them for soup.) Next cut the turkey lengthwise into 3 parts. Cut each of the 2 tender side sections diagonally into 3 parts, beginning with the neck and working toward the legs. Then, having left the breast bone with the meat intact on both sides, cut lengthwise: that is, cut away from the spine the full length of the turkey. Finally, quarter both the breast bone and the spine, making a total of 20 parts in all.

Carve a goose exactly the same way. If the goose or turkey weighs more than 5 lbs, then increase the number of tender, diagonally cut pieces, and cut the spine and breast bone into 10 or 12 pieces, instead of 8.

Carve a hen, capon, or fattened fowl (*puljarka*) into 12 parts: Remove the wings and legs and cut the bird lengthwise into 5 parts. Halve the middle section crosswise (that is, cut the breast bone so there is meat on both sides). Treat the spine the same way.

Capon and fatted fowl are best at 8 months and taste best from September to February. They should be fed barley kasha and pork fat for the final 2 weeks before slaughtering.

To serve 7–9 persons, increase the proportions by 1½. To serve 10–12 persons, double the proportions, or prepare 6 lbs. To serve 13–18 persons, triple the proportions, or prepare 9 lbs. To serve 19–24 persons, quadruple the proportions, or prepare 12 lbs.

*Molokhovets seems to contradict herself in these remarks, first telling us to hang the birds for several days, but then several lines later, advising us to cook them immediately after slaughtering.

**Tsyplenok was a young chicken, kuritsa was an older bird or hen; although I have mostly tried to retain the differences, a rigid translation sounds stilted since the distinction is being lost nowadays in English as well as in Russian. In modern Russian cookbooks, the favored designation seems to be kuritsa.

***The capercaillie (Tetrao urogallus) is the largest member of the grouse family in Europe. The *bird has handsome plumage, but likes to feed on pine needles which impart a flavor of turpentine to the flesh. If a young bird is promptly drawn and then hung for at least a week, the flavor of turpentine apparently becomes imperceptible. Old cocks, on the other hand, are all but inedible.*

*****The Russian writer and poet Nadezhda Teffi mocked this tucking of the gizzards and liver under the wings of a chicken in her 1912 spoof of Molokhovets, "Paskhal'nye sovety molodym khozjajkam" [Easter advice to young housewives]. In Teffi's eyes, a chicken garnished in this fashion "appeared as if it were setting out on a long journey and had taken in hand all that was necessary."*

## 779 Stuffed pigeons

### (Farshirovannye golubi)

Pigeons are much tastier if they are stuffed as follows: Cut a thin crust from a 5 kopeck French roll. Soak the roll in bouillon or milk, squeeze it out, and salt lightly. Add 2 eggs, 1 spoon butter, ¼ glass currants, and nutmeg. Mix thoroughly and use to stuff the abdominal and crop cavities of the pigeons. Tie them up with string and roast in the oven on a stoneware plate (*latka*), basting frequently with butter until the pigeons are brown and tender. Serve, pouring on the juices in which they cooked. Garnish with boiled potatoes. Serve a salad of fresh cucumbers separately.

Boiled pigeons are served with rice and cauliflower.

INGREDIENTS

| | |
|---|---|
| 6 pigeons | nutmeg |
| 1 French roll | ½ lb butter |
| ¼–½ glass currants | 2 eggs |

## 781 Stewed turkey, stuffed with liver

### (Zharkoe-indejka, farshirovannaja pechenkoju)

Clean a turkey as indicated in the Remarks. Place 1–2 onions, ½ parsley root, ½ celery root, 1 carrot, 2–3 bay leaves, 4–6 allspice berries, ¼–½ lb sliced pork fat or butter, and a little boiling water in a saucepan. Add the turkey and stew, covered, for 1½ hours on top of the stove over a low fire, turning the bird frequently. Brown the turkey, uncovered, in the oven for 15 minutes before serving. Prepare the stuffing as follows: Wash a calf's liver and fry it lightly in a stewpan with pork fat or butter, a bay leaf, and allspice. Chop the liver fine, pound in a mortar, and rub through a sieve, or grate the liver after it has cooled. Add 1 French roll soaked in milk, water, or bouillon and squeezed out, 1 spoon butter, 1 spoon sugar, salt, and ½ glass currants, if desired. Mix in 2–6 raw eggs, using the larger number if the turkey is to be served hot, so that the stuffing will be dense enough. If it is to be served cold, use fewer eggs. [Before roasting the turkey,] use your fingers to carefully separate the skin from the breast and slip some stuffing into the pocket. Do not pack it too tightly because the stuffing will expand. Sew the skin closed with thread. Stuff the abdominal cavity in the same manner, also sewing it closed.

Pour on brown sauce. This turkey serves 6 persons for 2 days.

INGREDIENTS

a fat turkey
¼ lb butter, or ½ lb pork fat
1–2 onions
½ parsley root
½ celery root
1 carrot
2–3 bay leaves
5–6 [sic] allspice

*For the stuffing*
1 calf's liver

⅛ lb butter, or ¼ lb pork fat
2–6 eggs
1–2 pieces sugar
2–4 bay leaves
2–4 allspice
1 5 kopeck French roll
1 glass milk
⅛–¼ lb butter
(½ glass currants)

## 785 Roast turkey, stuffed with walnuts

*(Zharenaja indejka farshirovannaja gretskimi orekhami)*

Shell 1 lb walnuts, scald the nutmeats, and remove the inner membranes. Pound the nuts until they form a paste. Add 1 lb calf's liver, fried in butter, pounded, and sieved, ½ white roll soaked in milk, 2–4 raw eggs, and ⅛ lb butter. Mix everything together, stuff the turkey, and roast as usual. To serve, slice the meat and pour on brown sauce with Madeira.

INGREDIENTS

a 3 lb turkey
1 lb walnuts
1 lb calf's liver
2–3 spoons butter
½ French roll
2 eggs

*For sauce*
⅓ glass flour
3–4 pieces sugar
½ lemon
¼–½ glass Madeira

## 790 Turkey fillet with cherry purée

*(Filej indejki s pjure iz vishen')*

Take a turkey fillet, remove the tendons, trim, and pound slightly. Add salt and drizzle on ½ wineglass of Madeira. Place in a flat-bottomed stewpan greased with 1 spoon butter. Fifteen minutes before serving, fry on both sides over a low flame until done. Arrange on a platter and cover with the pan juices diluted with bouillon. Fill the center of the platter with cherry purée, prepared as follows.

Stone 6 glasses of cherries, add various spices, and simmer over a very low fire, covered, until tender. Rub the cherries through a fine sieve. Pound 15–20 cherry stones* and bring to a boil in 1 wineglass water. Strain and add to the purée with some sugar. Bring to a boil, arrange the purée on a platter, and surround with sippets of white bread, fried in butter.

INGREDIENTS

turkey
½ wineglass Madeira
1 spoon butter

*For the sippets*
1 French roll
1 spoon butter

*For the cherry purée*
6 glasses (2 lbs) cherries
2 cloves
½ *vershok* stick cinnamon
2 cardamom pods
⅛ teaspoon nutmeg
½ glass or more sugar

*The kernels in cherry stones are almond-flavored, but they contain varying amounts of prussic acid, a deadly poison. A little almond essence will help intensify the flavor without immediately jeopardizing one's health. Alternatively, one might add a little Kirschwasser.*

### 791  Turkey or chicken patties*

*(Kotlety iz indejki ili kuritsy)*

Cut off the fillets from 1 turkey or 2 chickens, remove the membranes, and chop the meat fine. Add ⅛ lb butter, less than ¼ teaspoon nutmeg, salt, and ½ French roll, soaked in milk and squeezed out. An egg may be added as well. Mix everything together and pound in a mortar. Shape into small patties, dip in egg and rusk crumbs, and fry in 2 spoons butter. Arrange the patties on a platter and pour on the following sauce: Add the juice of ¼ lemon and ¾ wineglass of Madeira to the pan in which the patties were fried. Add a few capers, dilute with 1 glass bouillon, and bring to a boil.

Or pour on a sauce made of field mushrooms or truffles.

Or, arrange the patties around the edge of the platter and fill the center with fresh or dried peas.

If the patties are being prepared for a large number of people, arrange them in two rows lengthwise down the middle of the platter, and pour on one of the sauces mentioned above. Serve various vegetables separately on another platter. Arrange them across the platter in diagonal rows, dividing each vegetable with a strip of pastry. Appropriate vegetables (*zelen'*)** are green beans, boiled potatoes with butter and greens, chestnuts, fried sausages, carefully cut carrots or turnips, etc.

Or serve with mushroom sauce, or with greens or root vegetables, etc.

Save the leftover bones and meat of the turkey or chickens to make soup for the next day.

INGREDIENTS

| | |
|---|---|
| 1 turkey or 2 chickens | 5–6 rusks |
| 3 spoons butter | |
| ¼ teaspoon nutmeg | *For the sauce* |
| ½ French roll | (¼ lemon) |
| ½ glass milk | (¾ wineglass Madeira) |
| 2 eggs | ½ jar capers |

*These patties are usually called Pozharski cutlets after the inn of that name which used to exist in Torzhok on the road from Moscow to Novgorod. Pushkin recommended them in a whimsical culinary guide that he wrote for his friend S. A. Sobolevskij in November 1826. (A. S. Pushkin, Polnoe Sobranie Sochinenij, XVIII, 302–303.)*

**The English word "greens" has a more restricted meaning than the Russian zelen'. In this context, a better translation might be "garnishes."*

### 793a  Spit-roasted capon or fattened fowl, another way

*(Kaplun ili puljarka zharenye na vertele drugim manerom)*

Clean the fowl and attach it to the spit. Baste with butter and roast the bird before the fire, gently turning the spit, for 45 minutes before serving. When the bird begins to brown, lightly sieve flour onto the bird, using a small tea strainer. Drizzle with butter and continue cooking. After five minutes, flour the bird again and drizzle on more butter. Then strew with grated bread crumbs and let brown. Finally, detach from the spit and remove the threads. Transfer to a platter, pouring on the juices. Serve with fresh or marinated salad, or with cherry purée.

INGREDIENTS

| | |
|---|---|
| capon or fattened fowl | ½ glass flour |
| ¼ lb butter | 2–3 rusks |

### 795  Spit-roasted capon or fattened fowl with juniper berry sauce

*(Zharenyj kaplun ili puljarka s sousom iz mozhzhevelovykh jagod)*

Pound together in a mortar ½ spoon juniper berries, 1 glass grated bread crumbs, 1 spoon butter, 2 eggs, and 2 spoons ordinary cheese. Rub the mixture through a fine sieve and fill the capon with this stuffing. Pound and sieve an additional tablespoon of juniper berries. Rub the berries over the capon and a sheet of paper, tie the bird up in the paper, and cook it on a spit, basting with butter. Remove the paper, strew the bird with pounded rusks, and baste with the pan juices. When the bird has browned, transfer it to a platter. Pour on butter, browned with 2 spoons ground rusks.

INGREDIENTS

| | |
|---|---|
| capon | 2–3 spoons butter |
| ½ spoon juniper berries | 3 spoons ground rusks |
| 1 French white roll | salt |
| 2 eggs | [an additional tablespoon juniper |
| 2 spoons ordinary cheese | berries to rub over the bird] |

## 804  Fattened fowl boiled with tarragon

### (Puljarka razvarnaja s estragonom)

Clean and draw a fattened fowl, wash, and place in a stewpan. Cover with cold water and add ⅛ lb dry tarragon, salt, 2 slices of lemon, and various root vegetables. Boil until done. Pick over the leaves of another ⅛ lb of tarragon, cover with 3 glasses of strong bouillon, add ⅛ lb butter, and bring to a boil. Set the sauce aside to infuse. Cut the fattened fowl into serving portions and arrange them on a platter to resemble a whole bird. Pour on the sauce and serve.

INGREDIENTS

| | |
|---|---|
| 1 fattened fowl | 1 parsley root |
| ¼ lb tarragon* | 1 celery root |
| 2 lemon slices | ⅛ lb butter |
| 1 carrot | salt |

*Two varieties of tarragon (Artemisia dracunculus) are cultivated in kitchen gardens; of the two, French tarragon is much preferable to Russian tarragon (var. inodora) which is coarser and less flavorful. I do not know which variety of tarragon Molokhovets used but, whatever the variety, the excessive quantity in this recipe must have made the dish all but inedible.

## 807  Spit-roasted hen

### (Zharkoe kuritsa)

Pour a dessertspoon of vinegar down the gullet of a live hen. Slaughter it after 2 or 3 hours, then clean and draw the bird. Or, after slaughtering the hen, soak it in cold water for an hour, and then bury in sand for a full 24 hours. Pluck, draw, and salt the bird, then cook it on a spit or on a dripping pan, basting with butter and rich bouillon. Fry 2 crushed rusks in 1 spoon melted butter and mix with the strained pan juices. Arrange the meat on a platter, cover with the sauce, and serve with salad.

INGREDIENTS

| | |
|---|---|
| 1–2 hens, that is, 3 lbs | 2 spoons butter |
| 2–3 rusks | salt |

## 809  Hen with prunes in puff pastry

*(Kuritsa s chernoslivom na vol'vante)*

Clean and salt 1 large hen. Place ¼ lb butter, root vegetables, and spices in a stewpan. When the butter begins to bubble, add the hen and stew, covered, until tender, turning it and adding a little water. When the hen is cooked, remove and cut into parts. Return the pieces to the pan, add 3 glasses bouillon, and cook for another ½ hour.

Meanwhile, fry 1 spoon flour in butter, dilute with the hen bouillon, and add a little vinegar or lemon juice and 1–2 pieces sugar. Bring the sauce to a boil, strain, and pour over the hen. Add prunes that have been boiled in water, covered, left to stand 1–1½ hours, and removed from the water with a slotted spoon. Bring everything to a boil once more.

Serve in a vol-au-vent. That is, bake a circle of dough with sides, using puff pastry or short pastry. Transfer the baked pastry shell onto a platter, arrange the hen with prunes on top, and pour on a little sauce. Serve the remainder of the sauce separately. To economize, make soup from the hen and serve the boiled flesh in the vol-au-vent.

INGREDIENTS

| | |
|---|---|
| 1 large hen | 2–3 bay leaves |
| 2 spoons butter | 1 spoon flour |
| 1 carrot | vinegar or ½ lemon |
| 1 parsley root | 1–2 pieces of sugar |
| 1 celery root | ½ lb prunes |
| 1 onion | 10–15 allspice |

## 815  Chickens prepared like hazel grouse

*(Tsypljata na maner rjabchikov)*

Feed 3 chickens pounded juniper berries mixed with flour for several days, and then slaughter them. Store the birds, still feathered, on ice for a few days, then pluck, draw, and salt them. Strew the chickens with ½ spoon ground allspice, rub with a handful of ground juniper berries, and set aside for 15 hours. Wash the birds thoroughly, lard with pork fat, and truss with wooden spills like hazel grouse. Chop off the feet, wings, and head, pour on 2 spoons of vinegar, and cook the birds in a stewpan. When they are done, add 2–3 spoons sour cream. Let them brown and then strew with grated rusks. To serve, strain the sauce and pour over the meat.

Or cook on a spit, basting with 1–2 spoons butter. Serve with a salad of some kind.

INGREDIENTS

| | |
|---|---|
| 3 chickens | 2–4 spoons butter |
| juniper berries | 2–3 spoons sour cream |
| flour | 2–3 rusks |
| black peppercorns | ¼ lb pork fat |
| allspice | about 2 spoons vinegar |

## 820  Chickens with green peas

*(Tsypljata s zelenym gorokhom)*

Clean and halve or quarter 3 chickens. Place the chicken in a stewpan, cover with water, and add salt, 5 glasses freshly shelled green peas, and ½ spoon butter. Cook until done, then remove the chicken pieces. Add to the peas 2–3 pieces of sugar, ½ spoon flour, and finely chopped parsley and dill and cook, covered with a lid. ½ glass cream may also be added. Boil until the peas are tender and the sauce has reached the desired thickness. Alternatively, the chickens may be dipped in egg and rusk crumbs and fried. Serve garnished with the peas.*

INGREDIENTS

| | |
|---|---|
| 3 chickens | ½ glass cream |
| 5 glasses freshly shelled peas | 1 egg |
| 2–3 pieces sugar | 4–5 rusks |
| ½ spoon flour | 2 spoons butter |

*If these directions are followed exactly, the peas would be cooked long before the chicken. Either the strain of peas available in nineteenth-century Russia was much tougher than our own, or perhaps Molokhovets simply preferred mushy peas. Molokhovets gives no indication of the time required for cooking peas in the vegetable chapter, but in general vegetables were cooked longer then than now.*

## 823  Chickens in cauliflower and crayfish sauce

*(Tsypljata pod sousom s tsvetnoju kapustoju i rakami)*

Cut 3–4 well-cleaned chickens into parts and cook them in water with salt, 1 onion, ½ celery root, and ½ parsley root. Arrange the chicken on a deep platter and cover with the following sauce: Melt 1½ spoons butter in a stewpan, stir in 1½ spoons flour, dilute with 2 glasses strong bouillon, and bring to a boil. Add 1 glass good cream, a little salt, some nutmeg, and ½ spoon finely chopped parsley. Bring to a boil again, then add 25–30 crayfish tails, a head of cauliflower, boiled and cut into pieces, and ½–1 lb of asparagus, also boiled and cut into pieces. Thoroughly boil all this together and serve.

1–1½ spoons of crayfish butter may be substituted for the Finnish butter.

### 828 Roast goose in the Lithuanian style with apples

*(Zharkoe gus' po-litovski s jablokami)*

Remove from the goose any extra fat, which may be used for frying dough-nuts, etc. Rub the goose inside and out with ½ spoon ground caraway mixed with salt. Stuff with small apples that have been sliced and sprinkled with salt and marjoram. Cook in a roasting pan strewn with a handful of finely chopped onions. In the beginning, pour on bouillon, 2 or 3 spoons at a time, and then later baste the bird with its own juices. Bake 6–8 good apples separately. Cut up the goose, arrange it on a platter, and surround with the large baked apples. Skim any excess fat from the sauce, add ½ spoon flour, and dilute with bouil-lon. Bring the sauce to a boil, strain, and pour over the goose. Use the goose giblets for soup or sauce.

INGREDIENTS

| | |
|---|---|
| goose | 6–8 large apples |
| ½ spoon caraway seed | 1 spoon flour [total] |
| salt | (marjoram) |
| 2 onions | 12 small apples |

### 828a Roast goose stuffed with sauerkraut

*(Zharkoe gus' s kapustoju)*

In a covered saucepan, stew until tender 4 glasses finely shredded sauerkraut, 1–2 spoons butter, and 4 onions (if desired). Rub a raw goose with salt and caraway seed and stuff with the sauerkraut mixture. Cook as indicated above. Any leftover fat from the goose may be given to the servants to be eaten with their kasha.

INGREDIENTS

| | |
|---|---|
| a 3 lb goose | 1–2 spoons butter |
| ½ spoon caraway | (4 onions) |
| 4 glasses, or 2 lbs, sauerkraut | salt |

### 829  Roast goose stuffed with Italian macaroni

*(Zharkoe gus' s ital'janskimi makaronami)*

Split the back of a cleaned goose and carefully remove the backbone. Rub the flesh with salt and ½ teaspoon of ground black pepper and allspice. Stuff as follows: Boil ¾ lb Italian macaroni in salted water and drain in a coarse sieve. Mix the macaroni with butter, 2 egg yolks, less than ¼ teaspoon mace, and 2 spoons sour cream. Stuff the goose, sew it up, and cook in a roasting pan on a bed of cut up root vegetables. Turn the goose frequently. Baste at first with butter and later with its own juices. When the goose is cooked, transfer it to a platter. Add 2 glasses bouillon and 1 spoon flour to the pan juices and bring to a boil. Strain the sauce, remove any excess fat, and add ½ small jar of capers or olives. Bring to a boil once more and pour over the goose.

INGREDIENTS

| | |
|---|---|
| a 3 lb goose | 1 parsley root |
| salt | 1 leek |
| black pepper and allspice | (1 onion) |
| ¾ lb Italian macaroni | 1 spoon flour |
| 2 egg yolks | (½ small jar capers or olives) |
| nutmeg | ⅛ lb butter |
| 2 spoons sour cream | 1 carrot |

### 831  Goose with mushroom sauce

*(Gus' s gribnym sousom)*

Clean a young, lean goose and cut into parts. Cook until tender in a pan with water, root vegetables, spices, boletus mushrooms, and salt. In another pan, melt 1½ spoons butter, sprinkle on flour, and dilute with 3–4 glasses bouillon. Stir in ½ to 1½ glasses sour cream, or enough to make 5 glasses of sauce, and finely chopped mushrooms. Bring to a boil and pour over the goose. Boiled potatoes may be added also.

This is usually served on a deep platter for breakfast or for supper.

*Remarks:* If the goose is large enough, then 3 dishes, each serving 6–8 persons, may be prepared from it. Soup may be prepared from the goose giblets and blood. On the next day the goose itself may be cooked and served with some kind of sauce, and any bouillon remaining from this sauce may be used the following day to make soup.

Also soup with potatoes or kasha may be made from the leftover goose bones and sauce.

INGREDIENTS

goose                         ⅛ lb boletus mushrooms
salt                          ½–1½ glasses sour cream
1 carrot                      1½ spoons butter
1 parsley root                ¾ glass flour
1 leek                        parsley and dill
2 onions                      8–10 allspice
1–2 bay leaves

## 832  Goose giblet sauce

*(Sous iz gusinykh potrokhov)*

Clean the goose liver together with the other giblets. Cook with water, root vegetables, and spices. Beat about 1 glass of goose blood with 1–2 spoons vinegar and strain it into 3–4 glasses of the giblet broth. Add 2–3 pieces of sugar, 2 ground cloves, and 5–6 allspice berries and bring to a boil, stirring constantly. Add the giblets and let them heat through. Serve in a deep bowl.

INGREDIENTS

goose giblets                 1 spoon flour*
1 carrot                      1 spoon butter*
1 parsley root                1 glass goose blood
1 leek                        3 pieces of sugar
3 onions                      2 cloves
8–10 allspice                 5–6 allspice
2–3 bay leaves

*Neither the flour nor the butter is mentioned in the body of the recipe, but presumably they were intended to thicken the sauce.*

## 840  Duck with veal forcemeat

*(Utka s farshem iz teljatiny)*

Cut open a duck along its spine and remove the backbone. Prepare the follow-ing stuffing: Mix together 1½ lbs [minced] veal, 1 spoon washed Finnish butter, 1 white French roll soaked in milk and squeezed out, ¼ nutmeg, 10 ground allspice, and 1–2 raw eggs. Add an omelet made with 4 eggs, an onion, and butter. Pound everything together in a mortar, rub through a fine sieve, stuff the duck, and sew it up. Fry the stuffed duck in a covered stewpan, lined with ¼ lb finely sliced pork fat, root vegetables, and spices. When the duck and vegetables have browned, pour in bouillon, 2–3 spoons at a time, turning the duck occasionally. When the duck is cooked through, remove it from the pan, cut it up, and arrange it on a platter. Add ½ spoon flour to the sauce and mix over the fire. Dilute with 3 glasses bouillon, bring to a boil while stirring, and strain. 3–4 sliced truffles may be added along with a wineglass of Madeira. Bring the sauce to a boil once more and pour over the duck. Surround with pieces of cow's udder, boiled in salted water and cut up to resemble small cutlets.

INGREDIENTS

a 2½ or 3 lb duck
1½ lb veal
2½ spoons butter
1 white French roll
1 glass milk
5–6 eggs
1 onion
nutmeg
¼ lb pork fat
1 carrot
1 leek

1 onion
1 celery root
20 allspice
2–3 bay leaves
1 spoon flour
(2–4 truffles)
1 wineglass Madeira
(cow's udder)
salt
1 parsley root

# WILD FOWL

## (Dikija ptitsy)

*Remarks:* Pluck dry wild fowl without using any water. Then use a knife to extract any feathers remaining in the skin. Singe and rub the skin with flour, bran, or simply a towel. Draw the fowl and soak in cold water for an hour or more.

Cut greyhens lengthwise into 5 pieces, but if they are very large, cut them into 7 pieces, with each piece containing part of the breast bone and meat on both sides. Partridges are cut lengthwise also, but into only 3 pieces. Hazel grouse are halved lengthwise.

To preserve and salt wild fowl, see Chapter 30.

### 847 Fried capercaillie

#### (Zharenyj glukhar')

Soak a cleaned capercaillie for 8–10 hours in vinegar boiled with spices. Lard the bird with ¼ lb pork fat and roast on a dripping pan, basting with 2 spoons butter. When the bird is almost done, pour on 2 spoons vinegar and turn it frequently. Baste the bird with the pan juices as they are released and, at the end, pour on sour cream. Cut up, arrange on a platter, and pour on the strained sauce. Serve with creamed beets, stewed potatoes, or fresh or marinated salad.

Tsar's family at a picnic after a hunt. From Joseph Favre, *Dictionnaire universel de cuisine pratique*, vol. 3 (Paris, 1894).

If the capercaillie will be served cold, omit the sour cream.

To tenderize the bird, some people bury it in good earth in the garden for 24 hours.

INGREDIENTS

capercaillie
¼ lb pork fat
2 spoons butter

2 spoons vinegar
(½ glass sour cream)

### 848  Cold capercaillie or greyhens

*(Kholodnoe iz glukharja ili teterki)*

Line the bottom of a glazed pot with several pieces of pork fat, 2 bay leaves, 3 cloves, a stick of cinnamon ⅓ *vershok* long, and 1 large onion. Cut the birds into pieces and place them in layers in the pot, strewing them with more of the above-mentioned spices, pork fat, and salt. Pour on a bottle of very light red wine and bind up the pot with a cloth. Seal with dough and place in the oven after baking bread. Leave it there overnight, then remove the birds, arrange them on a platter, and keep on ice.

INGREDIENTS

capercaillie or greyhens
½ lb pork fat
2 bay leaves
3 cloves

⅓ *vershok* stick cinnamon
one whole onion
1 bottle red wine

## 853  Pheasant*

### (*Fazan*)

Hang a pheasant for 5–8 days before plucking it. After plucking, cut off the head and set it aside. Using a lighted paper, singe off all the down and, while the flesh is warm from the flame, rub the entire pheasant briskly with a piece of pork suet or with butter wrapped in an old cloth to remove the roots of the down and the pin feathers. Lard the breast with pork fat and cook in butter in a stewpan, basting constantly with hot fat diluted with 2–3 spoons boiling water and smearing the breast with sour cream. For juicy flesh, prick the bird with a fork to allow the fat to penetrate the meat. The liver and other giblets are not used in this recipe. When the pheasant is cooked, baste once more with butter and sprinkle with rusk crumbs. Keep it over a low fire so that the crumbs will bake. Arrange on a platter and mount the head with its feathers on a short stick. Attach this to the neck. Decorate [the neck] with a paper ruff and attach the tail feathers to the roast. Transfer to a serving dish and pour on the pan juices.

Or roast the pheasant on a spit, after larding it with ¼ lb of pork fat. Wrap it in an additional ¼ lb of sliced pork fat and then in buttered paper. Cook at first over a high flame, then over a low one, basting with butter. When done, strew with rusk crumbs and serve with salad.

INGREDIENTS

1 pheasant
½ lb pork fat

¼ lb butter
3–4 rusks

*This recipe, and particularly the presentation, is reminiscent of the medieval ceremonial presentation of a peacock in full plumage.*

## 858  Spit-roasted stuffed hazel grouse

### (*Rjabchiki zharenye farshirovannye*)

Clean 3–4 hazel grouse and stuff with finely ground rusks mixed with lemon juice and butter. Sew up the birds, surround with thin slices of pork fat, and wrap in paper greased with 1 spoon butter. Cook the grouse on a spit, basting with butter.

Pour any leftover fat into a glazed bowl, as usual, and give it to the servants for their kasha, potatoes, etc.

INGREDIENTS

| | |
|---|---|
| 3–4 hazel grouse | 4 spoons butter |
| 1½ glasses rusks, or 24 purchased | juice of 1 lemon |
| rusks | 1½ lb pork fat |

### 859  Fried hazel grouse

*(Zharenye rjabchiki)*

Clean and salt 3–4 hazel grouse and lard, if desired, with ¼ lb pork fat. Melt ½ lb butter in a saucepan until it bubbles, add the hazel grouse, and fry, uncovered, over a very high flame. Watch that they do not burn. Remove the birds when they have browned on all sides, which will take about 15 minutes. Cut them up, arrange on a platter, and sprinkle with rusk crumbs and ½ spoon finely chopped parsley. Add 2 spoons each bouillon and fresh or sour cream to the butter in the pan, bring to a boil, and pour over the hazel grouse.

Serve with a salad of some sort.

*Remarks:* If the hazel grouse are not fresh, pluck, draw, and soak the birds in cold water. Then put into cold fresh milk and bring the milk to a boil.

INGREDIENTS

| | |
|---|---|
| 3–4 hazel grouse | 2 spoons sour cream |
| ¼ lb pork fat | 2–3 rusks |
| ½ lb butter | parsley |

### 863  Hazel grouse à la Maréchal*

*(Mareshal' iz rjabchikov)*

Remove both fillets from the hazel grouse, cutting off the wings at the first joint. Make a slit lengthwise on the underside of the fillets. Stuff them and sew them up. Dip the fillets in egg and deep fry, or dip them in eggs and crumbs and fry on a gridiron.

Stuff with the following: Prepare a brown sauce using ⅛ lb butter and ½ glass flour and dilute with 1½ glasses bouillon. Add salt and bring to a boil 2 or 3 times. Add a wineglass of Madeira, 6 chopped raw field mushrooms, and 1–2 truffles. Bring to a boil 4 more times, cool, and stuff the fillet pieces with this mixture.

Arrange the hazel grouse around a platter and fill the center with the following ragout: Prepare a white sauce using ⅔ glass flour, 2 spoons crayfish butter made from crayfish shells, and 2 glasses bouillon. Add 12 washed, raw field mushrooms and 25 crayfish tails. Boil together thoroughly about twice and add 1–2 chopped truffles.

INGREDIENTS

3–4 hazel grouse
1 egg
(5–6 rusks)
(1 lb fat for deep frying)

*For the brown sauce*
½ glass flour
⅛ lb butter
6 fresh mushrooms
1–2 truffles

1 wineglass Madeira

*For the ragout*
⅔ glass flour
salt
12 field mushrooms
25 crayfish
1–2 truffles
¼ lb butter [2 spoons]

*The name Maréchal, used descriptively in a culinary sense, indicates a refined dish belonging to French haute cuisine. Today, it usually refers to chicken or fish fillets dipped in egg and bread crumbs and fried in butter, garnished with asparagus tips and truffles, and served with a rich truffled sauce. (Dictionnaire de l'académie des gastronomes II, 107.) Molokhovets' recipe was unusually elaborate; in particular, stuffed fillets were uncommon, although nineteenth-century preparations under this name varied considerably.*

## 864 Hazel grouse soufflé*

   *(Sufle iz rjabchikov)*

Bone 3 raw hazel grouse. Chop the meat and add 1 French roll, soaked in milk and squeezed out, ¼ lb butter, and salt. Pound all this thoroughly and rub through a fine sieve. Stir in 4 eggs, 2 glasses cream, 4 chopped truffles, and a little nutmeg. Butter a ring mold with a large center opening and pour in the soufflé. Five minutes before dinner, start steaming the soufflé. When cooked, turn it out onto a platter.

Bring to a boil 1 spoon butter, 1 spoon flour, and 1 glass bouillon. Wash and peel 20 field mushrooms, bring them to a boil twice in ¼ glass bouillon, and add the juice of ½ lemon. Remove the field mushrooms from the broth, chop them fine, and stir into the sauce, adding the mushroom bouillon as well. Sprinkle with salt and bring to a boil. Pour the sauce over the soufflé and fill the center with celery root purée.

INGREDIENTS

3 hazel grouse
1 French roll
1 glass milk

3½ spoons butter
4 eggs
2 glasses cream

| | |
|---|---|
| 4 truffles | *For the celery root purée* |
| nutmeg | 1½ lb celery root |
| 20 field mushrooms | root vegetables |
| salt | 2 spoons butter |
| ½ lemon | |
| 1 spoon flour | |

*The lack of beaten egg whites in this dish suggests more of a pudding than a soufflé.

### 869   Spit-roasted snipe

*(Bekasy zharenye)*

Pluck the snipe, but do not eviscerate, which is unnecessary. Wash and salt them and wrap them first with ¼ lb pork fat and then in paper greased with 1 spoon butter. Sew them up with strong thread and cook on a spit, basting with butter. When the snipe are cooked, remove the paper and transfer the birds to a platter. Do not cut off the heads. Alternatively, cook the snipe in a roasting pan in the oven. Serve with a salad of some kind.

*Remarks:* (Method for preserving fresh snipe from autumn to January.) After bringing the snipe from the fields, immediately pluck, but do not eviscerate them. Wrap them in fresh cabbage leaves, and plaster them all over with thick dough. Bake in the oven only long enough to cook the dough. Place the birds in a barrel, pour on melted fat, and cover and seal the barrel. This fat may be used later for greasing carriage wheels.*

INGREDIENTS

| | |
|---|---|
| 6 snipe | 2–3 spoons butter |
| ¼ lb pork fat | |

*The German traveler Kohl wrote in his memoirs about the difficulty of procuring tar in the Ukraine and the steppes of Russia. "In its absence fat bacon is often used as a substitute for greasing the wheels, and we have more than once purchased from a wagoner, for this purpose, a lump that he was just going to eat for his breakfast. The dogs seem to be aware of the custom, for whenever a travelling-carriage stops at a post-station, a whole pack of dogs often gather around to amuse themselves by licking the axletrees of the wheels" (Kohl, Russia, 406). Canadians and Americans in the mid nineteenth century had the same problem but greased their wheels with a salve made of "hog's lard, wheat flour, and black lead (plumbago)" (The British American Cultivator, 143).*

### 872   Teal or woodcocks with sippets

*(Svisteli\* ili val'dshnepy s grenkami)*

Teal, like woodcocks and thrushes, are not eviscerated, but fried with their legs and heads. Pluck 12–15 teal, wash and salt them, and cook in a stewpan with 3 spoons butter. Set each cooked bird on a sippet made of white bread, fried in butter, and dried out in the oven. Arrange the birds and sippets on a platter and pour on the butter in which the birds were cooked.

Teal have large livers, which may be removed, chopped fine, and fried together with the birds. If the liver is used, arrange the ducks in the middle of the platter, and garnish with sippets spread with the finely chopped cooked liver. Pour on the sauce.

INGREDIENTS

| | |
|---|---|
| 12–15 small teal, or 3 woodcocks | 1 French roll |
| ½ lb butter | |

*Svisteli *appears to be a dialect word for* svistunok (Anas crecca), *the name deriving from the bird's distinctive whistling cry. Although teal are larger than woodcocks and thrushes, in the nineteenth century, teal was a common term for several species of small freshwater ducks. Here Molokhovets was clearly referring to a particularly small variety.*

## 876 Sandpiper ragout

*(Ragu iz kulikov)*

In a stewpan, fry 12–15 cleaned sandpipers, without heads and stomachs, in 1½–2 spoons butter. Slice the fillet from the bones. Pound the wings, legs, and bones in a mortar and, in a separate saucepan, fry them with 1 spoon butter and 1 chopped onion. Stir in 1 tablespoon flour, the juice of 1 lemon, and 1–1½ glasses bouillon. Let the mixture boil thoroughly, rub it through a sieve, and pour the sauce over the fillet slices. Finely chop the innards of the sandpipers, excluding the stomachs, with little lumps of butter. Place the mixture in a saucepan, add 1 spoon sour cream, and boil thoroughly. Spread this mixture on slightly dried slices of French roll and use them to garnish the platter containing the ragout of sandpipers.

This ragout may be made using cold sandpipers that have been fried previously; just add them to the sauce and bring it to a boil before serving.

## 879 Livers of hens, geese, ducks, hares, etc., in Madeira sauce

*(Pechenki kur, gusej, utok, zajtsa i proch. pod sousom s maderoju)*

Where many domestic fowl are available [i.e., constantly eaten], the livers of all of the birds mentioned above may be collected and mixed together to prepare the following dish.

Soak 10 livers of various sorts in milk for 6 hours until they swell and whiten. Fry ½ spoon flour in 1 spoon browned butter and dilute with 1 glass bouillon. Boil thoroughly and pour in 1 wineglass Madeira. Flour the unsalted livers lightly (salting them earlier would harden them), add them to the sauce, and stew, covered, for 5–10 minutes over a low fire. For those who like them, 1–2 sliced onions or several truffles boiled in bouillon may be added to the sauce. When the sauce is served at the table, add salt and mix.

INGREDIENTS

10 livers
½ spoon flour
1–2 spoons butter

1 wineglass Madeira
3 glasses milk
(1–2 onions, or 2–3 truffles)

# SALADS TO ACCOMPANY COOKED FISH AND MEAT
### (Salaty k zharkomu rybnomu i mjasnomu)

### 881 Salad with sour cream

*(Salat so smetanoju)*

Remove the outer green leaves from 6 heads of garden lettuce. Pick over the remaining leaves and wash thoroughly. Either cut these leaves into several pieces or leave them whole (especially the small leaves), and salt them. One half hour before serving, pound 2 hard-boiled egg yolks until smooth and add a little salt and, if desired, sugar. Stir in ½ or 1 glass very fresh sour cream, 2–3 spoons vinegar, and dill. Add the prepared lettuce leaves and 1–2 peeled and very finely sliced fresh cucumbers. Decorate the top with quartered hard-boiled eggs or with attractively cut colored aspic.

### 886 Potato and beet salad to accompany boiled beef

*(Salat iz kartofelja i svekly k razvarnoj govjadine)*

Boil 18 potatoes and bake 3 beets. Slice the potatoes and beets and add ¼ lb white beans boiled in salted water. Mix the vegetables with salt, a little pepper, 3 spoons olive oil, vinegar, and chopped greens.

### 888 Marinated beets

*(Svekla marinovannaja)*

Cool boiled or baked red, sweet beets, then peel and slice them. Place in a jar and strew with grated horseradish. Marinate in plain vinegar for 3 to 24 hours, or use a spiced vinegar boiled with bay leaf, allspice, salt, and cloves.

### 889 Cress salad

*(Kress-salat)*

Cut cress from the roots. Cover with water and use a slotted spoon to skim off any seeds that rise to the surface. Drain the cress in a fine sieve or colander. Just before serving, place the cress in a salad bowl. Add salt, olive oil, and vinegar, and mix before serving. The salad may be garnished with quartered hard-boiled eggs.

[*Translator's note:* Molokhovets here included #897, Marinated Salads, which was simply a reference to the recipes for marinated and pickled fruits, mushrooms, and vegetables given in Chapter 28.]

# 7
# Fish and Crayfish

## (Ryby i raki)

*Remarks:* It is important to assure that the fish is fresh because only fresh fish is tasty and healthy. If the flesh around the gills is red, the fish is fresh, but if the flesh is very dark or pale, the fish should not be used. The eyes must be whole and clear, not cloudy and sunken. The skin must be firm. Any fish should be discarded as unfit if, when slitting the fish lengthwise from head to tail, the flesh falls away from the bones. Fish should not be killed until it is needed; instead, keep it in fresh water, changing the water frequently. If it is impossible to keep the fish in water for a long time, kill the fish with a blow on the head, slit it from head to tail, and clean it immediately. Rub it inside and out with fine salt and even with some black pepper, cover the fish, and set it aside in a cold place. Before using the fish, wash it thoroughly and dry with a towel, especially if the fish will be used for a *pirog.* When cleaning the fish, remove the gall bladder carefully.

In order to cook thoroughly a large, whole fish always begin by putting the fish into cold water or cold bouillon, then boil over a high flame, gradually adding cold water. The fire under the pan should be strong enough to envelope the sides as well. Drop small fish into boiling water. The fish is done when the eyes whiten and turn outward. To prevent a marshy flavor, add 2–3 red-hot birch coals to the water while boiling the fish.*

To boil frozen fish, it must be started in cold water without fail. When boiling fish, add the usual root vegetables plus allspice, black pepper, and bay leaves. But do not add anything to freshly caught fish because the flavor of such fish is superb by itself.

Boil a whole fish in a fish kettle, adding only enough water or bouillon to just cover the fish.

After removing a large, boiled fish from the fish kettle, arrange it on a serving platter with the backbone on top, carefully pressing and at the same time extending the abdominal part. By adjusting the backbone to remain in the center, it is easy to remove the flesh from both sides. Fish that will be masked in aspic** is set out in the same manner.

*Which fish are tastiest in which months:* Salmon (*semga*) and eel, from July to

August; carp, from September to April; trout, from May to August; pike, from February to April; burbot in January; tench, from May to July; and crayfish, from May to August.

The proportions are intended for 6 people. For 7–9 people, increase the amounts by 1½. For 10–12 people, double the amount of fish and increase the sauce by 1½. For 13–18 people, double both the fish and sauce. For 19–24 people, double the fish and triple the amount of sauce.

*So-called "bottom fish" like carp and tench feed on the muddy bottom of still water which often imparts a distinctive marshy flavor to their flesh. Despite this occasional drawback, the Chinese regard carp as a symbol of good fortune, abundance, and wealth, and have cultured the fish in ponds since the fifth century B.C. Likewise, Europeans have esteemed the carp for centuries and the fish still remains popular, especially in Eastern Europe where supplies fall short of demand. In England, on the other hand, carp is rarely eaten today although it used to be more favored. Carp ponds were maintained by wealthy English households in the fifteenth century to ensure a steady supply of fresh fish for the many fast days dictated by the Church, and eighteenth-century English cookery books still commonly included a variety of recipes for both carp and tench. Carp has never been particularly popular in America—nineteenth-century American cookery books rarely included more than one recipe for carp—and even today the commercial sale is small and mostly limited to people of Eastern European ancestry. (Simoons, Food in China, 343–345; Wilson, Food and Drink in Britain, 36–37; and McClane and deZanger, The Encyclopedia of Fish, 51–53.)

**See Chapter 9 for a discussion of the terminology for the different types of aspics used by Molokhovets.

### 902 Stuffed pike rolls

(Zrazy iz shchuki)

Split a large pike lengthwise, spread out the fish, and cut crosswise into thin slices, as for cutlets. Salt the pieces lightly and spread each slice with a bit of stuffing. Roll up the fish, dip in egg and sifted rusk crumbs, and fry until golden in

Pike, carp, and eel. From *Entsiklopedicheskij slovar'* (St. Petersburg, 1898).

clarified butter. To serve, add water or bouillon to the butter in which the fish rolls were fried and pour the sauce over the fish. Serve with dried green peas.

To prepare the stuffing, finely chop 6 onions and squeeze out the excess moisture through a cloth. Rechop the onions, fry them in hot butter, and let them cool. Add grated roll crumbs and a little ground pepper, beat in a raw egg, and mix everything together.

INGREDIENTS

| | |
|---|---|
| 3 lbs pike | ½ glass grated roll crumbs |
| 6 onions | pepper and salt |
| 2 eggs | 2–3 spoons butter |

## 905  Stuffed baked pike

*(Farshirovannaja shchuka pechenaja)*

Clean a pike and slit it along the backbone. Carefully remove the skin without piercing it. Set aside the head and tail, then separate the flesh from the bones. Salt the flesh and finely chop with 1 onion and several cleaned Black Sea sprats. Add a roll that has been soaked in milk and squeezed out and mix in 1 spoon butter. Add a little nutmeg, pepper, salt, and 1–2 eggs. Pound the mixture in a mortar, stuff the pike skin, and sew it up. Grease a roasting pan with butter. Lay the pike on wooden spills and tie up with string. Transfer the fish tied in its spills to the roasting pan, pour on butter and sour cream, and set in the oven. Baste the fish several times with this sauce while it is cooking. When the pike has browned on both sides, carefully transfer it to a platter and remove the string and the wooden spills. Pour the pan juices over the fish.

INGREDIENTS

| | |
|---|---|
| 3 lbs pike | 2–3 spoons butter |
| 1 onion | 1–2 eggs |
| parsley | salt |
| 6–7 Black Sea sprats | 1–½ glasses sour cream |
| ½ white French roll | nutmeg |
| allspice | |

## 906  Pike in gray sauce*

*(Shchuka pod serym sousom)*

Clean a pike and cut it into moderate-sized pieces. Wash and salt the pieces and set aside for an hour. Remove and reserve the fish skin, and prepare a force-meat from the flesh. Mix the fish with ½ white French roll soaked in water and squeezed out, a little pepper, salt, and nutmeg. If desired, add a chopped onion that has been fried in olive oil. Fill the reserved pieces of skin with forcemeat,** arrange the pieces in a stewpan, and pour on 3–4 glasses of strong bouillon made from root vegetables and spices. Add 1 glass table wine and ½ wine glass vinegar, according to taste. Then add ¼ glass olive oil, ½ lemon, sliced, and ½ glass raisins. Boil, covered, over a high flame. When the fish has thoroughly cooked, transfer the pieces to another stewpan and set the pan over steam to keep warm while preparing the sauce. To prepare the sauce, mix together 1 glass of grated *sitnik* bread crumbs, 1 chopped carrot, 3–4 sour apples, a little fine cinnamon and cloves, 2–3 pieces of sugar, and some water. Cook the mixture until it turns into a thick kasha or porridge, rub it through a sieve, and dilute with the bouillon in which the fish was cooked. Reduce until the consistency of a sauce and pour over the fish arranged on a platter.

This fish may be garnished with slices of boiled fish forcemeat.

## INGREDIENTS

| | |
|---|---|
| 3 lbs pike | 20 allspice |
| ½ French roll | ½–1 glass table wine |
| pepper and salt | vinegar |
| nutmeg | ¼ glass olive oil or Finnish butter |
| 1 parsley root | ½ lemon |
| 1 celery root | ½ glass raisins |
| 1 onion | ½ lb grated *sitnik* bread |
| 3 carrots | 2–4 apples |
| 1 leek | about 2 pieces of sugar |
| 2 onions | cinnamon |
| 2–3 bay leaves | 2–3 cloves |

*The sitnik *bread crumbs gave a grayish cast to the sauce. Sitnik *bread was made from sieved wheat flour, but not necessarily white flour. It was more expensive and considered more stylish than the ordinary bread made from rye flour. See Chapter 27 for recipe.*

**Although Molokhovets does not identify this dish as Jewish, the practice of wrapping a fish forcemeat in a piece of reserved fish skin has long been associated with gefilte fish in European Jewish cuisine. (For more on this topic, see Toomre, "A Note on 'Fish in the Jewish Style' in Nineteenth-Century Russia," Jewish Folklore and Ethnology Review, 36–37.)*

## 910 Pike with sauerkraut

*(Shchuka s kisloju kapustoju)*

Rinse 2 lbs of shredded sauerkraut and cook, densely packed, in a small quantity of water until tender. Meanwhile clean and bone a 2–3 lb pike and strew with a little fine salt. Cut the flesh into small pieces, dip in egg and rusk crumbs or flour, and fry slightly in 1 spoon butter. Grease a ring mold or a deep clay dish with butter, line the mold with a layer of sauerkraut, and dot with several small pieces of butter. Grate a little cheese on top, add a layer of fried pike pieces, and pour on some sour cream. Continue adding additional layers of sauerkraut, butter, cheese, pike, and sour cream until the pan is filled. Finish with a layer of sauerkraut dotted with bits of butter and grated cheese. Strew with rusk crumbs and bake in the oven for an hour. [Ingredients:] 2–3 spoons butter, 3–4 rusks, 1 glass of sour cream, 1/4–1/2 lb cheese, 2 lbs sauerkraut, and 2 eggs.

### 912  Pike in the Jewish fashion with saffron

*(Shchuka po-zhidovski\* s shafranom)*

Clean a 4–5 lb pike, cut into pieces, strew with salt, and set aside for at least an hour. Place in a saucepan and add 1/4 glass vinegar and, if desired, 1 glass table wine. Add 1/2 glass or more sultanas, 2–3 lemon slices, seeded and trimmed of pith, and root vegetables, half-cooked in water. Barely cover the fish with the water in which the root vegetables were boiled and cook over a high flame, covered, until done. To serve, pour on the following sauce: Mix 1 1/2 spoons each flour and butter, 1/2 teaspoon ground saffron, and 1 teaspoon of fine sugar. Mash these ingredients together and dilute with strained bouillon. Bring to a boil several times and, if desired, add 1/2 spoon honey or 1 spoon treacle. Bring to a boil once more and pour over the fish. Strew with boiled sultanas and slices of fresh lemon.

INGREDIENTS

| | |
|---|---|
| 4–5 lb pike | 1/2 celery root |
| 1 lemon | 1 1/2 spoons flour |
| 1 glass table wine | 1 1/2 spoons butter |
| 1 wineglass vinegar | 1–2 pieces sugar |
| 1/2 glass sultanas | 1/2 teaspoon saffron |
| 1/2 carrot | 1/2 spoon honey, or 1 spoon treacle |
| 1/2 parsley root | |

*\*Note that Molokhovets used the pejorative term* po-zhidovski *instead of the more neutral term* po-evrejski. *It is a bit like calling the dish "Yid fish." Alexis Soyer in the ninth edition of his well-known* Gastronomic Regenerator *(1861) gave three recipes for fish "in the Jewish style," but all three recipes called for saltwater fish, whereas Molokhovets used only freshwater fish for this genre. The greater availability of saltwater fish in England allowed English Jews to readily substitute them for freshwater varieties. Since the Russian and East European shtetls were landlocked for the most part, Jews from Eastern Europe were dependent on local fish for sustenance. Soyer suggested sautéing breaded brill filets (p. 103), frying breaded smelts in oil (p. 134), or stewing cod slices in a mixture of chopped onions, butter, Harvey sauce, essence of anchovies, and chili vinegar (p. 121). If the recipes in both of these books are typical, and for many reasons we must assume they are, they show a marked contrast between the fish dishes associated with the English Jews and those of Eastern Europe.*

### 914  Pike in the Italian fashion

*(Shchuka po ital'janski)*

Surround the edge of a plate with a rim of an unleavened short pastry made by preparing a stiff dough from 1 very small egg, ¼ lb butter, and ½ lb flour. If the butter is unsalted, add some salt. Roll out the dough and form a rim of dough around the edge of the platter. Chop 10 sardines or anchovies as fine as possible and mix them with a handful of chopped field mushrooms and ¼ lb of the very best fresh butter. Line the platter with half of this forcemeat and strew with 2 handfuls of ground rusk crumbs and 1 handful of Dutch cheese. Slice the fish, remove as many bones as possible, and arrange the fish slices on top of the forcemeat, one piece tightly against another. Squeeze the juice of two lemons over the fish, strew with salt and pepper, and pour on ½ glass of table wine. If the wine does not cover the fish, add some bouillon. Top with the rest of the forcemeat, strew with the same quantity of crumbs and Dutch cheese, and dot with ¼ lb butter. Cover the platter with paper and bake in a hot oven for ½ hour.

INGREDIENTS

3–4 lb pike
10 sardines or anchovies
1 handful of field mushrooms
1 glass of fine rusk crumbs
¼ lb Dutch cheese
½ lb butter
2 lemons

½ glass of wine

*For the pastry*
1½ glasses flour
1 egg
¼ lb butter

### 919  Patties from pike, zander, and perch

*(Kotlety iz shchuki, sudaka i okunej)*

Usually patties are prepared from pike, zander, and perch because of the binding properties of their flesh (*vjazhushchee mjaso*). For this reason, do not add eggs to the forcemeat. Clean the fish, remove the bones, and finely chop the flesh. Fry 1 finely chopped onion in 1 spoon butter, add the fish, and fry lightly. Add ½ French roll soaked and squeezed out, 1 spoon butter or 3–4 spoons thick cream, ¼ teaspoon or more nutmeg, and 5–6 ground black peppercorns. Mix and pound in a mortar. Grease a pan or skillet with 1½ spoons butter. Shape the fish paste into patties and strew lightly with flour or rusk crumbs. Place the patties in the pan and strew with finely chopped parsley and thin lemon slices. Cover the fish with a paper greased with butter and place a lid on top of the pan. Bake in a hot oven for 10 minutes.

INGREDIENTS

| | |
|---|---|
| 2–3 lbs pike, zander, or perch | ½ lemon |
| ¼ teaspoon mace | parsley |
| 5–6 allspice | 2 spoons flour, or 3–4 rusks |
| 3 spoons butter | |

## 919a [Fish patties,] another way

*(Drugim manerom)*

Clean and bone a fish, strew with salt, black pepper, and allspice, and chop the fish fine. Fry a finely chopped onion in 1 spoon butter, mix with the fish, and add a roll soaked in milk and squeezed out and 1–2 spoons thick cream. Pound everything together in a mortar and rub through a colander. Pour a little flour onto the table and shape the forcemeat into oblong patties. Instead of bones, insert little pieces of parsley root or carrot. Dip each patty in egg and crumbs, fry in hot butter, and arrange on a platter.

Patties, however prepared, are served with one of the following: green peas; brown sauce with wine and capers, diluted with bouillon made from the leftover fish bones; Dutch sauce; Milanese rice with crayfish sauce.

INGREDIENTS

| | |
|---|---|
| 3 lbs fish | 2 spoons flour, or 5–6 rusks |
| 1 onion | 2–3 spoons butter |
| black pepper and allspice | (3–4 spoons thick cream) |
| ½ white French roll | 1 parsley root or carrot |

## 922 Boiled carp with red wine

*(Varenyj karp s krasnym vinom)*

Carp may be boiled with its scales or without. Some people find that it is tastier if cooked with its scales, although it is not nearly as attractive. When killing a carp, immediately drain its blood into salted, boiled vinegar. Clean the carp, cut it into pieces, and rub with dry salt.* Do not discard the soft roe or caviar, both of which are very tasty. Meanwhile boil in beer 1 parsley root, 1 celery root, 1 leek, 1 carrot, and 1 dried mushroom. Add 2 onions, allspice, black pepper, bay leaves, and 2–4 cloves. Place the carp head in another stewpan, top with the pieces of fish, and add lemon zest and a crust of rye bread. Pour on the strained beer boiled with the root vegetables and boil over a high flame, watching that the fish does not burn. Fry 1 spoon flour in 1 spoon butter, let it cool, and then pour in the carp blood and vinegar and some caramelized sugar. Dilute with the bouillon in which the carp boiled. Add ½ glass of red wine, a little sugar to taste, and a handful of scalded raisins or sultanas. Add lemon juice to taste and 15 marinated cherries. Bring to a boil several times, but do not let the sauce reduce very much. Arrange the carp on a platter and strew with lemon slices and raisins. Pour on the sauce and serve.

Tench and bream are prepared in the same manner.

INGREDIENTS

| | |
|---|---|
| a 3–4 lb carp | crust of bread |
| 1 parsley root | ¼ glass vinegar |
| 1 celery root | 2 bottles beer |
| 1 leek | 1–2 spoons butter |
| 2 onions | 1 spoon flour |
| 3–4 black peppercorns | 5–6 pieces of sugar |
| 5–6 allspice | ½ glass red wine |
| 2–3 bay leaves | ½ glass raisins |
| 1 lemon | 15 marinated cherries** |
| 2–3 cloves | lemon zest |
| [1 carrot] | |

*Salt used to be sold from open barrels, and readily absorbed moisture from the atmosphere. In this case, Molokhovets is merely reminding the reader to dry out the salt before using it.
**See Chapter 28 for marinated cherries.

## 928  Fried eel in sauce

(Ugor' zharenyj pod sousom)

Prepare the eel as follows: Slit the skin around the head, pass a needle with string through the eyes, tie the string, and hang up the eel. Turn back the skin from the head with a knife, then, using your hands, pull off the skin entirely. Wash and slice the eel, sprinkle the pieces with salt, and wipe them dry with a napkin. Dip the pieces in egg and crumbs and fry in butter in a skillet.

Fry 1 spoon flour in 1 spoon butter with finely chopped onion and parsley. Dilute with 2 glasses of bouillon and add 3 ground black peppercorns, 3 ground allspice, and ½ lemon, sliced and seeded. Boil the sauce thoroughly, add the fried eel, and bring to a boil once more. Two to three egg yolks may be added to the sauce. Pour the sauce over the eel arranged on a platter.

INGREDIENTS

| | |
|---|---|
| 3 lbs eel | black pepper and allspice |
| 1½ spoons butter | 2 eggs |
| 1 onion | 3–4 rusks |
| 1 parsley root | ½ lemon |

1 spoon flour                                    fish or meat bouillon
(2–3 egg yolks)

### 930  Stuffed eel

(*Ugor' farshirovannyj*)

Clean the eel as indicated in #928. [Remove the flesh from the bones, reserving the backbone in one piece.] Pound the flesh in a mortar and add ½ French roll, soaked and squeezed out, and 1 onion and parsley root, both finely chopped and fried in ½ spoon butter. Add some salt, ground black pepper and allspice, 2–3 eggs, 2–3 spoons chopped truffles or fresh field mushrooms, and 2 spoons sour cream. Mix thoroughly and pack this forcemeat around the reserved backbone. Strew with crumbs and bake on a skillet in the oven, basting with 1 spoon butter.

Transfer to a platter and pour on Strong sauce #302 or Brown sauce #278.

INGREDIENTS

3 lbs eel                                        2–3 eggs
1 parsley root                                   1½ spoons butter
½ white French roll                              2 spoons sour cream
1 onion                                          2–3 spoons truffles or field
3–4 allspice                                        mushrooms
3–4 black peppercorns

### 934a  Baked salmon, another way

(*Lososina zharenaja drugim manerom*)

Grease a tin pan or roasting pan with Finnish butter. Strew with grated bread or rusk crumbs, top with thin pieces of fresh salmon, and strew the fish with grated rusk crumbs, chopped green onions, pepper, and salt. Add another layer of fish slices, crumbs, etc. Dot the top with Finnish butter and cover with sour cream. Strew with grated crumbs and bake in the oven for 15 minutes before serving.

### 935  Salmon in papillotes

(*Lososina v papil'otakh*)

Scale a salmon, thinly slice, and strew with salt, pepper, and finely chopped onions. Drizzle with olive oil and set it aside for several hours. Grease a sheet of clean paper with Finnish butter, or on fast days, with olive oil. Cut the paper into quarters, place a piece of salmon on each piece of paper, and spread the salmon with sprat or sardine butter. Fold the paper attractively, place the packets on a greased roasting pan, and brown in a hot oven. Serve the salmon in the paper papillotes.

INGREDIENTS

3 lbs salmon  
1 onion  
¼ lb Finnish butter  

pepper and salt  
¼ glass, that is, 1 wineglass, olive oil  
6 spoons sprat or sardine butter  

## 945  Zander in the Capuchin style, with rum

*(Sudak po kaputsinski, s romom)*

Clean a zander, sprinkle with salt, lard with ham, and stud all over with parsley. Fold a clean napkin into four, grease it with Finnish butter, wrap the fish in the napkin, and tie it up with string. Lower the wrapped fish into boiling bouillon and add allspice, black pepper, and ¼ glass vinegar. Boil the fish over a high flame for at least 15 minutes. Meanwhile prepare the following sauce: Pour ½ glass of good rum into a small saucepan and set it afire. After several minutes, add ½ glass olive oil, 1 glass strong bouillon, boiled field mushrooms or boletus mushrooms, and 2–3 seeded lemon slices. Bring the sauce to a boil. Remove the zander from the napkin, [arrange the fish on a platter,] and pour on the hot sauce.

INGREDIENTS

3–4 lbs zander  
¼ lb ham  
parsley root  
½ lb butter  
10 peppercorns  

¼ glass vinegar  
½ glass rum  
½ glass olive oil  
2–3 lemon slices  

## 967  Sturgeon with bechamel

*(Osetrina pod beshemelem)*

Cut a sturgeon into pieces or slices and strew with salt and pepper. Dip in flour and fry in butter until done. Set aside to cool. Arrange a border of dough around a plate, arrange the fish on the plate, and strew with grated cheese and breadcrumbs. Pour on a bechamel sauce made from strong bouillon, flour, cheese, cream, and nutmeg and bake in the oven. When it has finished cooking, decorate the top with field mushrooms and serve yellow sauce separately in a sauceboat.

### 969 Cod

(*Treska*)

Freshly salted cod must be soaked for a full 24 hours with frequent changes of water. And then, before it is served, it should be boiled in two waters.

Air-dried cod or stockfish* is prepared as follows: Place a dried cod in a wooden vessel, pour on a strong alkaline solution, and change the solution once a day for the next four days. Then pour away the alkaline solution, cover the fish with water mixed with quicklime, and set aside for a day until the fish just turns white. Rinse again and soak for another day in river water, changing the water thrice during the day.

In winter, it is practical to prepare enough fish for several occasions, using what is immediately necessary and setting the rest aside. To cook the fish, cover a 4–5 lb piece with water and place it over a moderate fire on top of the stove. When the water becomes warm, pour it off, and cover the fish with fresh water. Repeat as often as necessary until the water is no longer sticky. Then heat the water but do not let it boil, which will toughen the stockfish. Drain the fish in a coarse sieve, salt it slightly, and transfer to a platter. Cover to keep warm until it is served.

Another, faster, way of preparing stockfish is as follows: In the evening pound the stockfish thoroughly with the butt end of a wooden ax or cleaver. Soak the fish overnight in river water and, the next day, boil it in salted water.

Best of all is the third method: Cut up a dried cod, wash the pieces in two waters, and soak the pieces for a week in a very strong brine, i.e., in very salty cold water. Then, remove the cod from the brine and press slightly. Bring fresh, slightly salted water to a rapid boil, add the cod, immediately set the pan over a low fire, and let it boil for 3 hours. Serve with butter, eggs, etc.

Fresh cod, of course, is the tastiest.

*According to Alan Davidson, the air-drying of codfish reduces its water content to about 16 percent. More moisture is retained if the fish is salted before drying. Simple drying without salt is the older method, and cod and other fish preserved by this method are called stockfish. (Davidson, North Atlantic Seafood, 54.) Dried stockfish was already being imported into England from western Norway in the ninth century. The hardness of the fish was legendary; it had to be beaten, often for a full hour, and then soaked before cooking. In Elizabethan England, the stockfish hammer was a familiar kitchen utensil. (Wilson, Food and Drink in Britain, 30, 44.) The Church calendar with its many fast days, the poverty of the people, and the lack of alternatives all help explain the widespread consumption of stockfish in medieval and early modern Europe despite the difficulty of preparation and, all too frequently, the unpalatability of the result. The same religious and economic factors were still operative in nineteenth-century Russia.

### 977 Cod with cherry and red wine sauce

(*Treska s sousom iz vishen' i krasnago vina*)

[Soak fresh or lightly salted dried cod in water for 2 hours, wash the fish, and boil in two changes of water. Rinse the fish with fresh hot water. Pour on enough boiled whole milk to barely cover the fish and cook until done.]

Pour off the milk, scald with boiling water, and drain the fish. Fry ¾ glass of cherry purée in 1 spoon butter and dilute with 1½ glasses water or bouillon. Strew with a little sugar, and, if desired, 2–3 ground cloves. Add a little cinnamon and 1 teaspoon potato flour mixed with 1 spoon water, bring to a boil, and pour in ½–1 glass of red wine. Heat until the sauce is very hot and pour over the cod.

### 983  Baked bream stuffed with sauerkraut

*(Leshch pechenyj, farshirovannyj kisloju kapustoju)*

Rinse 2–3 glasses of sauerkraut in water and squeeze out the excess moisture. Fry the sauerkraut and 1 finely chopped onion in 1½ spoons butter. Add some salt, 3–4 ground black peppercorns, and 3–4 ground allspice berries. Stuff the fish, sew it up, and place on a skillet greased with butter. Mix 1–3 egg yolks and 1 spoon flour with 1 glass sour cream and pour over the bream. Strew with 2–3 spoons grated cheese and 1 spoon rusk crumbs. Drizzle with rich bouillon and place in the oven for slightly more than 30 minutes. When the fish has browned, transfer it carefully to a platter. Add 1 glass bouillon to the skillet, stir the sauce, and bring to a boil on top of the stove. Pour the sauce onto the platter, but not over the fish.

INGREDIENTS

| | |
|---|---|
| 3 lbs bream | 1 glass sour cream |
| 2–3 glasses sauerkraut | 1–3 egg yolks |
| 1 onion | 1 spoon flour |
| 3–4 allspice berries | 2–3 spoons grated cheese |
| 3–4 black peppercorns | 1 spoon rusk crumbs |
| 2 spoons butter | |

### 984  Baked bream stuffed with buckwheat kasha

*(Leshch pechenyj nafarshirovannyj grechnevoju kasheju)*

Scale and clean a bream, rub with salt, and stuff as follows: Fry 1–2 finely chopped onions in 1 spoon butter and stir in a plate of leftover boiled,* thick buckwheat kasha. Fry lightly and add 3–4 chopped hard-boiled eggs and some greens. Stuff the fish and sew it up. Melt butter in a skillet, add the fish, and strew with a mixture of half flour and half rusk crumbs. Pour on butter and about 2 spoons water and bake in the oven, basting frequently with the pan juices.

To serve, dilute the sauce with a little bouillon and 2–4 spoons sour cream. Bring to a boil and pour over the fish.

INGREDIENTS

| | |
|---|---|
| 4 lbs bream | greens |
| 2 onions | (2–4 spoons sour cream) |
| ½ lb buckwheat groats (1¼ glasses) | 3–4 eggs |
| 1 spoon flour | ⅜ lb butter |
| 2–3 rusks | |

*The literal translation is "boiled the day before."

## 985 Boiled bream with horseradish and apples

(Leshch varenyj s khrenom i jablokami)

Clean and salt the bream and cut it into pieces. Place the fish in a pan, pour boiling light vinegar over the fish, cover for several minutes, and then remove the fish from the vinegar. In a separate pan, boil root vegetables and spices, strain the bouillon, and pour it over the fish arranged in a stewpan. Boil over a high flame and transfer the fish to a platter. Garnish with lemon slices and a sauce made by mixing together grated horseradish, grated sour apples, a little vinegar, sugar, and some of the pan juices.

INGREDIENTS

| | |
|---|---|
| a 3–4 lb bream | a large horseradish root |
| 1 parsley root | 4–6 apples |
| 1 celery root | ½ lemon |
| 1 leek | vinegar |
| 2 onions | 2–4 pieces sugar |
| allspice | bay leaf |
| black pepper | |

## 998 Boiled crucians with sour cream sauce and quenelles

(Karasi varenye s sousom iz smetany i s knel'ju)

Clean and salt the fish, set them aside for a full hour, and then transfer to a stewpan. Pour on just enough cold bouillon made from root vegetables, onion, and spices to barely cover the fish. Set the pan on top of the stove and boil for 15–20 minutes over a very high flame. Meanwhile, bring to a boil 1 spoon butter with 1 spoon of the very best flour and add 4 spoons of very fresh, thick sour cream, 1 small lump of sugar, and finely chopped dill. Dilute with enough fish bouillon to make a rather thick sauce. Boil thoroughly and pour over the fish arranged on the platter. Garnish with sliced quenelles that have been wrapped in a cloth moistened in butter and boiled like a sausage.

INGREDIENTS

3–4 lbs crucians
root vegetables
onion
allspice and black pepper
1 spoon butter

1 spoon flour
dill
4 spoons thick sour cream
ingredients for quenelles
1 bay leaf

### 1011  Sterlet in champagne

*(Sterljad' na shampanskom)*

Clean a 3–4 lb sterlet and cut it into pieces. Wash in cold water and wipe dry with a clean napkin. Arrange in a single layer in a silver saucepan, failing that in a casserole or sauté pan. Add ¼ lb butter, salt, the juice from ½ lemon, and 2 glasses of champagne. Five minutes before serving, place on top of the stove to boil and immediately serve in the same pan.

### 1012  An unusually tasty fish platter, made from sterlet in white table wine

*(Rybnoe bljudo neobyknovenno vkusnoe, v osobennosti iz sterljadi s belym stolovym vinom)*

Take 3–4 lbs of fish, preferably sterlet. Wash the fish thoroughly and wipe dry with a towel. Cut it into pieces and place in a stewpan. Half-cover the fish with any type of white table wine, only not too strong. Add about ⅛ lb of very fresh Finnish butter and a whole lemon, seeded and sliced like an apple. Cover the stewpan, light a spirit lamp under it, and, in 15 minutes, this wonderful dish will be ready. Other fish with few bones, like sturgeon, whitefish, and zander, are prepared in the same manner.

INGREDIENTS

3–4 lbs fish
½–1 bottle wine

⅛ lb butter
1 lemon

### 1017  Meat and herring casserole

*(Forshmak\* iz mjasa)*

Chop 1½ lbs of cooked veal or wild fowl or boiled beef and add 2–3 soaked and cleaned herring and ½ French roll soaked and squeezed out. Chop everything as fine as possible and add 3–5 black peppercorns, 3–5 allspice berries, some nutmeg, 1 medium onion finely chopped and fried in butter, ½ glass sweet or sour cream, 2–4 eggs, and 1 spoon butter. Mix all this together and pile into a stewpan greased with butter and strewn with rusk crumbs. Bake in the oven for 30 minutes and serve, transferring to a platter.

The sour cream may be increased to 2 glasses, in which case the *forshmak* should be served in a tin or silver casserole.

INGREDIENTS

| | |
|---|---|
| leftover meat | 3–5 black peppercorns |
| 2–3 herrings, or 10–12 sardines | 3–5 allspice berries |
| ½ French roll | 2 eggs |
| 1 onion | 1 glass sweet or sour cream |
| 2 spoons butter | 2 rusks |

*Forshmak comes from the archaic German word* Vorschmack, *meaning foretaste or foreboding. Now known as a typical Russian appetizer, this baked dish, usually served hot, is made by mixing chopped cooked meat, herring, onion, raw eggs, and spices. Potatoes were less commonly added in the nineteenth century than now. Molokhovets used them in only two out of her five recipes for forshmak.*

## 1020  Crayfish with Smolensk kasha in sauce

*(Raki so smolenskoju krupoju pod sousom)*

Rub 1 glass of Smolensk kasha with an egg and let the kasha dry thoroughly. Bring to a boil 1½ glasses water and 1 spoon butter and stir in the kasha briskly. Add finely chopped parsley and dill, some nutmeg, and 1 piece sugar. Cover the pan with a lid and bake briefly in the oven. Cool and beat an egg into the kasha before stuffing the crayfish shells, which of course, have first been cooked in salted water with dill.

Arrange the stuffed crayfish in a stewpan, interlayering the tails and claws. Pour on the following sauce:

Fry 1½ spoons flour in 1½ spoons crayfish butter and dilute with 2–3 glasses of bouillon and 1½ glasses of very fresh sour cream. Add dill and a little nutmeg; mix and pour over the crayfish. Cover the saucepan and cook on top of the stove for ½ hour.

INGREDIENTS

| | |
|---|---|
| 60 crayfish | 1½ glasses sour cream |
| 1 glass Smolensk kasha | 1 piece sugar |
| 2 eggs | nutmeg |
| 1 spoon butter | ½ glass flour |
| 1½ spoons crayfish butter | parsley and dill |

### 1023  Marinated crayfish tails

*(Rakovyja shejki marinovannyja)*

Wash crayfish until clean, boil in salted water with dill, and let them cool. Clean the tails and press thoroughly in a napkin to remove any excess moisture. Place in a jar and pour on crayfish butter.

Or dry them slowly in the oven and, before using, soak them in water for several hours.

Or place the boiled and cooled crayfish tails in a jar and cover with cooled vinegar that has been boiled with spices, but no sugar.

In general, crayfish tails cannot be kept for long. Wash crayfish backs, that is the shells, as clean as possible, dry them, store them in a jar, and stuff them for serving. Also wash the shells left from the small claws and tails. Dry and pound them and store in a jar. Use this powder to prepare crayfish butter as indicated in the next recipe because crayfish butter may be prepared from either fresh or dried shells.

### 1024b  Zander patties with rice, *à la Milanese,* with crayfish sauce

*(Kotlety iz sudaka s risom po milanski, s rakovym sousom)*

Soak 1 glass of rice in cold water for several hours, then drain in a colander. Cover the rice with cold water, bring once to a boil, drain, and rinse with cold water. Melt ¼ lb Finnish butter in a saucepan with ¼ lb finely chopped bone marrow. Bring to a boil, add 1 onion, and fry until golden. Remove the onion, add the rice, fry lightly, and add 1 glass of white wine. When the rice thickens, strew with 2 pinches of powdered saffron, and gradually add a little hot bouillon without drowning the rice in the liquid. Stir to prevent the rice from burning and cook until the rice is done, but not overcooked. Serve immediately, strewn with a large quantity of grated Parmesan cheese. Garnish with zander patties and pour on crayfish sauce.

To prepare the patties, clean and bone 2–3 lbs zander, chop fine, and strew with salt and 3 ground black peppercorns. Add a roll soaked in milk and squeezed dry and 2 spoons thick cream. Pound everything in a mortar and rub through a colander. Form into round patties, sprinkle with flour, and fry in butter.

To prepare the sauce, boil 30 crayfish with salt and dill. Clean the claws and tails. Dry and pound the shells. Fry the pounded shells in 2 spoons butter until golden, add ½ glass flour, and dilute with 3 glasses bouillon. Boil thoroughly, strain, and add 2–3 spoons sweet or sour cream. Add a little lemon juice, the crayfish tails and claws, and bring to a boil once more. Or garnish the dish with marinated crayfish tails and pour on a white sauce made with very fresh sour cream.

INGREDIENTS

*For the patties*
2–3 lbs zander
½ French roll
pepper
¼ glass flour
½ glass milk
2 spoons thick cream

*For the sauce*
30 marinated crayfish tails, or 30 live
   crayfish
¾ glass flour
2–3 spoons or ⅓–½ glass sour cream

*For the rice*
1 glass rice
¼ lb bone marrow
¼–½ lb Parmesan cheese
1 glass white wine
lemon juice
1 onion
2 pinches saffron
¾ lb butter in all
Total of ¾ lb butter for rice, patties,
   and sauce

# 8
# *Pirogs* and *Pâtés*

*(Pirogi i pashtety)*

[*Translator's note: Pirogs* (filled pastries) have always beens essential for Russian festivities. "*Pirog* Day" (*Pirozhnyj den'*), the third day after a marriage, was traditionally the time when the young bride offered guests a selection of *pirogs* and *pirozhki*. The quintessential *pirog* in Russian culture, of course, was the one envisioned by Chichikov, the protagonist of Gogol's *Dead Souls*. No real *pirog* has ever quite matched its grandeur or indigestibility. *Pirogs* usually were round, but Molokhovets preferred rectangular ones. *Pirozhki* are small *pirogs*. Whether large or small, they come in many shapes and sizes with the doughs as varied as the fillings (cf. Chapter 2). Some have special names. *Karavaj*, for instance, is a large, round loaf that was part of the traditional offering of bread and salt, the Russian gesture of hospitality; *rastegai* is a small open-faced pastry with a fish filling that was customarily served with *ukhas* and other fish soups; *kurnik* is another festive pie, one that was often served at weddings. The Russian word *pashtet* comes from the German *Pasteten* via Polish. Originally this meant a rich forcemeat baked in pastry (*pâté en croûte*), but with the passage of time the emphasis has shifted to the forcemeat itself (*pâté en terrine*), which is commonly known as pâté. Molokhovets' *pirogs* encased the filling in pastry; with a few exceptions, her pâtés just had a top layer of pastry or none at all. Her *pirogs* tended to include pieces of meat, fish, or poultry with grains and vegetables and almost no forcemeat; by contrast, forcemeat fillings predominated in the pâtés. (For a good discussion of savory and sweet *pirogs* and of their role in Russian culture, see Kovalev, *Rasskazy o russkoj kukhne*, 140–145.)]

## DOUGH FOR *PIROGS, PIROZHKI,* AND PÂTÉS
### *(Testo dlja pirogov, pirozhkov i pashtetov)*

*Remarks:* The important rules for making dough are the following: If the dough is prepared for fast days, use approximately 1 lb fine wheat flour for each glass of water with yeast. More precise instructions are impossible since some flours are better than others, some are moister, and some are drier. If butter and eggs are added to the dough, use less than 1 glass of water for each lb of flour. 1½ lbs of flour is sufficient for a *pirog* for 6–8 persons since this amount of dough is enough for 8 large pieces or 15–18 small *pirozhki*. For each lb of flour use at least 1 *zolotnik* dry yeast. Dissolve the yeast in ¼ glass water mixed with 1 teaspoon flour, let the mixture rise slightly, and then prepare the dough. If the dough must be prepared quickly, dilute the yeast in warm water and after 15 minutes, prepare the dough. If the dough is needed early in the morning, start the yeast the night before. Do this by mixing the yeast with flour and cold water and letting it stand overnight in a heated* room, so that it will not turn sour.

Various recipes for dough are given below. *Pirogs* themselves are prepared as follows: After the dough has been mixed and has risen, knead the dough, without adding flour. Roll it out with a rolling pin, sprinkling the dough only lightly with flour. Arrange a rectangular piece of dough on a clean baking sheet, greased with butter. Place the prepared stuffing on the dough and turn up all four sides to shape the *pirog* into an even rectangle. Pinch the edges together and set it aside for at least half an hour. Paint the top but not the sides with an egg beaten with 1 spoon water. Rusk crumbs may be sprinkled on top. Place in a hot oven for half an hour, but if the *pirog* is big or stuffed with fish, then bake for an hour. Some people prefer a thin and dry crust and a lot of stuffing, while others like more pastry. In the latter case, more flour will be required. For any dough, the longer it is beaten, the better it will be.

Serve butter separately with *pirogs* made from yeast doughs, which are not as rich.

The amount of dough in the following recipes is sufficient for either one *pirog* or 15–18 *pirozhki*. *Pirozhkis*, however, require half the stuffing necessary for a *pirog*. To make *pirozhki*, cut off pieces of dough and roll each piece into a smooth ball, stretch it in your hands, fill it with ½ spoon stuffing, pinch it together, even it out, and set it to rise on the table or on a baking sheet greased with butter. When they have risen, paint with egg yolk beaten with water and place in the oven for approximately 20 minutes.

Or fry them in butter, omitting the egg wash. Serve sprinkled with fried parsley.

The proportions are sufficient for 6–8 persons. For 9–12 persons, increase the proportions by 1½. For 13–15 persons, double the proportions. For 16–18 persons, increase the proportions by 2½. For 19–24 persons, triple the proportions.

*More precisely, "in a room of ordinary temperature" (v komnate obyknovennoj temperatury), or about 60° F. Since contemporary American homes are warmer (about 68–70° F.), cooks today are advised to let their yeast breads rise slowly in the refrigerator overnight.*

## 1025  Puff pastry

*(Sloenoe testo)*

Prepare puff pastry. When the oven is ready, roll the dough out thin and place the stuffing on top. Shape into a rectangular *pirog* and paint with egg. Rusk crumbs may be strewn on top. Transfer from a cold place directly into a hot oven.

Another way: Pour 2 eggs and ½ wineglass of rum into a glass, add fresh sour cream, and pour into the flour. Knead the dough until it can be rolled thin. Place ½ lb of good, firm Finnish butter in the middle and cover with a circle of dough. Pinch together and roll into a long oval. Cover and let stand in a cold place for at least 15 minutes. Fold the dough into three, roll out, and again let it stand, being sure to cover the dough with a napkin. Roll out again and repeat 6 times in all. Make *pirozhki* from the dough, stuff them, and paint with egg. Transfer from a cold place directly into the oven.

*Remarks:* This amount of puff pastry, rich pastry, or short pastry, etc., is sufficient for a *pirog* or *pirozhki* for 6–8 persons; half the amount will be enough to cover a small deep dish of pâté, providing that the dish is not lined with dough.

INGREDIENTS

| | |
|---|---|
| 2 glasses flour, or ⅔ lb | 1 egg to paint the dough |
| ½ lb butter | (2 rusks) |

## 1027  Choux pastry

*(Testo zavarnoe bez drozhzhej)*

Bring to a boil 1¼ glasses water and ½ glass butter, immediately sprinkle on 1½ glasses flour, and mix until smooth. Beat 4 eggs, or preferably, 4 egg yolks, into the hot mixture and add salt. Immediately make about 18–20 *pirozhki*, sprinkling them lightly with flour (not more than 1 spoon). Bake them in the oven on a baking sheet strewn with flour. This dough should not be painted with egg.

INGREDIENTS

| | |
|---|---|
| ⅜ lb butter | 4 eggs |
| 3 glasses flour | salt |

## 1032  Yeast dough that rises in cold water

*(Drozhzhevoe testo podkhodjashchee v kholodnoj vode)*

In the evening dilute 3 *zolotniki* dry yeast in warm water and stir in 2 teaspoons flour to make 1 glass in all. Set the mixture aside to rise overnight and the next the morning mix this glass of very liquid yeast with 1 glass milk and ¼ lb clarified butter mixed with enough milk to make 1 glass. Add 2 lbs flour, 5 large eggs (that is, 1 glass of eggs), and 1 spoon salt. Knead as well as possible, working the dough for about an hour. Transfer the dough to a napkin and tie it up, leaving enough room for the dough to double in bulk. Submerge the napkin with dough into a barrel of cold water.

When the dough rises to the surface after several hours, beat the dough and use half of it to form a *pirog*. Stuff the *pirog* and place on a sheet to rise. Paint with egg, sprinkle with rusk crumbs, and bake in the oven for ½ to 1 hour, as indicated in the Remarks. Use the rest of the dough to make buns, sprinkling ½ glass fine sugar into the dough.

INGREDIENTS

| | |
|---|---|
| 3 lbs flour | (½ glass sugar) |
| ¼ lb butter | 3 *zolotniki*, or 1 kopeck, dry yeast |
| 6 eggs | about 2 glasses milk |

### 1033  Ordinary yeast dough

*(Testo na drozhzhakh obyknovennoe)*

Prepare a dough, as usual, from 1¼ glasses warm milk or water together with yeast and half the flour. Set the dough in a warm place and, when it rises, beat thoroughly with a small wooden spatula. Add salt, 2 spoons butter, 2 eggs, 2–3 egg yolks, and enough flour to make a thick dough. Knead the dough until it no longer sticks to your hands and [set it aside for the second rising.] After it has risen a second time, form a *pirog* as indicated in the Remarks.

INGREDIENTS

| | |
|---|---|
| 1¼–1½ glasses milk or water together with the yeast | 1½–2 lbs flour |
| 1½–2 *zolotniki* yeast | ¼ lb butter |
| 1 egg to paint the dough | 2 rusks |
| | 2 eggs |

If egg whites are needed for the next dish, then use only egg yolks in the dough, and save the egg whites for the other dish, such as meringues.

### 1038  Rye and wheat dough for pâtés

*(Testo rzhanoe i pshenichnoe dlja pashtetov)*

Mix 1½ glasses each sifted rye and wheat flours, pour in ½ glass boiling water and ¼ glass hot fat, mix, and let stand for several minutes. Beat in 2 eggs, add a little wheat flour, and knead into a stiff dough, as for noodles. Grease a mold with butter and line it with this dough. Sprinkle with crushed barley and bake in the oven. When it has cooked, pour out the barley, carefully remove the dough from the mold, and fill it with the pâté stuffing. Cover with a lid of dough and bake. Then carefully cut off the lid and serve. If the pâté will be served cold, decorate the top with chopped aspic.

This same mold may be used for hot pâtés. Prepare them from just wheat flour, or from puff pastry, rich pastry, or short pastry.

Grease with butter the interior of a tin mold resembling a flower pot, the two halves of which must separate. Line with a circle of pastry, fill with the stuffing and layers of roast wild fowl, lemon, capers, and truffles. Cover with a lid of the same dough and bake. After removing the pâté from the oven, arrange it on a platter and release it from the mold. To serve, cut off the top crust, pour in a little sauce, and pass the remaining sauce in a sauceboat.

For 9–12 persons, increase the proportions of dough for a mold of this size by 1½; for 13–24 persons, double the proportions.

## INGREDIENTS

1½ glass rye flour
1½ glasses wheat flour or 1⅛ lbs of wheat flour alone

¼ glass melted fat
2 eggs

# PIROGS

## *(Pirogi)*

*Remarks:* Any kind of dough that is handy, as indicated above, may be used for *pirogs* and *pirozhki*.

*Fish* [for *pirogs*] must be cleaned thoroughly, washed, and boned. Add salt, sprinkle with a little ground black pepper, and wrap in a napkin for an hour. Then cut into thin slices.

*Sago* for *pirogs* is prepared as follows:

Cover the sago with cold water in the evening and pour off the water the next morning. Pour the sago into a saucepan with a rather large amount of boiling water. Immediately begin to boil it, stirring with a spoon. When the sago has become tender, but before it turns mushy, turn it into a colander or coarse sieve and rinse with cold water. After the water has been drained completely, transfer the sago to a stoneware bowl and stir in salt, good butter, chopped eggs, chopped sturgeon marrow (*viziga*), pepper, and greens. Place half the stuffing on the rolled out dough, then the fish, then the rest of the stuffing. Cover with dough and let it rise. Paint with egg and bake in the oven for ¾–1 hour.

*Rice* is prepared as follows: Wash in cold water and drain. Add just enough fresh cold water to barely cover the rice. Boil until the rice is tender and drain in a sieve. Rinse with cold water, drain completely, and transfer to a stoneware bowl. Add butter, hard-boiled eggs, and other ingredients, depending on what else will be served with the *pirog*.

*Sturgeon marrow* is prepared as follows: In the evening soak it in cold water. The next day, [drain,] cover it with clean water and boil until tender with parsley root and an onion. Turn into a sieve, rinse with cold water, finely chop, and add salt and a little ground black pepper, etc.

### 1039 Pirog with sturgeon marrow, rice, eggs, and fish

*(Pirog s vizigoju, risom, jajtsami i ryboju)*

Boil the sturgeon marrow as indicated in the Remarks, finely chop, and add salt, black pepper, 2–4 chopped hard-boiled eggs, and rice boiled in water with 1 onion, 1 parsley root and 1 spoon butter (cf. Remarks). Add 1 spoon rich bouillon, parsley, and dill, mix everything together, and spread ¾ of this stuffing on the rolled out dough. Top with very thin slices of boned and lightly salted pike, zander, bream, salmon (*lososina* or *semga*), sturgeon, or whitefish. Sprinkle on a little finely chopped allspice, cover with the remaining stuffing, and then the dough. Let the *pirog* rise, paint with egg, and bake in the oven for 1 hour.

Serve additional butter separately with the *pirog*.

Similar *pirogs* may be made with: (1) sturgeon marrow, eggs, and fish (⅜ lb sturgeon marrow, 2 lbs fish, 2–3 eggs); (2) sturgeon marrow, rice, and eggs (½ lb rice, ¼ lb sturgeon marrow, 2–3 eggs); (3) rice and eggs (1 lb rice, ¼ lb butter, 3–4 eggs, greens).

## INGREDIENTS

*For the dough*
1¼—1½ glasses water or milk
together with yeast
2–3 eggs
¼ lb butter
salt
1½–2 lbs flour
1 egg
2 rusks

*For the stuffing*
⅛–¼ lb sturgeon marrow

3–4 eggs
(½–¾ glass rice)
1½–2 lbs fish
dill
parsley
1 parsley root
1 onion
¼ lb butter
about 3–4 black peppercorns
salt

### 1044  Pirog with sauerkraut and fish (for meat or fast days)

*(Pirog s kisloju kapustoju i ryboju) (Skoromnyj ili postnyj)*

Fry 1 finely chopped onion in ⅛ lb butter or oil. Add 3 glasses sauerkraut and finely ground black pepper and allspice, and stew, covered, until tender, adding rich bouillon and stirring so that it does not burn. Cut thin slices of cleaned, salted, and boned fish, such as salmon (*lososina* or *semga*) or sturgeon, etc., and fry the fish in 1 spoon butter. Place a layer of sauerkraut on the dough, then a layer of fish, then cover with the sauerkraut and dough, etc.

Finely chopped, dried mushrooms fried in butter or oil may be substituted for the fish.

For *pirozhki*, prepare only half the stuffing.

INGREDIENTS

3 glasses, or 1½ lbs, sauerkraut  
¼ lb butter, or ½ glass fast day oil  
[5 allspice berries]*  
1½ lbs fish  

2 black peppercorns  
1 onion  
separate ingredients for the dough

*\*Allspice was called for in the body of this recipe, but was omitted from the list of ingredients. Instead, Molokhovets gave two entries for black pepper, which I assume was a mistake or typographical error. I have therefore changed the larger peppercorn entry to allspice to reflect her usual proportion of spices for this type of recipe.*

### 1046  Pirog with veal pluck

*(Pirog s teljach'im liverom*

Boil the veal pluck, including the heart but not the liver, and chop fine. Melt 2 spoons butter in a skillet, add a finely chopped onion, and fry lightly. Add the chopped pluck and fry again, stirring so that the mixture does not burn. Add a little pepper, salt, 3–4 finely chopped hard-boiled eggs, parsley, and dill. Mix and fill the *pirog*. For a large *pirog*, a little boiled beef may be added.

For *pirozhki* make half the stuffing.

INGREDIENTS

veal pluck without the liver weighing  
   about 2½ lbs  
1 onion  
3–4 eggs  
greens  

salt  
¼ lb butter  
pepper  
separate ingredients for the dough

### 1050  Russian coulibiac with fish

*(Russkaja kulebjaka s ryboju)*

Prepare a dough using 1½ lbs flour, ⅜ lb Finnish butter, 3 egg yolks, 1 cup milk, 1 spoon good yeast, and ½ teaspoon salt. Begin the dough as usual, dissolving the yeast in milk. When it has risen, add the butter, eggs, salt, and remaining flour, and let it rise again. Meanwhile, prepare the following stuffing. Cut up and bone 1½ lbs zander and fry the pieces of fish in 1 spoon butter with 1 chopped onion and chopped fresh or dried dill. Chop everything together with the fish. Mix 1¼ glasses Smolensk buckwheat with 1 egg, let the buckwheat dry, and rub through a coarse sieve. Bring 1¼ glasses water to a boil with ¼ lb butter. When it begins to boil, sprinkle on the buckwheat groats, stirring briskly. Add salt. Place briefly in the oven to brown lightly, then mix it as well as possible with the fish stuffing. Slice 1 lb prepared* sturgeon and ½ lb salmon. Make a long or round coulibiac. Place half the stuffing with the kasha in the middle, cover with the sliced sturgeon and salmon, and top with the remaining kasha and stuffing. Pinch the edges of dough together and let the *pirog* rise for ½ hour. Paint with egg and place in the oven. This is a real Russian coulibiac.

INGREDIENTS

*Dough for 6 people*
1½ lb flour
1 glass milk
⅜ lb butter
3 egg yolks
2 *zolotniki* dry yeast

*For the stuffing*
1½ lb zander

1 onion
1 lb sturgeon
½ lb salmon
1¼ glasses Smolensk buckwheat
1 egg
¼ lb butter
dill

*By "prepared," Molokhovets *probably meant cleaned and boned, but not cooked.*

### 1052  Old-fashioned kurnik, or chicken pie

*(Starinnyj kurnik)*

Prepare a rich or short dough, make a round *pirog*, and fill with the following stuffing.

Boil a fresh chicken in a small quantity of salted water. [After it has cooked], remove it from the pot and cut it into pieces, as for soup. Mix 1¼ glasses fine buckwheat with 1 egg, let it dry, and rub through a sieve. Bring to a boil 1½ glasses water with 2 spoons butter, scatter on the buckwheat briskly, stirring constantly to prevent lumps from forming, and boil about 5 minutes. Place briefly in the oven to dry out slightly. Mix with 4–5 finely chopped hard-boiled eggs and greens and add salt. Place half the kasha on a flat circle of dough, add pieces of boned chicken, cover with the remaining stuffing, and sprinkle the top with dill. Before setting it in the oven, pour strong chicken broth into the middle. Cover with another small flat round of dough, pinch the edges together, paint with egg, and immediately put into the oven. Serve instead of pâté or *pirog*.

Serve the remaining chicken bouillon the next day for breakfast.

INGREDIENTS

*For the stuffing*
1 chicken
1½ glasses buckwheat groats
5 eggs
¼ lb butter
dill

1 egg to paint the dough

*For the dough*
½ lb butter
1 wineglass rum
1 lb flour

### 1053 Carrot *pirog*

*(Pirog s morkov'ju)*

Prepare puff pastry, a rich dough, or a yeast dough. Fill with the following: Wash and peel 12 medium carrots, boil in salted water or bouillon, and finely chop. Mix with 2 spoons butter, lightly fry, and add hard-boiled eggs and salt to taste. Prepare only half of this stuffing for *pirozhki*.

(Information about *pirozhki* is given in Chapter 2.)

## HOT AND COLD PÂTÉS

*(Pashtety gorjachie i kholodnye)*

*Remarks:* The dough for pâtés may be prepared from puff or choux pastry or rich, short, or rye pastry. Yeast dough is not used for pâtés.

*Fish forcemeat for pâtés.* Clean, gut, and wash 1½ lbs pike, zander, or perch. Cut up and bone the fish, finely chop, and add salt. Fry 1 finely chopped onion in 1 spoon butter, add the chopped fish, and fry lightly. Add salt, 3–5 finely ground peppercorns, and the soft interior from half a 5 kopeck French roll soaked in water, bouillon, or milk and squeezed out. Add another spoon of fresh, washed butter and ½ glass bouillon or ½ glass or more thick fresh cream. Mix, finely chop, pound in a mortar, and rub through a fine sieve. Eggs are not added to a forcemeat made from the above-mentioned fish, but if the forcemeat is prepared from whitefish or other fish, then it must be bound with 3–4 eggs.

*Liver forcemeat.* Wash ½ calf's liver and fry with ½ lb fresh unsalted pork fat, 1 carrot, 1 parsley root, 1 leek, 1 celery root, 1 onion, 1 bay leaf, and 5 allspice berries. When the liver has cooked, let it cool and then grate it. Rub the liver through a fine sieve together with the fried pork fat and root vegetables. Add ½ lb finely chopped raw veal, the soft interior of half a 5 kopeck French roll soaked in water and squeezed out, about 3 spoons bouillon, 4–5 eggs, and salt. Pound in a mortar and rub through a fine sieve.

## 1063 Pâté from partridges, hazel grouse, teal, capercaillie, hare, or other game, with puff pastry

*(Pashtet iz kuropatok, rjabchikov, svistelej, glukharja, zajtsa ili drugoj dichi s sloenym testom)*

Using ¼ lb sliced pork fat, lard one of the following: 3 partridges, 3 hazel grouse, 3 pigeons, 12 teal, or 1 small hare. Add salt and fry in a saucepan with 2 spoons butter until half done. Cut into parts and, if using a hare, remove the bones. Prepare a forcemeat from liver and veal as indicated in the Remarks and add 4–6 field mushrooms, sliced into long pieces. Arrange on a platter a layer of forcemeat, a layer of game, 2–3 or even 4 spoons finely sliced truffles boiled in Madeira, and more forcemeat. Cover with dough, paint with egg, and bake in the oven for an hour. Cut off the top crust before serving and pour in a glass of sauce made by degreasing the pan juices in which the game was fried, diluting with bouillon, and adding a little lemon juice.

Serve French truffle sauce in a sauceboat, Strong sauce #302, brown truffle sauce, or red wine sauce.

If the pâté is made with capercaillie, cut it into portions and arrange the pieces on a platter, pasting them together with forcemeat so that they appear whole in the pâté. Surround with the remaining forcemeat, cover with dough, paint with egg, and bake in the oven for 1½ hours. Before serving, cut off the upper crust, pour in a little sauce, and serve.

INGREDIENTS

| | |
|---|---|
| 3 partridges, 3 hazel grouse, 12 teal, 3 pigeons, or 1 small hare | salt |
| | nutmeg |
| ¼ lemon | about 5 allspice |
| ¼ lb pork fat | 4 field mushrooms |
| 4–5 spoons butter | 4–6 eggs |
| ½ calf's liver, or 1½ lbs | 2–3 or 4 spoons truffles |
| ½ lb veal | separate ingredients for the dough |
| ½ white French roll | |

## 1064  Turkish mutton pâté*

*(Pashtet turetskij iz baraniny)*

Salt 2 lbs boneless fatty mutton and boil until tender with spices, root vegetables, and ½ lb smoked ham. Remove the meat, strain the bouillon, and let it cool a little. Skim the fat from the bouillon, add butter, and bring to a boil. Pour in 1 glass rice, and stew, covered, until the grains are tender and separate easily. Sprinkle nutmeg on the rice. Butter a platter and strew with rusk crumbs. Cut the ham into small oblong pieces and mix with the rice. Spread a layer of ham and rice on the platter and top with a layer of mutton. Repeat the layers. Smooth the top, paint the edge of the platter with egg, cover the entire pâté with dough, and bake in the oven. Prepare a sauce using 2½ glasses of the bouillon in which the ham and mutton were cooked, add 1 spoon flour, and bring to a boil. Pour 1 glass into the pâté just before serving and serve the remaining sauce in a sauceboat, adding lemon slices or capers, and, if desired, a little sherry.

Separate ingredients [will be needed] for puff pastry or another dough.

If the ham is too salty, it should be soaked before using.

INGREDIENTS

| | |
|---|---|
| 2 lbs boneless mutton | 1 bay leaf |
| ½ lb ham | 1 glass rice |
| 1 carrot | ½ lb butter |
| 1 parsley root | nutmeg |
| 1 celery root | 2 rusks |
| 1 leek | 1 spoon flour |
| 1 onion | ¼ lemon, or 1 spoon capers |
| 10–15 allspice | |

*The name of this dish and the ingredients seem somewhat incongruous. Although rice and mutton have long been associated with Turkish cuisine, nineteenth-century Turks, who were Muslims, would not have eaten ham. On the other hand, the Ottoman Empire included many non-Muslim people. This dish seems more Armenian or Georgian and, from a Russian perspective, vaguely came from "somewhere down there near Turkey." The same kind of geographical fuzziness has led to our calling our native American bird, the Meleagris gallopavo, a turkey.*

## 1072  Cold pâté for traveling

*(Kholodnyj pashtet dorozhnyj)*

Lard 6 hazel grouse with ¼ lb pork fat and fry with ¼ lb butter, 30 allspice berries, 6 bay leaves, 1 parsley root, 1 leek, 1 celery root, and 1 onion. Take the hazel grouse from the pan, cool, remove the bones, and cut the meat into small pieces. Finely chop the bones and fry them once more in the same butter. Pound them together with the fried root vegetables and spices and pass through a fine sieve.

Slice 1 calf's liver and ¼ lb pork fat. Add salt, fry in 3 spoons butter until golden, and chop fine. Pound in a mortar and add ¼ lb washed Finnish butter, ½ white French roll soaked in water and squeezed out, nutmeg, salt, and 2–4 eggs. Pound, pass through a fine sieve, and add 3–4 spoons chopped truffles.

Prepare a very stiff dough from 1½ lbs flour and 4–5 eggs and use it to line the bottom and sides of a saucepan that has been greased with butter and strewn with rusk crumbs. Spread a layer of calf's liver forcemeat on the dough, add a layer of hazel grouse meat, and top with the purée made from the bones and root vegetables, diluted with 1 glass rich bouillon. Cover with dough and bake in the oven for 1 hour.

After removing the pâté from the oven, let it cool by cutting off the top crust. Cover the pâté with a saucepan lid and in this manner it may be taken on journeys.

INGREDIENTS

6 hazel grouse
½ lb pork fat
30 allspice
6 bay leaves
1 parsley root
1 leek
1 celery root
1 onion
1 calf's liver
1 lb Finnish butter

½ white French roll
nutmeg
salt
2–4 eggs
3–4 spoons truffles, or a ¼ lb jar
2 rusks

*For the dough*
1½ lbs, or 4½ glasses flour
4–5 eggs

## 1074  Hazel grouse butter for breakfast

*(Maslo iz rjabchikov k zavtraku)*

Clean 3 hazel grouse, fry in ⅛ lb butter, and cool. Remove the meat from the bones and chop and pound the meat. Add nutmeg, (⅛ lb grated Parmesan for those who like it,) 3–4 spoons chopped truffles, and ⅛ lb butter. Rub all this through a fine sieve, mix until it thickens, and transfer to a butter dish. To keep this butter for a long time, pack it in a stoneware bowl and pour on melted beef fat.

INGREDIENTS

3 hazel grouse
cayenne pepper or nutmeg
3–4 spoons chopped truffles

1 lb butter
(½ lb Parmesan cheese)
(melted fat)

## 1077  Hare cheese for breakfast

*(Syr iz zajtsa k zavtraku)*

Skin a hare and fry in 1 spoon butter. When half cooked, chop into parts and place in a saucepan. Add ⅛ lb butter and stew, covered, until tender. Remove the bones and finely chop the meat. Add an omelet made from 5 eggs, ¼ lb cheese, and ½ lb butter. Pound everything together and rub through a fine sieve. Add a little nutmeg, dried bouillon diluted in 1 spoon bouillon, ¼ glass wine, and chopped truffles. Mix everything thoroughly. Grease a saucepan with butter, strew with cheese, fill with the prepared forcemeat, and bake. Slice when cool. Serve with vinegar and olive oil.

INGREDIENTS

| | |
|---|---|
| 1 hare | 3–4 truffles |
| 5 eggs | almost 1 lb butter |
| ⅜ lb cheese | about 3 *lots* dry bouillon |
| 1 wineglass wine | |

# 9

# Aspics and Other Cold Dishes

*(Majonezy, zalivnyja i prochija kholodnyja kushan'ja k obedu
i k zavtraku)*

[*Translator's note:* Aspics were one of the glories of the nineteenth-century Russian table and were prepared in several different ways, each with its own name. The English and American traditions are poor by comparison. The Russian words *studen'*, *zalivnoe*, and *majonez* all indicated some kind of aspic, while a related dish, *rulet*, usually meant boned and rolled meat or fish decorated with chopped aspic. *Studen'* was the simplest version, being a molded mixture of only jellied meat or fish broth and small pieces of meat or fish. *Zalivnoe* required a more deliberate arrangement of slices or pieces of meat or fish in a mold with small bits of egg, dill, cucumber, or lemon embedded in the aspic. The dish was unmolded for serving and decorated with chopped aspic or other small garnishes. *Majonez*, the most elaborate of the three aspics, was often the showpiece of a grand banquet. What Molokhovets called *majonez*, we call galantine, using the French term. Frequently the meat or fish was stuffed with a forcemeat before it was arranged on a platter either whole or in slices. Oil was beaten into the liquid aspic as if making mayonnaise, hence the name. The resulting mousse, as it was called, was usually colored with cochineal, saffron, cornflowers, or spinach before it was poured over the meat or fish and set aside to gel before serving. Sometimes a single dish was masked with aspics of several different colors. This use of the term *majonez* seems to have died out in modern Russian; the first meaning of the word *majonez* now refers to the classic French sauce, while the second meaning indicates a cold dish of meat, fish, or vegetables covered with that same sauce. One last bit of confusion is that the French sauce made from egg yolks, oil, vinegar, and spices that we know as mayonnaise was called Provençal sauce in Russia at that time. (Most of this paragraph appeared earlier in my article "Schuyler's 'Diner à la Russe': Some Reflections and Recipes," 13–14.)]

# MEAT AND FISH ASPICS
## (Majonezy mjasnye i rybnye)

*Remarks:* Meat Aspics are prepared as follows: Thoroughly clean 1 calf's head, 4 calf's feet, or 2 ox feet, cover with fresh water, and boil.

The cooked calf's head or feet may be used for such preparations as fried or boiled calf's head or feet, calf's feet fried in batter, or calf's head with prune sauce.

If these dishes are being prepared for 6 to 8 persons, use 6 calf's feet instead of 4, or 1 very large calf's head. If the calf's head is small, add 2 calf's feet. Do not overcook, but boil just until done and remove the meat from the bones. The bouillon should then be boiled longer with the remaining bones, chopped up. Add beef bones or bones from a turkey, chicken, etc. and use to prepare aspic. As with bouillon, so with aspic—the longer meat is cooked in it, the tastier it will be. In this aspic, 2–3 bay leaves, 1–2 carrots, 1 parsley root, 1 celery root, and 2 onions should be added at the very beginning. Salt should not be added. When the meat is tender, set the saucepan aside and let it cool slightly. Completely remove any fat from the surface. Add 2–3 fresh, beaten eggs and return the pan to the top of the stove on the edge of a very low fire so that the pan with bouillon boils very gently just on the side closest to the fire.* Pour in ½ glass each sherry and ordinary vinegar. Cover the saucepan and frequently stir slightly. When the aspic has cleared, reduce it as required. Strain through a napkin. This should yield nearly 4 glasses after straining. If when remeasuring by the glass it is somewhat less, add cold water that has been boiled.

Four calf's feet weighing 4 lbs will yield 4 glasses of aspic in summer and 5 in winter.** A cleaned calf's head weighing 5½ lbs will yield the same amount of aspic. Pour off nearly 1 glass from the 4 glasses and color it with red gelatin to give it a good crimson color. If this color is not very clear, pour this glass of aspic back into the saucepan, clarify it with an egg white, strain, pour it into a bowl, and let it stand on ice to congeal.

No later than an hour before dinner, make a mousse from the remaining 3 glasses of prepared aspic as follows: Add ½ glass olive oil and salt to taste. When the mixture begins to cool, beat it with a spoon over ice until it turns into a thick foam. Then pour it over the wild fowl, turkey, fish, etc., arranged on a platter or in a shallow mold. When the liquid has set, decorate it attractively with various shapes cut or chopped from the colored aspic, and with sprigs of parsley. Garnish with heaps of marinated cornichons, marinated beans, capers, olives, chopped hard-boiled eggs, crayfish tails, marinated cauliflower, lemon slices, etc.

Or divide the mousse into several parts and color it red, blue, and other shades. Mask a piece of chicken, turkey, or fish in one color mousse, another piece in a different color, and so forth. Arrange on the platter like a wreath. Some kind of aspic [salad] may be arranged in the middle of the platter, but only if the platter is intended for 12, 18, or more persons. After setting out the aspic on the platter, pour on a little mixed sauce, serving the remainder in a sauceboat. Surround the edge of the platter with salad, such as green and white beans, cauliflower, potatoes, asparagus, each boiled [separately] in salted water, or baked beets or fresh cucumbers. Cut all these into even pieces, season each vegetable separately with 2–3 spoons olive oil, 3–4 spoons vinegar, salt, and pepper. Strew with parsley and dill, tarragon, chervil, etc.

*Unable to make fine adjustments of the heat of wood-burning stoves, cooks moved the pans around the top of the stove to take advantage of hot and cold spots, either closer to the fire for faster cooking, or further away if slower cooking was desired.*

**With no adequate refrigeration, more of the liquid had to be evaporated in the summer in order for the aspic to hold its shape. In the winter, the same amount of gelatin would congeal a greater amount of liquid.*

*Mousse may be made in five colors:*

a) natural white

b) red: Color with red gelatin.

c) yellow: Add a little saffron.

d) blue: Boil a handful of cornflowers in 2–3 spoons of boiling water, cover, and let stand for an hour. Squeeze through a clean cloth and pour a teaspoon or more into the mousse.

e) green: Pound in a stone mortar a handful of spinach that has been picked over, washed, and dried with a napkin. Squeeze dry and add 1 or more spoons to the mousse, or add ¼ glass of boiled and sieved spinach.

*Remarks for fish aspic.* Fish aspic is prepared from large fish such as tench, salmon, whitefish, trout, sturgeon, white salmon, pike, etc. Clean and lightly salt 3–4 lbs of very fresh fish. Wrap the fish in a clean napkin and set it aside for about 2 hours. Meanwhile, add root vegetables to the fish kettle: (carrots, parsley roots, celery roots, 2 onions), 2–3 bay leaves, and 1 lb of small fish, especially eels. Fill with cold water, add the large fish, and cook until done, but do not overcook. Cool the fish in this bouillon, then transfer it to a platter. Let it dry off and cool.

Pour ½ glass each of sherry and ordinary vinegar into the remaining bouillon. Add 3–4 *zolotniki* of white gelatin and cook until it softens and dissolves. Clarify with 2–3 fresh egg whites beaten with 2–3 spoons cold water or ⅛ lb pressed caviar beaten with water. Let it boil gently until it is reduced to 4 glasses. Then strain through a napkin. Pour off 1 glass into a small saucepan, add 2 *zolotniki*, or 2 sheets, of red gelatin, and boil until it softens and dissolves. Strain, pour out onto a platter, and cool. Cut this aspic into various shapes and decorate the aspic (*majonez*) with it. Or instead of using red gelatin, color this glass of aspic with caramelized sugar, let it cool, and then finely chop.

Prepare a mousse from the 3 remaining glasses as follows: Add ½ glass olive oil and salt to taste. When it begins to cool, beat it with a small whisk until it thickens. Coat the fish with the aspic and let it cool. Decorate the top with capers, small saffron milk-cap mushrooms, and colored aspic. Surround the fish with small heaps of boiled white beans, baked beets cut into small cubes, cubed potatoes, carrots, salad, etc. All these should first be moistened with Provençal sauce and mixed with the remaining mousse or mustard sauce.

Both fish and meat aspic are served with Provençal sauce, which is a kind of mousse, prepared as follows: Mix in a stoneware bowl 2 egg yolks, a teaspoon prepared *Sareptskaja* mustard, and 1 small piece fine sugar. Add ½ lb or more olive oil by the teaspoon until it thickens. Serve this sauce separately in a sauceboat.

The proportions are intended for 6–8 persons. For 9–12 persons increase the proportions by 1½. For 12–18, and even for 24 persons, double the proportions, in which case use 1 calf's head and 4 calf's feet.

## 1080 Stuffed turkey in aspic

*(Majonez iz farshirovannoj indejki)*

Clean 1 small turkey and cut off the head, wings, and legs. Slit the turkey along the backbone and carefully bone. Stuff as follows: Finely chop ¾ lb veal or the fillets from another turkey. Add salt, ½ French roll soaked in milk and squeezed out, 1½ spoons butter, (1 onion fried in ½ spoon butter, if desired), allspice, and 1–2 eggs. Pound all this together in a mortar and rub through a fine sieve. Thinly slice ¼ lb boiled ham or tongue.

Prepare an omelet from 2 egg yolks, ½ spoon butter, 1 ground allspice berry, and some parsley. Make another, similar omelet out of the 2 egg whites.

Stuff the turkey as follows: Arrange in layers the stuffing, ham, omelet, cornichons, etc. Then sew up the turkey firmly, wrap it in a napkin, and tie with strong thread. Boil until tender in bouillon for at least 3 hours. Then remove, cool thoroughly, and weight lightly. Slice and arrange on an oblong platter an hour before serving. Cover with mousse and decorate the top, or cool in a mold.

Prepare the mousse as indicated in the Remarks, namely, boil all the turkey bones, the head, wings, and legs (except the liver and gizzards), root vegetables, and 1 bay leaf with the bouillon in which the stuffed turkey was cooked. An additional lb of beef may be added. Boil 4 calf's feet or 2 ox feet in it until tender, or add white gelatin. Reduce to 4 glasses, etc.

Serve with mustard sauce, tartar sauce, or Provençal sauce.

INGREDIENTS

1 small 3 lb turkey*
¾ lb veal or turkey
½ French roll
(1 onion)
3–4 eggs
⅜ lb butter
¼ lb ham or tongue

parsley
allspice

*For the mousse*
4 calf's or ox feet, or 7 *zolotniki*
  gelatin
1 lb or more beef
2 carrots

| | |
|---|---|
| 1 parsley root | ½ glass vinegar |
| 1 celery root | ½ glass olive oil |
| 1–2 onions | 1 piece sugar |
| 1–2 bay leaves | 1–2 leaves red gelatin |
| ½ glass sherry | Other ingredients for decoration as |
| 2–3 egg whites | indicated in the Remarks |

*Turkeys, of course, originated in the New World and some of those wild birds could be very large indeed. In the early seventeenth century forty-pound wild male birds cost four shillings in Boston markets. Turkeys raised in captivity were much smaller. Molokhovets' recipes commonly specified turkeys that were no larger than 3 to 5 lbs. (Cronon, Changes in the Land, 99.)

### 1086 Stuffed suckling pig in aspic

*(Majonez iz farshirovannago porosenka s zalivnym)*

Clean a small, fat suckling pig. Cut off the head and feet, slit the body lengthwise along one side, and carefully bone. Salt the interior, scrape off any meat from the bones, and chop it fine with the liver from the suckling pig. Add ½ calf's liver and ½ lb or more raw veal. Fry all this lightly in 2 spoons butter and add 1–2 ground black peppercorns, ½ French roll soaked and squeezed out, and 3–6 eggs. Chop everything very fine, pound, and rub through a colander. Spread this forcemeat over the interior of the suckling pig, which has been spread out on the table. Arrange 3–6 sliced hard-boiled eggs over the forcemeat. Pieces of freshly boiled tongue are a good addition. Roll the suckling pig into a long tube, wrap it in a napkin, and tie it with string. Boil until done in bouillon prepared from the leftover bones, head, and feet of the pig, together with carrots, parsley root, celery root, 3 onions, 1–2 bay leaves, ½ glass each vinegar and sherry, and a little salt. When the meat roll has thoroughly cooked, which will take approximately an hour, remove and cool it. Press it with light weights for 2 hours, slice, and arrange the slices around a platter. Mask each piece with mousse. A shallow mold of aspic containing the same meat roll with the tongue, brains, ears, and other soft parts of the suckling pig's head may also be unmolded in the middle of the same platter. Serve Provençal sauce in a sauceboat (cf. the end of the Remarks on fish aspics).

The mousse and aspic for the molded dish are prepared as follows: Add enough separately prepared strong beef bouillon to the bouillon in which the suckling pig has cooked to make 6 glasses in all. Divide into two parts.

Add 4 leaves of white gelatin to the 3 glasses of liquid intended for the mold. Color with a piece of burnt sugar or with 1 spoon of pan juices from roast beef, or add a fourth leaf of red gelatin. Clarify with 2 egg whites beaten with 2 spoons cold water and strain through a napkin tied to an overturned bench.* Cool in a shallow mold; specifically, first pour in a little aspic, and when it has almost set, add slices of the stuffed suckling pig and pieces of the brains, tongue, ears, etc., as indicated above, and pour in what is left from the first 3 glasses of bouillon.

Prepare a mousse from the other 3 glasses as follows: add 2 leaves of white gelatin to the bouillon, bring it to a boil, and strain through a napkin. When it begins to thicken, pour in ½ glass of olive oil and begin to beat the mixture with a whisk until it turns into a thick foam. Use it to mask each slice of the meat roll of the suckling pig which garnishes the molded aspic.

Serve Provençal sauce separately.

*Essentially Molokhovets tied the napkin to whatever was handy; sometimes it was an over-turned bench, at other times an overturned stool.*

### 1089 Aspic of fish with salad and green sauce

*(Majonez iz ryby s salatom i zelenym sousom)*

Take 3 lbs of any kind of fish, such as tench, pike, salmon, a large perch, or whitefish. Cut the fillets into slices the thickness of a finger. Arrange them on a dripping pan in 1½ spoons melted butter and add salt, 1 wineglass wine, and the juice of ½ lemon. As soon as the fillets turn white on one side, turn them over. Watch that the fish is not raw, but do not let it darken. Transfer the fish onto a round platter to cool.

Prepare an aspic from the fish bones, scales, fish gelatin, and other small fish. Add root vegetables, spices, vinegar, and 5–6 field mushrooms. Clarify with 2–3 egg whites or caviar (cf. Remarks on fish aspics), reduce the mixture to 3½ glasses, strain through a napkin, and cool. Add ½ glass olive oil to the aspic and beat the mousse as indicated in the Remarks. Dip each piece of fish in this mousse and arrange the pieces on a platter in a circle. Surround with salad and fill the center with the following sauce:

Pit 10 olives and chop them with 10 anchovies, 10 cornichons, 1 spoon capers, and 10 hard-boiled egg yolks. Pound everything together in a mortar and rub through a fine sieve. Beat 2 raw egg yolks in a stoneware bowl with a teaspoon

Overturned stool used as an impromptu strainer. From Jules Gouffe, *Royal Book of Pastry and Confectionary* (London, 1874).

of prepared *Sareptskaja* mustard until they turn pale. Add olive oil drop by drop, 1 teaspoon vinegar, about 2 pieces fine sugar, some salt and spinach essence, and 1 spoon chopped greens, such as dill, chervil, and tarragon. Mix everything together.

[Prepare] the following salad: Slice green beans evenly and boil them in salted water until tender. When cooked, turn them into a colander, rinse with cold water, and set them on ice. In exactly the same manner boil asparagus, potatoes, and cauliflower. After they have been rinsed with cold water, mix them with the beans. Also add fresh peeled cucumbers, baked beets (all of these sliced or cut into pieces), parsley, dill, tarragon, and chervil. Season with 2–3 spoons vinegar, olive oil, salt, a little mustard, and sugar.

## INGREDIENTS

3 lbs large fish
3 lbs small fish and about 2 *zolotniki*
    fish glue if the aspic is for a fast
    day, or 1 calf's head and 4 calf's
    feet, if for a meat day, or 5–6 leaves
    white gelatin
1½ spoons butter
1 wineglass wine
½ lemon
2 carrots
1 parsley root
1 celery root
1 leek
3 onions
5–7 allspice
1–2 bay leaves
5–6 field mushrooms
½ glass olive oil
½ glass sherry
½ glass vinegar
⅛ [lb] pressed caviar, or 2–3 egg
    whites

*For the sauce*
10 olives

10 anchovies
10 cornichons
1 spoon capers
10 eggs*
2 egg yolks*
¾ glass olive oil
1 small spoon vinegar
greens
2 handfuls spinach
about 2 pieces sugar

*For the salad*
about 12 green beans
about 6–9 stalks asparagus
about 6 potatoes
1 beet
1 head cauliflower
2 cucumbers
vinegar
greens: parsley, dill, tarragon, etc.
olive oil
mustard
about 2–3 pieces sugar

*The 10 whole eggs and 2 egg yolks in the above recipe replace the 11 egg yolks of the first edition. The change may have been a culinary decision or it may have been that in a smaller household it was harder to use up the extra egg whites.*

### 1092  A whole stuffed baked fish in aspic

*(Majonez iz tsel'noj farshirovannoj zharenoj ryby)*

(Proportions are for 18–24 persons.) Clean a 5–6 lb fish, such as pike, zander, or salmon, and cut along the spine to take out the backbone. Add salt, remove the other bones, and stuff as follows:

Finely chop 3 lbs of boneless fish. Place in a mortar and add 1½ French rolls soaked in milk and squeezed out, 2½ spoons butter, 10 allspice, salt (2 finely chopped onions fried in 1 spoon butter), ½ nutmeg, and 6–10 eggs. Pound everything together and rub the mixture through a sieve with a wooden spoon. Stuff the fish, sew it up, and place it on a roasting pan greased with 1 spoon butter. Sprinkle with salt and finely chopped parsley, onion, and leek. Pour over ½ to 1 glass rich bouillon and cover with a clean cloth, folded in two and soaked in rich bouillon. Roast the fish in the oven, basting it frequently with that same sauce.

When the fish has cooked, remove it, brush it off, and let it cool. Arrange the fish on an oblong platter and decorate with mousse, colored aspic, and other decorations, as indicated in the Remarks.

Serve with Provençal sauce, mixed sauce, or mustard sauce.

INGREDIENTS

| | |
|---|---|
| a 5–6 lb fish | 1½ parsley roots |
| 3 lbs boneless fish | 1½ leeks |
| 1½ French rolls | 2 carrots |
| 1 glass milk | 2 celery roots |
| allspice | about 4–6 onions |
| salt | 10 allspice |
| nutmeg | 2–3 bay leaves |
| 6–10 eggs | 1 glass sherry |
| ½ lb butter | 1 glass vinegar |
| (2 onions) | 1½ glasses olive oil |
| | 2–3 leaves red gelatin and other decorative ingredients |

*For the mousse*
3 *zolotniki* fish glue and 6 lbs small fish, bones, and scales, or 1 calf's head and calf's feet


# JELLIED MEATS AND FISH, ASPIC SALADS, AND MARINADES

*(Zalivnoe rulet, vinigret i pr. marinaty)*

*Remarks:* Meat aspics for 6 persons are prepared as follows: Thoroughly clean

1 medium calf's head and 4 calf's feet, cover with water, and add the bones of the feathered game or fish from which the aspic will be made. If desired, add 1 lb beef. Add 2 carrots, 1 parsley root, 1 celery root, 1 leek, (2 onions), 10 allspice, and 1–2 bay leaves. Simmer over a very low fire.

When the feet have cooked, remove the bones and set the meat aside for another dish. Cook the bones longer, strain the bouillon, and cool slightly. Remove the fat and add at least ½ glass vinegar. If you wish the aspic to have a dark color, pound 1 piece of sugar, pour it onto a small skillet, set it alight, and add 1 spoon water. Bring to a boil, mix, and pour into the aspic as needed, so that it will not be too dark. Clarify with 2–3 egg whites mixed with water, ⅛ lb pressed caviar beaten with water, 1 lb minced beef, or chopped fried hazel grouse or hare (with bones) mixed with 2–3 spoons water and 2 fresh egg whites (cf. the Remarks for soups). Reduce to 4 glasses and strain through a napkin tied to an overturned stool.

Decorate the bottom and sides of a mold with ½ lemon, seeded and cut into half slices, 1 sliced hard-boiled egg, 1 carrot, parsley, red and white currants, gooseberries, capers, mushrooms, pickles, crayfish tails, and greens. Pour a little aspic over the bottom and let it cool. Before serving, dip the mold in hot water for a moment, wipe the mold, and turn the aspic out onto a platter.

These proportions will serve 6–8 persons. For 9–12 persons, increase the proportions by 1½. For 13–18 persons, double the proportions; use 1 calf's head and 4 calf's feet and reduce to 7–8 glasses.

## 1095 Hare in aspic

*(Zalivnoe iz zajtsa)*

Clean a small hare and lard it, if desired, with ⅛ lb pork fat. Fry it on a griddle with 1 spoon butter, slice, cool, and place it in a ring mold with a large center opening. Prepare an aspic from calf's feet, bones from the hare, 1½ lbs beef, etc., as indicated in the Remarks, and cover the hare with the aspic. When it has set, turn it out onto a platter and pour mixed sauce or mustard sauce into the center. Pour the remainder of the sauce into a sauceboat and serve separately.

INGREDIENTS

| | |
|---|---|
| 1 small hare | 20–30 allspice |
| ⅛ lb pork fat | 3–4 bay leaves |
| 1 calf's head, or 4 calf's feet | ½–1 glass vinegar |
| ⅛ lb butter | 2–3 eggs |
| 1–1½ lbs beef | (1 piece sugar) |
| 2 carrots | (various decorations) |
| 1 parsley root | 1 celery root |
| 1 leek | (2 onions) |

## 1098 Calf's head in aspic

*(Zalivnoe iz golovki teljach'ej)*

Remove the brains from 1 large calf's head and boil them in salted water with vinegar and spices. Remove, cool, and slice. Boil the calf's head with root vegetables, spices, and ½ glass vinegar, as indicated in the Remarks. Add, if desired, a piece of beef. Remove the calf's head when cooked and cut off the meat. Return the bones to the aspic and reduce it to 4 glasses in summer, but to 5–6 glasses in winter. Clarify with egg whites and strain. Decorate the interior of a mold with seeded lemon slices, pour in a little of the prepared aspic, and cool. Add the brains and thinly sliced oblong pieces of the calf's head, tongue, and ears, carefully cleaned of hair. Cover with aspic, cool, and turn out onto the platter.

Serve with mustard sauce or with vinegar, olive oil, and mustard. Or serve with sprat or sardine sauce.

INGREDIENTS

| | |
|---|---|
| 1 cleaned calf's head, about 5½ lbs (the bones may be added) | 1–2 bay leaves |
| | ½–1 glass vinegar |
| 2 carrots | (1 piece sugar) |
| 1 parsley root | 2 egg whites |
| 1 celery root | (various decorations) |
| 1 leek | 5 allspice |

## 1104 Stuffed hazel grouse in aspic with vegetable salad

*(Rod zalivnago iz farshirovannykh rjabchikov)*

Clean 3–4 hazel grouse, slit them along their backbones, and carefully remove the bones without piercing the skin. Chop off the wings and feet and stuff the birds with the following liver forcemeat.

Slice 1 calf's liver and fry it in a saucepan with 1 bay leaf, 5 *zolotniki* allspice, ½ lb pork fat, and root vegetables. Chop the mixture fine and add ½ white French roll soaked and squeezed out, 3–6 eggs, and salt. Pound all this and rub through a colander. Stuff the hazel grouse, place them in a sauté pan greased with butter, and roast in the oven. Cool, slice, and arrange them on a platter over a mound of beets, potatoes, etc. Sprinkle with chopped aspic and greens. Serve mustard or some other sauce separately.

The mound of vegetables is prepared as follows: Take several beets and potatoes, having baked the first and boiled the second. Peel, finely chop, and mix with 2 spoons each capers and olives. Add 1 teaspoon mustard mixed with 2 spoons each olive oil and vinegar. Mix all this together until it holds its shape. Form the vegetables into a round or oblong-rectangular mound two fingers high and the size of the platter. Smooth the top and sides as well as possible.

[To prepare the aspic, see the Remarks at the beginning of this section or at the beginning of the chapter.]

INGREDIENTS

3 hazel grouse
1 small calf's liver
3–4 bay leaves
5 allspice
½ French roll
½ lb pork fat
5–6 eggs
salt
⅜ lb butter

*For the vegetable salad*
2–3 beets
10–12 potatoes
about 2 spoons capers

about 2 spoons olives
a small spoon prepared mustard
about 2 spoons olive oil
about 2 spoons vinegar

*For the aspic*
½ lb beef
1–2 bay leaves
¼ glass vinegar
bones from a calf's head
¼ glass sherry
1–2 egg whites
salt
(reduce this to 2 glasses)

## 1106  Eel and crayfish in aspic

*(Rod zalivnago iz ugrja i rakov)*

Cut off the head of a live eel. When the blood has drained away, rub the eel with coarse sand and salt,* rinse, wipe dry, and cut into pieces. Add salt and boil the eel in a small quantity of water with root vegetables. When it has completely cooked, remove the skin. Strain the bouillon, clarify with eggs or caviar, and cool slightly. Meanwhile, boil crayfish and peel the crayfish tails and claws. Pour several spoons fish broth from the eel into a mold for the aspic. Let cool and add pieces of eel, layering them with crayfish tails and claws and sprigs of parsley and dill. Pour on the remaining fish broth. To serve, unmold onto a platter. The dish may be garnished with whole boiled crayfish.

INGREDIENTS

3 lbs eel
1 onion
½ parsley root
½ carrot
2–3 black peppercorns
6–8 allspice

2–3 bay leaves
dill
parsley
24 small crayfish, and, if desired, 12
    large crayfish

*See Chapter 7 for remarks on cleaning eels.

### 1108  Marinated beluga

*(Beluzhina marinovannaja)*

Remove the spinal column and cartilage from ½ pood fresh beluga. Prepare a pail of vinegar and add ⅛ lb peppercorns, 5 *zolotniki* ginger (not crushed, but in pieces), and if desired, 5 heads of garlic. Cut the fish into pieces, add to a large pan, and cover with the vinegar to which may be added 5 *zolotniki* tarragon, marjoram, savory, and about 2 large handfuls of salt. Boil until the fish is done, remove from the fire, and cool. Arrange the fish in a large jar or clay pot, strain the broth, and pour it over the fish. Remove and discard the herbs from the spices that [were earlier tied up] in a napkin,* retie the spices in a cloth, and add them to the top of the jar. Cover the fish with a wooden disk, place a small stone on top to ensure that the fish will always be covered with vinegar, and store in a cold place.

*Although Molokhovets directed the reader to remove the spices from a napkin, she neglected to instruct the reader earlier to tie up the spices in a napkin before adding them to the broth.*

### 1113  Marinated fish in the English fashion

*(Marinovannaja ryba po-anglijski)*

Use fish such as sturgeon, beluga, pike, burbot, or sterlet; in general, choose fish with few bones. Slice, dip in crumbs, and fry in butter, but not so that the fish becomes very oily. Cool, place in a jar, and cover with cold vinegar that has been brought to a boil with allspice, cinnamon, cloves, nutmeg, and salt. Layer the fish with tarragon, basil, marjoram, and rosemary, of which add the most. Add enough vinegar to cover the fish completely, covering the top with herbs. Tie the jar with a bladder and bury the jar of fish in ice.

### 1116  Herring with olive oil and vinegar for hors d'oeuvre*

*(Seledka s provanskim maslom i uksusom, podavaemaja k zakuske)*

a) Soak 2 Dutch or Scottish herring in water or, preferably, milk, *kvass*, or beer. Remove the heads and tails, clean, wash, and slit them lengthwise. Separate the meat from the bones and put both halves together again. Cut into diagonal pieces and arrange them on a plate. Attach the cut-off heads and tails, which have had the tip ends cut off. Pound the soft roe in a mortar with 1 spoon fresh butter and rub through a fine sieve. Add nutmeg and turn the mixture out onto the table. Shape into a flat rectangle and cut it into thin strips. Surround the herring with the strips and garnish with a boiled, attractively cut potato and beet and pour on 2 spoons olive oil. If desired, sprinkle the top with white and green onions. The herring may also be garnished with capers and various pickles.

b) Soak herring in water for about 3 hours, and then for about 2 hours in raw milk, or even boiled milk that has been cooled, or in tea.

Clean the herring, slit them lengthwise, remove the backbones, and put both halves together, or place each half separately on an oblong plate. Slice diagonally, attach the heads and tails, and pour on ¼ spoon vinegar mixed with 1 spoon olive oil. Sprinkle with greens.

c) Or slice the herring as indicated above and surround with vegetables as follows: Place small saffron milk-cap mushrooms on opposite sides of the herring and on the other two sides, arrange peeled, halved, and sliced salted cucumbers and a baked beet, sliced in the same manner. Add green onions in two other places, then green capers. Pour olive oil and vinegar over everything and strew with finely chopped greens.

d) Peel and slice a beet, as indicated in the beginning. Pour mustard sauce over it, prepared as follows: Using a small wooden spatula, mix in a teacup 1 teaspoon prepared *Sareptskaja* mustard, a little salt, and ¼ teaspoon olive oil. When the mustard thickens, add ¼ teaspoon vinegar. Mix, add ¼ teaspoon olive oil and more vinegar. Continue to the end, always mixing with the small spatula until there is ¼ cup or more of sauce. Then pour it over the herring and serve.

e) Surround one side of a cleaned and sliced herring with white sliced onions and the other side with sliced potatoes. Pour on olive oil and vinegar.

*The phrase "for hors d'oeuvre" was not part of the title in the first edition.

### 1118  Vinaigrette*

(Vinigret)

Take various cooked meats: game or wild fowl; veal or beef; or boiled fish, such as sturgeon, pike, or salmon. Add 1–2 boiled or baked beets, 1 spoon cornichons, 1 salted or fresh, large, peeled cucumber, 1 herring, 2 hard-boiled eggs, 5–6 marinated saffron milk-cap mushrooms, 1 spoon pickles, 5–6 boiled, finely chopped potatoes, 2 spoons capers, 3 spoons sauerkraut, ½ glass white beans, boiled in salted water, and 20 pitted olives.

Cube all these ingredients and pour on mustard sauce, made by mixing together salt, pepper, ½ glass or more vinegar, about 2 spoons olive oil, 1½ spoons prepared mustard, and 2–3 pieces sugar, if desired. Mix the sauce with the vegetables, arrange on a platter, and surround with attractively sliced boiled potatoes and beets. Place parsley all around or decorate with variously colored aspic, lemon, and hard-boiled eggs.

For fast days, omit all meat and dairy products.

*Internationally this salad and others like it have become known as "Russian salad," while in Russia they are often called "Olivier salad," after the French chef of that name who in the 1880s ran a fashionable Moscow restaurant called the Hermitage. (See Chamberlain, The Food and Cooking of Russia, 51–53.)

# 10
# Puddings

## (Pudingi)

*Remarks:* Puddings are prepared in various ways. Some are boiled in a napkin and others are steamed in a mold. A third kind are baked in the oven in a mold and then turned out onto a platter, and a fourth kind, the so-called soufflés, are served from the same dish in which they are baked.

a) *If the pudding is boiled in a napkin,* rinse the napkin (washed without soap) several times in cold water, wring it out thoroughly, and spread unsalted butter over the middle of the napkin, covering an area the size of a large round plate. (Use ½ spoon butter for a pudding to serve 6 persons.) Arrange the pudding mixture on the greased napkin and tie it up tightly with string, leaving a space of 2–3 fingers between the knot and the pudding mixture. That is, leave not too much space and not too little, because in the first case, the pudding will be flat and may fall to pieces, and in the second case, it will be too hard because it does not have room to rise. Lower the tied-up napkin into a saucepan filled with salted water, which must then boil vigorously for 1½ to 2 hours, depending on the kind of pudding. Tie the ends of the napkin to a stick, which should be placed on the rim of the saucepan so that the entire pudding will be submerged in water without resting on the bottom of the pan. Frequently replenish with boiling water so that the water in which the pudding is cooking does not stop boiling at any time during the cooking process. Remove the pudding from the water, drain in a coarse sieve, then untie the napkin and remove it from the top of the pudding. Cover the pudding with a dish, overturn with the sieve, and carefully remove the sieve and napkin.

b) *If the pudding is steamed in a mold over water,* which is preferable to baking in the oven, use a copper or tin mold with a detachable base and a tube in the middle. Grease the mold with melted butter (½ spoon), strew with finely ground rusks (1–2 rusks), and set the mold aside until the butter congeals. Fill the mold with the prepared mixture, but not to the very top. Cover tightly with a lid and set the mold in a saucepan of vigorously boiling water. Steam for 1½ or 2 hours, adding more boiling water as necessary. To serve, turn out onto a platter.

c) *If the pudding is baked in the oven,* use a copper or tin mold with a fixed base.

Grease with melted butter (½ spoon), strew with 1–2 rusks, cool, and fill the mold with the prepared mixture. Bake in the oven for ½ hour or more. To serve, turn out onto a platter.

In general, when preparing puddings, make sure to stir and beat the pudding with a spatula until the mixture is smooth and forms blisters. Then, in a cold place, whip very fresh egg whites until stiff, fold them gradually into the batter, mixing carefully from the top down, and immediately place in the oven.

It is best to beat the egg yolks first with sugar until white.

The proportions are for 6 persons. For 7–9 persons, increase the proportions by 1½. For 10–12 or even 18 persons—that is, for one large dish—double the proportions.

### 1125 [Cornmeal pudding covered with meringue]

*[Pirog iz maisovoj muki]** 

Mix together as well as possible 1 glass each fine sugar and fine wheat flour, ½ glass each melted butter, milk, and cornmeal, and 2 teaspoons dry yeast dissolved in the aforementioned milk. Add 5–6 beaten egg whites and bake in two shallow tin pans greased with butter and strewn with rusk crumbs. Stack the layers on a platter, one on top of the other, and sprinkle with grated coconut or ground almond paste mixed with wild strawberry or raspberry syrup to form a thick paste. Spread 3 egg whites beaten with ⅓ glass fine sugar over the top and brown briefly in the oven. To serve, pour on raspberry or wild strawberry jam.

INGREDIENTS

| | |
|---|---|
| 1⅓ glasses fine sugar | 5–6 eggs |
| ½ glass melted butter | 1 glass sweet almonds or coconut |
| ½ glass milk | ¼–½ glass syrup |
| 1 glass fine wheat flour | 2 teaspoons dry yeast |
| ½ glass cornmeal | |

*The title given here comes from the Table of Contents, but none is provided with the recipe itself.*

### 1127 Cheese pudding with short pastry

*(Puding iz tvoroga s razsypchatym testom)*

Beat ¼ lb butter until white. Beat in 6–8 egg yolks and add 1 lb of very fresh, weighted* farmer's cheese (*tvorog*), 1 glass fresh sour cream, a little salt, ½ glass or more sugar, and vanilla. Mix thoroughly.

Prepare short pastry from 1 lb flour, ½ lb butter, ½ glass fine sugar, 1 egg, 1 spoon sour cream, and salt. Add rum or vodka diluted with water, about ⅓ glass in all, or enough to knead the dough and roll it out. Line the bottom of a wide, shallow pan with this pastry and make a rim of dough. Pour in the prepared mixture and bake in a hot oven for no longer than 20 minutes. To serve, strew with sugar. Some people pour on melted butter.

INGREDIENTS

¼ lb butter
6–8 egg yolks
1 lb weighted farmer's cheese
½ glass, or ¼ lb, sugar
1 glass sour cream
vanilla

½ lb butter
½ glass sugar
1 egg
about 1 wineglass rum
1 spoon sour cream
(sugar and butter)

*For the dough*
3 glasses flour

*Fresh cheese was often compressed under weights for several hours or overnight to rid it of excess moisture.*


## 1133  Sour cream pie

(Smetannik)

Prepare puff pastry, roll it very thin, and line a saucepan or the bottom and sides of a mold with it. Spread 1½ glasses jam without syrup over the dough. Dilute ¾ glass ground almonds with enough milk to make a thick porridge and stir in 1 *zolotnik* cinnamon and 3 spoons very fresh sour cream mixed with 1 egg yolk. Mix thoroughly and pour into the saucepan lined with dough. Cover with dough and bake in the oven. This is a very tasty pastry. Cherry and raspberry jam are best of all.

INGREDIENTS

2 glasses flour
½ lb butter
1½ glasses jam
¼ lb almonds

2 small spoons cinnamon
3 small spoons sour cream
1 egg yolk


## 1137  Pudding made from cookies and rusks

(Puding iz biskvitov i sukharej)

Cut into several pieces about 10 homemade* or confectionary shop (*kanditer-skij*) cookies and about 10 homemade round rusks. Prepare a syrup from ⅓ glass sugar and 1 glass water, add ¼ glass each large raisins and shelled grated almonds, and let the syrup stand for at least ½ hour. Grease a saucepan with butter and strew with crumbs. Line the bottom with a layer of cookies and pour on the prepared syrup. Add a layer of rusks, again syrup, another layer of cookies, and finish with a layer of rusks. Beat 6 egg yolks with 2 glasses cream, sprinkle on a little cinnamon, and pour over the pudding. Bake for an hour in an oven that is not too hot. To serve, turn out onto a platter and pour on syrup or cover with a meringue prepared from the leftover egg whites beaten and mixed with 3 spoons sugar. Set in the oven for about 10 minutes. To serve, decorate with jam.

Extra syrup will be needed for serving or, if covering the pudding with meringue, an additional ½ glass sugar and ¼ glass jam for mixing with the egg whites.

INGREDIENTS

10 cookies
10 round homemade rusks
¼ glass raisins
¼ glass almonds
cinnamon

6 eggs
⅓ glass sugar
2 glasses cream
½ spoon butter
1 full spoon rusk crumbs

*By homemade cookies, Molokhovets meant the following (#1684): Beat 6 egg yolks with 6 teaspoons sugar, fold in 6 beaten egg whites, and gradually add 6 teaspoons potato flour. Bake in paper casings.*

## 1142 Spinach pudding

*(Puding iz shpinata)*

Clean and wash ½ lb spinach that has been well picked over. Drop the spinach into boiling salted water, bring to a boil, turn into a colander, and rinse with cold water. Squeeze all the moisture from the spinach, chop it fine, and rub through a fine sieve. Pour boiled cream or whole milk onto a stale roll, let stand at least ½ hour, and then beat thoroughly. Add the prepared spinach, nutmeg, and 1 spoon butter beaten with sugar and 6 egg yolks until white. Fold in 6–9 beaten egg whites, transfer to a buttered mold strewn with coarsely pounded sugar, and steam for a full hour. Pour on sabayon sauce.

Sometimes 30 or 40 crayfish tails are added to this pudding, in which case crayfish butter is poured over the pudding.

INGREDIENTS

½ lb spinach
½ lb white bread (soft part)
almost 2 glasses milk or cream
½ glass sugar
6–9 eggs

nutmeg
1½ spoons butter
(30–40 crayfish and at least ¼ lb crayfish butter)
Or sabayon sauce

### 1147 Plum pudding

*(Plum-puding)*

(Proportions for 18 persons.) Place in a stoneware bowl ¼ lb finely chopped mixed candied citrus rind, ½ lb picked over, washed, and dried sultanas, ¼ lb currants, 1 grated 5 kopeck French roll, 1 lb kidney fat, trimmed of veins and finely chopped, ½ lb bone marrow, ½ lb flour, ¾ lb fine sugar, the zest of 1 lemon, and nutmeg. Mix everything together, beat in 9 eggs, and dilute with 2 wineglasses each Madeira and Malaga and 1 wineglass rum. Stir and transfer to a napkin greased with butter. Simmer for 4 hours over a low fire, covering the saucepan with a lid. Carefully turn out onto a platter before serving. Cut off the crust all around, pour on rum, set it afire, and serve at the table, flaming. Or serve rum and sabayon sauce separately.

Ingredients are given for 6 persons. For 7–9 persons, increase the proportions by 1½. For 10–12 persons, double the proportions.

INGREDIENTS

| | |
|---|---|
| ¹⁄₁₂ lb candied citrus rind | ¼ lb, or ½ glass, fine sugar |
| ⅙ lb, or ½ glass, sultanas | zest of ⅓ lemon |
| ¹⁄₁₂ lb, or ¼ glass, currants | nutmeg |
| ⅓ French roll | 3 eggs |
| ⅛ lb kidney fat* | ⅔ wineglass Madeira |
| ⅙ lb bone marrow | ⅔ wineglass Malaga |
| ⅙ lb, or ½ glass, flour | ⅓ wineglass rum |
| rum for the sabayon sauce | |

*Since Molokhovets called for 1 lb of kidney fat in the full recipe, this should read ⅓ lb kidney fat, not ⅛ lb.

### 1151 Coffee pudding

*(Puding kofejnyj)*

Roast ½ glass of the very best coffee, and while still hot, pour into 2 glasses hot cream. Bring to a boil, set aside, and cover. Strain the cream after it has cooled.*

Mix ¼ lb butter and 1 glass flour, dilute with the flavored cream, boil thoroughly, add sugar, and then cool. Beat in 6 egg yolks, add 6–8 beaten egg whites, transfer to a mold greased with butter and strewn with sugar, and bake. Pour on almond or vanilla sauce.

INGREDIENTS

2½ spoons butter                    ½ glass coffee

2 glasses cream

1 glass flour

¼ lb sugar

6–8 eggs

*No mention is made of grinding the beans. Barbara Wheaton brought to my attention a recipe by Mrs. A. B. Marshall for a very delicate White Coffee Cream Ice using freshly roasted "coffee berries." (Marshall, Ices Plain and Fancy, 13.)*

## 1153  Chocolate pudding

### (Puding shokoladnyj)

Grate ¼ lb chocolate and mix with 5 egg yolks and ½ glass sugar. Dilute with ½ glass cream and cook thoroughly. Cream ⅛ lb butter and ½ glass flour until smooth, pinch off small pieces, add to the chocolate, and stir on top of the stove until the flour is incorporated, but do not let the mixture boil. It may then be strained through a fine sieve. Cool, mix with 10 beaten egg whites, and transfer to a mold greased with butter and strewn with rusk crumbs. Intersperse with strawberry jam, oranges, apples, cherries, etc. Bake in the oven for ½ hour.

To serve, turn out onto a platter and pour on red wine syrup prepared as follows. Bring to a boil ½ lb, or 1 glass, sugar and 1 glass red wine. Cool.

INGREDIENTS

¼ lb chocolate

½ glass sugar

½ glass cream

1½ spoons butter

½ glass flour

5 egg yolks

10 egg whites

2 rusks

1 orange

2 apples

⅓ glass cherries, etc.

*For the syrup*

1 glass red wine

1 glass, or ½ lb, sugar

## 1156  Pancake pudding

### (Puding iz blinov)

Prepare pancakes (Chapter 11). After beating the egg whites [and folding them into the batter], fry the pancakes on both sides. Spread each one with any kind of syrup, roll into a tube, and cut into 3–4 pieces.

Grease a saucepan with butter, sprinkle with rusk crumbs, and arrange the pieces of pancake in the pan. Stir together 2 glasses cream, 4 egg yolks, and ¼ lb sugar. Fold in 4 beaten egg whites, pour the mixture over the pancakes, and bake in an oven that is not too hot.

INGREDIENTS

*For the pancakes*
3 glasses milk
2 glasses, or ⅔ lb, flour
2–4 eggs
2 spoons butter

[*For the pudding*]
½ glass syrup
2 glasses cream
4–5 eggs
½ glass sugar

## 1160  Pear pudding

*(Puding iz grush)*

Peel and slice 12 pears and sprinkle the pieces with ¼ glass sugar, a little cinnamon, and 3–4 ground cloves. Add ¼ glass water and ½ glass wine and place the mixture in a covered saucepan over a high fire. When the sauce boils away, remove the pears from the fire and cool. Beat 6 egg yolks until white with ¼ glass sugar. In another bowl beat 1 spoon butter until white with a little lemon zest and ¼ lb roll soaked in milk and squeezed out. Add the eggs and sugar and fold in 6 beaten egg whites. Pour half of the batter into a mold, add the prepared pears, top with the rest of the batter, and bake.

INGREDIENTS

12 pears
½ glass wine
¼ lb bread, or ⅔ French roll
½ lb butter
6 eggs
⅓ glass milk

3–4 cloves
lemon zest
cinnamon
½ glass sugar
½ spoon butter
2–4 rusks

## 1168  Smolensk buckwheat pudding with apples and jam

*(Puding iz smolenskikh krup s jablokami i varen'em)*

Bring 3 glasses milk to a boil and pour in 1 glass Smolensk buckwheat, stirring. When the mixture thickens, cool and beat in 6 egg yolks. Add ½ spoon unsalted butter, 1 spoon sugar, and, finally, 6 beaten egg whites. Mix everything together. Grease a mold and add a layer of kasha, spread with jam, top with another layer of kasha, and cover with chopped apples. Sprinkle the layers with sugar, etc.

Steam the pudding. To serve, pour on syrup or sweet sauce.

INGREDIENTS

3 glasses milk
1 glass Smolensk buckwheat

6 eggs
½ glass sugar

2–3 apples

½ glass jam

2 rusks

(syrup or ingredients for sauce)

## 1172  Rice pudding

*(Puding iz risa)*

Wash 1 glass rice in cold water and drain. Barely cover the rice with fresh water, boil until half cooked, drain, rinse with cold water, and drain completely. Pour the rice into a saucepan, add 3 glasses whole milk, and boil until cooked, but not overcooked. The grains should remain separate. Add ⅛ lb butter and let cool. Sprinkle on ½ glass or more sugar and 1 spoon chopped candied peel, beat in 6 egg yolks, and add 6 beaten egg whites. Pour into a mold and bake in the oven. To serve, turn out onto a platter, strew with sugar, and pour on syrup or sauce [see Sauces for Puddings, Chapter 3].

INGREDIENTS

1 glass rice, that is, ½ lb

3 glasses cream or whole milk

¼ lb candied peel

⅛ lb butter

½ glass sugar

5–6 eggs

about 4 pieces sugar

½ spoon butter

## 1173  Two-colored rice pudding

*(Puding iz risa dvukh tsvetov)*

Boil 1½ glasses rice until half cooked. Bring to a boil 4 ½ glasses milk and 1½ spoons butter, add the rice, and boil until fully cooked. Divide the rice in half. To one half, add ⅛ to ¼ lb grated chocolate mixed with 2 spoons hot water and ⅓ glass sugar. Mix ⅓ glass sugar and 1 wineglass saffron infusion with the other half of the rice. Arrange alternate layers of rice in a mold greased with butter and strewn with rusk crumbs, making 6 layers in all.* Bake in the oven for fifteen minutes. To serve, turn out onto a platter and strew with sugar and cinnamon. Pour on chocolate, rum, or vanilla sauce.

INGREDIENTS

1½ glasses rice

4½ glasses milk

⅔ glass sugar

⅛–¼ lb chocolate

½ zolotnik saffron

1½ spoons butter

*This combination of saffron and chocolate is very unusual.

Puddings

### 1177 Cold rice with fresh or sour cream

*(Ris kholodnyj so slivkami ili smetanoju)*

Boil fluffy rice as indicated in #1172. Mix with ½ glass sugar and cinnamon, vanilla, or preserved orange rind. Grease a mold with olive oil or moisten it with cold water; then strew the interior with coarse sugar. Transfer the rice to the mold and cool. To serve, turn out onto a platter and cover with whipped sweet cream or fresh sour cream mixed with sugar and cinnamon,* vanilla, or lemon zest. Decorate the top with raspberry or cherry jam. Instead of molding, this rice may be arranged in a ring around a platter. Fill the center with whipped cream or sour cream and pour jam or syrup over it all.

INGREDIENTS

| | |
|---|---|
| 1 glass rice | 1 glass sour cream or very thick sweet |
| ¾ glass sugar | cream |
| orange rind, cloves,* or vanilla | jam |

*In the body of the original recipe Molokhovets called for cinnamon, but in the ingredients cloves.

### 1180 Rice with apples, jam, and meringue

*(Ris s jablokami, varen'em i meringoju)*

Boil 1 glass rice, as indicated in #1172, making sure that the grains remain separate. Add 1 spoon butter, ½ glass sugar, and a little cinnamon. Grease a platter with butter and strew with rusk crumbs. Add a layer of rice, then a layer of apples or pears, finely chopped and lightly fried with butter, sugar, and cinnamon, and then another layer of rice. Smooth the surface and top with jam or a fruit purée of some kind. Cover with meringue; that is, whip 4 egg whites, stir in ½ glass sugar, and brown lightly in the oven.

INGREDIENTS

| | |
|---|---|
| 3 glasses milk | 6 apples, or 8–12 pears, or about 20– |
| 1 glass rice | 30 plums |
| cinnamon | ½ glass jam |
| 2 spoons butter | 4 egg whites |
| ¾ glass sugar | |

### 1183 Sago pudding

*(Puding iz sago)*

Cover ½ lb white sago with cold water, set aside for 2 hours, then drain. Transfer the sago to a saucepan, stir in a large quantity of boiling water, and boil until the sago is half cooked. Drain the sago in a sieve and rinse with cold water. Pour the sago into a saucepan, add 3 glasses of boiling milk, and boil until tender, but do not let it overcook. Cool and add 1 spoon butter and 5–6 egg yolks beaten until white with ½ glass fine sugar. Fold in 5–6 beaten egg whites and transfer to a mold greased with fresh unsalted butter and strewn with rusk crumbs. Either bake the mold in the oven or boil it in water for about an hour.

Ten ground bitter almonds, 1 full spoon finely shredded preserved orange rind, or 1 spoon rum—or all of these—may be added to this pudding for flavoring.

To serve, pour on one of the following sauces: sabayon, chocolate, red wine, cherry, plum, raspberry or wild strawberry, almond, vanilla, cranberry, or rum sauce. Or, serve with cream, sugar, and cinnamon; almond milk with cherry jam; or a sauce made from fruit syrup.

If any pudding is left, then prepare pancakes the next day and interlay them with the leftover pudding diluted with 2–3 spoons cream. Add preserved orange rind and bake as a round loaf (*karavaj*).

### 1190 Baked stuffed apples

*(Pirog iz farshirovannykh jablok)*

Peel and core 10–12 apples. Finely chop 2 of the apples and mix with 1 spoon sugar, ¼ glass each raisins and finely pounded sweet almonds, and 6–7 bitter almonds. Fill the cored apples with this mixture, or simply fill them with jam, and bake. When they are cooked, beat 4–5 egg yolks with 2 spoons sugar and 1½ glasses cream. Sprinkle on a little cinnamon and ¾ glass sieved rusk crumbs and fold in 4–5 beaten egg whites. Pour over the apples arranged in a small deep dish and bake for a short time.

INGREDIENTS

| | |
|---|---|
| 10–12 apples | 1½ glasses cream |
| ¼ glass raisins | ⅓ glass sugar |
| ¼ glass sweet almonds, plus 6–7 bitter almonds, or ½ glass jam | ¾ glass rusk crumbs cinnamon |
| 4–5 eggs | |

### 1195 Apple pie à la reine

*(Jablochnyj pirog à la reine)*

Beat 5 egg yolks and ¼ lb sugar until white. Add 2 glasses flour, ¼ lb butter, a little lemon zest, and 1 spoon rum, if desired. Knead thoroughly and roll out on the table to the thickness of the blunt side of a knife. Cut out 2 rounds of dough and line the bottom of a tin pan with one. Also cut out a strip of dough and press this strip against the interior wall of the pan. Fill the pastry casing with apples, prepared as follows:

Peel and thinly slice 10 medium or 5 large apples, pour on 1 spoon table wine, and stew slightly. Mix with ¼ glass raisins, (⅓ glass ground sweet almonds and several bitter almonds,) ½ glass fine sugar, 1–2 spoons cherry jam, and preserved orange rind. Cover this mixture with the other round of dough. Crimp the edges, paint with egg white, sprinkle with rusk crumbs and sugar, and bake for 1½ hours.

Turn out onto a platter an hour before dinner. Let the pie cool a little, then cover it with 3 egg whites beaten with ¼ lb sugar. Brown in the oven and serve after decorating the top with jam.

INGREDIENTS

| | |
|---|---|
| 5 large or 10 medium apples | a little preserved orange rind |
| (1 spoon rum) | ⅔ lb, or 2 glasses, flour |
| (¼ glass raisins) | 1 very full glass fine sugar |
| (⅓ glass sweet almonds, plus 10 bitter almonds) | ¼ lb butter |
| | 5 egg yolks |
| 1–2 spoons cherry jam | |

### 1196  Apple charlotte with black bread

*(Sharlotka iz jablok s chernym khlebom)*

Peel, slice, and seed 6 apples. Add ½ glass* sugar, ¼ glass currants, ½ teaspoon or more fine cinnamon, ⅛ glass* ground bitter almonds, lemon zest, and ¾ glass white wine. Stew slightly, but do not overcook the apples. Meanwhile, mix about 1½ glasses black bread, ¼ lb* melted Finnish butter, [the remaining] 10 ground bitter almonds, lemon zest, [the remaining] ¼ glass sugar, finely ground cinnamon, vanilla, or 2–3 cloves. Grease a mold with [the remaining] butter, strew with rusk crumbs, and add half the black bread mixture and then the apples. Top with the bread mixture, place the mold on an baking sheet, and bake for 1 hour, turning the mold so that it browns evenly.

INGREDIENTS

| | |
|---|---|
| 6 apples | ¾ glass white wine |
| ¾ glass* sugar | 1½ glasses bread |
| ¼ glass currants | ⅓ lb* butter |
| cinnamon | lemon zest |
| 2–3 cloves | 2–3 rusks |
| ¼ glass* bitter almonds | |

*Usually in the list of ingredients Molokhovets indicated the amount for each separate use of an *ingredient as it occurred in the body of the recipe. In this case, however, she gave the total amount of sugar, bitter almonds, and butter required to make the charlotte.*

### 1199 Apple pudding with rusk sippets

*(Puding iz jablok s grenkami iz sukharej)*

Butter a mold and strew with rusk crumbs. Line the bottom and sides of the mold with plain small rusks that have been dipped in milk or cream. Fill any empty spaces with grated black bread or roll mixed with sugar and butter. Add a layer of finely chopped apples, strew with sugar and cinnamon or vanilla, and dot with small pieces of butter. Cover with a layer of rusks soaked in cream, interspersing them with more of the grated roll mixture. Add another layer of apples and continue in this manner to the end. Meanwhile, beat 4 egg yolks with ⅓ glass sugar until white, fold in 4 beaten egg whites, mix, and pour this over each layer of apples.* Bake and serve by turning out onto a platter. The more sugar, vanilla, and butter used, the tastier this pudding will be.

INGREDIENTS

| | |
|---|---|
| 24 rusks | ½ lb butter |
| 1 5 kopeck roll or black bread | ½ vanilla pod |
| up to 10 apples | 4 eggs |
| 1 glass sugar | |

*This is an excellent example of the wisdom of reading a recipe through to the end before beginning work. The instructions for making the egg yolk mixture logically belong before the directions for layering or composing the pudding.*

### 1202 Omelet with jam

*(Omlet s varen'em)*

Beat 7 egg yolks with ⅓ glass sugar until white. Add the zest of ½ lemon or, preferably, cinnamon, 3 spoons melted butter, ⅓ glass flour, and 7 beaten egg whites. Pour 1 spoon melted butter onto a large skillet and heat until very hot. Pour on the batter and bake in the oven for 10–15 minutes. As soon as it is cooked, immediately add jam without syrup—cherry or, even better, black currant. Roll the omelet into a tube and return it to the oven for 5 minutes. To serve, cut into diagonal slices, arrange them on a platter, and strew with sugar, or arrange them around a platter like a garland and fill the center with a meringue made as follows. Fold 1 glass cherry syrup into 6 beaten egg whites, strew with sugar, and bake for several minutes.

Pour on vanilla or sabayon sauce.

Or cook on small skillets,* place one layer on top of another on a platter, spreading the layers with jam, and serve.

INGREDIENTS

⅓ glass fine sugar
7 eggs
⅓ glass flour
¼ lb butter

zest of ½ lemon or cinnamon
1 glass jam
1 glass cherry syrup
6 egg whites

*These are small cast iron plates, usually stored in a stack. They have removable handles that are used to grip the plates and move them around the stove.*

## 1208  Bechamel soufflé

### (Sufle iz beshemelja)

Dilute ⅛ lb butter and ½ glass flour with 2 glasses cream. Add ½ ground vanilla bean and bring to a boil 2–3 times. Remove from the heat and add ¼ glass sugar, 4 egg yolks, and then 4 beaten egg whites. Prepare 8 small skillets, heat them until burning hot, grease them with butter, and place them on top of the stove. Divide the prepared mixture among the 8 skillets. Bake the soufflés in the oven and turn them out onto a platter, interlayering them with jam. Beat 4 egg whites and spread over the soufflé. Strew with sugar and bake for 5 minutes.

Soufflés, baked and arranged in this manner, may be served without the meringue. In that case, douse them with rum sauce or with a cold syrup prepared from 2 glasses red wine and ½ glass sugar.

INGREDIENTS

¼ lb butter
½ glass flour
3 glasses cream
4 egg yolks
¼ vanilla pod

½ glass sugar
1 glass jam
1 egg white
¼ glass sugar or 2 glasses red wine
    and ¼ lb sugar

## 1209  Meringue pie*

### (Pirog iz meringi)

Beat 8 egg whites into a thick foam. Bring to a boil 6 glasses milk and drop spoonfuls of the beaten egg whites into the milk. Cover with a lid and boil for several minutes. Using a slotted spoon, transfer the cooked meringues to drain on a fine sieve. Beat the egg yolks with sugar until white and dilute with the cooled milk. Sprinkle on ½ teaspoon cinnamon or about 2 drops bergamot oil.** Cook on top of the stove, stirring, until the mixture thickens. Arrange the boiled meringues on a platter, pour on the milk sauce, sprinkle with sugar and cinnamon, and place in an oven that is not too hot for 10 minutes.

INGREDIENTS

2 bottles milk  
¼ lb sugar  
8 eggs

about 2 drops bergamot oil, or  
cinnamon

*What Molokhovets called "Meringue pie" is what we call "Floating island." See the section on Milk soups in Chapter 1 for more variations on the same theme.*  
**For more on bergamot oil see the Glossary.*

## 1212  Apple soufflé*

*(Vozdushnyj pirog iz jablok)*

Bake 6 medium apples and rub them through a fine sieve. Beat 6–7 egg whites until stiff and fold into the apple purée, sprinkling on, or preferably, sifting on, ½ glass fine sugar. Transfer to a glazed earthenware dish, sprinkle the top with ¼ glass sugar, and bake for 10 minutes while the main course is being served. Serve as soon as the soufflé rises and browns; otherwise it will fall.

Serve with cream.

*With this recipe, I return to the issue of tangled culinary nomenclature—a separate treatise might well be written on the subject of puddings and soufflés. A soufflé, strictly defined, is a hot mixture of butter, flour, and beaten egg whites served directly from the oven. The name for any particular soufflé comes from the added ingredients, either crushed or puréed, or from a liquid or powdered flavoring. Since none of Molokhovets' fruit-based "soufflés" were made with a roux-like base, their consistency and texture differed considerably from the classic French preparation. Her hybrid soufflés—what we might call baked whips—are in fact close cousins of the German Aufläufe, which resemble puddings more than soufflés. Aufläufe contain very heavy ingredients and, although raised by whipped egg whites, they are not as light as a real soufflé. (For more on the differences between Aufläufe and soufflés, see Sheraton, The German Cookbook, 353–366.)*

## 1217  An outstanding soufflé made from homemade jam

*(Prevoskhodnyj vozdushnyj pirog iz domashnago varen'ja)*

Add 5 very fresh large egg whites to 1¼ glasses thick raspberry, wild strawberry, or black currant jam. There should be more berries than syrup. Beat with a spoon in one direction for at least an hour, until the mixture turns almost white and is very thick, or until a spoon can stand upright in it. Transfer to a deep platter and set in a cold place. When the main course is being served, sprinkle the soufflé with 1 spoon sugar, and bake it in a fairly hot oven. As soon as the soufflé rises and browns, serve it immediately at the table with cream.

This soufflé is so good that it does not fall as others sometimes do when prepared as indicated in #1212. It is more substantial and tastier, although it requires more work.

Puding iz vina

# Puddings

## 1220  Wine pudding

*(Puding iz vina)*

Fry 2 glasses grated stale roll crumbs in 1 spoon melted butter, pour on 1 glass boiling hot table wine, and mix until smooth. [In a separate bowl], beat 1 spoon butter until white and mix with 6 egg yolks, 3 spoons fine sugar, and cinnamon. Combine the eggs and sugar with the roll crumbs, add 6 beaten egg whites, transfer to a mold, and bake.

One wineglass rum may be added, in which case, use a little less wine. Pour on rum sauce.

INGREDIENTS

¼ lb butter
2 glasses grated roll, or 1 white French
   roll
6 eggs

½ glass fine sugar
¾–1 glass wine
(1 wineglass rum)
2 rusks

## 1225  Carrot pudding*

*(Puding iz morkovi)*

Grate enough raw carrots to make 4 glasses and squeeze out the juice to the last drop. Fry the carrots in ¼–½ lb butter until they turn brown, remove the saucepan from the fire, and set it on ice. Beat the carrots with a small spatula until they turn pale, then add 3 egg yolks, and again beat everything thoroughly. Add ½ cup sugar, 2–3 teaspoons sieved cinnamon, and 5 beaten egg whites. Mix thoroughly and pile into a buttered mold strewn with rusk crumbs. Steam a full hour, turn out onto a platter, and pour on sabayon sauce. This pudding is very tasty, and it is hard to guess that it is made of carrots. [Alternatively,] pour on butter or vanilla sauce.

INGREDIENTS

carrots
5 eggs
¼–½ lb Finnish butter
½ glass sugar

2–3 teaspoon cinnamon
additional butter, or ingredients for
   sauce

*Carrot puddings were common in eighteenth-century England and America. Both Hannah Glasse and E. Smith included recipes for carrot puddings made from a mixture of grated carrots, bread crumbs, eggs, butter, cream, and sack (the sixteenth-century English name for white wines imported from Spain and the Canary Islands) and baked in pastry. Amelia Simmons' American recipe, which omitted the bread crumbs, sack, and pie crust, was not only simpler than the English recipes, but also remarkably similar to that of Molokhovets. (Glasse, Art of Cooking, 107; Smith, The Compleat Housewife, 126, and Simmons, First American Cookbook, 27.)*

### 1228  Rice pudding with crayfish

*(Puding iz risa s rakami)*

Boil a thick rice porridge in milk after scalding the rice with boiling water. Boil 40 crayfish, peel the tails and claws, and chop fine. Discard the bile, dry the shells, and pound until fine, making enough to fill 1 glass. Prepare crayfish butter from the shells after frying them in 3 spoons Finnish butter. Add all the remaining [shells] to bouillon, boil for 15 minutes, and strain. Beat 1½ spoons crayfish butter until white and mix with the rice porridge, the finely chopped crayfish, and 6 egg yolks. Add salt, a little nutmeg, and 6–7 beaten egg whites (or 3–4 whole eggs). Mix and boil in a napkin for 1½ hours. To serve, pour on the following sauce. Mix ⅛ lb crayfish butter with 1 spoon flour. Dilute with 3 spoons cream and 1½ glasses crayfish bouillon, bring to a boil 2–3 times, stirring, and sprinkle on salt and nutmeg. Before serving, beat in 2 egg yolks and heat until very hot, but do not boil.

INGREDIENTS

½ lb, or 1 glass, rice
⅜ lb butter
40 crayfish
1 bottle milk
1 spoon flour

3 spoons cream
salt
4–8 eggs
nutmeg

### 1229  Pudding of calf's brains

*(Puding iz mozgov teljach'ikh)*

Soak the brains from 2 calf's heads in water for 15 minutes or more. Remove the membrane, boil the brains in salted water with a small amount of vinegar, and drain in a colander. After the brains have cooled, rub them through the colander, adding 1½ spoons melted butter, a little salt, pepper, nutmeg, and 5–6 egg yolks. Mix thoroughly and add the reserved egg whites, beaten until stiff. Transfer to a buttered mold strewn with rusk crumbs and bake in a hot oven for 30 minutes. To serve, pour on crayfish, mushroom, or rum sauce.

### 1233  Pudding from leftover domestic or wild fowl

*(Puding iz ostavshejsja dichi)*

Gather together the leftovers from yesterday's main course, including turkey, chicken, duck, or any kind of wild fowl. Add about ¼ lb beef marrow and 3 hard-boiled eggs. Finely chop all this and pound in a mortar. Whip ¼ lb butter until white, beat in 6 egg yolks one by one, and gradually add the puréed game mixture. Add 3 spoons grated roll, a little lemon zest, and nutmeg. Stir all this thoroughly in one direction and then add 6 beaten egg whites. Butter a mold, strew with rusk crumbs, line with parsley leaves, and fill with the prepared mixture. Bake for 1 hour. Pour on brown sauce.

INGREDIENTS

| | |
|---|---|
| leftover roast meat | lemon zest |
| 6 eggs | nutmeg |
| almost 1/4 lb beef marrow | salt |
| 1/4 lb butter | parsley |
| 1/2 white French roll | |

## 1235  Calf's liver pudding

*(Puding iz teljach'ej pechenki)*

Boil and grate the calf's liver. Finely chop 1 onion and fry in 1 1/2 spoons butter. Cool, mix with 3 egg yolks, and add 3/8 lb white bread soaked in milk and squeezed out, at least 1/2 glass currants, salt, nutmeg, the grated liver, and 1 wineglass cognac. Beat all this as well as possible in a stoneware bowl. Add 4 beaten egg whites and boil in a napkin 1 1/2 hours.

Serve with the following sauce: Fry 1 spoon flour in 1 spoon butter and dilute with 1 1/2 glasses bouillon and 1/2 glass wine. Bring to a boil, strain, and add lemon juice, a little sugar, lemon slices, and 1/4 glass raisins. Bring all this to a boil and pour over the pudding.

INGREDIENTS

| | |
|---|---|
| 1/2 calf's liver | *For the sauce* |
| 1 onion | 1 spoon butter |
| 1/4 lb butter | 1 spoon flour |
| 4 eggs | 1/2 glass wine |
| 3/8 lb white bread | 1–2 pieces sugar |
| 1 glass milk to soak the bread | 1/2 lemon, or 1 spoon capers, or |
| 1/2 glass currants | gooseberry juice |
| nutmeg | 1/4 glass raisins |
| salt | |
| [1 wineglass cognac] | |

# 11
# Crêpes, Pancakes for Butter Week, Sippets, and Eggs

*(Blinchiki, bliny na masljanoj nedele, grenki, jajchnitsy, omlet, jajtsa)*

## CRÊPES
*(Blinchiki)*

**1236 Ordinary pancakes, otherwise known as crêpes***
*(Bliny obyknovennye, inache blinchiki)*

(Proportions for 6–8 persons)

a) Mix until smooth 2 eggs and 2 glasses flour and gradually add 3 glasses milk and some salt. Strew a skillet with salt, heat it, and wipe with a towel. Grease with refined oil or a piece of pork fat, reheat the pan, pour on 1 spoon batter to cover the bottom of the skillet, and place on top of the stove. When the pancake begins to rise, loosen it from the skillet and remove it after it has cooked on one side. Grease the skillet with a feather, pour in more batter, etc. These crêpes are served with any kind of filling, such as meat, farmer's cheese, etc. Crêpes must be thoroughly fried on both sides before being used for any kind of round loaf (*karavaj*) or pudding.

b) To serve crêpes for dinner without filling and with only sugar and jam, prepare the batter from 4–5 eggs or 4–5 egg yolks with the whites beaten separately. Add 2 glasses flour, 2½ glasses milk, and salt. Fry the crêpes in a skillet and, after all have been fried, fold each into quarters and refry. ¼ lb butter, beaten until white, may be added to these crêpes. In that case fry the crêpes on both sides in small skillets. To serve, sprinkle with fine sugar scraped with lemon zest or serve with jam.

These proportions will yield about 20 crêpes.

INGREDIENTS

For Crêpes #a
3 glasses milk, or 1 ordinary bottle
2 glasses flour
2 eggs
salt
¼ lb butter to fry crêpes

For Crêpes #b
2 glasses, or ⅔ lb, flour

2½ glasses milk
4–5 eggs
salt
⅛ lb butter
(¼ lb butter to fry crêpes)
(sugar or jam)

*Blinchiki *are similar to French crêpes. They are very thin unleavened pancakes that may be filled or not, according to circumstances. Filled *blinchiki *are known as blintzes among the American Jewish community.

### 1239 Crêpes with jam, fruit purée, or bechamel

(Blinchiki s varen'em ili marmeladom i beshemelem)

Prepare large Crêpes #1236 and spread each crêpe with any kind of jam without syrup or with plum or apple purée. Roll up into a tube, dip in egg and rusk crumbs, and fry in butter. Or simply fold in quarters and fry. To serve, sprinkle with sugar.

The second frying may be omitted for Crêpes #1236b, provided the crêpes are well fried at the start so that they are lightly browned and not raw. Spread with jam or fruit purée, roll into a tube, heat, and serve covered with a sweet bechamel, made as follows: Cream thoroughly ½ spoon very fresh butter and ½ glass flour, dilute with 2 glasses cream or whole milk, boil several times, and sprinkle on 2–4 pieces fine sugar. For flavoring, add a little cinnamon, lemon zest, bitter almonds, or chocolate. Pour the sauce over the crêpes.

INGREDIENTS

3 glasses milk
2 glasses flour
2–4 eggs
1 glass jam or fruit purée

1 egg
4–6 rusks
2–3 spoons butter

### 1244 Pancakes with liver

(Bliny s pechenkoju)

Prepare Crêpes #1236a and stack them in a saucepan greased with butter after spreading each pancake with the following mixture. Boil ½ of a calf's lung and ½ of a calf's liver with root vegetables, spices, and salt. Remove the meat and chop very fine. Fry 1 finely chopped onion in 2 spoons melted butter. Add the liver and lungs and fry, stirring. Mix in salt, allspice, black pepper, nutmeg, and 4–5 finely chopped hard-boiled eggs. Cool the filling, [spread it over the pancakes, stack them in the pan,] and bake for 1 hour. To serve, turn out onto a platter and pour on brown sauce.

These pancakes made into a round loaf (*karavaj*) are also served with *shchi*.

INGREDIENTS

For the crêpes
3 glasses milk
2 glasses flour
2 eggs
salt
¾ lb butter

For the filling
½ of a calf's liver
½ of a calf's lungs

1 carrot
1 parsley root
1 onion
4–5 eggs
1½ spoons butter
nutmeg
black pepper and allspice
ingredients for the sauce

## 1247  Dutch pancakes

### (Bliny gollandskie)

a) Cool ⅜ glass melted butter and beat until white. Beat in 3 egg yolks and sprinkle on 4–5 pieces sugar and nearly 1 glass flour. Stir until smooth and gradually add 1⅛ glass cream and some salt. Mix and add 6 beaten egg whites. Heat a skillet until it is very hot. Pour on 1 teaspoon melted butter and then about 2 spoons batter, so that the pancakes are thicker than ordinary crêpes and thinner than Russian pancakes. Bake in the oven on coals and next to flaming coals. When the pancakes have cooked, spread them with jam and transfer them to a saucepan greased with butter. Bake for about 10 minutes. To serve, turn out onto a platter and pour on sabayon or any kind of sweet sauce or syrup. Or cover with a meringue made from 4 egg whites and ⅛ lb sugar and bake for about 10 minutes.

b) These pancakes are cooked the same way, but use a different proportion of ingredients. Beat 5 egg yolks until white with ½ glass sugar and pour in almost ½ glass cream. Add a little lemon zest and ¾ glass dry, sieved flour. Mix until smooth and add 5 beaten egg whites. Place the bowl with this batter in cold water so that the whites do not fall and bake the pancakes as indicated above.

Pour on sabayon or sweet sauce, cover with meringue, or sprinkle with sugar and cinnamon and pour on syrup.

INGREDIENTS

5 eggs  
¾ glass flour  
½ glass cream

¾–1 glass jam  
⅜ lb butter  
¼ lb sugar

## 1249 Round loaf of crêpes with rice and bone marrow

*(Karavaj iz blinchikov s risom i mozgami)*

Prepare Crêpes #1236a. Tie up 1½ glasses rice in a cloth and boil in salted water until half-cooked so the grains remain separate. Choose a saucepan the same size as the crêpes, butter the pan, and strew it with rusk crumbs. Stack the finished crêpes in the pan, covering each one with some rice, a few small pieces of bone marrow *(mozgi iz kostej)*, and some currants. Cover with the saucepan lid and bake. Serve separately sugar or brown sauce.

INGREDIENTS

*For the crêpes*  
2 eggs  
3 glasses milk  
2 glasses flour  
¼–½ lb butter  
2–3 rusks

*For the filling*  
1½ glass rice  
½ glass currants  
½ lb bone marrow  
(sugar, or ingredients for brown sauce)

# RUSSIAN PANCAKES
### *(Russkie bliny)*

*Remarks:* For Russians, pancakes are an essential component of Butter Week [= Carnival]. During this holiday, pancakes are as necessary to the Russians as doughnuts are to the Catholics and German rolls to the Lutherans. Russian pancakes may be varied by using just buckwheat flour, just wheat flour, or equal parts of each. Yeast is the usual leavening, but some pancakes are made with soda instead.

Although garnishings vary, all pancakes are prepared the same: After the last rising, the batter must not be mixed or it will fall. To prepare the skillet for frying the pancakes, strew it with fine salt, then heat the skillet, wipe it with a towel, and grease it with butter using a feather or cotton wool. After the skillet has been prepared and is burning hot, spoon batter over the bottom of the pan. Fry the pancakes on top of the stove or, preferably, bake them on hot coals in a Russian stove. (If baking them in a Russian stove, the fire must be kept constant.) When the pancakes begin to rise and brown, drizzle butter over them. If they are fried on top of the stove, turn them over to finish cooking and stack them up by the side of the stove to keep warm.

In general, pancakes should be cooked just before serving. Always grease the skillet generously with a feather dipped in butter before pouring on fresh batter. The batter must be a little thicker than for ordinary, unleavened crêpes (*blinchiki*) which uses 2 glasses flour for every 3 glasses milk. For Russian pancakes, use equal parts of flour and liquid, that is, for 3 glasses of water with milk and yeast, use the same amount of flour, or 3 glasses. These are just approximate proportions. It is hard to be more precise since flours differ and some are much easier to incorporate than others. Just as these pancakes must be much thicker than ordinary crêpes, they also must be lighter and more porous.

Cooking pancakes requires a special knack and skill acquired only by experience and practice.* Success depends most of all on the yeast, on beating the batter, and on knowing how to cook pancakes. For 4 glasses of flour (to yield 25 pancakes), use ½–2 *zolotniki* dry yeast. Use more yeast for pure buckwheat and "scalded" (*zavernye*) pancakes and less for pure wheat pancakes. Ideally, the batter should be prepared 5–6 hours before serving. The earlier the batter is prepared, the less yeast will be needed, while a later preparation will require more yeast.

"Scalded" pancakes are made by adding water or milk that has been brought just to the point of boiling but has not yet boiled.

Nearly 1 glass of melted butter will be needed for cooking this amount of pancakes.

After the batter has been poured on the skillet, the pancakes may be sprinkled with hard-boiled eggs, finely chopped onion, smelts that have been washed and wiped dry, or fluffy Smolensk buckwheat kasha.

The very best melted fresh or Finnish butter, very fresh sour cream, and fresh caviar are served separately with all these pancakes. Since both sour cream and fresh caviar are rather expensive in some places, economize by using the following preparations for the family and servants during Butter Week: Add 1 lb or 1⅔ glasses very fresh, thick sour cream to 3 bottles whole fresh milk. Beat the cream thoroughly with the milk and set it in a warm place. Let the mixture stand just until it has turned into yogurt, mix it all thoroughly, and store it in a cold place until needed. Buy pressed caviar instead of fresh. Mash it with a wooden spoon, adding boiled or fresh cream, and beat it thoroughly until it is as thick and smooth as fresh caviar.

*The Russians have a saying, "Pervyj blin da komom" (*lit.: "The first blin is a lump"*) or, more colloquially, "Practice makes perfect."

### 1250  Pure buckwheat pancakes

(*Chisto-grechnevye bliny*)

5 or 6 hours beforehand, prepare a batter from 4 glasses buckwheat flour, 3 glasses warm milk or water, 1 tablespoon melted butter, 2 egg yolks, and 1½ or 2

*zolotniki* dry yeast or 2–4 spoons fresh yeast. Mix and beat with a small spatula as well as possible. After the batter has risen, beat it again. Add a level spoon of salt and pour on 1½–2 glasses hot milk or water, as indicated above, and beat again. Two beaten egg whites may be added. Mix and let the batter rise. After it has risen, and without stirring the batter further, which would cause it to fall, carry it carefully to the appointed place [i.e., to the stove]. Ladle it out with a spoon and fry, as indicated in the Remarks.

### 1252  The very best pancakes

*(Bliny samye luchshie)*

Prepare a batter from 1½ glasses wheat flour, 2½ glasses buckwheat flour, 2½ glasses warm water, and 3–4 spoons yeast. After it has risen, sprinkle on 1 glass buckwheat flour and let the batter rise. When the stove is lit, an hour before cooking, pour 2 glasses boiling milk onto the batter all at once and mix until smooth. When it cools, add salt. (2–3 eggs and ⅛ lb butter may be added also.) Let the batter rise and, without stirring further, fry the pancakes as indicated in the Remarks. Yield: 25 pancakes.

INGREDIENTS

2½ glasses, or 1 lb, buckwheat flour
3–4 spoons yeast
1½ glasses, or ½ lb, wheat flour
2 glasses milk
salt
[1 extra glass buckwheat flour]
(3 eggs and ⅛ lb butter)

½–1 glass butter to fry the pancakes

*Serve separately*
butter
caviar
sour cream

### 1260  The Tsar's pancakes

*(Tsarskie bliny)*

Melt ½ lb butter and strain through a finely woven napkin into a stoneware bowl. When the butter has cooled a little, add 6 egg yolks and mix thoroughly in one direction with a small spatula. Add 1 teacup sugar and stir on ice until the mixture begins to foam. Meanwhile, prepare the following bechamel: Dilute ¼ lb, or ¾ glass, flour with ½ bottle cream. Boil thoroughly, stirring constantly until the bechamel is as thick as pancake batter. After removing from the fire, stir the bechamel over ice until it cools. Then add it to the butter, egg yolk, and sugar mixture and pour in ½ spoon orange flower water. Stir the mixture again in the same direction. Add ½ glass thick cream beaten into a foam, and, as soon as the table is set, pour the batter onto medium size skillets and cook over a low fire. Without using a knife, carefully overturn the skillets to stack the pancakes on a platter, sprinkling each one with sugar and a little lemon juice. After arranging the pancakes in this manner, one on top of another, trim the edges and decorate the top with jam or jelly.

INGREDIENTS

½ lb butter
6 egg yolks
1 cup sugar
¼ lb flour
½ bottle thick cream

½ spoon orange flower water
¼ glass thick cream
lemon juice
(jam or jelly)

# TOASTS OR SIPPETS
## (Grenki)

### 1262  French toast with fruit purée

*(Grenki iz belago khleba s marmeladom\*)*

Slice 1½ loaves of white French bread. Spread fruit purée on one side and cover with another slice. Dip in milk mixed with eggs and fry on both sides in hot butter. To serve, sprinkle with sugar.

INGREDIENTS

1½ loaves white French bread
¾ glass fruit purée [or jelly]
2 spoons butter

2–3 eggs
2 glasses milk
sugar

*\*For Molokhovets, marmelad was simply a fruit purée. In modern Russian, the word refers to a semi-solid confection made of fruit.*

### 1263  French toast with ground almonds

*(Grenki s mindal'noju massoju)*

Peel ¼ lb sweet almonds and 5–6 bitter almonds. Pound not too fine, pouring on 1 spoon of rosewater drop by drop. Stir the ground almonds in a saucepan over coals until they dry slightly. Melt 1 spoon butter and add 2 egg yolks, 2 eggs, the almonds, sugar, and 1 spoon sieved rusk crumbs. Mix, add 2 beaten egg whites, and spread this mixture on slices of white bread. Arrange the slices in pairs, dip them in milk mixed with eggs and sugar, and fry in butter on both sides.

INGREDIENTS

| | |
|---|---|
| 1½ loaves white French bread | 1 spoon rosewater |
| ¼ lb or ¾ glass sweet almonds | 6 eggs |
| 5–6 bitter almonds | 2 glasses milk |
| 1 spoon rusk crumbs | ⅓ glass sugar |
| 2–3 spoons butter | |

### 1265  White bread sippets with wine

*(Grenki iz belago khleba s vinom)*

Slice 1½ loaves of French bread, each slice as thick as 1½ fingers. Or lay 12–18 fast day rusks in a deep dish. Pour on white wine and keep basting the rusks with the wine until they are thoroughly moistened. Then dip the rusks in fine sugar, arrange them on a platter, and dry them in the oven. To serve, pour on fresh wine and spread jam on each slice. [Ingredients:] About 1 glass wine, ⅔ glass sugar, and about ½–1 glass jam or fruit purée.

## EGG DISHES

*(Kushan'ja iz jajts)*

### 1270  Scrambled eggs with herring or sprats

*(Jajtsa na skovorode s seledkoju ili s sardel'kami)*

Finely chop 2 boned herring or 12–15 boned sprats and mix them with 9–12 eggs. Melt ¼ lb butter and, when it is very hot, pour on the eggs and fish. Finely chopped ham (½ lb) may be substituted for the herring.

### 1276  Jam omelet with bechamel cream sauce

*(Omlet s varen'em i s beshemelem iz slivok)*

Thoroughly beat 12–15 very fresh eggs. Butter a skillet, but not excessively, and pour on the beaten eggs in batches to make several thin pancakes. Flip each pancake onto a plate and, while the pancake is still hot, immediately spread it with jam (raspberry is best) and fold into fourths. When all the pancakes have been fried, arrange them in a circle around a platter. Keep them warm in the oven without letting them cool. Serve covered with a bechamel sauce made with cream. To make the sauce, stir together ½ spoon very fresh butter, ¼ glass flour, and 2 pieces sugar, and dilute with 2 glasses cream. Mix thoroughly and sprinkle with lemon zest, a little cinnamon, or vanilla. Boil thoroughly, pour over the pancakes (*omlet*), and serve.

INGREDIENTS

| | |
|---|---|
| 12–15 eggs | 2 spoons butter |
| ¼ glass flour | 2 glasses cream |
| 2 pieces sugar | |

### 1279  Baked goose eggs*

   (*Gusinyja jajtsa pechenyja*)

   Drill holes in 6 eggs and empty out all the contents. Melt 2 spoons butter [in a skillet], pour on the eggs, and cook into thick scrambled eggs. Rub the scrambled eggs through a sieve and add 1 spoon grated roll, ¼ teaspoon mace, and 1 spoon finely chopped green onions. Stir in 3–4 [raw] chicken eggs, mix thoroughly, inject back into the shells with a fine hypodermic needle or syringe, and bake.

INGREDIENTS

| | |
|---|---|
| 6 goose eggs | ¼ teaspoon mace |
| 2 spoons butter | green onions |
| 1 spoon grated roll | 3–4 chicken eggs |

   *This is a very unusual recipe for several reasons. For one thing, the technique is unwieldy, being both fussy and labor intensive. Molokhovets' only other use for blown eggs was to fill the emptied shells with orange gelatin for dessert (cf. #1496). Dishes featuring eggs as the main ingredient were uncommon in traditional Russian cuisine, although of course they were often used as a component of other dishes. Also, goose eggs are not mentioned elsewhere in the book. All these factors make it possible, but unlikely, that this is an old Russian recipe. Barbara Wheaton noted its resemblance to a medieval favorite, Oeufz rostis en la broche (quoted in Tirel, called Taillevent, Le Viandier, 68). The general antecedents of the Russian recipe are clear enough, but the exact source remains a puzzle since Molokhovets included it in the first edition of her book (1861), a good thirty years before Pichon and Vicaire published their edition of Le Viandier.

# 12
# Filled Dumplings, Macaroni, and Kasha

*(Kolduny, pel'meni, makarony, vareniki, kashi, i proch.)*

The amounts indicated are for 6–8 persons. For 9–12 persons, increase the proportions by 1½. For 13–15 persons, double the proportions. For 16–18 persons, increase the proportions by 2½.

## FILLED DUMPLINGS, RAVIOLI, AND PASTRIES
### *(Kolduny, pel'meni, vareniki, vatrushki, and pezy)*

### 1281  Dough for *kolduny* and *pel'meni*

*(Testo na kolduny i pel'meni)*

Prepare a stiff dough from 3 glasses flour, 2 eggs, and 7 spoons, or almost ½ glass, water mixed with 1 full teaspoon salt. Roll out until the dough is thin but without holes. Arrange balls of filling in rows on the dough. Enclose the filling securely by folding over the dough and pressing down firmly around each ball. Then cut out *pirozhki* in the shape of half moons with a mold or with a pastry knife* [*formoju ili reztsom*]. This amount of dough will yield 60 *kolduny* but only about 40 *pel'meni*, which should be cut out with a larger mold. Drop into boiling salted water (for this amount of *kolduny*, *vareniki*, etc., add 1 full tablespoon salt to the boiling water) and test after 10 minutes. With a slotted spoon, carefully transfer the cooked dumplings from the water onto a platter.

INGREDIENTS

3 glasses, or 1 lb, wheat flour
salt

2 eggs
water

*It is not clear what this cutting instrument was; it could have been a special knife or perhaps a pastry cutting wheel.

### 1282  Dough for noodles, dumplings, and wafers

*(Testo na lapshu, lazanki i laman'tsy)*

Knead a stiff dough from 3 glasses flour, 3 eggs, and 4–5 silver spoons salted water, or nearly ⅓ glass. Roll out thinly, let the dough dry, and finely shred for noodles, but cut into lozenges for dumplings.

INGREDIENTS

1 lb, or 3 glasses, flour
water

3 eggs
salt

### 1283  Lithuanian kolduny

*(Kolduny litovskie)*

Very finely chop ¾ lb raw beef filet, rump, or round, etc., with ¾ lb kidney fat. For those who like very rich *kolduny*, double the amount of kidney fat. Add salt, 5 black peppercorns, 10 allspice, and 2 spoons finely chopped onions fried in ½ spoon butter, or simply bake an onion and chop it fine. Add, if desired, ½ teaspoon sieved marjoram and 1–2 spoons rich bouillon. Mix, prepare the dough as indicated in #1281, and cut out *kolduny* half the size of a small glass. Drop into boiling salted water and test after 15 minutes. When they are cooked, transfer them carefully with a slotted spoon onto a platter. Serve hot before bouillon. Eat strewn with salt and sifted* black pepper.

INGREDIENTS

¾ lb beef
1 onion
¾ or 1½ lbs kidney fat
5 black peppercorns
10 allspice
(½ spoon butter)

(marjoram, if desired)
salt

*For the dough*
3 glasses, or 1 lb, flour
2 eggs

*The need to sift black pepper suggests that it was being pounded in a mortar rather than ground in a pepper mill.

### 1289  Real Siberian *pel'meni*

*(Nastojashchie sibirskie pel'meni)*

Using a knife, scrape 1½ lbs first-quality beef from the short loin. Add 1 finely chopped and squeezed-out raw onion, sieved black pepper, and salt. Use this filling to make *pel'meni* as indicated in #1281. If the beef is lean, use 1 lb beef and ½ lb finely chopped kidney suet. Boil the *pel'meni* in salted water or in bouillon in a separate saucepan. Serve the *pel'meni* in strong clear bouillon combined with some of the strained bouillon in which they boiled. Or, after removing the *pel'meni* from water with a slotted spoon, serve them separately on a platter with vinegar.

These *pel'meni* are best made the size of *kolduny* or shaped like small ears (*ushki*).

To serve *pel'meni* in bouillon, only half the amount of forcemeat and dough is needed.

Siberians prepare *pel'meni* for several occasions at once, sprinkling them lightly with flour so they do not stick together. Then they are frozen and boiled in salted boiling water as needed.

INGREDIENTS

| | |
|---|---|
| 1½ lbs beef, or 1 lb beef and ½ lb kidney suet | *For the dough* |
| | 3 glasses flour |
| black pepper | 2 eggs |
| 2 onions | |

### 1293  Yeast *pirozhki* with farmer's cheese

*(Pirozhki na drozhzhakh s tvorogom)*

Mix thoroughly 4 egg yolks, ¼ lb melted butter, a little milk, and 1 spoon sugar. Heat, add 3 glasses wheat flour, stir until smooth, and add ½ wineglass thick white yeast. Beat the dough thoroughly and set in a warm place. After the dough rises, turn it out onto the table to knead. Divide into 6–9 parts, grease 6–9 quarter sheets of paper with butter, and place a piece of rolled-out dough on each. Spread the dough with farmer's cheese mixed with sugar, egg yolks, and cinnamon, or with any kind of jam. Fold each paper in half—that is, bend it—transfer to a baking sheet, and set in the oven. When the paper browns and the *pirozhki* are baked, remove [from the oven] and take off the paper. Arrange the *pirozhki* on a platter, sprinkle with sugar and cinnamon, and serve with melted butter or sour cream.

INGREDIENTS

| | |
|---|---|
| 4 egg yolks | ¼ lb butter |

½ wineglass yeast
1–2 spoons sugar
3½ glasses flour
2 spoons butter to grease the paper

*For the filling*
1½ lbs farmer's cheese
¼ glass sugar
cinnamon

½ glass currants
2 egg yolks
Or instead of all this, 1½–2 glasses
　jam

------------
sugar and cinnamon
serve separately 2–3 spoons butter, or
　1½ glasses sour cream

## 1296  Vareniki with cherries

*(Vareniki s vishnjami)*

Prepare the dough as usual for *vareniki*. Try to make the edges of the dough thin, since pinched edges of thick dough are very unattractive. Prepare the fruit beforehand by stoning the cherries and sprinkling them with sugar. Add 1½ cups sugar for every 4 cups of stoned cherries and set the fruit in the sun. After 3 or 4 hours, pour the juice released by the cherries into a saucepan and fill the *vareniki* with the cherries. Boil as for *vareniki* stuffed with farmer's cheese. The cherries must be thoroughly drained in a coarse sieve, otherwise the juice will leak through the dough. Bring the drained cherry juice to a boil several times and serve it cold with the *vareniki* and sour cream. Or dilute the drained cherry juice with water, bring to a boil, and cook the *vareniki* in it.

INGREDIENTS

3 glasses flour
2 eggs
1 lb, or 3 glasses, cherries

1½ cups sugar
sour cream

## 1301  Vareniki with sauerkraut

*(Vareniki s kapustoju)*

Wash 4 glasses sauerkraut in water, place in a saucepan, cover with water, and cook until tender. Turn into a colander to drain and cool. Finely chop 2 onions, fry in ¼ glass butter, and add the cabbage. Mix, lightly fry, and add salt, pepper, and nutmeg.

Prepare the dough and, in general, continue as indicated in #1281. To serve, fry a finely chopped onion in butter and pour over the *vareniki*. (If desired, omit the onion from the butter.)

INGREDIENTS

4 glasses, or 2 lbs, sauerkraut

2–4 onions

| | |
|---|---|
| salt | 3 glasses flour |
| pepper | 2 eggs |
| nutmeg | 3–4 spoons butter |

### 1305  Yeast buns

*(Pezy)*

Prepare a dough as usual from 1 glass milk with yeast and half the indicated amount of flour. Let the dough rise and then knead in the remaining flour. Add salt, 2 spoons butter, and 2 eggs to make a dough thinner than that used for rusks. Beat the dough as well as possible with a small spatula and set to rise again in a warm place. When the dough doubles in bulk, shape it into small round buns the size of walnuts. Dip each bun into melted butter and set each one to rise in a small, individual mold. [After the buns have risen], place the molds in boiling water and steam for about 30 minutes, or bake them in the oven. Turn them out onto a platter and serve hot. They are also served from the saucepan.

Finely chop 2 onions, fry them in 2–3 spoons butter until golden, and serve separately.

These buns may also be stuffed with beef or jam.

INGREDIENTS

| | |
|---|---|
| nearly 1 glass milk or water | 2 spoons yeast |
| 3 glasses, or 1 lb, flour | 2 onions |
| 2 eggs | ¾ lb butter in all |
| salt | |

# ITALIAN MACARONI, NOODLES, DUMPLINGS, AND WAFERS

*(Ital'janskie makarony, lapsha, lazanki, laman'tsy)*

### 1308  Macaroni with ham and Parmesan cheese

*(Makarony s vetchinoju i parmezanom)*

Boil 1 lb macaroni in salted water, turn into a coarse sieve, and rinse with cold water. Finely chop 1 lb boiled ham or corned beef and grate a piece of Parmesan cheese. Grease a platter or a tin or silver saucepan with ½ spoon butter, sprinkle lightly with Parmesan, and add a layer of macaroni and then a layer of ham. Lightly sprinkle with cheese, dot with bits of butter, and add another layer of macaroni and ham. Sprinkle the top with Parmesan, add butter, and bake.

INGREDIENTS

1 lb macaroni

1 lb ham or corned beef

⅛–¼ lb Parmesan cheese

3–4 spoons butter

### 1310  Macaroni with hazel grouse

*(Makarony s rjabchikami)*

Fry 2 fat hazel grouse, remove the bones, and cut the meat into small pieces. Add 5 glasses ordinary beef bouillon to the bones, boil them thoroughly, and strain. Bring [this bouillon] to a boil, sprinkle on broken macaroni, and boil 10 minutes. Drain the macaroni in a fine sieve, transfer to a silver saucepan or to a platter, and mix with the hazel grouse and ¼ lb grated Parmesan cheese. Add 1 spoon butter and a little of the same bouillon [in which the macaroni was cooked]. Bake for a short time to brown the top lightly. The drained bouillon may be added to soup.

INGREDIENTS

1 lb macaroni

2 hazel grouse

5–6 glasses bouillon

¼ lb butter

¼ lb Parmesan cheese

salt

### 1317  Vermicelli in milk with vanilla

*(Vermishel' na moloke s vanil'ju)*

Prepare homemade noodles or use 1 lb of purchased vermicelli. Bring 4½ glasses milk to a boil and add 1 spoon butter, 4–5 pieces sugar pounded with vanilla, and salt. Add the noodles and, when they boil and begin to thicken, cover with a lid and set in a hot oven for ½ hour. Remove from the oven and spoon out onto a platter, each time dipping the spoon into boiled cream. Drizzle cream on top and pour cream onto the platter. Place in a hot oven and continue to drizzle with cream until the vermicelli browns.

INGREDIENTS

4½ glasses, or 1½ bottles, milk

1 spoon butter

4–5 pieces sugar

½ *vershok* vanilla

1 glass cream

1 lb purchased Italian vermicelli, or 2
   glasses flour, 2 eggs, and salt for
   homemade noodles

### 1321 Wafers with poppy seeds and honey

*(Laman'tsy s makom i medom)*

Prepare a stiff dough from 1 spoon fast day oil, salt, 7 silver tablespoons water, and flour. Knead, roll out thinly, and arrange on a baking sheet strewn with flour. Cut into rectangles, like *lazanki*, with a sharp knife, and set in the oven to brown and dry out. Remove and break along the marked lines. Scald 2 glasses of white or, preferably, gray poppy seeds with boiling water, pour off the water, rinse in cold water, and drain. Grind the poppy seeds in a stoneware bowl with a wooden pestle until they whiten and all the seeds are mashed. Add ⅔ glass of lime honey* or sugar and 1 ground bitter almond. Stir in nearly 1 glass boiling water. Transfer to a bowl, stud the top with the dried wafers placed upright, and serve. Or, 2 minutes before serving, arrange the wafers in a sieve and pour boiling water over them. Add them to the poppy seeds, mix, and serve immediately.

INGREDIENTS

flour

2 glasses poppy seeds

several bitter almonds

1 spoon fast day oil

⅔ glass honey or sugar

*Lime honey is made not from the citrus fruit but from the flowers of the linden tree (Tilia) which in bloom will perfume an entire neighborhood. According to the herbalist Mrs. M. Grieve, "honey from [linden] flowers is regarded as the best flavoured and the most valuable in the world." (Grieve, A Modern Herbal, 485.) In France especially, its flowers and leaves are infused to make a kind of tea.

## KASHA, CAUL SAUSAGES, AND GRAIN PATTIES

*(Kashi, sal'niki i kotlety iz krup)*

[*Translator's note:* There is no one way to prepare kasha, one of Russia's oldest and most traditional dishes. In medieval Russia the word "kasha" was used to mean a feast. Any grain preparation—buckwheat, cornmeal, barley, millet, rice, semolina—that is cooked with water, milk, or broth, either in the oven or on top of the stove, is kasha. It can vary in consistency from soft and moist to firm and dry, and in flavor from sweet to savory. It may be eaten at any meal at any time of the day, from a simple peasant supper to a lavish formal banquet, and it may fill a *pirog*, serve as a side dish, or be transformed into an elegant dessert.]

### 1322 Fluffy Smolensk buckwheat kasha

*(Kasha razsypchataja iz smolenskikh krup)*

Mash 2 glasses Smolensk buckwheat with 2 eggs, dry, and rub through a fine colander to separate the grains.

Bring 2½ glasses water or milk to a boil with 2 spoons butter and a little salt. Sprinkle on the grain all at once, stirring briskly. Cook over a high flame for about 5 minutes and then, covered, over a low fire for 10 minutes. Stir after 10 minutes to prevent lumps. Sprinkle with currants that have been washed, scalded with boiling water, and dried. Stir in fine sugar, 1 teaspoon cinnamon, and butter. Bake for 20 or 30 minutes and stir with a spoon 2 or 3 times so that the kasha browns lightly and evenly. Turn the kasha out onto a platter and sprinkle with sugar or pour on any kind of syrup. Or serve separately cream or a sauce made from 3 egg yolks beaten until white with 3 pieces of sugar and diluted with ¾ glass fresh, unboiled cream.

If this kasha is to be served with meat patties or cutlets, use smaller proportions and prepare in exactly the same manner except omit the currants, sugar, and cinnamon. [Ingredients:] 1¼ glasses Smolensk buckwheat or very fine buckwheat, 1 egg, ¼ lb butter, salt, and 1¼ glasses water or bouillon.

INGREDIENTS

2 glasses Smolensk buckwheat
⅜ lb butter
2½ glasses water or milk
2 eggs

½–1 glass currants
5–6 pieces sugar
1 teaspoon cinnamon (for the sauce)

## 1330  Chestnut purée with whipped cream*

*(Kasha iz kashtanov so sbitymi slivkami)*

Cover 1 lb fresh chestnuts with water and set to boil. When the water boils, drain and peel the chestnuts, rub them through a colander, and mix with ½ glass fine sugar and 1 spoon cream. Rub through a coarse sieve to resemble fluffy kasha and pile around a small circular platter without pressing the purée. Fill the center with 1½ glasses thick whipped cream mixed with ½ glass fine sugar and vanilla.

*\*This elegant and luscious dessert is called* mont blanc *by the French and* monte bianco *by the Italians. I do not know whether the Russians ever called it* belaja gora, *but certainly Molokhovets herself favored descriptive names over poetical ones.*

## 1333  Ordinary Smolensk buckwheat kasha not too thick for the children's breakfast

*(Kasha obyknovennaja iz smolenskikh krup ne slishkom gustaja, podavaemaja detjam k zavtraku)*

(Proportions for 6 bowls):

a) *In water:* Bring 4 bottles water to a boil, pour on ½ lb, or 1¼ glasses, Smolensk buckwheat, salt, and ¼ lb butter. Boil for a rather long time.

b) *In milk:* 3 bottles milk, 1¼ glasses, or ½ lb, groats, salt, and ⅛ lb butter.

This same kasha may be baked after adding 2 eggs, 2–3 pieces sugar, cinnamon, and ½–1 glass raisins. Serve at the table in the same saucepan. In this case, 2 bottles milk are sufficient.

c) *In bouillon:* 9 glasses bouillon, 1½ glasses groats, salt, and ½ spoon butter.

### 1341  Buckwheat kasha

*(Lemeshka ili kasha iz grechnevoj muki)*

Pour ¾ lb of the very best buckwheat flour onto a clean skillet. Roast the flour in the oven, stirring as often as possible so that it does not burn but browns slightly and evenly. Pour the browned buckwheat into a saucepan, add 4 glasses boiling milk, and stir briskly to prevent lumps. Bake, and when the mixture [lit., *testo*] rises, it is ready to be served. Eat with fresh butter or fry in butter like a fritter.

### 1344  Green rye or wheat kasha

*(Kasha iz zelenoj rzhi ili pshenitsy)*

When rye or wheat grains are plump but still not ripe, cut the sheaves and drop the ears into boiling water for several minutes. Dry them in the oven and grind like any grain. To serve, boil in water or in milk and add salt and butter.

### 1347  Pumpkin and rice kasha, baked in pumpkin

*(Kasha iz tykvy i risu, zapechenaja v tykve)*

Cut off the top of a pumpkin, discard the seeds, and scrape out the interior with a spoon, leaving the walls as thick as a finger. Lightly boil 1 glass rice and add to half of the removed pumpkin flesh. Add 1 glass fresh sour cream, ¼ lb butter, ground cinnamon, ¼ glass sugar, 1 glass of mixed sultanas and currants, 5 egg yolks, and 5–6 beaten egg whites. Mix everything together, fill the pumpkin, cover with the cut-off top, bake in the oven, and serve on a platter.

### 1351  Caramelized semolina

*(Karmel'naja kasha iz manny)*

Bring 2 bottles cream or whole milk to a boil and sprinkle on 1 cup semolina and ½ lb walnuts ground with ½ cup sugar. Boil the kasha, stirring to prevent lumps and to keep it from burning. When cooked, transfer to a sauté pan and bake in the oven until a crust forms on top. Sprinkle 1 cup sieved sugar over the top crust. Then heat a tile or a piece of metal (*plitka*) until it is very hot and hold it over the kasha until the sugar caramelizes like candy (*ledenets*).*

INGREDIENTS

| | |
|---|---|
| 2 bottles cream or whole milk | 1½ cups sugar |
| 1 cup semolina | ½ lb walnuts |

*The heated tile or piece of metal served as a salamander. Today we would broil the pudding briefly.

### 1352  Russian kasha or so-called Guriev kasha*

*(Kasha russkaja pod nazvaniem Gur'evskaja)*

Scald 1 lb walnuts or hazelnuts and 10–20 bitter almonds with boiling water. Remove their skins and finely chop, adding water. Pour 5 glasses cream into a large, flat saucer and set before coals, skimming off into a dish the rosy skin that forms. When enough skins have accumulated, pour 1⅛ glasses semolina into the remaining cream and boil into a rather liquid porridge. Stir the ground nuts and sugar into the hot semolina. Make a rim of dough on a platter and fill the center with alternate layers of milk skins and semolina. Sprinkle the top with sugar and rusk crumbs and bake for a short time in the oven. To serve, decorate with jam. Layers of fruit and jam may be interspersed in this kasha.

INGREDIENTS

| | |
|---|---|
| 5 glasses cream or whole milk | 2–3 rusks |
| 1⅛ glasses semolina | ½ glass jam |
| 1 lb nuts | (add, if desired, ½ glass fruit or berry |
| ¾ glass sugar | jam) |

*It is believed that this dish was invented by Count Dmitri Alexandrovich Gur'ev (1751–1825), Tsar Alexander I's Minister of Finance, to commemorate the Russian victory over Napoleon in 1812. (Goldstein, A la russe, 114; Pokhlebkin, O kulinarii, 50.) According to another version of the story, however, the dish was an inspiration of the chef of Count Alexander Dmitrievich Gur'ev, who was governor of Odessa from 1822 to 1825. (Zakharova and Tolchinskaja, Puteshestvie v stranu Kulinariju, 79–80.)

### 1356  Guriev buckwheat kasha

*(Kasha Gur'eva iz grechnevykh krup)*

Prepare thick buckwheat kasha in an earthenware pot with boiling mushroom bouillon. Remove the kasha from the pot when it is almost cooked. Wash the pot so that the sides are clean and wipe dry. Fill the pot with alternate layers of kasha and beef bone marrow, ending with a layer of bone marrow. Cover the pot and let the kasha stew in the oven until the grains separate. Watch that it does not burn.

INGREDIENTS

1½ lbs buckwheat groats                    ¼ lb dried mushrooms
¾ lb bone marrow


### 1359  Fried rice patties with chocolate sauce

*(Kotlety risovyja zharenyja s shokoladnym sousom)*

Wash 1½ glasses rice, cover with cold water, and bring once to a boil. Turn into a colander, rinse with cold water, and return to the saucepan. Add 1 bottle of milk or cream, 1 spoon each butter and sugar, and ½ vanilla bean. Boil until tender. Let the rice cool, then add 2 eggs. Form into small pear-shaped patties, dip in egg and rusk crumbs, and drop into hot fat. When they have browned, remove with a slotted spoon to a colander. Dip the patties in warm chocolate and arrange on a platter. Pour on the following chocolate sauce. Beat 2 egg yolks until white with 2 pieces fine sugar, sprinkle on 2 spoons grated chocolate, and mix with 2 glasses boiled and slightly cooled milk. Place on top of the stove and stir with a spoon until it thickens, but do not let it boil. Pour over the patties.

Jam without juice may be added to these same patties. Roll a little of the prepared rice into a ball, make a small indentation, stuff with jam, and then, carefully rolling the ball, form into a pear-shaped cutlet, etc.

INGREDIENTS

1½ glasses rice                            *For the sauce*
1 bottle milk or cream                     2 egg yolks
1 spoon sugar                              2 pieces sugar
½ vanilla bean                             2 glasses milk
⅛ lb butter                                ⅛ lb, or ½ chocolate bar
2–3 eggs                                   (½ cup jam)
5–6 rusks
½ lb fat or Russian butter


### 1360  Buckwheat and liver caul sausage

*(Sal'nik iz grechnevoj krupy s pechenkoju)*

Wash large buckwheat groats in cold water, place them in a saucepan, and mix with very finely chopped raw calf's liver. Add salt, ⅛ or ¼ lb butter (depending on the fattiness of the caul), and 2 eggs. Line a saucepan with a mutton caul (*sal'nik*), arrange the prepared kasha on it, and cover with that same caul. Bake for 1 hour and turn out onto a platter to serve.

INGREDIENTS

1 lb, or 2½ glasses, large buckwheat groats

1 large calf's liver

1 mutton caul, or even a calf's caul

⅛ or ¼ lb butter

2 eggs

salt

# CHEESE AND OTHER DUMPLINGS
## (Syrniki, Kletski)

### 1362 Boiled cheese dumplings

(Syrniki varenye)

Thoroughly beat 3 lbs of ordinary, freshly pressed farmer's cheese in a stoneware bowl. Add 1 spoon butter, salt, 6 eggs, and ½ glass flour. If the farmer's cheese is very thick, add 2–3 spoons sour cream. Mix as well as possible and form into long, thick strips on a table strewn lightly with flour. Slice obliquely into pieces 1 *vershok* long. Drop them into salted boiling water, and when they float to the surface, transfer them with a slotted spoon onto a platter. Pour on 2–3 spoons melted butter fried with 2–3 pounded rusks.

INGREDIENTS

3 lbs farmer's cheese

6 eggs

salt

(2–3 spoons sour cream)

1 glass flour

nearly ½ lb butter

2–3 rusks

### 1370 Saxon dumplings

(Kletski saksonskija)

Beat 1½ spoons butter with 5 egg yolks until white, add 1 spoon water, and sprinkle on enough flour to make a rather thick dough. Mix as well as possible and add salt and 5 beaten egg whites. Cut up ¼ lb boiled ham and ¼ French roll into very small pieces, fry in 1 spoon butter, and mix with the dough. Shape the dough into large balls and drop them into boiling salted water or bouillon. Turn out onto a platter and pour on browned butter.

INGREDIENTS

5 eggs

½ lb butter

¼ lb ham

¼ white French roll

2 glasses flour

# 13
# Waffles, Wafers, Doughnuts, and Fritters

*(Vafli, trubochki, oblatki, ponchki, khvorost, olad'i, drachena i raznorodnyja sladkija kushan'ja)*

Proportions are for 6–8 persons. For 9–12 persons, increase the proportions by 1½. For 13–18 persons, double the proportions.

## WAFFLES, LITTLE HORNS, AND WAFERS
### *(Vafli, trubochki, oblatki)*

*Remarks:* For best results, waffles should be baked on hot coals. Grease the waffle iron only when the waffles stick to it. After baking the waffles, do not wash the waffle iron with water, but just wipe it with cotton wool or blotting paper. To make successful waffles, the melted butter must be beaten in a cold room until it whitens and the egg whites must be extremely fresh and thoroughly beaten.

### 1372 Ordinary waffles
#### *(Vafli obyknovennyja)*

Cool ½ glass melted butter and beat until white. Beat in 4 egg yolks, add 4–5 pieces sugar and 1¼ glasses flour, and mix until smooth, gradually pouring in almost 1 glass milk or cream. Gradually fold in 8 beaten egg whites, stirring carefully from top to bottom. Bake the waffles without greasing the waffle iron. Cinnamon or grated lemon zest may be added for flavoring. The fresher the egg whites and the better beaten, the more waffles there will be, so these proportions will produce from 12 to 16 large waffles.

These waffles are served with sugar, jam, or whipped cream.

¾ glass, or ¼ lb, sweet almonds and 5–6 bitter almonds may be added to the waffles for flavoring. In that case, add about 2–3 spoons milk or cream or reduce the amount of flour. Instead of milk, 1 glass water or sour cream may be added.

INGREDIENTS

3 spoons, ⅜ lb, butter
4–5 pieces sugar
1¼ glasses flour

1 glass milk, cream, or sour cream
8 eggs
(cinnamon or lemon zest)

### 1378  Little horns with wine

*(Trubochki s vinom)*

Thoroughly mix ¾ glass flour, ½ glass fine sugar, ¾ glass wine, and 3 egg whites. Heat a wafer iron until it is very hot, grease with white beeswax,* and pour in 1 scant tablespoon batter. Cover tightly and place over the fire. After 2 minutes, turn over the wafer iron and hold over the fire for 2 more minutes. When it is cooked, carefully remove from the iron and immediately fold into a tube. Lay on a platter in the oven, regrease the wafer iron with wax, and bake the next one.

Fill with whipped cream, or fill the center of the platter with whipped cream and surround with the horns, which may be filled with jam.

Yields 35 little horns.

Little horns for fast days are prepared in exactly the same manner, only without the egg whites and with 2 spoons of some kind of good fast day oil.

INGREDIENTS

*For the little horns*
¾ glass flour
¾ glass light inexpensive wine
½ glass fine sugar
3 egg whites
piece white beeswax

*For the whipped cream*
1¼ glasses thick cream
4 pieces sugar
zest from 1 lemon, or ½ *vershok*
    vanilla, or cinnamon
(1 glass jam)

*For centuries the Russians have been avid beekeepers. Most domestic manuals containing instructions on managing one's estate or farm contained a section on beekeeping. Molokhovets used honey extensively in her recipes and a natural by-product of processing honey is the wax. Insoluble in water, the wax has "an agreeable honey-like odor, and a faint, characteristic taste," some say a faint balsamic taste, but nothing that would impart an off-flavor to the baked pastries. (The Hive and the Honey Bee, 537–538.)*

### 1381  Cream wafers

*(Oblatki slivochnyja)*

Beat 1 egg with 1 glass cream, sprinkle on approximately 1 glass flour, 1 spoon sugar, salt, and 1 egg yolk, and mix thoroughly for 15 minutes. With butter or beeswax, grease a wafer iron for little horns. Cover the surface evenly with a little batter and bake like little horns.

Mix together about 2 spoons fine sugar, cinnamon, finely pounded sweet almonds, and 5–6 bitter almonds. When the wafers are cooked, spread each with butter, sprinkle with the prepared almonds, arrange in pairs, and place in a buttered wafer iron, cover, and hold over the fire for 2 minutes.

These wafers are served with tea and coffee. Yield: 20–25 pairs.

INGREDIENTS

| | |
|---|---|
| 2 eggs | 1 glass sweet almonds |
| 1 glass cream | 5–6 bitter almonds |
| 1 glass flour | 2 spoons sugar |
| 1 spoon sugar | cinnamon |
| salt | 1/2 spoon butter |
| white beeswax | |

# BUNS, PASTRY STRAWS, FRITTERS, AND BATTERS
### (Pyshki, khvorost, olad'i, drachena)

### 1383  Buns or doughnuts
*(Pyshki ili ponchki)*

About 5 hours before dinner prepare a dough as usual from 1 glass milk, yeast (1 *zolotnik* will cost 1/2 kopeck), and 2 glasses flour and set in a warm place to rise. After the dough has risen (in about 2 hours), beat thoroughly with a small spatula and add salt, 1/8–1/4 lb firm butter that is not too cold, 4 egg yolks beaten with 1 spoon sugar, and the remaining flour, saving a little to sprinkle on the table. Add 1/2 teaspoon cinnamon or 5–6 cardamom seeds, lemon zest, or vanilla, and about 2 spoons maraschino [liqueur], Kirschwasser, or rum. Beat the dough thoroughly with your hands or a small spatula, and set in a warm place for 1/2–1 hour. The dough must be thick enough so that it can barely be rolled out on the table, lightly sprinkled with flour.

After 1/2–1 hour, spread the prepared dough on the table, roll out into two circles almost the thickness of a finger, and sprinkle lightly with flour, as already indicated. Place half-teaspoons of jam without juice in little piles on one of these sheets, so that this amount of dough yields 24 buns. Cover evenly with the other sheet and cut out the doughnuts with a glass. Place the doughnuts on a baking sheet lightly strewn with flour and set in a warm place to rise for 45 minutes. The lightness of the buns depends on not leaving them for too long—if they rise too much on the baking sheet, the dough will lose its strength and turn leaden when put into oil because it will not be able to rise further.

Bring to a boil equal proportions of goose or pork fat and Russian butter.* Drop in 5–6 doughnuts at a time, and fry over a low fire, covered, so that the fat and butter boil steadily and do not burn. When the doughnuts have browned and are cooked, remove them from the fat with a slotted spoon. Immediately sprinkle them with sugar mixed with cinnamon and place them in a sieve on blotting paper. Then arrange them on a platter and serve hot.

The doughnuts are better still if the dough is thinner, but since that makes it more difficult to roll out on the table, simply spread out the dough on the table and cut it into 24 pieces. Stretch the pieces into small flat cakes in your hands. (If necessary, lightly grease your hands with oil or butter so that the dough does not stick to them.) Place jam on each piece, pinch shut, roll into a ball, and smooth all around, etc.

Applesauce may be used instead of jam: Bake 3 apples, rub through a sieve, add 1/4 glass sugar, and boil, stirring until the mixture thickens.

INGREDIENTS

| | |
|---|---|
| 1 glass milk together with yeast | 1/2 glass jam without juice |
| 1 spoon sugar | 1 1/4 lbs flour in all |
| 1/8–1/4 lb butter | For sprinkling on the doughnuts, 4–5 |
| 4 egg yolks | pieces sugar and 1 teaspoon |
| salt | cinnamon |
| 1 1/8 teaspoons cinnamon or some | 1 lb butter and 1 lb pork or goose fat |
| other flavoring | for frying the doughnuts |

*At this point Molokhovets recommended adding "1–2 spoons spirits (to prevent the doughnuts from becoming too greasy)." Let me warn readers against that practice, however, since it is extremely hazardous to add either water or alcohol to boiling fat. The liquid will cause the fat to splatter or even catch fire.

## 1387 Yeast doughnuts

*(Ponchki zavarnyja na drozhzhakh)*

Boil 2 glasses flour with 1 glass hot milk. When cool, pour in 1/2 glass milk mixed with 1 *zolotnik* yeast. Beat thoroughly, let rise in a warm place, and then beat the dough again with a spatula. Add salt, 4–5 egg yolks beaten with 1/2 glass sugar until white, 1/2 glass melted butter, 5–6 ground bitter almonds, and enough flour so that the dough can barely be rolled with a rolling pin. Add 4–5 beaten egg whites, mix, and let rise for 30 to 45 minutes. Sprinkle a little flour on the table and roll out 2 sheets, etc., as indicated in #1383. Yields 25–30 doughnuts.

INGREDIENTS

1½ lbs flour
1½ glasses milk
⅓ *lot* yeast
½ glass sugar
salt
4–5 eggs

½ lb butter
5–6 bitter almonds
½ glass jam without juice
1 lb butter and 1 lb pork fat
For sprinkling on top, 1 full spoon
    sugar and 1 teaspoon cinnamon

## 1389  Apple fritters

*(Ponchki s jablokami bez drozhzhej)*

Peel and carefully core 9–12 small apples. Fill the cavities with drained jam.

Beat 6 egg yolks and 6 teaspoons sugar until white. Gradually add 6 beaten egg whites, sprinkling on 6 teaspoons flour. Dip each apple in this batter and drop into boiling fat made of half butter and half pork or goose fat. When the apples have browned, remove them with a slotted spoon, sprinkle with sugar and cinnamon, and pour on syrup or sabayon sauce.

INGREDIENTS

9–12 apples
6 eggs
6 teaspoons sugar
6 teaspoons flour

(1 spoon sugar and cinnamon)
1½ or 2 lbs fat, half butter and half
    fat
1 glass syrup or sabayon sauce

## 1393  Pastry straws with fruit purée

*(Xhvorost zharenyj s marmeladom)*

Prepare a dough from 2 eggs, 1 glass flour, 1 tablespoon sugar scraped with lemon zest,* and 1 glass milk. Just before serving, heat an iron mold for pastry straws** in hot fat or butter. Wipe with a napkin, dip in batter, and drop into the hot fat. When the batter has fried and colored, turn the pastry straws into a sieve. Redip the mold in the fat, then into the batter, and continue in this manner to the end. Before serving, spread the pastry straws with any kind of fruit purée, arrange in pairs, sprinkle with sugar, and serve hot.

INGREDIENTS

2 eggs
1 glass flour
1 glass milk

2½ lbs fat or oil
⅓ glass fruit purée
1 spoon sugar scraped with lemon zest

*Since sugar was purchased in cones and not ground until needed, it was a common procedure for Molokhovets to scrape off the zest from a lemon or orange with a piece of hard sugar and then add the flavored sugar to the rest of the ingredients.

**This iron mold was like the Swedish rosette iron that is used to make fried batter cookies.

### 1395  Poured pastry straws

*(Khvorost lityj)*

Make a liquid batter by mixing 1 glass dry flour, 2 spoons sugar, and a little cinnamon with 1 glass milk or a little more. Stir in 4 egg yolks and 4 beaten egg whites. Using a small funnel, swirl the dough into boiling fat in threads in various directions to form a net of straws. Brown on both sides and turn into a sieve* lined with blotting paper. Serve hot and sprinkle on sugar or juice.

INGREDIENTS

| | |
|---|---|
| 1 glass flour | a little cinnamon |
| 4 eggs | 1 glass milk or wine |
| 2 spoons sugar | 1 lb butter |

*Molokhovets used the classic European drum sieves with a level surface of horsehair or wire held within a tall, thin wooden rim. Lining these wide, flat sieves with blotting paper made them ideal for draining, whereas our own concave wire nets attached to a metal rim hardly serve the purpose at all.

### 1401  Smolensk buckwheat fritters with jam

*(Olad'i iz smolenskikh krup s varen'em)*

Bring to a boil 3–4 glasses milk, sprinkle on 1¾ glasses Smolensk buckwheat, bring to a boil, and mix until smooth. Cool, beat in 2 eggs, sprinkle on sugar, and spread rather thinly on a baking sheet or platter.

When the kasha has cooled completely, cut out 26–28 scalloped circles or simply cut out with a glass. Spread half the cut-out circles with drained jam and cover with the remaining circles. Pinch the edges all around, dip in egg and rusk crumbs, and fry in butter on both sides. Transfer to a baking sheet and bake for a short time in the oven.

INGREDIENTS

| | |
|---|---|
| 3–4 glasses milk | 3 eggs |
| 1¾ glasses Smolensk buckwheat | 6 rusks |
| 4 pieces sugar | ⅔ glass jam |
| 2–3 spoons butter | |

## 1402  Carrot fritters

*(Olad'i iz morkovi)*

Grate 5 rather large carrots, add 2 raw eggs, and enough flour to make a batter as thick as for fritters. Heat oil in a skillet and fry the fritters as usual.

Similar fritters may be made from raw potatoes.

## 1403  Baked pancake

*(Drachena)*

Beat ⅛ lb butter until white, mix with 3–6 eggs, sprinkle on 2 glasses flour, and dilute with 2 glasses milk. Mix until smooth. Melt 1 spoon butter in a skillet and heat until very hot. Pour in the prepared batter and bake in a hot oven for 20–30 minutes. When the pancake has baked and browned, serve immediately sprinkled with sugar. The egg whites may be beaten and added separately.

Another variation: Beat 10 eggs until white, sprinkle on 1½ glasses flour, and mix, gradually adding 1 glass cream. Beat the batter for at least a half hour. Melt 1 spoon butter on a skillet, pour in the prepared mixture, and bake in the oven for 20 minutes.

# VARIOUS SWEET DISHES

*(Raznorodnyja sladkija kushan'ja)*

## 1407  "Monks"

*(Mnikhi)*

Pour boiling water over small, dry, purchased *krendels** until they swell slightly, but do not let them turn mushy like porridge. Drain off the water, add salt, and pour on browned or ordinary butter.

Or soak the *krendels* in red wine. When they swell, fry in butter. To serve, sprinkle with sugar and cinnamon.

These "monks" are prepared at roadside stations** where it is difficult to find any kind of provisions.

*Krendels *are pretzel-shaped loaves of sweetened yeast bread. Except for the shape, they are similar to* kuliches *and are often served at Russian name day celebrations. The word comes from the German* Kringel, *not via Polish, but via the German bakers who, according to Goldstein, "were numerous in Russia from the late thirteenth century on, especially in the merchant town of Novgorod" (Goldstein, A la Russe, 146). Molokhovets included over a dozen recipes for krendels. The large ones were like* kuliches *as described above, but most of the small ones were like bagels in that the yeast dough was boiled before it was baked. Those made of short pastry were baked without boiling. Several recipes for small krendels called for a further drying out in the oven after the initial* *baking. Presumably it was this latter sturdy variety of krendel that Molokhovets was recommending for travelers.*

*\*\*Most Russian traveling was done overland with either carriages or sledges. Almost all the memoirs, letters, and diaries of Europeans visitors to Russia in the nineteenth-century tell of the horrors and discomforts of traveling in Russia—the awful weather, the terrible roads, the lack of facilities at the roadside inns, and, most repugnant of all, the lice and cockroaches that infested the furniture and bedding even in private homes.*

## 1408 "Worms"

*(Chervjachki)*

Prepare a dough as for noodles and chop fine like worms, i.e., shred the dough. Fry until golden in fresh butter. Transfer to a platter and pour on a sauce prepared from eggs, sugar, cinnamon, and sour cream.

## 1409 Batter-fried apple slices

*(Jabloki zharenyja v teste ili kljare)*

Just before frying, mix together 1½ glasses flour, almost 1 glass milk or ½ glass each sour cream and beer (1 spoon yeast may be added), and 4 egg yolks. Whip 4 egg whites until stiff (or beat in whole eggs, that is, do not beat the whites separately) and fold into the mixture just before frying. Peel, slice, core, and seed 5 medium apples. Dip each slice in the batter and drop it into hot fat or butter. Fry on both sides and sprinkle with sugar when serving.

INGREDIENTS

almost 1 glass milk, or ½ glass sour    5 medium apples
   cream and ½ glass beer    ½ lb butter
4 eggs    1½ glasses flour

## 1411 Pastry coils

*(Vertuta)*

(A Greek pastry.) Prepare a rather thick dough from 2 eggs, 2 egg shells of water, and approximately 1½ lbs flour. Roll out very thinly into a long strip and spread the entire surface with the following mixture: Scald 1 lb sweet almonds and 2 lbs walnuts with boiling water and skin the nutmeats. Pound fine, pouring in just a little water, dilute with ½ lb good lime honey, and stir to make a thick mixture. Roll the dough into a tube that resembles a long sausage. Place in a skillet greased with 1 spoon butter, wrapping the pastry tightly into a coil. Spread 1 spoon butter on top, sprinkle on 1 spoon fine sugar, and bake in the oven.

## 1412 Turin Pastries*

*(Pirozhnoe turinskoe)*

Bring to a boil ½ glass each melted butter and milk. Immediately add 1 glass flour all at once, stirring briskly over a low fire. When the mixture is smooth and separates from a spoon, set it aside to cool. Beat in 3 eggs one by one and continue beating with a spatula until the dough becomes elastic. Place water on the stove to heat and, when it begins to boil, use a canvas pastry bag to press small, finger-length sticks of dough into the water and boil the sticks over a low fire. When they float, drain in a colander and rinse with cold water. Arrange the sticks in a buttered mold and cover with the following sauce: Mix 2 glasses milk or cream, 2 egg yolks, 2 spoons sugar, and 2 beaten egg whites. Pour this over the pastry and bake in the oven for 1 hour.

*These pastries sound like a sweet version of gnocchi made with pâte à choux and topped with a sweet cream sauce instead of a Mornay sauce with Parmesan cheese. (Luigi Carnacina's Great Italian Cooking, 217.)*

## 1414 Scottish wedding cakes*

*(Shotlandskija, svadebnyja lepeshki)*

Heat slightly ⅜ lb fresh unsalted butter, being careful not to let it boil. Add ½ lb fine wheat flour, ½ cup fine sugar, ½ cup finely chopped, blanched almonds, and ½ egg white. Knead, beat thoroughly, and roll out into a flat cake ½ vershok thick. Cut into 6–8 parts. Prick liberally with a fork and bake in the oven on a baking sheet. The oven must not be too hot since the pastry must dry out in the oven for a long time.

INGREDIENTS

| | |
|---|---|
| ⅜ lb butter | ½ egg white |
| ½ lb, or 1½ glasses, flour | ⅜ glass fine sugar |
| 1½ glasses, or ½ lb,[sic] almonds | |

*This is really a recipe for shortbread. According to Fitzgibbon, shortbread was often served at weddings in the Shetland Islands, especially an elaborate version called the "bride's bonn(ach)," which was baked with a comfit the size of a sixpence in the middle. Traditionally, each unmarried guest had to break off a piece of cake; whoever touched the comfit was reputedly doomed to remain single. (Fitzgibbon, Food of the Western World, 429.)*

*It is not as surprising as it might seem for Molokhovets to know about and include a recipe for a Scottish wedding cake. In late Tsarist Russia, members of the upper class were very cosmopolitan, perhaps even more than their European and English counterparts. They were well read and usually were fluent in several European languages including French, German, and English. Much of this fluency was due to the efforts of foreign governesses, who were widely employed in wealthy households from the end of the Napoleonic Wars to the Bolshevik revolution. Pitcher, who has written about English governesses in Russia, estimates that thousands of English-speaking governesses, including a very large number of Scots and Irish, lived with Russian families during this hundred year period. (Pitcher, When Miss Emmie Was in Russia, xi.) Along with language skills, a good govern-*

*ess would also acquaint her charges with some aspects of her culture, especially life-cycle events like weddings. Such information would have spread rapidly in the society; young women have an avid interest in such matters, as folklorists readily attest.*

### 1416  German buns

*(Nemetskija bulochki)*

Prepare a dough as indicated above for doughnuts (*ponchki*). After it has risen twice, roll out the buns so that after they have risen on top of the stove and in the oven, they will be as large as a good turnip. Paint the buns with egg beaten with water just before setting them in the oven. Let them cool a bit after removing them from the oven, then cut off the tops with a very sharp knife. Scoop out the soft interior with a spoon into a stoneware bowl and scald it with good cream. Add a little of the very best butter, sugar, cinnamon, 1–2 eggs, and currants that have been scalded with boiling water and dried. Mix thoroughly until the mixture resembles a thick porridge. Fill the rolls with this mixture, replace the cut-off tops, and paint lightly with egg. Strew with rusk crumbs and sugar and bake for ½ hour. Serve the rolls with cream or a sauce made with milk and egg yolks.

These buns are served as a last course during Butter Week.

# 14
# Ice Creams, Mousses, Kissels, and Compotes

(Morozhenoe, kremy, zefiry, mussy, blanmanzhe, kiseli, kompoty, molochnye zavarnye kremy)

## ICE CREAMS
### (Morozhenoe)

*Remarks:* Freeze ice cream in a narrow, tall pail with a small opening below (*vnizu*) [the level of the lid containing the cream]* which will allow the water from the melted ice to drain off. Cover the bottom of the pail with chopped ice, sprinkle on some salt, and set the mold in the pail, surrounding it with more ice and salt. A mold for 6 persons will require 3 lbs, or 6 glasses, salt, a mold for 12 persons, 6 lbs salt, and a very large mold will require 7 to 8 lbs salt.

If the pail is rotated by hand, the ice cream will freeze in ¾ of an hour, but if a mechanical crank is used, it will freeze in 10–15 minutes.

Ice cream is prepared as follows. Use cream that is very fresh, but not too thick or it will be too fatty [to freeze properly]. Lacking cream, use whole milk. Beat the egg yolks until white with fine sieved sugar, mix with the cream, and place in a saucepan over the fire. Stir until the mixture thickens, but do not let it boil. Test with a small spatula—the cream has cooked sufficiently if it no longer flows freely from the spatula, but adheres to it like thin sour cream. Remove from the heat and cool, stirring. Strain through a sieve into a mold that has been thoroughly dried. Cover with paper, place the lid on top, and rotate on ice.

After 15 minutes, wipe off the lid, and carefully remove it without letting any salt or ice fall into the cream. Thoroughly scrape the sides and bottom of the mold with a wooden spatula and stir the frozen cream into the rest of the mixture. Beat with the spatula as well as possible. Replace the paper and lid and rotate the mold for several more minutes, then mix again with the spatula as indicated above. Repeat at least five or six times until the ice cream has turned into a thick and smooth mass, similar to Finnish butter. Continue rotating the mold several more times. Serve immediately or if it is ready beforehand, cover the mold with salt and ice until needed. The more the ice cream is mixed with a spatula, the better it will be. This is the secret of good ice cream.

As the ice melts, drain the water and add fresh ice.

To make enough ice cream for 6 persons, use 3 glasses cream or milk, no more than ⅝ lb sugar, and a proportionate amount of the other ingredients. If using small dishes, these same proportions will serve 12 people. For ices from juice, use 3½ glasses juice and ¾ lb, or almost 1½ glasses, fine sugar.

Doubling the proportions (6 glasses cream, 1¼ lbs sugar, etc.) will yield 12 large or 24 small servings.

To remove the ice cream from the mold, dip the mold in hot water, wipe it thoroughly, and turn the ice cream out onto a platter covered with a napkin. Garnish with pastries.

*Although Molokhovets did not describe where the opening was, usually drainage holes were situated just below the level of the lid of the inner container to help prevent any salt water from seeping into the ice cream. At the same time, the opening needed to be fairly high on the container because the cold water, mixed with the ice, helped to freeze the mixture in its metal pail.*

### 1417  Ice cream

*(Morozhenoe slivochnoe)*

Pound and sieve the sugar and beat with egg yolks until white. Shave ½* *vershok* vanilla bean with a knife, add the shaved vanilla and the cream to the sugar and egg yolks, and stir on top of the stove until the mixture thickens but do not let it boil. Strain and cool, stirring occasionally. Pour into a mold and proceed as indicated in the remarks. If using lemon zest, add it to the cream after it has cooled.

INGREDIENTS

| | |
|---|---|
| 3 glasses cream | 1½* *vershok* vanilla bean or lemon |
| 3–4 egg yolks | zest |
| 1 full glass, or ⅜ lb, fine sugar | 3 lbs, or 6 glasses, salt |

*The discrepancy is in the original text. To judge by the other editions, ½ vershok of vanilla is probably the correct amount.*

### 1418  Coffee ice cream

*(Slivochnoe morozhenoe s kofe)*

Beat egg yolks and sugar until white, dilute with cream, and stir on top of the stove until the mixture thickens. Sprinkle on ⅛ lb of the very best, freshly roasted coffee. Remove the cream from the fire, cover, and let it cool. Strain into a mold, etc.

INGREDIENTS

3 glasses cream  
4 egg yolks  
⅝ lb, or 1 full glass, sugar

⅛ lb, or ½ glass, roasted coffee  
3 lbs, or 6 glasses, salt

### 1423  Caramel ice cream

*(Slivochnoe morozhenoe—Crème brûlée)*

Caramelize the sugar, that is, grind 3–4 pieces sugar, pour onto a small skillet, add 1 teaspoon water, and heat on top of the stove. When the sugar darkens, pour in 2 spoons cream and bring to a boil. Mix with the remaining cream and the egg yolks beaten until white with sugar. Stir on top of the stove until it thickens, etc.

INGREDIENTS

3 glasses cream  
1 full glass sugar, or ⅝ lb  
3–4 egg yolks

(½ *vershok* vanilla bean)  
about 3 lbs salt  
4 pieces sugar

### 1424  Orange, mignonette, or jasmine flower ice cream

*(Slivochnoe morozhenoe s pomerantsovym, rezedovym ili zhasminnym tsvetom)*

Pour 1 tablespoon orange, mignonette [*Reseda odorata*], or jasmine flowers into hot cream. Cover and strain after an hour. Mix with egg yolks beaten until white and place on top of the stove, etc.

INGREDIENTS

1 tablespoon orange, mignonette, or  
 jasmine flowers  
3 glasses cream

3–4 egg yolks  
⅝ lb sugar  
about 3 lbs salt

### 1425  Pistachio ice cream

*(Slivochnoe morozhenoe iz fistashek)*

Shell ¼ lb pistachios, leaving the green inner skin. Pound in a mortar as fine as possible with 1 spoon orange flower water amd stir in 3 glasses cream. Beat 3 egg yolks with sugar until white, mix with the cream and 1 teaspoon vanilla powder,* and stir on top of the stove until it thickens. Strain, rub through a sieve and, [for coloring,] add 1 spoon boiled spinach rubbed through a very fine sieve.

INGREDIENTS

| | |
|---|---|
| ¼ lb pistachios | ¾ *vershok* vanilla |
| 3 glasses cream | 3–4 egg yolks |
| 1 full spoon orange flower water | nearly ½ lb spinach |
| ⅝ lb, or 1 full glass, sugar | about 3 lbs salt |

*Molokhovets did not explain how vanilla powder was made. Usually she used vanilla beans or vanilla-flavored sugar.*

## 1428  Cultivated strawberry, raspberry, or wild strawberry ice cream

*(Slivochnoe morozhenoe iz klubniki, maliny ili zemljaniki)*

Combine 2 glasses cream with egg yolks beaten with sugar until white and stir on top of the stove until the mixture thickens. Remove from the stove and cool, stirring. Add 1 glass puréed, fresh [uncooked] cultivated or wild strawberries or raspberries, mix everything together, and strain into a mold, etc.

INGREDIENTS

| | |
|---|---|
| 2 glasses cream | 1 lb, or 2½–3 glasses raspberries or |
| 3–4 egg yolks | wild or cultivated strawberries |
| ⅝ lb, or 1 full glass, sugar | 3 lbs, or 6 glasses, salt |

## 1433  Pineapple water ice*

*(Morozhenoe iz ananasov)*

Bring to a boil almost 3 glasses water, ⅔ lb sugar, the juice of 1 lemon, and ¼ lb grated pineapple. Squeeze through a napkin, cool, pour into a mold, and freeze.

INGREDIENTS

| | |
|---|---|
| ⅔ lb fine sugar | 1 lemon |
| ¼ lb pineapple | about 5 glasses salt |

*In Tolstoy's War and Peace, when the young heroine Natasha Rostova begs her mother to reveal the dessert that will be served at her name-day party, the answer is pineapple water ice. Since the novel (1864–69) appeared not long after the cookbook (1861), it may not be too fanciful to imagine that the pineapple ice served at Natasha's party was similar to the one in this recipe. Pineapples were introduced into Russia in the eighteenth century and were still an expensive rarity in Molokhovets' time. She used the fruit sparingly; modern readers may want to increase the amount of pineapple.*

### 1434  Apple or pear water ice

*(Morozhenoe iz jablok ili grush)*

The best fruit to use for water ice is Rennet or Pineapple apples and Beri or Bergamot pears. If none are available, ordinary apples and pears may be used.

Cut up 7 peeled apples or pears, cover with 1½ glasses water, boil until tender, and strain. Bring to a boil 2¾ glasses of this juice and ¾ lb sugar. Cool and add the juice from ½ lemon and ½ glass champagne or ½ wineglass rum.

Add cinnamon and 1 clove or the zest from ¼ lemon when cooking apples; add ½ *vershok* vanilla when cooking pears.

INGREDIENTS

*For apple water ice*
7 apples
1½ glasses, or ¾ lb, sugar
½ lemon
cinnamon
½ glass champagne, or ½ wineglass
  rum
----------
about 6 glasses salt

*For pear water ice*
7 pears
¾ lb sugar
½ *vershok* vanilla
juice from ½ lemon
½ glass champagne, or ½ wineglass
  rum

### 1443  Black bread water ice

*(Morozhenoe iz chernago khleba)*

Dry ½ lb rye bread into rusks, pour on boiling water, cover, let stand for ½ hour, and drain. Mix ¾ lb sugar with 3 glasses of this "bread water" and bring to a boil. Add the juice of 1 lemon, strain, and cool. Pour into a mold and rotate on ice. When the mixture thickens, add ½ lb of soft rye bread, rubbed through a sieve. Mix and freeze.

INGREDIENTS

1 lb rye bread
¾ lb sugar, or 1½ glasses

1 lemon
about 6 glasses salt

### 1447  Imperial ice punch from wild strawberries and other fruits

*(Punsh imper'jal' morozhenyj iz zemljaniki i proch. fruktov)*

Pick over wild strawberries, rinse the berries, and rub them through a fine sieve into a stoneware bowl. Use ½ lb sugar for every lb of purée. Mix, dilute with ½ bottle Rhine wine, and pour into a mold for water ice. Rotate, scraping the edges of the mold so that the water ice does not freeze, but resembles slush. Divide into goblets or small dishes and serve.

INGREDIENTS

1 lb wild strawberry purée
½ lb, or 1 glass, sugar*

½ bottle Rhine wine
about 5 glasses salt

*Elsewhere in this chapter Molokhovets equated ⅝ lb sugar with 1 glass, although generally she used 2 glasses to 1 lb sugar. See Appendix, Weights and Measures.*

### 1449  Royal punch glacé

*(Korolevskij punsh glacé)*

Take several pineapples, 1 bottle each Rhine wine and champagne, ¼ bottle maraschino, ½ bottle arrack or Jamaica rum, the juice from 6 lemons and 3 oranges, and 2–3 lbs sugar.

First boil the sugar with lemon juice and a small quantity of water until it turns into a transparent syrup. Pound the pineapple in a mortar until it turns into a soft pulp, place in a bowl, and pour on the boiled syrup. Add the arrack or rum, cover, and cool. Add the strained lemon and orange juice, the wine, maraschino, champagne, etc. Strain everything through a napkin and chill on ice until it turns into an icy slush.

## CREAMS
### (Kremy)

*Remarks:* Isinglass (fish glue) or gelatin (the glue from calf's feet) is used for all creams. Use 3–5 *zolotniki* of either isinglass or gelatin for a mold to serve 6 persons.

Prepare isinglass as follows. Use 5 *zolotniki* in the summer, but 3 *zolotniki* of isinglass are sufficient in the dead of winter. Tear up the sheets of isinglass as finely as possible, cover with 2–3 glasses cold water, and simmer over a low fire. Add 1 piece sugar, reduce to ½ glass, and strain through fine linen. While still warm, mix with several spoons whipped cream and immediately add to the remainder of the cream, constantly beating with a whisk over ice so that the isinglass does not congeal before it is combined with the cream mixture. Gelatin from calf's feet may be dissolved in cold or hot water, but do not let it boil, because then it will not combine with the other ingredients and will form an unpalatable jelly under the cream.

There are two varieties of cream: Cream made from raw sweet or sour cream and that made from cream which has been scalded. The preparation of the latter demands great care because once the cream is mixed with egg yolks, it must not be allowed to boil. If it boils, the cream will turn. If it is not heated enough, the cream will not be incorporated and the consistency will be too heavy. After the mixture has cooked, pile it into a mold which has been dipped in cold water and sprinkled with sugar. Set the mold on ice or in snow, or lacking that, in cold water. Just before serving, dip the mold into warm water, wipe it off, and turn the cream out onto a platter. The cream [used for these recipes] must be very thick.

The recipes will serve 6 persons. For 7–9 persons, increase the proportions by 1¼. For 10–12 persons, increase the proportions by 1½. For 13–18 persons, double the proportions.

### 1450  Cream made from fresh cream

*(Krem iz syrykh slivok)*

Beat 1½ glass raw, very thick, cold cream with a whisk over ice until it forms soft peaks. Beat 3–4 egg yolks with ¼ lb fine sugar until white, dilute with ½ glass [thin] cream, and scald it, stirring. Remove from the fire and beat with a whisk. When it has cooled, mix with the beaten cream and ½ glass warm* isinglass and set in a cold place.

One of the following may be added to the cream: Two to three drops lemon oil or the zest rubbed from 1 lemon, ¾ *vershok* vanilla bean finely pounded with 1 piece sugar, or ½ wineglass white rum.

This cream is sometimes served with syrup or garnished with meringue prepared from ½ lb sugar and the 4 remaining egg whites.

Alternatively, take 12 preserved plums, remove the pits, and cut each plum into several pieces. Arrange on a platter and cover with 2⅓ glasses of whipped cream with sugar. (For 6 persons.)

INGREDIENTS

1½ glasses thick cream
½ glass thin cream
3–4 egg yolks

¼ lb, or ½ glass, sugar
3–5 *zolotniki* isinglass

---

*\*Be careful that the isinglass (or gelatin) is not too warm or it will deflate the beaten cream. Isinglass is difficult to find in the United States these days although it still is occasionally sold in specialized food emporiums. Unflavored gelatin may be substituted.*

### 1452  Cream from sour cream

*(Krem iz smetany)*

Beat 2¼ glasses thick, fresh sour cream with a whisk over ice until it forms soft peaks. Sprinkle on ¼ lb sugar, mix with ½ glass warm isinglass, and set in a cold place.

Sometimes the sour cream is combined with an equal amount of thick fresh cream. Mix the creams with isinglass, sugar, and berries from jam without juice.

INGREDIENTS

2¼ glasses sour cream
¼ lb, or ½ glass, sugar
3–5 *zolotniki* isinglass

lemon oil, or vanilla, or rum may be
added, as indicated in #1450

### 1453  Apricot cream

*(Krem iz abrikosov)*

Drop 8–10 apricots into boiling water, remove immediately, and turn into a sieve to drain. Skin, halve, remove the pits, and place the fruit in a saucepan. Add ⅜ lb sugar, cover with a lid, and boil until tender. Rub the apricots through a fine sieve, place on ice, and stir until the purée cools and thickens. Add ½ glass isinglass, mix with 1½ glasses or more of whipped cream, stir thoroughly, then pile into a mold and set on ice.

INGREDIENTS

8–10 apricots
1½ glasses very thick cream

¾ glass sugar
3–5 *zolotniki* isinglass

### 1459  Sabayon cream

*(Krem iz sabaiona)*

Rub ½ lb sugar over the zest of ½ lemon, pound the sugar, and beat with 5 egg yolks until white. Dilute with 1½ glasses light white wine, add the juice from ½ lemon, and place the mixture on top of the stove. Beat with a whisk until it thickens, remove from the fire, and set on ice, constantly beating with the whisk. Add 1 glass isinglass and, if desired, ½ wineglass white rum. Whip again, then pile into a mold, and set on ice.

INGREDIENTS

½ lb sugar
5 egg yolks
1½ glasses, or ½ bottle, table wine

3–5 *zolotniki* isinglass
½ lemon
(½ wineglass rum)

### 1465 Chocolate cream

*(Krem shokoladnyj)*

Pour ½ grated chocolate tablet into a saucepan, add 3 spoons cream, and place on top of the stove. Stir until the chocolate dissolves, then remove from the heat. Beat 3–4 egg yolks with sugar until white, mix with the chocolate and ½ glass cream, and stir over the fire until it thickens. Remove and cool, beating constantly with a whisk over ice. Separately whip 1½ glasses cream and fold into the chocolate mixture. Add ½ glass isinglass, pile into a mold, and set on ice.

INGREDIENTS

½ chocolate bar, or ⅛ lb
3–4 egg yolks
1½ glasses very thick cream
(¼ *vershok* vanilla)

½ glass thin cream
⅓ glass sugar
3–5 *zolotniki* isinglass

# ZEPHYRS OR CREAMS WITHOUT GELATIN AND *PLOMBIÈRES*

*(Zefir ili krem bez kleja i plombir)*

*Remarks: Plombières* is almost exactly the same as cream, except that gelatin is not added and it is frozen almost like ice cream. That is, freeze boiled cream with egg yolks in a mold until half ready, then mix with whipped cream, cover tightly with a lid, and set on ice with salt. Sprinkle more salt and ice all around, cover, and set aside for two or three hours. Before serving, dip the mold into hot water, wipe it off on all sides, turn out onto a platter, and serve immediately. Zephyr is the same except, just before serving, whip it over ice into a foam, pile onto a platter, smooth it out, and serve at once.

The cream must be very thick.

These proportions will serve 6–8 persons. For 9–12 persons, increase the proportions by 1½. For 13–18 persons, double the proportions.

### 1468 Cream zephyr

*(Zefir slivochnyj)*

Whip 3 glasses very thick cream over ice until the cream forms soft peaks. Add ⅓ lb sugar, 3–4 drops lemon oil, the zest from ¾ lemon, or 1 *vershok* pounded vanilla bean. Mix 1½ glasses fresh wild or cultivated strawberries or ¾ glass of any kind of red jam without juice with the cream and pile onto a platter. Smooth the surface or freeze in a mold as indicated in the remarks about *plombières*. Garnish with cookies (*biskviti*), meringues, etc.

A similar and very tasty dessert is made by folding meringue cookies into the center of the zephyr. Only be sure that they are very dry and crisp.

### INGREDIENTS

3 glasses, or 1 bottle, very thick cream
almost 1 glass sugar
1½ glasses wild or cultivated
 strawberries, or ¾ glass jam

3–4 drops lemon oil or lemon zest, or
 1 *vershok* vanilla bean
(ingredients for cookies or meringues)

## 1477  Whipped cream with rice

### (Sbityja slivki s risom)

Boil fluffy rice in milk or water as indicated in #1172. Whip 1 glass thick cream, sprinkle on sugar, mix with the rice, and pile onto a platter. Decorate the top with jam and syrup and serve. One *vershok* vanilla bean or lemon zest may be added as flavoring. To serve unmolded on a platter, add ⅓ glass [liquid] gelatin boiled from 3–4 *zolotniki* gelatin to the rice and cream. To serve, pour on syrup.

It is very attractive to prepare this cream as follows. Cook ½ glass raspberry jelly or ½ glass hot, thick *kissel* from raspberry syrup [cf. *Kissels*, below]. Pour this *kissel* into a smooth (*gladkij*) mold having moistened the interior with water. Tip the mold in all directions to allow the *kissel* to lightly congeal on the walls of the mold. After the *kissel* has congealed fairly well on the bottom of the mold, add rice and whipped cream prepared as indicated above with the addition of ⅓ glass gelatin boiled from 3–4 sheets of gelatin plus sugar and a little finely sieved vanilla bean. When the cream sets, turn out onto a platter and serve after pouring on raspberry syrup. The rice is sometimes lightly pounded in a mortar to break the grains in half.

### INGREDIENTS

1½ glasses rice
1 glass thick cream
½ glass fine sugar
½ glass jam

½ glass syrup
vanilla bean or lemon zest
(3–4 *zolotniki* gelatin)

## 1482  Tea *plombières*

### (Plombir chajnyj)

Bring to a boil 1 glass thin cream, add 1 tablespoon green tea, bring to a boil, let stand, and strain. Beat 5 egg yolks with ¾ glass sugar and dilute with the boiled and cooled cream. Heat, stirring, but do not boil. Pour into a mold, freeze until half ready, mix with 2 glasses whipped thick cream, and cover with ice and salt.

INGREDIENTS

| | |
|---|---|
| 1 glass thin cream | ¾–1 glass sugar |
| 1 tablespoon green tea | 5 egg yolks |
| 2 glasses thick cream | salt |

### 1483  Almond *plombières*

*(Plombir mindal'nyj)*

Pound very fine ¼ lb sweet almonds and 5–6 bitter almonds, adding water to prevent the oil from separating. Dilute with 1 glass whole milk, and squeeze out enough liquid to make 1 glass of almond milk. Mix with ¾ glass sugar and 5 egg yolks and heat, stirring, but do not boil. Pour into a mold and freeze until half ready. Mix with 2 glasses whipped cream, and cover with ice and salt, etc.

INGREDIENTS

| | |
|---|---|
| ¼ lb, or ¾ glass, sweet almonds | 1 glass whole milk |
| 5–6 bitter almonds | 5 egg yolks |
| 2 glasses thick cream | about 2½ lbs, or 5 glasses, salt |
| ¾–1 glass sugar | |

# JELLIES OR GELATINS
## *(Zhele)*

*Remarks:* Add either isinglass or gelatin to the jelly. If using gelatin, it must be boiled separately until softened and reduced to no more than ½ glass. Add water and sugar and bring to a boil. Pour in the wine or juice, strain, and pour into a mold. Set in a cold place or on ice or snow to gel. To remove from the mold, dip the mold briefly in hot water, wipe off, and turn out onto a platter.

If the [liquid] jelly is not completely clear, it may be clarified with white paper.* Bring the paper to a boil in cold water, finely pound it in a mortar, and drop into the jelly. Bring to a boil and pour onto a napkin, stretched out and tied to the ends of an overturned stool. Let the liquid drain gradually. Or clarify by dropping an egg white into the jelly. Cook over a very low fire, so that it boils from one side only, then strain.

To color the jelly golden, caramelize a piece of pounded fine sugar moistened with a teaspoon of water in a skillet. Dilute with 2 spoons water, bring to a boil, pour into the jelly, and strain. Add red gelatin to color the jelly red. For every 6 sheets of white [gelatin], use 4 of red.

Four glasses of jelly will serve 6 persons. When preparing jelly, it is best to pour 4 glasses water into the saucepan in which the jelly will be cooked and mark the height of the water on a spill. Discard this water and pour all the ingredients for the jelly into the saucepan. Cook and reduce the jelly until it is level with the mark on the spill when done.

For 6 persons and 4 glasses of jelly, add approximately 10 *zolotniki* or 10 sheets of gelatin in winter and 12 sheets of gelatin in summer. For 7–9 persons, use 1¼ the indicated proportions and reduce to 5 glasses. For 10–12 persons, increase the proportions by 1½ and reduce to 6 glasses. For 13–15 persons, increase the proportions by 1¾ and reduce to 7 glasses. For 16–18 persons, double the proportions and reduce to 8 glasses. The proportions for blancmange are increased in the same manner.

If serving a jelly of 2 colors with equal amounts of blancmange or mousse, use half the indicated amount of jelly and of blancmange, etc.

If serving the jelly or blancmange at a dinner for 24 persons, it is more convenient to serve it on 2 platters. In which case, almost treble the proportions to make 12 glasses of jelly, that is 6 glasses for each plate. Of this amount, use 4 glasses to fill a single small mold, and use the remaining 2 glasses to fill 6 very small molds, which can be halved when turned out onto the platter. Or instead of the small molds, garnish the jelly with compote.

*Paper at this time was made with cotton or rags. A good modern substitute would be paper filters for coffee.*

## 1485  Wine jelly

### (Zhele iz vina)

Pour 2½ glasses water into a saucepan and measure with a spill. Add ¾ lb sugar in pieces, that is 2¼ glasses, the zest of 1 lemon, and 10 sheets of broken gelatin. Boil until the gelatin dissolves and add the juice from 2 lemons, strained through very fine muslin so that no pits fall in. Measure with a spill. If necessary cook a little longer, otherwise immediately strain. Add 1½ glasses any kind of white wine, sherry, Madeira, sauternes, or Rhine wine to make a total of 4 glasses of liquid. Pour into a mold and set it on ice or snow.

To color this jelly golden, add a piece of caramelized sugar; to color it red, add 7 sheets white gelatin and 3 sheets red.

INGREDIENTS

10–12 sheets gelatin
¾ lb, or 2¼ glasses, sugar pieces
2 small lemons

1½ glasses wine
1–2 egg whites
(1 piece sugar to caramelize)

## 1487 Multicolored jelly*

*(Zhele neskol'kikh tsvetov)*

This jelly is made of 2, 3, or 4 colors, using half mousse or half blancmange. But these varicolored jellies must not be too firmly congealed, because the layers may separate and slide off each other on the platter.

COMBINATIONS

*Jelly of 3 colors*
a) Red jelly
b) White blancmange
c) Chocolate or coffee blancmange

*Multicolored jellies*
a) Raspberry jelly
b) White blancmange
c) Cornflower jelly
d) White blancmange
e) Lemon jelly
f) White blancmange
g) Cornflower jelly, etc.

*Blancmange of 2 colors*
a) White blancmange
b) Coffee or chocolate blancmange

*Jelly of 2 colors*
a) Yellow jelly
b) Coffee or chocolate blancmange

*Jelly of 2 colors*
a) Red jelly
b) White blancmange
Or make 9 stripes of these, 4 white and 5 red stripes

*Jelly of 3 colors*
a) Red jelly
b) Lemon mousse
c) White or dark blancmange

*Jelly of 2 colors*
a) Light jelly
b) Raspberry jelly

*Mousse of 2 colors*
a) White lemon mousse
b) Lemon mousse, apricot-colored

*Hannah Glasse was making varicolored jelly, or "Ribband Jelly" as she called it, in the mid eighteenth century. By the late nineteenth century, jellied desserts had soared in popularity in Europe, England, and America. Both Mrs. Beeton and Mrs. A. B. Marshall illustrated their books with a plethora of complicated molds that could be used this way. Although I cannot think of any reason for a special association of these jellies with Russia, Mrs. Marshall included a recipe for Russian Jelly that was tricolored, coloring it red with liquid carmine, green "with a very little sap green," and the white was left plain. (Marshall, Mrs. A. B. Marshall's Larger Cookery Book, 28–31 and 497.) Variegated jellies are still being made today, but the wide availability of commercial powdered and flavored gelatins in America has banished conceits such as these from most banquet menus. Recipes can still be found, however, in community cookbooks, promotional booklets, and the occasional ethnic or national cookbook.*

## 1488 Jelly from apple skins

*(Zhele iz jablochnoj kozhitsy)*

Wipe off thoroughly and peel 10 fresh, fragrant, sour apples. Use the fruit for apple compote and prepare the following jelly base from the peels. Place the peels in a saucepan, cover with 3 glasses water, add ¾ lb sugar and 1 *vershok* vanilla bean, and boil thoroughly. Add ½ glass isinglass prepared from 10 *zolotniki* isinglass and clarify with egg whites or paper as indicated in the remarks. Reduce to 4 glasses, strain, and chill.

INGREDIENTS

| | |
|---|---|
| 10 apples | 10–12 *zolotniki* isinglass |
| vanilla bean | ¾ lb sugar |

## 1494  Cornflower jelly

*(Zhele iz vasil'kov)*

Scald ¼ lb cornflowers [*vasilek = Centaurea Cyanus*] with boiling water. Let stand and strain. Add sugar and gelatin, boil until soft, and clarify with an egg white. Add the juice of 2 lemons and 1 wineglass maraschino, strain, and chill.

INGREDIENTS

| | |
|---|---|
| ¼ lb cornflowers | 2 small lemons |
| ¾ lb sugar | 1 wineglass maraschino |
| 10 *zolotniki* gelatin | 1 egg white |

## 1496  Orange jelly

*(Zhele apel'sinnoe)*

Boil gelatin until it softens, add sugar and the finely cut zest from 2 oranges, clarify with an egg white, and reduce to 3½ glasses. Squeeze the juice from 3 oranges and let the juice stand. Then pour it off, strain, and mix with the syrup. Restrain the liquid and chill in a mold. If desired, add 1 glass maraschino to the jelly after it has been clarified with an egg white. In that case use 1 glass less water. When preparing a large quantity of jelly, garnish a large mold with small ones. The orange jelly may be poured into halved orange rinds* instead of small molds or may be chilled in eggs as follows. Make a small hole in the egg shell, empty out the egg, rinse, fill with jelly, and chill. To serve, crack the eggs and remove the shells.

INGREDIENTS

| | |
|---|---|
| ¾ lb sugar | 1 egg white |
| 3–4 oranges | (1 glass maraschino) |
| 10 *zolotniki* gelatin | |

*Molokhovets' suggestion is reminiscent of the French chef Carême's presentations. Carême*

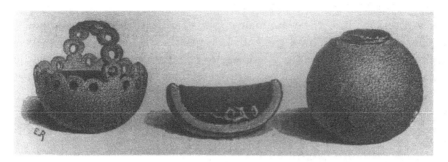

Orange rinds used as containers for jelly. From Gouffe, *Royal Book of Pastry and Confectionary* (London, 1874).

*hollowed out oranges, filled the shells with orange gelatin, and either served the fruit whole or in quarters. He also halved the oranges and made little handles of some extra peel to form minature baskets. Another of his presentations was to fill the shells with alternate layers of orange jelly and blancmange.*

### 1503  Jelly from various berries and fruits

*(Zhele iz raznykh jagod i fruktov)*

Take 2 glasses of various jams with juice, such as peach, apricot, pineapple, plum, pear, Bergamot pear, grape, cultivated or wild strawberry, raspberry, gooseberry, apple, currant, etc. Remove the berries and fruit from the jam and pour the juice into a saucepan. Dilute with water, pour in 1 glass gelatin, and add ¼ glass wine, if desired, and sugar if it is not sweet enough. Clarify with an egg white, reduce to 3 glasses, and strain through a napkin. Pour a little of this jelly into a mold and when it cools, add part of the berries and fruit. Cover with a little jelly, chill, and continue in this manner to the end.

INGREDIENTS

2 glasses jam                                   (¼ glass wine, sugar)
10 *zolotniki* gelatin

### 1504  Jelly from various berries and fruits in watermelon

*(Zhele iz raznykh jagod i fruktov v arbuze)*

When this jelly is made in a large quantity, it is sometimes served in a watermelon. Halve the watermelon, carefully cut away the flesh, remove the seeds, slice, and put in a cold place. Scoop out the remaining soft part of the watermelon with a spoon, place in a bowl, and sprinkle with fine sugar. Meanwhile, prepare double the amount of jelly as indicated above [cf. #1503]. Add the watermelon slices to the fruits and berries from the jam and the juice from the watermelon scraps to the jelly. After clarifying the jelly with egg whites, pour a little jelly into the watermelon, placed on ice. When it sets, add fruit, then again jelly, and so until the end. Less gelatin is added to this jelly because it will not be turned out of a mold, so 16–18 *zolotniki* of gelatin are sufficient for a large amount.

# MOUSSES
## (Muss)

*Remarks:* Mousse* is prepared exactly the same as jelly, except that it need not be clarified with egg whites, but only strained through a napkin. When it has slightly cooled, begin to beat it with a whisk over ice until it thickens and foams. Then pile into a mold and set on ice. For 6 persons, the proportions are the following: not 4 glasses, as indicated for jelly, but only 3 glasses, and 4 *zolotniki* gelatin in winter and 5 *zolotniki* in summer. To turn out onto a platter, dip the mold into hot water, wipe off the mold, and invert the mousse onto the plate.

For 7–8 persons, increase the proportions by 1¼. For 10–12 persons, increase the proportions by 1½. For 13–18 persons, double the proportions.

*By contrast with today's dense chocolate dessert, Molokhovets' mousses are no more than flavored sugar syrups whipped with gelatin.*

## 1506 Lemon mousse
### (Muss limonnyj)

Dilute almost ⅝ lb sugar with 5–6 glasses water, add the gelatin and the finely peeled zest from 1 lemon, and boil until the gelatin dissolves and the liquid is reduced to 3 glasses. Squeeze the juice from 1 large lemon through a strainer into the jelly. While still warm, begin to beat the mousse with a whisk over ice until it thickens and whitens. One wineglass rum may be added, then pile into a mold and set on ice.

This mousse may be colored with cranberries, squeezing the juice through a cloth so that it is a very light apricot color. Or divide the mousse into 2 parts and color one part red, leaving the other white.

INGREDIENTS

1 glass, or nearly ⅝ lb, sugar
1 large lemon
(1 wineglass rum)

4–5 *zolotniki* gelatin
(1 spoon cranberries)

### 1517  Mousse from rye rusks

*(Muss iz rzhanykh sukharej)*

Dry out black bread until it browns but do not let it burn. Break up the bread, pour one glass of the crumbs into a stoneware bowl, add 3 glasses of boiling water from the samovar, and cover with a plate for 15 minutes. Immediately strain through a fine sieve, measure and, if there is less than 3 glasses, add more boiling water, pouring it over the bread in the sieve. Add ½ lb sugar and 5 isinglass or 5 sheets gelatin and bring to a boil to dissolve the gelatin. Pour into a soup tureen and let it cool. When it begins to set, beat with a whisk over ice until it foams, transfer to a mold, and chill, etc.

# BLANCMANGES

*(Blanmanzhe)*

*Remarks:* To prevent the gelatin from separating it must be dissolved only in cold or warm water, but on no account let it come to a boil.

### 1518  Cream blancmange

*(Blanmanzhe slivochnoe)*

Scald ½ lb sweet almonds and 20–30 bitter almonds, peel, and pound in a mortar, pouring in about 2–3 spoons cream. Dilute with 3 glasses boiled cream which is still hot. Let stand an hour or more, strain through a napkin, sprinkle with sugar, and pour in ½ glass gelatin or enough to make exactly 4 glasses. Heat slightly, then pile into a mold and set on ice.

INGREDIENTS

| | |
|---|---|
| 1½ glasses sweet almonds | 3½ glasses thin cream, or milk |
| 20–30 bitter almonds, or 1 full spoon orange flower water | 10 sheets gelatin |
| | ⅜–½ lb sugar |

### 1519  Chocolate blancmange

*(Blanmanzhe shokoladnoe)*

Grate ⅛ lb chocolate, pour into a saucepan, and stir over the fire until it darkens. Prepare almond milk from ¼ lb sweet almonds, 10 bitter almonds, and 3 glasses milk. Pour the milk into the chocolate, strain, and sprinkle on ⅜ lb sugar. Add ½ glass gelatin, then pile into a mold and set on ice.

INGREDIENTS

| | |
|---|---|
| ¼ lb chocolate | ⅜ lb sugar |
| ¾ glass sweet almonds | 10 sheets gelatin |
| 10 bitter almonds | ½ *vershok* vanilla bean or more may |
| 3 glasses milk or cream | be added |

# KISSELS
## *(Kiseli)*

*Remarks:* For 6 glasses juice or milk, use 1 glass sieved potato flour diluted with 1 glass cold juice or milk. Bring to a boil 5 glasses juice and pour the flour mixture into the boiling liquid, stirring briskly over the fire for 4–5 minutes, but no longer. Stir until smooth so that no lumps remain.

Rinse a mold in cold water, pour in the *kissel*, and set on ice. To serve, turn out onto a platter.* For 6 glasses juice, 1 glass potato flour is sufficient if the flour is dry and of the highest quality. Otherwise, more flour must be added.

The amounts indicated wil! serve 6–8 persons. For 9–18 persons, increase the proportions by 1½.

*\*Kissel is a semi-solid dessert pudding traditionally made with berries, water, and sugar and thickened with potato starch. Its consistency varies; it can be thick enough to cut, semi-stiff, or even runny. Most of Molokhovets' kissels were stiff enough to be molded and turned out onto a platter.*

## 1524  Apple kissel

### (Kisel' jablochnyj)

Finely cut up 6–8 large Antonov apples, boil in water with a piece of cinnamon, and strain through a sieve. Mix 5 glasses of this juice with ¼ lb sugar pieces scraped over lemon zest. Add the juice from ½ lemon, bring to a boil, and pour in the flour diluted with 1 glass water, etc.

INGREDIENTS

| | |
|---|---|
| 6–8 apples | ½–1 glass sugar pieces |
| cinnamon | 1 glass potato flour |
| ½ lemon | sugar and cream to serve separately |

## 1526  A very tasty gooseberry kissel

### (Ochen' vkusnyj kisel' iz kryzhovnika)

Separate very fresh, ripe gooseberries from twigs and flowers and pour 9 glasses of clean berries into a saucepan. Barely cover the berries with water and add 1 or 3 glasses fine sugar and ½ *vershok* vanilla bean. Cook, stirring, for a long time until the berries soften, but do not let them burn. Near the end pour 1 heaping table-spoon potato flour mixed with ½ glass cold water into the berries. Mix, boil thoroughly, pour into a dish, and chill.

INGREDIENTS

3 lbs gooseberries
½ or 1½ lbs sugar
½ *vershok* vanilla bean

1 tablespoon potato flour
(sugar and cream)

### 1530  *Kissel* from raspberries, red or black currants, cherries, or plums

*(Kisel' iz maliny, krasnoj ili chernoj smorodiny, iz vishen', iz sliv)*

Crush the berries with a spoon, dilute with water, and strain. Pour ¼ or ½ lb sugar scraped over lemon zest onto 5 glasses of this juice, bring to a boil, and pour in the flour diluted with 1 glass cold water, etc.

To preserve a good color, all these *kissels* must be cooked in a stoneware pot or copper basin. This recipe produces a very thick *kissel*.

INGREDIENTS

2½ glasses, or 1 lb, cleaned currants
   or 4–5 glasses raspberries
½–1 glass sugar

1 glass sieved potato flour
lemon zest
sugar and cream to serve separately

### 1535  A pretty dessert—or a *kissel* with whipped cream like a torte

*(Krasivoe pirozhnoe, kisel' so sbitymi slivkami v rode torta)*

Cook a thick gooseberry *kissel* and pour it onto a round platter. Or pour the *kissel* into a smooth flat mold, chill, and turn out onto a platter. To serve, cover with whipped cream (¼–½ bottle) and sugar. Decorate the top with star-shaped biscuits and a border of small fancy-shaped chocolates.

### 1537  Cornstarch *kissel*

*(Kisel' iz maisovoj muki)*

Bring to a boil 5 glasses milk, pour in ½ glass cornstarch mixed with 1 glass cold water, add a little salt and 4 tablespoons fine sugar, and bring to a boil twice, stirring briskly.

# COMPOTES
## (Kompoty)

*Remarks:* The syrup which is poured over a compote must be very dense like a thick syrup from jam. Therefore for 1½ glasses of syrup, ¾ lb, or 2¼ glasses, of sugar pieces should be used. For a simpler compote for just the family, ¼ lb is sufficient.

The proportions will serve 6–8 persons. For 9–12 persons, increase the proportions by 1½. For 13–18 persons, double the proportions.

### 1538  Apple compote
*(Kompot iz jablok)*

Peel 6–12 apples and stick them with cloves. Quarter large apples, halve medium apples, and leave small ones whole. Core the apples and cook in a thin syrup with cloves and a piece of stick cinnamon. When the apples have thoroughly cooked (but do not let them disintegrate), turn them into a sieve. Strain the syrup and add the remaining sugar, ½–1 glass French wine, and the zest and juice from ½ lemon. Reduce the syrup to 1½ or 2 glasses, as desired, and pour it over the apples arranged on a platter, in a bowl, or in stemmed glasses (*v stekljannyja vazy*). Serve cold, topped with cherry jam or red or black currant jelly-jam. This compote may be served with roasts, in which case it does not have to be very sweet and wine need not be added.

INGREDIENTS

6–12 apples
¼–¾ lb, or 2½ glasses sugar in pieces (for those who do not like a very sweet compote ¼ lb sugar is sufficient)

10–20 cloves
cinnamon, a *vershok* or more
½–1 glass white French wine
½ lemon

### 1543  Plum compote
*(Kompot iz sliv)*

Make an incision in plums that are not completely ripe and remove the stones. Drop into boiling water until the skin splits, turn into a coarse sieve, and peel. Drop the peeled fruit into a boiling syrup prepared from ½ lb sugar, 4 glasses water, 10–20 cloves, and a piece of cinnamon or vanilla bean. When the plums have thoroughly cooked, transfer them with a slotted spoon to a serving dish. Strain the syrup, reduce to the appropriate thickness, cool, and pour over the plums.

If the plums are ripe, boil them up only once. Skin, arrange on a platter, and pour on the cold syrup prepared from sugar, cloves, cinnamon, or vanilla bean. Do not skin white plums or greengages.

INGREDIENTS

40–60 plums

¼–¾ lb sugar

6–12 cloves

cinnamon stick or vanilla bean

## 1549  Compote from odds and ends

### (Kompot iz raznostej)

Thoroughly wash and cook dried pears, apples, prunes, apricots, or peaches (*sheptala*), and figs. Cook raisins and currants separately. Finally, peel, core, and boil fresh apples separately in water with sugar. When cooked, remove the apples and strain the apple syrup through a napkin. Add the remainder of the sugar to the strained apple syrup and reduce to the requisite thickness, that is, to 1½ or 2 glasses, as desired. Strain the syrup again. Arrange a high mound of dried apples, pears, prunes, and raisins on a platter, sprinkle the top with currants and cherries taken from jam, and surround the mound of dried fruit with a ring of freshly boiled apples, interspersing them with halved figs. Pour on the remaining syrup cooked with finely shredded lemon or orange zest for flavoring. One-half wineglass sherry may also be added.

INGREDIENTS

3 [fresh] apples

8 dried figs

8 dried pears

9 dried apples

2–3 spoons dried cherries

18 prunes

½ glass raisins

1 spoon cherries, taken from jam

¼–¾ lb sugar

orange or lemon rind

(½ wineglass sherry)

9 dried apricots or peaches

¼ glass currants

# BOILED MILK CREAMS

## (Molochnye zavarnye kremy)

*Remarks:* Proportions are intended for 6–8 persons. For 9–12 persons, increase the proportions by 1½. For 13–18 persons, double the proportions.

### 1553 Almond milk cream

*(Molochnyj zavarnoj krem mindal'nyj)*

Peel 6–8 bitter almonds and ½ glass sweet almonds, pound the nuts, and dilute with 3 glasses whole milk. Strain, squeeze out, and sprinkle with sugar. Beat 12 egg yolks, mix with the almond milk, and strain through a sieve into a mold or bowl. Set the bowl in a pan of boiling water on top of the stove and immediately lower the flame to prevent the water from boiling further. When the milk is thick enough to cut with a knife, quickly remove the mold from the water and set it in a cold place, preferably overnight. To serve, turn out onto a platter and pour on syrup, vanilla, or chocolate sauce.

Use the leftover egg whites the next day for a soufflé or meringues. ¼ glass of bitter almonds may be substituted for the sweet almonds.

INGREDIENTS

| | |
|---|---|
| 3 glasses milk | 10–20 bitter almonds |
| 12 egg yolks | ½ glass sugar |
| ½ glass sweet almonds | syrup or ingredients for sauce |

### 1558 Crème caramel

*(Molochnyj zavarnoj krem s karmel'nym siropom)*

If the cream will be served with caramel syrup, prepare it as follows. Stir together 3 glasses milk, ½ glass or more fine sugar, and 12 egg yolks. Strain the mixture. Pound fine 12–16 pieces sugar, pour in 1 spoon water, and caramelize in a clean skillet, stirring constantly so that the sugar takes on the taste of sugar burnt over a candle. Add 2 spoons water, bring to a boil, and while still hot, pour immediately into a moistened mold or small moistened cups. Mask the entire interior with this sugar syrup, adding more on the bottom. Immediately pour in the prepared milk, cook as indicated in #1553, and cool. For this reason, it should be cooked the day before it will be served. To serve, dip the mold briefly into hot water, wipe it off, and turn the cream out onto a platter. One to two spoons boiling water may be poured into the sugar which remains in the mold, rinsed out, and poured over the cream. Thickly stud the top of the cream with finely sliced sweet almonds so that the almonds stick up like stubble.*

This cream may also be prepared very simply and served hot. Mix 3 glasses milk, ½ glass fine sugar, finely pounded lemon zest, and 12 egg yolks. Strain, pour into a stoneware or earthenware bowl, and bake for ½ hour before serving. When it thickens, serve hot in that same bowl.

INGREDIENTS

3 glasses whole milk                    ½ glass fine sugar, and up to ½ lb
12 egg yolks                            sugar in pieces

*The studded cream resembled a hedgehog, which was a popular image in Europe as well as Russia. Even in the Soviet era, the remains of the Easter paskha were still occasionally fashioned into a small hedgehog for the children. French and English recipes for dishes resembling hedgehogs date back at least to the fifteenth century.*

### 1559 Boiled fermented milk with silver leaven

*(Varenets\* s serebrjanoju zakvaskoju)*

Dip 1 silver 20 kopeck coin or a silver teaspoon into 1 bottle milk and set in a warm place for 4 days. Add almost 1 glass of this silver leaven to 5 bottles of thin cream. Place the cream in a warm oven and stir as often as possible. After 4 hours, the *varenets* will be ready. Transfer it carefully into another bowl without the whey and set it to cool on ice. Serve with sugar and with finely pounded and sieved rye rusks.

Silver leaven may be kept on ice for about 2 weeks.

INGREDIENTS

1 bottle milk                           (sugar and rye rusks)
5 bottles thin cream

*The word varenets comes from the same stem var- as in the verb varit', to boil. The basic preparation, without the silver leaven, is a very old Russian dish; its long popularity was partly due to the construction of the traditional Russian stove, the slow heat of which was ideal for clotting the cream. The addition of the silver must have mainly been for "good luck" since the reaction of silver is so slow that its presence would not materially affect either the chemical composition or the taste of the final product. Silver is a relatively inert metal; its slow reaction with the acid in the milk eventually precipitates out the milk's protein, making silver proteinate. This silver leaven is sweeter than milk that had soured on its own since natural clotting results from an organism reacting with the milk and increasing its acidity, but any effect of the silver leaven would be marginal in comparison with the natural clotting that occurs simultaneously, especially with unpasteurized milk and cream. Just as silver utensils and pans were used without ill effect, the silver reaction with the milk was not toxic. If anyone wants to experiment with this recipe, the silver should be polished first so that the metal is as clean as possible.*

### 1560 Boiled fermented milk, or Greek milk\*

*(Varenets ili grecheskoe moloko)*

Pour 4 bottles whole milk into a wide earthenware basin (*krinka*) and set in the oven in front of the coals to simmer slowly. When a colored skin forms on top, push it to the bottom with a spoon, and repeat the process several times, pushing down the skins as they form. Remove the pot from the oven, cool slightly, add ½ or 1 glass cream, and set in a warm place for the cream to sour. Cool and serve with sugar.

*The Greek connection here is unclear, but the process of clotting cream and letting it form skins is a very old one. In England, a mid seventeenth century recipe called for sprinkling sugar, rosewater, and orange flower water between the layers of clotted cream; this dish was called "cabbage cream" because the skins were heaped in a dish like a head of cabbage. (See Brears, The Gentlewoman's Kitchen, 89, and Wilson, Food and Drink in Britain, 169.)*

## 1561  Yogurt

### (Prostokvasha)

In winter, yogurt is prepared quickly as follows. Mix 3–4 bottles whole milk and several spoons fresh sour cream and set in a warm place for 24 hours. When it thickens, cool and serve with sugar and crumbs of finely pounded, dried black bread. In summer, it may be prepared in 24 hours even without sour cream, but before serving, it should be cooled on ice. Serve with sugar and rye rusks.

## 1562  Yogurt pudding with raisins

### (Arkas)

(Proportions for 10 persons) Thoroughly beat yogurt, sour cream, and eggs, pour in milk, and add washed and dried raisins and a little salt. Mix as well as possible and bring to a boil, stirring, so that the milk curdles. Pour into a napkin to let the whey drain off. Mix the curds with sugar, tie up the napkin, and hang in the cold cellar to chill. To serve, turn out carefully onto a platter and pour on whipped sweet or sour cream with sugar and cinnamon.

INGREDIENTS

| | |
|---|---|
| 1 *garnets* or 12 glasses milk | 1¼ glasses very thick sweet or sour |
| 1½ glasses yogurt | cream |
| 1 glass sour cream | ¼–⅓ glass sugar |
| 1 glass raisins | cinnamon or vanilla bean |
| 8 eggs | ½ glass sugar |

## 1563  Butter in the English fashion*

### (Maslo po-anglijski)

Beat 3 glasses very thick, fresh sour cream with a whisk over ice. When it begins to thicken, sprinkle with sugar and a little ground vanilla bean, or any kind of oil for flavoring, or rosewater. Mix, place in a napkin, tie up, and hang overnight in the cold cellar. The next day, turn out onto a platter and pour on a sauce made with cream, egg yolks, and sugar.

INGREDIENTS

| | |
|---|---|
| 3 glasses, or almost 2 lbs, sour cream | vanilla bean or rosewater, or any oil |
| ¼–½ glass sugar | for flavoring |
| | (ingredients for vanilla sauce) |

*For centuries the English have been fond of all sorts of curds and creams. Soft cheeses, clotted creams, fools, syllabubs, custards, and trifles are all part of the English heritage. The variety is staggering and the nomenclature confusing. Often the mixtures were sweetened with sugar, enriched with eggs, and flavored with sweet wines, sherry, lemon peel, spices, and other flavorings. Molokhovets' directions for whipping the cream over ice and letting the mixture hang overnight to solidify are similar to those found in Mrs. Beeton's recipe for Whipped Cream (#1492). The ingredients differed, however, since Mrs. Beeton incorporated a beaten egg white, a glass of sherry, and the zest of half a lemon into her sweetened cream. (Beeton, Book of Household Management, 752.)*

# 15
# Tortes

## (Torty)

*Remarks:* The important rules for baking tortes and other pastries are the following:

a) If clarified butter (*rastoplennoe maslo*)* is to be added to the pastry batter, it should be placed on top of the stove over a very low fire. When the foam rises, remove the butter from the stove and let it stand. Pour off the liquid on top and strain carefully through a fine sieve, so that the salt and other milky parts remain on the bottom of the pan. Then begin to mix this butter in one direction in a cold place, on snow or ice, until it whitens.

If non-clarified butter is to be added, as for puff pastry, it must be only the very best fresh butter. Soak the butter in water with ice, squeeze it dry in a napkin, and mix with a spatula in a cold place until it turns completely white.

b) Separately beat the egg yolks with sugar until white, add the butter, sprinkle on the flour, and mix only until the flour is incorporated. If beaten egg whites are to be added to the batter, it is best to sprinkle on the flour gradually when adding the egg whites, carefully folding from top to bottom. Then immediately transfer the batter to a pan and bake in the oven.

c) The sugar must be good, very fine, and bolted through a silk sieve.

d) Wheat flour must be used for tortes and pastries; it must be both dry and of the highest grade.

e) The eggs must be very fresh and whole.

f) If the torte is baked in a tin pan, the pan should be buttered and sprinkled lightly with flour and rusk crumbs. If a paper casing is used, grease the paper with unsalted butter, sprinkle with rusk crumbs, chill, and half fill the casing, that is, not to the very top, but with enough room left for the dough to rise.

g) Almonds must first be scalded with boiling water, then peeled, dried, and pounded in a mortar, moistening them with water or egg white to prevent the oil from separating.

h) Most important in the baking of pastries, of course, is the oven; the temperature can be determined as follows: Several minutes after lighting and sweeping the ashes out of the oven, place a sheet of paper in the middle of the oven. If the paper immediately turns yellow and burns, the oven is still too hot; if it curls up and turns yellow gradually, the pastry may be set in the oven with confidence.

i) The pastry must be set in the oven with great care so that it does not touch anything. Do not move it from place to place, because the dough may fall from shaking, and the pastry will not be successful.

j) Stick a straw or very thin spill into the pastry to see if it is done. If no batter adheres, the torte is ready.

k) Sometimes tortes are prepared from several layers, in which case they are filled with jam without juice, or preferably, with either fruit or berry purée. Nowadays biscuit tortes (*biskvitnye torty*) are filled with raspberry jam, or with wild or cultivated strawberry jam with juice, which soaks into the biscuit, making it moist and tasty.

l) To finish pastries—and especially tortes—attractively, they must be iced. If it is a plain torte, glaze it, sprinkle it with pieces of colored sugar, variously colored poppy seeds,** or finely chopped pistachios, and dry slightly in the oven. Or, glaze the cake, set in the oven for 10 minutes, and decorate with icing, using a paper cone as a pastry bag. Fill any gaps in the design with candied peel, various fruits, or jam.

Or instead of glazing the torte, decorate it with a meringue made from 2 beaten egg whites and ¼ lb sugar, or a pistachio mixture, or chocolate icing.

m) A torte for 6 persons is usually round and almost 5 *vershok* in diameter; that is, make a round paper casing for the torte from a half sheet of paper. Fasten on a circular rim of paper 2–3 fingers high. Today, rectangular tortes are also made.

n) In the text of the torte recipes, full proportions are given; that is, these amounts will yield a torte large enough for 18, or even 24, persons. The list of ingredients, however, is intended to serve only 6 people—therefore, they must be doubled for 12 people and tripled for 18.

*This term ordinarily means melted butter, but the process described by Molokhovets results in what we know as clarified butter. I have occasionally used the expression "melted and clarified," where it seemed appropriate to remind the reader of the process.
**See the Glossary for more on poppy seeds.

### 1566 Orange or lemon glaze

*(Glazur' apel'sinnaja i limonnaja)*

For a torte for 6 persons. Scrape the zest from an orange with ¼ lb sugar. Pound the sugar, add ¾ tablespoon freshly squeezed orange juice, sprinkle on lemon salt* the size of half a pea, and stir in a porcelain mortar until the mixture thickens. Spread over the torte, dry out a little, and decorate with jam, fruits, etc.

Lemon icing is also prepared the same way; that is, scrape off lemon zest with ¼ lb sugar and add ¾ spoon freshly squeezed lemon juice.

For a torte triple the size (for 18 persons), double the ingredients for the icing, that is, use ½ lb sugar, etc.

*Presumably this was crystalized citric acid.*

### 1571 Pistachio icing (green)

*(Glazur' iz fistashek—Zelenaja)*

Finely pound ⅛ lb shelled pistachios and add ¼ lb sugar, ¾ spoon orange flower water, and lemon salt. To color the icing green, pick over a handful of spinach, tear off the stems, wash the leaves, and drop them into boiling water. Boil uncovered, pour off the water, squeeze out, rub through a sieve, and add a little of this purée to the icing.

### 1578 Orange flower water glaze

*(Glazur' prozrachnaja s pomerantsevoju vodoju)*

Mix together ¼ lb, or ½ glass, very finely pounded and sieved sugar, ¾ spoon orange flower water, and lemon salt the size of 2 peas.

### 1579 Icing for designs

*(Glazur' dlja uzorov)*

Mix ¼ lb, or ½ glass, sugar, ½ egg white, and several drops lemon juice until the mixture whitens and thickens. Fold a sheet of writing paper into a tube, fill it with this mixture, and cut off the tip of the tube so that the opening is as thick as a shoelace. Take whatever drawing you wish, and follow the design, pressing out the icing, which will begin to harden immediately. Fill any gaps with fruits, berries, candied peel, etc.

### 1580 Marzipan and [Chocolate almond torte]

*(Mindal'naja massa)*

Peel 1½ lbs sweet almonds and ¼ lb bitter almonds. Pound very, very fine, adding 7 egg whites and 1 lb fine sugar. Transfer all this to a saucepan on top of the stove and cook until it begins to boil, stirring so that it does not burn. Cool, transfer to a clean paper casing, and set in the oven to dry. After removing the casing of baked almond paste from the oven, turn it out onto a wire rack and spread the bottom with egg white in order to detach the paper from the almond paste. Sandwich this almond layer between a biscuit torte and a chocolate torte, after spreading each layer with jam. Namely, lay a chocolate torte on the platter, spread it with a thick fruit purée such as applesauce or cherry purée, add the marzipan layer, press it down lightly, spread it with more fruit purée, add the biscuit torte, ice it, and decorate the top with icing, jam, etc.

For 6 persons use ⅓ of the indicated amount.

INGREDIENTS

| | |
|---|---|
| 1½ lb sweet almonds | 1 lb sugar |
| ¼ lb bitter almonds | 7 egg whites |

### 1586  Sweet layered Russian pirog*

*(Sloenyj sladkij russkij pirog)*

(For meat or fast days.) Beat 6 eggs, or 1 glass eggs, in a wooden bowl. Add 3 glasses sweet water, that is, ⅓ lb sugar dissolved in water, 1 wineglass vodka, and ½ teaspoon salt. Mix thoroughly, sprinkle on 4½ lbs sieved fine wheat flour gradually, beating with [the end of] a rolling pin** as well as possible until the dough begins to pull away from the rolling pin.

Transfer the dough onto a table sprinkled with ½ lb of the remaining flour. Cut the dough into 60 pieces, lightly roll each piece into a small bun, and then, sprinkling with flour and using a rolling pin, roll out each bun into a flat cake the size of a small dish. Pile these flat cakes one on top of another, sprinkling thoroughly with flour so that they do not stick together. Using a cloth or a small feather, grease a large round platter with clarified butter. Take one cake and stretch it out in your hands, using your fingers to work the edges first so that they are not too thick, and then work on the center, stretching the dough over your fists so as not to tear it. Stretch the dough out onto the platter, tuck in the edges, and grease this layer with a buttered cloth. Top this with the next stretched layer, grease with butter, etc.

Add 25 sheets in this way and spread the top layer with jam and fruit without the least bit of juice, using 1 lb or a little bit more. Turn up the edge of this layer so the jam does not leak out (this layer of pastry must not have the slightest hole). Add 35 more layers on top of the jam, greasing each with butter and tucking the edges under the platter.

Trim off the extra dough from under the edge of the platter (*krendels* can be made from this dough), grease the cake with butter, and bake it for half an hour in an oven that is not too hot. To serve, the edges may be trimmed again with a sharp knife. Sprinkle with sugar. This *pirog* may be made in the evening, kept in a cold place overnight, and baked the next day. It will keep for more than a month in a cold place. It is unnecessary to reheat it before serving.

For 6–8 persons, prepare the *pirog* from half the indicated proportions, make 45 layers in all, place 20 under the jam and 25 over the jam, and stretch out on a glazed dish.

Do not add even a drop of butter to the dough; use it only to grease the layers.

A *pirog* for fast days is prepared in exactly the same way, but the eggs are omitted. Instead of using eggs, add 1 glass water for the large proportions and ½ glass for the small *pirog*, and substitute poppy seed or sunflower seed oil for the butter.

INGREDIENTS (*for a large pirog*)

| | |
|---|---|
| 5 lbs flour | about 1½ glasses, or nearly 1 lb, |
| 6 eggs | clarified butter |
| ⅔ teaspoon salt | not less than 1 lb, or 1½ glasses, jam |
| ⅓ lb sugar | 1 wineglass vodka |

*According to Barbara Wheaton, Lancelot de Casteau gave a recipe for a similarly layered pastry in his Ovverture de Cuisine that was published in Liège in 1604.
**By turning a rolling pin or skalka on end, it could be used for beating or pounding.

### 1593  Torte of short pastry

(*Tort razsypchatyj*)

Thoroughly knead ½ lb butter, 1 lb flour, 1 spoon rum, 1 egg, 1 spoon sour cream, ½ glass sugar, and lemon zest or 12 bitter almonds. Roll out on a table, transfer to a skillet, attach a rim of pastry around the circumference, paint with egg, and bake. Fill with berries, apples, or jam, and top with whipped cream.

INGREDIENTS (*for 6 persons*)

| | |
|---|---|
| ½ lb butter | 1 wineglass rum |
| 3 glasses flour | 1 spoon sour cream |
| ½ glass sugar | (1 egg) |
| lemon zest or bitter almonds | |

### 1596  English torte

(*Tort anglijskij*)

Beat 1 lb fresh, unsalted butter until white. Sprinkle on 1 lb sugar and 1¼ lbs flour, mixing constantly. Finally beat in 8 eggs, add 10–12 bitter almonds or lemon zest for flavoring, and mix as long as possible. Spread this dough onto 2 circles and set in the summer oven. When baked, spread 1 layer with thick cranberry* syrup, cover with the other layer, top this with the same cranberry syrup, and place in the oven for 10 minutes.

Small pastries also may be made from this dough by spreading the prepared mixture with a knife onto a baking sheet dusted with flour. Set in the summer oven to bake. When the sheet of pastry is half cooked, cut it into rectangles without removing them from the sheet, and return the sheet to the oven. When they have finished baking, spread with fruit purée or cranberry syrup, stick them together in pairs, and cover each pair of cookies with icing.

INGREDIENTS (for 6 persons and for 2 layers)

⅓ lb butter
⅓ lb sugar
⅓ lb, or ⅔ glasses, sugar
5/12 lb, or 1⅓ glasses, flour
2⅔ eggs

5–6 bitter almonds, or lemon zest
½ glass cranberry juice and 1½ glasses fine sugar
ingredients for icing

*The European cranberry (Vaccinium oxycoccus var. palustris) is smaller than the American cranberry (Vaccinium macrocarpon), but its flavor is said to be superior. Although the plant is native to Britain, Northern Europe, and Siberia, the name cranberry, or craneberry, is comparatively recent in English and seems to have been adopted by the American colonists and brought back to England along with the larger American berries. Although cranberries were clearly known in England from an early date, references to them, under any name, are uncommon in English cookery books. They may have still been gathered and preserved in rural areas, but they seem to have disappeared from English middle class recipes by the nineteenth century. Why Molokhovets called for cranberries in an English torte is somewhat of a puzzle.

## 1597 Cream torte*

### (Tort slivochnyj)

Beat 8–10 egg whites into a foam, sprinkle on 1 lb finely sieved sugar, and mix thoroughly. Cut out several paper circles, fold a piece of paper into a tube, fill with the beaten egg whites, and cut off the sharp end of the tube. Press out the beaten egg whites around the edge of the circles, making a kind of wreath, and cover one circle entirely with egg whites, about one-half a finger thick. Place in the summer oven. After the meringues have dried out, remove the circles from the oven and carefully detach the rings from the paper. Arrange them one on top of the other on a platter and fill the interior with whipped cream made by beating with a whisk 4 glasses very thick cream over ice and sprinkling on ½ lb sugar with vanilla. Place the single filled disk of meringue on top and decorate with fruits, jelly, etc.

INGREDIENTS (for 6 persons)

4–5 egg whites
½ lb, or 1 glass, sugar
1⅓ glass thick cream

½ glass sugar and vanilla
fruits, jelly, etc.

*The French name for this confection is vacherin; often fresh berries are folded into the whipped cream filling.

### 1599  English wedding cake

*(Anglijskij svadebnyj pirog)*

Beat 1 lb butter until white. Also beat until white ½ lb sugar and ⅔ lb eggs (the eggs must be weighed together with their shells). Mix the sugar and eggs with the butter. Sprinkle on ½ lb finely pounded almonds and 1⅓ lb currants which have been sorted over, washed, and wiped dry. Add 1 *zolotnik* each nutmeg, ground cloves, and cinnamon, plus a little ginger. Mix all this as well as possible, sprinkling on ⅔ lb flour. Add ½ glass each Malaga and French wine.\* Cut out the hair mesh from a small sieve and set the sieve rim on a baking sheet lined with buttered paper.\*\* Add the prepared dough and place in the oven.

INGREDIENTS *(for 6 persons)*

| | |
|---|---|
| ½ lb butter | ½ *zolotnik*, or 1 teaspoon, cinnamon |
| ¼ lb, or ½ glass, sugar | a little ginger |
| ⅓ lb eggs, or 3 medium eggs | ⅓ lb, or 1 glass, flour |
| ⅙ lb, or ½ glass almonds | ¼ glass Malaga |
| ⅔ lb, or 2 glasses, currants | ¼ glass red wine\* |
| ½ *zolotnik*, or 1 very small, nutmeg | ½ spoon butter to grease the paper |
| ½ *zolotnik*, or 35, cloves | |

   \**Molokhovets did not specify the color of the wine in the body of the recipe, only in the list of ingredients.*
   ·\*\**With these instructions Molokhovets is simply improvising a flan ring. She did not mention lining the sieve drum with buttered paper, but she would have done that to prevent the batter from sticking. Aside from the absence of candied citron and candied orange and lemon peel, Molokhovets' recipe is similar to one given by Mrs. Beeton for Rich Bride or Christening Cake. Molokhovets' recipe omitted the traditional English finishing of almond paste and Royal icing. (See Beeton,* Book of Household Management, *854.)*

### 1600  Italian biscuit torte

*(Tort ital'janskij biskvitnyj)*

Beat 21 egg yolks and 1 lb sugar until the mixture whitens. Separately beat 21 egg whites into soft peaks and carefully fold into the egg yolks, gradually sieving on nearly ½ lb flour. Pour the mixture into 3 paper casings and place in a rather hot oven after baking bread. Remove from the oven, cautiously peel off the paper casings, and cool the layers on coarse sieves. Carefully stack the layers on top of each other, after spreading them with black or red currant jam, fruit purée, or an almond or poppy seed mixture. Glaze the top and decorate with fruits, jelly, etc.

   Cherry or apricot purée goes very well with this torte. Spread the purée between the layers and over the top layer. Coat the purée on top with a thin layer of rum icing and let the icing dry out. In this case it is not bad to add a little rum to the apricot purée.

Nowadays biscuit tortes are also filled with raspberry or wild strawberry jam with syrup, so that the syrup permeates almost all the biscuit. Decorate the top with a ring of pears halved lengthwise. Fill the pear cavities with jam from cultivated strawberries, and cover everything with a thin layer of thick, hot, wild strawberry *kissel*, prepared from syrup and potato flour, or with only just boiled and slightly cooled red jelly with gelatin, which will set completely when poured on the torte.

INGREDIENTS *(for 6 persons or for 2 layers)*

7 eggs  
⅓ lb (⅔ glass) sugar  
nearly ⅙ lb (nearly ⅓ glass) flour

¾ glass jam  
ingredients for icing

### 1605  Torte from rye bread

*(Tort iz rzhanago khleba)*

Beat as well as possible 30 egg yolks, 1 lb sugar, 1½ *zolotniki* or 3 teaspoons cinnamon, 1½ *zolotniki* [ground ?] star anise [*bad'jan = Illicum anisatum*], and ¾ *zolotnik*, or 50 [ground ?] whole cloves. Add ¾ glass pure rye bread, dried and sieved, and ½ glass fine wheat flour and stir all this in one direction for a full hour. Fold in 30 beaten egg whites and pour into a paper casing greased with unsalted butter and strewn with rye rusk crumbs. Place in the oven after bread, then stack the layers,* spreading them with jam or fruit purée, and glaze.

INGREDIENTS *(for 6 persons)*

10 eggs  
⅓ lb (⅔ glass) sugar  
½ *zolotnik* (1 teaspoon) cinnamon  
½ *zolotnik* star anise  
¼ *zolotnik* cloves (16 pieces)

¼ glass rye bread "flour"  
⅛ glass fine wheat flour  
¾ glass jam or marmalade  
ingredients for icing

*Molokhovets presumably intended the torte to be sliced horizontally into several layers of a convenient thickness. The thickness of the torte, of course, depends on how well the egg whites are beaten and how they are folded into the batter.

### 1607  Lemon torte

*(Tort limonnyj)*

[For 6 layers.] Boil 6 lemons in water until tender enough to be pierced easily with a straw. Do not overcook them or let them lose their juice.

After removing the lemons from the water, wrap them in a napkin folded into several layers. When the lemons have cooled, remove the seeds and beat the lemons [both pulp and juice] in a stoneware bowl until smooth, add 4 glasses sugar, and beat in 36 egg yolks one by one. Stir until the mixture whitens, rub through a fine sieve, mix again, and add 36 beaten egg whites. Mix lightly, pour into buttered paper casings,* and bake in the summer oven, but watch that the torte neither dries out nor browns. When cool, spread the layers with jam or fruit purée and stack the layers on top of each other. These 2 tortes, lemon torte and rye bread torte are sometimes served together, that is, the rye bread torte is sandwiched between layers of lemon torte after spreading each layer with jam or fruit purée.

INGREDIENTS *(for 6 persons and for 1 layer)*

1 large lemon
1/3 glass sugar
6 eggs

1/2 spoon butter to grease the casing
ingredients for icing and decorating
   the torte

*Molokhovets is inconsistent in her directions in that she speaks about one casing, but several layers. Here I changed the singular to the plural form under the assumption that the cake would rise better if it were baked in several layers. Also it is not clear whether she intended all six layers to be used in one torte or whether they were to be distributed among several different tortes.*

### 1608  Open-faced sweet pie with apples or fresh berries

*(Pirog sladkij s jablokami, ili svezhimi jagodami)*

Prepare a yeast dough. Peel 6–9 apples, chop them fine, and fry them lightly with 1/2 glass sugar, a little cinnamon, and 1 spoon butter. Add a wineglass or 2 of wine, finely chopped lemon zest, and, if desired, scalded currants. Stew all this until the mixture thickens. After the dough has risen, roll out a thin circle, top it with the prepared apples, surround with a thin rim of pastry, cover with a lattice of that same dough, paint with egg, and bake. Or, instead of the apples, cover the dough with jam or fresh berries and sprinkle with sugar. Serve sugar separately. This same pie may also be made from short or puff pastry.

INGREDIENTS *(for 6 persons)*

6–9 apples
(lemon zest, 1/4 glass currants)
1/2 glass sugar
cinnamon
1/2 spoon butter
(1–2 wineglasses wine)
Or, 1 lb, or nearly 3 glasses, fresh
   berries and 1/2 glass sugar

*For the yeast dough*
3/4 glass milk

1–2 spoons yeast, or 1 *zolotnik* dried
   yeast
1 lb, or 3 glasses, flour
1/4 lb butter
2–3' egg yolks
1/8 glass sugar and cinnamon or 3–4
   ground cardamom seeds
1 egg to paint the dough
Or, ingredients for short or puff pastry

### 1610  Eugenia torte

*(Tort Evgenija)*

(For 12 persons.) Beat 8 eggs, 4 egg yolks, and 1½ lb sugar until white. Add 22 *lots* potato flour, finely chopped orange rind, 6 *lots* blanched pistachios, and ½ lb sweet almonds. (Very finely chop half [the nuts], and shred the other half into oblong pieces.) Mix everything together as well as possible. Bake 2 thin layers. Spread jam over one layer, top with the other, and glaze the torte.

INGREDIENTS *(for 6 persons)*

| | |
|---|---|
| 4 eggs | 1 full spoon orange peel |
| 2 egg yolks | 3 *lots* pistachios |
| ¾ lb, or 1½ glasses, sugar | ¼ lb, or ¾ glass, sweet almonds |
| 11 *lots* potato flour | ingredients for icing |
| ¼ glass jam | |

### 1613  Dresden pyramid torte

*(Tort drezdenskij piramidal'nyj)*

Weigh 12 eggs (with their shells) and use the same weight each of flour, butter, and sugar. Thus, if the eggs weigh 1½ lbs, use 1½ lbs each of butter, flour, and sugar.

Beat washed and dried butter until white, add sugar, eggs, a little nutmeg, and cinnamon gradually, and finally add the flour. Mix until smooth. Cut several circles from paper, 6 to 8 or 10, each one smaller than the previous one. Spread this mixture, as thick as a finger, on each circle. Bake in an oven that is not too hot. When cooked, spread each circle—except the smallest one—with jam. Arrange them one on top of another so that the smallest is on top. Decorate the torte with various colored icings and arrange marzipan (made from almond dough) flowers or fruit on the very top.

INGREDIENTS *(for 6 persons)*

| | |
|---|---|
| 4 eggs, that is ½ lb | cinnamon |
| ½ lb, or 1 glass, sugar | ingredients for icing and other |
| ½ lb butter |     decorations |
| ½ lb, or 1½ glasses, flour | about 1½ glasses jam |
| nutmeg | |

### 1618  Torte from short pastry with fresh berries

*(Tort iz razsypchatago testa so svezhimi jagodami)*

Prepare a dough from short pastry, roll it out, place it in a paper casing, and top with 3 glasses gooseberries that are not completely ripe. Before using the berries, clean them, scald them with boiling water, cool, and drain them in a coarse sieve. Then arrange the berries on the torte after sprinkling them with ½ glass fine sugar and a little cinnamon. Bake and serve hot. Or, rinse in cold water 3 glasses of thoroughly picked over raspberries, wild strawberries, currants, or cherries, and turn into a fine sieve. After they have dried, mix them with sugar and cinnamon, arrange in the torte, and bake, having surrounded the torte with a rim of its dough. Or bake the torte first, add the berries, and bake again.

### 1620  Torte from short pastry with prunes

*(Tort iz razsypchatago testa s chernoslivom)*

Bake a very thin rimmed layer from short pastry.

Scald 1 lb prunes with boiling water, cover and set aside for awhile, then drain in a coarse sieve. Stone and finely chop the prunes. Boil a thick syrup from 1 lb sugar and ¾ glass wine and add 1 lb scalded and coarsely pounded almonds. Add the prunes, finely chopped lemon zest, and a little fine cinnamon and cloves. Place on coals, stirring, so that all this dries out slightly. Cool, fold in 6 beaten egg whites, pile into the baked layer of short pastry, and place in the summer oven. After removing it from the oven, cool, glaze, and decorate with jelly, fruits, etc.

INGREDIENTS *(for 6 persons)*

| | |
|---|---|
| 1 glass, or ½ lb, prunes | *For dough* |
| 1 glass, or ½ lb, almonds | ½ spoon sour cream |
| ⅓ lb, or ⅔ glass, sugar | ¼ lb butter |
| ¼ glass wine | 1½ glasses flour |
| cinnamon and cloves | ½ egg |
| 2 egg whites | ¼ glass sugar |
| lemon zest | ½ wineglass rum |
| | ingredients for icing and decorations |

### 1625  Torte filled with sweet bechamel*

*(Tort napolnennyj sladkim beshemelem)*

Bake 2 layers, one with a rim, and fill the rimmed layer with sweet bechamel. For 6 persons, mash ½ spoon very fresh butter with ½ glass flour, dilute with 2 glasses cream, and add lemon zest and ⅓ glass fine sugar. Boil thoroughly to thicken, remove from the fire, and immediately beat in 2 egg yolks, stirring briskly. Pass the sauce through a fine sieve and let it cool. Fill the torte with the bechamel, cover with the other layer, glaze, and serve.

The bechamel may be varied as desired. Instead of lemon zest, vanilla or cinnamon may be added, or orange flower water, or finely pounded bitter or sweet almonds or pistachios. Or instead of 2 glasses cream, use 1 glass cream and 1 glass strong coffee, and instead of ½ glass flour, use ¼ glass flour and ⅓ lb grated chocolate, etc.

This same torte may be baked from either short pastry (above) or biscuit dough. Glaze with an appropriate icing; for example, chocolate icing goes with bitter almonds, vanilla, or rum, while icing with orange flower water goes with bechamel and sweet almonds, etc.

*This recipe, which is unusually flexible, demonstrates an easy familiarity with both the processes and ingredients involved. Molokhovets clearly was comfortable with substitutions and recognized that the recipe could be adapted readily to whatever supplies were available.*

### 1628  Chinese torte*

*(Tort kitajskij)*

Beat 1 lb butter until white, adding 8 eggs and 8 egg yolks one by one. Add ¼ lb blanched, grated sweet almonds, 1 lb sugar, 12 hard-boiled egg yolks rubbed through a fine sieve, the zest from 2 lemons, ¼ *lot* cinnamon, and ½ lb flour. Mix all this as well as possible and bake 5 round layers on paper. [Set the layers aside to cool,] then stack them one on top of another, interspersing them with the following cream: Mix together 1½ glasses sour cream, ½ glass sugar beaten until white with 8 egg yolks, a little cinnamon, and the zest from 1 lemon. Place in a saucepan on top of the stove and beat with a whisk until it thickens, but do not let it boil. Remove from the fire, spread this cream over the layers, cover with saffron icing, and decorate with fruits, etc.

INGREDIENTS

| | |
|---|---|
| ⅓ lb butter | For the cream |
| 3⅔ eggs plus 2⅔ egg yolks | ½ glass sour cream |
| ¼ glass almonds | about 6 pieces sugar |
| ½ lb, or ⅔ glass, sugar | 3⅔ egg yolks |
| 4 hard-boiled egg yolks | cinnamon |
| ½ teaspoon cinnamon | zest from ⅓ lemon |
| ⅙ lb, or ½ glass, flour | ingredients for saffron icing and for |
| zest from ⅔ lemon | designs |

*Although there is nothing Chinese about either the ingredients or the preparation of this torte, its name—as often happens—might have derived from a torte that was served in the Café Chinois on Nevskij Prospect (#18, at the Police Bridge by the Mojka Canal). A café of that name was founded in 1830 by two Swiss bakers from Davos, Tobias Branger (Béranger) and Salomon Wolf, and the business continued until 1876. It was also known as the Café Wulf [sic] et Beranger, and later as Frères Wolf au Pont de la Police. It was at this café that the poet Pushkin stopped off to meet his second on the way to his fatal duel with d'Anthès. (Kaiser, Fast ein Volk von Zuckerbäkern? 145; Blue Guide Moscow and Leningrad, 269.)*

### 1641  Biscuit torte

*(Tort biskvitnyj)*

Beat 12 egg yolks with 1 glass fine sugar until white. Add the zest from 2 lemons, sprinkle on ¾ glass potato flour and ½ glass wheat flour, and mix everything thoroughly. Fold in 12 beaten egg whites, pour into a buttered paper casing or a tin form lined with buttered paper, and pop into the oven. For 24 persons, bake 1 layer from these proportions, and stack with a chocolate torte and a layer of marzipan.

For 6 persons, halve the ingredients.

INGREDIENTS

12 eggs
½ lb sugar
¾ glass potato flour

½ glass wheat flour
zest from 2 lemons

# 16
# Mazurkas and Other Small Pastries

## (Mazurki i prochee melkoe pirozhnoe)

### MAZURKAS
#### (Mazurki)

*Remarks:* The same rules for baking tortes, such as beating the butter, egg yolks, and sugar until white, etc., apply to baking mazurkas and other small pastries.

A mazurka should be a flat rectangle, half as thick as your finger, and as large as a half- or full-sheet of paper,* according to the proportions. A mazurka for 6–9 persons should be no bigger than a half-sheet of paper, and perhaps even smaller. It may be surrounded with a narrow rim of the same or some other pastry. The top is covered with icing and decorated with fruits, jam, etc., or it may be served without icing, simply covered with shredded almonds, currants, and sugar. If small pieces of pastry are desired, the mazurka should be removed from the oven after it has baked but before it has completely dried out. Cut it with a sharp knife into rectangles or other shapes and return them to the oven to dry out. (Proportions are for 6–9 persons. For a large mazurka, double the proportions).

*The standard size of a piece of paper must have been at least nine inches wide and perhaps double that length. This we know from Molokhovets' direction to cut a circle with a diameter of 5 vershok (8.75 inches or 22 cm) from a half sheet of paper. (See Chapter 15, Remarks on Tortes.)*

### 1647 Marzipan mazurka
#### (Mazurek iz martsipana)

Slightly dry out ½ lb blanched sweet almonds and pound them in a mortar with 2 egg whites and ⅜ to ½ lb sugar. Transfer to a saucepan and add enough egg whites to moisten the mixture without letting it become too thin. Place over hot coals and stir until the mixture becomes hot. Remove from the fire, turn out onto paper dusted with sugar, roll up, and set aside until cool. Remove from the paper and roll out onto a half sheet of paper, sprinkling with sugar. Trim the edges, roll out the scraps again, cut into strips, and surround the mazurka with them. Transfer to a baking sheet and bake until golden. Remove from the sheet, glaze, dry out [in the oven], and decorate with jam, fruits, etc.

INGREDIENTS

½ lb, or 1½ glasses, almonds
⅜ lb, or ¾ glass, sugar
3–4 egg whites

ingredients for icing and other
   decorations

### 1650  Mazurka from boiled egg yolks
*(Mazurek iz varenykh zheltkov)*

Beat 10 hard-boiled egg yolks until smooth, add about ⅜* glass cold, clarified butter, ½ glass sugar, the zest from ½ lemon, ¾ glass flour, and 1–2 raw eggs. Mix for an hour or more. Place ½ sheet of buttered paper on a baking sheet, spread the dough on top, and set in the oven after baking bread. Glaze and decorate, or simply cover with jam.

INGREDIENTS

10 egg yolks
½ glass clarified butter*
½ glass sugar
zest from 1 lemon

¾ glass flour
ingredients for icing and other
   decorations, or 1–1½ glasses jam

    *The discrepancy is in the original text.*

### 1653  Mazurka with wine
*(Mazurek s vinom)*

In a cold place knead together 1 glass fresh sour cream, ⅓ lb sugar, ½ glass wine, 1⅓ eggs, the juice and zest from ½ lemon, and flour. Roll out, place on a buttered baking sheet, paint the top with wine, sprinkle with coarsely ground sugar and chopped almonds, and bake.

INGREDIENTS

1 glass sour cream
⅓ lb, or ⅔ glass, sugar
½ glass wine
1½ eggs
½ lemon

nearly 2 glasses flour
½ spoon butter
½ glass almonds
1 spoon sugar

### 1658  Mazurka from store goods*

*(Mazurek iz bakalij)*

Thoroughly combine 1 cup each raisins, sultanas, sugar, and whole blanched almonds, and 1 cup [total] of finely chopped dried figs, candied peel, and lemon rind. Stir in a little ground clove and cinnamon, almost 1 cup flour, and 3 small eggs. Spread the mixture as thick as a finger on wafers arranged in several rows. Dry out in a summer oven and cover with chocolate icing.

*\*This recipe exemplifies the sharp distinction that was made between goods that were produced at home on one's own estate or farm and those which had to be purchased.*

## PETITS FOURS OR SMALL BAKED GOODS
### *(Melkoe pirozhnoe)*

Proportions are for 6 persons. For 12, 18, or more persons, do not increase the proportions but bake several sorts of cookies.

### 1662  English biscuits, another way

*(Pirozhnoe anglijskoe inache)*

Prepare a dough from ¼ lb fresh butter, ¾ lb flour, ¼ lb sugar, and 1½ eggs. Divide the dough in half, roll out each half, paint with egg, sprinkle with sugar, and bake. Remove from the oven and spread one sheet of pastry with thick apple, cherry, or bergamot [pear] fruit purée. Cover with the other half, cut into portions, and serve.

INGREDIENTS

¼ lb butter
¾ lb, or 2¼ glasses, flour
¼ lb, or ½ glass, sugar

¾–1 glass fruit purée
1 spoon sugar
2 eggs

### 1665  Almond pastries with pistachios

*(Pirozhnoe mindal'noe s fistashkami)*

Blanch ⅙ lb sweet almonds, 6–7 bitter almonds, and 1/12 lb pistachios. Chop very fine, adding ½ spoon orange flower water and, if necessary, 1 egg white. Sprinkle on a little vanilla powder and ⅕ lb sugar. Mix thoroughly, add beaten egg whites (7 egg whites in all), and pour into paper casings. When the pastries are half cooked, cut them into various shapes and return them to the oven.

## 1670  Cream cookies

*(Pirozhnoe slivochnoe)*

Beat 3 spoons clarified butter until white. While continuing to beat, add 1 egg, 1 egg yolk, 6 spoons cream, 4 pieces sugar, 1½ glasses flour, and, if desired, a little cinnamon or lemon zest. Set aside in a cold place. Roll out the dough to the thickness of the blunt side of a knife and transfer to a buttered baking sheet. Cut, or more exactly, mark rectangles on the dough with a knife and paint them with 1 egg yolk beaten with 1 spoon cream. Sprinkle with finely chopped almonds and currants that have been scalded with boiling water and dried. Take the sheet of pastry directly from the cold and set it in a hot oven to bake briefly, just enough to brown and dry out slightly. Let the pastry cool, then break it carefully along the marked lines.

Or roll out the dough, cut into various shapes, place on a buttered baking sheet, and paint with cream beaten with an egg yolk. Transfer from the cold directly into a hot oven for a short time to brown the cookies and dry them out slightly. Sprinkle with sugar and cinnamon. Yields 24 pieces.

INGREDIENTS

| | |
|---|---|
| 3 spoons, or ⅑ lb,* butter | ⅛ lb, or ¼ glass, sugar |
| 2 eggs | 1½ glasses flour |
| 6 spoons cream | 1 spoon cream |
| (lemon zest, or cinnamon, or | 1 spoon sugar and cinnamon |
|   almonds) | (½ glass each almonds and currants) |

*According to Molokhovets' own Table of Weights and Measures, 1 spoon butter equaled ⅛ lb.*

## 1672  Poppy seed cookies

*(Pirozhnoe s makom)*

Prepare dough #1670, roll out until thin, stamp out circles with a glass, transfer them to buttered paper, and cover with the following mixture: Scald ½ glass poppy seeds with boiling water, cover, and set aside 1 hour. Pour off the water, squeeze the poppy seeds dry in a napkin, grind in a stoneware bowl, and add ¼ lb sugar, some cinnamon, and 2 eggs. Mix, spread on top of the dough, and bake.

## 1679  Anise cornets

*(Trubochki s anisom)*

Beat ⅜ lb sugar and 4½ eggs with a whisk on top of the stove until the mixture whitens and thickens. Remove from the heat and cool, beating constantly. Sprinkle on a little anise and ⅜ lb flour. Mix thoroughly, spread thinly on a buttered baking sheet, and bake. After removing the sheet of pastry from the oven, cut it into several pieces. Roll each piece gently into a tube, dry out, and sprinkle with sugar.

INGREDIENTS

3/8 lb, or 3/4 glass, sugar
5 eggs
1 spoon anise*

3/8 lb, or 1 1/3 glasses, flour
1/2 spoon butter

*In the twentieth edition, the words for pineapple (ananas) and anise (anise) have been confused, a mistake not made in the first edition. Although this seems to be a large amount of anise for the flour—1 lozhka being about 2 American tablespoons—Molokhovets clearly had a variable image of the term, sometimes meaning a small spoon but mostly a large one. In this case, I assume she meant a small spoon.

## 1683 English cheese cookies*

(Syr anglijskij)

Beat 1/4 lb fresh unsalted butter until white. Add 1/4 lb sugar, 8 egg yolks, 1/2 large wineglass rum, 1/4 lb of the very best flour, a handful of washed and dried currants, and, finally, 8 beaten egg whites. Mix, fill small buttered paper casings or tin pans, and bake in a hot oven.

INGREDIENTS

1/4 lb butter
1/4 lb, or 1/2 glass, sugar
8 eggs
1/2 wineglass rum

1/4 lb, or 3/4 glass, flour
3/4 glass currants
1/2 spoon butter

*I have not found an explanation of why these were called English cheese cookies.

## 1687 Apples in puff pastry

(Jabloki v sloenom teste)

Prepare puff pastry from 1/2 lb butter and 2/3 lb flour. Roll out the dough until very thin and cut it into rectangles. Peel and core apples. (If the apples are large, halve or quarter them.) Place a piece of apple on each rectangle of dough and bring together the edges of the dough into a kind of envelope, or fold like a book. Paint the top with egg, but not the sides. Sprinkle with coarsely pounded sugar mixed with ground rusk crumbs and bake in a hot oven.

For 12 people double the proportions, and for 18, triple them.

INGREDIENTS

½ lb butter                          4–6 apples
⅔ lb, or 2 glasses, flour            1 egg
¼ glass sugar                        1 rusk

### 1688 Cookies, like *pirozhki*, from puff pastry with jam or sabayon*

(*Sloenye pirozhki s varen'em ili sabaionom*)

Prepare puff pastry from ½ lb butter and ⅔ lb flour. Roll out the dough, stamp out round *pirozhki* with a pastry cutter or glass, and stack in pairs. Leave the lower disk whole, but cut out a small circle from the center of the upper one. Paint everything with egg, including the small cut-out circles, and bake in a hot oven.

After the cookies are baked, fill the hollows with jam or fruit purée, or fill with the following sabayon: Beat 2 egg yolks, sugar, and 1 wineglass wine with a whisk on top of the stove until it thickens. Remove from the heat and set aside on ice. After it has cooled, fill the hollows with this cream. Cover with the small baked circles, decorate the top with jam or jelly, and sprinkle with sugar.

INGREDIENTS

½ lb butter                          1 wineglass wine
⅔ lb, or 2 glasses, flour            3 pieces sugar
(1 egg)                              1 spoon sugar
½ glass jam                          jelly
Or 2 egg yolks [for the sabayon]

*These cookies resemble certain pirozhki in shape, hence their name. Cf. Chapter 2.

### 1689 Cookies with meringue

(*Pirozhnoe s meringoju*)

Beat ¼ lb unsalted butter and ⅛ lb sugar until white and add ⅜ lb flour and ½ egg. Mix all this as well as possible, spread thinly on paper, and bake. Cool, spread with fruit purée, and cover with beaten egg whites mixed with ¼ lb sugar and vanilla. Using a sharp knife, cut into oblong *pirozhki*, sprinkle with sugar, sieving it through muslin, and bake for 5 minutes, or just enough to brown the tops very lightly.

INGREDIENTS

¼ lb butter                          ⅜ lb, or 1⅛ glass, flour
⅛ lb, or ¼ glass, sugar              1 egg

¾–1 glass fruit purée
4 egg whites
¼ lb, or ½ glass, sugar

about ¼ teaspoon vanilla
1 spoon sugar

### 1690 Viennese chocolate doughnuts or buns

*(Pyshki ili ponchki venskija shokoladnyja)*

Mix 6 egg yolks with ⅜ lb sugar until white. Add ⅜ lb flour and 6 beaten egg whites. Mix carefully, press out from a paper tube or canvas bag to form small round *pirozhki*, sprinkle with sugar, and bake. Or, to keep the pastry from spreading and to ensure that the circles are the same size, bake them in small round pans (1 *vershok* in diameter). After they have finished baking, hollow out these buns (*pirozhki*) from underneath and fill with whipped heavy cream and sugar (½ glass cream, about 2–4 pieces sugar, and, if desired, a little vanilla). Stack in pairs, dip in chocolate, lay on a wire rack, and place in the summer oven for several minutes.

Prepare the chocolate as follows: Bring to a boil ⅛ lb chocolate, ½ lb sugar, and 2 glasses milk. Strain and reboil until the mixture thickens and is reduced to 1½ glasses. Remove from the fire and beat with a wooden spoon until the liquid cools and begins to form a thin membrane. Dip the buns in this chocolate. Yields 13–15 pairs.

INGREDIENTS

6 eggs
⅜ lb, or ¾ glass, sugar
⅜ lb, or 1¼ glasses, flour
½ glass very thick cream

⅓ or ¼ lb chocolate, that is, ½–1
   tablet
½ lb sugar
2 glasses milk

### 1691 Oblong pastries with coffee bechamel

*(Prodolgovatoe pirozhnoe s kofejnym beshemelem)*

Bring to a boil 4 spoons clarified butter and 8 spoons milk, add 12 level spoons flour, and mix until smooth. Remove from the heat, cool, stir in 2 eggs, and beat the dough with a spatula until it begins to leave the sides of the pan. Turn the dough out onto the table and roll it into 24 cylinders, each 2 *vershok* long. Sprinkle them lightly with flour (in all ¼ spoon, not more), arrange them on a baking sheet, and place it in the oven.

Make a roux from 2 spoons clarified butter and ¼ glass flour, dilute with ½ glass strong coffee mixed with 3 spoons cream, and add 4 pieces of sugar. Bring to a boil, stirring; remove from the stove and cool. Cut each piece of pastry in half lengthwise, spread each half with the prepared coffee bechamel, and stick the halves back together. Meanwhile, in a very small saucepan on top of the stove, cook ½ lb sugar with 1 glass strong coffee until the syrup thickens and is reduced to 1 glass. Cool, stirring with a spatula until the color dulls,* then add the squeezed juice from ½ lemon, stirring constantly. Dip each piece of the prepared pastry in this mixture and place on a wire rack. After the pastries have dried, arrange them on a napkin on a platter and serve. These pastries may be served with any kind of mousse.

INGREDIENTS

| | |
|---|---|
| ¼ lb butter | 3 full teaspoons ground coffee |
| 8 spoons milk, or ⅓ glass | 2 eggs |
| 1½ glass flour | ½ lb sugar |
| juice from ½ lemon | 3 spoons cream |

*Literally, Molokhovets wrote "until the mixture turns gray" (poka massa ne sdelaetsja serago tsveta).

### 1693 Almond wreaths, another way

*(Mindal'nye venchiki drugim manerom)*

Finely chop ⅔ lb blanched sweet almonds, dry them, and add ⅛ lb fine sugar, 2 spoons orange-flower water, and 2 beaten egg whites. Mix everything together, press out wreaths from a tin cookie press (*iz zhestjannoj formy*)* onto a baking sheet greased with white [bees'] wax, and set in the oven.

*Since Molokhovets did not specify the type of "tin form," I am assuming that she meant a cookie press such as is used for making spritz cookies.

### 1695a Chocolate pastries with poppy seeds

*(Shokoladnoe pirozhnoe drugim manerom)*

Finely pound ⅛ lb blanched sweet almonds with 1 egg white and ¼ lb each sugar and grated chocolate. Add 1 spoon water, mix everything together, and add 2 spoons finely ground rye rusk .crumbs. Form into small ringlets, sprinkle with some more rusk crumbs, and bake. When the ringlets have dried, glaze them with a white icing, sprinkle with variously colored poppy seeds and return to the oven for several minutes. Yields 18 pieces.

INGREDIENTS

| | |
|---|---|
| ¼ lb chocolate | *For the icing* |
| ¼ lb sugar | ¼ lb sugar |
| ⅛ lb, or ⅜ glass, almonds | 1 egg white |
| 1 egg white | juice from ½ lemon |
| ⅔ glass rye rusk crumbs | ⅛ glass colored poppy seeds |

### 1696  Choux pastry

*(Petishu zavarnoe)*

Place in a saucepan on top of the stove ²⁄₃ glass clarified and melted, pure, fresh Finnish butter and enough water to make 2 glasses of liquid. Add a piece of sugar, bring to a boil, and pour on all at once 1½ glasses flour, stirring briskly until smooth. Keep on top of the stove, but not on the open fire, for at least ½ hour so that the flour thoroughly cooks, and stir the dough frequently with a wooden spoon. Then, right there on top of the stove, beat 6 very good, whole eggs (on no account use less than 6 eggs) into the hot dough, and stir until smooth. Immediately spoon out small heaps of dough onto a lightly buttered baking sheet. Moisten your finger with water and make holes in each mound of dough so that it resembles a pretzel (*krendel'*). Sprinkle with fine sugar and bake for 15 minutes. Yields 24 pieces. Some people cool the dough before adding the eggs and then beat the dough for a long time.

Lemon zest may be added to the dough, and the pastries may be sprinkled with finely chopped almonds (¼ glass or more) in addition to sugar.

These may be served at dinner instead of cookies and are also good with tea or coffee.

INGREDIENTS

| | |
|---|---|
| ½ lb Finnish butter | (¼ glass almonds) |
| 1½ glass flour | 6 pieces sugar |
| 6 eggs | |

### 1699  Apple kisses

*(Beze\* jablochnoe)*

Bake 5 large apples, rub through a fine sieve, and add 1½ glasses, or ¾ lb, fine sugar and 1 egg white. Surround the pan with ice or snow and stir for at least 2 hours in a saucepan until the mixture whitens and thickens sufficiently for a spoon to stand upright. Then spoon out small heaps onto paper or fill small paper cases 2 *vershok* long and almost ¾ *vershok* wide and high. Dry out the kisses in a low oven, then remove the papers, arrange the cookies on a platter, and keep them in a warm oven until served. Yields 40 pieces.

\*Beze *comes from the French* (baiser, *to kiss*).

### 1702  Meringues with whipped cream\*

*(Beze so sbitymi slivkami)*

Whip 4–5 egg whites and fold in ½ lb sugar. Divide the meringue in half, spread each half smoothly on a quarter sheet of paper, making it ½–2 fingers thick, and bake for several hours to dry out completely.

Whip ¾ glass thick cream, add ⅛ lb sugar and a little vanilla, and spread over 1 layer. Cover with the other layer, cut with a very sharp knife into 12–14 pieces, and serve.

*In France these are called* Meringues Chantilly.

### 1704  Cookies with wine custard

*(Pirozhnoe s zavarnym kremom)*

Beat until white 6 egg yolks, 6 spoons sugar, and the grated zest from ½ lemon. Stir in 2 full spoons clarified butter and 5 level silver spoons flour. Finally, fold in 6 beaten egg whites.

Butter a copper baking sheet or a shallow paper casing made from a half sheet of paper. Pour in the mixture, smooth it out, and bake. When the batter is half cooked, remove from the oven, mark out rectangles, and return to the oven to finish baking. Take out of the oven, cut into pieces with a thin knife, and remove from the baking sheet. Hollow out the bottoms slightly, leaving the edges intact, and fill with wine custard. Level off and stick together so that the custard is not visible. Set in a warm oven; then arrange on a napkin on a platter.

### 1705  Wine custard

*(Krem zavarnoj)*

Beat with a whisk over the fire 4 egg yolks, ⅜ lb fine sugar, the zest from ¼ lemon, the juice from 1½ lemons and 2 oranges, ½ wineglass Madeira, and 1 spoon white rum until the mixture thickens. Then set [the pan] on the edge of the stove and beat constantly while someone else uses a spoon to fill the cookies with the custard, as indicated above.

### 1706  Ringlets with cinnamon

*(Kolechki\* s koritseju)*

Mix 5 hard-boiled egg yolks, ⅛ lb fresh butter, ¼ glass sugar, 1 raw egg, ¾ glass flour, and finely ground cinnamon. Beat everything together, first with a wooden spoon and then with your hands for at least 15 minutes. Form into ringlets, dip them in cinnamon and sugar, and place on a baking sheet dusted with flour. The heat must be very low for baking these cookies. Yields 24 ringlets.

Or make flat, round cakes from the dough, paint with egg, and sprinkle on finely pounded almonds.

INGREDIENTS

⅛ lb butter                                         5 eggs

½ glass sugar in all

¾ glass flour

1 full teaspoon cinnamon

[1 raw egg]

*What were called pretzels (krendel'ki) in the first edition have become ringlets (kolechki) in the twentieth. Otherwise the recipes differ only slightly, with the raw egg and the final suggestion for alternative shaping added in the later edition.*

### 1714 Short pastry covered with apples and glazed with applesauce or a purée of apricots and prunes

*(Pirozhnoe iz razsypchatago testa, pokrytoe jablokami i jablochnoju ili abrikosnoju massoju s chernoslivom)*

Knead an ordinary thick dough from ⅔ lb (or 2 glasses) flour, ⅓ lb butter, and approximately ½ glass water, including a little rum. Roll out the dough until it is rather thin and shape it into a long rectangular pie shell with turned-up edges. Peel 3–5 sweet apples and cut into very thin half slices. Arrange rows of apple slices on the dough, overlapping them attractively. Sprinkle ¼ glass sugar over the apples, paint the rim of dough with egg, and bake. Meanwhile, finely shred 2–3 peeled tart apples or 6 apricots and place them in a saucepan. Add ⅓ lb scalded prunes, a little lemon zest, 1 finely torn up sheet of gelatin, ½ glass sugar, 1½–2 glasses water, and, if desired, 1 spoon rum. Boil until the mixture softens and thickens, rub though a fine sieve, and spread over the baked pie. To serve, cut with a very sharp knife into even, oblong pieces.

The same pie may be covered with jam, applesauce, or a purée made from cherries, fresh plums, or boiled sieved prunes. Using the same dough, prepare a lattice for the top, paint with egg, and bake. Cut into oblong pieces, sprinkle with sugar, or cover with a meringue made from 2 egg whites and ¼ lb fine sugar, and return briefly to the oven.

INGREDIENTS

⅔ lb, or 2 glasses, flour

⅓ lb butter

¾ glass fine sugar

1 egg to paint the dough

3–5 sweet apples

2–3 tart apples, or 6 apricots and ⅓ lb, or ¾ glass, prunes

(1 spoon rum, lemon zest)

### 1716 Marzipan, another way

*(Martsipany drugim manerom)*

Scald, peel, and dry 1 lb sweet almonds, including several bitter almonds. Finely pound and sieve the almonds and repound any large pieces that remain with the sugar. Finely pound 1 lb sugar, sieve, and mix with the almonds. Thoroughly beat this mixture, moistening it with rosewater. As soon as possible, put the mixture into small heart-shaped pans and leave until it dries out, otherwise it will break. Set the pans on a baking sheet, cover with another convex baking sheet, place hot coals on top, and bake.

For the icing, finely pound ¼ lb sugar or a little more, mix with 2 spoons rosewater or *pois de senteur*,* [sic] and beat with a spoon for 2–3 hours. When the marzipan are cool, cover them with this icing, dry out a little in the oven, and decorate with white icing, pressing it out from a paper tube into various designs. Fill any gaps in the designs with fruits, jelly, etc. Instead of white icing, the pastry may be given an attractive rim of that same dough, using a special utensil. Lacking [that gadget], incisions may be made in thin strips of dough with a penknife to give the strips the appearance of a braided or waving ribbon (*vid ploenoj lentochki*). Surround the confections with them and decorate with fruits, jelly, etc.

*This sounds like an erratum. Pois de senteur is a legume or variety of pea, which seems like a novel and not very effective way to flavor a marzipan. Eau de senteur, on the other hand, seems more plausible since it includes flavorings such as rosewater and orange flower water.*

### 1720  Buns in the Hamburg style

*(Zavarnyja pyshki po-gamburgski)*

Bring to a boil ⅔ bottle milk and ⅓ lb butter. Add 2 glasses flour and mix until smooth and until the dough thickens and begins to pull away from the sides of the saucepan. Let the dough cool, then add ¼ glass sugar, 1 *zolotnik* cinnamon, and the zest from ½ lemon. Beat in 5 large eggs, mix, press out ringlets with a canvas pastry tube, sprinkle with sugar and chopped almonds, and bake in the oven.

### 1721  Sour cream pastries, baked in small pans

*(Pirozhnoe iz smetany ispechenoe v formochkakh)*

Prepare a yeast dough from 1 full glass milk, ½ glass soft Finnish butter, a small spoon salt, ½ spoon very thick yeast, and approximately 1 lb flour. Mix well, knead, and let the dough rise once thoroughly.

Butter 12–15 small, round, smooth pans, or rings without bottoms. Roll the dough rather thinly, cut out flat cakes with the rings, and set them (with the rings) onto a lightly buttered baking sheet. When the cakes have risen, cover them with the following mixture (i.e., fill the pans): Beat 5 egg yolks until white with ½ glass finely sieved sugar and sprinkle on the finely ground seeds from 3 cardamom pods, 1–1½ pieces ground mace, ⅓ glass currants (scalded with boiling water, cleaned, and dried), 1⅓ glasses very fresh sour cream, and ⅓ glass flour. Mix thoroughly and, finally, fold in 5 beaten egg whites. Mix, fill the pans, and bake.

INGREDIENTS

*For the dough*
1 full glass milk
½ glass soft Finnish butter
½ spoon very thick yeast
salt
1 lb flour

*For the topping*
5 eggs

½ glass fine sugar
3 cardamom pods
1 or 1½ pieces mace
⅓ glass currants
1½ glasses sour cream
⅔ glass flour

# 17
# Babas, Buns, Rusks, and Small Baked Goods

*(Baby malorossijskija i pol'skija na drozhzhakh, baby na sbitykh belkakh, bulki i kulichi, strutseli, mazurki, pljatski, sukhari, krendeli i prochee melkoe pechen'e k chaju, kofe ili shokoladu)*

[*Translator's note:* This chapter on babas and pastries is distinctive as much for its variety of recipes as for its prodigious use of ingredients. The recipes evoke a vanished era. No homemaker today would use 70 egg yolks in a single cake. Aside from considerations of health and expense, we no longer have the equipment for baking such large babas, nor do we ordinarily expect to feed so many people.

Babas, cakes, and pastries were adopted by the Russians only in the eighteenth century, although yeast had been used in Russia since ancient times. German and Polish influences are particularly strong in this type of baking. It is perhaps not surprising that Americans are unfamiliar with the variety of babas and *kuliches* that were well known to Molokhovets—Russian cookbooks for Americans rarely contain more than a single recipe for each kind of yeast cake. But Russian cooks also are in danger of losing this aspect of their culinary heritage, which now appears mostly in specialized books on baking. In part, the nomenclature has changed (*pirogi* has broadened in meaning), but mostly altered tastes and circumstances have diminished the interest in baking. Most Russian cookbooks now devote relatively little space to recipes for cakes and pastries; among the few that are included, recipes for Eastern pastries and for frosted European cakes have replaced those for sweet yeast cakes and buns. As a case in point, the recent Soviet reprint of a selection of Molokhovets' recipes for sweet dishes included none of the recipes from the present chapter.]

# YEAST BABAS
## (Baby na drozhzhakh)

*Remarks:* The success of babas depends most of all on the yeast, then on the oven, and finally on the dryness of the flour.

Only the very best white and thick yeast should be used, and it must be corked up and stored in a cold place. Making yeast babas requires approximately 6–7 hours: for example, if the dough is prepared at nine o'clock in the morning, then the babas will be ready to be taken from the oven at three or four o'clock. Buns require just as much time.

If using dry yeast, take 4, or even 5, *zolotniki* for every 4 lbs of flour. Where I have indicated ½ glass of fresh yeast, substitute dry yeast dissolved in ½ glass of milk. One *garnets* of flour equals approximately 5 lbs.

The oven must be made extremely hot and then allowed to cool a little before using. For babas, the oven must be hotter than for ordinary buns.

The flour must be the very best, both dry and sieved.

The yolks must be carefully separated from the whites. They should be beaten thoroughly, then strained and beaten in a churn* until white, or mashed like butter in a stoneware bowl.

Almost all yeast babas must rise three times as follows: Prepare a dough from yeast, flour, milk, and eggs. Beat it with a spatula for half an hour, then cover, and put in a warm place until the yeast barely begins to proof. Beat the dough again with a spatula. Gradually add all the remaining ingredients, beating the dough after each addition and spending in all ¾ to 1 hour. Cover and put in a warm place until the dough doubles in bulk. Then beat it again with a spatula or knead it with your hands for 10 minutes or more. Pile the dough into a baking pan filling it no more than ¼ to ⅓ full. Set it in a warm, but not hot, place. Let the dough rise to fill ¾ of the pan. Then, being as careful as possible not to shake the pan (because then the dough will immediately fall and harden), put it in the oven directly in its designated place so that the pan need not be moved.

Let it bake in the oven a full hour or even an hour and a half if the baba is very high, but do not remove it from the oven before it is fully cooked. Some people, when pouring the dough into the pan, carefully insert 2 thin wisps of straw into two places and gently set the pan with its wisps in the oven. After an hour and 10 minutes, reach into the oven and remove 1 wisp of straw. If it is completely dry and no dough clings to it, the baba is done; otherwise, let the baba remain in the oven a little longer. When it is done, remove it from the oven very carefully. If it was baked in a paper casing, immediately place it on its side on a soft down pillow, covered with a medium-size napkin. Carefully remove the pan and the paper, turning the baba gently from side to side until it is cool; if it rests on just one side, it may become lopsided. Special pans for babas are made of copper or tin ¾ *arshin* high. Some are collapsible, others not, but all have handles and are a little nar-

Baba mold and raisin baba. From Gouffe, *Royal Book of Pastry and Confectionary* (London, 1874).

rower at the base than the top. Sometimes the pans are very attractive with 6 or 8 sides. In that case, the sides of the baba may be glazed in stripes, with various colored icings. Casings for babas are also pasted together from thick paper, 6 *vershok* in diameter and ¾ *arshin* high. Grease the casing with butter, sprinkle with rusk crumbs, and set on a flat lid of a saucepan (i.e., on a sauté pan). Small babas may be baked in a saucepan lined with buttered paper. Let them cool in the saucepan before removing. Similarly, if the baba is baked in a copper or tin pan, do not remove it until it cools, and again, place it on its side on a pillow without disturbing it. Turn it carefully because if it stands upright it may fall over.

In general, the dough for babas should not be thicker, and may even be a little thinner, than that for waffles.

For the third rising, the dough should rise some, but not too much because in that case babas would be hollow, while buns would fall in the oven.

After a baba has risen in a pan in a warm place and has been put into the oven, it must be protected from the cold and from drafts. To avoid any doors being slammed, no one should be allowed into the kitchen while a baba is baking.

The sugar for babas, buns, and other pastries must be very finely pounded and sieved.

Baking babas requires great skill. They often do not succeed even when someone bakes them frequently and skillfully; therefore, sometimes it is difficult to explain the reason for their failure. But since these babas are very tasty with tea and coffee and may be baked at any time, it is better to work with smaller proportions, such as ⅓ of the recipe. That is, bake a baba only 3–4 *vershok* high because, first, it is easier to bake them and they are more likely to succeed, and second, if they fail, it is not such a big loss.

Lemon zest, bitter almonds, cinnamon, cardamom, nutmeg, lemon, bergamot [pear], or rose oil may be added to the dough for flavor and aroma.

The amount of yeast indicated in these recipes refers to white, thick yeast—in a word, to the very best available. If the yeast is not so good, add more and reduce the amount of milk.

Babas may be glazed all over with whatever icing you wish, but mostly they are covered with the following inexpensive icing: for every 3 glasses of fine, sieved sugar, use 1½ glasses of very dry, sieved potato flour, the juice of 1 lemon, and 5 egg whites or a little more. Beat all this in a stoneware bowl until the mixture whitens and thickens. In general, this icing should not be too thick, because a thick icing is hard to spread evenly. This icing, when dry, will crack and fall off.

When babas and buns are baked only from egg yolks, one must devise dishes for dinner to use up the leftover egg whites, such as some sort of soufflé or meringue. Alternatively, bake a snow baba, buns of beaten egg whites, or mazurka, etc.

*In the days before electric beaters, churns of various sizes were a convenient implement for beating the numerous egg yolks that were called for in many of these recipes.

## 1723  Rum baba

### (Baba s romom)

For 6 people prepare a dough from [flour], ⅔ glass warm milk, and a little less than 1 zolotnik dry yeast. Cover, set in a warm place, and, when it has risen, beat as well as possible with a spatula. Add ½ small spoonful salt, beat in 12 whole eggs one by one, and sprinkle on ½ glass sieved sugar. Add ½ lb of the very best soft, but not melted, Finnish butter. A little lemon peel may also be added. Beat with a spatula, the longer the better. Cover, return to a warm place, and, when it has risen, beat thoroughly and pour into a greased pan. Let the dough rise slightly, then place in the oven for ½–¾ hour. Meanwhile, bring to a boil a sweet but watery syrup. Add rum to taste, enough to produce a sufficiently powerful aroma. Remove the baba from the oven and, while still hot, place on its side on a platter, and pour on the hot syrup. Carefully turn the baba several times to absorb the rum. Leave it on the platter to dry out, transfer to another dish, and serve.

INGREDIENTS

⅔ glass milk, nearly 1 zolotnik dry yeast, 1 lb flour, 12 eggs, ½ lb butter, ⅓ glass sugar, and lemon zest. For the syrup: ⅓ glass fine sugar, 1 glass water, and 2–4 spoons rum.

## 1728  Boiled baba

### (Baba zavarnaja)

(¼ arshin high). Scald ¼ garnets flour with ¼ garnets, or 3 glasses, boiling milk and stir until smooth and cool. Mix 6 glasses, or nearly 70, strained egg yolks with 1 lb sieved sugar and beat until white. Stir the beaten eggs and sugar into the dough along with 1½ glasses thick white yeast. Mix, cover, and set in a warm place to rise. Add salt, ½ glass raisins, cinnamon, finely chopped bitter orange rind, 3 glasses melted butter, and enough flour to form a rather liquid dough, as is usual for light babas. Beat a full hour, cover, let rise, and again beat thoroughly. Pour into a baking pan and, when it has risen, set carefully in a hot oven for 1¼ hours. For 6 persons use ⅓ the amount, namely: 1 glass flour, 1 glass milk, 2 glasses, or 24, egg yolks, ⅓ lb sugar, ½ glass yeast, ⅙ glass raisins, 1 glass melted butter, and about another 3 glasses flour.

### 1729  Ukrainian baba

*(Baba ukrainskaja)*

(¾ *arshin* high). Beat 3 glasses unfertilized egg yolks* and ¾ glass egg whites in a butter churn for a full hour. Meanwhile, scald 2⅓ glasses flour with 2¼ glasses boiling milk, cover with a napkin, and set aside for a half hour. Pour 1⅓ glasses yeast into the churn with the eggs and mix. Stir the scalded flour until smooth and add the eggs and yeast from the churn, straining them through a fine sieve. Mix thoroughly, sprinkle the top lightly with flour, cover, and let rise. Add 1 teaspoon salt and 4 to 4½ glasses flour, depending on its dryness, and knead for ½ hour. Add 1⅛ glasses melted butter, 1⅓ glasses sugar, and ⅛ glass bitter almonds or the zest from 1–1½ lemons. Knead until blisters appear in the dough, cover, and let rise. Prepare a casing from thick paper, place it in a saucepan, grease with butter, and pour in the dough, filling the casing ⅓ full. Set in a warm place and, after it has doubled in bulk, bake in a hot oven for 1 hour. After removing the baba from the oven, place it carefully on its side on a pillow, and continue as indicated in the Remarks. (Use ¾ *garnets* flour in all and 5–6 *zolotniki* dry yeast.) For 6 persons, use ⅓ the indicated proportions.

*\*Unfertilized egg yolks were desirable because they would not be marred by spots of blood or, worse yet, by embryo chicks.*

### 1733  Sacramental baba

*(Baba sakramentka)*

(¾ *arshin* high.) Beat 90 strained egg yolks with 2 cups sugar until white, sprinkle on 6 cups flour, and stir constantly for a full hour. Add 2 cups thick yeast and the zest from 1 lemon. Pour into a baking pan, filling only ⅓ of it. When the dough has risen to fill ⅔ of the pan, set in a hot oven for 1 hour. (For 6 persons, use ⅓ the indicated proportions.)

### 1738  A sturdy baba that does not get stale quickly

*(Baba tjazhelaja, kotoraja ne skoro cherstveet)*

[Ingredients:] 1 *garnets* flour, 2¼ glasses melted butter, about 1½ glasses milk, about 1¼ glasses yeast, 30 egg yolks, 15 whole eggs, 1 lb sugar, ½ lb sweet almonds, 15–30 bitter almonds, 1 lb of the best seeded raisins, and ½ lb candied peel or bitter orange rind boiled in sugar.

Warm the milk, stir in the yeast and half the flour, and set aside to rise. Beat the eggs and stir them gradually into the dough. Add the remaining flour and knead until the dough pulls away from your hands. Finally, pour in warm clarified butter and sprinkle on sugar, salt, the almonds, raisins, and candied peel. Mix as well as possible and pour into a pan. When the dough has risen, set in a hot oven for 1¼ hours.

For 6 persons, use ⅓ of the ingredients: ⅓ *garnets*, or about 4 glasses, flour, ¾ glass butter, ½ glass milk, ⅜ glass yeast, 10 egg yolks, 5 whole eggs, ⅔ glass sugar, ½ glass almonds, 5–10 bitter almonds, 1 glass raisins, and ⅙ lb candied peel.

### 1743  Quickly prepared baba for coffee

*(Baba k kofe, prigotovljaemaja na skoruju ruku)*

Beat together 10 eggs, 1 glass cream, ½ glass yeast, 1 glass butter, ½ glass sugar, the zest from 1 lemon, and enough flour to make a dough as thick as that for waffles. Pour into a buttered baking pan or saucepan strewn with rusk crumbs. When the dough has risen, bake in a hot oven.

### 1747  Almond milk baba

*(Baba na mindal'nom moloke)*

Prepare 3¾ glasses almond milk from 1 lb, or 3 glasses, sweet almonds and ¼ lb bitter almonds. Add 4–5 glasses flour, pour in 1 glass yeast, mix, and let rise. Then beat thoroughly with a spatula and add 2 glasses egg yolks and 1 glass egg whites, beaten until white with 1 lb sugar. Add 1½ glasses melted butter, the zest from 1 lemon, and the remaining flour.* Beat the dough with a spatula for at least ½ hour, sprinkle on about ½ lb seedless raisins and some finely chopped bitter orange peel, and pour into a buttered pan strewn with rusk crumbs. When the dough has risen, bake in a hot oven for 1 hour.

For 6 persons use 1 glass sweet almonds, ¼ glass bitter almonds, 1¼ glasses [almond] milk, ⅓ glass yeast, ⅔ glass egg yolks, ⅓ glass egg whites, ⅓ lb sugar, ½ glass melted butter, the zest from ⅓ lemon, ½ glass raisins, bitter orange rind, and flour.*

*Although Molokhovets did not specify the amount of flour in this recipe, she assumed that her readers would know to add enough extra flour to form "a rather liquid dough" (cf. #1728).*

### 1748  Chocolate baba

*(Baba shokoladnaja)*

Pour 60 strained egg yolks into a churn, sprinkle on 1 glass grated chocolate, and beat for ½ hour. Add ¾ glass sugar and 3 glasses flour and beat for another ½ hour. Pour in ¾ glass white yeast, beat for yet another ½ hour, and fill a baking pan half full. When the dough has risen, bake in a hot oven for 1 hour. As soon as the baba has finished baking, immediately remove it from the pan, and place it on its side on a pillow, etc. For 6 persons, use ⅓ the indicated proportions, namely: 20 egg yolks, ⅓ glass chocolate, ¼ glass sugar, 1 glass flour, and ¼ glass yeast.

### 1750  Capricious baba

*(Baba kapriznaja)*

Beat 6 cups egg yolks, strain into a stoneware bowl, sprinkle on 6 full spoons sugar, and beat until white. Add 6 cups flour and 6 spoons very thick yeast, mix, and let rise. Add about 2 cups warm butter, 10 beaten egg whites, and something for flavoring. Beat the dough as well as possible and fill one-third of a baking pan. After it has risen, set in the oven for 1 hour. Remove from the oven, place on a pillow, etc. (For 6 people use ⅓ the indicated proportions.)

This baba is extraordinarily tasty when it succeeds, but it rarely succeeds.*

*This recipe, with its prodigal use of egg yolks (6 glasses = 70 yolks) and its kicker of a last line, is one of the most quoted in the book. For a modern reader, the image of those sixty leftover egg whites is sufficiently daunting; how many cooks would be intrepid enough to risk a second attempt? The outrageous inconsistency between Molokhovets's kopeck-pinching frugality and her occasional offhand extravagance—of which this recipe is the most notable example—is appealing in its timelessness.

### 1757  A high and very light baba

*(Baba vysokaja i ochen' legkaja)*

Mix together ½ garnets flour and ¼ garnets milk as well as possible. Stir in ¾ glass strained yeast, cover, and set in a warm place. When the yeast begins to act, beat the dough with a spatula until smooth. Add some salt and ¼ garnets egg yolks and beat again until smooth. Beat in 1½ glasses warm clarified butter and another ½ garnets flour. Finally, sprinkle on 2 glasses sugar, some cinnamon, ¼ glass or more finely chopped candied peel, and at least ½ glass each raisins and finely chopped bitter almonds. Mix and let stand in a warm place. When the dough has doubled in bulk, beat with a spatula, and pour into a greased pan, filling ¼ of it. When the dough has risen to fill ⅔ of the pan, set it carefully in the oven and leave it for 1¼ hours. (For 6 persons, use ⅓ the indicated proportions.)

## BABAS MADE WITH BEATEN EGG WHITES
*(Baby na sbitykh belkakh)*

*Remarks:* These babas must be baked in buttered paper casings and they must not be removed from the casings until they are cool.

These are not as high as yeast babas. Fill only ¾ of the casing with dough. Bake from ¾–1 hour. The same dough may be used for tortes—which will be flat. They will bake in 40 minutes. Tortes are best baked in tin pans and should not be removed from them until cool. Egg yolks must always be beaten separately with sugar until they whiten and thicken.

### 1761  Lemon baba

*(Baba iz limona)*

Boil 3 lemons until they can be easily pierced with a straw, but do not over-cook, which will release their juice. Dry them in a napkin, halve, discard the seeds, beat the lemons in a stoneware bowl, and rub through a sieve. Beat 18 egg yolks until white with 1½ glasses sieved sugar, mix with the lemons, and fold in 18 beaten egg whites. Mix, pour into a buttered tin pan dusted with flour, and place in an oven that is not too hot. (For 6 persons, use ⅓ the indicated proportions.)

### 1762  Baba made from rye rusks

*(Baba iz rzhanykh sukharej)*

Beat 30 egg yolks and 1 lb sugar until white, sprinkle on 3 *zolotniki* ground and sieved cinnamon, 1½ *zolotniki* each [ground] cloves and star anise, ¾ glass dry, sieved flour* made from rye bread, and 2 spoons fine wheat flour. Mix until smooth. Add 30 beaten egg whites, mix, and pour into a buttered casserole or pan strewn with crumbs made from rye bread. Fill ¾ of the pan and bake for 1½ hours.

¼ lb chocolate may be added to this baba, in which case the fine wheat flour is unnecessary. The rye flour is prepared as follows: Slice pure rye bread, dry it out, grind, and sieve. (For 6 persons, use ⅓ the indicated proportions.)

*Although Molokhovets used the word for flour (muka), the directions at the end of the recipe indicate that she meant dry bread crumbs.*

### 1764  Almond baba

*(Baba mindal'naja)*

Scald and remove the skins from 1 lb sweet and ¼ lb bitter almonds, grind the nuts, and mix in a stoneware bowl for 1 hour, beating in 60 strained egg yolks one by one. After each egg yolk, sprinkle on 1 spoon sugar, ultimately incorporating 1 full pound sugar or even a little more. Add a little nutmeg and, finally, 60 beaten egg whites. Pour into a pan greased with unsalted butter and strewn with rusk crumbs and place in a rather hot oven. (For 6 persons, use ¼ the indicated proportions.)

## 1767  Baba from sour-sweet bread

*(Baba iz kislosladkago khleba)*

(For 6 persons). Trim off the crusts from thin slices of sour-sweet bread, moisten the slices in Muscat de Lunel wine,* dry the slices in the oven without letting them burn, and then grind and sieve the crumbs. Beat 10 egg yolks until white with 1 glass sugar, add ½ teaspoon ground cardamom, ¼ lb finely chopped candied orange peel No. 2,** and ¼ lb, or ⅔ glass, ground sieved rusks; and mix everything together. Add 10 beaten egg whites, mix, pour into a pan, and bake.

*Muscat de Lunel is a sweet, unfortified dessert wine from Languedoc on the French side of the Pyrenees. According to the English wine expert Hugh Johnson, this wine was exported to Russia as early as the late seventeenth century. (Johnson, Vintage: The Story of Wine, 281.)

**This is obviously a prepared product; "No. 2" probably referred either to the quality of the candied orange peel or the quantity.

## 1770  Chocolate baba

*(Baba shokoladnaja)*

Beat 30 egg yolks until white with 1 lb, or 2 glasses, sugar. Gradually add 1 lb grated chocolate, another lb, or 2 glasses, sugar, 1 ground, sieved vanilla bean, and ¾ glass sieved rye rusk crumbs. Beat until smooth. When the mixture thickens and whitens, add 30 beaten egg whites and sprinkle on nearly ⅓ glass potato flour. Pour into a pan and bake. (For a small baba, use only ⅓ the indicated proportions.)

## 1773  *Baumkuchen* (or tree torte)

*(Baumkuchen) (Ili tort drevesnyj)*

Beat ½ garnets clarified butter in a stoneware bowl until white. In another bowl beat egg yolks and sugar until white, ½ garnets of each; then combine the egg yolks with the butter. Add ½ garnets of very dry, sieved flour, beat the reserved egg whites, and add them to the mixture. Bake as follows: Take a wooden mold the same size and shape as a large cone of loaf sugar. Wrap it with paper, wind with rows of thin cord, [and secure the cord.] A small lengthwise slit must be made in the middle of this mold, through which an iron rod or skewer can be passed for attaching the mold to its stand. Generously pour hot, clarified butter over the paper and string so that both are soaked through. Set the stand and mold near the fire and, when the butter grows warm, begin to pour the batter over the mold, placing a pan beneath to catch any drips of batter. Rotate the mold rather quickly, trying to make as many lumps as possible.*

*This decorative and distinctive cake has been made in Germany and Austria since the end of the seventeenth century when recipes for sponge doughs began to appear in cookery books. Initially adopted by the upper classes in Europe, it later became a favorite feast dish among the common people. It is still used at Christmas in Germany and at weddings and birthdays in Austria. To make

Apparatus for making
Baumkuchen. From Marii Redelin,
*Dom i khozjajstvo*, vol. 2 (St.
Petersburg, 1895).

*the cake, the dough was poured over a rotating stake and "turned on the spit like a meat-joint in
front of the fire." As the batter hardened it formed a series of thin layers so that a slice of cake
resembled the concentric rings of a tree stump. (See Gamerith, "Farinaceous Foods in Austria," 95,
115.) It was the custom in Germany at the turn of the century to imprison a small bird such as a
sparrow inside the cake, closing the opening at the top with a bouquet of fresh flowers. At the
moment of serving, the bouquet was removed and the startled creature was allowed to make its
escape. (Barthélemy, "Le gateau de broche," 365.) The lumps mentioned by Molokhovets gave the
finished cone of dough a more treelike appearance. Modern German directions for this cake require
that successive layers of batter be poured onto an overturned cake pan; each layer is baked before
being coated with fresh batter. This yields a solid heap or mound of dough, which is less crisp and
makes a less dramatic presentation than the traditional method described by Molokhovets.*

## BUNS AND *KULICHES*
### *(Bulki i kulichi)*

*Remarks:* The same rules apply for baking buns and *kuliches* as for baking
babas: good yeast, good dry flour, and a hot oven are essential. Although the
amount of flour is mentioned, it cannot be held to blindly because the quality and
dryness of the flour vary. The most important rules are the following:

a) The dough should not be too liquid or the buns will spread in the oven and
be flat. A dough that is too thick is also not good because the buns will be heavy;
they will not taste good and will become stale quickly. The dough must be thick
enough to be cut with a knife, without stretching out after it. Therefore, when
shaping buns or rusks, do not sprinkle on more flour but lightly grease your hands
with butter.

b) Knead the dough and beat it with a small spatula or with your hands as
long as possible, until it does not stick to your hands or the kneading trough or
table.

c) The flour must be very dry and sieved.

d) The dough must rise 3 times; first, when the dough is prepared; second, when it is kneaded; and third, on the baking sheet. Place it in a hot oven and shut the oven door to protect it from any drafts.

e) Set the dough to rise in a warm, but not hot, place where it will be protected from both the cold and drafts; stick spills into the trough, earthenware pot, or saucepan containing the dough and cover the top with a napkin folded several times.

f) When the buns are baked in buttered paper casings, the dough must be as thick as fritter batter.

g) Buns that are baked on sheets and not in paper casings must be painted with an egg beaten with ½ spoon water. Just before setting the buns in the oven, paint the tops with a feather, but not the sides because the egg will prevent them from rising. After removing the buns from the oven, immediately place them with one edge on the table and the other on a low rack, and cover them with a napkin soaked in water and wrung out.

h) If using dry yeast, allow approximately 3 *zolotniki* dry yeast, or 1 kopeck's worth, for every 4 lbs of flour. Additional milk must be added as required for the yeast.

i) *Kuliches* may be baked from any bun dough. Their traditional form is round, like a bun, with a large cross of the same dough on top. When the *kulich* rises, the top, but not the sides, must be painted with egg diluted with 1 spoon water. Sprinkle with chopped almonds, coarse sugar, rusk crumbs, and currants. To help the *kulich* rise evenly, insert a spill into the middle of the *kulich* and keep it there when the *kulich* is put into the oven. After 1 to 1½ hours, depending on the size of the *kulich*, remove the spill. If the dough sticks to it, the *kulich* is still raw; if the spill is completely clean, the *kulich* is done. After removing the *kulich* from the oven, place one end on the table and the other on a rack, allowing the bottom to cool.

### 1778  Buns that will not get stale quickly

*(Bulki, kotoryja dolgo ne cherstvejut)*

Scald 3 glasses, or ¼ *garnets*, flour with 3 glasses of boiling milk, mix until smooth, cover, and let stand for 1 hour. Pour in about 1½ glasses warm milk, ½ glass each thick yeast and sugar, and a little flour. Mix and let rise. Beat the dough thoroughly with a spatula, pour in 1½ glasses butter, and sprinkle on enough flour to make a rather thick dough. After it has risen, shape the dough into buns, and transfer them to a baking sheet. When they have risen, place in a hot oven. (1 *garnets* flour.)

### 1779  Buns that rise in cold water*

*(Bulki, podkhodjashchija v kholodnoj vode)*

Scald 1 glass flour with 1 glass milk. When cool, pour in 1 glass thick yeast, mix until smooth, and let rise. Add 2 glasses each milk and egg yolks, 1 glass whole eggs, and 1½ glasses sugar. Then add lemon zest, 1 glass warm clarified butter, and enough flour to make a non-sticky dough of the usual thickness. Transfer to a buttered linen napkin, tie up loosely to allow room for the dough to expand, and submerge in cold water for 3 hours. When the napkin of dough rises to the surface, remove it from the water, shape the dough into buns, and place them on a baking sheet. When they have risen, paint with egg and set in a hot oven.

*For more on the process of raising yeast doughs in water, see Cooking Techniques in the Introduction.*

### 1780  Leavened buns with wheat bran

*(Bulki na opare iz pshenichnykh otrubej)*

Scald ¼ *garnets* wheat bran with 2 glasses milk and beat thoroughly. When the mixture cools, pour in ½ glass yeast and let rise. Combine a little warm milk with ½ glass clarified butter, pour into ½ *garnets* flour, and mix thoroughly. Strain the leavening from the wheat bran into this dough, sprinkle on sugar and salt, and let rise until doubled in bulk. Form into buns, having greased your hands with butter. Let the buns rise on a baking sheet, paint them with egg, and set in a hot oven.

### 1782  Superb buns

*(Bulki prevoskhodnyja)*

Mix until smooth ¼ *garnets* warm milk, ½ *garnets* very dry flour, and 3 spoons very thick yeast. Set in a warm place to rise and then beat in 5 eggs and 10 egg yolks, beaten with a full teaspoon salt. Add 1 glass sugar, ¾ lb clarified butter, and enough flour to make a rather thick dough. Knead and let the dough rise. Form into buns, paint with egg after they have risen on the baking sheet, and set in a hot oven. (Use nearly 6 lbs flour, or 1¼ *garnets*.)

### 1788  [More] superb buns

*(Bulki prevoskhodnyja)*

Dry out the flour for at least 2 days before using. Pour 1 *garnets* of this well-dried flour into a trough and make a depression in the flour. Mix 1 glass yeast, or more if it is not very fresh, with 20 eggs and ¼ *garnets* milk. Strain into the flour, mix everything together, and let the dough rise for a half hour or more. Then begin to beat the dough with your hands, gradually adding 1 teaspoon salt, 1½ glasses each sugar and clarified butter, and, finally, the remaining flour. After each addition, beat the dough as well as possible until it no longer sticks to your hands. Cover with a piece of linen, but do not let it touch the dough, and set the covered dough in a warm place to rise. When the dough has doubled in bulk and blisters appear on top, form it into small buns without using flour. Instead, grease your hands lightly with butter to prevent the dough from sticking to them. Smooth the tops and set them well apart from each other on a baking sheet. When the buns begin to rise on the baking sheet and blisters appear, use a feather to paint the tops, but not the sides, with an egg wash. Set carefully into a rather hot oven. When they have finished baking, remove them carefully, placing them on the table with one end propped on a wire rack, and cover them with a napkin moistened with water and squeezed out.

If the buns spread in the oven, the flour was not dry enough. Therefore it is always better to prepare a thicker dough and to let it rise thoroughly on the baking sheet. But a dough that is too thick also is not good. (Consequently, use in all 1 glass yeast, 1/4 *garnets*, or 3 glasses, milk, 20 eggs, 1 1/2 glasses sugar, 1 teaspoon salt, 1 1/3 glasses clarified butter, and about 1 1/2 to 1 3/4 *garnets* flour.) If the yeast is dry, use 1 *zolotnik* yeast for every lb of flour, adding milk instead of the yeast liquid.

### 1794  Buns made with water

*(Bulki na vode)*

Prepare a dough from 1/2 *garnets* flour, 4 glasses warm water, and 3/4 glass thick yeast, or an extra 3/4 glass water plus 4 *zolotniki* dry yeast. When the dough has risen, add 1 level tablespoon fine salt, 1/2 glass or more butter, and half the remaining flour. Beat the dough thoroughly and set it in a warm place to rise slightly. Add the remaining flour, knead the dough as well as possible, and let it rise again. Form into buns, and, after they have risen on a baking sheet greased with 1 spoon butter, paint them with boiling water or beer, and place them in the oven. The dough may be made much thinner, in which case, bake the buns in buttered pans. These proportions will yield at least 6 1/2 lbs of buns after baking and cooling.

Poppy seed milk may be used instead of water. Poppy seed buns are made from this dough, the tops of which should be sprinkled with poppy seeds. Caraway seeds may be used instead of poppy seeds.

(Use 5 lbs flour, or 1 *garnets*.)

If these buns are baked for tea, beat 3/4 glass sugar with the butter [and add the sweetened butter to the dough after the first rising.]

### 1800  *Kulich*

*(Kulich)*

Prepare a dough from 6 lbs flour, 1/2 glass good yeast, and 5 glasses milk heated to the temperature of milk fresh from the cow, or a little warmer. When the dough rises, add 10 egg yolks, 5 whole eggs, about 1 lb melted Finnish butter, 2–3 teacups sugar, 1 teaspoon salt, and [for flavoring] ½ teaspoon finely ground cardamom, 10 drops lemon or rose oil, or 1 *lot* vanilla drops. Add about 1 glass each raisins and almonds, saving some for decoration. Knead everything together and let rise. The dough must be rather thick so that it does not stick at all to the table. When the dough has thoroughly risen, light the oven. Punch down the dough, shape it into *kuliches,* and set them to rise in a warm place until the oven is completely ready. There is no need whatsoever to hurry to set the *kuliches* in the oven. Before baking, they need to rise fully, which can take rather a long time because of the heavy dough. After the *kuliches* have risen, paint them with an egg beaten with milk and decorate with raisins and whole or shredded almonds. Almost everyone likes these *kuliches;* the dough is completely different from a bun dough (*bulochnoe*). Saffron *kulich* is made exactly the same, except the cardamom is omitted. For these proportions add ½ teaspoon saffron ground into a powder. Before using the saffron, wrap it well in paper so that it does not lose its fragrance and dry it out in a very warm oven. Mash with butter [when you use it]. More or less saffron may be added according to taste.

INGREDIENTS

| | |
|---|---|
| 6 lbs flour | 2–3 teacups sugar |
| 5 glasses milk | 1 teaspoon salt |
| ½ glass yeast | ½ teaspoon cardamom, or ½ *zolotnik* |
| 10 egg yolks | or more saffron |
| 5 eggs | 1 glass raisins |
| 1 lb butter | 2 eggs to paint the dough |
| 1 glass almonds | |

### 1803  Krendels or braids

(*Krendel'ki, pletenki*)

Mix until smooth ¼ *garnets* warm milk, salt, ¾ glass yeast, and half the indicated amount of flour. Let the dough rise in a warm place and, when the top cracks, beat in 10 egg yolks that have been beaten until white with ¾ glass sugar. Add 10 beaten egg whites and knead the dough, sprinkling on enough flour so that it can be cut on the table with a knife and so that the dough does not stick to the knife. Add 1⅛ glasses clarified butter and lemon zest and knead until blisters appear in the dough and it does not stick to your hands or the trough. Let the dough rise, then roll it out on the table with your hands into small ropes of dough a little thicker in the middle than at the ends. Form into pretzels, or braid them as hair is plaited (*kak kosa*). Place on a greased and floured baking sheet. When they have risen, paint with egg and strew with sugar and cinnamon, currants, and almonds. Bake for 15 minutes. Use in all 1 *garnets* flour and 1 glass thick yeast or 1 glass milk with 6–8 *zolotniki* dry yeast.

### 1806  Rolled cake filled with farmer's cheese for 6 persons

*(Strutseli s tvorogom na 6 chelovek)*

Prepare a dough as indicated above in #1803, using ⅓ the indicated proportions. Mix 1 lb dry farmer's cheese with 4 egg yolks, ½ glass sugar, ½ spoon butter, ½ teaspoon cinnamon, 1 spoon sour cream, and ¼ to ⅓ glass scalded raisins. Spread on the rolled-out dough, which has been lightly buttered, and roll into a tube, etc.

### 1808  Buns with caraway seeds or *Kümmelkuchen*

*(Bulochki s tminom ili Kümmelkuchen)*

These are made from the same dough as #1803. When the dough has risen, form it into small, flat buns, place them on a baking sheet, and make a small depression in the middle of each. Fill [each hole] with ¼ teaspoon caraway seeds, top with ¼ teaspoon fresh butter, paint with egg, and bake for ½ hour.

### 1811  Almond *krendel* or *kulich*

*(Krendel' mindal'nyj ili kulich)*

Beat until white 70 egg yolks, 10 egg whites, clarified butter, and cream. Blanch and pound almonds, pouring on several drops of water. Sift the almonds through a fine sieve to remove any large pieces and mix the sieved almonds with 3¾ glasses lightly sieved flour. Add the sieved flour and almonds to the egg yolk mixture, pour in thick yeast, beat the dough thoroughly, and let it rise. Then beat again, sprinkle on salt and sugar, and let the dough rise once more. Pour into a pan and, when the dough has risen, bake in a very hot oven. Use in all 1¼ lbs, or 3¾ glasses, sweet almonds, ¾ glass, or ¼ lb, bitter almonds, 70 eggs, ¾ glass each cream, butter, and thick yeast, 3 glasses, or 1½ lbs, sugar, some salt, and about 3¾ glasses flour.

### 1813  Pie with jam

*(Pirog s varen'em)*

Mix 1½ glasses flour, 1 glass each sugar and clarified butter, and 1 egg. Knead thoroughly, roll out 2 flat cakes, and place one on a skillet. Spread the cake with a layer of applesauce or 1½ glasses jam without syrup. Cover with the other flat cake, paint with egg, sprinkle on rusk crumbs and sugar, and bake in the oven.

### 1815  Cake rings with jam and fruit

*(Obertukh)*

Pour into a bowl or saucepan warm cream, strained yeast, salt, and half the flour. Prepare a dough and, when it has risen, add 5 eggs mixed with sugar, warm butter, and the remaining flour. Knead thoroughly and let rise.

Butter a saucepan, sprinkle with rusk crumbs, and place a tin tube in the middle. Roll out a piece of dough as thick as a finger and the size of the bottom of the saucepan. Cut out a circle in the middle for the tin tube to pass through.

Prepare several such circles and place them in the saucepan, painting each circle with clarified butter and sprinkling with sugar and cinnamon, dry jam or raisins, and finely chopped prunes or figs. Fill ¾ of the saucepan, let the layers rise a little, and then bake. Use in all 1½ glasses cream, 5 eggs, ¾ glass butter, ½ glass each yeast and sugar, ½ garnets flour, cinnamon, 2–3 rusks, jam, raisins, prunes or figs, and ¼ lb butter to spread on the circles. See the Remarks regarding yeast.

### 1817  A way to freshen stale babas, buns, and pies

*(Sposob otsvezhat' cherstvyja baby, bulki, pirogi)*

Wrap the stale baked goods in 2 sheets of waxed paper, soaked in water. Place in the oven for half an hour and serve immediately. Never wrap them in printed newspapers.

Stale buns, even two weeks old, can be refreshed if they are dipped into cold water and immediately set on a baking sheet in the oven for several minutes.

## YEAST MAZURKAS
### *(Mazurki na drozhzhakh)*

*Remarks:* Mazurkas are very thin and dry rectangular pastries, the size of a half or full sheet of paper. The top may be glazed and decorated as desired or strewn with currants, sugar, almonds, etc. They are served with dinner, tea, or coffee. Do not remove the mazurkas from the paper until they are cool. They are also decorated like *pljatski*; see the Remarks.

### 1818  Yeast mazurkas

*(Mazurek na drozhzhakh)*

Sieve very dry flour that has been placed in the oven overnight. Pour ¼ garnets of this flour into a saucepan and add 1 glass warm milk, ⅓ glass yeast, and about ⅜ glass clarified butter. Mix until smooth, cover with a napkin folded over several times, and set aside in a warm place. When the dough has risen, pour in ¾ glass, or 9 to 11 strained egg yolks and add ¼ glass sugar, ½ teaspoon anise, and salt. Knead thoroughly in a warm place, add another ¼ garnets flour, and knead until the dough pulls away from your hands. Cover and let rise a second time.

When the dough has risen, spread it out on the table, sprinkle lightly with flour, and with your hands stretch it out as thin as possible. Place on a buttered baking sheet dusted with flour, turn up the edges a little all around, and paint with egg whites beaten with sugar. Prick the entire mazurka with a fork and, without letting it rise, place immediately into the oven for 1 hour. When it has browned lightly, cover with paper. After removing from the oven, let it cool, but if it is not very dry, return it to the oven. Then glaze and dry in the oven. Order (*velet'*)* the oven to be lit as you begin kneading the dough. Instead of icing, the mazurka may be spread with ground almonds mixed with sugar and egg whites. (Use ½ *garnets* of flour in all.)

*This verb is a reminder that serfs, and later servants, were an integral part of large, wealthy households in nineteenth-century Russia.

## 1821 Mazurkas that rise in cold water

*(Mazurek podnimajushchijsja v kholodnoj vode)*

Mix together about ¾ glass each warm milk, butter, and egg yolks, 1 spoon yeast, and 1¼ lbs flour. Knead the dough until it does not stick to your hands, place in a buttered napkin, and tie it up, leaving enough room for the dough to rise. Submerge the bundle of dough in cold water overnight. The next day, when the dough has risen to the surface, remove it from the napkin and knead it thoroughly, incorporating ⅓ glass sugar. Cover the dough and leave it on the table for an hour to rise slightly. Roll out a thin sheet of dough and place it on a baking sheet lined with paper. When it has risen slightly, paint with egg and dry out in the summer oven.

## POLISH CAKES

*(Dzjad i pljatski)*

*Remarks:* These cakes (*pljatski* and *dzjad*) resemble mazurkas, but they are not as thin or dry. When they have risen on the baking sheet, paint them with egg and sprinkle with sugar, currants, almonds, and cinnamon. Bake in buttered paper casings, but do not remove them from the casings until they have cooled.

Ice the cakes informally (*domashnim obrazom*) as follows: Bake them on a large sheet of paper and cut into oblong pieces or squares 4 *vershok* on each side. Cut several rectangles in half to make triangles, coat them with white icing, and sprinkle the tops uniformly with sugar or cover them with piles of pink and yellow sugar, prepared as follows:

*Pink sugar:* Pound the sugar, sieve, and sprinkle into the dough. Whatever coarse sugar remains in the sieve should be resieved onto a small dish and moistened lightly with cochineal of a very attractive pink color until the sugar itself turns pink. Let the sugar dry out just a little, spreading it out on the plate to prevent lumps from forming. Instead of liquid cochineal, a sheet of red gelatin dissolved in water may be used.

*Yellow sugar:* Proceed exactly the same as with pink sugar, only instead of cochineal, moisten the sugar with saffron that has been infused in a wineglass of vodka and strained.

For these *pljatski* and mazurkas, make paper boxes and attach a ruff of white and pink cigarette paper to the sides. Cut the paper with scissors into fine strips and twist each piece with a penknife in the same way that feathers are curled.

The tops may be iced with chocolate, with red fruit drop stars (*monpans'e*),* and with colored sugar beans, which are made from a tragacanth dough dipped into either a thick chocolate mixture boiled over water or in cochineal or a saffron infusion.

Other *pljatski* are lightly covered with the thick syrup from jam boiled with gelatin and generously sprinkled with finely chopped blanched almonds, walnuts, or coconut.

*The name of these fruit drops comes from Monpensier, a French ducal family related to the Bourbons. Why the name became associated with candy in Russia and not the rest of Europe, I do not know. In classical French cuisine, à la Monpensier usually refers to asparagus tips and truffle slices sautéed in butter (sometimes served on artichoke hearts) used as a garnish for tournedos, sweetbreads, or suprêmes de volaille. (See Küchen-Lexikon, 334; Saulnier, Répertoire de la Cuisine, 13, 123, 134, 138, and 163; and Fitzgibbon, Food of the Western World, 280–281.)*

### 1825 Dzjad or pljatski for tea or coffee*

*(Dzjad ili pljatsek k chaju ili kofe)*

Prepare a yeast dough as usual, from 3¼ glasses milk, 4 lbs flour, ⅛ lb yeast, 1 lb sugar, 1 glass butter, 8 egg yolks, and lemon zest or ¼ lb bitter almonds.

When the dough is ready, divide it in half, roll it out, and place it on a baking sheet the size of a piece of paper or even a little larger. Spread a mixture of dried fruits on the dough, cover with another sheet of dough, and let rise. Paint with egg and bake. Prepare the fruit mixture as follows: Pour 1 glass of berry syrup into a saucepan, add ½ lb sugar and 5 apples, each cut into 5 parts, and cook them as for jam. While the apple mixture is still hot, add ½ lb sultanas and 1 lb each dates and finely chopped dried figs. Remove from the stove, let stand for an hour, and proceed as indicated above.

INGREDIENTS

For the dough
4 lbs flour
⅛ lb dry yeast
3¼ glasses milk
1 lb sugar
1 glass butter

8 egg yolks
lemon zest or bitter almonds

For the filling
5 apples
½ lb sultanas

| | |
|---|---|
| 1 lb dried figs | ½ lb sugar |
| 1 lb dates | 1 glass syrup |

*Molokhovets kept the distinction between dzjad and pljatski in name only. The recipes them-
selves either used both names or were cross-referenced one to the other. To lessen the confusion for
readers who do not know Russian, I will use only the plural form pljatski even when the singular, ·
pljatsek, is used in Russian.

### 1830  Pljatski with apples, plums, or cherries

*(Pljatsek s jablokami, slivami, ili vishnjami)*

[Mix together] 2¼ glasses sieved flour, 3½ eggs, ½ lb butter, ¼ lb, or ½ glass,
sugar, and a little water. Knead as well as possible, roll out thinly, and surround
with a rim of the same dough. Place on a baking sheet dusted with flour, paint the
top with egg, and bake. When the pastry is nearly done, spread stoned cherries on
it and sprinkle with sugar, or add applesauce and top with the following mixture:
Beat 2–3 egg yolks until white with 2 spoons fine sugar, add 2 spoons very fresh
sour cream, and fold in 2 beaten egg whites. Sprinkle on a teaspoon of wheat or
potato flour and bake for a short time.

## RUSKS, *KRENDELS*, AND OTHER SMALL BAKED GOODS
## FOR TEA, COFFEE, AND CHOCOLATE
*(Sukhari, krendeli i prochee melkoe pechen'e k chaju, kofe i shokoladu)*

### 1832  Rusks

*(Sukhari)*

Prepare a dough from yeast, half the flour, and warm milk or cream that was
previously boiled. Let the dough rise slightly in a warm place, then beat it thoroughly. Add 6 eggs, 1 teaspoon salt, ⅔ glass sugar, and butter. (If the dough is
prepared with cream, use ¾ glass butter; if prepared with milk, use 1⅛ glasses
butter.) Knead until the dough does not stick to your hands and let it rise a
second time. Form into small round buns, without sprinkling them with flour. If
the dough sticks to your hands, grease them lightly with butter. Place the buns on
a buttered baking sheet, let them rise, paint with egg yolk beaten with water, and
bake for 15 minutes. After removing from the oven, let them cool slightly, halve
them with a sharp knife, and immediately return them to the oven to dry out.

The cut surfaces of the rusks may be dipped in milk or wine. Sprinkle immediately with sugar and cinnamon, place on a baking sheet, and dry out in the oven.
Rusks that have already been dried out may be glazed with white or chocolate
icing and then returned to the oven for several minutes.

INGREDIENTS: 1 *garnets*, or about 5 lbs, flour, ¼ *garnets* or 3 glasses, milk or cream, 6 eggs, ⅔ glass sugar, cardamom or cinnamon, 1 teaspoon salt, ¾ or 1⅛ glasses butter, ½ glass yeast, and 2 eggs to paint the dough.

### 1835 Scalded rusks

*(Sukhari zavarnye)*

Scald ¼ *garnets* dry flour with ¼ *garnets*, or 3 glasses, [hot] milk, and mix until smooth. When cool, pour in 1¼ glasses yeast and let the dough rise slightly. Knead the dough, add 20 eggs or 40 unfertilized egg yolks, almost 1¾ glasses butter, 1 teaspoon salt, ½ glass sugar, and another *garnets* flour to make a rather thick dough. Continue as indicated for Rusks #1832.

(Use 1¼ *garnets* flour in all, or nearly 7 lbs.)

### 1840 Rusks made from yogurt

*(Sukhari na prostokvashe)*

Beat ¼ lb butter until white and add 7–8 egg yolks or 3–4 eggs, about 2 glasses yogurt, ⅓ glass or more yeast, and about 3 glasses flour. Mix and let rise. Beat the dough thoroughly and add salt, ½ glass sugar, and the remaining flour. Knead to make a rather thick dough and let it rise a second time. Continue further as indicated for Rusks #1832.

(Use ½ *garnets* flour in all.)

These proportions will yield about 50 buns, hence 100 rusks.

### 1846 Little braids for tea

*(Pletenki k chaju)*

Mix together ¼ *garnets*, or 3 glasses, warm milk, ¾ glass yeast, 20 egg yolks, and 1 *garnets* flour. Let rise and then add ¾ glass clarified butter, 1 teaspoon salt, and ¾ glass sugar. Knead thoroughly and let rise a second time until the dough has nearly doubled in bulk. Turn it out onto the table, divide into long strips, braid each group of three strips like a woman's plait, and place on a baking sheet. When the braids have risen, paint with egg yolk mixed with water, sprinkle with sugar and chopped almonds, and bake.

### 1850 Jewish bagels*

*(Krendeli evrejskie)*

Mix ½ glass yeast, 1 *garnets* flour, a generous amount of salt, anise, and enough warm water to make a thick dough. Knead well, cover, and let rise thoroughly. Shape into bagels, dip into black cumin seeds [*chernushka = Nigella sativa*]** or anise seeds, arrange on a bread peel, and dry slightly before the fire. Drop several bagels at a time into boiling, salted water, stirring with a small stick so that they do not rest on the bottom of the pan. With the same stick, remove the bagels as they rise to the surface, place them on a peel again, drizzle them thoroughly with cold water, and keep in the oven to dry out, then set them directly on the floor of a freshly swept oven.

*Pretsls *are a very old form of baked goods and were referred to in Jewish sources as early as the first half of the thirteenth century. (A bagel is simply a type of pretzel.) Bagels, with many local variations, were known throughout the historic territory of the Ashkenazi Jews. Although Jews had no monopoly on bagels, they seem to have been closely associated with them, baking them almost every day and distributing them to friends and relatives on special occasions such as a circumcision. (For more information on pretzels and bagels in Jewish sources see Kosover, Yidishe maykholim, 116.) According to Kosover, Jewish pretsls were baked without spices or other flavorings, a practice that makes Molokhovets' addition of black cumin or anise seeds questionable, not to mention the modern American habit of flavoring bagels with anything or everything and tinting them all the colors in the rainbow. I am indebted to Barbara Kirshenblatt-Gimblett for this information on pretsls.*

**Also known as fennel flower, nutmeg flower, nigella, or Roman coriander, black cumin seeds are native to Syria, were very popular with the Romans, and are still used for flavoring sweet breads and pastries in Cyprus, Lebanon, and Armenia. In India they are used for curries and, according to Mrs. Grieve, were sometimes substituted for pepper in the French spice mixture known as quatre épices or toute épice. The plant grows wild in the Caucasus and Central Asia and is cultivated in many regions including Lithuainia, Moldavia, and Ukraine. (See Grieve, A Modern Herbal, 297–298; and Rybak, Romanenko, Korableva, Prjanosti, 104–105.)*

### 1853  Pastries with jam or almonds*

*(Pirozhnoe v rode sloenago)*

Pour ¼ *garnets* flour and a little salt into a stoneware bowl and add 3 egg yolks, 1 egg, ¼ glass sugar, and the zest from ½ lemon. Mix everything thoroughly, add 2 spoons yeast, and enough cold milk to make a dough thick enough for buns. Knead thoroughly until the dough begins to form blisters and let it rise slightly, but not in a warm place. While the dough is rising, prepare ½ lb butter, washed and squeezed dry, and set it in a cold place. When the dough has risen, turn it out onto the table, roll it out into a circle, and place on top a circle of butter half as large as the circle of dough. Fold over the dough**, roll it out, and gather it up again. Repeat 3 times. After rolling it out the third time, cut the dough into various shapes and let them rise on a baking sheet. Paint with egg, sprinkle with almonds, or place jam in the middle. Do all this in a cold place and transfer the pastries directly from the cold into a hot oven.

*Krendels* may be made from this dough as follows: Cut the dough into long strips, twist pairs of them, and seal into a kind of *krendel*, etc.

*This recipe, which combines a yeast dough with the technique for making puff pastry, resembles what we now call Danish pastry. The finishing with almonds or jam reinforces the analogy.*

**The text is ambiguous at this point. Molokhovets instructed the reader to cover the butter with dough (pokryt' testom) but, without indication that a second circle of dough was to have been* *prepared, I assume she meant that the reader should fold the dough over the butter, which is the usual procedure when making puff pastry.*

## 1856 Royal bread

### (Khleb korolevskij)

Beat 7 eggs and ³/₈ lb, or ³/₄ glass, sugar until white. Add the zest from ½ lemon, ground cinnamon, cloves, finely chopped candied citrus peel, several walnuts boiled in sugar and cut into very thin, long pieces, some raisins and boiled cherries without juice, a handful of shredded almonds, and ¼ lb flour. Mix all this thoroughly, fill a large buttered tin pan or several small pans, and bake in the oven.

## 1862 German krendel with saffron

### (Krendel' s shafranom nemetskij)

Mix thoroughly 1¼ glasses warm milk, ⅛ zolotnik saffron soaked in rum, ⅓ glass fresh sour cream, 1–2 spoons yeast, and nearly 1½ lbs flour. Let rise and then beat the dough with a small spatula. Add ¼ lb butter, washed and beaten until white, 1 egg yolk, ⅓ glass sugar, ½ glass or more [mixed] raisins and currants, and a little cardamom. Knead the dough as well as possible, and let it rise again. Form into a large krendel, let it rise on the baking sheet, then paint it with egg and place it in a rather hot oven.

## 1870 Egyptian squares for tea or coffee*

### (Egipetskie kvadratiki k chaju ili kofe)

Beat 5 eggs in one direction** for at least half an hour. Add 1½ glasses fine sugar, the zest from 1 lemon, a little ground cinnamon and cloves, and enough flour so that after kneading, the dough can be rolled out to the thickness of your little finger. Cut into squares and bake in the summer oven.

*The Egyptian reference is mysterious, since the recipe does not differ markedly from others in this chapter. Recipes often got their names from current events or from some visiting dignitary. In this case it may have been a familial or personal association.

**Beating in one direction was a common practice when making cakes in eighteenth-century England and America. In Hannah Glasse's recipe for A Rich Seed Cake, called the Nun's Cake, she noted that "you must observe always in beating of Butter to do it with a cool Hand, and beat it always one Way in a deep Earthen Dish." E. Smith's The Compleat Housewife was popular in colonial America; when making a white cake, Smith advised the reader to "make a hole in the midst of the flour, and pour all the wetting in, stirring it round with your hand all one way till well mix'd." By the late nineteenth century, beating in one direction had gone out of style in America if we can believe Mrs. Lincoln, who was principal of the Boston Cooking School before Fanny Farmer. She rhetorically asked her readers, "Shall we stir only one way?" and then answered, "No; stir any way you please, so long as you blend or mix the materials." For today's kitchen scientists, the pendulum has swung back in favor of unidirectional beating. According to Howard Hillman, "some mixtures

*can be blended more quickly and easily and more uniformly if the cook stirs only in one direction,"*
*but he adds that "it doesn't make a hoot of difference whether you stir clockwise or counterclockwise*
*(unless you believe in that old superstition that stirring counterclockwise brings bad luck)." (Glasse,*
*The Art of Cookery, 139; Smith, The Compleat Housewife, 180; Lincoln, Mrs. Lincoln's Boston Cook Book, 34; and Hillman, Kitchen Science, 245.)*

### 1876 Prune buns*

*(Bulochki vengerskija)*

Beat ½ lb unsalted butter until white and mix with 7 egg yolks, 1 egg, and 20 *lots* flour. Add ⅓ glass thick yeast, ¼ glass sugar, and nutmeg. Beat the dough thoroughly, form into small buns, place them on a baking sheet, and set in a warm place to rise. Meanwhile, boil a glass of prunes, chop fine, and mix with 1 spoon sugar and some cinnamon. Make an indentation in each bun after it has risen, fill with the prune mixture or with some kind of jam, paint with egg, sprinkle with sugar, and bake in the oven.

*The Russian name of this recipe derives from the variety of plum known as* vengerka *or*
*Hungarian plum. These plums were highly regarded both fresh and when dried into prunes; especially prized were those produced in the Caucasus.*

### 1880 Chocolate patience cookies

*(Shokoladnoe pirozhnoe, Gedulds-Kuchen)*

Beat 5 egg whites and ½ lb, or 1 glass, fine sieved sugar until white as for icing, and add 1 spoon grated chocolate and ⅜ lb dry flour, or 1⅛ glasses. Mix, pour into a paper cone, and cut off the tip. Meanwhile, grease a baking sheet with beeswax, wipe it with paper, and dust it lightly with flour. Squeeze the dough into various small figures onto the prepared baking sheet, set in a warm place for an hour or two to dry out the tops, sprinkle with chocolate, and set in a summer oven as hot as after baking buns. When baked, cool slightly and remove the cookies from the sheet with a knife.

### 1883 Round cookies

*(Korzhiki)*

Beat until pale 10 egg yolks and a third that number of egg whites. Add a large wineglass of pure spirits drop by drop, 2 spoons thick cream, and 1 teacup finely pounded sugar. Mix everything together, add enough flour to form a rather stiff dough, and roll out to the thickness of your little finger. Cut out circles with a glass, paint with butter, and sprinkle on sugar mixed with cinnamon. Arrange on a baking sheet and bake until the cookies brown and dry out slightly. These are served for dinner, with coffee or tea, and are good to take along when traveling.

This recipe is enough for two meals, so halve it for one.

INGREDIENTS

1 large wineglass spirits, rum, or even
   vodka
1 teacup sugar
cinnamon

10 eggs
2 spoons thick cream
flour

### 1889  Excellent krendels from potato flour

(Otlichnye krendeli iz kartofel'noj muki)

Bring to a boil 1 cup clarified butter and 2 teacups milk and add 3 full cups potato flour, mixing constantly with a wooden spatula. When the mixture has boiled sufficiently, remove it from the fire and beat until cool. Beat 6 eggs into the dough one by one until the dough is as thin as that usually used to make *krendels*. These must—without fail—be rolled out on a napkin and then set on a baking sheet and popped into the oven.

INGREDIENTS

1 cup butter
2 cups milk
3 cups potato flour

6 eggs
salt and sugar to taste

### 1890  Quick pastry rings for coffee

(Bubliki k kofe skorospelye)

For each cup of cream, add 1 cup egg yolks, ½ cup butter, 1 cup sugar, and 1 cup pure birch lye. [Add flour,] knead the dough, roll into [ropes, and form into] rings (*bubliki, inache baranki*).* Bring milk to a boil, drop in the rings, and when they rise to the surface, gather them up with a stick and place them on a plank or board in the oven. After they have dried out, turn over the plank so that the rings are also turned over,** and leave them in the oven until they have finished baking.

INGREDIENTS

1 cup cream
1 cup egg yolks
½ cup butter

1 cup sugar
1 cup birch lye
flour

*Both these words refer to ring-shaped breads or rolls. The lye in the recipe served as a mild leavener; it also heightened the browning during the baking process and gave a gloss to the final product. See the Glossary for more on lye.

**This perplexing maneuver results in baking the rings on the oven floor covered by the plank. Perhaps it was difficult to remove the rings from the plank without breaking them until they had

Elena Molokhovets' A Gift to Young Housewives

*finished baking. Otherwise one wonders why Molokhovets did not turn them individually instead of as a unit, plank and all.*

### 1892   Real Vyborg twists*

*(Nastojashchie vyborgskie krendeli)*

Prepare a thin batter from a little flour, 3 glasses good milk, and 2 full spoons of the very best thick yeast (or 4–5 *zolotniki* dry yeast mixed in 2 spoons milk). Set the batter in a warm place to rise thoroughly, beat well, and add 4 eggs, 1 spoon butter, ½ glass milk, 2 heaping cups sugar, 1 teaspoon ground cardamom, and flour. Knead into a very thick dough, let rise again, then knead the dough for a very long time. Shape into Vyborg twists and let them rise on a baking sheet. Just before putting them into the oven, drop each twist into boiling water, then set them on hay spread over the oven floor.

*\*These twists are Molokhovets' version of viipurinrinkilä, a traditional Christmas bread named after the Finnish city Viipuri (now part of Russia and known as Vyborg). They are still made in Finland although now they are simply baked in the oven without the preliminary boiling and omitting the straw, which added a special flavor.*

### 1894   Vanilla sugar

*(Sredstvo pridat' sakharu zapakh vanili, rozovago masla, kofe i proch.)\**

It is good to sprinkle the tops of *kuliches* and other pastries with fragrant sugar, which is prepared as follows: Bury a vanilla bean in fine sugar in a tin box. Keep the box closed and, after using half the sugar, refill the box with fresh sugar. Mix and recover the box.

*\*The Russian recipe title is "Method for infusing sugar with vanilla, rose oil, coffee, and other flavors." Flavors other than vanilla are given in other recipes.*

### 1899   Sugar flavored with coffee

*(Sakhar s zapakhom kofe)*

Onto ¼ lb sugar, drizzle 3 spoons of strong essence made from the very best coffee. Dry out the sugar in a place that is barely warm. Pound and sieve the sugar, pour it into a jar, and cork it up.

# 18
## Paskhas and Colored Eggs
### (Paskhi i krashennyja jajtsa)

[*Translator's note: Paskha* (a sweetened cheese mixture) and *kulich* (a rich yeast bread with raisins and almonds) were the highlights of the Easter table. These distinctive desserts were especially savored as they marked the end of the long Lenten fast when all meat, eggs, and dairy products were forbidden to devout Orthodox believers. In the countryside especially, baskets containing colored eggs, *paskha*, and *kulich* were taken to the midnight Church service on Easter eve. As the worshippers gathered, they stood in the darkness, each with an unlit taper in hand, waiting for the service to begin. At midnight the priest lit the first taper to mark the resurrection of Christ. From this taper, all the others were lit, and soon the entire church was aglow. The priest then led a candlelit procession out of the church and circled the building three times; he finished by blessing all the dishes and baskets of foods that were arrayed inside and outside the church. The parishioners reclaimed their baskets and hurried home to begin the Easter festivities, for traditionally the Lenten fast was broken by foods that had been blessed by the priest. On Easter day, wherever people gathered, they kissed and greeted each other, exclaiming "Christ is risen," and exchanged colored Easter eggs.

In Court circles, the custom developed of exchanging elaborate "eggs," fashioned from rare materials and ornamented with jewels. The eggs made by the Russian court jeweler, Fabergé, are the most well known, but thousands of others were manufactured as well.]

### 1900 Ordinary *paskha*
#### (Paskha obyknovennaja)

For a medium-size mold, use 7–8 lbs fresh farmer's cheese. Weight the cheese (*tvorog*) for 24 hours. Rub the pressed cheese through a coarse sieve and add 1 glass very fresh sour cream, ½ lb very fresh butter, 2 teaspoons salt, and ½ glass or more sugar, according to taste. Mix everything as well as possible until no lumps remain, and pile into a wooden mold* lined with a clean, thin napkin. Cover with

Left: Wooden mold for making paskha.
Right: Paskha unmolded and decorated.
From Molokhovets, 1917.

a board or plank and place a heavy stone on top. After 24 hours carefully unmold the *paskha* onto a platter.

*Special tall, wooden, hinged molds were used for making paskhas. Usually they were shaped like a pyramid with the Cyrillic letters XB (standing for "Christ is risen") carved into one side. Often, but not always, the molds were collapsible. Clay flower pots are a good modern substitute for the traditional wooden molds.*

### 1902  Cream *paskha*

*(Paskha slivochnaja)*

Mix together 5 cups thick, fresh sweet cream and an equal amount of sour cream, add 2 cups boiled milk, and place in the oven for 10 hours. During this time the mixture must form curds. Pour everything into a napkin and hang the napkin in a cold place for the whey to drain off. Salt the curds, add 1 raw egg, and beat thoroughly until no lumps remain. Line a mold with a napkin, pile in the prepared cheese, and place a weight on top. When serving, add sugar to taste.

The above proportions are sufficient for a small mold. A large mold will require 30 cups each fresh cream and sour cream, 12 cups milk, 6 eggs, and sugar.

### 1904  Red *paskha*

*(Krasnaja paskha)*

Pour 3 bottles of milk into an earthenware jug and place in a hot oven until the milk heats and colors slightly. Frequently push the crust that forms down into the milk [so that another crust can form]. Remove the milk from the oven and cool until it is only slightly warm. Stir in 4 glasses very fresh sour cream to the milk and set the mixture aside to sour. Let it gradually curdle in the oven or set it for an hour on the edge of the stove after it has been stoked. As soon as the whey separates, pour everything into a napkin, without stirring, and hang it in the icehouse for the whey to drain off. Then rub the curds through a fine sieve and add salt to taste. For these proportions, stir in 3 fresh eggs, pile into a mold, and weight the mold in a cold place. After serving, return any leftover *paskha* to the icehouse.

### 1909  Sweet *paskha*

*(Paskha sladkaja)*

Bring 3 bottles of cream to a boil and skim off the foam into a separate bowl. To the remaining cream add a ladle of sour cream and return to a boil. As soon as any foam appears, immediately skim it off and add it to that already collected. Add another saucespoon of sour cream to the pan and set it to boil. If any foam appears, remove it. As soon as the cream begins to heat, stir it so that it does not burn, which will happen very easily if you are not careful. When the whey separates, pour everything into a napkin to let the whey drain off. Turn the curds out onto a platter, sprinkle on 1 glass of sugar, and add some kind of flavoring, such as vanilla, cardamom, lemon zest, or mace. Mix thoroughly, pile into a mold, and weight the mold.

### 1911  Royal *paskha*

*(Paskha tsarskaja)*

Place in a saucepan 5 lbs finely sieved fresh farmer's cheese, 10 raw eggs, 1 lb very fresh unsalted butter, and 2 lbs very fresh sour cream. Set on top of the stove, stirring constantly with a wooden spatula so that the mixture does not burn. As soon as the cheese begins to boil—that is, as soon as even one bubble appears—immediately remove from the fire, set on ice, and stir until it is completely cool. Add 1–2 lbs sugar ground with 1 vanilla bean, about ½ glass blanched ground almonds, and ½ glass currants. Mix everything thoroughly, pile into a large mold lined with a napkin, and add weights.

### 1915  Pink *paskha*

*(Rozovaja paskha)*

Mix 2 lbs of freshly pressed farmer's cheese with ½ lb of well-drained raspberry jam (which is one of the very best jams). Add ½ glass or more sugar, as desired. Press through a coarse sieve, add 3 raw eggs, ¼ lb very fresh butter, and 2 or even 3 glasses very fresh, thick sour cream. Mix thoroughly and transfer to a small wooden mold lined with a thin napkin. Cover with the ends of the napkin and set a board with weights on top. The jam imparts a slight pink color and a delicate aroma of fresh raspberries to the *paskha*. Such *paskhas* are better made in small molds because uncooked *paskhas* quickly spoil and it is better to have a variety of flavors prepared in different ways.

### 1916  Colored eggs for Easter

*(Jajtsa krashenyja dlja paskhi)*

a) Color the eggs in scraps of silk material of various colors. These scraps must first be shredded, then mixed together. Wash the eggs thoroughly, wipe them

New designs for Easter eggs. *Nov'*, vol. 3 (1885).

clean, and then moisten them again. Place pieces of blue sugar paper cut into designs on the eggs and then wrap them in the shreds of silk. Cover all this with an old cloth, tie with thread, and place the eggs in a saucepan with cold water. Boil for 10 minutes, counting from the moment when the water first begins to boil. Remove the eggs from the water, cool, and take off the cloth and silk.

b) Wash eggs until clean, wipe dry, wrap in old cloths, and tie up with several threads. With a small wooden stick, dab drops of ink on the eggs in several places. Submerge them in water, bring the water to a boil, and boil the eggs for 10 minutes. Remove them from the water, cool, and remove the cloths.

c) Color red as follows: Pour ¼ lb of sandalwood [chips ??] into a medium-size earthenware jug, cover with cold water, and set aside until the next day. Place the water on top of the stove and when it begins to boil, stir in ½ *lot* of alum. Immerse the eggs in the liquid and keep them on the edge of the stove until they turn color. Then set the jug over a high flame, boil for 10 minutes, and cool the eggs in the liquid. Remove them from the dye, wipe them with cotton wool soaked in olive oil, and dry them with a towel. Arrange the eggs on a platter lined with a napkin. One batch of dye will color two or three batches of eggs.

d) Eggs may be dyed yellow by boiling them in onion skins or the leaves of young birch trees.

For diversity, dip eggs that have been dyed red into yellow dye and those dyed yellow into red dye. Bring them to a boil once, etc.

e) These days eggs are dyed beautifully using powders, which are sold in chemical laboratories with instructions for coloring them.

f) Still better are the "Marke"* dyes, which stain the eggs bright red, violet, blue, yellow, green, and orange.

g) Marbled paper is sold at chemists' shops and chemical laboratories for 5 kopecks, with 10 sheets to an envelope.

h) Liquid dyes in 12 colors are sold at 10 kopecks per flacon.

i) "Mozaic effect"* is sold for dyeing eggs in brilliant colors at 20 kopecks per flacon.

j) Gold and silver paints for eggs are 5 kopecks a package.

k) Powders for dyeing eggs a variegated marble cost 5 kopecks a package.

l) Egg lacquer in 12 colors is sold for 10 kopecks per flacon.

All these dyes are sold with printed directions.

*The starred items were brand name products which apparently were readily available in the stores of St. Petersburg. I have found no further information about the firms or their wares.

# 19
# Gingerbreads

## (Prjaniki)

[*Translator's note:* Gingerbreads are among the oldest baked confections in Europe. No one knows when they were first made in Russia, but *prjaniki* are mentioned in folk tales and fairy tales and in numerous proverbs and folk sayings. Stamping designs on gingerbreads is an old tradition in Russia. Intricately carved gingerbread boards have been found in the excavations of the medieval city of Novgorod. In the sixteenth century, foreign visitors recorded seeing impressive examples of these cakes, and by the early seventeenth century cities like Tula, Gorodets, Moscow, Archangel, and Suzdal had become noted for their gingerbreads. These took many shapes: human figures, horses, fish, and birds, especially roosters and peacocks. Molded and three-dimensional figures were popular in the north, especially Archangel; elsewhere, stamped gingerbreads were more common. Gingerbreads were produced for name days, holidays, and other special occasions; at weddings the bride traditionally presented one to the groom. The carved boards were often exquisite—and won prizes for the artists—but size was also important. On the principle that the bigger the cake, the greater the honor, these ceremonial gingerbreads were embellished with appropriate inscriptions and could weigh several poods (1 pood = 36 lbs). An extensive collection of preserved gingerbreads and carved boards is in St. Petersburg's Museum of Ethnography. (See *Novgorod the Great: Excavations at the Medieval City*, 10; Kovalev, *Rasskazy o russkoj kukhne*, 145–148; and Smith and Christian, *Bread and Salt*, 24, 180.)

Gingerbreads were traditionally sweetened with honey—in fact Fitzgibbon mentioned that "the earliest form of gingerbread [in England] was not so much a cake as a solid block of honey baked with flour, ginger, and spices, which was then decorated to resemble a piece of tooled leather." (Fitgibbon, *Food of the Western World*, 177.) Initially Molokhovets relied upon honey for making gingerbread, but as she added recipes over the years, she grew to depend on sugar. The proportional decrease in the use of honey is striking: whereas honey was used in nearly two-thirds of the early recipes, that figure dropped to just over one-third in the later edition. During the second half of the nineteenth century sugar imports dropped and prices declined once beet sugar began to be produced and sold in Russia.]

Gingerbreads

Carved mold for making
gingerbread, 1805. From
*Sokrovishche russkogo
narodnogo iskusstva* (Moscow,
1967).

### 1919  Chocolate spice cakes

*(Prjaniki shokoladnye)*

Dissolve 1 lb sugar in slightly less than a full glass of water, mix with 1½ glasses honey, and boil in a large saucepan. Sprinkle on 3 *zolotniki* potash, a little cinnamon, cardamom, cloves, allspice, and ½ lb finely chopped unblanched almonds. After removing from the fire, sprinkle on 1½ lbs flour and mix until smooth. Turn the mixture out onto a table dusted with flour and knead the dough with your hands. If it is not thick enough, add more flour. Roll it out, cut into various shapes, place them on a baking sheet lightly greased with unsalted butter, and bake them in the summer oven. Remove from the oven when brown.

Bring 1½ lbs sugar and a little water to a boil twice. When the syrup becomes viscous, stir in ½ lb grated chocolate. Spread this mixture first on one side of the spice cakes and, after they have dried out in the oven, on the other side. Return them to the oven for further drying.

### 1920  Spice cakes with rosewater

*(Prjaniki na rozovoj vode)*

Bring to a boil 1 glass rosewater and 1 lb sugar. Cool slightly. Dissolve 1 dessertspoon potash in water, mix with the rosewater syrup, and sprinkle on 1 lb flour. Beat thoroughly with a spatula, cover tightly, and set in the oven overnight. Roll out the next morning, let the dough rise, and bake in an oven that is not too hot.

### 1922  Torun gingerbreads*

*(Prjaniki torunskie)*

Heat ½ *garnets*, or 6 glasses, honey until it darkens slightly. Skim, set aside, and gradually stir in ¾ glass spirits, taking care that the honey does not burst into flame. Sprinkle on ¾ glass boiled, finely chopped bitter orange peel, ½ *lot* each cloves, ginger, and allspice, and 1 *lot* each anise and fennel.** Mix and immediately pour the hot, almost boiling honey into 9 glasses of rye flour, finely sieved and lightly roasted. Stir briskly with a spatula for a long time until the mixture begins to whiten, a process that will take at least 2 hours. Distribute the dough among shallow paper casings, not filling them completely, and each time dipping your hands in beer boiled with honey before touching the dough. Paint the tops of the cakes with the same beer and honey mixture, set the paper casings on a baking sheet for the dough to rise slightly, stud the tops with almonds and pieces of candied citrus peel, and pop into the oven after baking bread. After they have finished baking, store them in a cold place to prevent them from drying out too much.

*Torun is a Polish town on the Vistula River where the astronomer Copernicus was born in 1473.

**More exactly, Molokhovets called for Italian dill (ital'janskij ukrop). Since one Russian name for sweet fennel is ukrop florentijskij (Foeniculum dulce), I assume she meant fennel in this instance.

## 1926 Gingerbreads without spices

(Prjaniki bez spetsij)

Bring 3 lbs honey to a boil, skim, cool to the temperature of milk fresh from the cow, and begin to beat with a wooden spatula. After beating for half an hour, add 20 eggs one by one, incorporating each egg thoroughly before adding another one. Beat continuously while the oven is heating* and then add enough flour to make a thick dough. Divide the dough into 20 parts and distribute among paper casings prepared earlier. After adding the flour, do not overbeat; just mix and pile into the casings.

*This instruction may sound deceptively simple, but it should be remembered that wood-burning ovens took a long time to heat up.

## 1928 [Gingerbread figures]

[No title provided in the original]

Mix together 5 lbs treacle, 1 lb Russian butter, and 1½ lbs fine sugar. Set on the fire and bring to a boil, stirring, until the sugar dissolves. When it has come to a full boil, immediately add 3 *zolotniki* ground cinnamon and 1 *zolotnik* cloves and pour into a large earthenware pot. Add 3–4 *zolotniki* potash, dissolved in a wineglass of warm water. Pour in gradually while stirring so that the mixture does not overflow, because foam will rise up from the potash. Stir until the foam subsides. Gradually add 5 lbs fine wheat flour and knead thoroughly or beat with a spatula for at least an hour, until the dough whitens. Set aside in a [heated] room for 3–4 days, stirring the dough each day. On the fourth day, turn the dough out onto a table, knead it, roll it out with a rolling pin, and cut into shapes, such as stars, horses, cockerels, or deer. Transfer the figures to a baking sheet dusted with flour, arranging them close to each other. Bake in the oven and remove them after they have risen and browned.

First cut out paper patterns of deer, horses, etc. Press the patterns into the dough and cut out the figures. These gingerbreads are frosted, if desired, with white icing, or they are gilded,* if they are intended for the Christmas tree.

*The gilding is another clue to the ancestry of these cakes. Plain gold leaf (without the paper backing) was used to decorate both sweet and savory banquet dishes in medieval England and France and is still used for garnishing on grand occasions in India. Gilding may be done more simply (and inexpensively!) by painting the dough with egg yolk to give it a golden color after baking, but Molokhovets probably cut out gilded paper in the same shape as the figures and stuck it on with a thin sugar icing. Gingerbread figures decorated in this manner are still sold in Germany and Scandinavia at Christmas.

## 1929  Raspberry gingerbreads

### (Malinovye prjaniki)

Pour a convenient amount of dried raspberries into a preserving pan (tasik), barely cover with boiling water, and place on top of the stove. Boil thoroughly until the berries are completely soft, remove the pan from the fire, and rub the berries through a sieve. The sieved raspberries must be as thick as sieved cranberry or red whortleberry purée. Measure the purée and, for each cup, add 1 cup of honey. Meanwhile, prepare rusks by toasting white bread until very dry but not burned, pound the rusks and an equal amount of dried raspberries, and mix them together. Bring the honey and raspberry purée to a boil and stir in the pounded rusks and dried raspberries to form a thick dough. Boil thoroughly to cook the dried, pounded raspberries. Shape the dough into flat cakes on a baking sheet, dry out in the oven, sprinkle with sugar, and store in a jar.

## 1938  Excellent sugar gingerbreads

### (Otlichnye sakharnye prjaniki)

Add 1¼ glasses water to 1¼ lbs fine, sieved sugar and set the mixture on the fire to boil. Finely shred the zest of 1 lemon, add it to the syrup, and cook until the juice is as thick as if it were for jam. Remove the syrup from the fire, pour it into a stoneware bowl, and let it cool slightly. Add 1 zolotnik each ground cinnamon and cardamom, stir in 1½ lbs of the very best fine wheat flour, and knead for 2 hours. Prepare sheets of paper, sprinkle with flour, and place a flat cake of dough on each sheet of paper. After the cakes have baked, they may be iced as follows: Beat 2 egg whites and 1½ glasses sugar until the mixture whitens and thickens and add cinnamon oil or 1 or more spoons lemon juice, according to taste. Mix thoroughly, spread on the cakes, and dry out in the oven.

# 20
# Jams, Jellies, and Syrups

*(Varen'e, zhele, sirop)*

## JAMS AND PRESERVES
*(Varen'e)*

*Remarks:* Berries or other fruits intended for jam must not be overripe. The weather must be clear and dry, not rainy, when they are gathered and they must be used the very same day. When preparing jam, first boil the syrup thoroughly, that is, the water with which the sugar is moistened. It is best to buy the sugar in pieces. Boil the syrup until, when cooled on a spoon, it pours off in a narrow ribbon. After removing the scum, sprinkle the berries into the boiling syrup while shaking the preserving pan. Let the berries come to a rolling boil three times, each time removing the pan from the fire and skimming the surface. Finish cooking over a low flame.

To test whether the jam is ready, take a little on a spoon. If the berries are translucent and plump and the syrup thick and clear and a thin membrane forms after chilling slightly on ice, the jam is done.

Acidic berries such as currants, barberries, etc., need less cooking than other berries. Use 1½ or 2 lbs sugar to 1 lb berries. To save money, it might seem better to use 1½ lbs for 1 lb berries (that is, 1 glass fine sugar for 1 glass berries) but this is really a false economy, since more juice forms with 2 lbs sugar, allowing each berry to float separately, whole and uncrushed. Moreover, jam from 1½ lbs sugar turns sour and must be recooked with additional sugar, which actually uses up more sugar besides robbing the jam of its nice appearance and color. Granulated sugar, which is much cheaper, may be used instead of sugar pieces. In that case use 4 teacups water for 1 lb granulated sugar. Bring to a boil, skim, pour into a bowl, and leave in a cold place for a full 24 hours. The next day, carefully pour the clear syrup into a saucepan, reduce it to the proper thickness, and add the berries. Different spoons should be used for cooking, packing, and testing the jam, both for the sake of cleanliness and to prevent spoilage from excess moisture.

The hot jam should not be poured immediately into jars because the berries will float on the surface and the juice will remain on the bottom. Cool the jam in a china basin—do not let it stand in a copper vessel because the jam will lose its natural color and will take on a metallic taste, harmful to the health. Do not cover the hot jam with a lid because the rising steam, which turns into water and falls into the jam, will cause mold and spoil the jam. If it is absolutely necessary to cover the jam (for example, to protect it from flies), use a thin piece of canvas to absorb any moisture which might fall into the jam. When the jam comes to a rolling boil, skim it with a spoon as carefully as possible, being sure not to press or disturb the berries. Shake the basin frequently so that the syrup covers all the berries. Jam ought to be cooked in a preserving pan, that is, in a [wide], flat, copper saucepan (not tin-plated, which spoils the color of the jam).

*If the jam sugars*, add 1 spoon cold water to the jam to compensate for overcooking. Place the jar, having discarded its bladder and paper wrapping, in a saucepan filled with cold water to the level of the jam. Set the saucepan on the fire and heat until the water nearly boils. Remove the saucepan from the fire and let the water cool before removing the jar of now-melted jam.

*If the jam begins to turn sour*, that is, if it has not cooked long enough, boil it again as soon as possible, sprinkling the top with fine sugar (jam which stands too long without being reboiled cannot be saved). Boil until no scum remains. Store the jam in a cold, dry place, in covered boxes half-filled with sand that is changed each year. In the summer, the jam may be kept in the stove where the heat does not reach it and where there is no moisture.

The jam should be poured into small, 1 lb jars, because once half the jam is consumed, the larger jars allow more air to enter, which soon spoils the jam. Tie up the jars with wax paper or with a bladder moistened and then wiped dry. Place a circle of paper soaked in rum under the bladder. Write the kind of jam and the number of the jar on a clean piece of paper and tie on top of the jar.

### 1941  Very green gooseberry jam

*(Kryzhovnik ochen' zelenyj)*

Seed and rinse green, unripe gooseberries that have been gathered between the 10th and 15th of June. Place the berries in a glazed earthenware jug, separating the layers with cherry leaves and a little sorrel or spinach. Fill the pot with spirits, cover with a lid, and seal with dough. Set the pot for several hours in an oven that is as warm as when bread has just finished baking. The next day, remove the gooseberries [from the oven] and pour them into cold water and ice. After an hour, change the water and bring the berries to a boil. Pour off the boiling water and immediately pour the berries into fresh cold water with ice. Reboil and again plunge into cold water with ice. The ice water must be changed several times, each time keeping the berries in the water 10 or 15 minutes until they no longer smell of spirits. Turn the berries into a coarse sieve, and after the water has drained off, spread them out on a tablecloth. When they have dried, weigh them. For every lb of berries, use 2 lbs sugar and 1 glass water. Prepare a syrup from ¾ of the amount of sugar, boil thoroughly, remove the scum, and sprinkle the berries into the hot syrup. When the berries and syrup begin to boil, sprinkle on the remainder of the sugar. Let the mixture come to a rolling boil 3 times and finish cooking over a low fire. It is not bad to add a piece of vanilla to the syrup.

### 1945 Green gooseberries preserved like cones of hops

*(Zelenyj kryzhovnik v vide shishek khmelja)*

Gather large, green gooseberries, tear off the stems, and at that point, partially cut each berry into four parts to resemble 4 leaves, keeping the ends of the berries intact. Carefully remove the centers, that is, the seeds, with a penknife, and then thread a twig from a currant bush with 4 or 5 of these cut up berries. Cook them with great care as indicated in the recipe for Gooseberry jam #1941. That is, set them in an earthenware jug in the oven, having interlaid them with cherry leaves and poured on spirits, etc.

### 1949 Wild raspberry jam

*(Malina lesnaja)*

In good, dry weather gather large raspberries that are not too ripe and arrange them on a plate. For 1 lb of berries weigh out 1½ lbs sugar. Immediately pound a quarter of the sugar and sprinkle it over the berries. Set the platter of berries on ice overnight. The next day prepare a syrup from 1 glass water and the remaining sugar. Cool the syrup, pour it over the berries and, after 3 hours, cook as usual. After the jam has cooked, pour it into a bowl and let it cool. Remove the berries with a wooden twig or teaspoon and pile them into a jar. Strain the syrup over the berries. Sprinkling the berries with sugar overnight strengthens the berries and prevents them from disintegrating in the syrup. Moreover, it is good to gather wild raspberries in the evening so that after sprinkling the berries with sugar, they will be ready for cooking the next day. 1½ lbs sugar is sufficient for 1 lb of good, large raspberries.

### 1951 American raspberry jam

*(Amerikanskaja malina)*

These berries are harder to cook because they are very tender. They must be gathered after several days of good weather. First they must be moistened with spirits and then sprinkled with sugar. The next day, cook as indicated in #1949, but for 1 lb of berries use 2 lbs sugar. The berries will be firmer and will have a lovely color if several drops of vitriol* are added to the jam [while it is cooking], only you must guard that the jam does not boil over.

*See Glossary.

"Making Jam." Oil on canvas by Vladimir E. Makovskij, 1876. State Tretjakov Gallery, Moscow.

### 1952 Cultivated strawberry jam

*(Klubnika)*

This is prepared exactly the same as raspberry jam, except that the green leaves should first be cut off carefully, leaving the stem ¼ *vershok* long. Dip each berry into spirits or white rum and arrange on a platter. Sprinkle on one quarter of the sugar and set the platter of berries on ice. The next day prepare a syrup as follows: For every lb of berries use 1 glass water and 2 lbs sugar, boil thoroughly, sprinkle on the berries, and bring to a boil 3 times, each time removing the preserving pan from the fire and carefully skimming while shaking the pan. Finish cooking over a low fire until the berries lose their acidity and the syrup begins to form a membrane.

### 1953 Sour and sweet cherry jam

*(Vishni i chereshni)*

Carefully stone sour and sweet cherries* without marring the berries, put them in a coarse sieve, and douse them with cold water and ice. Use 1½ or 2 lbs sugar for every lb of uncleaned berries and 1 glass water for every lb of sugar. Boil the syrup thoroughly, sprinkle on the berries, and cook as usual.

Or, after sprinkling the berries into the syrup, cook them for a short time, pour them out into a stoneware bowl, and set aside overnight. The next day, carefully pour off the syrup. Bring it to a boil, sprinkle on the berries again, and finish cooking. Pour the jam into a stoneware bowl, cool, and transfer to a jar, etc.

Or, after rinsing the berries with water and ice, transfer them to a stoneware bowl and cover with a thick syrup that has been boiled and cooled. The next day, pour off the syrup, bring to a boil, sprinkle on the berries, and cook until done.

*Vishnja (Prunus cerasus), the ordinary Russian word for cherry, is a sour cherry, also known as the morello cherry. Chereshnja (Prunus avium) is much sweeter and is known as the mazzard or sweet cherry. Since Molokhovets rarely used sweet cherries, sour cherries should be used in all her recipes unless otherwise noted.* (Macura, Russian-English Botanical Dictionary, 625, 80–81; and Bianchini and Corbetta, Complete Book of Fruits and Vegetables, 146–149.)

### 1959  Rose blossom jam

*(Rozovyj tsvet)*

Gather wild rosebuds that have only just blossomed, or, preferably, buds of cabbage roses [*Rosa centifolia*].* Cut off [and discard] the white ends of the petals, weigh out 1 lb of petals, transfer to a colander, and scald with boiling water, using a spoon to prevent them from floating. Plunge the colander into cold water with ice so that all the petals are covered, stirring and turning them around on all sides. Repeat this process three times, first scalding with boiling water and then rinsing with cold water. From this the jam will be thick and squeak on your teeth. Thoroughly squeeze out the water from the petals and place them on a dish. For 1 lb petals squeeze the juice from 2 large, thin-skinned lemons and sprinkle on 1 glass fine sugar. Thoroughly mash the petals with the lemon juice and sugar. Then take the remaining sugar, adding for each lb of petals at least 2 lbs sugar and 2 glasses of rosewater or, lacking that, ordinary river water. Boil the syrup thoroughly, skim, and add the prepared rose petals. Cook over a low fire. If the aroma is too weak, add 2 drops of rose oil. When the rose petals are tender and no longer float on top, the jam is done.

This recipe yields 2½ lbs jam.

*Roses vary in color and aroma as well as taste, much like different varieties of apples. Darker petals often have a stronger flavor than light petals, but for best flavor, all petals should be used as soon as possible after gathering and cleaning. Although the practice of cooking and preserving roses has pretty much disappeared from contemporary American cooking, rose petals were widely used in Elizabethan and Stuart England to make conserves, candies, and medicinal cordials.* (Wilson, Food and Drink in Britain, 355–356; for an extensive collection of recipes for rose preserves, see Gordon, Rose Recipes, 27–35.)

### 1964  Green Hungarian plums

*(Slivy Vengerskija zelenyja)*

At the end of August, gather still unripe Hungarian plums—that is, plums that will still be good in winter. Prick them in several places with a needle and toss them into cold water. Change the water and place the pan of plums on top of the stove. As soon as the water begins to boil and the plums float to the top, immediately remove the preserving pan from the fire. After the plums settle to the bottom, replace the pan on the fire. When the plums again begin to float, remove the pan from the fire and carefully turn the plums into a fine sieve. Good jam depends on following these instructions exactly. When the water drains away, pack the plums into a jar. For every 1 lb of plums use 2 lbs sugar and 2 glasses water. Begin by using 2 glasses water and 1 lb sugar and bring the syrup to a boil. Let it cool and pour it over the plums. After 24 hours, pour off the syrup, add another ½ lb sugar, bring to a boil, let cool, and pour over the plums again. On the third day, add the remaining ½ lb sugar. When the syrup comes to a boil, add the plums and bring the mixture to a boil 2–3 times. Finish cooking over a low fire, watching that the plums do not overcook.

These plums can be prepared another way: Peel the plums and toss them immediately into cold water, bring a syrup to a boil, drop in the plums, and cook until half done. Pour the plums into a glazed bowl and cover. The next day, pour off the syrup, bring it to a boil, add the plums, and cook over a low fire until done. Pack the plums into a jar. If the syrup is too thin, cook it a little longer, let it cool, and pour it over the plums. The plums may be cooked with a piece of vanilla bean, 1 *vershok* long.

Or take the very best plums, but neither fully ripe nor soft. For every lb of plums use 1 or 1½ lb sugar. Peel the plums, place them on a platter, sprinkle on ½ lb finely pounded and sieved sugar, and set them in an oven that is barely warm. When the plums release their juice, pour it off, [reserve the juice,] sprinkle the plums with another ¼ lb sugar, and leave them in the oven overnight. The next day, again pour off the juice from the platter, mix it with the first batch of juice, and pour into a preserving pan. Sprinkle with the remaining sugar, bring to a boil, add the plums, and cook over a low fire until done. Pour into a glazed dish, cool, and pack into a jar. To produce more juice, add to the platter several completely ripe plums, which may be discarded later.

## 1966 Peaches

### (Persiki)

Prick peaches that are not too ripe in several places, using thin wooden spills. Drop the fruit into warm water, boil lightly, remove from the fire and, after 10 minutes, turn into a fine sieve. Pour the water in which the peaches were boiled into a stoneware bowl and set it in a cold place overnight. The next day, bring the peaches to a boil in this same water, remove them from the fire, and turn them into a fine sieve. Weigh the fruit after it has dried off a little. For 1 lb of peaches, use 2 lbs sugar and 1¼ glasses of the water in which the peaches were cooked. Boil the syrup thoroughly and skim the surface. Remove the pan from the fire briefly, drop the peaches into the warm syrup, and then cook them over a low fire. If, after a short time, the syrup appears to be too thin, pour it off and bring it to a boil 2–3 times, adding sugar.

### 1970 Lemons, another way

*(Limony drugim manerom)*

Choose large, thick-skinned lemons and soak them for 12 days, changing the water daily. Then cover with cold river water and cook them until they can be pierced with a straw. Remove those that are cooked; let the others cook a little longer. As the lemons are removed, place them immediately in a deep bowl lined with a napkin folded several times. Cover the fruit with the napkin and then with a lid. After the lemons have cooled, cut them into oblong pieces with a sharp knife, discarding the seeds. Weigh the fruit and pack into jars. For 1 lb of lemons, make a syrup from 1½ lbs sugar and 2 glasses of the water in which the lemons were cooked. Bring to a boil, cool, and pour over the lemons. The next day, pour off the syrup, bring it twice to a boil, cool, and pour over the lemons. On the third day, reduce the syrup to the requisite thickness and, while it is still warm but not hot, pour it over the lemons. Lemons prepared in this manner will be tasty and tender.

### 1975 Korobovki apples

*(Jablochki-korobovki)*

Korobovki apples* are sold in St. Petersburg in September. They must be peeled, but keep the stems and leave them whole because they are not large. After peeling, immediately plunge them into cold water. Then drop them into boiling water. When they have come to a boil, remove them with a slotted spoon and immediately drop them into a large quantity of cold water. Let them stand awhile. Then weigh the apples and, for 1 lb of apples, use 1 lb sugar. Prepare a syrup using 1 glass water for every lb of sugar, adding lemon peel or vanilla. When the syrup has come to a boil, drop in the apples and cook them until they become translucent.

*Korobovki apples are an old Russian variety; the fruit is small, aromatic, and sweet with a slight tartness.

### 1982 Whole preserved pineapple

*(Varen'e ananasy, tsel'nye)*

Peel the pineapple by removing a very thin skin not thicker than postal paper from each pineapple "cone" (*shishechka*). Boil the pineapple in water, using as little water as possible. Cook until the fruit is tender enough to be pierced easily with a straw. Then pack the pineapple into a jar. If the pineapples are medium-size, allow 1½ lbs sugar for each pineapple. After the pineapple has finished cooking, prepare a thin syrup from the cooking water. Cool the syrup to the temperature of milk fresh from a cow, pour over the pineapple, and let stand for 2 days. Each day for a week, pour off the syrup, add sugar to it, [boil], and when cool, repour over the pineapple. When the syrup has become as thick and as sweet as it ought to be, bring the pineapple to a boil in it 4 times, each time removing the preserving pan from the heat, cooling, and letting it stand for 2 days before recooking. Continue until the pineapple becomes translucent.

### 1985  Ersatz ginger jam made from watermelon rind

*(Iskusstvennoe imbirnoe varen'e iz arbuznykh korok)*

Remove [and discard] the very green rind from a watermelon. Cut the [peeled] melon rind into small pieces and boil the pieces in water. Turn into a coarse sieve, and when the water has drained away completely, sprinkle these pieces with ground ginger. Use 1 tablespoon ginger for every glass of boiled rind and set it aside for 24 hours in a cold place. The next day, rinse off the ginger from the rind in lukewarm water, changing it several times so that no ginger remains on the rind. Then take several glasses of rind, the same number of glasses of fine sugar, and ¼ or ½ glass water for every glass of sugar. Cook up a syrup, drop in the rind, and cook thoroughly, as for any jam.

### 1986  Lettuce preserves with ginger*

*(Varen'e iz salata s imbirem)*

Gather very thick lettuce stalks. They absolutely must be very young so that they are crisp and are not at all woody. Scald them with boiling water, peel, and cut into small pieces. Sprinkle thoroughly with grated ginger so that all the pieces are covered and set on ice for 3 days. Remove, wash, and rinse in pure water. Boil like ordinary preserves, adding for each lb of sugar 1 sliced root of white ginger to cook with the jam. After cooking, remove the pieces of ginger. This jam will resemble imported ginger jam. If the syrup becomes watery, pour it off and recook it with more sugar. Pour over the jam when cool.

For every lb of lettuce, use 1 lb sugar, ½ glass water, 2 spoons of ground ginger, and a piece of whole ginger.

*According to Pokhlebkin, Russians first adopted the Tartar practice of preserving root vegetables with honey (and later sugar) in the seventeenth century following the Russian acquisition of the khanates of Astrakhan, Kazan, and Siberia under Ivan the Terrible. (Pokhlebkin, Natsional'nye kukhni, 9.) This date seems late, but one must be careful to distinguish between the adoption of a particular technique in a given cuisine and the known use of the technique in other cultures. Certainly honey was known as a preservative in the ancient world. Greek physicians valued its medicinal properties and the Romans used honey extensively in their cooking, even for seasoning and preserving lettuce and root vegetables, a practice that was continued in medieval England. (Wilson,

Food and Drink in Britain, *278; Edwards,* The Roman Cookery of Apicius, *10; and* Curye on Inglysch, *120–121.) Barbara Wheaton brought to my attention the fact that La Varenne was already preserving lettuce stalks in sugar in France in the 1650s, which is the same period that the Tartar preserves reputedly were introduced to Russian cuisine. (La Varenne,* Le Cuisinier françois, *491.)*

### 1987  Lingonberries with apples

*(Brusnika s jablokami)*

Although this jam does not look very attractive, it is tasty nonetheless and especially pleasing to someone recovering from an illness. For 1 lb of picked-over red bilberries [*Vaccinium vitis-idaea*],* use 4 sweet apples. Peel, slice, and core the apples, removing all the seeds. Dissolve 1½ lbs sugar in 1½ glasses water. Cook the lingonberries until half done in this syrup, and then add the sweet apples. Lemon zest or lemon peel boiled in water may also be added.

*These small, wild, red berries are called cowberries, red bilberries, or red whortleberries in England. Since none of those names is much used in America, I will settle for the marginally more familiar Scandinavian name, lingonberries. Like Molokhovets, the Russians today value these berries as much for their healing properties as for their taste. In folk medicine, the berries are used as a diuretic and the dried leaves are made into a hot tea to alleviate rheumatism and other illnesses. (See Forsell,* Berries, *102–104;* Sturtevant's Edible Plants of the World, *588; Dzhangaliev and Rodionov,* Dary prirody, *79–81; and Dudchenko and Krivenko,* Plodovye i jagodnye rastenija—tseliteli, *35–36.)*

### 1990  Rose hip preserves

*(Shipovnik)*

Gather large, ripe dog rose hips, make a small hole in the hips, and carefully remove the entire interior with a hairpin. Wrap a twig in linen and thoroughly wipe out the center of the hips. Wash the hips in several changes of water and once more wipe out the centers with linen. Next, bring water to a boil and sprinkle on the hips. When the water begins to boil, immediately turn the hips into a

Bag for straining jelly. From Gouffe, *Royal Book of Pastry and Confectionary* (London, 1874).

440

colander and rinse with cold water. Spread them out on a tablecloth, openings downward so the water drains off. Then weigh them. For 1 lb hips use 2 lbs sugar and ½ glass water. Boil the syrup thoroughly, remove the scum, sprinkle on the hips, and cook as usual, over a high and then a low fire.

# JELLIES
## (Zhele [Varen'e])

*Remarks:* It is very difficult to prepare successful, good jelly. If it is cooked insufficiently, it will be watery and will not hold its shape in layers. Overcooked jelly will be too stiff. While the jelly is cooking, it must be tested constantly as follows to see whether it is ready. Take a little jelly on a teaspoon and place on ice. If the jelly sets and does not spread out when cut with a pin, it is ready. Or take up 2–3 drops of hot jelly with a teaspoon, and if the drops, falling from the spoon, harden and stick to it, the jelly is ready. The pan must be removed from the fire when testing in this manner. The very best and easiest way to produce consistently successful jelly is to cook it according to measured volume, as follows:

*For red jelly,* pour 1 glass of strained juice into a small saucepan or preserving pan. Measure the height of the juice with a spill and notch the spill with a knife. Add 1 glass fine sugar (i.e., a little less than ½ lb); it is better to strew on the sugar in pieces. Mix and cook over a low fire, removing the scum, until the syrup is reduced to the mark on the spill. Immediately remove from the fire and strain through fine muslin into a hot jar. Cover lightly with a linen cloth until completely cool, tie paper or a bladder around the jar, and store in a cold, dry place.

*For white jelly,* such as that from apples or green gooseberries, etc., pour 1 glass of clear, strained juice into a saucepan or preserving pan and measure with a spill. Sprinkle on 2 glasses fine sugar or 1 lb sugar in pieces. Mix thoroughly. When the sugar has dissolved, measure with a spill and mark it. Then cook over a low fire and reduce the jelly almost to the midpoint of the two marks on the spill. Do not reduce it further.

*Red jelly for decorating tortes and other pastries:* Take sour berries, such as rowanberries, stone brambles [a form of blackberry: *Rubus saxatilis*], currants, barberries, or cranberries. Use 1½ glasses juice and 1 glass fine sugar, and reduce to the mark [on the spill].

## 1993  White jelly from gooseberries
### (Zhele beloe iz kryzhovnika)

Gather gooseberries that are still completely green (i.e., before June 15). Clean the berries and place them in a preserving pan, pouring on enough water just to cover them. Cook until the gooseberries are soft, stirring and mashing them with a spoon. Pour everything into a napkin or into a clean, thick, triangular linen bag* tied to an overturned stool so the juice can drain off gradually. Let it settle and then carefully pour off the clear juice. For 1 glass juice, use 2 glasses fine sugar, and reduce the syrup almost to the midpoint of the two marks, as indicated in the remarks. Finely chopped lemon zest may be added for flavor. Remove the zest when the jelly has thoroughly cooked.

*This is called a jelly bag in English or a chausse (*sleeve*) in French.

## 1995 Rose petal jelly

### (Zhele iz rozovago tsveta)

Boil green gooseberries until they are soft, as indicated in #1993, and strain the berries. Take rosebuds that are blossoming, cut off [and discard] the white ends of the petals, strew 2–3 handfuls of petals into a teapot, and cover with boiling water. After the petals have settled, take ½ glass of this rose infusion and 1 glass of gooseberry juice, sprinkle on 2 glasses fine sugar, and reduce almost to the midpoint of the two marks, as indicated in the Remarks.

## 2003 Yellow apple jelly

### (Zhele jablochnoe zheltago tsveta)

Use sour, reddish, almost-ripe apples of a single variety. Quarter each apple and remove the seeds, but do not peel them. Immediately drop the apples into cold water to keep them from darkening. Transfer the apples to a preserving pan, barely cover them with fresh water, and cook until the fruit becomes translucent and the water turns sour. Then strain the juice through a napkin. For 1 glass juice, use 1 glass fine sugar, and reduce to the first mark, having measured the level previously with a spill. It is good to cook a piece of vanilla bean with this jelly and then remove it.

## 2006 Pineapple jelly

### (Zhele iz ananasov)

Cut a pineapple into small pieces, mash thoroughly with a spoon in a stoneware bowl, and squeeze the juice through a napkin. For 1 glass of juice, use 2 glasses, or 1 lb, fine sugar. Cook covered, like Wild strawberry jelly #2011. Reduce almost to the midpoint of the two marks [on a spill].

## 2011 Wild strawberry jelly

*(Zhele zemljanichnoe)*

Place ripe, but not overripe, berries in a bowl, mash them with a spoon, and pile them into a linen bag. Tie the bag securely above the berries and hang it up so that the juice flows out gradually. Let the juice settle and carefully decant the clear juice into a preserving pan, filling it halfway. For 1 lb juice, use 1½ lbs finely pounded sugar (i.e., for 1 glass juice, use 1½ glasses sugar). Mix to completely dissolve the sugar. Cover the saucepan with a lid and set it over a rather high fire. When it begins to boil, which can be recognized by the jingling handles of the pan, raise the lid and watch that the juice boils thoroughly but does not boil over. Then remove from the fire and thoroughly wipe off the lid. When the syrup stops steaming, replace the pan on top of the stove, covered, and let it come to a boil. Repeat this three times and then finish cooking over a low fire, testing with a spoon so that it does not overcook and with a spill so that it does not reduce to the mark itself. Toward the end, the lid may be removed.

## 2012 Wild strawberry jelly, another way

*(Zhele zemljanichnoe, drugim manerom)*

Some people, instead of mashing the berries, sprinkle them into a glass jar with an opening on the bottom of the jar. [Plug the bottom opening], tie up the jar with paper, and set it in the summer oven after baking bread. When the juice is released and the berries float to the top, let out the juice through the bottom opening and cook as indicated above.

# SUGAR SYRUPS

*(Siropy sakharnye)*

*Remarks:* In general use 1, or preferably, 1½ lbs sugar for every 3 glasses, or 1 bottle, of strained juice. Boil 3 or 4 times until completely clear, remove the scum, strain, and cover with a linen cloth. When cool, pour into dry bottles that have been thoroughly washed several weeks before.* Fill only to the neck, cork, and tar the bottles well. Store in dry sand in a dry, cold basement. All syrups prepared as described below will be sweet and thick and will last without spoiling not only until the next berry season, but for a year and a half or more, provided the bottles are well corked and stored in a cold, dry place. If such a thick syrup is not wanted, dilute each bottle as it is taken out of storage with 1 or 1½ glasses of water. Bring to a boil, cool, and serve. Always use a copper preserving pan. It is best to make the syrup with pieces of sugar.

*The bottles were washed beforehand to allow ample time for them to dry thoroughly in the air.

### 2014 Wild strawberry syrup

*(Sirop zemljanichnyj)*

Pick over and clean ½ pail of berries, turn them into a coarse sieve, and rinse with clear water. Pour the berries into a large jar, strew with 1 lb, or 2 glasses, fine sugar, and set the jar on a sunny windowsill for a full 24 hours. Transfer the berries to a linen bag, tie it up, and suspend it so that the juice can drain off gradually. For every 3 glasses of juice, use 2 glasses, or 1 lb, fine sugar. Bring to a boil 3 or 4 times, cool, and pour into bottles, etc.

Sugar or honey may be added to the remaining purée. Bring it to a boil and use for filling pies.

### 2018 Cherry syrup, together with cherry purée

*(Sirop vishnevyj i vmeste pjure iz vishen')*

Stone the cherries, place them in a preserving pan (several pounded pits may be added), and bring to a boil twice. When the juice is released, use a spoon to ladle it into a napkin or bag attached to an overturned bench (*skamejka*). For 3 glasses of juice, add 3 glasses, or 1½ lbs, fine sugar. Bring to a boil 3 or 4 times, removing the scum. After the juice has cleared, strain it, etc.

Keep a little juice for the cherries that are left and recook the fruit, stirring until the pulp softens. Rub the cherries through a fine sieve into a preserving pan and cook over a low fire, stirring constantly until the purée thickens and pulls away from the sides of the pan. Sugar or honey may be added, according to preference and taste, using 1 lb or less of honey for 1 lb of purée. Transfer the purée from the pan to an earthenware jug and set it in the oven after baking bread. Remove from the oven, set in a cool place, and, after it has cooled, cover with paper and tie up.

### 2026 Another pineapple syrup for drinks and ice cream

*(Sirop iz ananasov drugim manerom dlja pit'ja i dlja morozhenago)*

Prepare a ripe, aromatic pineapple as for eating, cut it into small pieces, and pack it in a jar. Sprinkle with sugar, wrap the jar with paper, and set it in the sun for three days to dissolve the sugar. Strain the fruit in a fine sieve and pour the juice into bottles. Plug with velvety, boiled corks [i.e., good quality corks], and seal with a mixture of half resin and half lard. Save the pineapple to use in a compote.

## 2030  Rose syrup

*(Sirop rozovyj)*

Trim the yellow ends from roses that have just bloomed. Put 1 lb of these trimmed rose petals into a napkin, the corners of which have been attached to the four legs of an overturned stool. Pour 2 bottles of boiling water over the petals, letting the water flow into a bowl placed beneath the napkin. The rose petals in the napkin should be shaken from time to time, not pressed. Transfer the petals to a plate, drizzle them thoroughly with lemon or currant juice, and mash until juice is released from the petals. Pour 1½ glasses rosewater onto 1 lb rose petals, mixing, rubbing, and pressing the liquid through a napkin. Add 1 lb, or 2 glasses, of very fine sugar to the pressed juice. To retain the fragrance, cook the syrup briefly over a very low fire only until the sugar dissolves completely. To strengthen the aroma, add 2 drops of rose oil, and to enhance the color, a little cochineal.

## 2032  Cider or lemon sherbet* for tea

*(Sidr ili sherbet limonnyj k chaju)*

Use 1 lb of sugar for 5 lemons. Use the sugar to scrape off the lemon zest. Squeeze the juice, mix with finely ground sugar, and let stand for 24 hours. The next day bring the juice to a boil 3 times in a preserving pan, skim, cool, and pour into a jar. If well boiled, this syrup will harden and crystalize. Hold it on a teaspoon while drinking water or tea. Many people who like to drink tea while holding a piece of lump sugar in their mouths use this cider or sherbet instead.

*\*The word sherbet derives from the Arabic sharbât. According to Alan Davidson, early recipes show that it was "a sweetened drink, flavoured with fruit, vegetables or flowers; it might have a pleasing sweet-acid taste, be cooled with snow, and sometimes be medicinal." In the United States sherbet now means a fruit ice while in England it means a fizzy confection for children. Ushakov's modern Russian definition is quite close to the original Arabic (via Turkish), "an Eastern chilled drink of sweetened fruit juice or fruit syrup." All of this makes Molokhovets' recipes even more puzzling; they seem closer to current English rather than Russian usage, as if they had developed apart from the rest of the culture. (Davidson, as quoted by Laura Mason in "Dibs, Dabs, Lemons and Love Hearts," 31; Ushakov, Tolkovyj slovar', III, 1333.)*

## 2034  Lemon sherbet

*(Sherbet limonnyj)*

Using 2 lbs sugar, scrape the zest from 3 lemons. Squeeze the juice [and set aside]. Add 1 small glass of water to the sugar and heat over a low fire, stirring until the sugar dissolves. Add the reserved lemon juice and, after putting more wood on the fire, boil over a high flame until the mixture sticks to the fingers and begins to thicken as for jelly. Remove the pan from the fire and stir in one direction with a wooden pestle, skimming off the foam and adding lemon juice for whiteness, just a few drops at a time. Keep stirring until the mixture thickens.

Transfer to a wide-mouthed jar and tie up. Eat with a spoon when drinking water or tea.

### 2037  Sherbet from almond shells

*(Sherbet iz skorlupy mindal'nykh orekhov)*

Boil almond shells until the water turns brown. For every 2 ½ glasses of the water, add 3 lbs of sugar. Cook as indicated in the above recipes. Remove from the fire and stir. To enhance the flavor, add 2 teaspoons of lemon juice without any lemon zest.

# 21
# Sugarless Juices, Syrups, and Conserves

*(Sok bez sakhara, sok dlja morozhenago, konservy)*

## JUICES WITHOUT SUGAR
*(Sok bez sakhara)*

### 2038 Raspberry juice without sugar
*(Sok bez sakhara iz maliny)*

Place raspberries or wild strawberries in a jar with an opening below. Wrap paper around the top and set the jar in the oven after baking bread. When the berries rise and give off their juice, let the jar cool, and release the juice [through the bottom opening] into bottles with necks.

Some people set this juice in a window on the sunny side of the house for a full week before straining it into bottles. Stop up the bottles tightly and seal them with tar. In the summer keep the bottles in the cold cellar, and in winter in a dry basement, overturned so their necks are in dry sand. A similar juice may be prepared in winter for *kvass, kissel,* syrup, etc.

### 2043 Lemon juice without sugar
*(Sok limonnyj bez sakhara)*

[Remove the zest from lemons and set it aside.] Squeeze the lemons, discard the pits, and strain the juice through a flannel into a jar. After the liquid has settled, carefully decant the clear juice into another jar, let it settle again, and then pour it into bottles with necks. A little olive or almond oil may be poured on top. Stop up the bottles, seal them, and store them overturned, burying their necks in dry sand. Dry the reserved zest, pound it fine, and store it in a jar, wrapped in paper. Add the zest to dishes for aroma. Fresh lemon zest is a good addition to vodka.

### 2045  Gooseberry juice similiar to lemon juice

*(Sok iz kryzhovnika na podobie limonnago)*

Gather ripe gooseberries around June 15. Clean the berries, pound them thoroughly in a wooden mortar, squeeze the juice from the berries, and pour it into a large jar or carboy. Add 2–3 lemons, sliced and seeded, wrap the carboy tightly with a cloth, and place in a sunny window or even in the garden in the open air for 12 or 14 days. After the liquid has settled, carefully decant the clear juice, strain, and bottle, adding 1–2 lemon slices or the zest from a lemon to each bottle. Cork, seal, and overturn the bottles with their necks buried in dry sand. This juice will keep 2–3 years, and the longer it stands, the better it becomes, until finally it is barely distinguishable from lemon juice. It is good to prepare jelly from this juice, after adding a little water and, if desired, lemon juice. Also, it may be added to dishes in place of vinegar.

## TO PREPARE JUICES FOR ICE CREAM IN THE WINTER

*(Prigotovlenie sokov na zimu dlja morozhenago)*

### 2051  Black currant syrup for ice cream

*(Sirop iz chernoj smorodiny dlja morozhenago)*

Sprinkle finely sieved sugar into a large jar and add a layer of berries 1½ to 2 times thicker than the layer of sugar. Cover with more sugar and another layer of berries, and repeat until the jar is filled. The last layer must be sugar. Tie paper around the jar and let it stand in the sun for 3 days so that the sugar dissolves. Turn everything into a fine sieve and let the juice drain off completely. Immediately pour the juice into bottles, stop them up with the best velvety corks, boiled until soft, and seal them using tar prepared half and half with fat or tallow to make it more pliable. Such syrup completely replaces fresh berries. If the syrup is prepared for beverages, it is better to pour it into small bottles so that it will not stand long uncorked. Store the bottles on their sides in a chest or box filled with dry sand. Keep them on ice until the frost and then in a dry, cold basement.

Prepare fruit pastilles (*prjanichki*) from the berries that remain (cf. #2059), or use them for filling sweet *pirogs*.

### 2053  Syrup from wild strawberries, another way

*(Syrop iz zemljaniki drugim manerom)*

Rub very ripe and fresh wild strawberries through a fine sieve. Measure the purée and, for each glass, add 1 glass of fine, sieved sugar. Mix until all the sugar has dissolved, pour the mixture into strong champagne bottles, stop them up securely with boiled corks, and tie each cork with twine. Place these bottles in a kettle with cold water, interspersing straw (*soloma*) between the bottles [to prevent them from breaking]. Boil the bottles for a full hour, then remove the kettle from the fire and let the bottles cool. Remove the bottles from the water, seal them, and store as indicated in #2051.

### 2059  Fruit pastilles made from any fruit

*(Prjanichki iz vsjakikh jagod)*

When preparing jelly-jam (*zhele-varen'e*), syrup for drinks, or syrup for ice cream (cf. Chapter 20), thoroughly mash the berries that remain in the sieve with sugar. For 3 cups of berries, add another cup of fine sugar and boil the mixture until it leaves the pan or congeals on a spoon placed on ice. Pour the mixture onto a platter, smooth it over, cool, and cut up like fruit pastilles (*prjanichki*).

## BERRY AND FRUIT PRESERVES FOR COMPOTES, ICE CREAM, AND DESSERTS IN WINTER

*(Konservy iz svezhikh jagod i fruktov na zimu dlja kompotov, morozhenago i desserta)*

### 2060  To keep berries and fruit for winter

*(Pervyj sposob sokhranjat' na zimu jagody i frukty)*

Immediately after gathering fresh, ripe, firm raspberries, currants, gooseberries, or cherries, pick them over and pour into dry bottles, shaking them slightly. Stop up the bottles and place them in a saucepan with hay (*seno*). Cover with cold water, cook for an hour, and remove the saucepan from the fire. When the water has cooled, remove the bottles and bury them in dry sand. In the winter these berries are used to prepare compotes and ice cream.

### 2063  A fourth way [to preserve berries and fruits for winter]

*(Chetvertyj sposob)*

a) All berries and fruits intended for conserves (that is, for compotes in the winter), must be very ripe and of the highest quality.

b) Glass jars, called *compotiers* (*kompot'er*) are used for preparing such conserves. Such jars are wider at the bottom than at the top. Pour syrup over the berries and fruits before wrapping the jars in hay or straw and setting them in a saucepan with cold water.

c) Boil the jars for 15–20 minutes, counting from the minute when the water begins to boil.

d) Wrap the jars with a bladder and tie with twine before setting them in a saucepan with water. The bladder must be be soaked in salted warm water for a full hour and then washed thoroughly in fresh water before being wrapped around the jars. Place a piece of clean linen under the bladder. However, the jars may be wrapped with linen even without the bladder.

e) Fill the jars leaving a space 3 fingers wide at the top.

f) For 1 lb of berries or fruit, use 1 lb sugar and ¾ glass water. First boil a thick syrup, remove the scum with blotting paper, and cool before pouring over the berries or fruit packed in the jars.

g) The very best preserves are prepared from gooseberries, peaches, pears, "amber" apples [a variety of yellow crabapple], raspberries, apricots, plums, cultivated strawberries, sour cherries, grapes, and sweet cherries.

h) The syrup poured over the berries becomes very watery with time. When preparing a compote from these berries and fruit, remove the bladder and pour off several spoonfuls of the syrup from the top. Pour the remaining syrup into a pan, add sugar, and reduce until thick. Cool, pour over the berries and fruit arranged on a platter, and serve. But only white syrups from peaches, pears, plums, and grapes are used for compotes in this way. Compotes with colored syrups are served only with meats and they should be half as sweet [as ordinary syrups].

i) A compote of various berries and fruits, nicely arranged and doused with white syrup, makes a very attractive platter.

### 2067  Bilberry conserves for compotes and soups for the sick

*(Konservy iz cherniki dlja kompotov i supov dlja bol'nykh)*

Sprinkle ripe, whole bilberries [*Vaccinium myrtillus*] into a jar, cover them with cooled syrup, wrap the jar in a bladder, and cook for 15 minutes.

### 2073  Conserves from nuts

*(Konservy iz orekhov)*

Gather, shell, and skin fresh nuts. Pack them into a *compotier*, pour on thick syrup, and wrap the jar in a bladder. Set the jar in a saucepan with cold water and boil for half an hour, etc.

### 2075  Greengage and other plum conserves, except Hungarian*

*(Konservy iz renklodov i rasnago roda sliv, krome vengerskikh)*

Choose very ripe, unblemished fruit as listed above. Prick each piece of fruit in several places with a wooden hairpin, drop them into cold water, and place the pot on top of the stove. Heat the water until it is very hot, but do not let it boil. Pour off the water and transfer the fruit to cold cranberry water for 12 hours. Drain off the cranberry water and pour a rather thin, cooled syrup over the fruit. After 24 hours, pour off the syrup, transfer the fruit to a *compotier*, and cover with fresh, thick syrup. Wrap the jar with a bladder, boil it for 15 minutes, and remove from the fire. After the water has cooled, wipe the jars dry and store them in a cold, dry place, etc.

*It is not clear why Molokhovets excluded Hungarian plums from this preparation since elsewhere she observed that they were "the very best plums to use for conserves."*

### 2080 [Hungarian plum conserves], the first method

*(Pervyj sposob)*

Wipe the plums thoroughly with a towel, make an incision in them carefully to remove the stones, and pack the plums in a jar. Cover with thick, cooled syrup, prepared from 1 glass water and 1 lb sugar for each lb of plums. Wrap the jar with a bladder and boil it for 25 minutes, but it is better to cook these plums longer in the oven.

### 2085 Another way to preserve cherries for compotes

*(Eshche sberezhenie vishen' dlja kompotu)*

Discard any twigs and pour the cherries into bottles, filling them rather compactly, but do not mash the fruit at all. For each bottle sprinkle on a full cup of the best sieved sugar, stop up the bottles, and tie with cords. When white bread is removed from the oven, set the bottles in the oven, shut the oven door, and leave the bottles there until the oven cools.


## PRESERVES FOR DECORATING TORTES AND COMPOTES

*(Varen'e dlja ukrashenija tortov i kompotov)*

### 2087 Preserved walnuts

*(Varen'e iz gretskikh orekhov)*

Prick green walnuts all over with a wooden hairpin, soak them in soft water for 9 days, and then set them in the same soft water on top of the stove. Let them boil until they are tender enough to be pierced easily by a wooden hairpin. Drain the nuts in a fine sieve. For 1 lb nuts, weigh out 2 lbs sugar. Use half the sugar to prepare a syrup that is not very thick. Add a piece of cinnamon and several cloves.

Cool the syrup before pouring it over the nuts, let them stand in the syrup for 3 days, and then drain the nuts in a fine sieve. Add the remaining sugar to the syrup, bring once to a boil, cool, pour over the nuts, and let stand for another 3 days. Then again turn the nuts into a sieve, reduce the syrup to the necessary thickness, pour it over the nuts while still hot, and let stand for 9 days. Transfer to a jar and tie with a bladder.

### 2089 Clear carrot preserves

*(Prozrachnoe varen'e iz morkovi)*

Boil yellow or red carrots in water until they begin to soften. Drain, cut them up attractively into little stars, drop into thick syrup, and boil them until they become translucent. Since carrots are available at any time, it is unnecessary to stock up supplies of this jam and to waste sugar unnecessarily.* For immediate use, ½ lb sugar is sufficient for 1 lb carrots, but old carrots from last spring's crop are not suitable.

*More sugar was needed to store preserves for a protracted period. In this case, the extra sugar was unnecessary since the preserves were kept only for a short time.

# 22

# Fruit Liqueurs, Cherry Brandies, and Sparkling Wines

## (Nalivki, vishnjak, shipovka, voditsa)

### 2091  Fruit liqueurs
*(Nalivki)*

Fruit liqueurs are an acceptable replacement for grape wine of medium strength and may be prepared from any kind of berries or fruit as follows: First, it is crucial that berries be ripe, clean, and free from green leaves or roots (old or crushed berries, provided they are not moldy, will not spoil the liqueur). If apples are used, they should be sour, not sweet, and cut into pieces small enough to fit through the neck of the bottle. Second, good spirits are essential; if not French brandy, then distilled vodka with the strength of 25 degrees of Gess* [Hess] must be used, otherwise the fruit liqueur will have a nasty odor.

Add a suitable amount of clean, ripe berries or fruit to a large glass bottle or carboy. Cover the berries with spirits (use distilled vodka if French brandy is not available) until you have ⅓ more liquid than berries; for example, if the berries fill ⅔ of the bottle, fill the remaining ⅓ of the bottle, to the very top of its neck, with vodka. Cover the bottle with a good strong cloth, tie it with a cord, and seal the ends. Set the bottle of liqueur in a window with a southern exposure, that is, on the sunny side of the house, and leave it there for 2 or 3 months, shaking it every 3 or 4 days. The length of time (2 or 3 months) depends on the ripeness of the berries or fruit and their quantity. The riper the berries and the more of them, the less time needed. For instance, if only very ripe berries or fruit are used, and vodka covers the fruit by the height of only two fingers, the time may be shortened even to 1½ months.

After standing, the fruit liqueur must be refined or strained. Line a clean funnel with a piece of cotton, cover the top with a cloth, and strain, pouring directly from the carboy into smaller bottles that were prepared beforehand. Should the fruit liqueur still be cloudy, strain it again in the same manner, but this will happen very rarely if only clean berries were used and if all the fruit liqueur was passed through a piece of cotton. Fruit liqueur prepared this way is still quite strong; to use in place of grape wine, it should be diluted by adding 1 bottle of water for every 3 to 4 bottles of strained liqueur.

Sweeten the liqueur, or add syrup, as follows: make a syrup, using from 1/4–1/3 lb sugar, broken into small pieces, for each bottle of liqueur (including the additional water). That is, add the sugar to a good tin-plated saucepan large enough to hold all the liqueur. Pour in only enough water to dissolve the sugar, and place on the fire. When the sugar dissolves and comes to a boil, immediately add the liqueur, including the water used to dilute it, to the boiling syrup. Keep on the fire until the mixture barely begins to boil. Immediately remove the saucepan from the fire and transfer the contents to a stoneware or glazed bowl to cool.

When the liqueur has cooled, it is ready to be used. The liqueur must first be bottled, corked, and sealed, and then it may be kept as long as you like. A little plaque with a number and description should be attached to every bottle of liqueur, sparkling beverage, or syrup. To keep track of how many remain, always use the highest-numbered bottle first. The sugar required per bottle, from 1/4 to 1/3 lb, depends on the taste of the prepared liqueur and still more on the berries that were used. For example, black currants and cloudberries (from Archangel province) require less sugar than other berries—not more than 1/4 lb per bottle. The liqueur from these berries (especially cloudberries) is very tasty. If only ripe berries and good vodka are used, the liqueur will be exactly like old Hungarian wine** in both flavor and bouquet [sic].

The very best fruit liqueurs are made from cloudberries, black currants, cherries, raspberries, red currants, lingonberries, plums, and rowanberries. Gather the latter in the fall after the first frost; pick them over and add them to a carboy. Add vodka as indicated above and set in a window, but best of all on a cupboard in a heated room for 2 or 3 months.

*"Gess" is a unit of measurement denoting the strength of alcohol, named after the chemist Academician German Ivanovich Gess (1802–1850).

**Hungarian wine, which here I assume means Tokay wine, was a favorite of the Tsars and was held in the highest repute during the nineteenth century.

### 2092 A quick-ripening fruit liqueur

#### (Nalivka skorspelaja)

Fill a glazed bowl with berries, especially cherries, black currants, or raspberries, and cover the berries with good distilled vodka. Tie up the bowl with sugar wrapping paper* and pierce the paper in several places with a thin stick or fork. Put this bowl in the oven after baking rye bread and leave it there until the berries are well-stewed, which is indicated by their turning brown and becoming so soft that the cherry stones are loosened with the least pressure. Drain the berries in a coarse sieve and collect the juice in a bowl. Be careful not to crush the berries, only shake them slightly. The berry juice may be sweetened as desired using from ¼ to ¾ pound sugar per bottle.

This fruit liqueur can be prepared in 24 hours. The berries that remain in the sieve may be covered with water and distilled. The resulting liquid will be suitable for vinegar, for which the addition of vodka is not necessary.

*"*Sugar wrapping paper*" refers to the heavy blue paper that was ordinarily used to wrap sugar cones. It corresponds to the present-day heavy brown paper in America used for grocery bags.*

### 2096  Lingonberry liqueur

*(Nalivka iz brusniki)*

In the spring, pour a pail of vodka over ¼–½ pound dry wormwood and let it infuse. In the autumn, fill a carboy ⅓ full with very ripe lingonberries and top up with the wormwood-infused vodka. Let it stand in a [heated] room for about 2 months, then pour off and sweeten the liqueur, using from ¼–¾ pound of sugar per bottle.

[2099: Prepare exactly the same as #2096, except fill the bottle half-full with lingonberries and add plain distilled vodka instead of wormwood-infused vodka.]

# CHERRY BRANDY
## *(Vishnevka)*

### 2101  Cherry brandy

*(Vishnjak)*

This very tasty and healthy drink is prepared as follows: choose a good, strong, small barrel bound with 4 iron hoops. The cherries for this brandy must be ripe and clean, without twigs or leaves. Fill the barrel almost full, leaving a space of no more than 1–1½ *vershok* at the top. Cover the cherries with raw and pure honey from a beehive, without any wax and unadulterated by pollen-flour, such as often pollutes store-bought honey.* It is better if the honey is white rather than red. Pour it slowly, adding as much as needed to cover all the cherries and fill all the space between them. Stop pouring when the honey begins to cover the top layer, plug the barrel tightly, and pour resin over the cork. Tie the barrel around the cork with sturdy rope. It is best to seal the entire barrel with resin so that no air will come in contact with the cherries. Set the barrel in a cold place or in the cold cellar, but not on ice; or better yet bury it in the ground or in sand in the basement and leave it there for 3 months while the brandy ferments. If a barrel is flimsy or lacks iron hoops, it probably will explode.

After 3 months, the cherry brandy will be ready. Uncork the barrel and bottle the brandy, straining it through a piece of canvas. Cork the bottles securely and seal the necks with resin or sealing-wax. Cherry brandy prepared in this way will keep for several years. For a three-pail barrel, use 2 pails of cherries and 1 pail of honey.

*\*Pollen was sometimes referred to as tsvetochnaja-muka, or "flower-flour"; in this case Molokhovets omitted the qualifier tsvetochnaja.*

### 2102  Ukrainian cherry brandy
*(Malorossijskaja vishnevka)*

First prepare a board with a rim or edges. Arrange very ripe cherries, cleaned of twigs, on the board, with their holes upward to prevent the juice from escaping. Place the board with the cherries into a very slow oven [i.e., after the fire has been dampened] just until the cherries wilt and wrinkle slightly, but do not let them dry out. Let them cool before pouring into a prepared keg or carboy. Shake the carboy or roll the keg while filling so that more cherries can be added. When the barrel is full of fruit, top it up with the very best distilled vodka. Set the barrel in the cold cellar, but not in the icehouse, for 10 days. Then pour all the liquid into another carboy and cover the berries with vodka for a second time. Let stand for 2 weeks before pouring off [and reserving] this liquid. Cover the berries with vodka for a third time and let steep for 7 weeks. Mix the 3 infusions together and sweeten to taste, using from 1/4–3/4 pound sugar per bottle. Cork, seal with resin, and store in the cold cellar.


## SPARKLING AND OTHER HOMEMADE LIGHT WINES
*(Shipovki i pr. legkija domashnija vina)*

### 2104  Sparkling wines
*(Shipovki)*

Sparkling wines, like liqueurs, may be prepared from any kind of berry or fruit. The resulting drink, however, is much sweeter and more delicate than any kind of liqueur. It sparkles (*shipit*) like champagne, hence its name "sparkling" (*shipovka*). When preparing sparkling wines, attention must be paid to the choice of both the berries and the vodka. The berries must be completely fresh and ripe, and French brandy or cognac is essential (or "old" [*staraja*]\* good vodka, as it is still called in several places in the Western provinces).

To prepare this sparkling wine, pour 14 bottles, or 7 *shtof* of pure, raw [i.e., unboiled] water into a glass carboy, add 7 pounds of finely pounded good sugar, mix with a spoon until the sugar completely dissolves, and add 7 pounds of fresh, ripe berries or fruit. Pour in 2 bottles or 1 *shtof* of "old" vodka or French brandy, shake the carboy several times, and cover the neck with a thin piece of canvas. Tie it up and place in a sunlit window for 12 days. During this period thoroughly stir the berries every morning with a clean spatula, being careful not to crush them or, alternatively, shake the carboy several times. After 12 days in the sun, the berries will circulate up and down, and this shows that the sparkling wine is ready. It must now be strained through a canvas or napkin folded in four (but do not use cotton cloth, as for fruit liqueurs). Strain into another carboy and let stand on ice for 3 days. Note that juice should not be squeezed from the leftover berries and mixed with the already filtered sparkling drinks as is done when preparing fruit liqueurs.

After 3 days the fizzing will have settled down. The wine should then be strained once more through a piece of canvas folded in four and bottled carefully. Use only champagne bottles (other bottles will burst eventually) and do not fill them completely. The corks must be the very best, and they must be boiled before using.** Cork the bottles as securely as possible, driving the corks in with a wooden mallet. Use a thin wire or a strong cord to attach the corks to the necks of the bottles, as is done with champagne. Dip the necks of the corked bottles into resin or tar and store all the bottles in a cold place, but not on ice, with their necks downward, buried in sand. Let them stand in this manner for 1½–2 months. During this time the wine will ferment and, if a bottle or two bursts, then it proves that the sparkling wine is ready. You may expect many bottles to burst if you use inferior corks or ordinary bottles instead of champagne bottles. This beverage cannot be kept longer than 1½ years before turning sour. The very best sparkling wines are made of *kumaniki*,*** raspberries, black and red currants, ripe gooseberries, etc.

[A pleasing alternative to this sparkling wine is sparkling macédoine. It is made like the above recipe (#2104), but combines a variety of berries and fruits (especially cherries, black currants, raspberries, melons, peaches, and pineapple) either in equal parts, or by adding more of any preferred fruit. It has an inexplicable aroma, and many prefer it to all other sparkling wine.]

*Related to this "old" vodka is today's Starka vodka, which is a variety of strong vodka that is aged before bottling and is the same color as French brandy.*

**Bottles had to be securely stoppered to retard the spoilage of their contents. This led to a wide discussion in nineteenth-century domestic literature of the most suitable stoppers and corks. "The choice of corks is highly important. Some corks are very porous, and, although they stop the bottle well in appearance, they allow the wine to evaporate. Hard and dry corks have this effect. The best corks are those which are fine-grained, soft, yielding to the fingers, and showing few pores." (Good-holme's Domestic Cyclopaedia of Practical Information, 594; see also Godey's Lady's Book and Magazine, March 1856, 267–268.)*

***This is a regional word for a kind of blackberry. Kumanika can refer to any one of three different berries: (1) The European blackberry, Rubus fructicosus, (2) the European dewberry, Rubus caesius, or (3) Rubus nessensis. (Macura, Russian-English Botanical Dictionary, 262.)*

## 2107  Raisin wine*

*(Voda izjumennaja)*

Fill a small barrel with 10 pounds of raisins, which need not be of high quality. Add 3 pails of raw, unboiled water, the zest and pulp of 5 large lemons without pith or seeds, and 3 tablespoons of the very best yeast. Let the mixture ferment in a warm room for 3 days, shaking the barrel each day. If fermentation does not occur, add a little more yeast. Set the barrel on ice for 12 days, and then pour into bottles. Cork well, tar, and lay the bottles on their sides in sand in the ice house so that the corks are always covered with liquid. Test after 2 weeks. Place a teaspoon of fine sugar in a glass and stir with a spoon while pouring on the raisin water. If the mixture foams like soda, it is ready to be used. This is a very refreshing and pleasant beverage, especially in the hot summer weather.

*\*Raisin wine had been made for a long time in Russia and elsewhere. With the addition of treacle and barm, this was called raisin mead in eighteenth-century Russia. By the mid nineteenth century, recipes for both raisin mead (with treacle) and raisin wine (without treacle) were appearing in Russian cookbooks. One advantage of raisin wine was that it could be made anywhere at any season, which was one of the reasons why it was commonly used during Passover by the Jews of Eastern Europe.*

## 2115  Black currant wine, another way

*(Voditsa iz chernoj smorodiny, drugim manerom)*

Fill a glazed earthenware pot with very ripe black currants. Tie up the pot with blue sugar wrapping paper, prick the paper with a small twig, and set the pot in the oven immediately after baking bread. Remove when the berries are well-stewed, which is shown by their turning brown. Pour the berries into à sieve, letting the juice drain away completely. Bottle the strained berries and cover with boiled and cooled water. The berries need only half-fill the bottle, or even less, then fill the rest of the bottle with water. Store on ice until the frost, and after several days it will be completely ready. [As the liquid is drawn off from the bottle, it should be replaced with the same amount of boiled, cooled water.] A beverage prepared in this manner will not keep long and will mature quite soon. Use the juice which was first drained from the berries to prepare syrup.

## 2119  Seville orange wine

*(Voditsa pomerantsovaja)*

Boil 6 pails of water with 24 pounds of sugar until reduced to only 4 pails. Remove from the fire, pour into a six-pail keg, and let stand until cooled to the temperature of milk fresh from the cow. The barrel should be made of very sturdy oak bound with iron hoops. Cut very ripe Seville oranges into several pieces so the seeds can be easily removed and discarded. Toss the oranges into the barrel with 7 spoons of the very best yeast and a pail of white table wine (it can be the very cheapest of light wines). When the mixture has fermented 3 or 4 hours, plug and seal the bunghole, transfer the keg to ice, and keep it there for 14 days. Without removing the keg from the ice house, decant the orange wine into champagne bottles. Cork the bottles, bind the corks with wire, and seal. Keep the bottles in a cold place, packing them with sand in a box or trunk. In winter keep them in the cold cellar, in summer on ice.

### 2126 Birch drink*

*(Berezovik)*

In the spring, make a crosswise opening through the bark of a good, large, young birch tree, and tightly drive in a splint, similar to those used for rolling eggs, but shorter.** Attach a tub or vat to the splint to catch the flowing sap. A good tree may yield from 1–4 pails of sap, others none at all; therefore several trees should be tapped. Pour a full pail of birch sap into a one and one-half pail barrel, and add 3 bottles of cheap, light white wine, 1 bottle of low-quality Hungarian wine, 2 bottles of French brandy, 3–6 pounds of sugar, according to taste, and 3 pounds of good raisins. Plug the bunghole as tightly as possible, seal it all around, and set the barrel on ice for 2½ months. Bottle the birch drink, cork, seal, and place the bottles on their sides in sand in the cold cellar. After adding sugar, the birch juice must be shaken or stirred to dissolve the sugar.

*Birch wines were common in seventeenth- and eighteenth-century England and also were widely consumed in Colonial America. (Hartley, Food in England, 553–554; Martha Washington's Booke of Cookery, 384–385.)
**At Easter time Russian children played a game of rolling Easter eggs with a small trough-like piece of wood.

### 2131 Bishop of Seville oranges with Malaga

*(Bishof iz pomerantsev s malagoju)*

To make a dry bishop,* chop up 3 pounds of sugar as for tea. Scrape the zest off Seville oranges (it is impossible to say exactly how many) with the pieces of sugar until the sugar is yellow on all sides. Scrape the yellowed sugar onto a plate and continue rubbing the oranges with the sugar pieces until all the sugar has been yellowed and used up. Moisten the saturated sugar powder with orange juice until it is the consistency of *kissel*.** Pour the mixture into a jar and store in a dry place. When bishop is wanted, dilute with Malaga, according to taste, and serve.

*This recipe is related to the English drink of the same name. The English version calls for clove-studded oranges to be steeped in hot port with sugar and other spices. The earliest attested English-language reference is Swift's, who wrote in 1738, "[Oranges] well-roasted, with sugar and wine in a cup, They'll make a sweet bishop." In 1801 Coleridge referred to "Spicy bishop, drink divine." (Oxford English Dictionary, I, 878–879.)

**This direction is not very helpful since kissels can vary in consistency from stiff to semi-liquid.*
*They can also quiver like molded gelatin. See recipes in Chapter 14 for examples.*

### 2134 Limpopo (a Finnish drink)*

*(Limpopo [Finljadskij napitok])*

Thinly slice a 10 kopeck loaf of sour-sweet bread without candied peel, dry the slices as well as possible, and put them in a soup bowl. Meanwhile, scrape the zest from 2 lemons with 1½ glasses of sugar pieces. In a separate bowl, mix together the flavored sugar, the juice from the lemons, 3 bottles of the very best white beer, and a large wineglass of 2 ruble rum. Strain the mixture. Thirty minutes before using, pour the strained liquid over the dried rusks. Strain again before serving.

The leftover rusks are also very tasty.

*\*I have been unable to discover the origin of this drink, but the name recalls the traditional Swedish rye bread, limpa, that is made with molasses and candied citrus peel.*

# 23

# Sugarless Vodkas, Punches, and Fruit Drinks

*(Vodki bez sakhara, vodki sladkija, likery,*
*punshi i raznoe pit'e)*

## SUGARLESS VODKAS

*(Vodki bez sakhara)*

### 2140 Baked vodka

*(Vodka zapekanka)*

Distill ordinary vodka over dried lemon peels and pour 4 *shtofs* of this distilled vodka into a thick glass bottle. Pound 12 *zolotniki* cinnamon, 4 *zolotniki* star anise, and 5 *zolotniki* each cardamom and mace. Grate 2 nutmegs and add all the spices to the bottle. Spread rye dough, 3 fingers thick, over the bottle. For 4 days in a row, place the bottle in the oven overnight after baking bread, and remove it from the oven every morning. Then pour off the vodka and sweeten it, adding 1 lb sugar for each *shtof* vodka.

### 2142 To cleanse the odor from spirits

*(Ochishchat' spirt ot vsjakago zapakha)*

For 1 pail of spirits, add 1½ lbs of birch coals prepared as follows. Pour very hot, disintegrating coal embers into an earthenware pot, blow off all the ashes to make them as clean as possible, and tightly cover the pot with a lid so that the coals die out. Remove the coals from the pot, carefully blow off the ashes, cool, and pound, but not too fine. Pour the coals into a bottle and cover with the spirits. Set aside for 3 weeks and shake the bottle 3 or 4 times per day, then let the spirits stand undisturbed on the coals for another week. Prepare another bottle, add 1 lb good, large, yellow raisins, well picked over, and 8 *zolotniki* finely chopped orris root. Pour the spirits into the newly prepared bottle using a funnel lined with a white flannel. Set the spirits aside for 12 days, then re-strain through a flannel. Spirits prepared in this way may completely replace French brandy in fruit liqueurs. The vodka must be diluted with boiled, cooled water; otherwise, it will whiten. To determine the strength of this vodka, consult a spirit thermometer.

# SWEET VODKAS OR RATAFIAS
### (Sladkaja vodka ili ratafija)

### 2144  Peach pit ratafia
#### (Ratafija iz persikovykh kostochek)

Pound peach pits,* half fill a *shtof* container with them, fill the container up to the neck with good, old, French brandy, and set it in the sun or on a heated stove-bench (*lezhanka*) for 4 or 5 weeks. Pour off the liquid and, for 1 bottle of this ratafia, add 1 lb sugar. If a weaker ratafia is preferred, make a thick syrup by adding 1 glass boiling water to sugar and reduce the syrup to the desired consistency. Pour the syrup into the ratafia. To clear the ratafia, strain it through fine linen.

*Peach pits, like cherry pits, contain prussic acid and should not be used. A safer alternative is almond extract.*

### 2146  Raspberry vodka
#### (Vodka malinovaja)

Pour ripe, picked-over raspberries into a carboy, add just enough thrice-distilled vodka to barely cover the berries, and set the jar in the sun. Pour off the vodka after 2–3 days. For ¼ pail vodka, use 3 glasses water and 1½ lbs sugar. Bring the water and sugar to a boil twice, skim until clear, and gradually pour the vodka into the hot syrup, stirring with a spoon. Mix thoroughly and strain through a flannel. Or, strain through a funnel that has been lined with cotton wool, sprinkled with well-pounded coals that have not been slaked with water, and topped with a piece of flannel. Strain the vodka into a carboy in this manner, stopping before the neck of the bottle is filled. Cork the bottle as well as possible and set in a warm place for several weeks until the vodka settles. Then carefully pour off and bottle the clear vodka. If refined vodka is wanted in a short time, add 10–15 grains potash for every quarter-pail of vodka. Dissolve the potash in a wineglass of warm water, mix with the vodka, stirring vigorously, and set in a warm place. Strain as indicated above.

### 2153  Allspice vodka or pepper vodka

*(Vodka s anglijskim ili prostym pertsem)*

Pour 18 *zolotniki* coarsely pounded allspice berries or black peppercorns into
¼ pail vodka and set aside for 2 weeks in a warm place. Strain, dilute with a syrup
prepared from 3 glasses water and 1½–2 lbs sugar, and re-strain. Proceed further,
following the instructions for Raspberry vodka.


## VERY SWEET VODKAS, LIKE LIQUEURS
### *(Vodki ochen' sladkija, v rode likerov)*

*Remarks:* For ¼ pail thrice-distilled vodka, use 6–9 glasses water and 6 lbs
sugar. Prepare a syrup from this water and sugar and skim until clear. Let cool, stir
in the distilled and strained vodka seasoned with some kind of spice and then
strain through a flannel, as indicated in the directions for Raspberry vodka
#2146. Let liqueur settle for several weeks in a warm place, then carefully decant
and bottle.


### 2154  Rose liqueur

*(Liker rozovyj)*

Gather rosebuds that are just blossoming, cut off [and discard] the white ends
of the petals, and pour the petals into a carboy. Add enough thrice-distilled vodka
just to cover the petals. Set the carboy in the sun for 3 days, pour off the vodka,
and pour it over fresh rose petals. Repeat 3 times. Strain thoroughly. To heighten
the color, add several drops vitriol, but take great care because vitriol turns the
liqueur acid and readily causes it to overflow. Therefore, after every drop of vitriol,
shake [the liqueur] and observe the color. If color is sufficiently pink, do not add
any more vitriol. Dilute ¼ pail of this vodka with a syrup prepared from 6–9
glasses rosewater and 6 lbs sugar.


### 2159  Maraschino* liqueur

*(Liker maraskin)*

Pour into a carboy 5 bottles raspberry water, 1½ bottles cherry water, 1¾
bottles orange flower water, 15 lbs sugar, and 5–6 bottles of very strong grain
spirits, distilled over coals. Cork, tar, and set in the larder for 6 months. Then
carefully decant into another carboy and filter the sediment through a flannel into
a separate bottle.

Liqueur from arctic brambleberries (*Rubus arcticus*)** is prepared like Raspberry liqueur. It may be obtained ready-made at Chesnokov's store, 29 Great Konjushennaja Street.

*\*The name of this liqueur comes from* marasca, *Italian for the morello cherry.*
*\*\*For more on this elusive northern berry which seems to defy cultivation, see Forsell,* Berries, *48–51.*

# VARIOUS PUNCHES
## (Raznye punshy)

### 2161  Cold punch
*(Punsh kholodnyj)*

Break 3 lbs sugar into pieces of the usual size and use them to scrape off the zest from 10 lemons and 3 oranges. Remove and discard all the white pith from the lemons and oranges and cut the fruit pulp into pieces, discarding any seeds.

If possible, it is good to add other fruit, including a very small sliced pineapple. Place the cut-up fruit in a bowl and cover with 3⅓ bottles, or 10 glasses, boiling

Punch dispenser with glasses. Cover from *Banketnye i gastronomicheskie napitki* (St. Petersburg [1912]).

water. Add the sugar pieces and mix thoroughly. After the sugar has dissolved and the boiling water has cooled, pour 2 glasses cognac and 1 bottle French brandy into the syrup. Immediately cover the bowl with a lid or, preferably, with a napkin. Place a pillow on top to prevent the alcohol from evaporating. Strain after 3 hours, squeeze out the napkin, and store the punch in bottles, corked and tarred. This cold punch has a very pleasant flavor.

### 2164  Ladies' punch, another way

*(Punsh damskij drugim manerom)*

(For 6 persons). Pour boiling water over 1 teaspoon yellow tea* and let it brew. Squeeze the juice from 6 oranges. Add to each teacup 1 piece sugar, 1 teaspoon maraschino, 2 teaspoons white rum and the juice of an orange. Fill up [the cup] with tea.

*Yellow tea is a Chinese tea prepared from the youngest shoots of the plant, especially from the buds of the tea leaves. It is an exceptionally fine, delicate tea with an elusive aroma. Yellow Chinese tea is almost unknown in Europe; not only is it very expensive, but in the past the Chinese prohibited its export since the use of yellow tea was reserved for high officials at the Imperial Court and for religious ceremonies. (Pokhlebkin, Chai, ego tipy, svojstva, upotreblenie, 43–44.)*

### 2165  Sabayon punch

*(Punsh sabaion)*

(For 6 glasses). Beat together ⅔ glass fine sugar strained through a fine sieve and 6 very fresh egg yolks until completely thick and white. Bring to a boil 4 glasses Malaga, and while still hot, pour into the beaten egg yolks, stirring constantly. Beat with a whisk, as for chocolate, without letting the mixture boil, and serve hot.


# VARIOUS DRINKS
*(Raznoe pit'e)*


### 2171  To prepare chocolate bars

*(Sposob prigotovlenija samago shokolada)*

Hot chocolate will cost very little if you prepare your own chocolate bars. The quality of the chocolate depends solely on the freshness of the cocoa, which is indicated as follows: Break the bean, and if the interior is neither decayed nor rotten, the bean may be used. After purchasing very fresh cocoa beans, roast them like coffee beans in a brazier, a few at a time. When the beans begin to crack slightly, immediately pour them onto a clean table so that they barely touch one another. Be careful not to overcook them, because overcooked cocoa beans are as unfit for use as undercooked ones.

After the beans have cooled, skin them and grind as fine as possible. Then, in 1½ lb batches, grind the powder long and hard in an *iron* mortar. No other kind is suitable, for after pouring in the powder and beginning to pound it, you must immediately begin to heat the mortar until it becomes very hot. Set it on a very hot stove tile such as that used for resting an iron, and exchange the tile for a hot one as soon as it cools. But watch that the mortar does not get too hot and burn the cocoa, because in that case, everything will be wasted.

When the powder turns into a smooth, oily mixture, gradually pour in 1½ lbs finely sieved sugar, constantly pounding the mixture and stirring with a spoon. Finally, add ½ *lot* vanilla finely pounded with a piece of sugar and sieved. (If desired, ½ *lot* each cardamom and cinnamon also may be added.) But since vanilla generally is a rather harmful substance, the only good part being its fragrance, it is best to use sugar saturated with the odor of vanilla from having been stored in a glass jar with a piece of vanilla. These jars [of vanilla sugar] must be wrapped with a bladder or with paper.

Thoroughly stir the mixture of cocoa and sugar, and then pour it into tin molds, shaped like small bars of chocolate. These shallow molds must be wider on top and narrower on the bottom. When spreading this mixture, shake the molds thoroughly to distribute the chocolate evenly. Set the molds in a cold place, cover them with muslin to protect them from flies, and leave them to dry. When the tops have dried, remove the bars from the molds and spread them out on clean paper to dry thoroughly on the other side. Then wrap in paper. Good chocolate must be a very dark, reddish color; it must be very smooth and melt in the mouth.

### 2172  To prepare coffee

*(Kak varit' kofe)*

For 1 lb coffee use ¼ lb chicory. The coffee should be roasted not in a skillet but in a covered brazier, which should be shaken constantly. It is ready when the beans turn dark chestnut and are covered with moisture. Beware of overcooking. It is better to pound the beans rather than to grind them, and the finer the better. For each cup, use one full teaspoon of coffee blended with chicory. Pour into a flannel bag in a coffee pot, add boiling water measured by the teacup, and set the pot on top of the stove. Remove from the stove when the coffee comes to a boil and immediately add a spoon of cold water. After the coffee has settled, return the pot to the top of the stove. When it begins to boil, set it aside again and add another spoon of cold water. Again let it come to a boil, and again add a spoon of cold water. The fourth time, let it come to a boil, set aside to settle, and then serve.

Or, cook in the oven in an earthenware coffee pot, glazed on both sides. Use coffee water instead of regular water; that is, use water boiled down from the sediment from left-over coffee, adding to it a piece of fish glue or isinglass.* After cooking, let the coffee settle, decant it carefully into another coffee pot, heat, and serve. Heat the cream for coffee in small jugs with lids so a thick membrane will form.

*According to Mrs. Lincoln, one-time head of the Boston Cooking School, "Fish glue or inferior isinglass, which can be purchased at a druggist's, is a cheap and convenient article to use in clearing coffee. Egg shells should be saved and used for the same purpose. . . . Two or three shells contain albumen sufficient to clear a quart of coffee" (Lincoln, Mrs. Lincoln's Boston Cook Book, 114).

### 2176 Pistachio drink

(Fistashkovoe pit'e)

Scald ½ lb pistachios with boiling water, remove the skins, and pound the nuts fine. Add 4 glasses of boiled and cooled water to the nuts, pound several times, strain, and press. Add ½ spoon vanilla powder and 2 glasses water boiled with sugar.

INGREDIENTS (for 6 glasses)

½ lb pistachios                       ½ spoon vanilla powder
¼–⅓ lb fine sugar

### 2181 Home-style fizzy lemonade

(Limonad gazez domashnim obrazom)

Boil and cool 26 bottles of water. Pour the water into a large carboy and add ½ lb currant leaves, 6 lemons cut into small pieces (and seeded), about 8 lbs sugar, and 42 zolotniki cream of tartar. Shake all this thoroughly and keep it in the icehouse for 24 hours. Then set the carboy in the sun for 3 days, after which bottle, cork securely, and set on ice, where it should be kept until used.

# 24
# Kvass, Beer, and Mead

## (Kvas, pivo, med)

## KVASS
### (Kvas)

[*Translator's note:* Kvass is a lightly fermented sour-sweet beverage that is commonly made of black bread or grain with yeast and somewhat resembles beer in flavor. Both grain *kvass* and beet *kvass* are used for soup. Other more delicate varieties of *kvass* are made from fruits or berries. *Kvass*, along with mead and beer, has been drunk since Kievan Rus'. Whereas the nobility in earlier times preferred mead, the common people drank *kvass*. It was the most popular drink in nineteenth-century Russia, consumed by the rich as an occasional refreshment and by the peasantry on a daily basis. Like the gathering of mushrooms and berries, the eating of *prjaniki,* and the consumption of *shchi,* the drinking of *kvass* in late Tsarist Russia had become a culture-laden act that helped to define one's Russianness. Although *kvass* was easily made at home, the itinerant *kvass* peddler was a common figure in the streets and markets. Even today, it is not unusual to see a *kvass* truck parked at the curb while the driver dispenses drinks to a crowd of customers. *Kvass* is a relatively healthy drink, having a low alcoholic content (0.7 to 2.2%) and a good proportion of readily assimilable proteins and carbohydrates. (Dix, "Non-Alcoholic Beverages," 22.)]

### 2184  White grain kvass*
#### (Kvas khlebnyj belyj)

This simple white grain *kvass* is essential to the household, since it is drunk by the servants and used as a base (*zakvaska*) for borshch, *shchi,* etc., and for stewing beef. It is prepared as follows: Mix together 10 lbs rye flour and 1 lb each malt and buckwheat flour. Moisten with 1 *garnets* lukewarm water, mix, and pour on 1 *garnets* boiling water. After 30 minutes, add 2 more *garnets* boiling water. Do this 3 or 4 times. When a pail of boiling water has been added in this manner, mix and let cool slightly. Add ½ *garnets* or a little more *kvass* sediment [from an earlier batch], cover, and set in a rather warm place. The next day dilute the *kvass* with unboiled cold water, mix, and transfer to a cold place. Let it stand, and use as is or bottle. These proportions will yield 5 pails of *kvass*. When all the *kvass* has been consumed, set aside nearly 1 *garnets* of sediment remaining on the bottom for fermenting the next batch. Pour any extra sediment into the mash for the cows.

*This basic recipe for* kvass *is of mostly historical interest. For instance, one cannot tell from Molokhovets' instructions just how much water should be added at what stage of the process. For more on weights and measures, see the Appendix.*

### 2185 Grain kvass

*(Kvas khlebnyj krasnyj)*

[Ingredients:] 1 pood rye flour; 3 lbs each wheat flour and buckwheat flour; 1 *garnets* each barley malt, rye malt, and wheat malt; 2 glasses yeast; and ½ lb mint. These proportions will yield at least 12 pails *kvass*.

Pour the rye flour and the malts into a tub or vat. Set aside 1 lb each of the wheat and buckwheat flour and add the rest of the flour to the vat. Pour in enough warm water to make a thick dough. Bring a kettle of water to a boil, pour the boiling water into the dough all at once, and stir until smooth. When the oven has been heated, prepare 2 kettles, ladle cold water into them, immediately add the dough, and set in a very hot oven that has been swept out, but with hot coals left on both sides. Seal the oven [door] with clay. On the next day—that is, after 24 hours—remove the kettles and top them up with warm water. Set aside for 1½-2 hours, until the crusts are soaked. Return all the dough to the vat, mix thoroughly, and add 2 pails boiling water. Mix again, add 4 pails cold water, stir several times, add a small piece of ice, and let the mixture settle.

Meanwhile, prepare a leaven by pouring the remaining 1 lb each of wheat and buckwheat flour into 2 ladles of the just-settled wort. Add 2 glasses yeast, mix, cover, and set in a warm place to rise. When the must in the tub has completely settled, pour off the 6 pails of liquid into a 12–pail keg and add the raised leavened dough. Pour another 6 pails of cold water onto the dough that remains in the tub, mix several times, let settle again, and pour off into the same large keg.

Take a little of this *kvass*, add some mint, and bring to a boil. Remove from the stove, cover, and let cool. Strain into the keg or add the mint leaves as well. Plug the keg securely and transfer the *kvass* to the cold cellar in summer, or, in winter, to a dry basement where it will not freeze. The *kvass* may be used after 2 days.

### 2188 Excellent kvass

*(Kvas otlichnyj)*

Pour 4 lbs malted flour into 50 glasses cold water—that is, almost 17 bottles or 17 half-*shtofs*. [1 bottle = ½ *shtof*] Mix and add enough rye flour (approximately 1 pood) to form a thick dough, but a little thinner than for bread. Prepare this dough at 9 o'clock in the evening, and keep it at room temperature until 7 o'clock in the morning, at which time you must have prepared 4–5 pails of boiling water and have heated the oven hot enough for baking bread. (In summer the dough will be ready sooner.) Dilute the prepared dough with the boiling water and pour into glazed jugs or even into kettles—but the color will not be as clear if kettles are used. Cover tightly and set in the oven for a full 24 hours. Watch that the dough does not overflow, but if that happens, immediately set a kettle of cold water in the oven.

After 12 hours, remove the kettles without shaking them. Fill them with boiling water and return them to the same oven for another 12 hours. Meanwhile, prepare a trough with a small opening in the middle. Place a clean stick or spill over this opening, spread hay on top, and cover with a single layer of thick canvas. Remove the kettles from the oven, let them stand 2 hours, and then carefully pour the liquid into the trough, which must drain into a prepared vat. Remove all the sediment from the kettle to allow all the liquid to drain off.

While this wort is being strained, prepare a bunch each of rowanberries, mint, and black currant twigs (twice as large as the bunches of berries and mint). Beat 1 tablespoon bread leaven with rye flour and let rise for 2 hours. When it has risen, place the prepared bunches of herbs in a small saucepan, fill the saucepan with some of the strained wort, and bring to a boil. Pour the wort into 3-pail kegs and add 1–3 spoons of the prepared leaven, according to the acidity of the wort. Set the kegs in the kitchen in the winter for 7 hours, or, in summer, in the cold cellar for 12 hours. Then bottle, adding a raisin to each bottle.* Cork the bottles and place them on their sides in [a box of] sand on ice.

*A few raisins were traditionally added to home brews to monitor the fermentation process; when the raisins stopped bobbing around and floated on top of the liquid, the fermentation was finished.

### 2197 Apple juice or cider

(*Jablochnyj sok ili sidr*)

This drink, which costs almost nothing, is good to prepare where apples are plentiful. Pick sour apples from the tree, and sweet apples too, but keep them separate. Spread the apples on straw until they become soft but not rotten. Then chop them as for sauerkraut and squeeze out the juice using a press or vice. Squeeze the juice from the sour apples separately, and keep the juice in the ice house for 3 or 4 days, until the sediment settles. Pour off the liquid carefully and mix the sweet juice with the sour, adjusting the flavor. Bottle, adding 2 raisins to each bottle, cork securely, and tar. Store in the ice house and transfer to a dry, cold cellar for the winter. This cider will keep more than a year if it is stored in a cold place. Otherwise the bottles will burst.

# TO PREPARE MOSCOW *KVASS*

## (*Zagotovka Moskovskikh kvasov*)

*Remarks:* In order for Moscow *kvass* to be successful, the berries must be ripe and fresh; otherwise the *kvass* will not be tasty. These *kvasses* are the cheapest and most refreshing drinks in the countryside, where berries cost nothing. It is best to prepare them in carboys, because barrels and kegs sometimes leak. But *kvass* from raspberries and cultivated strawberries can be made only in tubs or vats with attached covers. And the kegs must always be covered and buried in ice.

### 2199 Moscow *kvass* from raspberries and cultivated strawberries

#### (*Moskovskij kvas iz maliny i klubniki*)

Moscow *kvass* from raspberries and strawberries is made in a special way. The barrel that is prepared for these berries must have a hole (½ *vershok* in diameter) drilled from the side close to the bottom of the barrel. This hole must be securely plugged with a wooden bung. The barrel must be lined to a depth 3 *vershok* higher than the bung hole with very clean, fresh straw, well rinsed and completely dried in the sun. This is done because these berries are very tender and quickly release a sediment. When moistened, the straw will retain the sediment, and the *kvass* will be clear. Fill the barrel with berries and pour on boiled water. After drawing off a bottle of *kvass* from the barrel, replace the liquid in the barrel with a bottle of boiled and cooled water. If the *kvass* is too strong, dilute it with water and sweeten to taste just before using. When all the *kvass* has been poured off—that is, when it becomes too weak through having been constantly diluted with water—discard it and begin another barrel of already-prepared *kvass*. It is essential to set the barrel on ice and, when the weather is hot, the barrel must be surrounded with ice. In winter keep the barrel in the cold cellar, because the *kvass* will spoil if it freezes.

### 2203 Moscow *kvass* from apples

#### (*Moskovskij kvas jablochnyj*)

Sour but ripe apples must be used. Cut off the blossom end (*travka*) of the apple and fill any handy barrel with the apples. Pour on boiled water and, in the summer and fall, place on ice, but in the winter, set the barrel in a dry cold cellar. Pour off the apple water and refill as indicated in #2199. Lemon zest may be added to the barrel since apples lack their own fragrance (*zapakh*)*. This *kvass* will easily keep for a year without spoiling at all. Anyone who has a lot of apples should substitute this *kvass* for grain *kvass*, which costs much more and is not always successful. This *kvass* never spoils, but be sure that each time you draw off *kvass*, you refill the barrel with exactly the same amount of water.

*\*This seems an odd observation given the strong odor of apples. Perhaps the fragrance depended on the varieties available.*

# BEER
## (Pivo)

### 2208  Home-brewed beer

*(Pivo domashnee)*

Mix warm water with 1 *garnets* each ground malted rye and rye flour. Bore a hole in a large earthenware pot for draining the wort, spread hay on the bottom, and transfer the dough to the pot. Cover the pot with a lid and set it in a very hot oven. The next morning, remove the dough from the pot, pour off the wort, fill the pot with boiling water, and again pour off. For this proportion, boil a handful of hops, add the hops to the wort, blend, and add 1 glass yeast. When the mixture has turned into beer, bottle and cork securely. These proportions will yield 25–30 bottles of beer.

### 2211  Beer in the English manner

*(Pivo na anglijskij maner)*

After removing bread from the oven, sweep out the floor of the oven thoroughly. Sprinkle 8 lbs of good barley or oats on the oven floor and dry out the grain, constantly mixing it with a wooden shovel. Take care that the grain does not burn or roast even slightly. Then pound the grain, pour it into a kettle or any dish, and cover with 1⅓ pails hot water (65 degrees).* Mix thoroughly, let stand for 3 hours, and carefully pour off the liquid. Pour another pail of hot water (72 degrees) over the pounded barley in the kettle and pour it off after 2 hours. Then pour on a pail of cold water and pour it off after 1½ hours. Mix together the waters poured from the grain in these 3 soakings. Dilute 15 lbs treacle with 2½ pails warm water and pour it into the prepared liquid. Add ½ lb of the best hops and bring to a boil, stirring. After 2 hours, when the liquid has cooled, add 2 glasses good yeast, mix as well as possible, and set somewhere where the temperature will not fall below 15 degrees. When the beer ferments, pour it into a barrel. Let it stand uncovered for 3 days, then drive in the bung, and after 2 weeks, you will have an outstanding beer.

*Remarks:* By the way, it is necessary to watch that the water poured on the

Sprig of hops. From W. Baxter, *British Flowering Plants*, vol. 5 (Oxford, 1840), by permission of the Library of the Gray Herbarium, Harvard University.

grains is not too hot, for it has already been mentioned that strongly boiling water is bad for the beer.

*Thermometers did not loom large in Molokhovets' cooking; she mentioned the Reaumur scale a few times in her recipes, but centigrade only once. She baked bread at 60 degrees Reaumur and heated milk for cheese at 40 degrees Reaumur, but she stored grapes over the winter in a room kept at a temperature between 1 and 7 degrees centigrade. Most likely, Molokhovets was referring to degrees Reaumur for preparing the beer. The Reaumur scale, devised by René de Réaumur in 1730, set the freezing point of water at 0 degrees and the boiling point at 80 degrees.*

# MEAD
## (Med)

### 2213 Sweetened mead*

(Med sakharnyj)

Boil together 6 pails water and 1 pood sugar until reduced to 5 pails, skimming off the foam. Remove from the fire, pour into a vat, cool to the temperature of milk fresh from the cow, and set in a warm room. Dip a French roll into yeast until it absorbs at least 1 glass yeast and add it to the syrup. When the mead begins to ferment, which will take about an hour, remove the roll. If the mixture does not ferment, add more yeast. Add ¼ lb sturgeon glue, ½ lb colored orris root, and the zest from 25 lemons. Pour everything into a very strong barrel, cork securely, and set on ice for 12 days. Then uncork, bottle, and store in the cold cellar. Let stand for 4 months before using. This drink is unusually pleasant.

*The name of this recipe is something of an anomaly since, traditionally, the primary ingredient of mead is honey. In Russian, the word* med *means both mead and honey. Recipes for mead tend to be very old and date from the time when sugar was either not known or was still a very expensive and rare ingredient.*

### 2218 Real monastery mead

(Prigotovlenie nastojashchago monastyrskago meda dlja pit'ja)

To prepare this mead, use the very best pure honey, unadulterated by wax.

Pour 1 *garnets* honey and 2 *garnets* water into a well-tinned iron or copper kettle. Mix and place on top of the stove. Boil for 3 hours over a low, even fire, counting from when the liquid first comes to a boil. Then add hops, tied in a thin cloth but not tied over the hops themselves. Sew a clean, small stone into the cloth to weight the bundle and to keep the hops on the bottom of the kettle. For every *garnets* of this liquid, add 2 *lots* of hops. One *garnets* honey and 2 *garnets* water, therefore, will require 6 *lots* hops in all.

[Mark the level of the liquid on a spill.] The honey and water must cook for 1 hour with the hops; then the liquid must be measured [again] with the spill.* If the liquid is below the level marked, fill up to the mark with hot, boiled water, or even add a little extra, because when honey boils, it usually rises, so that it amounts to much less when it is completely cool. After adding this water, bring to a boil once, then set aside and cover.

While it is still rather warm, strain the honey through a cloth or a fine linen into a wooden or glass dish, but fill it only four-fifths full. Cover with a piece of tulle and set in a warm place (18–20 degrees), in winter in the oven and in summer in the sun.

After 2 days the mead will begin to foam and ferment.

If the mead stands at a low temperature, then it will not ferment but will grow moldy and spoil. The warmer the place [for storage], the sooner the mead will be ready. Usually 3–5 weeks are necessary for this process. Listen after 3 weeks: if the mead is obviously noisy, leave it a bit longer. But if the noise has stopped and the odor and strength of the mead is already evident, then it is ready to be used.

In general, if a stronger mead is desired, it must stand quietly in a warm place until it stops hissing. But if a weaker and sweeter mead is desired, then it may be strained while it is still hissing.

Before straining, for every 3 *garnets* mead, add 1 glass tea essence prepared from 1 teaspoon good tea and 1 glass boiling water.

Do not stir the mead liquid, but carefully pour it off, straining through a flannel. Repeat several times, until the mead is completely clear and transparent. Mead strained in this manner is ready to be used, but it will be better in 6 months' time. After a year, it will be outstanding. In general, the longer it stands, the better it will be, even if it is kept for 20 years.

*Remarks:* If a sweeter and stronger mead is desired, use 1 *garnets* water instead of 2 for every 1 *garnets* honey. Measure with a spill and then add the other *garnets*.

Also less hops and more tea may be added.

No spices should be added since mead by itself has enough aroma.

If the mead matures well and will be strained after it ceases hissing completely, it may be bottled in ordinary thin bottles without bursting them. If bottled earlier, then stronger and thicker bottles must be used.

Mead ought not to be kept for long in barrels in the wine cellar because it will turn moldy and take on a musty odor.

Soft river water must be used for preparing mead. In an extreme case, well water may be used, but it must be such that soap lathers in it and such as would be used for washing linens.

The dishes used for preparing mead, must be, if not new, then completely clean, and the bottles must be completely dry. This means that they must be thoroughly rinsed and overturned several days before being used.

*Although Molokhovets does not say so, the liquid must have been measured before it was boiled; otherwise there would be no basis for comparison.

# 25

# Vinegars, Mustards, Fast Day Oils, Grains, and Starches

*(Zagotovka uksusa, gorchitsy, postnago masla, raznykh krup i krakhmala)*

## VINEGAR
*(Uksus)*

### 2219 Ordinary vinegar for marinated salads
*(Uksus obyknovennyj dlja marinovanija salatov)*

For 7 *garnets* spring water, use 1 *garnets* vodka. Pour into a barrel and add a sheet of ordinary paper that has been spread with 1 lb unmelted, fresh honey together with its wax, and rolled into a tube.

Prepare another 2 barrels in exactly the same way. In a warm and dry summer set all 3 barrels in the sun; in winter set them in a warm room not far from the oven but not beside it. Do not drive a bung into the barrels, but cover them with linen. Leave them undisturbed for 3 months, after which time the vinegar can be used. It is said that just one person should take charge of the vinegar and that person should be a man; the vinegar must be set out on a Friday in the new moon.*

The vinegar will be ready in 3 months on a Friday in the new moon, in the morning before breakfast [lit., "on an empty stomach" *(natoshchak)*]. At that time, draw out a month's supply of vinegar with a pipette, submerging it only a little so as not to spoil the mother. Replace the drawn-off vinegar with the same amount of liquid, using 7 parts spring water and 1 part vodka. But never refill with vinegar because that would cause the remaining vinegar to spoil. The next month, draw off vinegar in the same manner from the second barrel, and also refill. In the third month, still on a Friday in the new moon, draw off vinegar from the third barrel. In this manner, the vinegar will never run out and will always have 3 months to mature.

When drawing off vinegar from the barrel and refilling with water and vodka, a little honey may be added, but do not add any more paper, which is used only once, at the very beginning.

If the mother takes too long to form, the process can be hastened by dropping a fresh chicken egg into the vinegar. Before placing the egg carefully on its side in the vinegar, make a small hole in both ends of the shell and cover them with your fingers so as not to lose the white. In 2 to 3 weeks, a mother will begin to form near the egg, and the vinegar will begin to strengthen and improve.

*It is a widely held folk belief that the preparation of vinegar should be commenced on the first Friday in the new moon. Numerous attestations of this belief have been found not only in Europe, but all across the United States as late as the 1960s. The scientific principles of fermentation were only explained in the late nineteenth century; many people, however, traditionally viewed fermentation as a magical process that had to be protected from harmful influences. Menstruating women and pregnant women, who are themselves "fermenting," were regarded as particularly dangerous to other fermenting products. The advice to put a man in charge of the vinegar was essentially to protect the vinegar from these potentially harmful women. (Encyclopedia of American Popular Belief and Superstition, Vol. 7, s.v. vinegar.)*

### 2223  Wine vinegar

*(Vinnyj uksus)*

If you have 5–6 bottles of spoiled sour wine, pour them into a barrel and add 1 pail boiled and then chilled water, 2 lbs sugar or honey, and about 3 zolotniki tartar (*vinnyj kamen'*). Set in a warm place without corking, covering the bunghole with a towel. (Some people add an old swallow's nest to the barrel.*) In 2 months the vinegar will be ready. Decant into clean large carboys or bottles and cork.

*The nests of swallows are said to be a good natural source of calcium. For more, see Glossary.*

### 2225  Raisin vinegar

*(Izjumennyj uksus)*

A good oak 10-pail barrel, bound with iron hoops of course, is essential for this recipe. Test it for leaks and then crush 20 lbs of the lowest-quality raisins until they form a dough-like mass. Place them in the barrel and add 6 pails warmish river water, no warmer than milk fresh from the cow. Cover the bunghole with a cloth and set the barrel on a board on a warm stove so that it will not become too hot. After 8 days, add 10 lbs honey that has been thoroughly mixed with ½ pail water. After 4 months the vinegar will be ready. Decant the vinegar and pour 4 pails warmish water over the sediment left in the barrel. Add 5 lbs honey and 2 lbs pounded tartar. Set aside for 3 months, then decant the vinegar again. Keep repeating the process. When the vinegar weakens noticeably—that is, when the raisins lose their power—add 4 shtofs sparkling wine with the 4 pails water and 5 lbs honey. If these rules are observed, you will always have good vinegar. If the mother becomes too high in the barrel, leaving little room for the vinegar, pour out all the sediment from the barrel, detach one part of the mother, and pour the remaining sediment back into the barrel. Extreme cleanliness is essential when preparing vinegar; if anything extraneous falls into the barrel, the vinegar will spoil.

### 2227  Cider vinegar

*(Uksus iz jablok)*

Gather windfall apples even if they are not completely ripe. Pile them up, but watch that they only soften, but do not rot. Using a chopper, mince them as fine as for cabbage. Place them in a conical sack and squeeze out the juice in a press. Pour all the pressed juice into a tub and set on ice for 3 days. Without disturbing the sediment, carefully pour off the clear juice into a strong oak barrel. For each pail juice, add 1 glass honey and 2 glasses black treacle. Add a mother of vinegar if it is available; otherwise, add a sheet of writing paper spread with honey. Cover the bunghole with a cloth, seal, and set the barrel aside for 3 months. This vinegar takes a long time to mature. If honey is not added, the vinegar sometimes can take a full year to mature but then it becomes very strong and pleasant. But most importantly, it costs almost nothing if one owns an orchard, because it can also be made without honey, which like a mother is added for quickness. The marc which remains may be placed in garden beds, and if the apples were ripe, then in spring all the seeds will sprout and form a nursery.

### 2228  Berry vinegar

*(Jagodnyj uksus)*

Fill half a 5- or 6-pail barrel with any kind of berries that are handy, except wild strawberries or lingonberries. Add 3 pails boiling water and set aside for 2 weeks. Drive in the bung very gently and shake up the barrel several times a day [during this fortnight]. Spread honey on 1½ lbs rye bread (without the crust). Toss the bread and honey into the barrel along with 1 handful each white peas and oak chips,* a piece of cotton cloth the size of a glass, a sheet of white writing paper spread with honey, 5 glasses honey, and 3 *shtofs* sparkling wine. Cover the bunghole with a cloth and seal it. Decant the vinegar when it is ready, then pour on 3 more pails river water with the same quantity of honey and wine as indicated above. Mix the second batch of decanted vinegar with the first, because the first will be more aromatic. This vinegar may be constantly renewed in this manner. The berries may be discarded when they lose their flavor and strength, but the mother that has formed will always yield good vinegar.

*\*Vinegar aged in oak barrels has a more complex flavor than our modern commercially produced vinegars. Since this vinegar is decanted rather soon, the addition of the oak chips presumably*

*compensated for the flavor which the vinegar otherwise would have acquired by longer aging in the barrel.*

### 2236 Vinegar for marinated fish and meat

*(Uksus dlja marinovanija ryb i mjasa)*

For 1 bottle vinegar, add 2 level spoons salt, finely shredded celery root, parsley root, carrots, onions, a handful each of allspice and bay leaves, a little mace, and cloves. (Cinnamon, cardamom, and garlic may also be added, if desired.) Bring to a boil and cool.

# MUSTARDS

*(Zagotovka gorchitsy)*

### 2238 Long-lasting mustard

*(Gorchitsa ochen' prochnaja)*

For [every] 3 heaping tablespoons [powdered] mustard, add 1½ zolotniki ground cloves and 2 heaping spoons sugar. Pour the mixture into a small stoneware pot and stir in enough good vinegar until no lumps remain and the sauce is much thinner than ordinary mustard. Place the pan on top of the stove and reduce the mustard to the consistency of a very thick batter. Remove from the fire and dilute with cold vinegar to the usual consistency. Pour into jars and set on a warm stove for a full week.* This prepared mustard may be stored for more than a year. If it is too thick, stir in some vinegar.

*\*The reference here is to the bulky, traditional Russian stove used to heat the room as well as cook the food. Rather than keeping the mustard directly over the fire, it would have been set on the stove bench, where it would stay warm without any further cooking.*

### 2239 Mustard in the French manner

*(Gorchitsa na maner frantsuzskoj)*

To 1½ lbs gray or yellow [powdered] mustard, add ½ lb sugar, 4 tablespoons pounded and sieved rye rusks, 1 dessertspoon salt, ½ teaspoon ground pepper, a small jar each capers and olives, 2 Dutch herring,* and 4 tablespoons herring brine—without the slightest odor. Chop the herring, capers, and olives very fine and rub through a fine sieve. Mix with the mustard and the other ingredients and beat thoroughly, diluting with ½ bottle French vinegar. Then add enough of the best wine vinegar so that the mustard will not be too thick, because it will thicken with time. If yellow mustard is used, pepper need not be added.

*If anything, this sauce might be called Scandinavian, but it is hardly French. The Swedes, for instance, commonly serve herring in a mustard sauce, but I have not found elsewhere mashed herring used as an ordinary component of mustard.*

### 2241  Excellent apple mustard

*(Jablochnaja otlichnaja gorchitsa)*

Bake good sour apples and, while still hot, rub them through a fine sieve. For [every] 3 spoons yellow mustard, add 4 spoons sieved apples. Mix together and, for these proportions, add 2 heaping tablespoons sugar. Dilute thoroughly with vinegar boiled with spices as for marinating. Two teaspoons salt may be added. This mustard has an excellent flavor. Let it mellow for at least 3 days before using.

### 2248  Home-grown mustard

*(Gorchitsa domashnjaja)*

When home-grown mustard—that is, *Sareptskaja*—ripens in the kitchen garden, gather it and cast it onto a tablecloth. Thresh, sieve, and clean to remove any hulls. Pour into a small sack and store in a dry place. When you want to prepare mustard, wash the seeds and dry them in the oven after baking bread. When the mustard is completely dry, pound in a mortar or grind in a coffee mill, and pass through a fine sieve. Boil 1 glass honey on top of the stove until it changes color and browns, then pour on 1 glass milled or pounded mustard and dilute with boiled and cooled vinegar. Mix until smooth and cork immediately.

## FAST DAY OILS

*(Zapasy iz postnago masla)*

### 2250  Olive oil

*(Provanskoe maslo)*

The very best fast day oil is olive oil or *huile vierge* [sic]. It is whitish in color and pressed from olives that are not overripe and that have been grown on the islands of the Greek archipelago, on the shores of the Adriatic and Mediterranean Sea, and in Greece, Dalmatia, and southern France. Oil pressed from overripe olives is not as good and is more yellowish in color. Still worse is oil of a greenish color. Olive oil is used to prepare beefsteaks, salads, and mustard sauces. It is served with herring and is used for frying fish, etc. It costs about 60 kopecks a pound.

### 2253  Mustard oil

*(Gorchichnoe maslo)*

Mustard oil is prepared as follows. Use millstones to remove the hulls of lightly dried mustard seeds, as when preparing barley and millet for groats. Pound and sieve the seeds and pour them into a large tin can with a tight cover. Submerge the tin can in water, boil for 15 minutes, remove the mustard from the can, and pound the hot mustard in a mortar. Transfer to a conical sack and squeeze out the oil in a press, as usual. The pressed seeds should be returned to the tin can several times, heated in boiling water, and squeezed in a press until not a particle of oil remains in them. Mustard oil costs about 50 kopecks a pound and is used mostly for frying fish.

### 2257  To rectify hempseed oil

*(Kak ispravljat' konopljanoe maslo)*

Hempseed oil is prepared from hempseeds and costs about 14 kopecks a pound. It is used by poor people for cooking, but for the most part it is used for lighting. To remove its unpleasant aroma and flavor, take 6 medium onions for every bottle of oil. Peel and chop the onions, mix with the oil, and bring to a boil in a saucepan 5–6 times. During the last strong boiling, add 1 saucespoon cold water to the oil and immediately remove the saucepan from the fire. Be sure to use a very large saucepan, because the action of the ice water is so strong that the oil easily boils over.

# TO PREPARE GROATS, FLOUR, AND OAT FLOUR
*(Zagotovka raznykh krup, muki i tolokna)*

*Remarks:* 1 pood of rye will yield 35 lbs rye flour. 1 pood of wheat will yield 22 lbs of first quality flour, 9 lbs of second quality flour, and 5 lbs of bran. 1 pood of winter barley, which is better than summer barley, will yield 23 lbs coarse groats, or 21 lbs medium groats, or 19 lbs very fine groats. 1 pood of good dry oats will yield 10 lbs groats.

### 2263  Green groats

*(Zelenaja krupa)*

For these groats, the rye must be cut while it is still green, and the sheaves must not be more than 6 *vershok* in girth. Bring a kettle of water to a full boil, then toss in the spikes from 1 sheaf or, at most, from 2 sheaves so as not to cool the water. Leave them in the water no longer than 10 seconds. After removing the first batch, let the water come to a boil again, and continue to drop the remaining sheaves into the boiling water in this fashion. The water must be salted. Stick the sheaves on the fence to dry out in the sun. Then dry them in the oven, thresh them, and make into groats.

## 2268 Potato flour

*(Kartofel'naja muka)*

Potato flour is best prepared in autumn, because the potatoes are mealier when they are just dug out of the ground. Wash the potatoes, grate them, and immediately drop them into water. After grating as much as is convenient, mix them with water so that you have at least twice as much water as grated potatoes. Set aside for several hours or overnight. Squeeze out the potatoes over a coarse sieve, mixing and squeezing with your hands. Strain all the water through this sieve, constantly shaking it, because a sediment, which is the flour, will form on the bottom. Cover the leftover pressed potatoes with fresh, cold water, mix, and again let stand, stirring to wash off the flour, and continue as above.

Next pour off the water that has stood on the potatoes, and cover the potato mash on the bottom with fresh water. Shake thoroughly, strain through a sieve, and so proceed until the flour is completely white. Then, for the last time, pour off the water and take out the flour, which adheres in a thick mass to the bowl or tub. Lay it out in pieces on a thick sheet, and, after covering it with another sheet to protect it from dust, set it to dry in a warm room. When the flour is completely dry, pound it, sieve, and store in a dry place. Use this flour for *kissels*, biscuit tortes, and puddings. It is added to icings for covering tortes, etc.

# TO PREPARE STARCHES
*(Zagotovka krakhmala)*

## 2269 Wheat starch

*(Krakhmal pshenichnyj)*

Take, for example, 8 *garnets*, or 96 glasses, of wheat that has been cleanly picked over and sieved. Wash the wheat until the water is completely clear. Soak the wheat for 9 days, covering it first with warm water and then with cold water, each time using fresh water. (In cold weather, it must soak longer.) Continue soaking until the water whitens and the seeds begin to split. Pour the wheat into a sack made of new linen and tie it up, leaving a fair amount of slack. Place the sack in a trough and trample it with your feet. After some time, untie the sack, pour water on the wheat, and mix with your hands; then pour more water over the wheat, and pour off the water into a flat tray or pan. After settling, this water will yield a very nasty starch of the worst kind.

Retie the sack and trample it as before, untie the sack, pour on water, mix, add more water, and pour it off into another vessel. Each time, thoroughly rinse out the trough.

The third time the wheat will have to be trampled longer, since this third trampling will yield the very best starch. As before, pour off the water from the wheat into a separate vessel, straining it, as before, through a sieve covered with muslin. Let the water in all these vessels stand for 24 hours, then pour off the yellowish water on top as carefully as possible. Cover the starch that remains on the bottom with clean water, and knead thoroughly, washing the starch in this manner. Let it stand for 24 hours and repeat for five days, until the water remains completely clear. After pouring off the water for the last time, turn out the starch that remains on the bottom onto a sheet on a table either outdoors in the open air or in a warm, dry room. In sunny weather, the starch will dry out in five days. Eight *garnets* wheat will yield 4–4½ *garnets* starch, or about 50 glasses, which amounts to 20–25 pounds.

### 2271 Starch from immature apple and pears

*(Krakhmal iz nedozrelykh jablok i grush)*

This method for preparing starch from immature windfall apples and pears was published in German newspapers. Gather, peel, core, and thoroughly rinse the fruit. Grate, immediately dropping the grated fruit into a tub that has been two-thirds filled with water. The grated fruit must constantly be mixed with this water. When all the fruit has been grated, thoroughly mix it with the water once more, even using your hands, then let it settle. After the water has cleared on top, carefully pour it off. Pour on fresh water, mix, let it settle, and pour off again. After the second time, two types of starch will remain on the bottom: the top layer will be fibrous and the lower layer will be a greenish solid mass like a jelly. Remove both layers [together] with a large spoon onto a fine sieve and rub the starch through the sieve now by hand, and now with a brush, pouring on water from time to time. Let the mixture settle, pour off the water, and spread the starch out on a table covered with paper, and let it dry.

Pour the waters from the first two soakings into a tub and let it settle since it contains small particles of starch.

122 lbs apples will yield up to 20 lbs starch.

Apple starch should be prepared separately from pear starch.

# 26
# Butter, Cheese, Milk, Cream, and Eggs

*(Slivochnoe i proch. maslo, syr, moloko, slivki, jajtsa)*

## BUTTER
*(Maslo)*

### 2272 [To prepare Finnish butter]

One pail of good, pure sour cream without any yogurt or flour* will yield about 15 lbs of washed, unsalted** Finnish butter.

Butter must be washed clean in water as warm as river water in the summer, and the water must be changed until it remains completely clear. Then salt the butter with white, dried salt.

One pood of butter usually will take 4½ lbs salt. If the butter is to be stored for a year or longer, add 5 lbs salt.

It is best to pack the butter in an earthenware or glazed vessel. After sprinkling salt on the bottom, pack the butter in layers and compress it as well as possible. Pour highly salted water over the top to the depth of 2 fingers and cover with a clean cloth, tucking in the ends of the cloth so they do not hang down. As the water diminishes, pour on fresh water. The butter may be packed into small tubs of oak, maple, or even alder instead of earthenware vessels, but not into tubs of spruce, pine, or other resinous woods. The tubs must be strong and without cracks, to prevent the salt water from leaking. Old, or used, kegs are preferable to new kegs.

---

*Sour cream was sometimes adulterated either by adding yogurt, which was less expensive than the cream, or by thickening with flour, which masked an inferior, thin cream.*

**Salt was used in this recipe to help preserve the butter, but here Molokhovets was talking about the weight of the butter before it was salted.*

### 2275 To rectify spoiled Finnish or ordinary butter

*(Sposob ispravljat' isportivsheesja chukhonskoe ili slivochnoe maslo)*

Thoroughly wash the spoiled butter in several changes of water. Add salt and juice from carrots that have been grated and squeezed through a cloth. Mix until completely incorporated.

Carrot juice gives the butter a very delicate, pleasant taste, but it is better to add it just before serving, because this butter will only keep for a few days.

### 2278 A fourth way [to rectify spoiled butter]

*(Chetvertyj sposob)*

Pound good birch coals into small pieces in a mortar and sieve the pieces. For 5 lbs butter, use 2 teacups of the best pieces without ashes. Sprinkle them into butter that has been melted, but not boiled, on top of the stove. Set aside for a full 24 hours in a place warm enough so that the butter and coals will remain as thick as sour cream without congealing. The next day melt the mixture on top of the stove, but do not let it boil. Strain while still hot. By this method, the butter will lose its bitterness.

### 2283 Synthetic butter

*(Iskustvennoe maslo)*

Finnish butter may be replaced with the following: Finely chop 1 lb mutton fat, place in a saucepan, and cover with 1½ glasses whole milk. Bring to a boil several times to render the fat, then strain through a fine sieve. As the fat begins to cool, beat with a spatula until smooth. Fry 4 *lots* of dried bread crumbs made from the crusts of sieved wheat bread (*sitnyj*) with 1 *lot* tragacanth. Beat the fried crumbs and 2 finely chopped and sieved onions into the mutton fat. Fat prepared in this manner is very tasty, cheap, and convenient, since 1 lb of fat may replace 2 lbs of butter. Anything may be fried in it, and it may be used even to prepare doughs.

### 2288 Butter with almonds, walnuts, or pistachios

*(Slivochnoe maslo s mindalem, gretskimi orekhami ili fistashkami)*

Shell 1 lb walnuts, scald with boiling water, and remove the skins. Pound very fine, adding a little milk, and pour into a bottle (*grafin*).* Add a bottle of very thick cream and whip into butter. After churning, wash the butter thoroughly and rub through a fine sieve.

Proceed in exactly the same manner with 1 lb almonds, including 10–12 bitter almonds, or use 1 lb pistachios.

*For small amounts of cream, butter was sometimes shaken in a bottle instead of beaten in a churn.

### 2289  Inexpensive spread for bread

*(Deshevoe maslo s khlebom)*

Boil and peel 15 very clean, large potatoes. Rub them through a fine sieve into a butter churn, add 8 tablespoons very cold, thick sour cream, and mix thoroughly. Gradually add 1 teacup very hot water and continue to churn for about 5 minutes after the last drop of water has been added. Then, while still churning, gradually add cold water until butter forms. Next, wash the butter in cold water with ice, add a little salt, and serve.

If you do not have a butter churn, mix everything in a stoneware bowl or soup tureen, adding water in the same sequence as indicated above.

### 2291  Russian butter [or clarified butter]

*(Russkoe maslo)*

Butter used for frying, or so-called Russian butter, is processed as follows. Place 10 lbs of Finnish butter in a large, tinned saucepan, pour in 3¼ *garnets*, or about 40 glasses, water, and set over a low fire. Stir until the butter completely melts, remove the saucepan from the stove, and set in a cold place. When the butter has hardened, make a small hole at the side of the pan, piercing through to the bottom of the fat and pour off any water. Cover with fresh water and remelt the butter. Repeat 3 or 4 times until the water residue is completely clear. Then salt the butter as indicated above with very fine salt and pack into jugs or vats. Cover the butter with a cloth, fill the vessel with very salty water, and store in a cold, dry place. Butter prepared in this manner will not spoil for 3–4 years.

# CHEESES
## (Syry)

### 2296  Homemade white cheese made from curds and sour cream

*(Syr domashnij belyj iz tvorogu so smetanoju)*

Fresh, whole milk poured, as usual, into an earthenware jug will sour after standing for several days in a warm place and turn into yogurt, i.e., the whey will begin to separate [from the curds]. The soured cream may be blended with milk or, better yet, left undisturbed and put as is into a summer oven that is not too hot (about 40 degrees Reaumur), such as after baking bread. If the oven is too hot and causes the milk suddenly to turn into curd cheese, the resulting cheese will be reddish, crumbly, and foul-tasting.

Curd cheese prepared in this manner should be taken out of the oven and completely cooled in the same jugs before being transferred to a conical sack. Let the whey drain off, place the sack with the cheese onto a sloping table, and weight the sack with a wooden board and a stone—start with a light stone, and add a heavier one later. After several hours, when the whey has completely drained into a container placed below the edge of the sloping table, remove the cheese from the bag and salt it slightly. Add some caraway seeds, if desired, being careful not to disturb the layers. Then transfer the cheese to small triangular sacks [for shaping], tie them up, and place under a press again; i.e., cover with a board and stones for several hours.

If flaky cheese is desired, do not disturb the cheese by salting, but pack it directly into small triangular sacks. Later remove the cheese and salt the surface, or wrap it for 24 hours in a cloth dampened in salted water. Repeat this process several times.

Cheeses prepared by either method are dried during the summer in the fresh air, in the shade. In winter they are dried in a warm room but far from the oven, on shelves or poles* covered with straw. Cheese will crack if dried in the sunshine or near the oven. As mold appears, scrape it off with a knife and rinse the cheese in salt water. To protect the cheese from flies, dry it in baskets that allow the air to penetrate, or cover it with a thick net and turn the cheese frequently from one side to the other. Well-dried cheeses that have been cleaned and scraped with a knife should be packed with oat straw in large earthenware jugs, or the entire jug of cheese may be nestled in a bed of straw. As a rule, cheese should not be stored where it is too dry or too damp. In the first instance it will dry out, in the second, it will rot and spoil. If the cheese becomes moldy, rinse it with whey, salt it, and dry in the shade, turning it from side to side.

*Sometimes makeshift shelves were erected by placing several poles close together with supports at each end. This was an ideal storage system for the cheese, as it allowed the air to circulate freely.

## 2298  Dry cheese that is soft and sliceable like Dutch cheese

(Syr povidimomu sukhoj, no v seredine tak mjagok i tak razrezyvaetsja, kak gollandskij)

Heat sour milk without sour cream in the summer oven. Remove, and when completely cool, fill a sack with the curds. The next day, after the whey has drained off, mix the curds with salt, transfer to small sacks, and weight them for 48 hours.* Remove the cheeses from the sacks and cover them immediately with a thick piece of canvas to protect them from the air. Turn the cheeses daily until they are covered with mold, like mushrooms, and until they smell very strong and unpleasant—this will occur after 2 to 3 weeks. During this time do not open the windows in the room where the cheeses are kept; also do not light the oven.

Next, remove the canvas from the cheeses for one week. When the mold has dried, wash the cheeses in whey that has been heated to a temperature barely tolerable to the touch. Wash the cheeses and rub them gently with the palm of your hand, but do not scrape the mold with a knife or with your fingers. Change the heated whey several times until the cheeses are clean. Return the cheeses to the same room and place them on clean, dry shelves. Keep them uncovered and turn them twice a day. The windows may now be opened occasionally, and, in winter, the oven may be lit. After the cheeses have dried, pack them in dry rye.

Two or three hours before using the cheeses, wash them in hot water and let them dry slightly. It is best to prepare them soon after the Feast of Peter and Paul [July 12th]. On top they will be dry, and, inside, as soft as Dutch cheese. When sliced, they will not crumble like other cheeses.

*There is no mention of rennet in this recipe. Perhaps Molokhovets assumed that the reader would add the rennet or perhaps the omission was inadvertent.*

### 2299 Swiss cheese

*(Syr shvejtsarskij)*

RENNET STARTER #1: WHEY TO CURDLE FRESH MILK

Thoroughly wash the stomach of a freshly slaughtered calf and soak it in strong vinegar for 3 to 4 hours. Rinse well in whey, rub thoroughly with salt inside and out, stretch over two thin poles to dry completely, and store in a dry place. Three or four hours before using, soak the stomach in sour or fresh whey in a warm place. This whey is called a rennet starter (*podpushka*). When poured into milk fresh from the cow, it will curdle the milk. The same stomach may be used three times. However, after each use, remove the stomach from the whey, wash it out well, rub with salt, and dry over poles.

RENNET STARTER #2:

Clean the calf's stomach, wash it well, and rub with fine salt inside and out. After 2–3 days, rewash thoroughly, rub with salt, and stretch the stomach on poles to dry. Before making cheese, mix together 4 bottles each of sour and fresh milk and warm the mixture in the oven. When the whey separates, pour off the liquid and soak the stomach in it until the whey sours. This whey, like Rennet starter #1, may be used to make cheese.

PREPARATION OF THE CHEESE:

Pour 1 pail of milk fresh from the cow and the cream taken from 1 pail of the previous day's milk into a clean tin-plated pot and set over hot coals. Heat until slightly warmer than milk fresh from the cow. Add 2 bottles Rennet starter #2—whey in which a calf's stomach was soaked—and stir with a wooden spatula until the milk turns into curds and the whey separates from them. Remove the pot from the fire, pour off the whey, and press the solids carefully without disturbing the curds—the porosity of the cheese depends on this. Pack the curds into a rectangular wooden mold lined with a thin, damp cloth. The mold should be about 6 *vershok* long and 4 *vershok* wide; the height does not matter—whatever is convenient—but there must be 5 small holes on the bottom of the mold for drainage. Cover with a round barrel top, 1 *vershok* thick, and weight with stones, beginning with light ones and gradually increasing the weight. Keep the cheese in the mold until the whey has ceased dripping and the cheese has dried—at least 24 hours. Remove the cheese carefully and rub with fine salt on all sides. Place in a basket that will permit the air to circulate while protecting the cheese from flies. Turn the cheese twice a day and, for the first few days, rub the cheese with salt. After several weeks the 2 lb cheese will be completely ready, extraordinarily tasty, and almost indistinguishable from Swiss cheese. It will keep for 2 years in a slightly damp environment.

This kind of cheese is best prepared in May and June, because milk is most abundant then. Cheese prepared in winter is tastier but not as attractive or as porous. Since small cheeses tend to dry out quickly, it is better to make large cheeses by doubling or tripling the designated proportions. If the cheeses do dry out, wrap them in a cloth soaked in beer, salted water, or even white wine.

### 2302  Sour cream cheese for breakfast

*(Syr iz smetany k zavtraku)*

Pour 5–6 glasses thick, fresh sour cream into a new closely-woven napkin, tie it up just above the sour cream, and lower it into a small pit, ½ *arshin* deep, which has been dug in the ground in soil that is heavy and black but not sandy. Cover the top of the cheese with canvas to protect it from dirt, fill the hole with soil, even it out with your feet, and place a stone on top. After 24 hours carefully remove the napkin with the cheese, untie it, and transfer the cheese to a plate. This cheese is extraordinarily tasty, but it does not keep for more than 2 weeks. Some people add salt and 1 spoon caraway seeds to this cheese.

## MILK AND CREAM
*(Moloko i slivki)*

### 2308  To store milk

*(Sberezhenie moloka)*

The vessels must always be impeccably clean and dry because the least spot of old milk will sour and spoil fresh milk. Milk should be stored in uncorked glass or clay vessels in a dry, semi-dark cold cellar with a small opening for air. It is best to store milk in a separate cold shed since it spoils very easily and readily absorbs extraneous odors and flavors. Milk from the morning's milking is more suitable for sick people, for example, than that taken at other milkings during the day.*

*For more on the morning's milking, see the section on Health in the Introduction.

### 2309  How to judge the quality of milk

*(Sredstvo uznavat' kachestvo moloka)*

Good milk is somewhat heavier than water, because drops of good milk sink in water.* If whole, good milk is dropped on a fingernail, the round drops will hold their shape, but milk diluted with water will spread out. Good milk is thick and pure white, but adulterated milk is thin and falls in a bluish tint.

Rub some milk between your fingers to determine whether or not it is fatty.

Nutrients are lost from boiling milk. Milk for yogurt must sour at room temperature. If milk is set out in the morning during the summer, it will sour by the next afternoon; therefore it should be carried into a cold place an hour before dinner.**

*The specific gravity of milk is about 1.033, although the composition of milk varies according to its source and the season of the year. In unhomogenized milk, cream rises to the surface because the large fat particles are less dense than milk. (Pauli, Classical Cooking: The Modern Way, 104–108.)

**Presumably Molokhovets wanted to chill the yogurt before dinner, which usually was served about 3 or 4 p.m. (See Meals and Menus in the Introduction.)

## TO STORE EGGS
*(Sberezhenie jajts)*

### 2312  [To store eggs]

*(Pervyj sposob)*

Rub very fresh eggs with any kind of butter or fat and arrange them in rows with the pointed end downward in a box with oats. Stand them upright with a space between each egg and cover with enough oats to prevent one egg from touching another. Cover each layer of eggs with a layer of oats 2 *vershok* thick. The top layer of oats must be twice as thick.

After filling a box to the top with eggs in this manner, nail the box tightly closed and store in a dry, cold place.

Eggs are also stored in well-dried salt, in oak ashes, and in sand that has been dried out in the oven, standing the eggs in rows with all the noses (*nosik*) pointing downward.

# 27

# Yeasts and Bread

## (Drozhzhi i khleb)

## YEAST

### (Drozhzhi)

### 2317  Homemade dry yeast

#### (Sukhija drozhzhi domashnjago prigotovlenia)

Take yeast from freshly prepared beer, pour it into any kind of linen or clean napkin, surround with a thick layer of ashes on all sides, and squeeze tightly. The ashes will draw out all the moisture and a thick dough will form from the yeast after 24 hours. Shape this dough into thin, flat cakes and dry them out on coarse sieves in the sun or in a moderately warm oven. Grind them into flour and store in small sacks in the open air.

### 2318  Homemade yeast

#### (Drozhzhi domashnija)

Take ½ *garnets*, or 6 glasses, coarsely sieved wheat bran. Pour 4 glasses of the bran into a stoneware bowl, add just enough boiling water to make a thick porridge, and beat with a spoon for 2 minutes. Sprinkle a large handful of bran on top, cover with a napkin folded in half, and leave for 5 minutes, not longer. Add just enough boiling water to mix in the bran that was sprinkled on top, beat thoroughly, sprinkle on the remaining bran, and recover with a napkin for 5 minutes in order to ferment. Add boiling water for the third time, but be careful not to let it overflow; use just enough for the bran to form a dough as thick as that for bread. This time do not cover with a napkin, but mix with a spoon or spatula until it cools. Pour off the liquid, squeezing the bran in a napkin. Add ¾ glass hops to this liquid. (Pour 1 glass boiling water over 2 *lots* of hops, cover, let settle, and strain.) After all this has cooled, add 3 or 4 spoons old yeast. Divide this mixture into 2 bottles, filling them not more than ⅔ full, stop the bottles with paper, and set in a warm place for 5–6 hours. After the yeast has risen, cork the bottles and store in a cold place. This yeast will not keep very long and quickly sours. Therefore new yeast must be prepared frequently, using 3–4 spoons of the old. Add twice as much of this yeast to dough as beer yeast.

### 2322  A very good homemade yeast
*(Domashnija drozhzhi ochen' khoroshija)*

Mix together a big pinch hops, a full teaspoon yellow honey, and ½ glass water. Bring all this thoroughly to a boil and reduce it slightly. Pour into a jar and, after it has cooled slightly, add 1½ glasses fine wheat flour. Mix and set in a warm place. The yeast will be ready in 2 days. If ½ spoon old yeast is added, it will be ready the next day.

## BREAD
### *(Khleb)*

*Remarks:* Bread increases by a third during baking. For example, if bread takes

Detail from "Bakery," watercolor on paper by Boris M. Kustodiev, 1920. From *Rus': Russkie tipy V. M. Kustodieva* (1923).

9 lbs of flour, then after baking and cooling the bread will weigh 12 lbs; if it is made from 12 lbs of flour, the bread will weigh 16 lbs.

## 2326  Rye and sifted wheat bread

*(Khleba rzhanye, sitnye i reshetnye)*

When preparing bread, some dough always remains on the bottom and sides of the kneading trough. These scraps of leftover dough are enough to sour the next batch of bread. If you prefer a more sour dough, you must leave an additional piece of dough, the size of a goose egg, in the trough. Never wash the trough but keep it clean, always covered with a tablecloth and a round wooden plank. This way, the dough will not go flat and it will be protected from dust. The trough must be stored in a dry and clean place where the air is fresh, otherwise the bread may spoil. Do not use this trough for any other purpose. Sometimes it happens that the leaven in the trough spoils. In that case, the bread will fail to rise and, upon baking, will turn black, heavy, and hard. Some people rectify the trough as follows: turn it over and pour boiling water over the bottom, wipe the interior with an onion and salt, rinse with water at room temperature, and prepare dough as usual for fresh leaven. Always bake sieved rye bread with pure water, but sieved wheat bread may be baked with either whey or yogurt. Every type of bread, however, must have its own special trough. Using the wrong trough will cause the bread to spoil. It is impossible to indicate precisely the amount of flour and water needed. This depends on the quality and dryness of the flour, but the approximate proportions are as follows. For ¼ pail of water, whey, or yogurt, use 1 pail flour.

Flour intended for bread must first be thoroughly dried by spreading it out in front of the oven on a table covered with a cloth. In the evening prepare a dough; that is, take a piece of leaven, dilute it with water, and mix. Pour ⅓ or ½ of the intended flour into the leaven, dilute with the intended water, whey, or yogurt, which has not been boiled but heated to only 25 degrees Reaumur. Mix thoroughly with a paddle (*vecelochka*), sprinkle the flour on top, cover, and set in a warm place until morning. If using sifted wheat flour, the dough must be rather liquid, but if using ordinary rye, the dough will be thicker. By the next morning the dough will have risen (but only if the kneading trough has stood in a warm place) and the flour, which was sprinkled on top, will not be visible. Sprinkle on the remaining flour and some salt. Add caraway seeds if desired. Knead the dough as usual for at least half an hour. After the dough is well kneaded, i.e., when it no longer sticks to your hands, cover with a tablecloth and leave it in the kneading trough until it rises. It should rise in 1½ or 2 hours if it rests in a warm place and is well covered. Roll the dough into loaves. If the bread is made from sieved wheat flour, the loaves may be dropped into water (as cold as river water in the summer), where they must stay until they rise. When the loaves float on top of the water, set them in the oven. This method is good because one need not worry about the time required for the bread to rise; quite simply, when bread rises to the surface, set it in the oven. However, if the loaves rise on the table, a small piece of dough may be dropped into water as a test; when it rises, all the loaves should be set in the oven.

Or, after rolling out the loaves, set them on the table, covered, in a warm place, and let them rise. It will require 30–45 minutes and sometimes a little longer for the dough to rise as it ought to. In large part the success of the bread depends on this. If it has not risen enough, the bread will be heavy and dense, and if it has risen too much so that it cannot rise any more in the oven, the dough will fall and become hard.

To transfer the bread into the oven, set the loaf on a wooden bread peel* sprinkled with flour. Pour boiling water over the bread, smooth the surface, and set in a cleanly swept out oven. Bread that has risen in water need not have boiling water poured over it.

For bread made of sieved wheat flour, the temperature of the oven must be 60 degrees Reaumur, but the oven must be much warmer for ordinary rye bread. The oven can be tested by throwing a handful of flour into it. If the flour browns gradually, the temperature is suitable for baking. If it immediately burns or does not brown at all, then the oven is too hot or not hot enough. Close the damper after setting the loaves in the oven.

It is difficult to judge how long to leave the loaves in the oven. The time varies according to the heat and the size of the loaves. A 12 lb loaf should bake in 2½ to 3 hours and a 1 lb loaf in ¾ hour. Take one loaf from the oven to test whether the bread has baked long enough. The loaf is done if it is light and if, after tapping the lower crust with the middle joint of your fingers, a knock can be heard. When the bread has browned and is almost done, remove each piece one by one. Immediately pour boiling water over each loaf, right by the oven, and return the loaves to the oven. Rye loaves need not be doused with boiling water at all; only smooth them over when setting them in the oven, after dipping your hands in cold water. After they are done and have been removed from the oven, moisten them lightly with water. The loaves must be removed from the oven carefully. Place them on the table around a drum sieve; that is, place one end on the table and lean the other end against the sieve to allow air to circulate underneath and to cool both the upper and lower crusts at the same time. Let the bread cool before moving it to a cold place.

*A bread peel is a pole with a broad flat disk at one end used for thrusting bread and pies into the oven and removing them from it. One of the oldest baking tools, peels are still a necessary implement for large, deep ovens. In American commercial establishments, they are commonly used for baking pizzas.

### 2330  Sour-sweet bread

*(Kislosladkij khleb)*

For 20 lbs of sieved, finely ground rye flour, use 20 glasses boiling water. At 9 o'clock in the morning, scald part of the flour, adding water until the dough is thick enough to hold a wooden spoon upright. Beat the dough until it pulls away from the paddle, cover it, and set in a warm place. In the evening of that same day, add the remaining flour and knead the dough thoroughly. The next morning knead again and add 4 glasses of *kvass* lees and a piece of oak bark the size of your palm.* Near dinner time, knead again, and in the evening again knead. On the third morning, remove the oak bark, knead the dough, and add 2 handfuls finely chopped bitter orange rind, 2 tablespoons caraway seeds, 2 lbs treacle, and 2 spoons yeast. After this, punch down the dough, [form into loaves], smooth them over with wet hands, sprinkle with caraway, and set in a very hot oven. After an hour change the position of the loaves, moving the back loaves to the front and the front loaves to the back so that they all bake evenly.

*The tannin in the oak bark presumably enhances the complexity of the bread's flavor.*

### 2333  Excellent sour-sweet bread for tea

*(Otlichnyj kislosladkij khleb k chaju)*

Take 12 lbs of flour. At 8 o'clock in the morning, pour 12 glasses of boiling water into half of this flour, beat it as well as possible, and set in a warm place to ferment. At 8 o'clock in the evening, knead in the remaining flour and add 2½ glasses *kvass* lees and 1½ lb prunes. Before using the prunes, cover them with boiling water in order to remove their stones, but do not allow them to soften completely. Chop the prunes and add them to the dough with 1 lb sweet almonds, shelled and finely chopped, about 4 lbs treacle, and, if desired, ½ cup caraway seeds, or even more. Knead everything thoroughly and set in a warm place until morning. Roll out the loaves as usual, smooth them thoroughly with a wet hand, and set them in a very hot oven.

# 28

# Preserved Fruits and Berries

*(Raznye zapasy iz fruktov i jagod)*

## APPLE PRESERVES
*(Zapasy iz jablok)*

In August, after gathering apples in the country or after buying them in bulk when they are inexpensive, they may be preserved as follows.

### 2335  To keep apples fresh

*(Sokhranjat' jabloki svezhimi)*

Summer apples are the best kind to lay out on clean, dry, straw-lined shelves in a dry basement. Do not let the apples touch each other, and rub them frequently with a dry towel. All apples for storage must be cut from the tree and not allowed to drop from the tree.

### 2340  [To keep winter apples fresh]

Winter apples are also stored in rye and in fresh rye straw, which is not dried for the threshing of the rye, because after drying on the threshing floor it acquires a peculiar odor. It must be cut fine, the size of oats. Dry thoroughly on a hot, clean stove-bench, or even in the oven. Spread out the apples in the prepared boxes, thickly interspersing them with straw so that they do not touch each other at all. Keep them in the winter in the basement, inspecting them every month and a half. If the straw becomes damp, repack them with fresh straw prepared the same way.

### 2342  Apple cheese* with honey

*(Syr jablochnyj s medom)*

Peel and core sour apples, cut into pieces, place in a clay pot, and cover with a lid. Seal with dough or simply cover with a wet, clean cloth and bake in the oven.

Rub through a fine sieve. For every glass of apple purée, add 1 glass honey or sugar. Cook, constantly stirring, until the mixture thickens and pulls away from the spoon. Five minutes before the apples have finished cooking, add finely chopped preserved orange peel, some ground cloves or cinnamon, and if desired, ginger and allspice. Mix thoroughly, wrap in a damp napkin, tie the napkin with string, and place under a press. After two days the cheese will be ready. Store in a dry place and wipe it occasionally with a dry towel to prevent mold from appearing.

*This recipe resembles the family of English fruit cheeses that reduce a large amount of fruit to a fairly small quantity of semi-solid fruit pulp. Its odd name, therefore, may derive as much from the method of preparation as from the fact that the final product is served in slices or wedges, like cheese.*

### 2346 Marinated apples

*(Jabloki marinovannyja)*

Peel 20 apples and cut each into several pieces. Bring water to a boil with sugar or honey, drop in the apples, bring to a boil twice, and turn into a sieve. When they have dried, pack into a jar. Bring 4½ glasses vinegar to a boil with 1½ lbs sugar or honey, and add cloves, cinnamon, allspice, and salt. Cool, pour over the apples, tie up, and store in a cold place. Serve with meats.

### 2348 Soaked apples, another way

*(Jabloki mochenyja drugim sposobom)*

For one measure of apples, use 1 lb rye flour. Pour 1 pail boiling water onto the flour, mix, and let settle. Cool, pour off the water onto the apples, and place tarragon and other greens on top, etc.

### 2349 Soaked apples, a third way

*(Tret'im sposobom)*

For 1 pail water, add 1 or 2 lbs honey or sugar syrup, ¼ lb, or ½ glass, salt, tarragon, and basil. Boil all this at least half an hour, cool, pour over the apples, etc.

### 2351 Dried apples in a foreign manner

*(Jabloki sushenyja na zagranichnyj maner)*

Gather good, ripe, large apples, either sour or sweet, and peel off the skin as closely as possible. Core each apple by piercing with a small iron tube made for this purpose. It is good to have several of these iron tubes, both thicker and thinner, to match the size of the apples. After peeling and coring each apple, drop it immediately into cold water so that it will not discolor, but do not leave it in the water for more than half an hour. Thread the apples on a thick string or cord and dip them into boiling water for 5 seconds. Remove from the water, drain, and dry them in a low oven or, preferably, in the sun. To assure that the apples will be flat, remove them from the oven as soon as they soften and flatten them by placing a board and stone on top. Arrange them on a baking sheet to finish drying, but do not let them overdry. Pack into large jars, tie up, and store in a dry place.

These apples are used for compotes and for creams.

### 2354 Marinated apples, pears, and bergamots, another way

*(Jabloki, grushi, bergamoty, marinovannyja drugim manerom)*

Prepare good strong kegs and steam them thoroughly with black currant leaves. Gather good, ripe fruit. Pears and bergamots should be freshly picked, but apples must have lain on straw for 2 weeks. Pack the fruit into the kegs, sprinkling each layer with a mixture of black currant leaves, tarragon, savory, and marjoram. Place a thicker layer [of herbs] on the bottom and on top. Boil up a brine using 5 lbs honey or 7 lbs sugar, 1 lb salt, and ½ *garnets* good vinegar for each pail of water. Bring to a boil, cool, and pour over the fruit. Set aside some of the prepared brine, so that as the brine evaporates, the kegs may be refilled to the same level. To assure that the fruit is always covered by brine, place a round wooden plank on top with a stone.* Serve with meats.

*A similar method of marinating was used in Roman times and was recommended by Apicius for preserving hard-skinned peaches. (Edwards, The Roman Cookery of Apicius, 11.)

### 2356 Apple "soy" syrup

*(Jablochnaja soja)*

Lay sour apples on straw until they become juicy, but do not let them rot at all. Chop them very fine with a chopper and extract the juice in a press. In the same manner, chop sweet apples, very ordinary [i.e., no special variety], only without bitterness, and extract the juice in a press. For 2 parts sweet apple juice, add 1 part sour apple juice. Pour into a carboy and let the juice settle on ice for 3–4 days. Then decant carefully without disturbing the sediment and begin to cook the liquid. When the juice begins to thicken, stir it frequently with a wooden spatula so that it does not burn. Cook for a long time until, when it cools on a spoon on ice, it is as thick as fresh honey just removed from the hive. This soy* keeps in bottles for several years. It is used for sauces and is served in either salads or gravies and with veal, turkey, chicken, and beef.

*The word "soy" in this recipe must be understood analogously since this apple syrup, like soy sauce, is savory and keeps well. Its mildly tart flavor, however, obviously differs radically from the salty pungency of the sauce made from fermented soy beans. Naming by analogy is not uncommon in *culinary history. Our use of the word "ketchup," which now refers to a thickened, sweetened, and mildly spiced tomato sauce, derives from the Malay kechap which means fermented fish sauce.*

### 2359  Apple leather

*(Postila jablochnaja)*

Bake sour Antonov or Limonnyj apples on an iron sheet and rub them through a fine sieve. Measure out the purée by the glassful and stir in a stoneware bowl until the mixture whitens. For 2 glasses apple purée, use 1 glass honey, also beaten until white. Stir the apple purée and honey together until the mixture becomes white and crumbly (*rykhlyj*). Pour into paper casings to the height of 3 fingers and arrange them on an baking sheet dusted with bran. Dry out in the summer oven for several hours, remove from the oven, take off the paper, and pack in jars. Or place the leather in 2 or 3 layers, one on top of another, spreading them with honey, and return to the oven to dry out.

### 2362  Apple confections

*(Jablochnaja postila iz varenykh jablok)*

Fill a clay pot with large, ripe, sour apples, add water, and cook until the apple skins begin to split. Drain the apples in a sieve and let them dry overnight. The next day, rub the apples through a fine sieve. For 2 lbs of sieved apples, use 2½ lbs fine sugar and 3 egg whites. Mix everything together thoroughly and beat with a small whisk until the mixture whitens and thickens. Add about ⅛ lb ground bitter almonds and 1 spoon good, fragrant rosewater. Beat the mixture, then spread out in boxes made of pine slats, 1¼ *arshins* long, 6 *vershok* wide, and 1½ *vershok* high. These boxes must be lined on the bottom and sides with writing paper. Set them on small wooden blocks in a well-heated, cleanly swept out oven and leave them there for 24 hours. When, after some time, the apple mixture has dried out on top, remove the confections from the oven and set the boxes on the windowsill to cool faster. Remove the sweets from the boxes, turn onto clean boards covered with writing paper, and tear off the paper that has stuck to the bottom and sides. Return the confections to the oven on these boards to dry out evenly on all sides.

# PLUM PRESERVES

*(Zapasy iz sliv)*

### 2367  [To transport plums]

To transport plums,* place them in kegs, sprinkling them with bran or millet or layering them with dry moss.

*The importance of these directions derives from the fact that wealthy families like that of Molokhovets usually spent only the summer on their estates and in the winter moved back to the city, where they received regular shipments from the country.*

### 2368 "Drunken" plums

*(Likernye slivy)*

Cover plums with the best cognac or rum and let them stand for 2 days. Pour off the liquor and cover the plums with a boiled and cooled thick syrup made from 1½ glasses of the best fine sugar for each glass water and wineglass cognac.

### 2374 To keep plums fresh until Christmas

*(Kak sokhranit' slivy vengerskija svezhimi na zimu do Rozhdestva Khristova)*

At midday after the dew has dried in good, dry, warm weather, cut plums from the tree with scissors. Immediately place each plum into a jar, sprinkling with millet, or pack into a keg, interlayering the fruit with cherry leaves or millet. Wrap the jars with a bladder, seal the top with tar, and bury in the basement in the ground one *arshin* deep. If storing the fruit in kegs, the kegs must be tarred all over and submerged in water.

### 2375 Plum cheese without honey or sugar

*(Syr iz sliv bez medu i sakharu)*

Wipe plums dry, pack into a jar, and set in the oven after baking bread. Pour off the juice the next day and cook it over a low fire, constantly stirring. Test with a spoon over ice: if the juice begins to congeal like jelly, remove from the fire and immediately pour into a wide, glazed earthenware pot or into a jar. When it has cooled, tie it up and store in a cold, dry place. Slice like cheese and serve with vodka.

### 2378 Stuffed, dried plums

*(Slivy sushenyja, farshirovannyja)*

Use fresh plums that have lain aside for a while [i.e., not newly picked from the tree]. Slit the plums lengthwise, stone and stuff them, and thread on a very thin long spill, piercing the plums across to prevent them from disintegrating and the stuffing from falling out. Arrange the plums on a baking sheet covered with straw and dry out in the oven after baking bread. Repeat this several times, then pack into jars. They may be served with the spills, rather than removing them.

Any of the following fillings may be used.

a) Take some dried, pounded, and sieved rye bread, add some caraway seeds, and dilute with enough white honey to moisten the stuffing without making it runny.

b) Shell almonds (hazelnuts and walnuts may be added, if desired), chop fine, and dilute with white honey.

c) Finely chop peeled apples and add, if desired, cinnamon, cloves, and chopped orange rind. Dilute with white honey and use to stuff plums.

d) Stuff plums with finely chopped raw plums mixed with honey and caraway.

e) Stuff plums with grated almonds, chopped apples, and honey.

f) Stuff plums with a mixture of grated almonds, rosewater, and fine sugar. Then dry out the plums.

g) Finely chop sweet almonds, orange rind, and a few raw plums. Add sugar, dilute with water, and bring to a boil 2–3 times until the mixture thickens. When it is almost ready, add pounded cinnamon and cloves. Let the mixture cool, stuff the plums, and dry them in the summer oven on a baking sheet covered with straw. Repeat this several times until the plums have dried, but do not let them over-dry and become hard, which can happen if the oven is too hot. Serve with vodka and for dessert, like other dried preserves.


# PEAR PRESERVES

*(Zapasy iz grush)*


### 2379  To keep pears fresh

*(Grushi sokhranjat' svezhimi)*

Cut pears gently from the trees, because those that have fallen to the ground are not suitable for preserving. Arrange them with care in a small basket.

a) Store on ice in small, tinned copper saucepans with lids. Every 2 weeks, wipe off both the pears and the interior of the saucepan. Do not remove them from the ice house.

b) If you have a large quantity of pears, pack them in kegs with tight-fitting lids and bury them in ice. During freezing weather, set them at the bottom of the ice house to prevent them from freezing.

c) Lay out pears on clean, dry shelves in a cold, dry place so that the pears do not touch each other. Frequently wipe them dry with a towel.

d) Pears may be laid out on shelves covered with very dry straw, which should be changed if it becomes moist.


### 2381  Pears in honey

*(Grushi v mede)*

Peel and core large pears and boil them in a mixture of half water and half honey. They may also be boiled in a sugar syrup made from 5 glasses water for every 1 lb sugar. When the pears can be lightly pierced with a straw, remove them with a slotted spoon, flatten them, sprinkle them with sugar, place them on a dripping pan covered with straw, and set in the oven after baking bread. [Meanwhile, continue to cook other pears in the syrup.] After removing some pears from the syrup, drop in others until the syrup is reduced to the thickness of honey. Remove the pears from the oven, dip each into that same syrup, and return to the oven. Repeat this 3–4 times. The last time, dip the pears into the syrup and sprinkle lightly with cinnamon. Store in jars.

### 2388  Confections or dried pear preserves

*(Smokvy\* ili sukhoe varen'e iz grush)*

Choose very large pears that are not overripe. Peel them and toss them immediately into cold water to prevent them from darkening from the knife. Wash the peeled skins, cover them with water, add at least ten quartered pears (but not those that are intended for the confections), and cook over a high flame. After the water has sweetened and has become infused with the flavor of pears, add the pears intended for preserving. Cook them until they can be easily pierced with a straw, but do not overcook or let them fall apart. Drain the pears in a sieve, let them dry, and sprinkle them with sugar. Arrange the fruit with the stem end upward on a dripping pan covered with straw. Set in a summer oven for the fruit to firm, but do not let it dry out. Meanwhile, add ½ lb sugar for 1 lb pears to the water in which the pears were cooked and reduce until the syrup thickens. Remove the pears from the oven and, holding the fruit by the stem, dip each pear into the syrup. Sprinkle, if desired, with sugar and cinnamon, arrange on the dripping pan, and return to the oven. Repeat several times. When the pears have dried out sufficiently, sprinkle with sugar and pack into a jar after they have cooled.

*\*Smokva is usually translated as fig, but Molokhovets used the term for sweetened and dried fruit confections in general. See also the last section in this chapter.*

## CHERRY PRESERVES

*(Zapasy iz vishen')*

### 2390  A second way to keep cherries fresh

*(Vtoroj sposob sokhranjat' vishni svezhimi)*

Leave a short stem on each large, ripe cherry. Prepare a rather thin syrup from 1 glass each water and sugar. Keep the syrup in a basin on the coals and, holding each cherry by its stem, dip into the syrup and immediately roll in very finely pounded and sieved sugar of the best sort. Set the cherries on a platter so that one does not touch another. Dry out in a very low oven, pack into a jar, tie up, and store in a dry place.

### 2395  To dry cherries

*(Vishni sushonyja)*

Stone the fruit, dry it in the sun, and then in the oven. Or, lay out unstoned cherries in sieves lightly lined with straw and set them to dry several times in the summer oven.

### 2398  An excellent cherry salad*

*(Otlichnyj salat iz vishen')*

Use only firm, ripe, unblemished cherries. Prepare cherry juice from any crushed and overripe berries by filling a glazed pot with them, tying a cloth around the pot, and sealing with dough. Set in the oven before removing bread. If the bread is baked in the morning, the cherries may remain in the oven until evening. After removing the cherries from the oven, turn them into a sieve and let the juice drain off completely. Measure the juice and, for each glass of juice, add 1 glass sugar. Bring to a boil 5–6 times and cool. Pack the selected cherries into bottles and cover them with this juice. Cork and tar the bottles, place them on their side in a box, and set [the box] on ice. When the frost begins, carry the bottles into the basement and store them there, on their side, in sand. If desired, the juice may be boiled with spices, or with cinnamon and cloves, or with 3–5 pounded cherry pits, or with lemon zest (for 1 bottle juice, use the zest from ½ lemon).

*Molokhovets used the word "salad" to include fruit compotes that were served with meat.

### 2402  Cherries for ice cream

*(Vishni dlja morozhenago)*

Stone the cherries, pound several of the pits, and sew the crushed pits into a muslin bag. Add the muslin bag to the fruit so that after the juice has been drained, the broken pits will not prevent the cherries from being used for gingerbreads or fruit purées. Pour a layer of finely sieved sugar into a large jar and cover with a layer of cherries 1½–2 times thicker than the layer of sugar. Continue in this manner, adding alternate layers of sugar and cherries, until the jar is filled. Set the jar in the sun for 3 days for the sugar to dissolve, then drain in a fine sieve. Immediately pour the juice into bottles and cork with the best velvety corks that have been boiled until pliable. Seal with a mixture of half tar and half lard, which will not crack easily. This syrup is a good substitute for fresh cherries. Place the bottles on their side in chests and store on ice until the frost, and thereafter in the wine cellar. This juice is also good to serve for drinks, in which case it should be stored in small bottles. Purée the cherries that remain, bring to a boil, and use for filling *pirogs*, or for fruit pastilles.

# TO STORE GRAPES
## (*Zapasy iz vinograda*)

### 2408 [The usefulness of cotton cloth]

The latest tests show that cotton cloth will help significantly to preserve various foods. For example, if a bottle filled with meat bouillon is stopped up with cotton cloth, even if not quite securely, the bouillon will keep completely fresh for more than a year.

The same attributes of cotton will help preserve other items. But up until now, cotton has not been used in this way in Europe, whereas in America it has been used for a long time to preserve grapes and other fruits.

### 2410 [A new French way of preserving grapes]

Recently the following new method for preserving grapes was proposed in France.

Leave the grapes on the vines as long as possible, depending on the weather. When removing them, cut them off from the vine with a piece of stem above and below the bunch (roughly 2 nodes above and 3–4 below). Thoroughly coat the top end of the branch with wax and dip the lower end into a glass phial with water in which a little wood ash has been dissolved to impede any spoilage of the grapes. Cover the phial or paste it over with wax in exactly the same way. Carry the bunches of grapes in this condition to a cold location where they will be protected from frost, and set them on straw. Better still, hang them, which can be done easily if the phials or the glasses are well stopped. Thereafter, it is only necessary from time to time to pick off those grapes that have begun to spoil. The grapes can be kept for a very long time in this manner, especially if they are stored in the cold cellar, where the temperature is rather low and constant. Several times the inventor of this method has exhibited bunches of grapes which he has stored in this way. Observers have been startled by the freshness of the grapes.

Another way to keep grapes fresh is as follows:

To store grapes over the winter until May, choose a dry room on the second floor. This room should be in the middle of the building so that two of the walls and the floor adjoin the living quarters and the remaining two walls look outward and have at least one window each. These windows are essential to air the room in summer, when there is no fruit in the room. Upon filling the room with grapes, the windows must be immediately shut and, with the onset of frost, covered with felt and warm shields made from moss, or hay, or straw. During freezing weather, the adjacent rooms must be heated with stoves and the stove pipes vented into the room where the grapes are kept. In the room itself, the stove must never be lit for any reason, because it will change the air in the room and will spoil the grapes.

Set up supports 2 *arshins* apart along the walls and in the middle of this room. Along the supports attach shelves 5–6 *vershok* wide and set ¾ *arshin* apart. Every 6 or 7 *vershok*, make a semicircular excision along the shelves. In these holes place the necks of oblong glass jars with a capacity of 125 grams of water. Three days before placing the bunches of grapes in the jars, fill the jars to their necks with water and add 1 teaspoon powdered wood-ash to the water of each jar.

In general, it is best to select grapes from the upper branches of the vine for preserving. In France, grapes for this purpose are cut off on dry days when there is no dew, about October (20) 8.* The bunches of grapes are cut from the vine so that there are 3 buds below the bunches and 2 above. Usually, however, there are only 2 bunches on the branch that fulfill these conditions. After carefully cutting off the grapes, carry them into the room and stick the lower end of the branches into the jars so that the bunches of grapes hang freely in the air and touch neither the shelves nor each other.

After setting the bunches of grapes in the jars of water, the following rules must be observed.

a) Do not touch the jars.

b) Do not let either fresh air or light into the room.

c) The temperature of the room must be maintained between 1–7 degrees Centigrade.

d) Do not change the water in the jars, which will evaporate until only 5 or 6 centimeters remain by May.

e) While inspecting the grapes in winter, cut off any spoiled grapes carefully with scissors and discard immediately.

f) In case moisture appears in the room, set a barrel half-filled with quicklime at each end of the room. And in case the room begins to smell musty, it must be aired with ventilators,** but do this only in extreme circumstances. In a word, you should try not to circulate the air.

Grapes kept in this manner are so good that it is impossible to distinguish them from those just cut [from the vine], and therefore the price for them in both winter and spring is much higher than for grapes kept by other means.*** The expense of keeping them, which appears significant for the construction of shelves and the purchase of the jars, is repaid with interest by the high prices for the preserved grapes.

*The two numbers refer to dates in the old and new calendars.
**This probably meant nothing more than opening a window or vent to create a crossdraft. According to Ushakov, the first meaning of ventiljator is an air-hole or vent in the wall for circulation. It was only later that the word came to mean a fan with moving blades.

Rack for storing grapes. *Nov'*,
vol. 3 (1885).

***A similar, if somewhat simplified, plan for keeping grapes over the winter appeared in the*
*illustrated journal* Nov', *1885 (vol. 3), p. 499.*

### 2412 Marinated grapes for roasts and sauces

(*Marinovannyj vinograd k zharkomu and sousu*)

Pluck ripe but firm grapes from the stalk, or place whole, large bunches in a
jar. Pour on the following marinade: For 2 glasses water, use 1 glass of the best
wine vinegar, and for every 3 glasses of liquid, add 2 glasses fine sugar and the zest
from 1 lemon. Bring to a boil, stir, cool, and pour over the grapes. Place a round
piece of wood on top, tie up with a bladder, and set on ice until the frost. Then
store in a cold, dry basement where the grapes will not freeze.

## ORANGE PRESERVES

(*Zapasy iz apel'sin*)

### 2415 Candied orange peel

(*Tsukat iz apel'sinnoj korki*)

Cut good oranges into 4 or 6 pieces, remove the peel, and soak the peel in
water for about 3 hours. Change the water, cook the peel until it is tender enough

to be pierced with a straw, and soak again [in] cold water. For ½ lb of rind, use 1 lb sugar and 1 glass water. Prepare a syrup from 1 glass water and half of the weighed out sugar. Cool and pour over the rind packed into a jar that has been previously wiped dry. Cover with a napkin and pass a rolling pin over it, pressing rather hard. Pour off the syrup after 3 days, bring to a boil, add some sugar, and, when cold, pour over the orange rind. After 2 days repeat this same process, and finally, the fourth time, pour off the syrup, sprinkle the remaining sugar into it, and reduce until thick. Dip each piece of rind into the syrup, place on a dripping pan, and set in the summer oven for a short time, just long enough for the sugar to dry out. Repeat this several times, but do not over-dry the peel even once, otherwise it will be too hard.

### 2417  Orangeade

*(Oranshada)*

Remove the peel from 8 oranges and use for preparing candied orange peel. Divide each orange into several pieces and remove the seeds. Take another 2 oranges and cut them into several pieces, removing the seeds but not the peels. Place these 10 oranges in a stoneware bowl, pour on 5 lbs of fine sugar, and pound with a wooden pestle until the mixture turns into a watery mass, more or less. Transfer everything to a glass jar and wrap with a bladder. To make a drink, use 1 small spoon of this orange mixture for 1 glass water.

## MELON AND WATERMELON PRESERVES

*(Zapasy iz dyni i arbuza)*

### 2418  Marinated melon

*(Marinovannaja dynja)*

The melon must be a little underripe but not green. A very ripe melon will be fragile, but a green one will have no aroma. Peel, seed, and cut the melon into pieces as for eating. And to avoid having any thin ends, cut them off. Stud each piece of melon with several cloves, place in a basin, and cover with good vinegar. Set aside for 24 hours, then bring the melon to a boil in that same vinegar until the melon becomes a tiny bit tender. Line a sieve with a napkin folded into four, and pour on the melon to strain the vinegar. Prepare a thick syrup such as is made for jam, using 3 glasses sugar, 2 glasses water, and 1 glass strained vinegar. Cool and pour over the melon.

# PUMPKIN PRESERVES
*(Zapasy iz tykvy)*

### 2426  Marinated pumpkin, another way
*(Tykva marinovannaja drugim manerom)*

[Peel and seed a pumpkin and cut into pieces as you would a melon for eating.] Add the pumpkin pieces to the vinegar and boil until tender, but do not overcook. Then take good, thick treacle, but it must not be made from potatoes.* For every 3 glasses of treacle, add 1 glass wine vinegar and the zest from 1 lemon. Bring to a boil twice and, while hot, pour over the pumpkin. After it has cooled, pack into a jar, wrap with a bladder, and store in a cold place.

*Although treacle is usually a byproduct of sugar refining, it also may be produced from the juices of various trees and plants. The mention of potato treacle above is Molokhovets' only reference to this alternative kind of treacle.*

# GOOSEBERRY PRESERVES
*(Zapasy iz kryzhovnika)*

### 2433  Dried gooseberries for sauce
*(Sushonyj kryzhovnik dlja sousa)*

Gather very ripe gooseberries and dry them out in a very low oven. Such gooseberries are very tasty when added to a sour-sweet brown sauce to be served with beef and calf's feet or head. They replace raisins to some extent. Before using, they must be scalded with boiling water and left to soak.

### 2434  Gooseberry confections
*(Postila iz kryzhovnika)*

Around July 8, gather unripe, or even completely green, gooseberries of those varieties that would be green or white when ripe. Half fill a basin with the berries and fill up with water. Cook until tender enough to be rubbed through a fine sieve. Transfer them to a sieve, let the juice drain off, and rub the fruit pulp through the sieve while it is still hot. Measure the sieved pulp and, for every 2 glasses, add 1 heaping glass sugar. Beat with a spatula until it turns pale. To lighten and whiten the mixture, add one very fresh egg white for every 4 glasses of sieved purée. Divide into boxes and dry as indicated for apple confections and lingonberry pastilles.

# LEMON PRESERVES

*(Zapasy iz limonov)*

### 2436  To keep lemons fresh

*(Kak sokhranjat' limony svezhimi)*

Lemons are imported into Russia twice a year, in May and in September. Therefore one must stock up on lemons for an entire half year. Later they become too expensive or even difficult to obtain.

Thus, after purchasing lemons in May, use them in the following recipes.

### 2437  To keep lemons fresh, the first method

*(Vo pervykh sokhranit' svezhimi)*

Each lemon must be dried with a towel and wrapped in non-absorbent paper [i.e., not blotting paper]. Pack the fruit into a chest, interspersing with fresh green birch branches to prevent the lemons from pressing upon or touching each other, and store on ice. In this way the lemons will keep completely fresh for 2–3 months, but they must be inspected every 2–3 weeks. Dry them off, and rewrap in fresh paper. Use those lemons which have begun to spoil. Or, store the lemons in a dry place on shelves, arranging them so that one lemon does not touch another. Wipe them dry once a week and use those that have begun to spoil.

### 2442  To salt lemons

*(Solit' limony)*

Fill a jar with good, unblemished lemons. Liberally salt unboiled water so that a fresh raw egg dropped into it* will rise almost to the surface. Pour this water into the jar of lemons, top with a round plank (*donyshko*) and a stone, and store in a cold place. Lemons prepared in this way make a fine salad, especially on fast days with cooked fish, to which they impart a wonderful flavor. They are used in brown sauces and also in white sauces when fresh lemons are not available. They will keep for several months.

*A fresh raw egg in its shell was often used to determine the salinity of a brine solution. When pickling cucumbers, for instance, Hannah Glasse directed the reader to add enough salt to every gallon of water "as will make it bear an Egg" (Glasse, Art of Cookery, 132). The egg was only used for testing and was removed from the brine as soon as it floated.

## PINEAPPLE PRESERVES
### (*Zapasy iz ananasov*)

### 2444  Fresh pineapple with sugar
#### (*Svezhij ananas v sakhare*)

Slice pineapples and pack into a jar, interspersing each layer with sugar so that the layers of sugar are thicker than the layers of pineapple. The bottom and top layers must both be sugar. After filling the jar, tie a bladder around it, tar thoroughly, and store on ice. In this manner, pineapples will keep completely fresh and will retain their aroma. Before using, a little cognac may be added to the jar, according to individual taste.

## RASPBERRY PRESERVES
### (*Zapasy iz maliny*)

### 2446  To dry raspberries
#### (*Malina sushonaja*)

Pick over the berries and dry out in the oven. Repeat several times, if necessary. Use as a sudorific to treat colds. A simple jam may be prepared from these dried berries in winter. They are also used to prepare pastilles, Smolensk excommunicants, etc.

### 2448  Raspberry pastilles
#### (*Malinovyja prjanichki*)

Grind and pound 1 lb dried raspberries into a powder. Prepare a syrup from ½ lb sugar and a little water. After the syrup has boiled up several times, sprinkle on the raspberries and cook until thick enough for the syrup to congeal on a spoon when placed on ice. Form into small flat cakes, place them on a baking sheet, smooth them over, and let them cool. Dry them out in the oven.

### 2450  To keep [raspberries] fresh
#### (*Sokhranjat' svezheju*)

Gather fresh, ripe, firm raspberries, pick them over, and immediately pour into dry bottles. Shake the bottles, cork, and set in a saucepan with hay. Fill the saucepan with cold water, boil for an hour, and remove from the fire. After the water has cooled, remove the bottles, seal with tar, and bury in sand. These berries are used in the winter to prepare compotes or ice creams.

## NUT AND ALMOND PRESERVES
*(Zapasy iz orekhov i mindalja)*

### 2452  To keep nuts fresh, another way
*(Sokhranjat' orekhi svezhimi drugim manerom)*

Select good nuts and sprinkle them with very dry sand in a glazed clay pot. After filling the pot, tie round with a cloth and seal with clay prepared as for making bricks. Let the clay dry. If cracks appear, seal them, and store the pot in the basement or wine cellar. Nuts will keep in this manner for several years. It is best to store them in small vessels and to use them as soon as they are removed from the pot.

### 2456  Smolensk excommunicants
*(Smolenskie otluchentsy)*

Take equal parts of grated dry raspberries, ground dry nuts, and ground rye rusks. For 1 glass honey, add 3 glasses of this mixture. First bring the honey to a boil, then add the ground flours and cook thoroughly until the mixture congeals. Form into flat cakes on a baking sheet and dry out as indicated above for raspberry pastilles.

## LINGONBERRY PRESERVES
*(Zapasy iz brusniki)*

### 2459  Lingonberry jam for meats
*(Brusnichnoe varen'e k zharkomu)*

Pick over lingonberries, place in a sieve, and scald 3 times with boiling water. For 2 lbs lingonberries, use 1 lb honey or granulated sugar. Cook as usual, stirring with a spoon. Add apples, peeled and quartered, a peeled and thinly sliced pumpkin, halved pears, candied orange peel cut into small pieces, a piece of cinnamon, and 2–3 cloves. After the lingonberries have finished cooking, place 3–4 or more silver teaspoons in the saucepan. It is said that the silver removes any bitterness from the berries. This same jam may be made from cranberries.

If no honey is available when the lingonberries are gathered, cook the berries in their own juice without water. Pour the juice into a jug and, after it has cooled, cover and keep in a cold, dry place. Later it may be recooked with honey at any time, but in general it is tastier if it is cooked with sugar.

### 2463 To keep fresh lingonberries halfway through the winter
*(Svezhaja brusnika do poloviny zimy)*

Place small, crushed lingonberries in a glazed earthenware jug, fill it to the very top, cover with spills, seal with dough, and set in the oven to stew after baking bread. Remove the jug from the oven the next morning, turn the contents into a sieve, and drain off the juice, which may be used for *kissel*. Rub the berries through the sieve. Measure the sieved purée, and for 2 glasses of this purée, add 1 glass honey, 2 glasses sugar, or 1½ glasses treacle. Mix thoroughly with a spatula for at least half an hour, not less. Pour this thin purée over large, picked-over lingonberries, mix carefully so as not to smash the berries, cover, and store on ice until using. At the beginning of the frost, transfer to the wine cellar. In winter, these berries make a very pleasant and refreshing dessert by themselves.

# CRANBERRY PRESERVES
*(Zapasy iz kljukvy)*

### 2471 Cranberry confections
*(Konfekty iz kljukvy)*

For 1 egg white, add 1 cup finely [pounded] best sugar. Beat with a wooden spoon until white. Add 1 full dessertspoon lemon juice and mix with a spoon until the icing thickens and holds its shape. Carefully roll every berry in this icing and place on a platter greased with wax or very fresh unsalted butter. Let the berries dry out and pack them into jars, but they cannot be kept for long.

# PRESERVES FROM ROSE HIPS
*(Zapasy iz shipovnika)*

### 2473 Marinated rose hips*
*(Marinovannyj shipovnik)*

Select large, ripe, completely firm rose hips. If they are even a little soft, they are unsuitable. Clean them out carefully so that the slits are small. Place them in a basin and bring them to a boil several times in a juice prepared from cranberries or red currants (boiled in water until the berries whiten). Bring the rose hips to a boil 2–3 times in this juice without letting them soften at all, just long enough so that they are not completely raw. Turn them into a sieve to let the juice drain off. When they have cooled completely, pack them into a jar and pour over them some of the same vinegar used for marinating white plums.

*Rose hips are the fruit of the dog rose (Rosa canina). They contain large amounts of Vitamin C and are widely used for making preserves, syrups, and even wine. (Fitzgibbon, Food of the Western World, 398; Grieve, A Modern Herbal, 690–691.*

# PRESERVES FROM ROSE PETALS
### (Zapasy iz rozovago tsveta)

## 2475  Rose groats
### (Krupa iz rozovago tsveta)

Snip off the white ends of rose petals and finely pound the petals. Add potato flour and egg whites and beat in a stoneware bowl. When the dough thickens, knead it thoroughly, roll it out, chop it fine, and rub through a coarse sieve. After the groats have dried, rub them smooth with your hands to resemble rice. These groats are used to make a milk kasha with sugar or a steamed pudding.

## 2476  A superb confection from fresh, whole roses
### (Prevoskhodnye konfekty iz zhivykh roz)

Cut fragrant red or white centifolia roses, rinse them in pure water, and dry them out in the shade. Meanwhile buy some powdered cherry glue* and rosewater at the chemist's shop. Pour the rosewater into a basin, sprinkle on the cherry glue, set the basin on the fire, and stir until the water becomes as thick as liqueur. One at a time gently dip each dried rose into this warmish solution so that the entire blossom is evenly moistened. Carefully shake off the excess moisture and let the flowers dry. Sprinkle them with finely pounded sugar sieved through a very fine muslin. Arrange the blossoms carefully on a platter and set them in the sun. The sugar, warmed by the heat of the sun, will be absorbed by the rose petals and, after turning into tender crystals, will transform the flower into a confection. Roses prepared in this manner may be used in winter to decorate tortes and platters of fruit and grapes, which are very pretty and pleasant to the eye.

*Presumably, this was a powdered and flavored gelatin, although usually gelatin was sold in sheets.*

# WILD STRAWBERRY PRESERVES
### (Zapasy iz zemljaniki)

### 2482  Syrup from field strawberries for drinks and ice cream
### (Sirop iz polevoj zemljaniki dlja pit'ja ili dlja morozhenago)

Pour a layer of fine sugar into a large jar, then a layer of berries four times as thick as the layer of sugar. Continue adding alternate layers of berries and sugar until the jar is filled. The top layer must be sugar. Wrap the jar in paper and set in the sun for 2 days or more until the sugar dissolves. Transfer everything to a sieve, drain, and reserve the juice. To the strained juice, stir in the same amount of sugar that was poured earlier into the jar. Bottle, cork with the very best "velvet" corks, which first must be boiled tender, and seal. Prepare the tar half and half with lard, because then it will not crack so much. If this syrup is being prepared for drinks, pour it into small bottles so that it will not remain uncorked for long. Place the bottles on their side in a chest and store on ice until the frost, and then in the wine cellar. Make fruit pastilles from the berries that remain, or use them for filling sweet *pirogs*.

# BLACK CURRANT PRESERVES
### (Zapasy iz chernoj smorodiny)

### 2486  To keep currants almost as if fresh
### (Sokhranjat' smorodinu pochti kak by svezheju)

Prepare a thin syrup from 1 glass each water and fine sugar, keep it in the basin over the coals, and dip good branches of currants into the syrup. Immediately place on a platter, then dry in a low oven, pack carefully in a jar, tie up, and store in a dry place.

### 2491  Uncooked black currant jelly
### (Zhele varen'e iz chernoj smorodiny bez ognja)

Clean the berries and squeeze out the juice, but do not rub them through a sieve. Weigh 1 lb of this juice and 1 lb sugar, pounded as fine as possible and sieved. Begin to mix with a spatula, in one direction only, without fail, adding the sugar gradually. After 2 or 3 hours, it will form a jelly just like one that has been boiled, but with an incomparably better aroma.

## RED CURRANT PRESERVES
*(Zapasy iz krasnoj smorodiny)*

**2497 Red currants in "camisoles"**

*(Krasnaja smorodina v sorochke)*

Dip good full clusters of currants into egg white and immediately roll in sugar. Place on a platter or a baking sheet greased with wax and dry out in a low oven. These red currants are very tasty, but they will not keep for long.

## BARBERRY PRESERVES
*(Zapasy iz barbarisa)*

**2502 Salted barberries**

*(Barbaris solenyj)*

Gather whole bunches of barberries in late autumn. Pack into a jar and pour on boiled and cooled salted water. Tie up the jars. If mold appears, pour off the water and refill with a fresh batch of salted water. These barberries are used for garnishing dishes. They are also served with meats, instead of pickles. For 3 glasses water, use 9–12 zolotniki, or ¼ glass, salt.

## ROWANBERRY PRESERVES
*(Zapasy iz rjabiny)*

**2505 Rowanberries in honey**

*(Rjabina na medu)*

Pick over rowanberries gathered after the first frost, bake in the summer oven on a dripping pan, and add them to honey that has been boiled until golden. Cook like ordinary jam.

## PEACH PRESERVES
*(Zapasy iz persikov)*

**2510 To transport fresh peaches and other fruits**

*(Perevozka svezhikh persikov i drugikh fruktov)*

Choose the very best fruit and dip [each piece] in melted paraffin. After the paraffin has cooled, place the fruit in chests with straw. The fruit can then be transported anywhere you like in this manner. For instance, fruit from America arrives in Europe as if just gathered from the tree, despite the tossing and shaking of the journey.

# APRICOT PRESERVES
*(Zapasy iz abrikosov)*

### 2513  Marinated apricots to be served with meats
*(Marinovannye abrikosy k zharkomu)*

Pierce ripe but firm apricots in 10 places with a thin wooden needle and pack into jars, layering the apricots with marjoram. Pour on the following vinegar: For 2 glasses water, add 1 glass of the best wine vinegar and, for 3 glasses of this mixture, add 2 glasses fine sugar. Bring to a boil, while stirring, cool, and pour over the apricots. Place a round wooden plank and stone on top, tie up with a bladder, and store on ice until the frost.

# TOMATO PRESERVES
*(Zapasy iz pomidorov)*

### 2517  Salted tomatoes for stuffing
*(Solenye pomidory dlja farshirovan'ja)*

Wipe tomatoes* dry, pack them into an earthenware pot, and pour on cooled water that has been boiled with salt. (This water must be salted enough so that a fresh egg can float in it, that is, use 1 glass salt for 3–4 glasses water.) First place a small round plank on top of the tomatoes so that they are constantly immersed in the salted water and then cover the earthenware pot. Remove the mold frequently. Before using, the tomatoes must be soaked in water and washed thoroughly. They are used in soup.

*Green, but not red, tomatoes are usually preserved in brine. The modern process is still remarkably similiar to that outlined by Molokhovets. (See Stocking Up, 161–163.) In Chapter 1, Molokhovets gave a recipe for green tomatoes stuffed with veal forcemeat that were used as a garnish for soup.

### 2518  Marinated tomatoes or eggplants
*(Marinovannye pomidory ili baklazhany)*

Gather tomatoes when they have reached a fair size but are not yet ripe. Pack into a jar, interspersing each layer with fragrant herbs, such as marjoram, tarragon, and chervil. Place 6 chili peppers on the bottom of a half-pail jar and the same number in the middle and on top. Pour on good wine vinegar boiled with spices. Tie up the jar and store in a cold place. The tomatoes or eggplants will be good until the next summer only if the vinegar is good. In case it turns watery, pour off the old vinegar and add fresh vinegar.

# CONFECTIONS OR DRY PRESERVES AND HOMEMADE CANDIES
*(Smokvy ili sukhoe varen'e i domashnija konfekty)*

### 2520 Candied chestnuts
*(Zasakharennye kashtany)*

Bake thoroughly, peel off the skins, and pierce with a twig. Soak the chestnuts in a very thick caramel syrup (that is, boiled until golden) until they are saturated. Let the excess syrup drain off, lay the chestnuts on a baking sheet greased with very fresh, unsalted butter, let them dry out, and store in jars.

### 2522 Dry preserves from sweet flag
*(Sukhoe varen'e iz aira)*

Dig up sweet flag roots [*Acorus calamus*]* in May, wash, and toss them immediately into cold water. Soak them for 3 days, each day changing the water. Peel the roots with a knife and again soak in water overnight. The next day bring the roots to a boil in 2 waters [i.e., change the water once and bring the second water also to a boil]. Use a large kettle, because the more water, the sooner the bitterness will be boiled out of the roots. Each time after boiling the roots, toss them into cold water. After bringing the water to a boil the second time, soak the roots in cold water until the next day, changing the water several times. Finally, cut the sweet flag into pieces, cover with water, and keep changing the water until the roots are no longer bitter. Lay out the sweet flag on a napkin, cover with another napkin, pass a rolling pin over the roots, and press down firmly to squeeze out all the moisture. For 1 lb sweet flag, weigh out 2 lbs sugar and 1 glass water. Bring the syrup to a boil, cool, and add the sweet flag. Cook over a low fire, stirring with a spatula and removing the pan frequently from the fire so that the bottom does not burn. When the syrup has thickened enough so that it begins to coat the spoon, turn the sweet flag out onto a platter and sprinkle with sugar. To hasten the drying process, keep the platter in front of the fire. Then pack into a jar.

*Another way:* Peel the roots, cut into pieces, and drop them into cold water for 4 hours. Remove from the water, cover with milk, and cook for a long time.

Plunge them into cold water for another 5 minutes and cook in fresh milk until tender. Rinse them thoroughly, place in a napkin, cover with another, and pass a rolling pin over to press out all the moisture. For 1 lb sweet flag, weigh out 2 lbs sugar and 1 glass water. Proceed further as indicated above.

*For more on this fragrant root, see the Glossary.*

### 2524  Homemade tragacanth or gummy confections: wild strawberries, mint patties, and mushrooms

*(Domashnija tragantovyja konfekty: zemljanika, mjatnyja lepeshki, gribki)*

*Wild strawberries:* Place 10 kopecks' worth, or 2 *zolotniki*, tragacanth in a teacup, pour on just enough cold water to barely cover the pieces of this glue, and let them soak overnight. The next day, pour 2 lbs of sieved sugar, or 4 glasses, onto a board. Strain the tragacanth through a cloth onto the sugar, squeezing it with 2 sticks to extract all the liquid. Knead this dough, gathering in the sugar with a knife. The dough must be as thick as that for buns, so that it can be rolled out with a rolling pin. Add something for flavoring, either 3 drops of cinnamon oil or 3–4 drops of rose or lemon oil. Take small balls of this dough and shape into wild strawberries, pricking the middle of each strawberry with a sharp wooden twig. Dry out on a plate lined with paper. Then, holding each strawberry by its stick, dip it into prepared cochineal of a very soft color. Sprinkle immediately with fine white sugar left in a sieve [from a previous sifting]. Cochineal is prepared at the chemist's or at home as indicated in #2635. If no cochineal is available, 1 sheet of red gelatin may be dissolved in a wineglass of water.

*Mint patties:* Mint patties are prepared from the same mixture, adding 3–4 drops mint oil to the sugared dough. Roll out the dough with a rolling pin and cut out the patties with a thimble.

*Mushrooms* are prepared from the same dough, except that a little saffron powder must be added to tint part of the dough slightly yellow. Roll out small mushroom stems from this yellowish dough and let them dry out. Sprinkle a little chocolate into the remaining dough and form into mushroom caps. Immediately stick one of the dried stems into each cap.

# 29

# Preserved Vegetables and Greens

*(Zapasy iz ovoshchej i zeleni)*

## TO PRESERVE CAULIFLOWER

*(Zapasy iz tsvetnoj kapusty)*

### 2525 To keep cauliflower fresh

*(Sokhranjat' svezhuju tsvetnuju kapustu)*

Choose very firm heads of cauliflower, undamaged by frost. Tie string around the heads so that one does not touch another and hang them from the ceiling in the basement. If any yellowed leaves are picked off as they appear, the heads will keep until Christmas stored in this manner.

*Another way:* Before the frost, dig up heads of cauliflower with some earth and set them in a bed of earth or in sand in the basement. Pick off any yellow leaves and gently tie up the remaining leaves over the top with a thin cord. Inspect the heads frequently and tear off any leaves that are beginning to spoil. In general, dry out the basement frequently by opening the window in dry weather and closing it before sunset. Immediately cook, salt, or marinate any heads which begin to spoil. This method of storing cauliflower is so good that small heads continue to grow even in the basement.

## TO PRESERVE ORDINARY CABBAGE

*(Zapasy iz kapusty obyknovennoj)*

### 2529 Chopped cabbage

*(Shinkovannaja kapusta)*

There is no need to hurry and gather the cabbages before the frost while the weather is still warm. Just bring the cabbages into the vegetable cellar when the frost begins. First prepare chopped gray cabbage, and then, after waiting for the new moon, cut off the outer leaves from the firm, tightly closed heads, halve each head, and shred with a sharp knife or machine.

It has been observed that cabbage which is set to sour at the new moon is firm and squeaks on the teeth. Therefore, if soft cabbage is preferred, it should be set to sour in the last quarter of the moon. Place the shredded cabbage on a large coarse sieve and wash it thoroughly with clean, cold water. After draining off the water, fill a keg with layers of cabbage, sprinkling each layer with a small handful of washed salt* and a handful of caraway seeds. Press each layer down well and cram it in with a pounder made for this purpose until juice appears. To make more juice, pour 1 glass very salty water over each layer of cabbage and place carrots, apples, and lingonberries or cranberries between the layers. By the way, the cabbage should not be pressed down too much or it will become too soft.

After filling a keg in this manner, poke an oak or birch pole into the cabbage to the very bottom of the keg in 6 or 7 different places. This must be done twice a day without fail. These passages will allow a strong unpleasant gas to escape which, if it remained on the cabbage, would spoil it completely. After 2 weeks, cover the cabbage with cabbage leaves and place a round barrel lid and stone on top. Kegs of cabbage must be stored from the beginning in a rather cold place, where the cabbage may sour slowly and where it will not freeze in winter.

In general, all the kegs for fermenting cabbage must be washed clean and the interior chinks filled with a dough made from rye flour. The outside of the kegs must be tarred. A keg with a capacity of 15 pails will require almost 1 *garnets* salt. Gradually pour salted water over the layers of cabbage as indicated above, each time using 1 *garnets*, or ¼ pail, water with 1 lb salt. (For 15 pails of cabbage, use in all about 4½–6 glasses caraway.) This cabbage is used in *shchi* and is served with roasts or sausages instead of salad.

*Larger, coarser granules of salt were used for pickling than for the table. The pieces were big and dirty and needed to be rinsed off or washed. These granules were considered more "salty" than table salt and hence better for pickling.

### 2533 To prepare sauerkraut in a few days

*(Kak prigotovit' kisluju kapustu v neskol'ko dnej)*

In summer when no more sauerkraut is left and you need some quickly, you must first shred and wash fresh heads of cabbage. Plunge the shredded cabbage into boiling water, let it come once to a boil, turn it into a sieve, and cool by rinsing with cold water. After the water has drained off completely, salt the cabbage as indicated for Chopped cabbage #2529. Cooling the cabbage under running water makes the sauerkraut firm and squeaky.

### 2536  Stewed cabbage

*(Kapusta parenaja)*

Cabbage prepared in this way ripens very quickly but it does not keep well and therefore must be used sooner than others. Choose good, firm heads and trim off any greenish leaves. As soon as rye loaves are removed from the oven, immediately spread straw on the oven floor (the oven must not be very hot, otherwise the straw will burn), and place the heads on the straw one next to another. Close the oven and let the cabbage stew. When the cabbage has become tender, remove the heads from the oven. Cool them and pack into vats, thickly sprinkling each layer with chopped cabbage. Set the vat in the cold cellar to let the cabbage sour gradually. When the chopped cabbage has soured, the heads are ready. Cabbage prepared in this manner has its own special flavor which some people do not like, but its most important merit is that it ripens quickly.

### 2537  Chopped cabbage with wine

*(Kapusta shinkovannaja s vinom)*

Measure out 3 pails of chopped cabbage, pack it into a vat, salt it as usual (cf. #2529), and pound it thoroughly with a wooden mallet (*kolotushka*). For this amount of cabbage, add 1 bottle of white table wine. It does not matter what kind, only of course use the cheapest sweet wine available. Pour it over the cabbage, trying to cover all the cabbage evenly. It is best to pour it from a small watering can. Set the cabbage to sour in the usual manner in the cold cellar. Cabbage prepared in this way is unusually tasty.

## TO PRESERVE GREEN PEAS

*(Zapasy iz zelenago gorokha)*

### 2543  To keep peas fresh for the winter

*(Kak sokhranjat' gorokh svezhim na zimu)*

Choose young sugar peas with large, oblong seeds—this variety is called "Marrow" [sic]. Shell the peas, add salt, and let them stand overnight. (For 1 *garnets* peas, use ½ glass salt.) Pour off the juice the next day, pour the peas into dry, strong ale-house bottles, and cork immediately. Wrap up the bottles with hay, set them in a kettle with cold water, and boil for 1½ hours, not longer. Let the water cool completely before removing the bottles. Tar them and bury them in dry sand. These peas must be soaked in water for 2 hours before using. Add sugar and boil.

The flavor of peas prepared in this manner is barely distinguishable from that of fresh peas.

### 2549  To prepare dried green peas

*(Prigotovlenie sushonago zelenago goroshka)*

For 1 pail water, add 1 teaspoon butter and 1 lb salt. Bring to a boil and, while it is boiling strongly, add shelled green peas that are not yet completely ripe, as many as will fit into the pail. Set on the fire for 2 minutes, then turn the peas onto several coarse sieves. Let the water drain off, turn the peas out onto a sheet, fold the sheet over the top of the peas, and leave for 12 hours. Repour the peas onto the sieves and set in a low oven to dry out, but do not let them brown. Store in a dry place. The smaller and less ripe the peas are, the better they will be. Very ordinary field peas may be dried in this manner.

## TO PRESERVE ONIONS
*(Zapasy iz luka)*

### 2550  To store onions for winter

*(Luk sokhranjat' na zimu)*

After gathering the onions, string them by the hundred or by fifty on a thin cord and hang them on the wall in a warm, dry larder or in a shed or peasant's cottage (*izba*).

## TO PRESERVE MUSHROOMS
*(Zapasy iz gribov)*

### 2552  Fried saffron milk-caps

*(Ryzhiki zharenye)*

Wipe young saffron milk-caps dry and fry them in a large quantity of butter, but do not overcook them or let them dry out. Cool the mushrooms, stand them upright in a jar (as they grow with the caps on top), and pour on that same barely warm butter in which they were fried. The butter should completely cover the mushrooms and extend above them to a width of 3 or 4 fingers. Tie a bladder round the jar and store in a dry, cold place. Refry lightly when using the mushrooms in winter.

### 2555 Marinated saffron milk-caps

*(Ryzhiki marinovannye)*

For 1½ glasses salt, use ⅛ lot, or ½ dram, of saltpeter and 10 grains of alum. Dilute with 2½ lbs vinegar. Bring the mixture to a boil in a well-tinned saucepan and add the young saffron milk-caps that have been wiped dry. Let them come to a boil, then pour them into a deep, glazed earthenware dish. After they have cooled, arrange them standing upright in a jar and pour over them the same vinegar in which they cooled. Pour off the vinegar after 2 weeks and cover with fresh vinegar boiled with cinnamon, cloves, allspice, and black pepper.

### 2564 Dried boletus mushrooms, another way

*(Sushonye boroviki drugim manerom)*

After gathering the mushrooms, peel them, and separate the caps from the stems. Thread them separately, but not very tightly, on a thin string. Dry them out by setting them in the oven several times or by hanging them in the sun. These mushrooms are used to flavor borshch or sorrel *shchi*, or as forcement. They are also used to stuff dumplings.

In addition, they are served with vodka or with the main course (*zharkoe*)* instead of salad on fast days. Prepare them as follows: Choose good caps, wash them in warm water, and boil until tender in salted water. Half an hour before serving, arrange the mushrooms in a bowl and pour on vinegar and, if desired, olive oil.

*\*Zharkoe normally means a meat dish or the main meat course. This is an instance where its extended meaning of "main dish" must be assumed, since meat dishes per se were proscribed on fast days.*

### 2571 Salted boletus mushrooms

*(Belye griby solenye)*

Mushrooms may be stockpiled in spring for the summer and in autumn for the winter. Drop young boletus mushrooms into boiling water. After they have come to a boil once or twice, turn them into a coarse sieve and cool by rinsing them in cold water. Let them dry off in the same sieves, turning them over on all sides. Pack them into jars standing upright, sprinkle each layer with salt, cover the top layer with a dry, round piece of wood, and place a stone on top. If after several days the mushrooms have subsided, top up the jar with fresh mushrooms, and pour on melted beef fat or butter that is barely warm. Best of all, wrap a bladder around the jar and store it in a cold, dry place. Before using, soak the mushrooms for 1 hour in cold water. If they have been salted for a long time, they may be soaked for a full 24 hours. Wash them in several waters. The flavor of mushrooms prepared in this manner is barely distinguishable from that of fresh mushrooms, especially if they are boiled in bouillon with powdered boletus mushrooms. For 1 pail of boletus mushrooms, use 1½ glasses salt.

### 2575 Soy sauce from field mushrooms*

(*Soja iz shampin'onov*)

Salt 20 large field mushrooms, set aside for 24 hours, and then mash them with a spoon. Strain, bring to a boil, skim, and pour into bottles. Twenty field mushrooms should yield 1½–2 bottles of soy.

*Although mushroom soy sauce had an especially important role in Russian cuisine because of the large number of fast days, mushroom soy, or ketchup as it was called, was also commonly used in English cookery in the eighteenth century. The English ketchups, which derived from the East, were more highly spiced than Molokhovets' version cited above, and allowed an easy transition to tomato ketchup when that New World fruit became more widely available.*

### 2577 Milk-agaric mushrooms

(*Gruzdi*)

Select small milk-agaric mushrooms. Wash, but do not soak them, and let them dry off in coarse sieves. Pack them in large jars, interspersing them with dill. Dust each layer lightly with salt. Do not weight the mushrooms, but sprinkle a fair amount of salt on top and cover with a cabbage leaf. Soak before using.

### 2581 Marinated truffles

(*Marinovannye trjufeli*)

Wash off any dirt from the truffles, arrange them in a glazed earthenware jug, and sprinkle on a little salt, as you would season a dish while cooking. Cover the truffles completely with a mixture made from equal parts of red beer vinegar and red Médoc wine. Tie a cloth around the jug, seal with dough and, for 3 days in a row, set it in the oven after baking bread. Remove the jug every afternoon at 5 o'clock.* After four days remove the cloth and add enough water to cover the truffles completely. Drain the truffles in a fine sieve, reserving the liquid. Transfer the truffles to a bowl and the liquid to a saucepan. If necessary, add some salt according to taste and add a few spices, if desired. Bring twice to a boil and pour the hot liquid over the truffles in the bowl. Let them cool, then pack into jars with wide necks. Make sure that the truffles are covered completely by the liquid. Cork and tar the jars and place them on their sides so that the end of the cork is constantly covered by the liquid. Store in a cold, dry cellar. Truffles prepared in this manner may be added to brown sauces and pâtés.

*Aside from the major ingredient, this recipe is interesting for what it reveals about the daily rhythm of the household, with bread being baked every morning.*

### 2582  To cultivate field mushrooms

*(Razvedenie shampin'onov)*

Dig a ditch ¾ *arshin* deep and as wide as is convenient. Fill the ditch with horse manure, sprinkle ½ *arshin* of black earth on top, and level it thoroughly. Coarsely chop field mushrooms, including the roots and any earth that adheres to them, sow them on this bed, and cover with earth to a depth of 3 fingers. After 3 weeks, the earth will begin to rise in small lumps along the top of this bed, a sign that the mushrooms are growing. Planted in this manner, they will last a long time, especially if, when gathering them, you resow the bed each time with chopped roots and cover them up with earth.

# TO PRESERVE CUCUMBERS

*(Zapasy iz ogurtsov)*

### 2583  Salted cucumbers

*(Ogurtsy solenye)*

To have solid rather than hollow cucumbers, they must be salted immediately after they have been gathered, or at the latest, on the next day. To prevent them from drying out, it is best to drop them into cold water with ice as soon as they have been gathered.

Cover the bottom of a small barrel with oak, cherry, currant, and dill leaves and quartered garlic cloves. If not using garlic, add the leaves and shavings of horseradish roots. Stand the cucumbers upright one next to another on the bottom of the barrel and spread a handful of each of the above-mentioned greens on each layer of cucumbers. After filling the barrel in this manner, cover it immediately with another barrel bottom, in which two small holes must be drilled. One hole is to allow gasses to escape; insert a funnel in the other hole and pour in salted water as follows: Use 6 glasses salt and 1 spoon saltpeter for 2½ pails, or for 10 *garnets*, of river or well water. Mix the water and salts together and pour as is [without heating] over the cucumbers. Immediately cork and tar the barrel. It is good to intersperse the cucumbers with small watermelons, which are abundant in the southern provinces of Russia.

### 2584  Another method for salting [cucumbers]

*(Drugoj sposob solenija)*

For 2 pails cucumbers, use 1 pail water and 1 to 1¼ lbs salt. Bring to a boil, cool, and pour the brine over the cucumbers. When the barrel is full, drive bungs into both openings, tar the barrel all over, and submerge in water, attaching it to a stake hammered into something solid. Or store the barrel in the basement on wooden platforms, but not on the ground, and frequently wipe the mold off the barrel. The best method, however, is to bury the barrel or kegs of cucumbers in the ground in the basement or in the ice in the ice house. [First, bury the barrel] and, the next day, gather and wash the cucumbers. Pack them into the kegs, sprinkling on greens, and let them stand for two days. On the third day pour on a brine prepared as indicated above, cork, etc.

Vessels for salting cucumbers must be well washed and steamed with pure water, dill, chervil, and other fragrant herbs. Cucumber kegs or barrels must not be used for any other purpose; especially do not pour lye into them. It has been observed that salted cucumbers prepared during the last quarter of the moon tend to be hollow. Therefore, to have full and firm cucumbers, you must begin to salt them 5–6 days after the new moon and finish the salting before the next new moon.

### 2588  Marinated cucumbers with mustard, horseradish, etc.

*(Ogurtsy marinovannye s gorchitseju, khrenom i proch.)*

Peel fresh, green cucumbers and cut them lengthwise into four or more pieces. Wash the pieces, dry them carefully with a napkin, and pack them in a glazed earthenware jug. Bring to a boil enough vinegar to cover the cucumbers and, while still hot, pour it over them and set the jug aside for 2 days. Pour off the vinegar, bring it to a boil, and repour it over the cucumbers while still hot. Repeat this again after 2 days. Coarsely pound together a little white and black pepper, the same amount of cloves, and a little more allspice. Finely chop a little horseradish, 2 onions, and 1 or 2 heads of garlic. Add 4 *lots* of black mustard and mix all the seasonings together. Remove the cucumbers from the vinegar, roll them in the seasonings, and place them in a jar, sprinkling on any leftover horseradish, onion, and garlic. Pour on strong, just-boiled vinegar. When the liquid has cooled, wrap a bladder round the jar, and store in a cold place.

### 2593  Salted cucumbers, another way

*(Solenye ogurtsy drugim manerom)*

Dry out very clean river sand and pass it through a fine sieve. Spread a layer of this sand the thickness of your palm on the bottom of a barrel. Add a layer of clean black currant leaves, dill, and horseradish cut into pieces, followed by a layer of cucumbers. Cover the cucumbers with another layer of leaves, dill, and horseradish, topped with a layer of sand. Continue in this manner until the barrel is full. The last layer over the cucumbers must be currant leaves, with sand on the very top. Prepare the brine as follows: For 1 pail of water, use 1½ lbs salt. Bring to a boil, cool, and cover the cucumbers completely with the brine. Replenish the brine as it evaporates. Before any kind of salting, cucumbers must be soaked for 12–15 hours in water with ice.

### 2595  Nezhinskie* cucumbers

*(Nezhinskie ogurtsy)*

Remove one end of a small barrel with a 1½ pail capacity. Line the bottom of the barrel with 3 sprigs of tarragon, 3 large celery roots, and 3 large parsley roots, including all the green leaves from the root vegetables. The roots may be cut up and spread out. Fill half the barrel with washed and dried small cucumbers. Cover the cucumbers with the same amount of roots and greens and intersperse 3 red pepper pods among the greens. Wrap the peppers in greens so they do not touch the cucumbers, then fill up the rest of the barrel with cucumbers. Cover them with the same quantity of roots and greens and place 3 more red pepper pods on top. Next, add 1 glass salt to 1 pail of good vinegar and bring to a boil. Let the brine cool before pouring over the cucumbers. After the cucumbers have absorbed the brine, fill up the barrel with more of the same brine. Cork the barrel, seal with tar, and store in a cold place, but not on ice.

*The name for these cucumbers comes from Nezhin, a very old town in the Ukraine about 100 kilometers northeast of Kiev. An early settlement in this location was mentioned in the Russian chronicles of the mid twelfth century; by the mid seventeenth century, the town had become an important trading center.*

### 2598  Salted cucumbers in a pumpkin

*(Ogurtsy solenye v tykve)*

Cut off the top of a small pumpkin with care and clean out the interior, leaving the walls at least 1 *vershok* thick. Fill the pumpkin with cucumbers, interspersing them with tarragon, marjoram, and chervil, or other herbs as desired. Sprinkle with salt, using 1½ lbs salt for this amount of cucumbers. When the pumpkin is full, cover the cucumbers with the same fragrant herbs and replace the lid of the pumpkin that was cut off earlier. Attach it carefully with wooden tacks the size of a match. Place the pumpkin or pumpkins in small barrels so they do not topple over. Fill any crevices with cucumbers and pour on a cold brine, using 1½ lbs salt for 1 pail of water. For every 2 pails of salt brine, add 1 pail of a decoction of oak bark, prepared as follows: For 1 pail water, add 1 lb dry oak bark and boil until it is reduced by a fifth, measured with a spill.

### 2601  Warning about cucumbers

*(Predosterezhenie otnositel'no ogurtsov)*

Purchased cucumbers are sometimes very attractive, that is, green as a result of being prepared in an untinned copper vessel, which is extremely harmful to your health. To check whether the greenness of the cucumbers is really a result of this preparation, stick a clean steel needle into a cucumber. The needle will turn a copper color in a short time if the cucumbers have been adulterated.

# TO PRESERVE BEETS
### *(Zapasy iz svekly)*

### 2603  Soaked beets
*(Svekla mochenaja)*

Beets must be soured in the last quarter of the year when beets always tend to be soft. Scrape them with a knife, then wash thoroughly, and place in a large vat. When it is filled, pour on river water or, lacking that, well water. Replenish any brine that you pour off before Christmas with the same amount of water. But do not add any water to the vat after Christmas, because by then the beets are almost entirely saturated. If you wish to have constant supply of fresh beet brine for sauces and soups, soak only half the beets in the autumn and leave the other half fresh, souring them in batches every 3 weeks. If using beet brine which has been diluted with water, then, for a better flavor, boil it with 1 or 2 fresh beets before using.

# TO PRESERVE SORREL
### *(Zapasy iz shchavelja)*

### 2608  Salted sorrel
*(Shchavel' solenyj)*

When the mown grass begins to grow again in September, then sorrel also begins to send up fresh shoots and turn green. This is the time to gather it and preserve it for winter.

Clean and wash the sorrel and spread it on a tablecloth to dry in the fresh air. Place in small pails of non-resinous wood and sprinkle with salt. When the pails are full, cover the sorrel with a round board and weight with a stone. After the sorrel has subsided, add more fresh sorrel. Store in a cold place, but do not let it freeze. For 1½ pails sorrel, use 1½ glasses salt. This sorrel must be washed, chopped, and added to boiling bouillon just before serving.

# TO PRESERVE DILL, PARSLEY, TARRAGON, MARJORAM, AND HORSERADISH

*(Zapasy iz ukropa, petrushki, estragona, majorana i khrena)*

### 2611  Dried dill and parsley

*(Ukrop sushenyj i petrushka)*

Sow dill in mid-August. After it has grown in September, cut it off at the root and dry in the open air on a tablecloth. Or, tie it in bunches and hang them up in pairs to dry in the sun or in a warm room. After the dill has dried out, grind it into a coarse powder. Pour into glass jars and serve in soup and other dishes. Green parsley may be dried for winter in exactly the same way.

## CELERY AND ASPARAGUS

*(Zapasy iz sellerej i sparzha)*

### 2619  Salted asparagus

*(Sparzha solenaja)*

Place well-cleaned asparagus in a glazed earthenware jug. Add enough salt to the water to support a raw egg, that is, use 1 glass salt for 3–4 glasses water. Bring this salted water to a boil and cover asparagus completely with the boiling liquid. Let the water cool, wrap and tie a paper moistened with olive oil round the jug and tie a bladder over the paper. Two hours before using, soak the asparagus in cold water and boil in a large quantity of water.

## CAPERS

*(Zapasy iz kapartsy)*

### 2621  Homemade capers, another way

*(Kapartsy domashnie drugim manerom)*

Bring young nasturtium seeds to a boil once in salted water and turn into a coarse sieve to dry. Or, salt dried seeds and let them stand 24 hours, stirring them frequently. Dry them in a napkin, place in small jars, and cover with a boiled and cooled vinegar that is not too strong. After two weeks, pour off the vinegar and pour on a fresh, stronger vinegar that has been boiled with allspice, bay leaves, cloves, and cinnamon.

# PICKLES
## *(Pikuli)*

### 2622  Mixed pickles
*(Prigotovlenie pikuleg)*

Take young carrots cut into stars, small cucumbers, peeled young lettuce stalks, cauliflower and its young stalks, also peeled, finely sliced young Indian corn,* the pods of turnip seeds, and nasturtium seeds. All these must be very young. Add small, unripe muskmelons, watermelons, green plums, small saffron milk-cap mushrooms, asparagus, peeled purslane stalks, small peeled onions, young sugar pea pods, and green beans. Wipe off everything thoroughly with a napkin. For 3 glasses salt, use ¼ *lot* saltpeter and 20 grains alum. Dilute with 5 lbs, or 10 glasses, water, bring to a boil, skim, and cool. Add all the above-mentioned vegetables to this water, set on top of the stove, and let it come to a boil once. Turn into a coarse sieve to drain. When the vegetables have dried, pack them into small glass jars and cover with boiled and cooled vinegar. Pour off the vinegar after two weeks when it has become cloudy and pour on fresh, very strong, cold vinegar that has been boiled with tarragon, allspice, black pepper, and red pepper. Tie bladders around the jars and store in boxes in dry sand.

*Maize or Indian corn is a New World plant that was first domesticated by the Mexicans and was brought to Spain by Columbus in the late fifteenth century. During the next century, the plant gradually spread around the world, but mainly took hold in warm climates around the Mediterranean, especially Italy. By the late seventeenth century, corn meal had become a staple in Rumania and Moldavia, where it displaced wheat as the basic component in the national dish, mamal'ga, which resembles polenta. The use of corn spread less rapidly in Russia, however, no doubt in part because of the climate. As late as 1847, the Tsarist government authorized the distribution of free seed to encourage its cultivation in Russia. Since ground corn meal obviously keeps somewhat better and is easier to transport than fresh cobs, it is understandable why Molokhovets used corn meal frequently and easily, but seemed unfamiliar with methods for handling fresh ears. This is the sole recipe, in fact, in this edition to call for fresh corn, although the later undated German edition also included instructions for boiling corn on the cob. (Pokhlebkin, Natsional'nye kukhni, 111; and Guba, Tainy shchedrogo stola, 81.)*

# TO PRESERVE BEANS
## *(Zapasy iz fasoli)*

### 2628  Marinated beans
*(Fasol' marinovannaja)*

Soak young green beans in very salty water for several days until they turn yellow. Transfer them to a clean vessel and cover with strong, hot vinegar. Pour off this vinegar the next day, bring the vinegar to a boil, and repour over the beans while still hot. Repeat this process on the third and fourth days, that is, until the beans regain their natural color. For the last boiling, add a bay leaf and allspice to the vinegar.


# TO PRESERVE CARROTS
*(Zapasy iz morkovi)*


### 2631  Translucent carrot preserves to decorate tortes and babas

*(Varen'e prozrachnoe sluzhashchee dlja ukrashenija tortov i bab)*

Boil yellow or red carrots in water until they soften slightly. Remove from the water, cut up attractively into little stars, leaves, etc., drop into a thick syrup, and cook until they become translucent. Since carrots are available all year, there is no need to store up supplies of this jam, thereby wasting sugar unnecessarily. For a quick preparation, ½ lb sugar and 1 glass water will be sufficient for 1 lb carrots.


# EXCELLENT DRIED GREENS AND ROOTS FOR BOUILLON, CLEAR FISH SOUPS, AND SAUCES
*(Velikolepnaja sushonaja zelen' i koren'ja dlja bul'ona, ukhi i sousov)*

### 2632  [To dry vegetables for soups and sauces]

Wash carrots, parsley roots, celery roots, and leeks in the beginning of the autumn when root vegetables are fresh, young, and cheap. Clean them thoroughly with a knife, wipe dry, and slice very thinly. Spread them on a baking sheet lined with paper and dry them out in the kitchen on the stove or on shelves. But dry each of these root vegetables separately because some dry out more quickly than others. Dry very young shelled peas in the same manner. Mix everything together, but in equal parts, measuring with a cup. Store in glass jars in a dry place. When preparing bouillon for 6 persons, use 7 platefuls of water, a little salt, and 2 full tablespoons of these dried vegetables. Boil for approximately 30 minutes or even a little longer. Strain and add 2 teaspoons of Liebig's* extract or bouillon from Klechkovskij's wild fowls (according to the printed instructions attached to it). Bring to a boil and serve with fresh root vegetables, young carrots, groats, dumplings, meatballs, or *pirozhki.*

These dried root vegetables impart an extraordinary flavor to clear fish soups, quick *shchi*, etc. They may also be dried after stringing them on a stout thread.

*Justus von Liebig (1803–1873) was an eminent German chemist and biochemist. After making numerous contributions to inorganic chemistry, Liebig went on to investigate the chemistry of animal and vegetable life processes. His book, Researches on the Chemistry of Food (1847), was widely quoted among scientists and even among cooks. Liebig was concerned with the loss of juice (and nutrients) when meat was cooked and, on the basis of his research, he advocated heating the meat quickly to seal the juices inside. This revolutionized the way meat was cooked in English, French, and American homes. Fanny Farmer was still advocating his methods at the end of the nineteenth century. A secondary result of Liebig's research on animal tissue was the development of his world-famous extract of meat which continued to be sold throughout the century. (McGee, On Food and Cooking, 113–114; Encyclopaedia Britannica, XIV, 37–39.) I have not been able to find any information about Klechkovskij's wild fowls.*

### 2635  Cochineal

*(Koshenil')*

Mix together 3 *zolotniki* each cochineal and cream of tartar, 2 *zolotniki* potash, and 1 *zolotnik* alum. Pound fine in a clay mortar and store this powder in small jars, well tied up. Before using, scald a little powder with boiling water and strain through a cloth. For a small household, ⅓ of these proportions will be sufficient. This cochineal is very good.

# 30
# Preserved Fish and Wild and Domestic Birds

*(Sberezhenie, solenie, sushenie, marinovanie i kopchenie ryb, dichi i domashnikh ptits)*

[*Translator's note:* Readers are warned to approach traditional recipes for preserving food with caution. Not all of Molokhovets' recommendations are safe or practicable. Also, today's urban dwellers are in a double bind: they have mostly lost their forebears' easy familiarity with preserving methods while, all too often, they ignore modern rules of hygiene and sanitation. For instance, contemporary American newspapers publish warnings every November not to leave the stuffing overnight in the Thanksgiving turkey. It is only prudent, therefore, to follow standard modern practices for storing foods and, "when in doubt, throw it out."]

### 2637 To preserve fresh fish and to rectify spoiled fish
*(Sberezhenie svezhej ryby i ispravlenie isportivshejsja)*

To keep fish fresh for 12–15 days, rub it with powdered salicylic acid* and wrap in a clean napkin. Wash in several waters before using.

To rectify spoiled fish, rub the fish thoroughly with this powder and then wash in several changes of water.

Powdered salicylic acid is sold at the druggist's for 60 kopecks per ounce.

*See Glossary.

### To store fish, domestic birds, and wild fowl in the ice house
*(Kak sberegat' na lednike rybu, a takzhe domashnikh i dikikh ptits)*

Prepare a box with a close-fitting lid. Drill a hole in the bottom of the box, then bury the box completely in ice. Half-fill the interior of the box with pieces of ice, sprinkle salt on top, and pound the ice with a wooden mallet. Spread a thin layer of straw on top and cover the entire length and width of the surface with a simple oilcloth. Freshly slaughtered domestic birds, plucked and cleaned, may be stored on this oilcloth for several days.

Treat wild fowl in the same manner, but they will keep longer if they are not eviscerated. Arrange the birds in the box so that they do not touch one another. Fish are treated exactly the same.

### To transport live fish in summer
*(Perevozka zhivoj ryby letom)*

If you have caught a pike, for instance, immediately submerge it in the net into fresh water. Meanwhile drill holes into a board of the same width and length as the fish and knock together a box. Line the bottom with moss moistened with water. Place a piece of sponge moistened with French wine on the gills of the fish, set the fish on the moss, and cover with more moss. Hammer on a lid made from a board drilled with holes. Fish may be transported a great distance in this manner, only try to pour cold water over this box as often as possible. And, if possible, lower the box into a river or lake for a short time when an opportunity presents itself.

When transporting carp, cover the gills with the soft part of a roll moistened with French wine.

### To transport live fish in winter
*(Perevozka zhivoj ryby zimoju)*

Intersperse the fish with snow in a basket or in boxes drilled with holes. The fish will appear to have frozen, but will revive upon being lowered into fresh water. However, the fish must not be brought into a warm room.

### Another way to transport live fish
*(Eshche sposob perevozki zhivoj ryby)*

Cover the gills of a live and, of course, a large fish with white bread moistened with rum or spirits. Wrap the fish in a bast mat and, in that manner, it may be transported for 2 days or even longer. After arriving, remove the white bread, and drop the fish into a large washtub or bath with water.

### 2638  To keep domestic ducks fresh through half the winter
*(Svezhija domashnija utki sokhranjat' svezhimi do poloviny zimy)*

When the frost begins, wring the necks of fattened ducks so that they die immediately, but do not slaughter them in the usual manner. Hang the ducks by their necks on the walls in the ice house without removing their feathers or cleaning them. This method of preserving is very convenient because the ducks are always available and keep well until Christmas without [the expense] of feeding them.

Wild ducks also keep well in the same manner.

### To transport birds
*(Perevozka ptits)*

Slaughter the birds and immediately pluck the feathers and cleain the birds. Dry the birds, fill them with blotting paper, and freeze. Arrange them in vats, spreading straw between each layer.

### To freeze domestic and wild birds
*(Zamorazhivan'e domashnikh i dikikh ptits)*

In late autumn, eviscerate fattened birds, wash, and wipe dry. Tie up the birds in pairs, dip in water, and immediately hang in a cold place where they will freeze. Repeat several times. After the birds have frozen solid, arrange them in boxes and sprinkle with snow. A bird, frozen in this manner, may be kept all winter.

### To refresh spoiled hazel grouse
*(Osvezhit' isportivshiesja rjabchiki)*

Soak cleaned and eviscerated birds in cold water and then in cold milk. Set the pan with the birds on top of the stove, let it come once to a boil, remove, and fry the birds.

### To preserve hazel grouse and snipe
*(Sokhranenie rjabchikov i bekasov)*

Clean and evicerate the birds. Wash and dry them. Fry them in fat until half cooked and set aside to cool. Pour melted fat (*maslo*)* into the bottom of a small barrel. Let the fat cool completely, then pack the hazel grouse tightly into the barrel, one next to another. Pour melted fat over every layer. The top layer of fat should be 2 fingers thick. Let the fat cool, then nail up the barrel, seal with tar, and store on ice. Before using, stuff the hazel grouse, and finish frying them in some of that same fat [from the barrel].

*Although maslo can mean butter, fat, or oil, here Molokhovets almost certainly meant ordinary animal fat or lard, not the more expensive, and perishable, cow's butter. In a similar recipe, Molokhovets recommended using the leftover fat for greasing carriage wheels (cf. #869).*

### 2641 To turn heavily salted fish into freshly salted fish

*(Delat' iz samoj solenoj ryby svezheprosol'noj)*

Very salty fish, called *korennaja*,* must first be washed thoroughly. Since they tend to be covered with mildew, which is difficult to wash off, it is best to beat the fish with scraped willow switches while constantly pouring water over the fish. This is done most conveniently in a river or pond. When the mildew has been removed, rewash the fish thoroughly and cut into serving pieces. Pack the pieces into a tub, setting them on edge so the fish are not too compact and cover with the lees** of fresh, lightly fermented *kvass*. The sweeter the lees, the better. Set the fish aside for 4 days. Remove the fish from the *kvass*, wash it, and pack tightly in a vat, sprinkling each layer with hops. Take a good beer wort,*** and for each pail of wort, use 1 teacup of juniper berries, 2 *zolotniki* bay leaves, and 1 *zolotnik* allspice. Bring to a boil, cool, and pour the wort over the fish. Cover the vat with a lid and bury the vat in ice for 3 weeks. If, after marinating, the fish are still too salty and the brine must be poured off, then bring fresh wort to a boil without spices and pour it over the fish after it has cooled.

*\*Dal' defined korennaja ryba as a red fish caught in the summer and then heavily salted (Dal', Tolkovyj slovar', II, 163). The Russian term "red fish" refers to any fish whose flesh has a reddish tint, such as salmon.*
*\*\*Lees is the sediment that forms during the fermentation of an alcoholic beverage, usually wine or beer, but in this case kvass.*
*\*\*\*Wort, a clarified infusion of malt, is the liquid from which beer is brewed.*

### To salt salmon

*(Solenie semgi)*

Clean a fresh salmon, wipe it off with a napkin, and immediately salt, using ¾ *lot* saltpeter for every 1½ glasses salt. After 3–4 days, chop off the head, remove the backbone, and slit the salmon lengthwise into four parts. Dry the fish pieces in the fresh air, hanging them by the tail in the shade. After 2–3 months,* this salmon may be used for breakfast and in fast day soups and *pirogs*.

After removing the salmon from the salt, it may be smoked as indicated in #2651.

*\*Molokhovets did not indicate what was to be done with the fish in this 2–3 month interval. Was it returned to the salt for further brining, was it left hanging in the fresh air by its tail (which seems unlikely), or was it hung somewhere else for further drying?*

### To salt wild duck

*(Solenie dikikh utok)*

When the summer's hunting yields so many wild ducks that there is no room for them, clean and split them and pack them in small barrels with salt, using 1 lb salt for 1 *lot* saltpeter. Nail the lid shut, seal with tar, and bury in ice.

### 2648 To marinate goose rolls

*(Marinovanie ruleta iz gusja)*

Clean and draw a good goose, carefully remove the bones without tearing the skin, and spread the goose open. Chop together the goose liver, the liver from a small young calf, and 3 lbs veal meat. Pound like dough and add salt, black pepper, and allspice. Place chopped Polish truffles in the middle, or, lacking the truffles, use small marinated gherkins, halved or quartered lengthwise, according to their size. Stuff the goose with this mixture, roll up the goose, and wind round with strong thread. Sew into a napkin, drop into boiling water, and boil for 2½ hours. Remove, cool, and place in an earthenware jug. Prepare a marinade by boiling spices and a mixture of half vinegar and half water. This goose roll may be kept for about a month even if not marinated in vinegar, since some people may not care for the sourness.

### 2651 Home-smoked whitefish and other fish

*(Domashnee kopchenie sigov i proch. ryby)*

Gut fresh whitefish and other fish, wash, and salt for 24 hours. Wipe dry, pierce each fish with a spill, and place on a gridiron. Stack resinous wood in the back of a Russian stove and light the fire. Set the gridiron with the fish in front of the wood, close the damper of the oven against the handle of the gridiron, which will leave an opening below. As the smoke passes from the stove into the stove-pipe it will smoke the fish. As soon as one side has smoked and has turned golden, turn the fish over. Remove and serve the fish when it has finished both smoking and baking. This is an excellent method for smoking. Bream, crucians, perch, carp, *rjapushka* [*Corregonus maraenula*], smelts, etc., are also smoked in the same manner.

### Home-smoked fish, another way

*(Domashnee kopchenie ryby drugim manerom)*

Line a dripping pan, baking sheet, or skillet with a layer of straw that is not completely dry. Top with a layer of cleaned, salted, and wiped-off fish, prepared as indicated above. Set over a medium fire. From the glowing iron, the straw will begin to smolder, and from the resinous smoke, the fish will smoke and bake at the same time. The larger the fish, the more straw must be put under it, so that it smokes better and does not release its oil through contact with the hot dripping pan.

### To smoke eel

*(Ugor' kopchenyj)*

Cut along the backbone, remove the skin, and gut the eel. Cut off the head, salt thoroughly, and sprinkle with pepper, a bay leaf, and dry tarragon. After 2–3 days, wipe the eel dry, wrap and tie it round with paper, and smoke for 4–5 days.

# 31
# [Preserved Meats]

## BEEF, VEAL, AND LAMB PRESERVES
### (Zapasy iz govjadiny, teljatiny, baraniny)

*Remarks: To store fresh meat and to rectify spoiled meat:* If you wish to keep meat fresh for 12–15 days without an ice house or cold cellar, you must rub the meat with powdered salicylic acid, pack it into a vat, sprinkle more of the same powdered acid on top, and cover with a cloth.

This powder is sold at the druggist's for 60 kopecks a jar. One jar of powder will cure enough meat for a family of 6–8 persons for the 3 summer months. The acid is harmless and does not impart any odor to the meat. However, the meat must be washed in several changes of water before using. If steps have not been taken for preserving the meat and it has already spoiled, then sprinkle the meat with some of the same powder. Rub it on thoroughly, immediately wash in several waters, and boil. Another way to rectify spoiled meat: wash it and soak in clean water. Cover with fresh water, bring to a boil, and remove the scum. Throw several well-heated, glowing but not smoking, clean coals into this water and boil for 15 minutes. If the beef is really rotten, then pour off this water as well. Cover with fresh water, bring to a boil, and throw in a fresh batch of glowing coals. After 15 minutes, remove the meat, and prepare it as usual. Or pour ordinary home-made vinegar over the meat, and let it marinate for 20 hours.

### 2654 Dried meat bouillon
#### (Sukhoj bul'on mjasnoj)

Take 3½ lbs of beef that is not very fatty, cut it into pieces, and wash in cold water. Take 2 forequarters and hindquarters of veal, 4 ducks, 4 hares, 2 turkeys, and 6 chickens. Roast everything except the beef on a spit or in the oven on a dripping pan until half done. Do not add salt. [Transfer to a large pot] and add 2 large handfuls of washed leeks, 30 each of carrots, onions, celery roots, and parsley roots, and ¼ lb each allspice and cloves. Cover with water and cook continuously over a fairly high flame for a full twenty-four hours. Add additional water as needed and constantly remove the scum into a special saucepan. After the meat has cooked completely, drain off the liquid and squeeze any excess liquid from the meat. Return the meat to the saucepan, pour on water, boil for awhile, and again strain. Combine this second bouillon with the first, degrease, strain through a fine sieve and then through a napkin.

Boil this strained bouillon for some time, removing the scum. When the bouillon begins to reduce and thicken, sprinkle on 2 finely pounded nutmegs. Then begin to boil the bouillon over hot coals, stirring constantly to prevent it from burning. After boiling for an hour or two, pour into a mold or onto a platter or plate. Let the liquid congeal, remove from the mold, and dry in the shade in the fresh air. Wrap in paper and store in a cold, dry place. If you do not want to include the poultry, this bouillon may be prepared just from beef. But in that case, do not add salt to the bouillon, because then it will not congeal. The bouillon may be stored in large jars, wrapped in a bladder.

This amount of meat will yield at least 14 lbs of dried bouillon.

### 2656  Dried tomato bouillon

*(Sukhoj bul'on iz pomidorov)*

Squeeze out and discard the juice and seeds from tomatoes, place the tomato pulp in a saucepan, and boil without water for 30 minutes, constantly stirring. Rub the pulp through a fine sieve, return to the saucepan, and boil until it thickens. Spread thinly with a knife on a baking sheet greased with olive oil. Set in the oven after baking bread or dry in the open air in the shade. Cut into pieces, wrap in paper, and store in a cold, dry place. Use in sauces and other dishes.

### 2657  Corned beef

*(Solonina)*

Use a towel to immediately rub off any blood from freshly slaughtered beef. This must be done while the carcass is still warm because the blood very quickly spoils the meat. Remove the very large bones, weigh the meat, and rub it all over with salt that has been dried in the oven and mixed with saltpeter and spices. Lay out the meat on a table to cool completely. Then pack into small barrels, placing the large pieces in the middle and small half-pound pieces around the edges so as not to leave any gaps. Press the meat lightly with a pounder. Sprinkle salt, saltpeter, bay leaves, rosemary, and allspice on the bottom of the barrel and over each layer of meat as the barrel is filled. When the barrel is full, cover it with a lid, seal with tar on all sides, and keep in a [heated] room for 2–3 days, every day inverting the barrel, first on one end and then the other. Transfer the barrel to the cold cellar and then invert the barrel twice a week. After 3 weeks, store the barrel on ice.

Use the following proportions of salt and spices. For 1½ poods of meat, use 2½ lbs well-dried salt, 6 *zolotniki* saltpeter, and 3 *lots* each coriander, marjoram, basil, bay leaves, allspice, and black pepper. Add garlic if desired. Sprinkle a little extra salt into those barrels which will be used later.

The barrels must be small and made of oak, because when a barrel is unsealed and the meat is exposed to the air, it soon spoils. The barrels must be sealed all over to prevent the juice from leaking. Before salting the meat, the barrels must be soaked and disinfected.

# PORK PRESERVES

## (*Zapasy iz svininy*)

*Remarks:* Not every housewife wants to be present at the dismembering of a pig since it is such an unpleasant task. Therefore, to aid their understanding of the process, I am including a short description of this operation along with directions for preserving the meat and recipes for several dishes which may be prepared from both fresh and salted pork.

After slaughtering a fattened pig and completely removing all the hair and bristles (*sherst'*), carry the animal into a room set aside for dividing the carcass and dressing the meat. Hang up the carcass or place it on a wide bench. Weigh and record each piece intended for salting as it is cut off.

## 2662 First cut off the head

### (*Sperva otrezyvaetsja golova*)

Set aside a fine, whole head with attractive ears for Easter. Salt and smoke the head; halve less attractive ones. Salt and smoke the lower jaws which are extraordinarily tasty for garnishing sauces (cf. #529). Or, use them to prepare Jowls #2686. Remove the brains from the upper part of the head and use them while they are still fresh. Use the head itself for jellied meat (*studen'*).

## 2663 Tongues

### (*Jazyki*)

Tongues are eaten while fresh, or salt or smoke them.

## 2664 [The scrag]

Cut off the head a little higher than usual so that the tender piece of scrag may be cut off separately. Salt it together with the fillets and tongues, then smoke. Serve for hors d'oeuvre.

### 2665 [The blood]

When cutting off the head,* place a large, clean, earthenware jug underneath to catch the blood. Carry the jug into a cold place and use the blood while it is still fresh for blood sausages and in pig's blood soup. Any fillets and tongues intended for smoking should be soaked in the blood for several days.

*Molokhovets made no mention of piercing the throat before cutting off the head, which is the usual practice as it makes collecting the blood easier.

### 2666 [The feet]

Cut off the feet at the knee joint and use them to prepare jellied meat (studen').

### 2667 [Lard]

Cut off the Bauchshpeck [sic = "belly lard" in German], a large oblong piece of the outer, thin lard weighing 12–20 lbs. Salt and smoke it, but it is better to cut it into pieces and salt in a barrel, as indicated in #2676.

Then remove the layer of the very best lard (salo), which covers the entire interior. In a well-fed fatty pig, this lard may weigh up to 40 lbs. Use part of it for making pomade and melt the rest. The lard may be mixed with goose fat and butter and used for frying doughnuts, buns, fritters, pastry straws, etc. Knead the remaining lard with your hands until it turns into a smooth mass like butter. Add salt, using 3 lots salt for 1 lb lard, sew into a pork caul, and use it in dishes for the servants. To use the lard, prepare it as follows: Take 3 lbs of this pork lard, weigh out each pound separately, divide each pound into 8 parts, and roll each part into a small ball before distributing.

### 2668 [Organ meats]

Remove the organs. The lungs, heart, spleen, and liver are used fresh and in sausages. Place the intestines immediately in a washtub with snow and cover them with more snow. Clean them out and wash as well as possible. Carefully cut off the fat which adheres without making any holes in the intestines, which are used for frankfurters and sausages.

### 2669 [The fillets]

After removing the organs, cleanse the cavity of blood. Wipe it clean with a towel and cut off the small tenderloins from each side, which are used fresh or chopped up for sausages.

### 2670 [Brisket]

Cut off the brisket. Use it fresh or salt in a barrel (cf. #2676). Leave it whole without cutting it up so it will not get mixed up with the other parts.

### 2671 [Fore and hind quarters]

Cut off the shoulder and hind quarters to the fat sides of the pig, which are left for the bacon. Trim these quarters with a knife and use the fatty scraps for sausages or forcemeat. Salt the trimmed fore and hind quarters in small barrels (cf. #2676), leaving them whole or cut them into pieces. Leave the outer fat and skin on the hams which are to be smoked. Salt them in separate barrels. They are served at the table both cold and hot, boiled or, preferably, baked in rye dough #764. The best hams for smoking are those of 1½ year or 2 year old young pigs.

### 2672 [Ribs]

Cut off the outer fat or lard from the ribs, chop them into pieces and salt in small barrels (cf. #2676), or use fresh.

### 2673 [Lard or bacon]

Remove the large sides of lard or bacon (*shpik*), each of which will weigh from 40–50 lbs. Trim them, cut off the thin parts, and salt in large deep wash-tubs. Smoke them lightly. They are used for larding meats, hare, wild fowl, etc. Leave whole as many sides as desired for bacon and cut the remaining sides into pieces which may then be used for boiling. Salt them in small barrels (cf. #2676) because salted bacon is tastier and more economical. One third of the weight is lost in smoking.

### 2674 [Loins or fillets]

Cut off the outer large fillets from both sides of the rib bones. Use them fresh or salt them for smoking.

### 2675 [No title]

Chop the backbone into portions. When dividing up young pigs, do not remove the large sides of pork fat. Without detaching the pork fat or outer thick skin, cut off the fore and hind quarters to the knee bone. These pieces are best salted and smoked. Also cut off the ribs with the outer skin and fat. Salt or smoke them, but some people use them fresh.

### 2676  To salt hams in small barrels

*(Solenie vetchiny v bochenkakh)*

Separate all the parts intended for salting, weigh them, and divide into pieces. Leave some parts whole, such as the shoulders and briskets. Divide the pork into ½ lb portions, but the lard and bacon into ¼ lb portions.

For 100 lbs pork, use 5 lbs pounded and sieved dry salt, 5 *lots* each saltpeter, allspice, and bay leaves, 3½ *lots* cloves, and 10 *lots* coriander. Pound everything together except the coriander and marjoram. Add garlic and white onion according to taste, but do not pound with the other spices. For meat that will be salted, immediately wipe off any trace of blood with a dry towel while the flesh is still warm. Lay the meat on a table prepared with salt and saltpeter, etc., and rub the meat with the spices. Let it cool, then pack into small barrels or tubs. Sprinkle the prepared salt and spices on the bottom of the barrels. Add a layer of meat cut into pieces, then salt, another layer of meat pieces, salt, then a whole ham. Continue packing small pieces of meat around the larger pieces until the barrel is filled. Hammer the lid of the barrel on securely and keep the barrel in a [heated] room for 2 days, inverting it twice a day from one end to the other. Then seal the barrel with tar and transfer to a cold place, inverting it once a week. Finally, in the spring pack it in ice in the cold cellar. Indicate on the barrel the approximate weight and number of portions it contains.

### 2679  To salt sides of bacon

*(Solenie polotkov shpika)*

Salt sides of bacon in deep tubs without adding any other pieces of pork. For 1 lb bacon use 2 *lots* dry, sieved, fine salt, but do not add either pepper or saltpeter. Cut several slits in a side of bacon, sprinkle salt over the surface, and rub it in. Place skin side down in the barrel and top with the other half, skin side up. Continue layering in pairs until the barrel is filled. Cover the top with a board and stones and set aside for 2 or 3 weeks, frequently basting the sides of bacon with their own brine. Occasionally shift the pieces from top to bottom. Remove the sides from the brine, dry, and lightly smoke. Or, preferably, pack them in large chests, wrapping each piece in hay dried out in the oven. If moisture is found on the bacon after awhile, wipe off the bacon, hang it up for 2 days to dry off, and rewrap in fresh hay. Cover tightly with a lid and store in a cold, dry place.

### 2682  To preserve pork fat for various ointments and pomades

*(Kak sokhranjat' vnutrenoe svinoe salo dlja raznykh mazej i pomad)*

Remove the interior pork fat, place it in a saucepan, and set in another pan of hot water. Boil the water until the lard dissolves. Strain the melted lard through a napkin into a stoneware vessel, or, preferably, into a heated glass jar. Let the lard cool, tie a bladder round the jar, and store in the ice house. Lard prepared in this manner will keep for a year and is eminently suitable for ointments and various creams. Lard intended for consumption should be salted.

### 2686  Head cheese from a pig's lower jowl
*(Golovizna iz nizhnej cheljusti kabana)*

Clean the fresh lower jaw of a pig and boil until tender in salted water with an onion, bay leaves, allspice, and black pepper. When the flesh is tender, carefully remove the skin without piercing it. Cut the meat and fat into small cubes, sprinkle with salt and ground allspice, and mix everything together. Clean the skin on both sides, [spread it out,] and cover with the seasoned meat and fat. Roll up the skin to resemble a log, tie it up in a cloth, and place under weights. Let the roll cool, then slice and serve for *zakuski*. Serve with vinegar, olive oil, and mustard. Store in a cold place, but no longer than two weeks.

# SAUSAGES
*(Kolbasy i sosiski)*

### 2690  Fresh sausages
*(Sosiski svezhija)*

Take 10 lbs each lean pork and fatty scraps. If the pork is fresh, scrape it with a knife [i.e., purée the meat]. If it is slightly frozen, finely chop until it resembles buckwheat groats. Prepare a bouillon from 3–4 lbs of leftover scraps and sinews. Add allspice, bay leaves, and ½ lb or more finely chopped onion. Strain and cool the bouillon after it has finished cooking. Pour 5–6 glasses of the bouillon over the chopped pork mentioned above. Add 3 *zolotniki* ground allspice, 1½ *zolotniki* black pepper, and, if desired, 3 *zolotniki* marjoram. Mix thoroughly with your hands and pipe the mixture into thin pork intestines with a canvas bag [i.e., pastry tube]. Tie up in ¾ *arshin* lengths and at both ends. Hang in a warm place for several hours to dry off, then transfer to a cold place. These sausages will not keep longer than three weeks. Before serving, place them in a saucepan, barely cover them with water, beer, or beet brine, and cook until the sauce boils away. Then fry them on both sides on top of the stove or in the oven. A little pork fat may be added, sprinkle them with rusk crumbs, and serve with fresh cabbage or sauerkraut or with mustard.

### 2692  Lithuanian smoked sausages

*(Kolbasy litovskija kopchenyja)*

Take 10 lbs of trimmed pork, 3 lbs beef, and 2 lbs game, chamois, or elk. The fresher this meat, the finer it can be cut up with a knife. Discard the sinew and chop with a chopper (*sechka*). Some people freeze the meat to make it easier to chop, but frozen meat loses its taste and juiciness. Pound fine about 20 *lots* dry salt, 2 *lots* black pepper, 1 *lot* each allspice and saltpeter, and ½ *lot* each cloves, marjoram, and bay leaves. Sieve the spices, mix with the meat, add ¾ glass spirits, and pound the mixture with a wooden mallet. Cut ½ lb of the outer pork fat from the scrag into thin oblong pieces and add the fat to the meat. Firmly stuff thick beef intestines (the thicker the better) with this mixture, smoothing it with your hand to fill any gaps. Be careful, however, not to burst the intestine. Tie up into links, place between 2 boards with a light weight on top, and keep in a heated room for 2 days. Transfer them to the pantry and cover with a board and stones, gradually increasing the weight over a period of two weeks. Remove them from the press, hang in a cold place, and smoke for nearly two weeks, hanging them first from one end and then the other. After smoking, hang them in a draft in the loft for 2 weeks. Clean them and store in dry rye, hops, hay, or in ashes.

### 2696  Blood sausages

*(Krovjanyja kolbasy)*

Remove the brains from a pig's head. Place in a large pot the cleaned head, the lungs, heart, spleen, and all the pork belly fat or *Bauchspeck*, which will weigh nearly 12–15 lbs. Cover with water and boil for 1½ hours. Add the pork liver and cook for another 30 minutes. Chop the liver, lungs, hearts, and spleen; cut the pork fat, the ears, and the meat from the head into pieces that are not too small. Add ¾ glass salt, 1 *lot* black pepper, ¼ *lot* allspice and, if desired, marjoram. Mix everything together and dilute with nearly 3 glasses strained pork blood so that the mixture is not too thick. Fill ⅔ of a beef intestine or thick pork intestine, tie it up, smooth out the segments, and boil in water for 30 minutes. The sausages are done if the juices are fatty instead of bloody when pierced with a fork. Wash the sausages thoroughly in cold water, lay them out on a table, and flatten them with a board for an hour or two. Transfer to a cold place. If these sausages are to be used very soon, a little finely chopped white onion fried in butter may be added to the mixture. Omit the onion if the sausages will be kept for later use. They must be smoked in a light cold smoke for ten days. It is best to hang them in the chimney.

These same sausages are prepared from just the pig's head. Very finely chop half of the meat and cut the other half into pieces.

Or, they may be prepared from only the livers, lungs, and belly fat.

Fry fresh blood sausages in butter before serving and set in the oven, but serve smoked sausages cold.

### 2699 Blood sausages from Smolensk buckwheat or buckwheat flour

*(Kolbasy krovjanyja iz smolenskikh krup ili grechnevoj muki)*

Pour ¼ *garnets* Smolensk buckwheat groats or flour into a stoneware bowl, add 2¼ glasses boiling pork fat, and mix thoroughly. Add at least ¼ *lot* each black pepper and allspice, some cloves, marjoram, and salt and stir in 5¼ glasses of fresh, strained pig's blood. Stuff cleaned pork intestines, leaving ¼ of the intestine empty. Tie up the intestines, place in a saucepan, cover with cold water, and set over a high fire, uncovered. Boil the sausages for ¾ hour, frequently turning them with care. Remove from the water and set in a cold place.

Shortly before serving, fry the sausages on both sides in a skillet with butter or pork fat. They may be sliced. Serve before bouillon, or for *zakuski*, or for breakfast. For six persons, one-third of the recipe will be sufficient.

### 2701 Finnish *pal'ten** from rye flour

*(Finljandskija pal'ten iz rzhanoj muki)*

For 1 bottle of strained pig's blood, use 1½ lbs finely cut up pork kidney fat, 1 tablespoon fine salt, and 2½–3 lbs sieved rye flour. Beat the dough thoroughly—it must be rather thick, as for bread. Moisten your hand in warm water, form the dough into balls the size of good apples, and boil in salted boiling water. Remove, cool, and store in a cold place, wiping off the mold on top from time to time. To use, slice and fry in a skillet in butter with apple slices, which is very tasty. Serve for dinner, breakfast, or supper. They are also eaten just boiled with butter. They will keep in the cold for a month. Sometimes they are made from beef blood and kidney fat, but these are considered less tasty.

Fry them also without apples.

*According to Hilkka Uusivirta, the word pal'ten derives from old Swedish and the name is used mostly in the western and southwestern regions of Finland where there is a significant Swedish population. Elsewhere in Finland, the dish is known under various local names. The dish itself is associated with pagan sacrifices and also with the adoption of Christianity by the Finns. Uusivirta's modern recipe is more elaborate than that of Molokhovets and includes chopped onion, milk (or kvass), pepper, and both barley and rye flours as well as salt and the pig's fat and blood. Instead of making dumplings which are sliced and later fried, Uusivirta fries or bakes the mixture into a single large, flat cake and serves it with lingonberries, cranberries, milk sauce, or cold kvass or beer. (Uusivirta, Finskaja natsional'naja kukhnja, 61–62.)*

### 2702 White sausages from Smolensk buckwheat

*(Kolbasy belyja iz smolenskikh krup)*

Rub 3 glasses, or ¼ *garnets*, Smolensk groats with 2 eggs, let the groats dry, and rub them through a fine sieve. Bring to a boil ½ *garnets*, or 6 glasses, milk and ¼ *garnets*, or 3 glasses, melted pork fat. Add the groats, set over a low fire, cover with a lid, and stir frequently with a spoon. When the groats are cooked, cool, and beat in 8 eggs. Add ¾ glass boiled milk, a little cinnamon, 1 glass currants, about 4 pieces sugar, a few sweet almonds, and 4–5 bitter almonds. Mix and gently fill intestines evenly so that they will not burst when boiled. After they have cooked, store them in a cold place. Fry on both sides before serving. Serve for *zakuski* or before soup. One-third of the indicated proportions will be enough for one meal for six persons.

### 2708  Brain sausage links

*(Sosiski iz mozgov)*

Wash and boil 2 veal brains in salted water and chop them with bread soaked in cream and squeezed out. Add ¼ lb butter, a little salt, black pepper, and nutmeg. Beat all this until white. Stir in 8 egg yolks and the cream in which the roll soaked, stuff intestines that have been prepared in advance, and boil in a mixture of half milk and half water. To serve, fry in Finnish butter.

# 32
# Fast Day Soups

## (Postnye supy)

### HOT FISH FAST DAY SOUPS
#### (Postnye supy, gorjachie rybnye)

*Remarks:* The same principle holds for *ukha* and fish soups as for meat bouillon; the more flesh in the soup, the tastier it will be. A very good *ukha* for 6–8 bowls requires at least 6 lbs of fish; a middling *ukha* may be made from 3 lbs of fish.

Fast day soups are prepared just like meat soups, only substitute some kind of fast day oil, such as sunflower, poppy seed, or nut oil for the animal fat. If the fish is very fresh and has just been caught, do not add anything to the soup except salt and greens, because the flavor of fresh fish is extraordinary. To recognize fresh fish, see the Remarks for Chapter 7.

To cook small fish or pieces of a large fish, bring the water to a rapid boil before adding the fish. To cook a whole fish weighing more than 2 lbs, start it in cold water and let it come to a boil. Otherwise it will not cook through.

### 2712  Clear fish soup with *pirozhki*
#### (Ukha iz ershej s pirozhkami)

Prepare 9–12 glasses fish broth from root vegetables using 1 carrot, 1 parsley root, 1 celery root, 1 leek, 1–2 onions, 5–15 black peppercorns, 2–3 bay leaves, and 3 to 6 lbs ruff. Boil a full hour until everything is very tender, then strain the broth. To serve, garnish with parsley and dill. Add several seeded lemon slices and, if desired, ½ or 1 glass sauternes or champagne or even Madeira or sherry. Serve *pirozhki* separately.

INGREDIENTS

| | |
|---|---|
| 3–6 lbs ruff | 1 celery root |
| 1 parsley root | ½ lemon without seeds |

2 onions

5–20 [sic] black peppercorns

1–2 [sic] bay leaves

(½–1 glass wine)

### 2734 Sauerkraut *shchi* with sturgeon or sturgeon's head

*(Shchi iz kisloj kapusty s osetrovoju golovoju ili prosto osetrinoju)*

Wash 3 lbs of fresh sturgeon's head, cover with water, and skim as the liquid begins to boil. Add an onion and spices, cook until the meat separates from the bones, and strain the bouillon, reserving the fish. Lightly squeeze 3 glasses sauerkraut and fry in 3–4 spoons poppy seed oil with 1–2 onions. Add the sauerkraut to the strained bouillon, cook until tender, and thicken with 1 spoon flour diluted with cold water. Boil thoroughly, pour into the soup tureen over the fish, and sprinkle with greens.

### 2735 Beluga or sturgeon soup with sauerkraut

*(Soljanka iz beluzhiny ili osetriny)*

Cut 2–3 lbs beluga or sturgeon into small pieces and wash thoroughly. Squeeze out 3–4 glasses sauerkraut and fry slightly in a saucepan in 2 spoons poppy seed or sunflower seed oil. Heat 2 spoons oil in a separate pan and fry 1–2 onions and the fish dipped in flour. Mix everything together, cover with about 10–12 glasses boiling water, and add 2–3 bay leaves, 2–3 black peppercorns, and ¼–½ lb unpressed black caviar. Cook until done and serve.

## OIL-BASED FAST DAY SOUPS

*(Postnye supy, masljanye)*

### 2739 Borshch from fried beets

*(Borshch iz zharenoj svekly)*

Peel and shred 5 large beets. Grease a large skillet with sunflower or mustard seed oil and heat the pan. Add the beets, moisten them with 3 spoons vinegar, and fry, stirring. Sprinkle on 1 spoon flour, mix, and continue frying until the beets are almost cooked while adding root vegetable bouillon by the spoonful. Transfer the beets to [a pan of] strained bouillon and cook until done. To serve, season with greens and 2–3 shredded small mushrooms.

INGREDIENTS

| | |
|---|---|
| 5 large beets | ½ parsley root |
| 3 spoons vinegar | ½ celery root |
| 1–2 spoons oil | ½ leek |
| 2 carrots | bay leaves |
| 2 onions | allspice |
| 2–3 small mushrooms | greens |
| 1 spoon flour | |

### 2741  Borshch with fried herring

*(Borshch s zharenoju seledkoju)*

Prepare a bouillon from root vegetables and ⅛ lb dried boletus mushrooms. Strain the bouillon. Bake 1 lb beets, peel, chop, and place in a saucepan. Cover with the strained bouillon, pour on beet brine that has been boiled separately, and add salt, pepper, greens, and finely chopped mushrooms. Heat until very hot. Soak and clean 3 Scottish herring, roll them in flour, fry them in oil, and add them to the bouillon. Bring the borshch to a boil and serve.

### 2744  Mushroom noodle soup with vermicelli or macaroni

*(Lapsha gribnaja s vermishelem ili makaronami)*

Boil ⅛–¼ lb dried mushrooms with 1 onion and a little allspice. Strain the bouillon and finely chop the mushrooms. Fry 1 finely chopped onion in 1 spoon sunflower seed or nut oil, add the mushrooms, barely fry them, and dilute with the mushroom bouillon. Meanwhile, drop homemade noodles or Italian macaroni into boiling water, drain in a colander, and rinse with cold water. Let the mushroom bouillon come to a boil, then add the noodles and cook until done. To serve, sprinkle with greens. Potatoes, boiled separately, may be added to these noodles.

INGREDIENTS

| | |
|---|---|
| ⅛ or ¼ lb mushrooms | 2 carrots |
| 1–2 onions | 1 celery root |
| ¼ lb macaroni, or 1⅓ glasses flour for the noodles | 1 parsley root |
| | 1 leek |
| (12 potatoes) | 10–15 allspice berries |
| 2–3 bay leaves | 1–2 spoons oil |
| greens | black pepper |

### 2752  Puréed yellow pea soup

*(Sup pjure iz zheltago gorokha)*

Boil 1 lb, or 2 glasses, peas with 2 onions and 2 spoons good fast day oil. (If desired, the onion may be fried beforehand in the oil.) Do not add salt so the peas will cook faster. When the peas are tender, thicken them with ½ spoon flour, that is, mix the flour with 3–4 spoons cold water and pour into the peas. Bring to a boil and add enough boiled water to make 9–12 glasses. Strain, rub through a fine sieve or colander, and pour into a soup tureen. Serve with croutons.

A smoked fish, cut into pieces and boned, may be brought to a boil with the peas. Serve in the soup.

Or, add mushroom bouillon to the pea soup and sprinkle with boiled and finely chopped, dried mushrooms, ⅛ lb or more, which may be fried beforehand with an onion.

### 2758  Puréed tomato soup

*(Sup pjure iz pomidorov)*

Boil root vegetables using [1] carrot, 1 parsley root, 1 celery root, 1 leek, 1–2 onions, and 5–10 black peppercorns. Strain the bouillon. Discard the seeds and juice of 3–5 very ripe tomatoes and chop the flesh fine. Place in a saucepan, add 2–3 spoons nut oil, and stew until tender, but do not let the tomatoes burn. Stir in ½ spoon flour, cover with a little bouillon, and boil thoroughly. Rub through a colander and add as much bouillon as necessary. Add ½ glass pearl barley boiled separately and whiten with almond, walnut, or coconut milk. Serve with croutons.

## HOT, SWEET FAST DAY SOUPS

*(Postnye sladkie, gorjachie supy)*

### 2763  Almond milk soup with rice or sago

*Sup iz mindal'nago moloka s risom ili sago)*

Pour boiling water over 1 lb sweet almonds, cover, and let stand. Peel, pound in a mortar as fine as possible while pouring on water, and strain through a napkin. Pound again several times, adding enough fresh boiled water to make 6–8 bowls of milk. Add sugar to taste using 1–2 pieces of sugar per glass. Boil without fail in a silver saucepan or stoneware pot, but not by any means in a copper saucepan. Or, pound the almonds, cover with 9–12 glasses boiled water, and boil thoroughly. Strain, squeeze the almonds, and pour into a soup tureen. Add fluffy rice or sago that has been boiled separately (½ glass) with ½ to 1 glass sultanas or blue raisins.* Sprinkle with sugar and serve. Boil the rice and sago as indicated in the remarks for Chapter 8 regarding *pirogs*.

*See the Glossary for more on raisins.*

### 2769  Almond soup in the chocolate manner

(*Sup mindal'nyj na maner shokoladnago*)

Prepare 7–9 glasses almond milk (cf. #2763). In a clean skillet fry ¾ glass of the very best fine-ground flour, previously dried out. Stir constantly until it darkens, but do not let it burn. Bring the almond milk to a boil with a piece of cinnamon or vanilla, sprinkle on the flour, and boil thoroughly. Before serving sprinkle on 9–12 pieces fine sugar. Serve with small, fast day sugar rusks coated with thick chocolate, prepared by melting chocolate and sugar in water with a piece of fish glue or gelatin.

### 2779  Beer soup

(*Sup iz piva*)

For 2 bottles good beer, use 2 glasses water. Add 1 glass sugar or treacle and 1 teaspoon caraway seeds or lemon zest and bring to a boil. Serve with croutons from sour-sweet bread made with raisins and orange rind.

## COLD, SWEET FAST DAY SOUPS
(*Postnyj sladkij kholodets*)

### 2784  French beer soup

(*Frantsuzskij sup iz piva*)

Remove and shred the zest from ½ orange and ½ lemon. Cut off the pith and slice the orange and lemon. Boil 3 bottles of white beer with cinnamon, cloves, and sugar and pour the spiced beer over ½ glass raisins, 3–4 dried figs, 1–2 fresh apples, and 1–2 pears, cut into several pieces. Bring everything to a boil several times, pour into a soup tureen, and serve cold or hot. Pour 1 wineglass rum or sherry into this soup.

# 33

# Fast Day Accompaniments
# for Soup

*(Postnyja prinadlezhnosti k supu)*

*Remarks:* Pirozhki are made from the same dough as *pirogs*. They may also be fried in oil. They require half as much stuffing as a *pirog*.

### 2786  Fish forcemeat

*(Rybnyj farsh)*

Take 1 lb of boned pike, zander, ruff, or perch since these fish have a binding quality. Sprinkle with salt, a little black pepper, 1 finely chopped onion fried in ½ spoon oil, and a 3 kopeck roll soaked in water and squeezed out. A little nutmeg may be added, if desired. Finely chop the mixture, pound it, and rub through a fine sieve. Sprinkle flour on the table, roll the forcemeat into a sausage, tie it up in a clean cloth, and tie with a string. Drop the roll of forcemeat into fish bouillon, boil it, cool, and remove the cloth. Slice, place in a soup tureen, and cover with *ukha*. This same forcemeat is used to stuff *pel'meni* and *pirozhki*. It is also used for pâtés.

### 2795  Fast day yeast dough for *pirozhki* and *pirogs*

*(Postnoe testo na drozhzhakh dlja pirozhkov i pirogov)*

Pour 1½ zolotniki dry yeast into a glass and add enough warm water to make 1½ or 1¾ glasses liquid. Mix with 2 glasses sieved, fine-ground wheat flour and beat until smooth and blisters appear. Set in a warm place to rise. After it has risen, beat thoroughly and add 1 teaspoon salt, 2–3 spoons poppy seed, sunflower seed, or nut oil, and the remaining flour. Beat thoroughly until the dough leaves your hands and let it rise again. Roll out the dough, transfer to a baking sheet greased with oil, add the stuffing, pinch the edges closed, and let rise. Paint with boiling water or with oil mixed with cold water and a little flour or beer. If making sweet *pirogs*, paint them with honey. Set in a hot oven. Paint them with oil after removing them from the oven.

INGREDIENTS

1½–2 lbs flour
1½ or 1¾ glasses water
1½ *zolotniki* yeast
¼ glass oil, sunflower seed, poppy
    seed, or nut oil

beer, or something else to paint the
    dough

### 2796  Fast day yeast dough fried in oil

*(Postnoe testo na drozhzhakh zharenoe v masle)*

Prepare a yeast dough as indicated above, except make a thinner dough so that the *pirozhki* must be made in your hands. Dip your hands in flour, fill the *pirozhki*, and let them rise on a table sprinkled with flour. Fry them in 1 glass boiling sunflower seed or nut oil. The *pirozhki* may be dipped individually in batter before frying them in the hot oil.

### 2797  Quick dough with cream of tartar*

*(Testo na skoruju ruku s kremertartarom)*

Mix together 6 glasses flour, ½ tablespoon salt, and nearly 2 glasses warm water including 2–4 spoons of any kind of fast day oil, but preferably either nut oil or poppy seed oil. Beat thoroughly until smooth and until blisters appear. Add 1 teaspoon cream of tartar and ½ teaspoon bicarbonate of soda, mix thoroughly, and immediately turn out onto a table. Divide the dough into equal parts, stretch out the dough with your hands to form circles the size of a small saucer, place some of the prepared stuffing on each round of dough, and pinch shut. Set on a baking sheet greased with oil, paint with oil mixed with water, and place in the oven.

*This is really a quick-rising dough made with baking powder, which is made by mixing cream of tartar with bicarbonate of soda. See the Glossary under Bicarbonate of Soda.

### 2799  Pirog with sturgeon marrow, rice, and fish

*(Pirog s vizigoju, risom i ryboju)*

Soak the sturgeon marrow overnight in water, wash the next day, cover with fresh water, and boil until it becomes tender and translucent. Add salt, allspice, ½ parsley root, and ½ onion. Turn out into a coarse sieve, (if desired, rinse with cold water,) finely chop, and add salt. Separately prepare rice (see the Remarks for

Chapter 7) by boiling the rice in water with 1 onion, 1 parsley root, and 1 spoon oil. Mix the boiled rice with 1 spoon fish bouillon, dill, parsley, and the chopped sturgeon marrow. Roll out the dough, place ¾ of this stuffing on the dough, and top with very thin slices of boned fish, slightly salted, sprinkled with black pepper, and dried in a napkin. Use pike, zander, bream, salmon (*lososina* or *semga*), sturgeon, or whitefish. Cover with the remaining stuffing, place the dough on top, and bake in the oven for approximately 1 hour.

INGREDIENTS

*For the dough*
1¼–1½ glasses water together with yeast
3 spoons oil
salt
1½–2 lbs flour

*For the stuffing*
⅛–¼ lb sturgeon marrow
1 glass rice

1½–2 lbs fish
dill
parsley
¼ glass oil
1 parsley root
1 onion
2 black peppercorns
salt

## 2803  Pirog with sago and salmon

*(Pirog s sago i semgoju)*

Boil 1 glass white sago in water as indicated in the Remarks about *pirogs* in Chapter 7. Turn the sago into a coarse sieve, rinse with cold water, drain, and add salt. Mix with 2 spoons oil and some dill. [Prepare the dough and roll it out; clean and slice the fish.] Place a layer of sago on the dough and top with a layer of salmon. Sprinkle with pepper, add the remaining sago and, finally, cover with the rest of the dough. Paint with water or oil, sprinkle with rusk crumbs, and bake in a hot oven.

INGREDIENTS

1⅛ glasses white sago, or ½ lb
¼ glass oil
1½ lbs salmon
dill

salt
pepper
separate ingredients for the dough

## 2806  Pirog with sauerkraut and fish

*(Pirog s kisloju kapustoju i ryboju)*

Fry 1 finely chopped onion in ¼ or ½ glass oil. Add finely ground black pepper, allspice, and 3 glasses squeezed-out sauerkraut. Stew, covered, until tender, stirring so that it does not burn. Thinly slice a cleaned, salted fish such as salmon (*lososina* or *semga*) or sturgeon, etc. Remove the bones and fry in 1 spoon oil. Mix with the cabbage and fill the *pirog*.

*Pirozhki* will require only half the amount of stuffing.

INGREDIENTS

| | |
|---|---|
| 3 glasses (1½ lbs) sauerkraut | 1½–2 lbs fish |
| ⅓ glass fast day oil | 5 allspice berries |
| 5 black peppercorns | separate ingredients for the dough |
| 1 onion | |

### 2808 Pirog with fish forcemeat, sturgeon marrow, and fish

*(Pirog s tel'nym, vizigoju i ryboju)*

Use 2–3 lbs of zander or pike for the flesh, i.e., for fish forcemeat. Remove the bones and fry the fish slightly in 3–4 spoons nut or mustard oil. Finely chop and add 1–2 finely chopped onions which may be fried beforehand in the same oil. Sprinkle on salt, black pepper, dill, and if desired, a little nutmeg. Soak ⅛ lb sturgeon marrow overnight in cold water. The next day boil the sturgeon marrow in fresh water with a carrot, an onion, and 2–3 allspice berries. Drain, finely chop, add salt, and mix with the fish forcement. Add oil, place this forcemeat on the rolled-out dough, and top with whatever fish you like. To prepare the fish, wash and clean it, sprinkle with salt and black pepper, and wrap tightly in a clean napkin to squeeze out the moisture. Cover the top of the fish with more of the fish forcement and continue as indicated in #2795.

INGREDIENTS

| | |
|---|---|
| *For the forcement* | 1–2 onions |
| 2–3 lbs zander or pike | salt |
| 3–5 spoons mustard or nut oil | black pepper |
| dill | |

### 2813 Pirog with buckwheat kasha, mushrooms, or fish

*(Pirog s grechnevoju kasheju, s gribami ili ryboju)*

Pound 1 lb groats lightly and cook into a thick porridge. Boil ¼ lb dried boletus mushrooms and finely chop. Lightly fry 2–3 finely chopped onions in ⅓ glass oil and add the mushrooms. Mix with the buckwheat and stuff the *pirog*. Or instead of mushrooms, mix finely chopped fish with the buckwheat, using pike, zander, or perch (in all, 1½–2 lbs). Add salt and pepper to the fish and fry everything slightly with a finely chopped onion.

### 2830 *Rastegai* with fish forcemeat and salmon

*(Pirozhki rastegai s rybnym farshem i semgoju)*

Prepare Forcemeat #2808 and slice 1 lb salmon. Prepare a yeast dough, roll out circles, and place a little forcemeat on each. Top with a slice of salmon, cover with more forcemeat, and pinch the edges together leaving a little of the filling exposed. Bake as usual. To serve, sprinkle the salmon with black pepper.

### 2831 Fish *rastegai* with fried onion

*(Pirozhki rastegai s zharenym lukom)*

Prepare a yeast dough and roll out into circles. For the stuffing, fry some finely chopped onion in oil with salt and a little pepper (12–15 onions and ½ glass oil). Place some of the chopped and fried onion on each round of dough and proceed as indicated in #2830.

### 2833 Pirozhki with carrots

*(Pirozhki s morkov'ju)*

Peel 5–6 medium carrots, boil until tender in water, drain, and finely chop. Add salt, mix with 1 spoon good oil, and stuff the *pirozhki*.

# 34

# Fast Day Sauces

## (Postnye sousa)

*Remarks:* For fast day sauces use oil—nut, sunflower seed, poppy seed, olive, or almond.

*Basic white sauce:* Pour 3–4 spoons nut oil or any other fast day oil into a saucepan, add ½ glass fine wheat flour, and fry slightly, stirring. Dilute gradually with 2⅓ glasses fish or mushroom bouillon, constantly stirring. Or use a bouillon prepared from root vegetables. The sauce should be no thicker than thin sour cream. Boil thoroughly and strain through a fine sieve. Then add lemon juice, seeded lemon slices, apple juice, a little mushroom soy, or 5–6 finely chopped field mushrooms, depending upon how the sauce will be used.

### 2835  White sauce for boiled fish

*(Sous belyj k varenoj rybe)*

Bake 2–3 onions, peel, finely chop, and fry slightly in 2 spoons sunflower seed or nut oil. Stir in 2 spoons flour, fry, and dilute with 2½ glasses fish bouillon. Add vinegar, lemon or gooseberry juice, or apple soy, and 2–4 pieces sugar to give the sauce a pleasant sour-sweet flavor. Boil thoroughly, strain, pour some sauce over the fish, and serve the rest in a sauceboat.

### 2837  Brown sauce with truffles

*(Sous krasnyj s trjufeljami)*

Bring to a boil 1 spoon fried flour with 2 spoons oil, dilute with 2½ glasses fish bouillon, and add caramelized sugar. Boil thoroughly and add 2–3 pieces sugar, the juice from ⅓ lemon, and 5–6 finely chopped truffles. Boil thoroughly and pour over boiled zander, etc.

### 2841  Herring sauce

*(Sous iz seledki)*

Soak 1 Dutch herring, remove the bones, and finely chop with 1 onion. Mix 2–3 spoons oil with 1 spoon fried flour and the herring and onion. Fry the fish mixture, pour in 2½ glasses fish bouillon and a little lemon juice, and bring to a boil. Strain and pour over boiled potatoes, potato patties, etc.

### 2843 Mustard sauce for fish

*(Sous gorchichnyj k rybam)*

Mix 1 spoon mustard, ½ spoon flour, and 1–2 spoons oil with 2 glasses water boiled with an onion, root vegetables and spices. Stir until smooth, bring to a boil, strain, and add ¼–½ glass table wine, lemon slices, and 2–3 pieces sugar. About 2 spoons capers may be added. Bring the sauce to a boil and pour over zander, tench, sturgeon, trout, etc.

### 2845 Sauce for cauliflower and asparagus

*(Sous dlja tsvetnoj kapusty i sparzhi)*

Mix together 1½ spoons each flour and whatever fast day oil you like, but either nut oil or olive oil is preferable. Dilute with 1 glass water, boil thoroughly, and add half a bottle white wine, the juice from half a lemon, and about 2–4 pieces sugar. Bring to a boil, strain, and pour over cauliflower, asparagus, etc.

### 2847 Sour-sweet onion sauce

*(Kislosladkij sous iz luka)*

Boil 3 large, finely chopped onions in 2 glasses water. Lightly fry 1 spoon fried flour with 2–3 spoons oil, stir in the onions and water, and add vinegar, salt, and caramelized sugar. Bring to a boil, rub through a fine sieve, and sprinkle with greens. This sauce should be sour-sweet. Serve with boiled potatoes, fish patties, etc.

### 2848 Dutch sauce

*(Sous gollandskij)*

Mix ½ glass flour with 2–3 spoons oil, dilute with 3 glasses fish bouillon, and boil thoroughly, constantly stirring, until the sauce thickens. Strain and add salt, 2–3 lemon slices or 2 spoons marinated gooseberries, and ¼ nutmeg or ¼ small spoon mace. Bring to a boil and pour over boiled pike, zander, or any other large fish.

### 2853 Red currant sauce for baked fish*

*(Sous iz krasnoj smorodiny k zharenoj rybe)*

Rub 1½ glasses cleaned red currants through a fine sieve and add ¼–½ glass wine, 1 glass of the pan juices left after baking a large fish, a little cinnamon, and

½ glass sugar. Stir in 1 teaspoon potato flour mixed with 1 spoon cold water, bring to a boil, strain, and pour over the baked fish.

*This recipe is an excellent example of the difficulty of translating zharenyj out of context. The title would seem to indicate fried fish, but the directions are clearly for baked (pechenaja) fish. For more on this topic see Issues of Translation in the Introduction and my comments under Beef and Cooked Beef in Chapter 5.

# 35

# Fast Day Vegetables and Greens

*(Postnyja kushan'ja iz ovoshchej i zeleni)*

### 2876  Stuffed turnips with sour-sweet sauce

*(Repa farshirovannaja s kislo-sladkim sousom)*

Trim the shoots from 6–9 turnips or rutabagas, wash the roots thoroughly, and boil them in water without peeling. When they are done, cut off the tops and carefully scoop out the interiors with a spoon, leaving the walls. Mash half of the removed soft pulp and add at least ½ glass of "*Sarachinskoe* wheat,"* which has been washed in several changes of hot water and boiled separately in water. Add 2–3 spoons nut oil, salt, and a little sugar. Mix, stuff the turnips, replace the lids, and paint each with oil. Place in a sauté pan greased with oil and bake in the oven for 20 minutes. To serve, pour on sour-sweet sauce or mushroom sauce.

*See Glossary.

### 2881  Stuffed cabbage with mushroom sauce

*(Farshirovannaja kapusta s gribnym sousom)*

Trim 1–2 heads of cabbage, bring to a boil twice, and drain in a coarse sieve. For the stuffing, boil ½ lb buckwheat groats into a thick kasha and add ⅛ glass nut or poppy seed oil, a little salt, and finely shredded mushrooms. Fill the cabbage leaves with this kasha,* tie up with thread, and place on a skillet greased with oil. Paint the cabbage with oil, sprinkle with rusk crumbs, and fry. To serve, pour on the following sauce: Boil 6 dried boletus mushrooms with salt, an onion, and 2–3 black peppercorns. Fry 2 spoons oil with a finely chopped onion and 1 spoon flour, dilute with 2¼ glasses mushroom bouillon, and boil thoroughly. Add the shredded mushrooms, bring to a boil, and pour over the cabbage.

*From the directions, it is not clear whether the whole cabbage was stuffed or whether the leaves were broken off and stuffed individually. I think Molokhovets intended the former, but either interpretation is possible.

### 2888  Potato croquettes
*(Kartofel'nyja krokety)*

Peel and boil ¾ *garnets* potatoes and immediately mash them with a wooden pestle while they are still hot. Add ⅓ glass flour and some salt and form into croquettes, that is, into oblong *pirozhki*. Dip them into ground rusk crumbs and fry in ⅓ glass oil or serve them as flat patties. To serve, pour on one of the following: mushroom sauce, herring sauce with dill, sour-sweet sauce with raisins, sour-sweet sauce with onion, cherry sauce, red currant sauce, or sprat or anchovy sauce. Or serve them with green peas.

### 2889  Potatoes with salmon
*(Kartofel' s lososinoju)*

Slice 30 raw potatoes and 1 lb raw salmon, add salt, and arrange the potatoes and salmon in layers in a sauté pan. Sprinkle each layer with ground fast day rusks, pour on 3–4 spoons hot oil, and bake. Serve pepper separately.

### 2895  Broad beans
*(Sous iz russkikh bobov)*

Pour 2 glasses white haricot beans or broad beans [*Vicia faba*] into boiling water, bring to a boil, and pour off the water. Cover with a little hot water, add salt and about 2 spoons oil, and stew, covered, over a low fire. When the beans are almost cooked, add 2 seeded lemon slices or a little vinegar and 1–2 pieces sugar and cook until done. Sprinkle with greens and serve with fish patties or simply for breakfast.

### 2897  Stuffed artichokes
*(Farshirovannye artishoki)*

Clean 12–15 artichokes, cook in boiling water with a little salt, remove from the water, and take out the chokes. To prepare the stuffing, peel and chop ½ lb shallots and 10–12 fresh field mushrooms and fry in a saucepan in 3–4 spoons poppy seed oil. Add chopped dill, salt, a little lemon juice, and enough ground roll crumbs to make a mixture that is not very thick. Mix everything thoroughly and fill the artichokes with this stuffing. Place on an oiled baking sheet, drizzle the artichokes with oil, sprinkle them with ground roll crumbs, and brown them [in the oven]. Serve with the following sauce: Pour 3–4 teaspoons sugar into a skillet, moisten with water, and while constantly stirring, cook slightly over the fire until brown. Then add 3 spoons water and shredded truffles that have been fried in oil. Boil thoroughly, pour in 1 glass Madeira or white wine, and serve in a sauceboat.

### 2898 "Worms" from dried white peas*

*(Chervjachki iz sushonago, belago gorokha)*

Boil 2 lbs, or 4 glasses, ordinary peas, drain, and let them dry slightly. While still hot, rub the peas through a coarse sieve directly onto a platter. Add salt and pour on mustard sauce with green onions and pepper.

*This dish strikes me as a savory poor cousin to the French dessert called Mont-blanc, which is chestnut purée topped with crème Chantilly. Often, but not always, the "mountain" is formed by pressing the cooked chestnuts through a ricer directly onto the serving platter.*

### 2901 Mushrooms for vodka or pancakes

*(Griby k vodke ili blinam)*

Wash dried boletus mushrooms, boil in water, and finely chop. Mix with nut oil, salt, and black pepper. Pour the mushrooms into a small saucer and garnish with finely chopped white or green onions.

# 36

# Fish for Fast Days

## (Ryby)

*Remarks:* See the Remarks for Chapter 7.

### 2913  Fish patties

*(Kotlety iz ryby)*

Clean and bone 2–3 lbs pike, zander, or perch. Chop the flesh fine, pound in a wooden mortar, and add a 3 kopeck roll, soaked in water and squeezed out. Stir in 2 spoons mustard oil, salt, 2–3 ground black peppercorns, and mace. Form into patties, roll in flour or finely pounded and sieved rusk crumbs, and fry in a skillet in ¼–⅓ glass fast day oil such as poppy seed, sunflower seed, olive, nut, or mustard oil. If desired, sprinkle with finely chopped parsley and [¼] finely cut up and seeded lemon. Place an oiled paper over the patties, cover the pan with a lid, and bake in a hot oven for 10–15 minutes.

Serve with the same sauces as for Baked fish loaf #2914.

INGREDIENTS

| | |
|---|---|
| 2–3 lbs fish | ¼ teaspoon mace |
| 1 French roll | ⅓ glass oil |
| 2–3 allspice berries | (parsley) |
| 2–3 black peppercorns | (¼ lemon) |

### 2914  Baked fish loaf

*(Rod zharenoj bulki iz rybnago farsha)*

For this recipe, prepare Forcemeat #2913 and shape it into an oblong loaf instead of patties. After rolling it out, spread on top boiled and finely chopped sturgeon marrow mixed with oil, salt, and a little allspice. Roll up the forcemeat and smooth it into an oblong, rather flat loaf. Transfer to a skillet greased with oil and sprinkle on sieved rusk crumbs, finely chopped parsley, and a finely cut up and seeded lemon. Drizzle on hot oil and add some oil to the pan [so that it will not be dry.] Bake in the oven, frequently basting with the fish juices, to which 2–3 spoons of fish broth may be added. When it is cooked, transfer carefully to a platter and slice. This fish loaf is served mostly as a third course instead of a main meat dish.

Both fish patties and this baked loaf are served with the following sauces and salads: salad or green cucumbers; fried potatoes and cucumbers; dried green peas; compote of apples, cherries, apricots, etc.; mushroom sauce; salted cucumber sauce; cherry sauce; red currant sauce; sour-sweet sauce; sprat sauce; herring sauce; onion sauce with or without caraway; stewed cabbage; sauerkraut with mushrooms; fried milk-agaric mushrooms; strong sauce essence, diluted with fish broth; brown sauce.

### 2915 Fried or baked fish

*(Ryba zharenaja ili pechenaja)*

Take 3 lbs of a large fish such as zander, pike, whitefish, bream, tench, carp, vimba, white salmon, sturgeon, etc. Clean and wash the fish, slit lengthwise, and remove the bones. Cut into even pieces, salt for 1 hour, then wipe dry and roll in flour or rusk crumbs. Heat a skillet, pour in ¼–½ glass poppy seed, sunflower seed, olive, mustard, or nut oil and, when it begins to boil, add the fish. Fry on both sides, sprinkling with more rusk crumbs and pricking with a fork. To fry the fish more evenly, make several incisions in the thick portions of the flesh. Serve immediately. All the oil should be added to the skillet in the beginning, because if it is added gradually, the fish will not fry well and may burn. After arranging the fish on a platter, sprinkle with parsley.

Many people find baked fish tastier than fried. In that case, the fish must be cleaned, washed, salted, and wiped dry. Paint the entire fish thoroughly with oil and set it on a dripping pan in the oven. When it has baked slightly, generously sprinkle with rusk crumbs, and baste it frequently with its own juices until done. But only large fish are suitable for baking. Small fish such as navaga, smelts, cisco, crucians, graylings, perch, etc.* must be fried whole on top of the stove as indicated above, after making 3–4 slits along the spine of each fish. To serve, sprinkle with parsley and arrange in a circle, like a well.

Serve fried potatoes and one of the following with the fish: salted cucumbers; lettuce salad; beet salad; marinated beets; chicory salad; fresh cucumber salad; apple, cherry, plum, and apricot compote; potato salad; potato and beet salad; shredded cabbage; cherry sauce; red currant sauce; walnut sauce; strong sauce; brown sauce; sour-sweet sauce.

*For the Latin and Russian names of these fish, see the Appendix.

Fish vendor. Pen and ink by Boris M. Kustodiev, 1923. From
Vsevolod V. Vojnov, *B. M. Kustodiev* (1925).

### 2916  Boiled pike with pressed caviar

*(Shchuka varenaja s pajusnoju ikroju)*

Boil 3–4 lbs pike in a fish kettle with root vegetables, 2 onions, 2–3 bay leaves,
and 5–10 black peppercorns. After the fish has boiled, let it dry off on a platter,
then cover it with good pressed caviar (½ lb) mashed with 2–3 spoons olive oil.
Add a little lemon juice, a little ground black pepper, and serve immediately,
generally for breakfast.

### 2921  Carp in field mushroom sauce

*(Karp pod sousom s shampin'onami)*

Fry 2 grated onions and 12–20 cleaned and finely minced field mushrooms in
2–4 spoons nut or mustard oil. Pour in 1½ glasses boiling water or fish bouillon
and 1 glass red wine. Add 2–3 black peppercorns, ½ spoon chopped parsley, and
3–4 lbs carp, cleaned, washed, rubbed with ½ teaspoon salt, and cut into pieces.
Cover with a lid and boil over a high flame. When the fish is cooked, thicken the
sauce with ½ spoon flour mixed with ½ spoon olive oil, boil thoroughly, and
serve.

### 2936 Trout with fresh mushrooms and crayfish sauce

*(Forel' so svezhimi gribami i rakovym sousom)*

Boil the trout. Soak a plateful of cleaned, fresh boletus mushrooms in vinegar and boil them in crayfish broth. Arrange the trout on a platter, surround with the mushrooms, and pour on the crayfish sauce. To prepare the sauce, mix 1–2 spoons olive oil or nut oil with ½ glass flour, fry lightly, and dilute with crayfish or fish bouillon. Boil thoroughly and add 20 cleaned crayfish tails, 1 spoon capers, and some salt. Bring to a boil and pour over the fish and mushrooms.

### 2953 Fried small zander with salad

*(Sudachki zharenye s salatom)*

Take 3 lbs of small zander, split each fish in half, spread it out, and remove the backbone. Salt the fish, set it aside for a little while, and wipe dry with a napkin or blotting paper. Paint with mustard oil, dip in flour or rusk crumbs, and fry the fish on both sides in a hot sauté pan with ½–1 glass of mustard oil. To serve, sprinkle with finely chopped parsley fried in 1 spoon oil. Serve with any kind of salad.

### 2965 Baked cod

*(Treska zapechenaja)*

Prepare cod as indicated in #969. Grease a tinned saucepan with olive or mustard oil, add a layer of boiled and sliced potatoes, and sprinkle them with chopped parsley and dill, 1 spoon finely chopped shallots, a little allspice, and nutmeg. (If desired, chopped garlic shoots may be added.) Pour on 1 spoon olive oil, place the cut-up cod on top, and cover with another layer of potatoes, etc. Pour on oil or batter, sprinkle with a grated roll, and brown in the oven.

Cod is also served in the following ways: with white table wine, prepared like carp; with tomato sauce, but omit all meat day ingredients; or with cherry and red wine sauce.

INGREDIENTS

| | |
|---|---|
| 3 lbs cod | 2–3 rusks |
| ½ *garnets* potatoes | ¼–½ glass mustard or other fast day |
| ¼–½ lb shallots | oil |
| 5–10 allspice berries | (garlic) |
| nutmeg | (ingredients for batter) |
| parsley and dill | |

### 2967  Herring patties

(*Kotlety iz seledki*)

Soak 4–5 ordinary or Dutch herrings, remove the bones, chop fine, and stir in 1–3 finely chopped onions fried in oil. Add 1 French roll soaked and squeezed out or 12 boiled potatoes. Form into patties, sprinkle with flour, and fry in ¼ glass oil. Serve with sour-sweet sauce.

### 2975  Fried sterlet with sour-sweet sauce

(*Sterljad' zharenaja s kislo-sladkim sousom*)

Clean 3–4 lbs sterlet, remove the sturgeon marrow, salt the fish, and set it aside for awhile. Wipe the fish dry, coat with poppy seed, nut, or mustard oil, sprinkle with rusk crumbs, place in heated oil, and fry on both sides. Meanwhile, prepare the following sauce: Boil 1 glass each prunes and raisins. Fry 1 spoon each flour and poppy seed or olive oil almost until golden and dilute with 2 glasses boiling water or fish bouillon. Add the prunes and raisins, the juice from half a lemon, 1–2 bay leaves, 1–2 cloves, and 2–3 pieces sugar, or honey, or treacle. Boil for at least 15 minutes and pour over the fish on a platter. A little caramelized sugar may be added to the sauce.

### 2978  Stuffed perch

(*Okuni farshirovannye*)

Clean and salt a large perch weighing about 3 lbs, and carefully cut out the backbone with a knife. Stuff as follows: Remove the skin and bones from 1 lb pike or zander, pound the flesh, and fry in 1–2 spoons mustard oil. Add salt, 2–4 black peppercorns, 1–2 allspice berries, a little nutmeg, a handful of chopped dill, the soft center of half a French roll, soaked in water and squeezed out, and a full saucer of cleaned, half-boiled, and finely chopped field mushrooms. Mix everything together, stuff the perch, sew it up, and boil in bouillon. To prepare the bouillon, boil in water 1 carrot, 1 parsley root, 1 celery root, 2 onions, 1–2 bay leaves, and 3–5 black peppercorns.

While the fish cooks, prepare the following sauce: Fry 2 spoons flour in 2 spoons olive or nut oil, dilute with 2½ glasses fish bouillon, boil thoroughly, and strain. Add the juice from ½ lemon, 2–4 pieces sugar, and 20–30 cleaned crayfish tails. Bring to a boil and pour over the fish arranged on a platter and garnished with greens.

Use the fish bouillon for *ukha* or fish soup.

### 2983 Boiled burbot

*(Nalimy varenye)*

Clean and gut a 3–4 lb burbot. Cut off the head, which is not served at the table. Pour wine vinegar over the fish and set aside for an hour. Boil 2 onions, ½ parsley root, half a handful of parsley, and 2–4 black peppercorns in water. Bring the broth to a rapid boil and add the fish. When the burbot has cooked, transfer it to a platter and garnish with parsley, the sliced burbot liver, and large, boiled crayfish. In a sauceboat, serve White sauce #2835, Sauce #327, Field mushroom sauce #286, or Tomato sauce #303.

On meat days, it is good to serve the burbot with crayfish sauce.

### 2984 Burbot liver

*(Pechenka nalima)*

Burbot has a very tasty liver. Add the liver to the fish bouillon when the burbot is almost done because the liver toughens with prolonged boiling. Slice the boiled liver and garnish the platter with it. To increase the size of the burbot liver, gastronomes rub the live burbot with salt and flog the fish with birch rods.

### 2986 Boiled crayfish

*(Raki varenye)*

Rinse 30–60 live crayfish in cold water and drop them into rapidly boiling salted water, in which dip a piece of iron heated until red. Also add a bunch of dill, cover with a lid, and boil for at least 30 minutes. Using a slotted spoon, transfer the fish onto a platter and serve.

### 2987 Potato and herring casserole

*(Forshmak)*

Fry 2–3 onions in 2–3 spoons oil, mix with ¾ glass boiled rice, 12–18 boiled and mashed potatoes, and 2 cleaned and finely chopped herring. Pile the mixture into a tinned saucepan, brush with oil, and sprinkle with rusk crumbs. Brown in the oven and serve.

# 37

# Pâtés, Aspics, and Other Cold Dishes for Fast Days

*(Pashtety, maionezy, zalivnoe, i prochija kholodnyja kushan'ja)*

## PÂTÉS
*(Pashtety)*

### 3003 Dough for pâtés

*(Testo dlja pashtetov)*

Prepare a dough from ¾ glass water, 1–2 spoons each oil and rum, salt, and 3 glasses flour. Roll out the dough rather thinly.

Grease the interior of a tin mold shaped like a flower pot or a small saucepan, line the mold with dough, and fill with raw forcemeat. Cover with a lid of the same dough and bake. Remove from the oven and unmold onto a dish. (The form must be made so that each half may be removed separately.) Cut off the top crust, pour in a little sauce, and serve with the filling exposed. Pass extra sauce in a sauceboat.

### 3004 Fish forcemeat for pâtés

*(Rybnyj farsh dlja pashtetov)*

Bone 1½ lbs pike, whitefish, or zander, salt the fish, and sprinkle on a little black pepper, allspice, nutmeg, and ½ finely chopped onion fried in ½ spoon oil. Chop everything fine, pound in a mortar, and add ½ French roll soaked in water or fish broth and squeezed out. Stir in ½ glass fish bouillon and 1–2 spoons oil, and rub through a fine sieve.

### 3005 Salmon pâté

*(Pashtet iz lososiny)*

Fry a chopped and squeezed out onion in 3–4 spoons oil in a sauté pan, add 2 lbs cleaned salmon, salted and cut into pieces, and fry, covered, on one side so that the fish does not cook completely. Add ½ glass French wine, about 2 spoons vinegar, and a little water. Sprinkle on salt, 5 allspice, 5 black peppercorns, and 2 bay leaves. Bring all this to a boil over a high flame, remove the fish, and cool. Meanwhile, prepare Forcemeat #3004 and Dough #3003. Line a mold with the dough. Add alternate layers of forcemeat and fish, finishing with a layer of fish. Pour on a glass of the strained sauce in which the fish was boiled. Cover with dough and bake in the oven for 1 hour. Serve the fish paté with a sauce [made from fish stock, crayfish essence, and either truffles or ripe salted olives.] Pass the sauce separately in a sauceboat.

# ASPICS

## (Zalivnoe)

### 3017  Whole cold fish in aspic

*(Tsel'naja kholodnaja ryba s vinigretom i lanspikom)*

Boil a zander or trout, cool, and place on a platter with the backbone upper-most. Flatten the fish and cover with clear aspic. Cut up baked beets, red carrots, potatoes, and beans into very fine even pieces to make them extremely attractive. Mix the vegetables together and strew them over the platter of fish. Serve mustard sauce separately. Fish prepared in this manner is mostly served for breakfast.

### 3018  Aspic from fried navaga

*(Zalivnoe iz zharenoj navagi)*

Clean, gut, and wash 12–16 navaga. Salt the fish, sprinkle with a little ground pepper, and wipe with a napkin. Cut each fish into thirds, dip into flour, fry in 2–3 spoons of some kind of fast day oil, and cool. Prepare an aspic from 2 lbs small fish and 2 *zolotniki* fish glue. Clarify the aspic with caviar by pounding the caviar and boiling it together with the aspic. Strain through a napkin tied to the legs of a stool. Pour a little aspic into a mold and cool it. Add lemon slices, greens, and 15–20 boiled and shelled crayfish tails, top with pieces of navaga, and cover with aspic. Cool and turn out onto a platter.

### 3019  Royal marinated sterlet

*(Marinovannaja sterljad' po-korolevski)*

Boil a sterlet in lightly salted boiling water, turn into a coarse sieve to cool, then cut into pieces. Meanwhile, boil vinegar with bay leaves, pepper, cloves, cinnamon, and 1 tablespoon prepared mustard. In another saucepan, place several dried figs, dates, raisins, and several skinned and seeded lemon and orange slices. Add the cut-off citrus zest, shredded into strips, and 2–3 quartered Crimean apples. Strain the spiced vinegar over the fruit, bring it all to a boil twice, and cool. Arrange pieces of sterlet in a jar, interspersing them with the boiled fruit, cover with the almost cooled vinegar, and pour a spoon of olive oil on top. Set the jar aside for 4 hours, tie it up with waxed paper and then with ordinary paper. Store in a cold place.

### 3020  Fish roll

*(Rulet iz ryby)*

Take 4 lbs raw fish such as 2 lbs each of white salmon and sturgeon or 2 lbs each of beluga and salmon (*semga*), ½ small jar each of capers and olives, 10 anchovies, and, if desired, 10 small onions. Stone the olives and finely chop. Also chop the capers and anchovies and mix together all the chopped ingredients. If you are adding onions, they must be chopped as well. Cut the fish into very thin slices, spread out the slices [i.e., cover the surface of a napkin with overlapping slices], sprinkle them first with salt and pepper and then with the chopped capers, olives, and anchovies. If desired, strew chopped onions on top. Roll up carefully into a tube, wrap well in the napkin, tie round with a cord, and boil twice as long as a large fish is usually boiled. Cool the fish in the water without removing it from the napkin. When cool, place the fish, still wrapped in the napkin, under a heavy weight for 3 days. Remove the fish roll carefully from the napkin and, when it is time to eat the fish, slice it like sausages. Serve vinegar, olive oil, and mustard separately.

INGREDIENTS

| | |
|---|---|
| 4 lbs fish | 10 anchovies |
| ½ jar capers | 10 small onions |
| ½ jar olives | salt and pepper |

### 3022  Cold white salmon

*(Kholodnoe iz belorybitsy)*

Cut the salmon into pieces, dip in olive oil and fast day crumbs, and fry on a gridiron. Prepare a green sauce from olive oil, mustard, vinegar, salt, pepper, nutmeg, lemon zest, mashed and finely chopped green parsley, and mashed anchovies. Pour this sauce over the fish and decorate with marinated plums.

### 3023a  Fast day ham—Fish zakuski

*(Postnyj okorok—rybnaja zakuska)*

Clean fish such as carp, tench, eel, or salmon (*semga*). Remove the meat from the bones, take the roe from the carp, and chop everything thoroughly. Pound with salt, black pepper, nutmeg, and olive oil. Form the mixture into a bun [to look like a ham], sew it tightly in a napkin, and boil in a mixture of half red wine and half water, adding cloves, bay leaves, and pepper. After it has cooked, cool in the same wine. To serve for hors d'oeuvre, slice and decorate with greens.

### 3036 Boletus mushroom salad

*(Vinigret iz belykh gribov)*

Soak 12–18 large boletus mushrooms, wash, boil in salted water, and drain. Dry them slightly with a towel and dip them in batter. Sprinkle them with rusk crumbs, fry in ¼ glass fast day oil, and cool. Arrange on a platter, decorate with salted lemons, plums, capers, and olives, and pour on cold mustard sauce.

### 3037b Laberdan*

*(Labardan)*

Peel 30 boiled potatoes, cool, and chop fine. Mix with 2 chopped herring or ⅛ lb dried, boiled, and chopped white mushrooms. Add green and white onions, dilute slightly with fish or mushroom bouillon, and mix. Form into an oblong bun and pour on mustard sauce with pickles, small mushrooms, finely chopped salted cucumbers, and finely chopped onions, which are essential (use 1 glass in all).

*\*Laberdan, a corruption of Aberdeen, is the name of a particularly fine salt cod, the process for which was first developed in that Scottish seaport. (Fitzgibbon, Food of the Western World, 243.) This recipe is interesting in that Molokhovets adopted the name but did not use salt cod or even specify Scottish herring.*

# 38

# Fast Day Puddings

*(Postnye pudingi)*

### 3042 A *pirog* made from whole apples, covered with applesauce

*(Pirog iz tsel'nykh jablok, pokrytykh jablochnoju massoju)*

Peel and core 10 apples. Bring to a boil twice in water, turn into a coarse sieve, and cool. Stuff with finely ground almonds mixed with raisins and sugar or fill with jam.

Arrange the apples on a platter and cover with the following purée. Bake 5 large apples, rub them while still hot through a fine sieve, sprinkle on ½ glass sugar, and beat until white. Spread the purée over the whole apples and bake in the oven for 15 minutes.

INGREDIENTS

15 rather large apples
½ glass each almonds and raisins

¾ glass sugar or 1 glass jam

### 3046 Rice with wild strawberry purée

*(Ris s zemljanichnym pjure)*

Boil rice with pieces of vanilla and arrange the rice in a ring on a platter. Smooth over the surface and fill the center with wild strawberry purée.

To make the purée, pick over 2 lbs, or 5 glasses, of wild strawberries, rub the berries through a fine sieve, and stir in ½–¾ glass fine sugar.

INGREDIENTS

1¼ glasses rice
¾ *vershok* vanilla bean

2 lbs, or 5 glasses, wild strawberries
¾–1 glass sugar

### 3050 Rice with chocolate sauce

*(Ris s shokoladnym sousom)*

Boil 1½ glasses rice until the rice is cooked, but the grains are still separate (cf. Remarks on puddings). Add ½ glass sugar flavored with vanilla (cf. #1894), 5 ground bitter almonds, and 15 ground sweet almonds. Or, instead of vanilla, add 1 spoon rosewater or 3 drops rose oil. Pour on the following sauce. Dissolve ⅛–¼ lb chocolate in a mixture of 2 glasses boiling water and 2–4 pieces sugar. When the chocolate begins to boil, add 1 teaspoon potato flour, ordinary [wheat] flour, or cornstarch mixed with 1 spoon water and bring the sauce to a boil, stirring.

### 3051 Rice pudding with fresh fruits

*(Puding iz risa so svezhimi fruktami)*

Boil 1 glass rice and stir in ¼–½ glass sugar and 1 wineglass liqueur or maraschino. Peel and quarter 3 apples, 4 pears, and 4 peaches. Add 8 stoned yellow or red plums and boil the fruit in a syrup made from 1 glass water and ¾ glass sugar. Cook the plums in the syrup for 5 minutes, but cook the peaches a little longer. Rinse with water a small mold shaped like a saucepan and sprinkle with coarsely ground sugar. Fill the mold with alternate layers of rice and cooked fruit, beginning and ending with a layer of rice. (A little gooseberry jam may be added to the fruit.) Cool and serve by turning out onto a platter. Surround with green and red* grapes, place a pear boiled in syrup on top, surround the pear with plums, and pour on the remaining syrup, adding a wineglass of liqueur.

INGREDIENTS

| | |
|---|---|
| 1 glass rice | 1 glass sugar |
| 3 apples | 2 wineglasses liqueur or maraschino |
| 4 pears | green and blue* fresh grapes |
| 4 peaches | 1 spoon gooseberries from jam |
| 8 plums | |

*The color discrepancy is in the original text.*

### 3055 Rice with cranberry purée

*(Ris s kljukvennym morsom)*

Boil 1 lb, or 2 glasses, rice tied up in a rag until the rice is tender and the grains are separate. Add 10–20 sweet almonds and 5 bitter almonds, all ground and mixed with sugar. To serve, pour on a thick purée of raw cranberries mixed with sugar. (Use ⅓ lb cranberries and 1 glass fine sugar.)

### 3056  Cold sago with red wine

*(Sago kholodnoe s krasnym vinom)*

Boil 1⅛ glasses sago until half done as indicated in #1183. Cover with 1½ glasses red wine, add a piece of cinnamon, and boil over a low fire. When the sago is almost cooked, sprinkle on ¾ glass sugar scraped with lemon zest, and cook until the mixture thickens, stirring frequently. Remove the cinnamon, transfer the sago to a platter, cool, and serve. Or, pile the sago into a moistened mold sprinkled with sugar and cool. To serve, turn out onto a platter and pour on cherry syrup. When filling the mold, ¾ wineglass rum may be added, or arrange the sago in small sections, dividing them with oranges.

INGREDIENTS

| | |
|---|---|
| 1⅛ glasses, or ½ lb, sago | zest from ½ lemon |
| ½ bottle red wine | (¾ wineglass rum may be added) |
| ¾ glass sugar | 2 oranges |
| cinnamon | (cherry syrup) |

### 3058  Prune dessert

*(Pirozhnoe iz chernosliva)*

Boil 1–1½ lbs prunes and rub through a fine sieve. Boil 4–6 apples that are not too sour with sugar in a very small amount of water. Sieve the apples, mix with the sieved prunes, and beat with a spoon for half an hour.

Prepare a syrup from ¾–1 glass sugar in pieces and ¾–1 glass water and stir the syrup into the purée. Before serving, heat on top of the stove, but not too hot. When serving, the purée may be surrounded with sippets.

INGREDIENTS

| | |
|---|---|
| 3–4½ glasses prunes | ¾–1 glass sugar in pieces |
| 4–6 apples | |

# 39

# Fast Day Pancakes, Buns, Dumplings, and Kasha

*(Postnye bliny, olad'i, grenki, bulochki, trubochki, oblatki, khvorost, nalivashniki, vareniki, kashi, i proch.)*

[*Translator's note:* The recipes in this chapter strongly resemble those in Chapters 11, 12, and 13. Often the only difference between a meat day and a fast day recipe is the substitution of fast day oils for animal fat and, of course, the elimination of all meat, dairy products, and eggs.]

### 3061  Russian buckwheat pancakes

*(Russkie bliny grechnevye)*

Very early in the morning prepare a dough from 1 lb wheat flour, 3 glasses warm water, and 2 *zolotniki* dry yeast. Mix and set in a warm place to rise. Or, prepare the dough the day before and let it rise overnight. After the dough has risen, beat it thoroughly with a spatula, add salt and 1 lb buckwheat flour, and let the dough rise again. Thirty minutes before cooking, pour 3 glasses boiling water onto the dough. Let the dough rise once more and cook as indicated in the Remarks for Russian pancakes in Chapter 11. Grease the skillets with olive, poppy seed, sunflower seed, or nut oil, etc.

As soon as the batter is poured onto the skillet and while it is still cooking, the pancakes may be sprinkled with white or green onions or smelts. Serve with caviar, Mushrooms #2901, salmon, oil, or heated honey.

### 3069  Buns with jam and rum

*(Bulochki s varen'em i romom)*

Cut off the tops of 12–18 ordinary, cheap buns, carefully remove the soft interior, and fill the cavity with thick jam or fruit purée. Replace the lids, dip in syrup prepared from ¾ glass water, 1 wineglass rum, and ¼ glass sugar, and dry out for a short time in the oven. (Use about ¾ glass jam.)

### 3072 Filled fritters

*(Nalivashniki)*

Knead thoroughly 1 lb flour, 1 glass water, 1 tablespoon nut or olive oil, and ¼ teaspoon salt. Roll out thinly, dot with small mounds of jam without syrup, and fold up like *pirozhki*. Pinch together, punch out with a glass or a [biscuit] cutter, and fry in a generous amount of oil, from ½–1 lb. Use a narrower saucepan than usual so that the fritters will be immersed in oil and swell up. Remove them when they have browned and drain on a coarse sieve lined with blotting paper. While they are still hot, sprinkle them with sugar and, if desired, a little cinnamon.

### 3074 Pelmeni with mushrooms

*(Pel'meni s gribami)*

Prepare a fast day dough from 1 lb flour, salt, ¾ glass boiling water, and 1–2 spoons sunflower seed oil. Roll out as thin as possible.

Wash ½ lb dried boletus mushrooms, boil until tender, and chop fine. Fry with a finely chopped onion in 2 spoons nut, sunflower, or mustard oil. Strew with salt and ground allspice, cool, and proceed as indicated in #1281.

### 3076 Vareniki with plums

*(Vareniki so slivami)*

Prepare Dough #3074. Scald 1½ lbs ripe plums with boiling water, halve each plum, remove the pits, and place the fruit in a saucepan. Add ¼–½ glass fine sugar and stew over the fire, constantly shaking the saucepan to prevent the plums from burning. Cool, drain the plums well, reserving the syrup, and stuff the *vareniki*. To serve, boil the *vareniki* and pour on the reserved syrup boiled with 1 glass water, ¼ glass sugar, and a piece of vanilla bean.

### 3086 Fluffy kasha made with mushroom bouillon

*(Kasha razsypchataja na gribnom bul'one)*

Wash 5–10 dried mushrooms in hot water and boil in water with salt, root vegetables, and spices. Remove and finely chop the mushrooms. Strain the bouillon. Pour 2½ glasses of this bouillon into a saucepan, add ¼ glass olive oil fried with an onion, bring to a boil, and add the groats all at once, stirring briskly. Set over a high flame for 5 minutes, then lower the flame and cover the pan. Mix after

10 minutes to prevent lumps, add more oil, sprinkle on the finely chopped mushrooms, and brown in the oven. To serve, turn out onto a platter.

This kasha also may be prepared for meat days, in which case the buckwheat groats should be rubbed with 2 eggs, dried out, and then strained through a colander.

INGREDIENTS

| | |
|---|---|
| 2 glasses Smolensk buckwheat, or rice | 1 carrot |
| 5–10 dried mushrooms | ½ parsley root |
| salt | ½ celery root |
| 3–4 spoons Finnish butter, or ½ glass | 1 onion |
|    olive or sunflower seed oil | ½ leek |
| 5–6 allspice berries | |

### 3092  Semolina with almond milk

*(Kashka mannaja na mindal'nom moloke)*

Scald ¼–½ lb sweet almonds and 5–10 bitter almonds with boiling water, remove the skins, and finely pound the nuts, adding water by the spoonful. Strain the nuts, pound them again, dilute with 4 glasses hot water, mix, and bring to a boil. Stir in 1⅛ glasses semolina. After the semolina has cooked and thickened, add ½ glass fine sugar. Transfer to a silver saucepan, strew with fine sugar, and glaze with a salamander. It is essential to cook the kasha in a stoneware saucepan and not to add the sugar earlier, otherwise the almond milk will spoil.

INGREDIENTS

| | |
|---|---|
| 1⅛ glasses, or ½ lb, semolina | 5–10 bitter almonds |
| ½ glass sugar | serve fine sugar separately |
| ¼–½ lb sweet almonds | |

### 3094  Semolina with cranberry juice

*(Kasha mannaja na kljukvennom morse)*

Prepare 6 glasses juice from 1 glass cranberries. Bring the juice to a boil and sprinkle on ½ glass semolina and at least ½ glass granulated sugar. Boil, cool, and serve with sugar.

### 3097  *Kut'ja* from baked wheat with poppy seeds or jam*

*(Kut'ja iz pshenitsy s makom ili s varen'em)*

Pick over 1 lb wheat, wash, and pour into boiling water. When the water begins to boil, turn the wheat into a colander, and rinse with cold water. Place in a saucepan, cover with water, and bring to a boil. Cover with a lid and bake in a hot oven for 4 hours until tender. Remove and set in a cold place. Meanwhile, wash 1 glass poppy seeds, scald with boiling water, pour off the water, and rinse in cold water. Drain, scald with boiling water once more, drain, pour on cold water, and drain. Grind in a stoneware bowl until the mixture whitens and the grains are pulverized. Add ½ glass sugar or about 2 spoons honey, add a little water that has been boiled and cooled, and mix with the wheat. Or, instead of poppy seeds, a glass of berries and fruit from jam, without the juice, may be added to the wheat. Dilute with sugar boiled with water.

*This has long been one of the obligatory dishes served in Ukrainian homes on Christmas eve. It is also a ritual funeral dish in some parts of Russia. Usually made with wheat, it could also be made with rice (#3099) or other grains. The word kut'ja is derived from a Greek word meaning seed or kernel.*

### 3099  Kut'ja or rice cooked with almond milk or jam

*(Kut'ja ili kasha risovaja s mindal'nym molokom ili varen'em)*

Boil 1 lb rice until the grains separate, mix with ½ glass sugar and, if desired, cinnamon. Add 1 glass sultanas and bring once to a boil. To serve, pour on almond milk.

Or, after having boiled the rice until the grains separate, add 1 glass berries and fruit from jam without the juice. Dilute with sugar boiled with water and add almond milk.

### 3103  Rice patties with sweet sauce

*(Kotlety risovyja so sladkim sousom)*

Boil 1½ glasses rice, sprinkle on ¼ glass sugar and lemon zest or preserved orange rind, strew with flour, and shape into patties. Fry the patties in oil. To serve, pour on rum sauce.

### 3105  Onion tarts

*(Vatrushki s lukom)*

Prepare yeast dough or short pastry. Cut the dough into pieces, roll out thin flat cakes, cover with finely shredded onion fried in nut oil with salt and a little pepper. Turn up and pinch the edges all around. Set aside to rise, paint with olive oil, and bake in the oven. To serve, brush on more olive or nut oil. [Ingredients:] 24 onions, ⅓ glass nut oil, and 1 lb flour.

# 40
# Fast Day Ices, Compotes, and *Kissels*

*(Postnoe morozhenoe, krem, blanmanzhe, zhele, mussy, kompoty, kiseli)*

*Remarks:* These fast day dishes are prepared like meat day dishes, except substitute fish glue for gelatin. Tear up the fish glue, soak in 1 glass of cold water for several hours, and then boil in the same water until the volume is reduced by half. Use the same amount of fish glue as you would gelatin.

[*Translator's note:* Since every "recipe" in this chapter simply refers back to its counterpart in Chapter 14, none has been included in this edition.]

# 41
# Fast Day Sweet Pirogs
# and Pastries

*(Postnye sladkie pirogi i pirozhnoe)*

### 3179  Fast day dough for sweet pirogs

*(Postnoe testo dlja sladkikh pirogov)*

For 6 persons. Early in the morning prepare a dough from 1½ glasses warm water, 1½ zolotniki dry yeast diluted in a little warm water, and 2 glasses fine wheat flour. Let the dough rise, beat thoroughly with a spatula, and add 1 teaspoon salt and 2 spoons poppy seed, sunflower seed, or olive oil beaten with ½ glass sugar. For flavoring, add 10 cardamom seeds, lemon zest, 2–3 drops rose or lemon oil, vanilla, or cinnamon. Add the rest of the flour and knead. Let it rise, shape into a rimmed circular pie, fill with apples, etc., decorate the top with strips of dough, and let rise. Paint with honey mixed with water and bake in the oven. (Use 1½–2 lbs flour in all.)

### 3190  Tarts with jam or apples

*(Vatrushki s varen'em ili jablokami)*

Prepare a fast day yeast dough (cf. #3179) or a very simple dough as for noodles, adding 1 spoon fast day oil and 1 wineglass rum or vodka. Roll out small flat cakes, top with some jam without juice or baked and puréed apples with sugar, and pinch the edges all around, etc. Or, peel 8–10 apples, thinly slice, and stew in a saucepan with ½ glass sugar, 1 spoon rum, and 2–3 spoons water.

### 3193  Small almond cakes

*(Mindal'nye lepeshechki)*

Scald and peel ½ lb sweet almonds including 10 bitter almonds. Wipe the almonds dry or dry them out slightly in the summer oven. Pound the nuts, gradually adding about 2 spoons rose water and stir in ½ lb or more fine sugar. Make small rectangular cakes from this dough and arrange them [on a baking sheet] lined with paper. Place a strip of candied lemon peel or bitter or sweet orange peel diagonally across the middle of each cake. Bake in an oven that is not too hot.

### 3195  Almond pastries

*(Pirozhnoe iz podzharenago mindalja)*

Blanch and peel ½ lb, or 1½ glasses, sweet almonds, rub them dry, and pound them as fine as possible until they form a dough, gradually adding rosewater. Meanwhile, pour 1 glass fine sugar into a saucepan, moisten with 3 spoons water, and stir on top of the stove until the mixture becomes golden. Add the almond paste, stir again slightly over the fire, and pour the mixture into small, oblong paper casings greased with olive oil. Transfer the casings to a baking sheet and bake in a low oven. Let the pastries cool, remove the papers, and serve.

### 3196  Almond balls

*(Mindal'nye shariki)*

Blanch and peel 1½ glasses sweet almonds, rub dry, and pound as fine as possible, adding rosewater gradually to prevent the oil in the nuts from separating. Stir in 1 glass fine sugar and the zest and juice of ½ lemon. [Using a spoon, scoop out] small heaps of the mixture onto a baking sheet greased with olive oil. Bake in the summer oven. When the balls have almost finished cooking, moisten your little finger with water, make a small indentation in each, and fill with jam—raspberries without syrup are best of all. Let them dry out slightly in the oven and then serve.

# 42

# Fast Day Small Baked Goods

### (Postnoe pechen'e k chaju i kofe)

*Remarks:* To flavor the dough for sweet buns (made from 5 lbs flour), add 1 spoon lemon zest or 10–15 drops lemon oil, ½–1 small, crushed vanilla bean, ½–1 *lot* of vanilla drops, 10–15 drops of rose oil, ¼ lb bitter almonds, 1 small spoon ground cinnamon, 10 drops of cinnamon oil, or 20–30 cardamom seeds. Also add raisins, finely chopped candied citrus peel, or candied orange rind.

For 5 lbs of flour, use 5 *zolotniki* of dry yeast. Dissolve the yeast in ½ glass warm water, add 1 small spoon flour, beat the mixture, set it aside overnight, and in the morning prepare the dough.

### 3201  Fast day buns

#### (Bulki postnyja)

Prepare a dough late in the evening or early in the morning from ½ *garnets,* or 7½ glasses, flour, 4 glasses warm water, and ¾ glass liquid yeast. Or dissolve 4 *zolotniki* dry yeast in an extra ¾ glass of warm water. When the dough rises, beat it as long as possible with a spatula and add 1 tablespoon salt. One half glass poppy seed, sunflower seed, or nut oil may be added. Pour in the remaining flour, beat thoroughly, and let it rise. Shape the dough into buns, let them rise on a baking sheet greased with a spoon of oil, paint them with beer or boiling water with oil or honey, and bake them in the oven. These proportions will yield at least 6½ lbs of buns after they have cooled. In all use 5 lbs flour, or 1 *garnets.* The tops of these buns may be sprinkled with sugar and caraway seeds. If these buns are baked for tea, add to the dough ¾ glass sugar beaten with the oil until white. A glass or more of picked-over, washed, and dried sultanas and candied orange peel may be added, or any kind of flavoring as indicated in the Remarks.

### 3206  Rolled cake with poppy seeds

#### (Strutseli s makom)

Mix together 2½ glasses warm water, 2–3 *zolotniki* dry yeast, and 3 glasses flour and let the dough rise. Beat the dough thoroughly and add salt and ¼ glass olive or sunflower seed oil. Mix until white with ½ lb sugar and 1 spoon good honey (which will make a crumbly, short dough). Add a little ground bitter almond and enough flour to make a dough of the usual consistency for buns. Knead until it leaves your hands and set the dough aside to rise. Meanwhile, scald 2 glasses poppy seeds with boiling water, cover, and set aside for a full hour. Squeeze the seeds until dry, grind them in a stoneware bowl, and add a few ground bitter almonds and 1 full spoon sugar and 1 spoon or so of honey to sweeten the mixture. Mix thoroughly. When the dough has risen, roll it out into several thin ovals, spread [each] with some of the poppy seed mixture, and roll up into a tube so that the ends are neat and even. Place on a baking sheet greased with olive oil and strewn with flour and paint the dough with honey diluted with water. Sprinkle with poppy seeds or sweet almonds and bake in the oven for 45 minutes. (Use 3 lbs flour in all.)

### 3211 Jewish bagels*

*(Krendeli evrejskie)*

Stir together ½ glass yeast, 1 *garnets* flour, a generous amount of salt, anise, and just enough warm water to make a stiff dough. Mix well, cover, and let rise thoroughly. Form into bagels, dip them in black cumin seeds (*chernyshki*) or anise, place them on an oven peel, and dry them out slightly before the fire. Drop several bagels at a time into boiling salted water, stirring them so that they do not stick to the bottom of the saucepan. As the bagels rise to the surface, remove them and place them on the oven peel. Drizzle them generously with cold water and keep them in the oven. When they have dried out, place them directly on the floor of a cleanly swept out oven.

*This recipe closely resembles #1850. The fact that it is included among the fast day recipes, surely an anomaly if there ever was one, shows how widely disseminated these bagels were among the Russian Orthodox community.*

Tea table with samovar, teapot, and pastries. Pen and ink by Boris M. Kustodiev. Illustration for N. S. Leskov, *Stopal'shchik* (1922).

### 3212  Fast day rusks and crackers

*(Sukhari postnye i postnye sushki)*

Prepare dough #3201. After it has risen a second time, spread it out on the table, cut into small pieces, and roll them into little buns. Let them rise on a baking sheet greased with oil, then paint them with warm water and bake. Cool, slice each in half with a sharp knife, place the pieces on a baking sheet, and dry them out in the oven. Before drying out the rusks, moisten the cut surfaces with white wine and sprinkle with sugar and cinnamon and finely pounded sweet almonds. Similar rusks are prepared from a dough made with almond milk. Before drying the rusks, moisten them with almond milk and sprinkle with sugar mixed with pounded sweet almonds. Only let them brown slightly. Best of all, set them in a hot oven and watch that they do not brown too much.

### 3218  Name day krendel for fast days

*(Postnyj imjaninnyj krendel')*

Bake an ordinary yeast dough using 3 lbs flour, a cup of the very best mustard oil, 1 cup sugar, ½ *zolotnik* saffron, a little salt, and some raisins. Just before setting the *krendel* into the oven, paint it with water and sprinkle it with almonds, currants, sugar, and dried fast day buns, pounded into crumbs.

# Complete List of Recipes in the Twentieth Edition

(Recipes marked with "!" appeared in the 1st edition of 1861)
(Recipes marked with "*" appear in the present edition)

## CHAPTER 1. SOUPS

### Hot Meat-based Soups

| | | | | | |
|---|---|---|---|---|---|
| * | i | Utensils for bouillon | ! | 10 | Clear white French soup |
| * | ii | The quality of meat | *! | 11 | Windsor soup made from calf's feet |
| * | iii | [No heading] | ! | 12 | White soup |
| * | iv | The quantity of beef | ! | 13 | Wallachian white soup |
| * | v | The quantity of water | ! | 14 | Royal soup |
| * | vi | The order of cooking | | 15 | Tripe soup |
| * | vii | Scum | *! | 16 | Salted cucumber soup or *rassol'nik* |
| * | viii | Root vegetables | ! | 17 | Young beet green soup |
| | ix | [Missing from the original] | *! | 18 | Cherry soup with Smolensk buckwheat |
| | x | [Missing from the original] | ! | 19 | Veal kidney soup |
| * | xi | The amount of salt | *! | 20 | Italian soup with macaroni |
| * | xii | How to correct unsavory bouillon resulting from inferior cuts of meat | ! | 21 | Soup with lemon, rice or pearl barley, and sour cream |
| * | xiii | How to color a clear bouillon | | 22 | Celery root soup |
| * | xiv | To clarify bouillon | ˈ! | 23 | German soup with cream and egg yolks |
| * | xv | The kinds of beef usually used for soup | ! | 24 | Fish soup with meat bouillon |
| *! | xvi | The basic recipe for a clear, strong bouillon for all kinds of soups | ! | 25 | Green *shchi* from nettles |
| | | | | 25a | *Shchi* from young green cabbage |
| | | | ! | 26 | Sorrel *shchi* |
| | | | ! | 27 | Sorrel *shchi*, another way |
| *! | [1] | Clear bouillon | ! | 28 | Quick *shchi* |
| ! | 2 | Brown bouillon | *! | 29 | Sauerkraut *shchi* |
| | 3 | Bouillon prepared from dried bouillon | ! | 30 | Sour *shchi* made from fresh cabbage |
| * | 4 | Bouillon for sick people | *! | 31 | Ukrainian borshch |
| * | 5 | Bouillon with rum for weak children and adults who must lead an active life and "be constantly on the go" | ! | 32 | Borshch, another way |
| | | | ! | 33 | Polish borshch |
| | | | | 34 | Borshch, another way |
| * | 6 | Beef bouillon for breakfast for sick people | ! | 35 | Borshch from baked beets |
| | | | ! | 36 | Celery root borshch |
| ! | 7 | Strong bouillon with wine, sometimes served in cups | ! | 37 | Soup with asparagus and spinach |
| | | | | 38 | Soup with rutabagas and crushed barley |
| ! | 8 | Wallachian brown bouillon with root vegetables | * | 39 | Fresh mushroom soup |
| | | | ! | 40 | Veal soup |
| *! | 9 | French julienne soup | ! | 41 | Lamb soup |

## Complete List of Recipes

### Meat-based Puréed Soups

### Fish Soups

### Butter-based Soups (without Meat)

Complete List of Recipes

## Pirozhki

## CHAPTER 3. SAUCES

# Complete List of Recipes

## Sauces for Meat Dishes

## Sauces for Vegetables

## Fish Sauces

## CHAPTER 4. VEGETABLES, GREENS, AND GARNISHES

### VEGETABLES AND GREENS

# Complete List of Recipes

## Kohlrabi

## Parsnips

## Green and White Beans

## Sorrel, Spinach, Cress, Goosefoot, and Radish Tops

## Beets and Beet Greens

## Cauliflower, Savoy Cabbage, and Brussel Sprouts

## Ordinary Fresh Cabbage and Sauerkraut

## Asparagus

# Complete List of Recipes

## Potatoes

## Mushrooms

## Stewed root vegetables

## Tomatoes

## Cucumbers

## Lentils

## Artichokes

## Onions

# Complete List of Recipes

## Jerusalem Artichokes

## Apples

## Celery Root

## Pumpkin

## Chestnuts

# VARIOUS GARNISHES FOR DISHES OF GREENS AND ROOT VEGETABLES

# CHAPTER 5. BEEF, VEAL, MUTTON, AND PORK

## Boiled Beef

## Stewed Beef

## Cooked Beef

# Complete List of Recipes

## Veal

## Mutton

## Suckling Pig

## Pork

## Ham

## Chamois, Venison, Elk, and Hare

# CHAPTER 6. DOMESTIC AND WILD BIRDS AND SALAD ACCOMPANIMENTS

## Domestic birds

## Wild Fowl

## Salads to Accompany Cooked Meat and Fish

## CHAPTER 7. FISH AND CRAYFISH

# CHAPTER 8. PIROGS AND PÂTÉS

## Dough for Pirogs, Pirozhki, and Pâtés

## Pirogs

# Complete List of Recipes

## Hot and Cold Pâtés

# CHAPTER 9. ASPICS AND OTHER COLD DISHES

## Meat and Fish Aspics

## Jellied Meats and Fish, Aspic Salads, and Marinades

# CHAPTER 10. PUDDINGS

## CHAPTER 11. CRÊPES, PANCAKES FOR BUTTER WEEK, SIPPETS, AND EGGS

### Crêpes

### Russian Pancakes

### Toasts or Sippets

### Egg Dishes

## CHAPTER 12. FILLED DUMPLINGS, MACARONI, AND KASHA

### Filled Dumplings, Ravioli, and Pastries

# Complete List of Recipes

## Italian Macaroni, Noodles, Dumplings, and Wafers

## Kasha, Caul Sausages, and Grain Patties

## Cheese and Other Dumplings

## CHAPTER 13. WAFFLES, WAFERS, DOUGHNUTS, AND FRITTERS

### Waffles, Little Horns, and Wafers

### Buns, Pastry Straws, Fritters, and Batters

### Various Sweet Dishes

## CHAPTER 14. ICE CREAMS, MOUSSES, *KISSELS*, AND COMPOTES

### Ice Creams

# Complete List of Recipes

## Kissels

## Compotes

## Boiled milk creams

## CHAPTER 15. TORTES

# Complete List of Recipes

## CHAPTER 16. MAZURKAS AND OTHER SMALL PASTRIES

### Mazurkas

### Petits Fours or Small Baked Goods

## CHAPTER 17. BABAS, BUNS, RUSKS, AND SMALL BAKED GOODS

### Yeast Babas

### Babas Made with Beaten Egg Whites

### Buns and Kuliches

# Complete List of Recipes

## CHAPTER 18. *PASKHAS* AND COLORED EGGS

## CHAPTER 19. GINGERBREADS

## CHAPTER 20. JAMS, JELLIES, AND SYRUPS

### Jams and Preserves

## Jellies

## Sugar Syrups

## CHAPTER 21. SUGARLESS JUICES, SYRUPS, AND CONSERVES

### Juices without Sugar

# Complete List of Recipes

## To Prepare Juices for Ice Cream in the Winter

## Fresh Berry and Fruit Preserves for Compotes, Ice Cream, and Desserts in Winter

## Preserves for Decorating Tortes and Compotes

# CHAPTER 22. FRUIT LIQUEURS, CHERRY BRANDIES, AND SPARKLING WINES

## Cherry Brandy

## Sparkling and Other Homemade Light Wines

## CHAPTER 23. SUGARLESS VODKAS, PUNCHES, AND FRUIT DRINKS

### Sugarless Vodkas

### Sweet Vodkas or Ratafias

### Very Sweet Vodkas, like Liqueurs

### Various Punches

### Various Drinks

## CHAPTER 24. KVASS, BEER, AND MEAD

### Kvass

### To Prepare Moscow Kvass

### Beer

### Mead

## CHAPTER 25. VINEGARS, MUSTARDS, FAST DAY OILS, GRAINS, AND STARCHES

### Vinegars

## Complete List of Recipes

## CHAPTER 27. YEASTS AND BREADS

### Yeast

### Bread

## CHAPTER 28. PRESERVED FRUITS AND BERRIES

### Apple Preserves

# Complete List of Recipes

# Complete List of Recipes

# Complete List of Recipes

## Preserves from Roses

## Wild Strawberry Preserves

## Preserves from Cultivated Strawberries

## Black Currant Preserves

## Red Currant Preserves

## Barberry Preserves

## Rowanberry Preserves

## Peach Preserves

## Apricot Preserves

## Tomato Preserves

## CHAPTER 29. PRESERVED VEGETABLES AND GREENS

### To Preserve Cauliflower

### To Preserve Ordinary Cabbage

### To Preserve Green Peas

### To Preserve Onions

### To Preserve Mushrooms

# Complete List of Recipes

[2573 No recipe]
!2574 Salted field mushrooms
*!2575 Soy sauce from field mushrooms
2575a Soy sauce from dried boletus mushrooms
!2576 Milk-agaric mushrooms

* 2577 Milk-agaric mushrooms
!2578 Powdered field mushrooms
!2579 Marinated field mushrooms
!2580 Truffles
* 2581 Marinated truffles
* 2582 To cultivate field mushrooms

## To Preserve Cucumbers

*!2583 Salted cucumbers
*!2584 Another method for salting [cucumbers]
!2585 Salted cucumbers, a third way
!2586 Very green salted cucumbers
!2587 To keep cucumbers fresh until late autumn
*!2588 Marinated cucumbers with mustard, horseradish, etc.
!2589 Cornichons
!2590 Cornichons, another way
2591 Long-lasting salted cucumbers

2592 Long-lasting salted cucumbers, another way
* 2593 Salted cucumbers, another way
2594 Salted cucumbers, a fourth way
* 2595 Nezhinskie cucumbers
2596 Nezhinskie cucumbers, another way
2597 Small cucumbers in vinegar
* 2598 Salted cucumbers in a pumpkin
2599 Fresh cucumbers in winter
2600 Cucumbers filled with mustard seeds
* 2601 Warning about cucumbers
2602 Cucumber water for the face

## To Preserve Beets

*!2603 Soaked beets
!2604 To store fresh beets
!2605 To preserve beet greens for winter

!2606 [Beet greens,] another way
!2607 [Beet greens, another way]

## To Preserve Sorrel

*!2608 Salted sorrel
!2609 Marinated sorrel

!2610 Dried sorrel

## To Preserve Dill, Parsley, Tarragon, Marjoram, and Horseradish

*!2611 Dried dill and parsley
!2612 Salted tarragon
!2613 Dried tarragon

!2614 Dried marjoram
!2615 Dried horseradish
2616 Dried horseradish, another way

## Celery and Asparagus

!2617 Celery for borshch
2618 Dried celery

*!2619 Salted asparagus

## Capers

!2620 Homemade capers

*!2621 Homemade capers, another way

## Pickles

*!2622 Mixed pickles
!2623 Pickles, another way

!2624 Pickles, a third way
!2625 Pickles for garnishing boiled beef

## To Preserve Beans

!2626 Salted beans
!2626a Salted beans, another way

2627 Dried green beans
*!2628 Marinated beans

## CHAPTER 32. FAST DAY SOUPS

### Hot Fish Fast Day Soups

### Oil-based Fast Day Soups

### Cold Fast Day Soups, with or without Fish

## CHAPTER 33. FAST DAY ACCOMPANIMENTS FOR SOUP

## CHAPTER 34. FAST DAY SAUCES

## CHAPTER 35. FAST DAY VEGETABLES AND GREENS

## CHAPTER 36. FISH FOR FAST DAYS

## Salads to Serve with Fish

## CHAPTER 37. PÂTÉS, ASPICS, AND OTHER COLD DISHES FOR FAST DAYS

### Pâtés

## Aspics

## Aspics

## CHAPTER 38. FAST DAY PUDDINGS

## CHAPTER 39. FAST DAY PANCAKES, BUNS, DUMPLINGS, AND KASHA

## CHAPTER 40. FAST DAY ICES, COMPOTES, AND KISSELS

### Ices

### Whips

### Jellies

### Mousses

# Bibliography

## WORKS BY ELENA IVANOVNA MOLOKHOVETS

*Podarok molodym khozjajkam, ili sredstvo dlja sokrashchenija raskhodov v domashnem khozjajstve* [Gift to young housewives, or the means for reducing housekeeping expenses.] Part I and Part II.

LIST OF EDITIONS

*1861 Kursk: Tip. gubernskago pravlenija (1st ed.) [no name or initials.]
*1866 St. Petersburg: Tip. Tovarishchestva "Obshchestvennaja Pol'za" (2nd ed., with additions) [E. M. . . . .ts listed as compiler.] Unless otherwise indicated, subsequent editions were published in St. Petersburg.
1868 (3rd ed.)
1869 V. Golovin (4th ed.) [Elena Molokhovets listed as compiler]
1871 (5th ed.)
1872 (6th ed., rev.)
*1875 O. I. Bakst (7th ed., rev.)
1878 (8th ed., 3 parts)
1881 (9th ed.)
1883 (10th ed.)
1884 Sheperdson (11th ed.)
*1886 (12th ed.)
1887 (13th ed.)
1888 (14th ed.)
1889 (15th ed.)
1890 Doma Prizrenija Maloletnikh Bednykh (16th ed.)
*1897 Doma Prizrenija Maloletnikh Bednykh (20th ed.)
1903 N. N. Klobykov (23rd ed.)
1909 (26th ed.)
1911 (Jubilee ed.)
*1914 Pervaja Sankpeterburgskaja Trudovaja Artel' (28th ed.)
1917 Pervaja Petrogradskaja Trudovaja Artel' (29th ed.)
*192? Berlin: Parabola
1932 Riga, Latvia: Praktiska biblioteka. [For details, see below.]
*196? New York: Izd. N. N. Mart'ianova, n.d.

*Sources of bibliographical information for this history of the editions are N. N. Golitsyn, Bibliograficheskij slovar' russkikh pisatel'nits (St. Petersburg: V. C. Valashev, 1889), 160, and C. I. Ponomarev, "Nashi pisatel'nitsy," in Sbornik otdelenija russkago jazyka i slovesnosti imperatorskoj akademii nauk, vol. 52 (St. Petersburg: Tip. imper. akademii nauk, 1891), 43. The* *title page of the fourth edition was reproduced in Lesley Chamberlain, "Some Russian Concepts of Food and Cooking," in Petits Propos Culinaires, 8 (June 1981), 43. I have seen and used the editions marked with an asterisk (\*); otherwise I have relied on Golitsyn, Ponomarev, and Chamberlain. Molokhovets turned eighty in 1911 and included a long introduction with many personal comments for the 1914 edition, but what happened after 1914 is unclear since the date of her death has not been recorded. Nor do I know any details about the history of the Parabola edition in Berlin, not even whether Molokhovets herself or someone in her family gave permission for its publication.*

## Translations and adaptations of *Podarok molodym khozjajkam*

*Geschenk für junge Hausfrauen oder Mittel zur Verringerung der Wirthschaftsausgaben.* Leipzig: Oswald Mutze, 1877. [The author is listed on the title page as Helene von Molochowetz.]

Bobrova, Nadezhda. *Povarennaja kniga; podarok molodym khozjajkam. Sostavleno po izvestnomu kulinarnomu trudu E. M. [sic] Molokhovets* [A cookbook; A gift to young housewives based on the well-known work of E. M. Molokhovets.] Riga: Praktiska biblioteka, 1932.

*Bobrova's book—224 pages—is only one quarter the length of Molokhovets' late editions. I have not seen this volume, but if it is a genuine adaptation, it would be interesting to know what was included and what was omitted.*

*I have seen references to a Polish translation in the nineteenth century and a French edition in the twentieth century, but I have not been able to find any details about those translations or even to verify their existence.*

*Famous Russian Recipes.* Selected and translated by Sasha Kashevaroff. Sitka, Alaska: Arrowhead Press, 1936.

*This small book (23 pp.) consists of twenty modernized recipes from the A Gift to Young Housewives. I do not know of any other English translation.*

## Other cookbooks by Molokhovets

*Prostaja obshedostupnaja kukhnja* [Simple, popular cooking]. St. Petersburg, 1883.

*Podarok molodym khozjajkam. 400 original'nykh retseptov sladkikh bljud* [Gift to young housewives. 400 original recipes for sweet dishes.] Vosproizvedeno s izdanija 1904 goda. Moscow, n.d. [1989].

*Iz kulinarnykh sovetov grafini Eleny Molokhovets: Vegetarianskij stol; Postnyj stol; Kulichi i paskhi* [Culinary advice from Countess Elena Molokhovets: vegetarian dishes; fast day dishes; kuliches and paskhas.] Moscow: Khudozh. lit., 1989.

*I have not yet seen this book, but the title alone is curious. For one thing, Molokhovets was not a countess; for another, it is an odd collection of recipes. The emphasis on vegetarian and fast day dishes and those associated with Easter suggests that the book's publication was a result of the resurgence of the Eastern Orthodox Church in the last years of the Soviet Union. During the period when people were not allowed to attend church or practice their religion, most books about Church observances were destroyed. Once it was no longer illegal to observe the Church holidays and fasts, it must have been decided that Molokhovets' recipes, even if outdated, would provide some welcome guidance for the new generation of Orthodox believers.*

## Other works by Molokhovets

*Golos russkoj zhenshchiny* [Voice of the Russian woman.] 1906.

*Aside from a few entries by Golitsyn, the bulk of this list of Molokhovets' works was composed*

# Bibliography

*from an advertisement that appeared opposite the title page of the 1914 edition of the Podarok. According to that advertisement, only the Podarok itself (meaning Parts I & II) was available from the bookseller, V. I. Gubinskij. The other titles, most of which were small, inexpensive pamphlets, were sold directly by the author from her home at 54 Suvorovskij Prospect, Apt. #17.*

*Golos zhenshchiny v zashchitu khristianskoj sem'i* [The woman's voice in defense of the Christian family.] Circa 1903.

*Jakor' spasenija dlja posjagajushchikh na bezverie, ubijstvo, samoubijstvo i krajnjuju besnravstvennost' (iz oblasti spiritizma)* [A sheet-anchor for those who struggle against disbelief, murder, suicide, and extreme immorality (in the realm of spiritualism).] 1911.

*Khram meditsiny* [The temple of medicine]. St. Petersburg, 1880.

*Kratkaja istorija Domostroitel'stva vselennoj s prilozheniem karty v kraskakh.* [A short history of the building of the universe with a supplemental map in color.] n.d.

*Monarkhizm, natsionalizm i pravoslavie* [Monarchism, nationalism, and orthodoxy.] Circa 1910.

*O tainstve pravoslavnago tserkovnago braka* [On the secret of Russian Orthodox church marriage.] n.d.

*Opyt istolkovanija XIV glavy prorochestva Isaija* [An attempt at explicating the 14th chapter of the Prophet Isaiah.] n.d.

*Podarok molodym khozjajkam. Domashnee, gorodskoe i sel'skoe khozjajstvo, gigiena i meditsina, zakljuchajushchaja v sebe 3000 domashnikh sredstve ot razlichnykh boleznej vsroslykh i detej i 1000 ukazanij na ukhod, otkarmlivanie i bolezni domashnikh ptits i zhivotnykh* [Gift to young housewives. Domestic and urban house-keeping, agriculture, hygiene, and medicine, including 3000 domestic remedies for various adult and childhood illnesses and 1000 instructions for the care and feeding of domestic birds and animals, also the curing of their diseases]. Part III. Circa 1880.

*Golitsyn (Bibliograficheskij slovar', 160) listed a Part III for 1878. Whereas Parts I and II were continually reprinted right through the Berlin edition of the 1920s, Part III was not included with the other two parts at least from 1897 onwards. Part III was never as popular as Parts I and II and seems to have dropped somewhat out of sight after its initial publication. According to the 1914 advertisement, the 1880 edition was sold out but a new edition was being prepared and would be sold privately by Molokhovets at a cost of two rubles apiece.*

*Pomoshch' vracham i vrachuemym* [Aid to doctors and patients.] St. Petersburg, 1883.

*Rajskoe chelovechestvo i ego padenie. Istorija Khrista-Boga kak Vracha ot posledstvij grekhopadenija* [Heavenly humanity and its fall. The history of Christ-God as healer of the consequences of the Fall.] 1911.

*Razdum'e* [Meditation.] Polka-mazurka. Circa 1854.

*Russko-frantsuzskie razgovory dlja detej, v vide malen'kikh stsenok* [Russian-French conversations for children in the form of short scenes.] Circa 1898.

*Russkoj zhenshchine, o velikom znachenii nashego vremeni i o budushchnosti synov eja* [To the Russian woman, on the great significance of our time and on the future for her sons.] Circa 1909.

*Russkomu narodu. Sobranie gigienicheskikh i poleznejshikh, prostykh, domashnikh vrachujushchikh sredstv ot razlichnykh boleznej vzroslykh i detej* [To the Russian people. A collection of hygienic and most useful, simple, domestic medicinal remedies for various illnesses of adults and children.] St. Petersburg, 1880; 2nd ed., 1880 [sic].

*Golitsyn gave 1880 as the dates of both editions (Bibliograficheskij slovar', 160).*

*Sokrovennyja istorii: Pravoslavnoj Rossii, katolichestva i protestantstva voobshche* [Secret stories of orthodox Russia, Catholicism, and Protestantism in general.] n.d.

*Stol dlja dukhovenstva* [Dishes for the clergy.] n.d.

*This title was not listed among the others advertised in the 1914 edition of A Gift to Young Housewives, but was mentioned in an article about Molokhovets and her works in Novoe vremja (May 20, 1911). In that same article, Molokhovets was quoted as having said that Constantine Pobedonostsev, a leading reactionary in late nineteenth century Russia who had instructed both Tsar*

# Bibliography

*Alexander III and his son Nicholas II, strongly approved of this work of hers and even liked the spirit (dukh) with which it was written. Although flattered by the praise, Molokhovets admitted that Pobedonostsev was a harmful influence on Russia.*

*Tajna gorja i smut nc shego vremeni* [Secret of the grief and disturbance of our time.] n.d.

*Vetkhozavetnaja istorija Iakova i sem'i ego, kak proobraz istorii khristianstva novozavetnago* [Old Testament story of Jacob and his family, as a prototype of the history of New Testament Christianity.] n.d.

*Znachenie obrjadnostej pravoslavnykh tainstv Kreshchenija i Miropomazanija* [Significance of the rituals of the Orthodox sacraments of baptism and anointing.] n.d.

*Znachenie pravoslavnoj panikhidy* [Significance of the Orthodox requiem.] 1910.

## SELECT BIBLIOGRAPHY

Acton, Eliza. *Modern Cookery, for Private Families* . . . London: Longman, Brown, Green and Longmans, 1855.

Aleksandrova-Ignat'eva, P. P. *Prakticheskija osnovy kulinarnago iskusstva: Rukovodstvo dlja kulinarnykh shkol i dlja samoobuchenija* [Practical fundamentals of culinary art: A handbook for culinary schools and self-instruction.] 9th ed. St. Petersburg: Ja. Trej, 1912.

Alexander, J. H. *Universal Dictionary of Weights and Measures, Ancient and Modern; Reduced to the Standards of the United States of America.* Baltimore: W. M. Minifie, 1850.

*Alexandre Dumas' Adventures in Czarist Russia.* Translated and edited by Alma Elizabeth Murch. Westport, Conn.: Greenwood Press, 1961.

*American Practical Cookery Book.* By a practical housekeeper. Philadelphia: John E. Potter, 1859.

Anderson, Oscar Edward, Jr. *Refrigeration in America: A History of a New Technology and Its Impact.* Princeton: Princeton University Press for the University of Cincinnati, 1953.

Andoh, Elizabeth. *An American Taste of Japan.* New York: William Morrow, 1985.

Anufriev, V., Kirillova, G., and Kiknadze, N. *Sousy i spitsii* [Sauces and spices.] 2nd ed. Moscow: Gosudarstvennoe izd. torgovoj literatury, 1959.

A[udot], L[ouis] E[ustache]. *La cuisinière de la campagne et de la ville: ou, La nouvelle cuisine économique.* Paris: Audot, 18—.

Austin, Thomas, ed. *Two Fifteenth-century Cookery Books: Harleian Ms. 279 (ab. 1430) and Harl. Ms. 4016 (ab. 1450), with Extracts from Ashmole Ms. 1429, Laud Ms. 553, and Douce Ms. 55.* London: N. Trübner for the Early English Text Society, 1888. Reprint. London: Oxford University Press for the Early English Text Society, 1964.

Avdeeva, Katerina Alekseevna. *Karmannaja povarennaja kniga* [The pocket cookbook.] St. Petersburg, 1846.

———. *Ruchnaja kniga russkoj opytnoj khozjajki* [Handbook of an experienced Russian mistress of the household.] St. Petersburg, 1842. 6th ed. St. Petersburg: Tip. voenno-uchebnikh zavedenij, 1848.

———. *Rukovodstvo dlja khozjaek, kljuchnits, ekonomok i kukharok* [Handbook for the mistress of the household, the housekeeper, steward, and cook.] St. Petersburg, 1846.

Avdeeva, Katerina Alekseevna and Avdeev, A. *Ekonomicheskij leksikon* [Steward's lexicon.] St. Petersburg, 1848.

Bainbridge, J. W. "Stocking Northumbrian Icehouses: An exercise in relating climate to history." *Industrial Archaeology,* vol. 9 (1972), 152–171.

Barthélemy, F. "Le gateau de broche." *Le journal des confiseurs et des patissiers,* December 1906, 365–370.

Beach, S. A. *The Apples of New York.* Albany: New York Dept. of Agriculture, 1905.

Beamon, Sylvia P. and Roaf, Susan. *The Ice-Houses of Britain.* London: Routledge, 1991.

Beard, James. *Beard on Bread.* New York: Alred A. Knopf, 1973.

Beck, Bruce. *The Official Fulton Fish Market Cookbook.* New York: E. P. Dutton, 1989.

Beck, Leonard N. *Two "Loaf-Givers."* Washington, D.C.: Library of Congress, 1984.

# Bibliography

Beecher, Catharine Esther. *Miss Beecher's Domestic Receipt Book.* 3rd ed. New York: Harper & Brothers, 1852.

Beeton, Mrs. Isabella. *The Book of Household Management.* London: S. O. Beeton, 1861. Facsimile reprint. London: Jonathan Cape, 1968. Paperback ed., New York: Farrar, Straus & Giroux, 1977.

Belov, Anatolij Vasil'evich. *Kogda zvonjat kolokola* [When the bells ring]. Moscow: Sovetskaja Rossija, 1977.

*The Best of Eliza Acton.* Edited by Elizabeth Ray with an introduction by Elizabeth David. London: Longmans, Green, 1968. Reprint. London: Penguin Books, 1974.

Bianchini, F. and Corbetta, F. *The Complete Book of Fruits and Vegetables.* New York: Crown Publishers, 1976.

*Blue Guide Moscow and Leningrad.* Edited by Evan and Margaret Mawdsley. New York: W. W. Norton, 1988.

Borisov, P. G. and Ovsjannikov, N. S. *Opredelitel' promyslovykh ryb SSSR* [Handbook of commercial fish in the Soviet Union.] Moscow: Pishchepromizdat, 1951.

Bourke, Richard Southwell. *St. Petersburg & Moscow: A Visit to the Court of the Czar.* London: Henry Colburn, 1846. Reprint (2 vols. in 1). New York: Arno Press and the New York Times, 1970.

Bradley, Richard. *The Country Housewife and Lady's Director.* 1736. Reprint. London: Prospect Books, 1980.

Braumejster, N. *Banketnye i gastronomicheskie napitki* [Banquet and gastronomic drinks.] St. Petersburg: V. I. Gubinskij, n.d. [1912?].

Brears, P. C. D. *The Gentlewoman's Kitchen: Great Food in Yorkshire 1650–1750.* Wakefield, England: Wakefield Historical Publications, 1984.

Brett, Gerard. *Dinner Is Served: A History of Dining in England, 1400–1900.* London: Rupert Hart-Davis, 1968.

*The British American Cultivator.* Edited by W. G. Edmundson. Vol. 3, New Series. Toronto: Eastwood & Co., 1847.

Brooks, Jeffrey. *When Russia Learned to Read: Literacy and Popular Literature, 1861–1917.* Princeton: Princeton University Press, 1985.

Brothwell, Don and Patricia. *Food in Antiquity.* New York: Frederick A. Praeger, 1969.

Brown, John Halit. "A Provincial Landowner: A. T. Bolotov (1738–1833)." Ph.D. diss., Princeton University, 1977.

Brown, Sanborn C. *Benjamin Thompson, Count Rumford.* Cambridge, Mass.: MIT Press, 1979. Paperback ed., 1981.

*Bul'ba: Entsiklopedicheskij spravochnik po vyrashchivaniju, khraneniju, pererabotke i ispol'zovaniju kartofelja* [Tubers: Encyclopedic guide for the cultivation, storage, treatment, and use of potatoes.] Minsk: Belorusskoj sovetskoj entsiklopedii imeni Petrusja Brovki, 1988.

Bynum, Caroline W. *Holy Feast and Holy Fast: The Religious Significance of Food to Medieval Women.* Berkeley: University of California Press, 1987.

Campbell, Susan. *Cooks' Tools.* New York: Bantam Books, 1981.

Carême, Marie Antonin. *Le maître d'hôtel français, ou Parallèle de la cuisine ancienne et moderne, considérée sous le rapport de l'ordonnance des menus selon les quatre saison: Ouvrage contenant un traité des menus à servir à Paris, à Saint-Petersbourg, à Londres et à Vienne.* 2 vols. Paris: Didot, 1822.

———. *The Royal Parisian Pastrycook and Confectioner.* Edited by John Porter. London: F. J. Mason, 1834.

Caro, Robert A. "Lyndon Johnson and the Roots of Power." In *Extraordinary Lives: The Art and Craft of American Biography.* Edited by William Zinsser, 199–231. Boston: Houghton Mifflin, 1986.

Carter, Susannah. *The Frugal Colonial Housewife.* First published as *The Frugal Housewife, or Complete Woman Cook,* 1772. Reprint. Garden City, N.Y.: Dolphin Books, Doubleday, 1976.

Chamberlain, Lesley. *The Food and Cooking of Eastern Europe.* London: Penguin Books, 1989.

———. *The Food and Cooking of Russia.* London: Allen Lane, 1982. Reprint. Penguin Books, 1983.

# Bibliography

———. "Ideology and the Growth of a Russian School of Cooking." In *Oxford Symposium Papers 1981*, 188–195. London: Prospect Books, 1982.

———. "Some Russian Concepts of Food and Cooking." *Petits Propos Culinaires*, 8 (June 1981), 41–48.

Chekhov, Anton Pavlovich. *Polnoe sobranie sochinenij i pisem v tridtsati tomakh* [Complete collected works and letters in thirty volumes.] Moscow: Nauka, 1974.

Child, Julia and Beck, Simone [and Bertholle, Louisette for Vol. 1]. *Mastering the Art of French Cooking*. 2 vols. New York: Alfred A. Knopf, 1961 and 1970.

Child, Mrs. [Lydia Maria]. *The American Frugal Housewife*. 12th ed. Boston: Carter, Hendee, & Co, 1833. Reprint. Cambridge, Mass.: Applewood Books in Cooperation with Old Sturbridge Village, n.d.

*The Collected Works of Count Rumford*. Edited by Sanborn C. Brown. 5 vols. Cambridge, Mass.: Belknap Press of Harvard University Press, 1968–1970.

[Collins, Samuel]. *The present state of Russia, in a letter to a friend at London; written by an eminent person residing at the Great Tsars court at Moscow for the space of nine years.* London: Dorman Newman, 1671.

*The Compact Edition of the Oxford English Dictionary*. 2 vols. Oxford: Oxford University Press, 1971.

Cookson, Caroline. "The Technology of Cooking in the British Isles, 1600 to 1950." Part I: "Before the Use of Gas." *Petits Propos Culinaires* [1] (1979), 23–41; Part II: "Gas and Electricity." *Petits Propos Culinaires*, 3 (November 1979), 45–54.

Cost, Bruce. *Bruce Cost's Asian Ingredients: Buying and Cooking the Staple Foods of China, Japan and Southeast Asia*. New York: William Morrow, 1988.

Crawforth, Michael A. "Weighing in the Kitchen." *Petits Propos Culinaires*, 17 (June 1984), 30–37.

Creasy, Rosalind. *Cooking from the Garden*. San Francisco: Sierra Club Books, 1988.

Cronon, William. *Changes in the Land: Indians, Colonists, and the Ecology of New England*. New York: Hill and Wang/Farrar, Straus & Giroux, 1983.

*Curye on Inglysch: English Culinary Manuscripts of the Fourteenth Century (Including the "Forme of Cury")*. Edited by Constance B. Hieatt and Sharon Butler. London: Early English Text Society/Oxford University Press, 1985.

Custine, The Marquis de. *Empire of the Czar: A Journey through Eternal Russia*. New York: Doubleday, 1989.

Czerny, Zofia. *Polish Cookbook*. Translated by Christina Cekalska and May Miller. Warsaw: Panstwowe Wydawnictwo Ekonomiczne, 1975.

Dal', Vladimir Ivanovich. *Tolkovyj slovar' zhivago velikorusskago jazyka* [Full dictionary of the living Russian language.] 4 vols. 1880. Reprint. Moscow: Russkij jazyk, 1989.

Dalal-Clayton, D. B. *Black's Agricultural Dictionary*. 2nd ed. Totowa, N.J.: Barnes & Noble Books, 1985.

Darby, William J., Ghalioungui, Paul, and Grivetti, Louis. *Food: The Gift of Osiris*. 2 vols. London: Academic Press, 1977.

David, Elizabeth. *English Bread and Yeast Cookery*. Introduction and Notes for the American Cook by Karen Hess. New York: Viking Press, 1980.

———. "Fromages Glacés and Iced Creams." *Petits Propos Culinaires*, 2 (August 1979), 23–35.

———. "Hunt the Ice Cream." *Petits Propos Culinaires*, [1] (1979), 8–13.

———. "Savour of Ice and of Roses." *Petits Propos Culinaires*, 8 (June 1981), 7–17.

Davidis, Henriette. *Praktisches Kochbuch für die gewöhnliche und feinere Küche . . . mit besonderer Berücksichtigung der Anfängerinnen und angehenden Hausfrauen*. Bielefeld: Velhagen & Klasing, 1851.

Davidson, Alan. *Mediterranean Seafood*. 2nd ed. London: Penguin Books, 1981.

———. *North Atlantic Seafood*. London: Macmillan, 1979.

———. *Seafood: A Connoisseur's Guide and Cookbook*. New York: Simon & Schuster, 1989.

———. "The Use of Copper in Cooking." *Petits Propos Culinaires*, 2 (August 1979), 20–22.

de Pomiane, Edouard. *The Jews of Poland: Recollections and Recipes*. Translated by Josephine Bacon. Garden Grove, Calif.: Pholiota Press, 1985.

# Bibliography

*Dictionary of Russian Historical Terms from the Eleventh Century to 1917.* Compiled by Sergei G. Pushkarev. Edited by George Vernadsky and Ralph T. Fisher, Jr. New Haven: Yale University Press, 1970.

*Dictionnaire de l'académie des gastronomes.* 2 vols. Paris: Editions Prisma, 1962.

Dix, Graham. "Non-Alcoholic Beverages in Nineteenth Century Russia." *Petits Propos Culinaires,* 10 (March 1982), 21–28.

*Domashnjaja spravochnaja kniga; sobranie nastavlenij, retseptov i—tak nazyvaemykh—sekretov, po raznym otrasljam khozjajstva i domovodstva* [Domestic reference book: a collection of instructions, recipes and so-called secrets, for various branches of housekeeping.] 2 vols. St. Petersburg: Tip. Shtaba Otdel'n, Korpusa Vnutren, Strazhi, 1855.

Driver, Elizabeth. *A Bibliography of Cookery Books Published in Britain, 1875–1914.* London: Prospect Books in association with Mansell Publishing, 1989.

Drukovtsov, Sergej Vasil'evich. *Povarennye zapiski* [Cooking notes.] Moscow: Tip. imper. moskovskago universiteta, 1779.

Dudchenko, Ljubov' Grigor'evna and Krivenko, Valerija Vsevolodovna. *Plodovye i jagodnye rastenija—tseliteli* [Medicinal uses for fruits and berries.] Kiev: Naukova dumka, 1987.

Dumas, Alexandre. *Le grand dictionnaire de cuisine.* 1873. Reprint. Paris: Pierre Grobel, 1958.

Dumbleton, C. W. *Russian-English Biological Dictionary.* Edinburgh: Oliver & Boyd, 1964.

Dunne, Patrick and Mackie, Charles L. "Clio's Table: Dining in the French Fashion." *Historic Preservation* (Jan.–Feb. 1991), 62–63.

Durande, Amédee. *Joseph, Carle et Horace Vernet: Correspondance et Biographies.* Paris: J. Hezel, [1863].

Dzhangaliev, Ajmak Dzhangalievich, and Rodionov, Boris Semonovich. *Dary prirody* [Gifts of nature.] Alma-Ata: Kajnar, 1978.

Edwards, John. *The Roman Cookery of Apicius.* Point Roberts, Wash.: Hartley & Marks, 1984.

*Encyclopedia of American Popular Belief and Superstition.* 7 vols. Berkeley: University of California Press, 1991–.

*Encyclopaedia Britannica.* 24 vols. Chicago: Encyclopaedia Britannica, 1960.

Engel, Barbara Alpern. *Mothers and Daughters: Women of the Intelligentsia in Nineteenth-Century Russia.* Cambridge: Cambridge University Press, 1983.

*An Englishwoman in Russia by a Lady Ten Years Resident in That Country.* New York: Charles Scribner, 1855.

*Entsiklopedicheskij slovar'* [Encyclopedia.] Edited by F. A. Brokgauz and I. J. Efron. St. Petersburg: I. A. Efron, 1898.

*Entsiklopedija vinogradarstva* [Encyclopedia of viticulture.] 3 vols. Kishinev: Glavnaja redaktsija Moldavskoj Sovetskoj Entsiklopedii, 1986.

Escoffier, Auguste. *Le guide culinaire: Aide-mémoire de cuisine pratique.* 1902. Reprint. Paris: Flammarion, 1985.

Farley, John. *The London Art of Cookery.* 1783. Reprint. Lewes, East Sussex: Southover Press, 1988.

Farmer, Fannie. *The Boston Cooking-School Cook Book.* Boston: Little, Brown, 1895. (rev. eds., 1906, 1918, 1923, 1930, 1941, 1965.)

Favre, Joseph. *Dictionnaire universel de cuisine pratique: Encyclopédie illustré d'hygiene alimentaire.* 4 vols. 2nd ed. Paris: the author, 1894.

Fedorov, Fedor Vladimirovich. *Griby* [Mushrooms.] Moscow: Rossel'khozizdat, 1983.

Fedorov, Vladimir Dmitrievich. *Vino dlja vashego stola* [Wine for your table.] Moscow: Izd. Pishchevoj promyshlennosti, 1969.

Feild, Rachael. *Irons in the Fire: A History of Cooking Equipment.* Marlborough, England: Crowood Press, 1984.

Fitzgibbon, Theodora. *The Food of the Western World: An Encyclopedia of Food from North America and Europe.* New York: Quadrangle/New York Times Book Co., 1976.

Fitzpatrick, Anne Lincoln. *The Great Russian Fair: Nizhnii Novgorod, 1840–90.* London: Macmillan, 1990.

[Florinus, Franciscus Philippus], pseud. *Ekonomiia* [Agricultural and household management.] St. Petersburg: Pri imp. akademii nauk, 1738.

# Bibliography

*Food Conservation: Ethnological Studies.* Edited by Astri Riddervold and Andreas Ropeid. London: Prospect Books, 1988.

Forsell, Mary. *Berries: Cultivation, Decoration and Recipes.* New York: Bantam Books, 1989.

Francatelli, Charles Elmé. *The Modern Cook (1846): 1462 Recipes by Queen Victoria's Chef.* Introduction by Daniel V. Thompson. Philadelphia: T. B. Peterson and Brothers, ca. 1880. Reprint. New York: Dover, 1973.

Frazer, Lynne Howard. "Calling the Kettle a Pot: Reviving Eighteenth Century Cooking Equipment Nomenclature." *Petits Propos Culinaires,* 26 (July 1987), 40–53.

Gal'kovich, Roman Stepanovich, and Sabirov, Arkadij Mikhajlovich. *Bljuda iz kuritsy* [Chicken dishes]. Perm': Permskoe knizhnoe izdatel'stvo, 1986.

Gamerith, Anni. "The Privileged Position of Farinaceous Foods in Austria." In *Food in Perspective: Proceedings of the Third International Conference on Ethnological Food Research.* Edited by Alexander Fenton and Trefor M. Owen, 83–117. Edinburgh: John Donald, 1981.

Garland, Sarah. *The Complete Book of Herbs and Spices.* New York: The Viking Press, 1979.

Georgacas, Demetrius J. *Ichthyological Terms for the Sturgeon and Etymology of the International Terms Botargo, Caviar, and Congeners.* Athens: Pragmateiai tes Akademias Athenon, Tomos 43, Athens, 1978.

Gerhart, Genevra. *The Russian's World: Life and Language.* New York: Harcourt Brace Jovanovich, 1974.

Girouard, Mark. *Life in the English Country House: A Social and Architectual History.* New Haven: Yale University Press, 1978; Penguin Books, 1980.

Glasse, Hannah. *The Art of Cookery Made Plain and Easy, Which Far Exceeds Any Thing of the Kind Ever Yet Published, by a Lady.* London: for the author, 1747. Reprint. London: Prospect Books, 1983.

Gogol, Nikolaj Vasilievich. *Dead Souls.* Translated by Bernard Guilbert Guerney. New York: Rinehart, 1942 and 1948.

———. *Polnoe sobranie sochinenij* [Complete collected works.] 14 vols. Moscow: Izd. akademii nauk SSSR, 1937–1952.

Goldstein, Darra. *A la russe: A Cookbook of Russian Hospitality.* New York: Random House, 1983.

———. "The Eastern Influence on Russian Cuisine." In *Current Research in Culinary History: Sources, Topics, and Methods.* Edited by Jillian Strang, Bonnie Brown, and Patricia Kelly, 20–26. Boston: Culinary Historians of Boston, 1986.

Golitsyn, Nikolaj Nikolaevich. *Bibliograficheskij slovar' russkikh pisatel'nits* [Bibliographical dictionary of Russian women writers]. St. Petersburg: V. C. Valashev, 1889.

Goncharov, Ivan Aleksandrovich. *Oblomov.* New York. E. P. Dutton, 1960.

———. *Sobranie sochinenij* [Collected works.] 8 vols. Moscow: Gosudarstvennoe izd. khudozhestvennoj literatury, 1952–55.

*Goodholme's Domestic Cyclopaedia of Practical Information.* Edited by Todd S. Goodholme. New York: C. A. Montgomery, 1887.

Gordon, Jean. *Rose Recipes: Customs, Facts, Fancies.* Woodstock, Vt.: Red Rose Publications, ca. 1958.

*The Gourmet Cookbook.* New York: Gourmet, 1950.

Gray, Camilla. *The Russian Experiment in Art, 1863–1922.* Rev. and enl. Edited by Marian Burleigh-Motley. London: Thames and Hudson, 1962.

*Great Soviet Encyclopedia.* Translation of *Bol'shaja Sovetskaja Entsiklopedija.* 3rd ed. (1974). New York: Macmillan, 1977.

Grewe, Rudolf. "The Arrival of the Tomato in Spain and Italy: Early Recipes." *Journal of Gastronomy,* vol. 3, no. 2 (Summer 1987), 67–82.

Grieve, Mrs. M. *A Modern Herbal.* Edited and introduced by Mrs. C. F. Leyel. London: Jonathan Cape, 1931. Reprint. London: Penguin Handbooks, 1984.

Grigson, Jane. *The Art of Charcuterie.* New York: Alfred A. Knopf, 1968.

Guba, Nikolaj Ivanovich. *Ovoshchi i frukty na vashem stole* [Vegetables and fruits for your table.] 3rd ed. Kiev: Urozhaj, 1987.

————. *Tainy shchedrogo stola* [Secrets of a Lavish Table.] 2nd ed. Dnepropetrovsk: Promin',
1978.

Guba, Nikolaj Ivanovich and Lazarev, Boris Georgievich. *Kulinarija* [Cookery.] 2nd ed. Kiev:
Vishcha shkola, 1987.

Guthrie, Katherine Blanche. *Through Russia: From St. Petersburg to Astrakhan and the Crimea.*
London: Hurst and Blackett, 1874. Reprint (2 vols in 1). New York: Arno Press and the
New York Times, 1970.

Gutsaljuk, Taisija Grigor'evna. *Ot arbuza do tykvy* [From watermelon to pumpkin.] Alma-Ata:
Kajnar, 1989.

*Handbook of Russian Literature.* Edited by Victor Terras. New Haven: Yale University Press,
1985.

Harris, Marvin. *Good to Eat: Riddles of Food and Culture.* New York: Simon & Schuster, 1985.

Hartley, Dorothy. *Food in England.* London: Macdonald, 1954.

Henisch, Bridget Ann. *Fast and Feast: Food in Medieval Society.* University Park: Pennsylvania
State University Press, 1976.

Herlihy, Patricia, "'Joy of the Rus': Rites and Rituals of Russian Drinking." *Russian Review,* vol.
50 (April 1991), 131–147.

Hillman, Howard. *Kitchen Science.* Boston: Houghton Mifflin, 1981.

*A History of Technology.* 8 vols. Edited by Charles Singer, E. J. Holmyard, A. R. Hall, and Revor
I. Williams. Oxford: Clarendon Press, 1956–58.

*The Hive and the Honey Bee.* Edited by Dadant & Sons. Hamilton, Ill.: Dadant & Sons, 1975.

*Honey: A Comprehensive Survey.* Edited by Eva Crane. London: Heinemann, 1975.

Ignat'ev, Mikhail. *Mjasovedenija dlja kulinarnykh shkol* [Meat-cutting for culinary schools.]
Published as part of P. P. Aleksandrova-Ignat'eva's *Prakticheskija osnovy kulinarnago is-
kusstva: Rukovodstvo dlja kulinarnykh shkol i dlja samoobuchenija.* 9th ed. St. Petersburg:
Ja. Trej, 1912.

*In the Russian Style.* Edited by Jacqueline Onassis with the cooperation of The Metropolitan
Museum of Art. New York: Viking Press, 1976.

Ivanits, Linda J. *Russian Folk Belief.* Armonk, N.Y.: M. E. Sharpe, 1989.

*Izvlechenie iz obshchago kataloga s risunkami na kukhonnuju posudu.* Sklada zagranichnykh
tovarov "Brat'ja Petrokokino." [Excerpt from the illustrated general catalog of kitchen
utensils from the storehouse of foreign goods of the Brothers Petrokokino.] Odessa: Tip.
E. I. Fesenko, 1897.

Jatsenkov, Nikolaj. *Novejshaja i polnaja povarennaja kniga* [Newest complete cookery book.] 2
parts. Moscow: Univ. tip. V. Okorokova, 1790–1791.

Johanson, Christine. *Women's Struggle for Higher Education in Russia, 1855–1900.* Kingston
and Montreal: McGill-Queen's University Press, 1987.

Johnson, Hugh. *Vintage: The Story of Wine.* New York: Simon & Schuster, 1989.

Johnstone, William D. *For Good Measure: A Complete Compendium of International Weights and
Measures.* New York: Avon Books, 1977.

*Joys of Jell-O (Gelatin Dessert).* 3rd ed. New York: General Foods Corp, n.d. [196?].

Jurchenko, L. A. and Vasil'kevich, S. I. *Prjanosti i spetsii* [spices.] Minsk: Pol'mja, 1989.

Kaiser, Dolf. *Fast ein Volk von Zuckerbäkern?* Zurich: Verlag Neue Zürcher Zeitung, [1985].

Kalakura, Marija Mikhajlovna. *Na vse vkusy* [For all tastes.] Kiev: Reklama, 1988.

Kalvik, Silvia. *Estonian Cuisine.* 2nd ed. Translated by Kristi Tarand. Tallinn: Perioodika Publishers, 1987.

Karlinsky, Simon. "The Vanished World of Elena Molokhovets." *University Publishing,* No. 8,
Fall 1979 (University of California at Berkeley), 1–3.

*Katalog russkago otdelenija knizhnago magazina Mavrikija Osipovicha Vol'fa. Sorokoletie russkoj
literatury, 1830–1870* [Catalog of the Russian department of M.O. Vol'f's bookstore.
Forty years of Russian literature, 1830–1870.] St. Petersburg: Tip. M. Ol Vol'fa, 1872.

Kengis, R.P. *Domashnee prigotovlenie tortov, pirozhnykh, pechen'ja, prjanikov, pirogov* [Home
preparation of tortes, small baked goods, pastries, gingerbreads, and pies.] 4th ed. Moscow: Agropromizdat, 1987.

Kirshenblatt-Gimblett, Barbara. "The Kosher Gourmet in the Nineteenth-Century Kitchen:

# Bibliography

Three Jewish Cookbooks in Historical Perspective." *The Journal of Gastronomy*, vol. 2, no. 4 (Winter 1986/1987), 51–89.

———. Review of *The Futurist Cookbook* by F. T. Marinetti. *Art Forum* (November 1989), 20–23.

Knechtges, David R. "A Literary Feast: Food in Early Chinese Literature." *Journal of the American Oriental Society*, vol. 106, no. 1 (Jan.-Mar., 1986), 49–65.

*Kniga o vkusnoj i zdorovoj pishche* [Book about tasty and healthy food.] Moscow: Pishchepromizdat, 1953.

———. 6th ed. Moscow: Pishchevaja promyshlennost', 1977.

———. 8th ed. Moscow: Agropromizdat, 1985.

———. 9th ed. Moscow: Agropromizdat, 1989.

Kohl, Johann George. *Russia.* 1842. Reprint. New York: Arno Press & The New York Times, 1970.

Korb, Johann-Georg. *Diary of an Austrian Secretary of Legation.* 1863. Reprint. London: Frank Cass, 1968.

Kosover, Mordecai. *Yidishe maykholim* [Food and beverages: A study in the history of culture and linguistics]. New York: Yivo Institute of Jewish Research, 1958.

Kotoshikhin, Grigorij Karpovich. *O Rossii v tsarstvovanie Alekseja Mikhajlovicha* [On Russia under Tsar Aleksei Mikhailovich.] St. Petersburg: Tip. E. Pratsa, 1895. Reprint. Text and commentary by A. E. Pennington. Oxford: Clarendon Press, Oxford University Press, 1980.

Kovalev, Nikolaj Ivanovich. *Rasskazy o russkoj kukhne* [Tales of the Russian kitchen.] Moscow: Ekonomika, 1984.

———. *Russkaja kulinarija* [Russian cookery.] Moscow: Ekonomika, 1972.

Kovalevskaya, Sofya. *A Russian Childhood.* Translated, edited, and introduced by Beatrice Stillman. New York: Springer-Verlag, 1978.

Kozak, Vasilij Timofeevich and Koz'jakov, Sergej Nikolaevich. *Vse o s"edobnykh gribakh* [All about edible mushrooms.] Kiev: Urozhaj, 1987.

Krekhova, Dina Pinkhusovna, and Ape, Tamara Konstantinovna. *Spravochnoe posobie konditera* [Confectioner's reference book.] Minsk: Vyshejshaja shkola, 1984.

*Küchen-Lexikon: Von Aachener Printen bis Zwischenrippenstück.* 8th ed. Munich: Deutscher Taschenbuch Verlag, 1988.

Kulakova, Elena Vasil'evna. *Kholodnye bljuda i zakuski* [Cold dishes and hors d'oeuvre.] Kishinev: Kartja moldovenjaske, 1983.

Kulzowa-Hawliczkowa, Helena. *Kuchnia polska* [Polish cookery.] Warsaw: Panstwowe Wydawnictwo Ekonomiczne, 1988.

*Kumys i shubat* [Fermented mare's milk and fermented camel's milk.] 3rd ed. Alma-Ata: Kajnar, 1979.

*Larousse Gastronomique.* Edited by Jenifer Harvey Lang. New York: Crown Publishers, 1988.

La Varenne, François. *Le cuisinier françois: Textes présentés par Jean-Louis Flandrin, Philip et Mary Hyman.* (Bibliothèque bleue) Paris: Montalba, 1984. (Reprint of *Le cuisinier françois*, Troyes: la veuve Pierre Garnier, 1738?; *Le patissier françois*, 4th ed., Troyes, Paris: Antoine de Rafflé, and *Le confiturier françois*, Troyes, Paris: Antoine de Rafflé)

Leibenstein, Margaret. *The Edible Mushroom: A Gourmet Cook's Guide.* New York: Fawcett Columbine, 1986.

Levenstein, Harvey. *Revolution at the Table: The Transformation of the American Diet.* New York: Oxford University Press, 1988.

Levshin, Vasilij Alekseevich. *Russkaja povarnja* [Russian kitchen]. Moscow: Tip. S. Selivanovskogo, 1816.

———. *Slovar' povarennyj, prispeshnichij, kanditerskij i distilljatorskij, soderzhashchij po azbuchnomu porjadku podrobnoe i vernoe nastavlenie k prigotovleniju vsjakago roda kushan'ja iz frantsuzskoj, nemetskoj, gollandskoj, ispanskoj i anglijskoj povarni* [An alphabetical dictionary of cooking, general assistance, confectionary, and distilling, containing detailed and reliable instructions for preparing all sorts of French, German, Dutch, Spanish, and English dishes.] Moscow: Univ. tip., 1795–1797.

# Bibliography

Lincoln, Mrs. D. A. *Mrs. Lincoln's Boston Cook Book: What to Do and What Not to Do in Cooking.* Boston: Roberts Brothers, 1889.

Ljakhovskaja, Lidija Petrovna. *Molodoj sem'e o kulinarii* [What a young family needs to know about cooking.] Moscow: Ekonomika, 1988.

Longone, Jan. "A Sufficiency and No More, A Graphic Description of the American Kitchen of the 1850s." *American Magazine and Historical Chronicle* (published by the Clements Library, University of Michigan), vol. 3, no. 1 (Spring-Summer 1987), 28–44.

*Luigi Carnacina's Great Italian Cooking (La Grande Cucina Internazionale).* Edited by Michael Sonino. New York: Abradale Press, n.d. [196?].

Lyle, David. *The Book of Masonry Stoves: Rediscovering an Old Way of Warming.* Andover, Mass.: Brick House Publishing, 1984.

Lyons, Marvin. *Russia in Original Photographs, 1860–1910.* Boston: Routledge & Kegan Paul, 1977.

McBride, Theresa M. *The Domestic Revolution: The Modernisation of Household Service in England and France 1820–1920.* New York: Holmes & Meier, 1976.

McClane, A. J., and deZanger, Arie. *The Encyclopedia of Fish.* New York: Holt, Rinehart & Winston, 1977.

Maclean, Virginia. *A Short-title Catalogue of Household and Cookery Books Published in the English Tongue 1701–1800.* London: Prospect Books, 1981.

Macura, Paul. *Russian-English Botanical Dictionary.* Columbus, Ohio: Slavica Publishers, 1979.

McGee, Harold. *On Food and Cooking: The Science and Lore of the Kitchen.* New York: Charles Scribner's Sons, 1984.

Maitland, Derek. *5000 Years of Tea.* New York: Gallery Books, 1982.

Mallos, Tess. *The Complete Middle East Cookbook.* New York: McGraw-Hill, 1979.

Makarenko, P. P. *Ocherki istorii vinogradarstva Bessarabii i levoberezhnogo podnestrov'ja* [Outline of the history of viticulture in Bessarabia and along the left bank of the Dniester.] Kishinev: Stiintsa, 1988.

Marinetti, F. T. *The Futurist Cookbook.* Translated by Suzanne Brill. Edited with an introduction by Lesley Chamberlain. San Francisco: Bedford Arts, 1989.

Markham, Gervase. *The English Housewife.* London: Nicolas Okes for Iohn Harison, 1631. Reprint. Edited by Michael R. Best. Kingston and Montreal: McGill-Queen's University Press, 1986.

Marsden, Christopher. *Palmyra of the North: The First Days of St. Petersburg.* London: Faber & Faber, 1942.

Marshall, Agnes Bertha. *Ices Plain and Fancy.* Reprint of A. B. *Marshall's Book of Ices.* London: Marshall's School of Cookery, ca. 1885. Edited by Barbara Ketcham Wheaton. New York: Metropolitan Museum of Art, 1976.

———. *Mrs. A. B. Marshall's Larger Cookery Book of Extra Recipes.* London: Marshall's School of Cookery and Simpkin, Marshall, Hamilton, Kent, 1902.

*Martha Washington's Booke of Cookery.* Edited by Karen Hess. New York: Columbia University Press, 1981.

Mason, Laura. "Dibs, Dabs, Lemons and Love Hearts: An Investigation into Sherbet Sweets." *Petits Propos Culinaires*, 35 (July 1990), 31–38.

*Le Ménagier de Paris.* Edited by Georgina E. Grereton and Janet M. Ferrier. New York: Oxford University Press, 1981.

Mendelson, Anne. "Hartshorn Salt and Potash." *Petits Propos Culinaires*, 20 (July 1985), 78–79.

[Menon]. *La Cuisinière bourgeoise.* Paris, 1746.

Miller, David W. "Technology and the Ideal: Production Quality and Kitchen Reform in Nineteenth-Century America." In *Dining in America, 1850–1900.* Edited by Kathryn Grover, 47–84. Amherst & Rochester, N.Y.: University of Massachusetts Press and Margaret Woodbury Strong Museum, 1987.

Mintz, Sidney W. *Sweetness and Power.* New York: Penguin Books, 1985.

Morineau, Michel. "The Potato in the Eighteenth Century." In *Food and Drink in History.* Edited by Robert Forster and Orest Ranum, 17–36. Baltimore: Johns Hopkins University Press, 1979.

# Bibliography

Nanobashvili, Iosif Dzhimsherovich. *Drevnjaja kul'tura lozy v Kiziki* [Ancient culture of the vine in Kiziki.] Tbilisi: Akademii nauk Gruzinskoj SSR, 1960.

*Nastol'naja kniga. Raznyja neobkhodimyja spravochnyja svedenija* [Manual. Various essential pieces of infomation.] St. Petersburg: S. Dobrodeev, 1895.

Nerhood, Harry W. *To Russia and Return: An Annotated Bibliography of Travelers' English-Language Account of Russia from the Ninth Century to the Present.* Columbus: Ohio State University Press, 1968.

Newall, Venetia. *An Egg at Easter: A Folklore Study.* London: Routledge & Kegan Paul, 1971; Bloomington: Indiana University Press, 1989.

Norman, Jill. *The Complete Book of Spices: A Practical Guide to Spices and Aromatic Seeds.* New York: Viking Studio Books, 1990.

*Novgorod the Great: Excavations at the Medieval City Directed by A. V. Artsikhovsky and B. A. Kolchin.* Compiled and written by M. W. Thompson. London: Evelyn, Adams & Mackay, 1967.

Ojakangas, Beatrice A. *The Finnish Cookbook.* New York: Crown Publishers, 1964.

Orlov, Aleksandr Sergeevich. *Domostroi: Izsledovanie, pt. 1* [Domestic management: Research, Part 1.] Moscow: Sinodal'naja tip., 1917. Reprint. The Hague: Europe Printing, 1967.

Orlova, Zhanna Ivanovna. *Vse ob ovoshchakh* [Everything about vegetables.] 2nd ed. Moscow: Agropromizdat, 1986.

"Orris Root." In *Bulletin of Miscellaneous Information,* Royal Botanic Gardens, Kew, No. 1 (1930), 91–93.

Osipov, Nikolai Petrovich. *Starinnaja russkaja khozjajka, kljuchnitsa i strjapukha* [Old-time Russian mistress of the household, housekeeper, and cook.] St. Petersburg: Imp. tip, 1790. Reprint. 1828.

———. *Novyj i polnyj rossijskoj khozjajstvennoj vinokur* [The new and complete Russian domestic vintner.] St. Petersburg, 1796. (This is an expanded version of *Rossijskoj khozjajstvennoj vinokur.* St. Petersburg: Imp. tip, 1792.)

———. *Rossijskoj khozjajstvennoj vinokur, pivovar, medovar, vodochnoj master, kvasnik, uksusnik, i pogrebshchik* [Russian domestic vintner, brewer, cellerer, and maker of spirits, kvass, and vinegar.] St. Petersburg: Imp. tip, 1792.

Papashvily, Helen and George. *Russian Cooking.* New York: Time-Life Books, 1969. Revised, 1971.

Parkinson, John. *A Tour of Russia, Siberia and the Crimea 1792–1794.* London: Frank Cass, 1971.

Pasternak, Boris. *Doktor Zhivago.* Ann Arbor, Mich.: University of Michigan Press, 1958.

Pauli, Eugen. *Classical Cooking: The Modern Way.* 2nd ed. New York: Van Nostrand Reinhold, 1989.

Perednev, V. P., Shapiro, D. K., Matveev, V. A., and Radjuk, A. F. *Plody i ovoshchi v pitanii cheloveka* [Fruits and vegetables in human nutrition.] Minsk: Uradzhaj, 1983.

Periam, Jonathan. *The Home and Farm Manual: A Pictorial Encyclopedia of Farm, Garden, Household, Architectural, Legal, Medical and Social Information.* 1884. Reprint. New York: Greenwich House, 1984.

Petit, Alphonse. *La Gastronomie en Russie.* Paris: Chez l'auteur, 1860.

Phillips, Roger. *Mushrooms and Other Fungi of Great Britain and Europe.* London: Pan Books, 1981.

Pitcher, Harvey. *When Miss Emmie Was in Russia: English Governesses Before, During and After the October Revolution.* London: Century Publishing, 1984.

*Podarok molodym khozjajkam i neopytnym khozjaevam* [Gift to young and inexperienced housewives.] St. Petersburg: Dom prizrenija maloletnikh bednykh, 1874.

Pokhlebkin, Vil'jam Vasil'evich. *Chai, ego tipy, svojstva, upotreblenie* [Tea, its varieties, properties, and use.] Moscow: Pishchevaja promyshlennost', 1968.

———. *Natsional'nye kukhni nashikh narodov* [The national dishes of our people.] Moscow: Pishchevaja promyshlennost', 1980.

———. *O kulinarii ot A do Ja: Slovar'-spravochnik* [Cookery from A to Z: An alphabetical guide.] Minsk: Polymja, 1988.

Ponomarev, S. I. "Nashi pisatel'nitsy" [Our women writers.] In *Sbornik otdelenija russkago jazyka i slovesnosti imperatorskoj akademii nauk*, vol. 52, 1–77. St. Petersburg: Tip. imper. akademii nauk, 1891.

*Popular Lithuanian Recipes*. 8th ed. Chicago: Lithuanian Catholic Press, 1981.

*A Portrait of Tsarist Russia: Unknown Photographs from the Soviet Archives*. Translated by Michael Robinson. New York: Pantheon Books, 1989.

Pouncy, Carolyn Johnston. "The Domostroi as a Source for Muscovite History." Ph.D. diss., Stanford University, 1985.

Preobrazhensky, A. G. *Etymological Dictionary of the Russian Language*. New York: Columbia University Press, 1951.

Ptushenko, E. S., Beme, R. L., Flint, V. E., and Uspenskij, S. M. *Spravochnik nazvanij ptits fauny SSSR na latinskom, russkom, anglijskom i nemetskom jazykakh* [Guide to the birds of the Soviet Union with their names in Latin, Russian, English, and German.] Moscow: Izd. Moskovskogo universiteta, 1972.

Pushkin, Aleksandr Sergeevich. *Eugene Onegin*. Translated by Walter Arndt. New York: E. P. Dutton, 1963.

———. *Polnoe sobranie sochinenij* [Complete collected works.] 17 vols. Leningrad: Akademii nauk SSSR, 1937–59.

———. *The Queen of Spades*. In *The Poems, Prose and Plays of Pushkin*. Edited by Avrahm Yarmolinsky, 556–589. New York: Modern Library, 1936 and 1964.

Radetskij, I. M. *Al'manakh gastronomov. Zakljuchajashchij v sebe tridtsat' polnykh obedov, oznachennykh zapiskami russkimi i frantsuzskimi* [Almanac for gastronomes, including thirty full dinner menus in Russian and French.] St. Petersburg: Tip. shtaba otdel'nago korpusa vnutrennej strazhi, 1852. (2nd rev. ed. St. Petersburg, 1877.)

———. *Khozjajka, ili Polnejshee rukovodstvo k sokrashcheniju domashnikh raskhodov* [Mistress of the household, or, the most complete guide to reducing household expenses.] 2nd ed., revised and enlarged. St. Petersburg: M. O. Vol'f, [187–?].

Radeva, Lilija. "Traditional Methods of Food Preserving among the Bulgarians." In *Food Conservation: Ethnological Studies*. Edited by Astri Riddervold and Andreas Ropeid, 38–44. London: Prospect Books, 1988.

Raffald, Elizabeth. *The Experienced English Housekeeper, for the Use and Ease of Ladies, Housekeepers, Cooks, etc., Wrote Purely from Practice, Consisting of Near 800 Original Receipts, Most of Which Never Appeared in Print*. Manchester: J. Harrop for the author, 1769.

Ragan, W. H. *Nomenclature of the Apple: A Catalogue of the Known Varieties Referred to in American Publications from 1804 to 1904*. Washington, D.C.: Government Printing Office (U.S. Dept. of Agriculture, Bureau of Plant Industry, Bulletin 56), 1905.

Randolph, Mary. *The Virginia Housewife*, 1828. Facsimile reprint. Historical notes and commentary by Karen Hess. Columbia: University of South Carolina Press, 1984.

Ranhofer, Charles. *The Epicurean*. 1893. Reprint. New York: Dover, 1971.

Riasanovsky, Nicholas V. *A History of Russia*. 4th ed. New York: Oxford University Press, 1984.

Ricker, W. E. *Russian-English Dictionary for Students of Fisheries and Aquatic Biology*. Bulletin 183. Ottawa: Fisheries Research Board of Canada, 1973.

Riely, Elizabeth. *The Chef's Companion: A Concise Dictionary of Culinary Terms*. New York: Van Nostrand Reinhold, 1986.

Rodil, Louis. *Antonin Carême de Paris, 1783–1833*. Paris: Editions Jeanne Laffitte, 1980.

Rombauer, Irma S. and Marion Rombauer Becker. *Joy of Cooking*. New York: Bobbs-Merrill, 1963.

Rosengarten, Frederic. *The Book of Spices*. Wynnewood, Pa.: Livingston Publishing Co., 1969.

Rumpolt, Marx. *Ein neu Kochbuch*. Frankfurt: S. Feyerabend, 1587.

*Russia, The Land, The People: Russian Painting, 1850–1910*. Washington, D.C.: Smithsonian Institution Traveling Exhibition Service in association with University of Washington Press, 1986.

*Russian Journal of Lady Londonderry, 1836–7*. Edited by W. A. L. Seaman and J. R. Sewell. London: John Murrary, 1973.

Rybak, Galina Mikhajlovna, Romanenko, Ljudmila Rodionovna, and Korableva, Ol'ga Anatol'evna. *Prjanosti* [Spices.] Kiev: Urozhaj, 1989.

Sabban, Françoise. "Insights into the Problem of Preservation by Fermentation in 6th Century

# Bibliography

China." In *Food Conservation: Ethnological Studies*. Edited by Astri Riddervold and Andreas Ropeid, 45–55. London: Prospect Books, 1988.

Sala, George Augustus. *A Journey Due North; Being Notes of a Residence in Russia*. Boston: Ticknor & Fields, 1858.

———. *Breakfast in Bed*. Boston: James Redpath, 1863.

Salaman, Redcliffe. *The History and Social Influence of the Potato*. 1949. Reprint. Cambridge: Cambridge University Press, 1986.

Saulnier, Louis. *Le répertoire de la cuisine*, 1914. Translated by E. Brunet. New York: Barron's Educational Series, 1976.

Scharfenberg, Horst. *The Cuisines of Germany*. New York: Poseidon Press, 1989.

Schumacher-Voelker, Uta. "German Cookery Books, 1485–1800." *Petits Propos Culinaires, 6* (October 1980), 34–46.

Schuyler, Eugene. "Diner à la Russe, 1868." *Petits Propos Culinaires, 28* (April 1988), 22–27.

Scully, Terence. *The Viandier of Taillevent*. Ottawa, Canada: University of Ottawa Press, 1988.

Serkoff, Vera, Countess. *Paper-Bag Cookery*. London: C. Arthur Pearson, 1911.

Seymour, John. *Forgotten Household Crafts*. New York: Alfred A. Knopf, 1987.

Shapiro, Laura. *Perfection Salad: Women and Cooking at the Turn of the Century*. New York: Farrar, Straus & Giroux, 1986.

Sheraton, Mimi. *The German Cookbook*. New York: Random House, 1965.

Shimolin, V. I. *Sladkoezhka* [Dishes for a sweet tooth.] Minsk: Polymja, 1985.

Shklovsky, Victor. *Lev Tolstoy*. Moscow: Progress Publishers, 1978.

Simmons, Amelia. *The First American Cookbook*. Facsimile of *American Cookery*, 1796. New York: Oxford University Press, 1958; New York: Dover Publications, 1984.

Simoons, Frederick J. *Eat Not This Flesh: Food Avoidance in the Old World*. Madison: University of Wisconsin Press, 1963.

———. *Food in China: A Cultural and Historical Inquiry*. Boca Raton, Florida: CRC Press, 1991.

*Slovar' russkogo jazyka XI-XVII vv* [Dictionary of the Russian language from the 11th to 17th centries.] 14 vols. Moscow: Nauka, 1975–1988. [Still in progress]

*Slovar' sovremenogo russkogo literaturnogo jazyka* [Dictionary of the contemporary Russian literary language.] 17 vols. Moscow: Izd. akademii nauk SSSR, 1950–1965.

*Slownik jezyka polskiego* [Dictionary of the Polish language.] Edited by Witold Doroszewski. 11 vols. Warsaw: Wiedza Powszechna, 1958–   .

Smith, E. *The Compleat Housewife: or, Accomplish'd Gentlewoman's Companion*. Reprint of 15th ed., London, 1753 and 18th ed., London, 1773. London: Literary Services and Production, 1968.

Smith, R. E. F. "Drink in Old Russia." In *Peasants in History: Essays in Honour of Daniel Thorner*, 43–54. Calcutta: Oxford University Press, 1980.

———. *Peasant Farming in Muscovy*. Cambridge: Cambridge University Press, 1977.

———. "The Russian Stove." *Oxford Slavonic Papers*, New Series, vol. XVIII (1985), 83–101.

———. "Whence the Samovar?" *Petits Propos Culinaires, 4* (February 1980), 57–72.

Smith, R. E. F. and Christian, David. *Bread and Salt: A Social and Economic History of Food and Drink in Russia*. Cambridge: Cambridge University Press, 1984.

Sokolov, Raymond. "Measure for Measure." In *Oxford Symposium on Food and Cookery 1988: The Cooking Pot*, 148–152. London: Prospect Books, 1989.

Soyer, Alexis. *Gastronomic Regenerator*. 9th ed. London: Simpkin, Marshall, 1861.

Soyer, Nicolas. *Soyer's Paper-Bag Cookery*. New York: Sturgis & Walton, 1911.

Spear, Ruth A. *Cooking Fish and Shellfish*. Garden City, N.Y.: Doubleday, 1980.

Spurling, Hilary. *Elinor Fettiplace's Receipt Book: Elizabethan Country House Cooking*. New York: Elisabeth Sifton Books/Viking Penguin, 1986.

Stallings, W. S., Jr. "Ice Cream and Water Ices in 17th and 18th Century England." *Petits Propos Culinaires, 3* (Supplement) [1979], 1–32.

*Stocking Up: How to Preserve the Foods You Grow Naturally*. Edited by Carol Hupping Stoner. Emmaus, Pa.: Rodale Press, 1977.

Stone, Sally and Stone, Martin. *The Mustard Cookbook*. New York: Avon, 1981.

# Bibliography

*Sturtevant's Edible Plants of the World.* Edited by U. P. Hedrick. New York: Dover Publications, 1972.

Sumarokov, Pankratij Platonovich. *Istochnik zdravija, ili Slovar' vsekh upotrebitel'nykh snedej, priprav i napitkov iz trekh tsarstv prirody izvlekaemykh* [Source of health, or Dictionary of all common foods, seasonings, and beverages derived from the three realms of nature.] Moscow: Univ. tip., 1800.

Svrcek, Mirko. *The Hamlyn Book of Mushrooms and Fungi.* London: Hamlyn, 1983.

Tarkovskij, Arsenij Aleksandrovich. *Stikhotvorenija* [Poems.] Moscow: Khudozhestvennaja literatura, 1974.

Tirel, Guillaume, called Taillevent. *Le Viandier.* Edited by Jérôme Pichon and Georges Vicaire. Paris: Techener, 1892.

Tolstoy, Lev Nikolaevich. *Polnoe sobranie sochinenij* [Complete collected works.] 90 vols. Moscow: Gosudarstvennoe izd. khudozhestvennoj literatury, 1928–58.

——— . *War and Peace.* Translated by Constance Garnett. New York: Modern Library, Random House, n.d.

Toomre, Joyce. "A Note on 'Fish in the Jewish style' in Nineteenth-Century Russia." *Jewish Folklore and Ethnology Review,* vol. 9, no. 1 [1987], 36–37.

——— . "Russia and Champagne," *Wine and Spirits,* vol. 7, no. 3 (June 1988), 26–27.

——— . "Schuyler's 'Diner à la Russe': Some Reflections and Recipes." *Petits Propos Culinaires,* 32 (June 1989), 11–18.

——— . "A Short History of 'Shchi.'" In *Proceedings of the Oxford Symposium on Food & Cookery 1984 & 1985,* 62–69. London: Prospect Books, 1986.

——— . "Three Hundred Years of Russian Fasting: Foreign Perceptions vs Native Practice." Presented June 1989 at the Eighth International Conference on Ethnological Food Research, sponsored by the Balch Institute for Ethnic Studies, Philadelphia, Pa. (Due to appear as part of the Conference Proceedings.)

*Tovarnyj slovar'* [Commercial dictionary.] 9 vols. Moscow: Gosudarstvennoe izd. torgovoj literatury, 1957.

Ude, Louis Eustache. *The French Cook,* 1828. Reprint. New York: Arco Publishing, 1978.

Ushakov, D. N. *Tolkovyj slovar' russkogo jazyka* [Full dictionary of the Russian language.] 4 vols. Moscow, 1934–1940. Reprint (4 vols. in 3). Cambridge, Mass.: Slavica Publishers, 1974.

Uusivirta, Hilkka. *Finskaja natsional'naja kukhnja* [Finnish cookery.] Translated by V. V. Pokhlebkin. Moscow: Legkaja i pishchevaja promyshlennost', 1982. [Original title: *Supisuomalaiset herkut.*]

Vall, Nell du. *Domestic Technology: A Chronology of Developments.* Boston: G. K. Hall, 1988.

Vakki, Eric and Summers, Diane. "Nest Gatherers of Tiger Cave." *National Geographic,* vol. 177, no. 1 (January 1990), 107–133.

*Van Nostrand's Scientific Encyclopedia.* 3rd ed. New York: D. Van Nostrand, 1958.

Varlamova, Raida. *Semejnyj magazin sovremennykh usovershenstvovanij k rasprostraneniju mezhdu vsemi klassami ljudej izjashchnago vkusa, porjadka i udobstva v domashnej i obshchestvennoj zhizni* [Family magazine of modern refinements to be disseminated among all classes of people of elegance, order, and comfort in domestic and social life.] 4 parts. Moscow: Tip. A. Evrennova, 1856.

Vasmer, Max. *Etimologicheskij slovar' russkogo jazyka.* 4 vols. Translated from German. Heidelberg, 1950–58. Moscow: Progress, 1964.

Vengerov, Semen Afanas'evich. *Istochniki slovarja russkikh pisatelij* [Sources for a dictionary of Russian writers.] 4 vols. St. Petersburg: Tip. imper. akademii nauk, 1900–1917.

*Ves' Peterburg na 1901 god: adresnaja i spravochnaja kniga g. S.-Peterburga* [All St. Petersburg for the year 1901: Address and reference book for the city of St. Petersburg.] St. Petersburg: A. S. Suvorin, 1901.

*Vinogradarstvo Moldavii i Ukrainy* [Viticulture of Moldavia and Ukraine.] Edited by T. F. Isak, A. G. Tsopa, N. D. Kolomysova, and V. N. Konskii. Kishinev: Kartja Moldovenjaske, 1976.

Visser, Margaret. *Much Depends on Dinner.* New York: Grove Press, 1986.

Visson, Lynn. *The Complete Russian Cookbook.* Ann Arbor, Mich.: Ardis, 1982.

# Bibliography

————. "Kasha vs. Cachet Blanc: The Gastronomic Dialectics of Russian Literature." In *Russianness: Studies on a Nation's Identity.* Edited by Robert L. Belknap, 60–73. Ann Arbor, Mich.: Ardis, 1990.

Völckel, Margaretha. *Neuestes Bayerisches Kochbuch.* Nuremberg: Jacob Zeiser, 1875. Reprint. Nuremberg: Lorenz Spindler Verlag, 1987.

Volokh, Anne. *The Art of Russian Cuisine.* New York: Macmillan, 1983.

Wasson, Valentine Pavlovna and R. Gordon. *Mushrooms, Russia and History.* 2 vols. New York: Pantheon, 1957.

Webster, Thomas, assisted by Mrs. Parkes. *An Encyclopaedia of Domestic Economy: Comprising Such Subjects as Are Most Immediately Connected with Housekeeping.* London: Longman, Brown, Green, and Longmans, 1847.

Weigley, Emma Siefrit. *Sarah Tyson Rorer.* Philadelphia: American Philosophical Society, 1977.

Wheaton, Barbara Ketcham. *Savoring the Past: The French Kitchen and Table from 1300 to 1789.* Philadelphia: University of Pennsylvania Press, 1983.

Wheaton, Barbara Ketcham and Kelly, Patricia. *Bibliography of Culinary History: Food Resources in Eastern Massachusetts.* Boston: G. K. Hall, [1987].

Wheeler, Alwyne. *Fishes of the World: An Illustrated Dictionary.* New York: Macmillan, 1975.

Willan, Anne. *Great Cooks and Their Recipes: From Taillevent to Escoffier.* London: Elm Tree Books, 1977.

*William Verrall's Cookery Book: First Published 1759.* [Reprint of William Verral, *A Complete System of Cookery.* London: Printed for the author, 1759] Lewes, East Sussex: Southover Press, 1988.

Wilmot, Martha and Catherine. *The Russian Journals of Martha and Catherine Wilmot.* Edited by the Marchioness of Londonderry & H. Montgomery Hyde. London, 1934. Reprint. New York: Arno Press & The New York Times, 1971.

Wilson, C. Anne. *The Book of Marmalade: Its Antecedents, Its History and Its Role in the World Today.* New York: St. Martin's/Marek, 1985.

————. *Food and Drink in Britain.* London: Constable, 1973.

Wilson, Francesca. *Muscovy: Russia through Foreign Eyes, 1553–1900.* London: George Allen & Unwin, 1970.

Winton, Andrew L. and Winton, Kate Barber. *The Structure and Composition of Foods.* 4 vols. New York: John Wiley & Sons, 1939.

Witteveen, Joop. "Potash and Hartshorn Salt." *Petits Propos Culinaires,* 21 (November 1985), 66–68.

Zakharova, Ljubov' Fedorovna and Tolchinskaja, Eva Iosifovna. *Puteshestvie v stranu Kulinariju* [Journey in Culinary Land.] 2nd ed. Kishinev: Timpul, 1987.

Zoshchenko, Mikhail. *Scenes from the Bathhouse and Other Stories of Communist Russia.* Translated by Sidney Monas. Ann Arbor, Mich.: Ann Arbor Paperbacks, University of Michigan Press, 1962.

# Index

Abbreviation: *GYH* = Gift to Young Housewives

Note: Underscored page numbers refer to recipes

Joyce Toomre is an Associate of the Russian Research Center at Harvard University and lecturer in culinary history at Radcliffe College. A cofounder of the Culinary Historians of Boston, she has published articles in *Petits Propos Culinaires*, *Journal of Gastronomy*, and *Wine and Spirits*.

EDITOR: Roberta Diehl
BOOK AND JACKET DESIGNER: Sharon L. Sklar
PRODUCTION: Harriet Curry
TYPEFACE: Goudy Old Style
COMPOSITOR: Shepard Poorman
PRINTER: Maple Vail Book Manufacturing Group